W9-BTZ-317

The Curriculum Studies Reader

Third Edition

In this much-anticipated third edition of the best-selling anthology, David J. Flinders and Stephen J. Thornton once again bring together the best scholarship in curriculum studies. From John Dewey's nineteenth-century creed to Nel Noddings' twenty-first century aims, this thoughtful combination of new and timely essays provides a complete survey of the discipline coupled with concrete examples of innovative curriculum and an examination of contemporary topics. New to this edition are additional historical and contextual pieces from Maria Montessori and Jerome Bruner, and a thoroughly updated collection of contemporary selections, reflecting issues such as standardization, high-stakes testing, and globalization.

Carefully balanced to engage with the history of curriculum studies while simultaneously looking ahead to its future, *The Curriculum Studies Reader* continues to be the most authoritative collection in the field.

David J. Flinders is Professor of Curriculum Studies in the School of Education at Indiana University, Bloomington.

Stephen J. Thornton is Professor and Chair of the Department of Secondary Education at the University of South Florida.

The Curriculum Studies Reader

Third Edition

Edited by

David J. Flinders and
Stephen J. Thornton

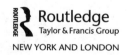

Routledge
Taylor & Francis Group

NEW YORK AND LONDON

First edition published 1998
by RoutledgeFalmer
270 Madison Ave, New York, NY 10016

Second edition published 2004
by RoutledgeFalmer
270 Madison Ave, New York, NY 10016

This edition published 2009
by Routledge
270 Madison Ave, New York, NY 10016

Simultaneously published in the UK
by Routledge
2 Park Square, Milton Park, Abingdon, Oxon OX14 4RN

Routledge is an imprint of the Taylor & Francis Group, an informa business

© 1998 Taylor & Francis
© 2004 Taylor & Francis
© 2009 Taylor & Francis

Typeset in Minion by RefineCatch Limited, Bungay, Suffolk
Printed and bound in the United States of America on acid-free paper
by Sheridan Books, Inc

All rights reserved. No part of this book may be reprinted or reproduced
or utilized in any form or by any electronic, mechanical, or other means,
now known or hereafter invented, including photocopying and recording,
or in any information storage or retrieval system, without permission in
writing from the publishers.

Trademark Notice: Product or corporate names may be trademarks or registered trademarks,
and are used only for identification and explanation without intent to infringe.

Library of Congress Cataloging in Publication Data
The curriculum studies reader / David J. Flinders, Stephen J. Thornton, editors. — 3rd ed.
    p. cm.
    Includes index.
    1. Education—Curricula–United States—Philosophy.   2. Curriculum planning—United States.
    3. Curriculum change—United States.   I. Flinders, David J., 1955–   II. Thornton, Stephen J.
    LB1570.C957 2008
    375.000973—dc22
    2008032515

ISBN10: 0–415–96321–4 (hbk)
ISBN10: 0–415–96322–2 (pbk)

ISBN13: 978–0–415–96321–3 (hbk)
ISBN13: 978–0–415–96322–0 (pbk)

Contents

Preface to the Third Edition

Like earlier editions of *The Curriculum Studies Reader*, this third edition is designed as a sourcebook to be used in the study of curriculum theory, practice, and research. As such, it brings together some of the field's most influential writings—works that have proved enduring and central to contemporary educational thought. In selecting this scholarship, our aim has been to identify the broad contours of the field and its characteristic landmarks. What types of problems interest curriculum scholars? What distinguishes the field? What are its central questions and recurrent themes as they relate to educational policy and practice? How do various lines of curriculum inquiry reflect social values, historical trends, and ideological points of view? How do these common values and points of view overlap? How do they differ?

While this third edition of the *Reader* takes a broad perspective on these questions, it does not attempt to assess the field "from above" or remove it from the fray of local and national debates over education. The readings that follow are very much a part of the arguments that mark any serious examination of what children should learn. For this reason, the collection represents highly diverse perspectives and beliefs. We have used this diversity to juxtapose dissimilar and often opposing positions, as our intent is to underscore the field's intricacies and its range of approaches. Whether we view curriculum as an arena of scholarship or as an area of educational practice, we are faced with a complex and often contentious undertaking. Indeed, the hallmarks of the field include unpredictability over inevitability, flexibility over rigidity, and sufficing over idealism. Curriculum studies is a very rich field, but also a messy one.

In addition to capturing the field's dynamic qualities, we also hope the *Reader* brings into focus the intellectual traditions on which contemporary work is built. Our day-to-day experiences of working in various educational settings—experiences of getting to meetings on time, planning projects, conducting lessons, meeting deadlines, getting grades in and the like—can distract us from the underlying foundations and historical traditions that define our profession. We hope that the readings that follow promote a renewed appreciation for the foundations and historical trends that have guided schools. These foundations and trends may be taken for granted, and thus not consciously recognized. However, such larger issues rest just below the surface of what we as educators must grapple with in order to get our work done. We hope the *Reader* draws attention to these issues and to the broad range of truly exceptional thinkers who have struggled to answer curriculum questions, including the perennial question of what knowledge is of most worth.

Several features of the third edition deserve mentioning briefly. As with the first and second editions, we have kept the book's chronological organization, adding only one (albeit an important) piece, by Maria Montessori to Part One. In Part Two we have added a *vs. Traditionalists e.g Tyler / Bobbitt*

reading by Jerome S. Bruner that focuses on *Man: A Course of Study*, a venture that became one of the best known (and most controversial) curriculum development projects of the 1960s. Part Three remains similar in its contents to previous editions, but we have moved excerpts from *How Schools Shortchange Girls* from its earlier placement in Part Four. Now excerpts from that report conclude Part Three. Our reasoning is that while this report remains highly controversial and relevant to contemporary issues, it is rooted in the 1970s and 1980s. These were the decades of the reconceptualist movement and its characteristic concerns over equity and social justice. We have revised Part Four, which focuses on current issues and research, more thoroughly than the other sections. The new additions are meant to update this section of the *Reader* as well as reemphasize the two themes of continuity and change that run throughout the entire collection. Our revisions also bring into sharp focus the more recent entrenchment of standards-based accountability and high-stakes testing. These trends were well underway at the times we published earlier editions of the *Reader*, but they have intensified and broadened their scope in recent years.

wikipedia ↓
William Pinar
Madeleine Grumet
(challenging)
tradition
(characterized by)
behavioral objectives, planning
an evaluation
↓ hub pages

Our final point concerns this development. Today's accountability movement combines standardized, high-stakes testing with the mandates of top-down curriculum planning. The early research and commentary on this trend are now in, but recent work has amplified uncertainties over how well state standards and similar accountability schemes will serve as a means for improving schools. If anything, it seems that the opposite is the case. In particular, recent studies point to the dangers of creating new inequalities and a curriculum marked by hours of mind-numbing test preparation (McNeil, 2000). Scholars increasingly worry that current policies fragment what students learn and thereby reduce schooling to forms of rote memorization. The result tends to remove curriculum from the lives of students and from the concerns of local communities. If teaching to the test becomes the default mode for classroom instruction, and if teachers have no other basis for decision-making, an entire generation of children could suffer. Consequently, these are not times when educators may confidently fall back on unquestioned practices and standard procedures. The dangers of doing so now make an understanding of curriculum traditions more, not less, important to the practical work of teaching, school improvement, and program evaluation.

Similar to Biology food webs

Reference

McNeil, L. M. (2000). Creating new inequalities: Contradictions of reform. *Phi Delta Kappan*, Vol. 81, No. 10, pp. 729–734.

Introduction

What do schools teach, what should they teach, and who should decide? Is the primary aim of education to instill basic skills or foster critical thinking? Should education aim to mold future citizens, transmit national values, engender personal development, or inspire academic achievement? Must education have an aim? And what beliefs, values, or attitudes are learned from the way classrooms are? That is, what lessons are taught but not planned, acquired but taken for granted? These are some of the perennial questions around which curriculum scholars have organized theory, research, teaching, and program evaluation. Collectively, such efforts constitute the academic study of curriculum and the focus of this book.

Although stating the book's focus implies a clearly delineated topic, the field of curriculum studies is anything but narrow. On the contrary, our topic sprawls out like the seemingly endless suburbs of a modern megalopolis. Its wide reach overlaps with every subject area; with cultural, political, and economic trends; with philosophical concerns; and with social issues. In addition, contemporary models of curriculum theory and research draw on increasingly diverse disciplinary perspectives and increasingly diverse inquiry methods. While this diversity can bewilder those unfamiliar with the field's intellectual terrain, others see both the need and the room for still greater diversity. Even without further development, the current range of work makes it useful to adopt broad perspectives from which to identify the field's various regions and familiar landmarks. No one can accurately represent the field from a single perspective. Yet, the trade-offs of accommodation are involved here as well. The more inclusive one's perspective, the more challenging it is to represent the field in ways that clearly illustrate its contributions to educational policy and practice.

Our choice in responding to this challenge is to portray the field, its various regions and familiar landmarks, through the genre of a "reader"—a collection of informed and influential writings. All of the writings in this reader are previously published articles, book chapters, research reports, or excerpts from larger works that sample the past and present trends of curriculum scholarship. The primary advantage of this approach is not comprehensiveness but rather the opportunity it allows for getting close to the ideas and debates that have inspired such wide interest in curriculum studies to begin with. Like other curriculum textbooks, this reader seeks to cast a broad net by attending to the field at large rather than to a certain type of curriculum work or area of specialization. However, the views and perspectives introduced in this collection do not stand above the fray of academic disagreements, arguments, and strongly held convictions.

On the contrary, the reader is intentionally designed to capture some of the contentious

[handwritten margin notes:] Karl Popper quote · trying to get used to / close to the original inspiration

[handwritten bottom notes:] Scientific theories are "nets cast to catch what we call 'the world.' We endeavor to make the mesh ever finer + finer" (Popper 1959 p 59) · SO: Reader looking at "the world" · in NRC pub

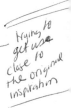

discourse and outright disputes for which the curriculum field is known. This animation of ideas and values plays an important role because it has nurtured the field in unlikely settings and through otherwise lean times. Surprisingly to some, the study of curriculum has held its own, even flourished, when no national crisis demanded an immediate educational response, when no vast infusion of federal dollars poured into research and development, when no mobs of angry parents clamored at the schoolhouse door, and when no technological marvels promised new ways to build better curricular mousetraps. All of these factors have had their day, and many are likely to recur in the future. Yet, with or without any added impetus, the questions of curriculum theory and practice are questions that have captured the imagination of educators and lay people from one generation to the next.

This enduring interest is found in both specific and general curriculum issues, and the writings in this volume also vary with respect to scope. Some readings are broadly conceived around the purposes and politics of schooling in general. Others focus on particular topics such as the use of instructional objectives, high-stakes testing, or heteronormativity. Even the most narrowly focused of these readings, however, illustrate recurrent themes and historical antecedents. Curricular debates, in short, represent intellectual traditions. Furthermore, the issues raised in curriculum studies often cut across a variety of subject areas and levels of education. One could reasonably argue that basic curriculum issues, or at least some of those issues, extend well beyond schooling to include the concerns of anyone interested in how people come to acquire the knowledge, skills, and values they do.

Be that as it may, our collection does focus mainly on the types of learning that are intended to take place in schools and classrooms. These institutional settings simply provide a window onto broader issues. Yet, our focus is still expansive, and as with any book of this kind, the difficult task has been to winnow down an extremely large body of material by selecting only a sample of that material. Having done so, we cannot claim to be representing the field in a comprehensive way. Our challenge reminds us of a common story told among cultural anthropologists. Seasoned ethnographers like to ask their fellow researchers just returning from fieldwork whether they have captured the entire culture of the particular group being studied. The question is asked tongue-in-cheek because all but the most naive know full well the impossibility of learning everything there is to know about other people. Like those returning anthropologists, we are unable to provide a complete or definitive account of all that is going on in the field—the norms, kinships, and relations of curriculum scholarship are simply too complex. This limitation of our work may sound harsh, but it can also be viewed together with another adage from ethnographic research—that we are not required to know everything in order to learn something.

To say that this book was created by sampling a much larger body of scholarship still leaves unanswered the questions of what criteria we used to select that sample. How did we choose some readings over others, and for what reasons? While this process was almost always more ambiguous than anticipated, three concerns stand out as having a prominent influence on our decisions. First, we sought to include work that is well recognized within the field. This criterion is not so much a matter of name recognition as it is a matter of a work's endurance or impact on how others think about curriculum issues. In a few cases, we have included authors (John Dewey or Paulo Freire, for example) who might not be considered curriculum scholars per se, but whose ideas have been so influential to curriculum studies that they can be considered part of the intellectual traditions on which others continue to build.

Writers who achieve this type of legacy also tend to be those who are grappling with

[Handwritten marginal notes:]

why b/c teachers in my opinion b/c of the belief in Quality

"from wikipedia View that involves that involves alignment of biological sex sexuality gender identity and gender roles"

[above] (annotation near "winnow")

ideas and problems that often surface in different areas of curriculum practice. Certain issues and problems are recurrent or even thematic to the point of being recognized as common to the field. We looked for writings that possess this thematic quality because they lend continuity to the particulars of practice, and without that continuity it would be difficult to connect the otherwise broad range of topics on which curriculum scholarship is carried out.

A second consideration in deciding the book's content has been our desire to include pivotal work. This consideration has played out in an effort to identify writings that most clearly signal turning points in the development of the field, or that serve as prototypes for exploring issues previously taken for granted. Exactly what constitutes ground-breaking work is conceptually difficult to pin down. Nevertheless, our aim is to represent not only the continuity of the field but also its dynamic qualities. The field is constantly changing, if not always in its underlying philosophical concerns, then in the field's ways of responding to concerns as they take on new shades of emphasis. Topics come and go as well, and some specific developments of current interest such as AIDS education or No Child Left Behind could not have been fully anticipated by earlier generations.

The first two considerations we have mentioned concern the conceptual foundations and development of the field. Our third consideration differs by emphasizing pedagogy. Because we teach curriculum courses at both the undergraduate and graduate levels, we often found our attention drawn to work that is accessible across a wide audience. In part, this means we have tried to select examples of scholarship that avoid the jargon of education and its associated disciplines. Much of the work in curriculum studies is and should be intellectually challenging, but some of that work (as in all fields) is challenging for reasons unnecessary to understanding its subject matter. We hope to have avoided the latter, sampling only from the most accessible work available.

The final issue we want to address concerns the organization of the book's content. Overall, the readings are divided chronologically into four parts. Part One, "Looking Back: A Prologue to Curriculum Studies," is centered on the work of five prominent figures: Franklin Bobbitt, Maria Montessori, John Dewey, Jane Addams, and George S. Counts. Their writings are brought together with a classic historical critique that introduces some of the early traditions of curriculum scholarship. Not only are all of these readings worth revisiting from time to time, but they also serve to provide enough historical information for new students of curriculum to start to appreciate the antecedents and changing social contexts in which the field's contemporary theories are rooted.

Part Two, "Curriculum at Education's Center Stage," sets out to illustrate the optimism and contradictions of an era marked by unparalleled national support for curriculum reform. Whatever complacency Americans had about education seemed to vanish with the launch of Sputnik I in 1957. For almost two decades after that event, hardly anyone questioned the need and urgency for large-scale curriculum reforms. Yet, this same period is remembered for an increasing sense of uneasiness within the field. Debates grew over how curriculum work should be carried out, earlier traditions became the targets of some criticism, and greater scrutiny was given to the field's underlying purposes.

These undertones of discontent were not short-lived. On the contrary, in many ways they presaged the soon-to-blossom critical and reconceptualist movements. Among other achievements, the reconceptualists, together with the open education movement, brought into focus the sociocultural and personal dimensions of curriculum with greater emphasis and clarity than had earlier generations. The efforts to achieve this are represented in Part Three, "Reconceptualizing Curriculum Theory." This section, however, is not limited to

[handwritten margin notes: recognized / thematic / Pivotal / Accessible]

reconceptualist thought, which in and of itself is quite diverse. While curriculum studies had taken a reflective turn that is today very much alive and well, the field's most conventional scholarship did not stop simply because other ways of understanding that scholarship were made more readily available. To put this another way, the field seemed to annex new territory rather than move its location.

This annexation of various topics, ideas, and perspectives is examined as a contemporary issue in Part Four, "After a Century of Curriculum Thought." Our aim in this section is to suggest the various ways in which current scholarship reflects both the change and continuity of the field. The readings we have selected to represent these perspectives may at first seem unbridled, which is exactly how some people have come to view curriculum studies. Topics range from postmodernism to the growing debate over national standards. We have selected these readings to illustrate in as concrete a way as possible the breadth of issues on which today's curriculum scholars work, and at the same time, how this work builds on previous traditions.

If we were pressed to summarize what this final set of readings has to say about the current state of the field and its future directions, we would have to fall back on the truism that "much changes while staying the same." But that comment is not at all meant to be glib. Changes in both the tenor and focus of contemporary work make a difference in what receives attention and what does not. In this way, such trends make a difference in discussions of educational policy and practice, and in the levels of sophistication at which these discussions are carried out. In current decision making at the levels of research, policy and practice, informed points of view are valued by those engaged in such work. If anything, the need for informed scholarship today seems by past benchmarks to be increasingly urgent.

Part One

Looking Back: A Prologue to Curriculum Studies

Introduction to Part One

Curriculum theorizing and development are as old as educating institutions because any educational program must have a content. Although theorists and practitioners have (perhaps without conscious awareness) dealt with curriculum questions since at least the time of Plato's design for education in his ideal state, the notion of curriculum as a professional or scholarly field is recent. Historically, curriculum decisions were largely left to that small, usually elite, portion of the public most directly concerned with the operation of schools. In the United States, curriculum began to emerge as a field of scholarly inquiry and professional practice only toward the close of the nineteenth century, a time that roughly coincided with the rise of public schooling for the masses.

The burgeoning population of the public schools at the dawn of the twentieth century was only one of a number of tumultuous and consequential developments in American life. One result of all this upheaval was the Progressive movement, a broad based effort aimed at assuring the realization of American ideals in an increasingly urban-industrial and pluralistic nation (Cremin, 1964, pp. 8–10). Thus, the first self-conscious curriculum scholars saw their work as part of this broader reformation of American life. The responses of the progressive educational reformers were to institutionalize many of the now characteristic features of school curriculum, including such practices as tracking, standardized testing, and civic education (Tyack, 1974).

Although early curriculum specialists frequently perceived themselves as "progressives," these educational reformers, like their fellow progressives in politics and other fields, worked with diverse, even contradictory, conceptions of what "progressive" meant (see Curti, 1959; Kliebard, 1995; Lagemann, 2000). Thus, from its earliest days, the curriculum field has been characterized by vigorous disagreements about its proper aims and practices. For example, the various meanings assigned by curriculum specialists to terms such as "learning" and "democracy" are not merely esoteric concerns without consequences for the world of practice. To the contrary, how one defines terms to a great extent determines the resulting character of education.

The first set of readings we introduce includes five of the early formulations of the curriculum field as represented in the work of Franklin Bobbitt, Maria Montessori, John Dewey, Jane Addams, and George S. Counts. Each of these formulations retains an important contemporary presence in curriculum scholarship (see Eisner, 2002). In this sense, conflicting conceptions of curriculum have never been an aberration in the field. On the contrary, differing views have been present since the very first generation of curriculum scholarship. Indeed, the work of the first three early scholars we will encounter, Franklin Bobbitt, Maria Montessori and John Dewey, exemplify how different archetypes of

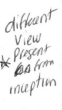

the meaning of "curriculum" result in radically different views of educational aims and practice.

When he wrote *The Curriculum* (1918), Bobbitt was a professor at the University of Chicago as well as a sought-after curriculum consultant to school districts across the nation. He is an apt starting point for tracing the development of professional curriculum scholarship and practice in North America as the essentials of his approach to curriculum have been dominant in practice ever since. Moreover, Bobbitt was a self-proclaimed pioneer of the field. He asserts in the excerpt reproduced in this volume to be writing the "first" curriculum textbook. Although it is not self-evident what constitutes the "first" curriculum textbook, Bobbitt's claim is often conceded. In any case, there is no doubt that Bobbitt's *The Curriculum* has had enduring influence, particularly in its insistence that curriculum developers begin with the identification of proper goals. "Pioneer" implies finding one's way in unfamiliar terrain, but Bobbitt seems to have had few doubts that he was headed in the right direction. He epitomized the "can-do" attitude of the new professional elites of the Progressive era, a time when professionals in a variety of fields were increasingly considered the preferred means by which a forward-looking society addressed its problems. Bobbitt was quite sure of what ailed curriculum making: for too long it had been in the hands of amateurs and it was high time it became a professional undertaking.

Bobbitt was convinced that professional knowledge applicable to curriculum work could be found in the logic of "scientific management," which had been applied to raising worker productivity in industry (Callahan, 1962, pp. 79–94). In a nutshell, Bobbitt believed that curriculum work, like work in industry, should be managed in the interests of efficiency and the elimination of waste. These same interests after all, it seemed obvious to Bobbitt and many of his contemporaries, in significant respects accounted for the world preeminence of United States manufacturing industry. Use of the same methods would bring the same world-class standards to the school curriculum.

Bobbitt's claim that curriculum work was out of date, having not kept pace with other advances in schooling, is almost poignant. *The Curriculum* was Bobbitt's solution to this unfortunate state of affairs. As he makes plain in the preface, he proposed to lay out how curriculum can be constructed in a manner that honors scientific procedures. For Bobbitt, "scientific" suggested a systematic series of procedures, carried out by curriculum professionals, prior to implementation in a school district (see Eisner, 1985).

The content of any given curriculum, according to Bobbitt, could be "discovered" by a process of surveying what successful adults know and can do (Bobbitt, this volume, Chapter 1). In turn, the results of this process of discovery would be used to formulate educational objectives from which the curriculum scope and sequence (i.e., what is taught and in what order) would be derived to address where students fell short of successful adults. After instruction with this kind of curriculum, he believed, students would be prepared to lead successful lives in their adult years.

Efficiency, of course, suggests not only smooth operating procedures but minimization of "waste" as well. Thus, in addition to scientific curriculum making, Bobbitt wanted to minimize sources of wasted instructional time. He believed that diagnostic testing and other procedures proposed by behavioral psychologists such as Edward L. Thorndike would make possible prediction of the kind of errors students typically made. This would enable more efficient curriculum making as well as prevent unnecessary time being spent on the costly business of instruction, especially grade-level retention of students which Bobbitt considered enormously wasteful. As in industrial enterprises, Bobbitt wanted to maximize output (i.e., student learning) at minimum cost (i.e., paying teachers).

[handwritten margin note: Couldn't corporate make the same argument now]

This outlook also held significance for the content of the curriculum. Bobbitt believed that "the shortcomings of children and men" in subjects such as spelling and grammar were "obvious" and hence these fields needed to be included in the curriculum. It was less apparent to Bobbitt, however, what shortcomings were overcome by "social" subjects such as literature, history, and geography. He urged attention to identifying significant educational objectives to which these social subjects could contribute (Bobbitt, this volume).

Because Bobbitt's approach to curriculum work was based, he argued, on a dispassionate analysis of what youngsters needed to lead productive lives as adults, he dismissed arguments about the interests of children as irrelevant to the educational process. Moreover, Bobbitt did not question whether the existing social and economic order was just; he merely took that for granted. Hence, he saw the aim of schooling as matching individuals with the existing social and economic order (Lagemann, 2000, p. 107).

The second reading in Part One is by Italian educator and physician Maria Montessori. This figure shares at least one interest with Bobbitt; that being the relationship between science and education. Like Bobbitt, Montessori took a progressive stance in wanting to help design more modern conditions for schools via "scientific pedagogy." She saw education as following in the footsteps of medicine to "pass the purely speculative stage and base its conclusions on the positive results of experimentation" (this volume, Chapter 2). In addition, systematic inquiry is at the heart of what today has become widely known as the Montessori Method. Beyond these points, however, the similarities between Bobbitt and Montessori end and their differences begin.

Unlike Bobbitt, Montessori explicitly cautions against the dangers of applying science too literally to the education of children. Montessori locates these dangers in a tension that would follow curriculum work throughout the twentieth century. This tension is found in the differences between the specialized interests of the scientist and the social interests of the educator. For Montessori, educators needed the science of the clinician, not the science of aloof professionals removed from the day-to-day practical affairs of working with children. In the most useful view of science, child study through the fields of anthropology and psychology could inform but not substitute for sound pedagogy. By way of example, Montessori cites the extreme practice of designing student desks based purely on the measurements of children's physical characteristics. The result is children rigidly fastened in straight rows of desks with little or no room for natural movement. For Montessori, such artificial arrangements invoked the image of a display box of butterflies mounted on pins in their perfect lifelessness. She uses this image to emphasize that any use of science in education must be guided by broader purposes—purposes which she argues can be found in the concept of social liberty.

Another contrast with Bobbitt is that Montessori's approach elevates and transforms the role of classroom teachers. In Bobbitt's system, teachers were given a curriculum prior to instruction, a curriculum designed by a new brand of professional known as curriculum developers or curriculum workers. Montessori's teachers, on the other hand, were charged with creating developmental activities and classroom arrangements based on careful observations of the children in their care. For Montessori, it was not a matter of technical methods but rather attentive observations and the desire to learn that signaled the true spirit of scientific pedagogy.

A final point of difference between these two educational thinkers concerns the place of student interests. For Bobbitt, the needs of the individual were determined by the demands of adult life. Thus, curriculum designers looked to society while individual interests were largely irrelevant to their task. For Montessori, personal interests and talents represented important opportunities for development, and as such they should be nurtured. She makes this point specifically in relation to the use of rewards and prizes as ways to motivate or control children. Montessori (this volume) writes:

> Everyone has as special tendency, a special vocation, modest perhaps, but certainly useful. The system of prizes may turn an individual aside from this vocation, may make him choose a false road, for him a vain one, and forced to follow it, the natural activity of a human being may be warped, lessened, even annihilated.

John Dewey's "My Pedagogic Creed," which follows Montessori's chapter, echoes similar concerns regarding the interests of students and their role in education. In doing so, Dewey's view of curriculum again provides a contrast with Bobbitt's industrial model. Where Bobbitt argued that adult society is the mold for the school curriculum, Dewey (this volume, Chapter 3) said such a view "results in subordinating the freedom of the individual to a preconceived social and political status." "True education," Dewey insisted, "comes through the stimulation of the child's powers by the demands of the social situations in which he finds himself." Reliance on behaviorist methods to Dewey signified external imposition whose effects "cannot truly be called educative." Indeed, Dewey pointed out the worth of subject matter could only be determined by its educational uses. For example, Dewey (this volume) questioned the value of history as school subject if it was the customary "inert" study of "the distant past." But Dewey maintained history "becomes full of meaning" if "taken as the record of man's social life and progress . . . as the child is introduced . . . directly into social life."

The distinctions Dewey drew, although consequential, are frequently subtle as Dewey spoke the unfamiliar language of reform, of education as a means of extending and reforming democratic, community life in the United States. The relative novelty of his language and views may help explain why Dewey's theory of curriculum has been often and widely misunderstood, even by those purporting to be his followers. In this regard, he wrote *Experience and Education* (1938) toward the end of his career because he believed, for example, his insistence on curriculum planning beginning with the experience of the child was being wrongly interpreted as disdain for the "progressive organization of subject-matter." Similarly, Dewey emphasized that starting with the experience of the child, far from producing laissez-faire classroom arrangements, increased rather than replaced the demands on judgment by the teacher in directing each pupil's learning toward worthwhile goals.

What would Dewey's ideal curriculum look like in practice? Although too lengthy a question to answer fully here, probably the most authentic answer can be obtained by examination of the laboratory school Dewey established and oversaw during his years at the University of Chicago (see Mayhew & Edwards, 1966; Tanner, 1997). In broad terms, Dewey's curriculum broke down the barriers, customary in schools a century ago as well as today, between children's life experiences and their experiences in the classroom. Hence, the heart of the curriculum would be activities based on a simplification of "existing social life." In this scheme of things, boundaries between traditional school subjects would be traversed. Children might, for example, examine how the local community deals with its problems and, in this context, develop measuring skills ordinarily assigned to mathematics, drawing skills ordinarily assigned to art, map skills ordinarily assigned to geography, and so forth. The logical organization of school subjects, Dewey insisted, was the organizational schema of adults; children require the "psychological" organization of subject matter, moving gradually toward adult modes of understanding associated with formal school subjects.

In sum, the school for Dewey was an integral part of community life; it was also an instrument for social reform. Whereas the followers of Bobbitt saw the school as an agent of social adaptation to the status quo, Dewey (this volume) portrayed "the school as the primary and most effective interest of social progress and reform." Just as there should be no strict boundary between the curriculum and community life, Dewey believed the curriculum held the potential for society to remake itself. ⚹

Jane Addams, friend and collaborator of Dewey, also saw no sharp boundary between the curriculum and democratic community life. In 1889 Addams and her longtime associate, Helen Gates Starr, established a social settlement, Hull House, in Chicago's West Side slums. While Dewey's curriculum thought was mainly directed at formal schooling, the primary site of Addams' work was Hull House and its adjacent community. As Richard Bernstein (1967, p. 34) observed, while Dewey brought "the theory and methods of social philosophy to bear on the concrete facts," Hull-House "provided him with the 'facts' ". Moreover, as Ellen Condliffe Lagemann (1994, p. xiii) has noted, Addams' location outside of the academy "enabled her to develop and sustain an approach to social analysis that was broad, synthetic, and problem- as opposed to discipline- or profession-centered."

Hull House reached out to immigrants, to laborers, to mothers and children, to all in an urban-industrial community who needed or wanted its educational and social programs. Celebrated almost from the beginning, Hull House aimed through its educational programs to address the range of problems and aspirations of ordinary and needy people in an era when public schools often appeared inadequate to the task. Although Addams wrote and spoke widely about education, she considered these activities no substitute for the direct caring she saw as necessary (Noddings, 2001, p. 184). As Addams wrote in her autobiographical *Twenty Years At Hull-House*, first published in 1910, she believed she was filling educational needs that were otherwise either unrecognized or unmet:

> It sometimes seems that the men of substantial scholarship were content to leave to the charlatan the teaching of those things which deeply concern the welfare of mankind. . . . A settlement soon discovers that simple people are interested in large and vital subjects. . . .
> (Addams, 1961, p. 282)

Hull House strove to value both the traditions immigrants brought to the United States and necessary adjustments to their new environment. "The ignorant teacher," Addams wrote, "cuts [immigrant children] off" from their parents and their parents' traditions, while "the cultivated teacher fastens them because his own mind is open to the charm and beauty of the old-country life." It is therefore not surprising that Addams understood that a one-size-fits-all curriculum to "Americanize" immigrants may not fit the needs of any individual. Coercion was not part of her stock in trade.

Rather, through provision of choice and individualization, the extraordinary breadth of Hull House curricular offerings aimed to both expand student horizons and connect to their aspirations and needs. But these ambitious goals were as far as possible harmonized with the community. Courses were offered in cooking, arithmetic, history, athletics, clay modeling, English for Italians, and many other subject matters. As well, classes were offered on writers such as Dante, Browning, and Shakespeare and a Plato club and Dr. Dewey lecturing on social psychology were made available to "groups consisting largely of people from the immediate neighborhood" (Addams, this volume, Chapter 4).

Although fully supportive of the exceptional community member who was college-bound, more fundamentally Hull House aimed to "connect him with all sorts of people by his ability to understand them as well by his power to supplement their present surroundings with the historic background" (Addams, 1961, pp. 284–285).

Since at least Addams' time, great significance and considerable disagreement has been attached to the connection of cultural pluralism and the school curriculum. The educational program enacted at Hull House in this regard has always held the potential to inform discussion of this issue. Its curriculum modeled how to foster intergenerational and intercultural communication, open-minded and balanced debate, and the relationship of education to community betterment. As Nel Noddings (2001, p. 185) writes:

> Life at Hull House was proof that people could cooperate, actually live together, despite differences of religion, nationality and economic status. There were no ideological tests at Hull House beyond the common commitment to improve the neighborhood, Chicago and, more generally, the lives of working people.

If building a more humane and democratic society was integral to Dewey's and Addams' theories of curriculum, it was almost the singular goal of George S. Counts. From the time of his earliest, major works in the 1920s, Counts was concerned with the injustices of democracy and capitalism in the United States, particularly as they played out in the context of schooling (see Kliebard, 1995, pp. 158–159). Like Dewey, Counts grew increasingly restive with "child-centered," progressive educators who appeared to be ignoring the social context of education in the business-dominated atmosphere of the 1920s. For Counts, the seemingly dominant stream of progressive education spoke to the "needs" of the child as though these had meaning outside of the society in which education unfolded.

The catastrophic economic slump of the 1930s ushered in a much more receptive environment for the disenchanted intellectual critics of the business civilization of the 1920s. American social thought became more polarized, and collectivist thought enjoyed possibly its most widespread popularity in the history of the United States (see Bowers, 1969). Counts (this volume, Chapter 5) caught the spirit of the times when he remarked in *Dare the School Build a New Social Order?* (1932) that "the so-called 'practical' men of our generation—the politicians, the financiers, the industrialists" had acted selfishly and bungled the well-being of Americans. Counts appealed for teachers to lead the schools and the public "for social regeneration." For Counts and his fellow social reconstructionists, several of the most prominent of whom such as Harold Rugg were Counts' colleagues at Teachers College, Columbia University, it seemed apparent that the age of collectivism had arrived.

Aspects of Counts' vision of a regulated and directed economy in order to serve more than society's elite were, of course, consistent with the more radical elements of the New Deal yet to come. Indeed, it is a sign of how Counts was in touch with the times that later some of his main ideas were to find their parallels in the words and policies of President Franklin D. Roosevelt during the early New Deal years. Nevertheless, given what he viewed as the failure of individualism in American life, Counts looked to school curriculum as a place to inculcate collectivist ideas. Counts maintained that all school programs already inculcated ideas, but those ideas had been ones that primarily served the interests of the ruling classes. As Counts (this volume) put it, "the real question is not whether imposition will take place, but rather from what source it will come."

Counts' theory of curriculum found a ready audience during the depths of the Great

Depression in the early 1930s. For example, he and his colleague, the historian Charles A. Beard, were dominant forces in the Commission on the Social Studies, which had been established by the American Historical Association to make recommendations for the schools. The commission's reports, although stopping short of formulating an actual curriculum, nonetheless leaned heavily toward an activist-oriented social studies curriculum consonant with the tenets of social reconstructionism. Furthermore, beginning in the 1920s, Rugg oversaw the development of social studies curriculum materials that were based to some extent on social reconstructionist principles. In contrast to most available materials, their explicit focus was on the problems of American life (see Thornton, 2001). Rugg's materials became bestsellers and were widely adopted across the United States, all the more remarkable given the economic hard times faced by school districts during the 1930s.

Rugg's social studies materials probably mark the greatest success of the social reconstructionists in the implementation of their ideas in school programs. As the Great Depression and the New Deal waned, however, Rugg's textbooks came under growing fire from conservative groups. For this and other reasons, the series eventually fell out of favor. Almost the same fate befell social reconstructionism itself as the 1930s wore on and World War II approached. Conservative criticism and the changing climate of educational opinion increasingly shifted Counts and other social reconstructionists from at or near the center of educational debate to a more peripheral position (Kliebard, 1995, pp. 176–178). Nevertheless, the flame of social reconstructionism in educational thought was never entirely extinguished and was, as we shall see, visible again in the 1970s and after.

Before leaving Counts, however, it should be noted that his view of curriculum attracted criticism not only from educational and political traditionalists. No less a progressive figure than Dewey, while sympathizing with some of Counts' collectivist goals, found parts of Counts' curriculum thinking worrisome. For example, Dewey always championed teaching students to think for themselves. From this perspective, the preordained ends of Counts' "imposition" seemed hard to distinguish from indoctrination.

To round out this first section, we have included a well-known essay by curriculum historian Herbert Kliebard (1975) dealing with the early years of the curriculum field. Kliebard's focus is the influence of "scientific" curriculum making. We have already noted that the scientific strain of curriculum thought has tended to be dominant ever since the field's inception, and although Kliebard's piece is now over thirty years old, it is particularly relevant today. Specifically, Kliebard concludes that "scientific" approaches to curriculum and other educational matters have come to pervade and continue to shape educational thought and practice—a conclusion that is as germane today as it was in the 1970s.

References

Addams, J. (1961). *Twenty years at Hull-House.* New York: Signet Classic.
Bernstein, R. J. (1967). *John Dewey.* New York: Washington Square Press.
Bowers, C. A. (1969). *The progressive educator and the Depression.* New York: Random House.
Callahan, R. E. (1962). *Education and the cult of efficiency.* Chicago: University of Chicago Press.
Cremin, L. A. (1964). *The transformation of the school.* New York: Vintage.
Curti, M. (1959). *The social ideas of American educators, with a new chapter on the last twenty-five years.* Totowa, NJ: Littlefield, Adams.
Dewey, J. (1938). *Experience and education.* New York: Macmillan.

Eisner, E. W. (1985). Franklin Bobbitt and the "science" of curriculum making. In E. W. Eisner (ed.), *The art of educational evaluation* (pp. 13–28). London: Falmer.

Eisner, E. W. (2002). *The educational imagination* (3rd ed.). Upper Saddle River, NJ: Merrill Prentice Hall.

Kliebard, H. M. (1995). *The struggle for the American curriculum, 1893–1958* (2nd ed.). New York: Routledge.

Lagemann, E. C. (1994). Introduction to the Transaction edition: "Why read Jane Addams?" In Jane Addams, *On education* (pp. vii–xvii). New Brunswick, NJ: Transaction Publishers.

Lagemann, E. C. (2000). *An elusive science: The troubling history of education research.* Chicago: University of Chicago Press.

Mayhew, K. C., & Edwards, A. C. (1966). *The Dewey school.* New York: Atherton.

Noddings, N. (2001). Jane Addams, 1860–1935. In J. A. Palmer (ed.), *Fifty major thinkers on education: From Confucius to Dewey* (pp. 182–187). London: Routledge.

Tanner, L. M. (1997). *Dewey's laboratory school.* New York: Teachers College Press.

Thornton, S. J. (2001). Harold Rugg, 1886–1960. In J. A. Palmer (ed.), *Fifty modern thinkers on education: From Piaget to the present* (pp. 10–15). London: Routledge.

Tyack, D. B. (1974). *The one best system.* Cambridge, MA: Harvard University Press.

1

Scientific Method in Curriculum-Making

Franklin Bobbitt

Since the opening of the twentieth century, the evolution of our social order has been proceeding with great and ever-accelerating rapidity. Simple conditions have been growing complex. Small institutions have been growing large. Increased specialization has been multiplying human interdependencies and the consequent need of coordinating effort. Democracy is increasing within the Nation; and growing throughout the world. All classes are aspiring to a full human opportunity. Never before have civilization and humanization advanced so swiftly.

As the world presses eagerly forward toward the accomplishment of new things, education also must advance no less swiftly. It must provide the intelligence and the aspirations necessary for the advance; and for stability and consistency in holding the gains. Education must take a pace set, not by itself, but by social progress.

The present program of public education was mainly formulated during the simpler conditions of the nineteenth century. In details it has been improved. In fundamentals it is not greatly different. A program never designed for the present day has been inherited.

Any inherited system, good for its time, when held to after its day, hampers social progress. It is not enough that the system, fundamentally unchanged in plan and purpose, be improved in details. In education this has been done in conspicuous degree. Our schools today are better than ever before. Teachers are better trained. Supervision is more adequate. Buildings and equipment are enormously improved. Effective methods are being introduced, and time is being economized. Improvements are visible on every hand. And yet to do the nineteenth-century task better than it was then done is not necessarily to do the twentieth-century task.

New duties lie before us. And these require new methods, new materials, new vision. The old education, except as it conferred the tools of knowledge, was mainly devoted to filling the memory with facts. The new age is more in need of facts than the old; and of more facts; and it must find more effective methods of teaching them. But there are now other functions. Education is now to develop a type of wisdom that can grow only out of participation in the living experiences of men, and never out of mere memorization of verbal statements of facts. It must, therefore, train thought and judgment in connection with actual life-situations, a task distinctly different from the cloistral activities of the past. It is also to develop the goodwill, the spirit of service, the social valuations, sympathies, and attitudes of mind necessary for effective group-action where specialization has created endless interdependency. It has the function of training every citizen, man or woman, not for knowledge about citizenship, but for proficiency in citizenship; not for knowledge about hygiene, but for proficiency in maintaining robust health; not for a mere knowledge of abstract science, but for proficiency in the use of ideas in the control of practical situations. Most of these are new tasks. In connection with each, much is now being done in all progressive school systems; but most of them yet are but partially developed. We have been developing knowledge, not function; the power to reproduce facts, rather than the powers to think and feel and will and act in vital relation to the world's life. Now we must look to these latter things as well.

Our task in this volume is to point out some of the new duties. We are to show why education must now undertake tasks that until recently were not considered needful; why new methods, new materials, and new types of experience must be employed. We here try to develop a point of view that seems to be needed by practical school men and women as they make the educational adjustments now demanded by social conditions; and needed also by scientific workers who are seeking to define with accuracy the objectives of education. It is the feeling of the writer that in the social reconstructions of the post-war years that lie just ahead of us, education is to be called upon to bear a hitherto undreamed-of burden of responsibility; and to undertake unaccustomed labors. To present some of the theory needed for the curriculum labors of this new age has been the task herein attempted.

This is a first book in a field that until recently has been too little cultivated. For a long time, we have been developing the theory of educational method, both general and special; and we have required teachers and supervisors to be thoroughly cognizant of it. Recently, however, we have discerned that there is a theory of curriculum-formulation that is no less extensive and involved than that of method; and that it is just as much needed by teachers and supervisors. To know what to do is as important as to know how to do it. This volume, therefore, is designed for teacher-training institutions as an introductory textbook in the theory of the curriculum; and for reading circles in the training of teachers in service. It is hoped also that it may assist the general reader who is interested in noting recent educational tendencies.

The technique of curriculum-making along scientific lines has been but little developed. The controlling purposes of education have not been sufficiently particularized. We have aimed at a vague culture, an ill-defined discipline, a nebulous harmonious development of the individual, an indefinite moral character-building, an unparticularized social efficiency, or, often enough nothing more than escape from a life of work. Often there are no controlling purposes; the momentum of the educational machine keeps it running. So long as objectives are but vague guesses, or not even that, there can be no demand for anything but vague guesses as to means and procedure. But the era of contentment with large, undefined purposes is rapidly passing. An age of science is demanding exactness and particularity.

The technique of scientific method is at present being developed for every important aspect of education. Experimental laboratories and schools are discovering accurate methods of measuring and evaluating different types of educational processes. Bureaus of educational measurement are discovering scientific methods of analyzing results, of diagnosing specific situations, and of prescribing remedies. Scientific method is being applied to the fields of budget-making, child-accounting, systems of grading and promotion, etc.

The curriculum, however, is a primordial factor. If it is wrongly drawn up on the basis merely of guess and personal opinion, all of the science in the world applied to the factors above enumerated will not make the work efficient. The scientific task preceding all others is the determination of the curriculum. For this we need a scientific technique. At present this is being rapidly developed in connection with various fields of training.

The central theory is simple. Human life, however varied, consists in the performance of specific activities. Education that prepares for life is one that prepares definitely and adequately for these specific activities. However numerous and diverse they may be for any social class, they can be discovered. This requires only that one go out into the world of affairs and discover the particulars of which these affairs consist. These will show the abilities, attitudes, habits, appreciations, and forms of knowledge that men need. These will be the objectives of the curriculum. They will be numerous, definite, and particularized. The curriculum will then be that series of experiences which children and youth must have by way of attaining those objectives.

The word *curriculum* is Latin for a *race-course*, or the *race* itself—a place of deeds, or a series of deeds. As applied to education, it is that *series of things which children and youth must do and experience* by way of developing abilities to do the things well that make up the affairs of adult life; and to be in all respects what adults should be. *[experience included]*

The developmental experiences exist upon two levels. On the one hand, there is the general experience of living the community life, without thought of the training values. In this way, through participation, one gets much of his education for participation in community life. In many things this provides most of the training; and in all essential things, much of it. But in all fields, this incidental or undirected developmental experience leaves the training imperfect. It is necessary, therefore, to supplement it with the conscious directed training of systematized education. The first level we shall call undirected training; and the second, directed training.

The curriculum may, therefore, be defined in two ways: (1) it is the entire range of experiences, both undirected and directed, concerned in unfolding the abilities of the individual; or (2) it is the series of consciously directed training experiences that the schools use for completing and perfecting the unfoldment. Our profession uses the term usually in the latter sense. But as education is coming more and more to be seen as a thing of experiences, and as the work- and play-experiences of general community life are being more and more utilized, the line of demarcation between directed and undirected training experience is rapidly disappearing. Education must be concerned with both, even though it does not direct both. *[2 definitions of curriculum]* *[Now its back "]*

When the curriculum is defined as including both directed and undirected experiences, then its objectives are the total range of human abilities, habits, systems of knowledge, etc., that one should possess. These will be discovered by analytic survey. The curriculum-discoverer will first be an analyst of human nature and of human affairs. His task at this point is not at all concerned with "the studies"—later he will draw up appropriate studies as *means*, but he will not analyze the tools to be used in a piece of work as a mode of discovering the objectives of that work. His first task rather, in ascertaining the education appropriate for any special class, is to discover the total range of habits, skills, abilities, forms of thought, valuations, ambitions, etc., that its members need for the effective performance of their vocational labors; likewise, the total range needed for their civic activities; their health activities; their recreations; their language; their parental, religious, and general social activities. The program of analysis will be no narrow one. It will be wide as life itself. As it thus finds all the things that make up the mosaic of full-formed human life, it discovers the full range of educational objectives. *[holistic]* *[① access what is needed to become educated citizen workers]*

Notwithstanding the fact that many of these objectives are attained without conscious effort, the curriculum-discoverer must have all of them before him for his labors. Even though the scholastic curriculum will not find it necessary to aim at all of them, it is the function of education to see that all of them are attained. Only as he looks to the entire series can he discover the ones that require conscious effort. He will be content to let as much as possible be taken care of through undirected experiences. Indeed he will strive for such conditions that a maximum amount of the training can be so taken care of.

The curriculum of the schools will aim at those objectives that are not sufficiently attained as a result of the general undirected experience. This is to recognize that the total range of specific educational objectives breaks up into two sets: one, those arrived at through one's general experiences without his taking thought as to the training; the other, those that are imperfectly or not at all attained through such general experience. The latter are revealed, and distinguished from the former, by the presence of imperfections, errors, shortcomings. Like the symptoms of disease, these point unerringly to those objectives that require the systematized labors of directed training. Deficiencies point to the ends of conscious education. As the specific objectives upon which education is to be focused are thus pointed out, we are shown where the curriculum of the directed training is to be developed.

Let us illustrate. One of the most important things in which one is to be trained is the effective use of the mother-tongue. It is possible to analyze one's language activities and find all of the things one must do in effectively and correctly using it. Each of these things then becomes an objective of the training. But it is not necessary consciously to train for each of them. Let an individual grow up in a cultivated language-atmosphere, and he will learn to do, and be sufficiently practiced in doing, most of them, without any directed training. Here and there he will make mistakes. *Each mistake is a call for directed training.*

The curriculum of the directed training is to be discovered in the shortcomings of individuals after they have had all that can be given by the undirected training. This principle is recognized in the recent work of many investigators as to the curriculum of grammar. One of the earliest studies was that of Professor Charters.[1] Under his direction, the teachers of Kansas City undertook to discover the errors made by pupils in their oral and written language. For the oral errors the teachers carried notebooks for five days of one week and jotted down every grammatical error which they heard made by any pupil at any time during the day. For the errors in writing they examined the written work of the pupils for a period of three weeks. They discovered twenty-one types of errors in the oral speech and twenty-seven types in the written. The oral errors in the order of their frequency were as follows:—

1. Confusion of past tense and past participle	24
2. Failure of verb to agree with its subject in number and person	14
3. Wrong verb	12
4. Double negative	11
5. Syntactical redundance	10
6. Wrong sentence form	5
7. Confusion of adjectives and adverbs	4
8. Subject of verb not in nominative case	4
9. Confusion of demonstrative adjective with personal pronoun	3
10. Predicate nominative not in nominative case	2
11. First personal pronoun standing first in a series	2
12. Wrong form of noun or pronoun	2
13. Confusion of past and present tenses	2
14. Object of verb or preposition not in the objective case	1
15. Wrong part of speech due to a similarity of sound	1
16. Incorrect comparison of adjectives	1

17. Failure of the pronoun to agree with its antecedent   0.3
18. Incorrect use of mood   0.3
19. Misplaced modifier   0.3
20. Confusion of preposition and conjunction   0.2
21. Confusion of comparatives and superlatives   0.1

Each error discovered is a symptom of grammatical ignorance, wrong habit, imperfect valuation, or careless attitude toward one's language. The nature of the deficiency points to the abilities and dispositions that are to be developed in the child by way of bringing about the use of the correct forms. Each grammatical shortcoming discovered, therefore, points to a needed objective of education. It points to a development of knowledge or attitude which the general undirected language experience has not sufficiently accomplished; and which must therefore be consciously undertaken by the schools.

Scientific method must consider both levels of the grammar curriculum. One task is to provide at the school as much as possible of a cultivated language-atmosphere in which the children can live and receive unconscious training. This is really the task of major importance, and provides the type of experience that should accomplish an ever-increasing proportion of the training. The other task is to make children conscious of their errors, to teach the grammar needed for correction or prevention, and to bring the children to put their grammatical knowledge to work in eliminating the errors. In proportion as the other type of experience is increased, this conscious training will play a diminishing role.

In the spelling field, Ayres, Jones, Cook and O'Shea, and others have been tabulating the words that children and adults use in writing letters, reports, compositions, etc. In this way they have been discovering the particularized objectives of training in spelling. But words are of unequal difficulty. Most are learned in the course of the reading and writing experience of the children without much conscious attention to the spelling. But here and there are words that are not so learned. Investigations, therefore, lay special emphasis upon the words that are misspelled. Each misspelled word reveals a directed-curriculum task. Here, as in the grammar, error is the symptom of training need; and the complete error-list points unerringly to the curriculum of conscious training.

In the vocational field, and on the technical side only, Indianapolis has provided an excellent example of method of discovering the objectives of training. Investigators, without pre-suppositions as to content of vocational curriculum, set out to discover the major occupations of the city, the processes to be performed in each, and the knowledge, habits and skills needed for effective work. They talked with expert workmen; and observed the work-processes. In their report, for each occupation, they present: (1) a list of tools and machines with which a workman must be skillful; (2) a list of the materials used in the work with which workers need to be familiar; (3) a list of items of general knowledge needed concerning jobs and processes; (4) the kinds of mathematical operations actually employed in the work; (5) the items or portions of science needed for control of processes; (6) the elements of drawing and design actually used in the work; (7) the characteristics of the English needed where language is vitally involved in one's work, as in commercial occupations; (8) elements of hygiene needed for keeping one's self up to the physical standards demanded by the work; and (9) the needed facts of economics.

Many of the things listed in such a survey are learned through incidental experience. Others cannot be sufficiently learned in this way. It is by putting the workers to work, whether adolescent or adult, and by noting the kinds of shortcomings and mistakes that show themselves when training is absent or deficient, that we can discover the curriculum tasks for directed vocational education.

The objectives of education are not to be discovered within just any kind or quality of human affairs. Occupational, civic, sanitary, or other activity may be poorly performed and productive of only meager results. At the other end of the scale are types of activity that are as well performed as it is in human nature to perform them, and which are abundantly fruitful in good results. Education is established upon the presumption that human activities exist upon different levels of quality or efficiency; that performance of low character is not good; that it can be eliminated through training; and that only the best or at least the best attainable is good enough. Whether in agriculture, building-trades, housekeeping, commerce, civic regulation, sanitation, or any other, education presumes that the best that is practicable is what ought to be. Education is to keep its feet squarely upon the earth; but this does not require that it aim lower than the highest that is practicable.

Let us take a concrete illustration. The curriculum-discoverer wishes, for example, to draw up a course of training in agriculture. He will go out into the practical world of agriculture as the only place that can reveal the objectives of agricultural education. He will start out without prejudgment as to the specific objectives. All that he needs for the work is pencil, notebook, and a discerning intelligence. He will observe the work of farmers; he will talk with them about all aspects of their work; and he will read reliable accounts which give insight into their activities. From these sources he will discover the particular things that the farmers do in carrying on each piece of work; the specific knowledge which the farmers employ in planning and performing each specific task; the kinds of judgments at which they must arrive; the types of problems they must solve; the habits and skills demanded by the tasks; the attitudes of mind, appreciations, valuations, ambitions, and desires, which motivate and exercise general control.

Facts upon all of these matters can be obtained from a survey of any agricultural region, however primitive or backward. But primitive agriculture is the thing which exists without any education. It is the thing education is to eliminate. The curriculum-discoverer, therefore, will not investigate just any agricultural situation. He will go to the farms that are most productive and most successful from every legitimate point of view. These will often be experimental or demonstration farms which represent what is practicable for the community, but which may not be typical of actual practices in that community. Where such general practices are inferior, agricultural education is to aim not at what is but at what ought to be.

When the farming practices are already upon a high plane, education has but a single function: it is to hand over these practices unchanged to the members of the new generation.

Where the practices of a region are primitive or backward, education has a double function to perform. It is not only to hand over to the new generation a proficiency that is equal to that of their fathers, but it is also to lift the proficiency of the sons to a height much beyond that of their fathers. Within such a region, therefore, agricultural education has the additional function of serving as the fundamental social agency of agricultural progress.

What we have said concerning agriculture is generally applicable throughout the occupational world. For discovering the objectives for a training course in bricklaying one will analyze not the activities of bricklayers in general, but those where bricklaying has been carried to its highest practicable level of efficiency—as this efficiency is judged on the basis of all legitimate standards. Education will aim, not at average bricklayers, but at the best types of bricklayers.

When stated in broad outline, the general principle is obvious. In practical application,

, employer + employee would have different opinions naturally

it presents difficulties. Men do not agree as to the characteristics of the most desirable types of work. The employers of the bricklayers will be inclined to use maximum productiveness as the criterion of superior work; and unquestioning obedience to orders and contentment with any kind of hours, wages, and working conditions as proper mental attitudes. The employees will judge otherwise as to some of the factors. The employers will invite the curriculum-discoverer to investigate situations where productiveness in proportion to costs is greatest; the employees, where the total welfare of the worker is considered alongside of the factor of productiveness. Both sides will agree that education should aim at the best and that scientific investigations as to objectives should seek to discover the characteristics of only the best. They disagree as to what is the best, and therefore where the investigations are to be made.

The general principle of finding the scholastic curriculum in the shortcomings of children and men is quite obvious and entirely familiar to teachers in its application to the curriculum of spelling, grammar, and other subjects that result in objective performance, such as pronunciation, drawing, music, computation, etc. It is not so clear in connection with the highly complex subjects of history, literature, geography, etc. What are the social shortcomings that are to be eliminated through a study of these social subjects? Our ideas are yet so vague, in most cases, that we can scarcely be said to have objectives. The first task of the scientific curriculum-maker is the discovery of those social deficiencies that result from a lack of historical, literary, and geographical experiences. Each deficiency found is a call for directed training; it points to an objective that is to be set up for conscious training. The nature of the objectives will point to the curriculum materials to be selected for these subjects. A major obstacle is lack of agreement as to what constitutes social deficiency. There is however no justification for scholastic training of any kind except as a gap exists between the training of general experience and the training that ought to be accomplished.

Society agrees sufficiently well as to many social shortcomings. Education needs to assemble them in as accurate and particularized a form as possible. They can then be used as the social symptoms which point to the objectives of history, literature, geography, economics, and other social studies. Society will disagree as to many suggested deficiencies. A program can be scientific, however, without being complete. The thousand spelling words presented by Mr. Ayres is a good list notwithstanding the fact that it presents not more than a quarter of the words needed. It is a secure beginning that can be completed by further studies. In the same way in our social training, we shall do very well if we can set up a quarter of the desirable objectives. That would be a great advance over none at all, as at present; and would provide the nucleus, the technique, and the vision of possibilities necessary for gradually rounding out the list.

a start can't force everything

The principle involves us in similar difficulties in its application to civic, moral, vocational, sanitational, recreational, and parental education. It is equally valid, however, in connection with each of these. Only as we agree upon *what ought to be* in each of these difficult fields, can we know at what the training should aim. Only as we list the errors and shortcomings of human performance in each of the fields can we know what to include and to emphasize in the directed curriculum of the schools.

use NCLB to make a new future
idea

Note

1.   Charters, W. W., and Miller, Edith. A Course of Study in Grammar based upon the Grammatical Errors of School Children in Kansas City, Missouri. University of Missouri, Education Bulletin, no. 9.

2

A Critical Consideration of the New Pedagogy in its Relation to Modern Science

Maria Montessori

It is not my intention to present a treatise on Scientific Pedagogy. The modest design of these incomplete notes is to give the results of an experiment that apparently opens the way for putting into practice those new principles of science which in these last years are tending to revolutionise the work of education.

Much has been said in the past decade concerning the tendency of pedagogy, following in the footsteps of medicine, to pass beyond the purely speculative stage and base its conclusions on the positive results of experimentation. Physiological or experimental psychology which, from Weber and Fechner to Wundt, has become organised into a new science, seems destined to furnish to the new pedagogy that fundamental preparation which the old-time metaphysical psychology furnished to philosophical pedagogy. Morphological anthropology, applied to the physical study of children, is also a strong element in the growth of the new pedagogy.

But in spite of all these tendencies, Scientific Pedagogy has never yet been definitely constructed nor defined. It is something vague of which we speak, but which does not, in reality, exist. We might say that it has been, up to the present time, the mere intuition or suggestion of a science which, by the aid of the positive and experimental sciences that have renewed the thought of the nineteenth century, must emerge from the mist and clouds that have surrounded it. For man, who has formed a new world through scientific progress, must himself be prepared and developed through a new pedagogy. But I will not attempt to speak of this more fully here.

Several years ago, a well-known physician established in Italy a *School of Scientific Pedagogy*, the object of which was to prepare teachers to follow the new movement which had begun to be felt in the pedagogical world. This school had, for two or three years, a great success, so great, indeed, that teachers from all over Italy flocked to it, and it was endowed by the City of Milan with a splendid equipment of scientific material. Indeed, its beginnings were most propitious, and liberal help was afforded it in the hope that it might be possible to establish, through the experiments carried on there, "the science of forming man."

The enthusiasm which welcomed this school was, in a large measure, due to the warm support given it by the distinguished anthropologist, Giuseppe Sergi, who for more than thirty years had earnestly laboured to spread among the teachers of Italy the principles of a new civilisation based upon education. "To-day in the social world," said Sergi, "an imperative need makes itself felt—the reconstruction of educational methods; and he who fights for this cause, fights for human regeneration." In his pedagogical writings collected in a volume under the title of "*Educazione ed Istruzione*" (Pensieri),[1] he gives a résumé of the lectures in which he encouraged this new movement, and says that he believes the way to this desired regeneration lies in a methodical study of the one to be educated, carried on under the guidance of pedagogical anthropology and of experimental psychology.

"For several years I have done battle for an idea concerning the instruction and education of man, which appeared the more just and useful the more deeply I thought upon it. My idea was that in order to establish natural, rational methods, it was essential that we make numerous, exact, and rational observations of man as an individual, principally during infancy, which is the age at which the foundations of education and culture must be laid.

"To measure the head, the height, etc., does not indeed mean that we are establishing a system of pedagogy, but it indicates the road which we may follow to arrive at such a system, since if we are to educate an individual, we must have a definite and direct knowledge of him."

The authority of Sergi was enough to convince many that, given such a knowledge of the individual, the art of educating him would develop naturally. This, as often happens, led to a confusion of ideas among his followers, arising now from a too literal interpretation, now from an exaggeration, of the master's ideas. The chief trouble lay in confusing the experimental study of the pupil, with his education. And since the one was the road leading to the other, which should have grown from it naturally and rationally, they straightway gave the name of Scientific Pedagogy to what was in truth pedagogical anthropology. These new converts carried as their banner, the "Biographical Chart," believing that once this ensign was firmly planted upon the battlefield of the school, the victory would be won.

The so-called School of Scientific Pedagogy, therefore, instructed the teachers in the taking of anthropometric measurements, in the use of esthesiometric instruments, in the gathering of Psychological Data—and the army of new scientific teachers was formed.

It should be said that in this movement Italy showed herself to be abreast of the times. In France, in England, and especially in America, experiments have been made in the elementary schools, based upon a study of anthropology and psychological pedagogy, in the hope of finding in anthropometry and psychometry, the regeneration of the school. In these attempts it has rarely been the *teachers* who have carried on the research; the experiments have been, in most cases, in the hands of physicians who have taken more interest in their especial science than in education. They have usually sought to get from their experiments some contribution to psychology, or anthropology, rather than to attempt to organise their work and their results toward the formation of the long-sought Scientific Pedagogy. To sum up the situation briefly, anthropology and psychology have never devoted themselves to the question of educating children in the schools, nor have the scientifically trained teachers ever measured up to the standards of genuine scientists.

The truth is that the practical progress of the school demands a genuine *fusion* of these modern tendencies, in practice and thought; such a fusion as shall bring scientists directly into the important field of the school and at the same time raise teachers from the inferior intellectual level to which they are limited today. Toward this eminently practical ideal the University School of Pedagogy, founded in Italy by Credaro, is definitely working. It is the intention of this school to raise Pedagogy from the inferior position it has occupied as a secondary branch of philosophy, to the dignity of a definite science, which shall, as does Medicine, cover a broad and varied field of comparative study.

And among the branches affiliated with it will most certainly be found Pedagogical Hygiene, Pedagogical Anthropology, and Experimental Psychology.

Truly, Italy, the country of Lombroso, of De-Giovanni, and of Sergi, may claim the honour of being pre-eminent in the organisation of such a movement. In fact, these three scientists may be called the founders of the new tendency in Anthropology: the first leading the way in criminal anthropology, the second in medical anthropology, and the third in pedagogical anthropology. For the good fortune of science, all three of them have been the recognised leaders of their special lines of thought, and have been so prominent in the scientific world that they have not only made courageous and valuable disciples, but have also prepared the minds of the masses to receive the scientific regeneration which they have encouraged. (For reference, see my treatise "Pedagogical Anthropology.")[2]

Surely all this is something of which our country may be justly proud.

Today, however, those things which occupy us in the field of education are the interests of humanity at large, and of civilisation, and before such great forces we can recognise only one country—the entire world. And in a cause of such great importance, all those who have given any contribution, even though it be only an attempt not crowned with success, are worthy of the respect of humanity throughout the civilised world. So, in Italy, the schools of Scientific Pedagogy and the Anthropological Laboratories, which have sprung up in the various cities through the efforts of elementary teachers and scholarly inspectors, and which have been abandoned almost before they became definitely organised, have nevertheless a great value by reason of the faith which inspired them, and because of the doors they have opened to thinking people.

It is needless to say that such attempts were premature and sprang from too slight a comprehension of new sciences still in the process of development. Every great cause is born from repeated failures and from imperfect achievements. When St. Francis of Assisi saw his Lord in a vision, and received from the Divine lips the command—"Francis, rebuild my Church!"—he believed that the Master spoke of the little church within which he knelt at that moment. And he immediately set about the task, carrying upon his shoulders the stones with which he meant to rebuild the fallen walls. It was not until later that he became aware of the fact that his mission was to renew the Catholic Church through the spirit of poverty. But the St. Francis who so ingenuously carried the stones, and the great reformer who so miraculously led the people to a triumph of the spirit, are one and the same person in different stages of development. So we, who work toward one great end, are members of one and the same body; and those who come after us will reach the goal only because there were those who believed and laboured before them. And, like St. Francis, we have believed that by carrying the hard and barren stones of the experimental laboratory to the old and crumbling walls of the school, we might rebuild it. We have looked upon the aids offered by the materialistic and mechanical sciences with the same hopefulness with which St. Francis looked upon the squares of granite, which he must carry upon his shoulders.

Thus we have been drawn into a false and narrow way, from which we must free ourselves, if we are to establish true and living methods for the training of future generations.

To prepare teachers in the method of the experimental sciences is not an easy matter. When we shall have instructed them in anthropometry and psychometry in the most minute manner possible, we shall have only created machines, whose usefulness will be most doubtful. Indeed, if it is after this fashion that we are to initiate our teachers into experiment, we shall remain forever in the field of theory. The teachers of the old school, prepared according to the principles of metaphysical philosophy, understood the ideas of certain men regarded as authorities, and moved the muscles of speech in talking of them, and the muscles of the eye in reading their theories. Our scientific teachers, instead, are familiar with certain instruments and know how to move the muscles of the hand and arm in order to use these instruments; besides this, they have an intellectual preparation which consists of a series of typical tests, which they have, in a barren and mechanical way, learned how to apply.

The difference is not substantial, for profound differences cannot exist in exterior technique alone, but lie rather within the inner man. Not with all our initiation into scientific experiment have we prepared *new masters*, for, after all, we have left them standing without the door of real experimental science; we have not admitted them to the noblest and most profound phase of such study,—to that experience which makes real scientists.

And, indeed, what is a scientist? Not, certainly, he who knows how to manipulate all the instruments in the physical laboratory, or who in the laboratory of the chemist handles the various reactives with deftness and security, or who in biology knows how to make ready the specimens for the microscope. Indeed, it is often the case that an assistant has a greater dexterity in experimental technique than the master scientist himself. We give the name scientist to the type of man who has felt experiment to be a means guiding him to search out the deep truth of life, to lift a veil from its fascinating secrets, and who, in this pursuit, has felt arising within him a love for the mysteries of nature, so passionate as to annihilate the thought of himself. The scientist is not the clever manipulator of instruments, he is the worshipper of nature and he bears the external symbols of his passion as does the follower of some religious order. To this body of real scientists belong those who, forgetting, like the Trappists of the Middle Ages, the world about them, live only in the laboratory, careless often in matters of food and dress because they no longer think of themselves; those who, through years of unwearied use of the microscope, become blind; those who in their scientific ardour inoculate themselves with tuberculosis germs; those who handle the excrement of cholera patients in their eagerness to learn the vehicle through which the diseases are transmitted; and those who, knowing that a certain chemical preparation may be an explosive, still persist in testing their theories at the risk of their lives. This is the spirit of the men of science, to whom nature freely reveals her secrets, crowning their labours with the glory of discovery.

There exists, then, the "spirit" of the scientist, a thing far above his mere "mechanical skill," and the scientist is at the height of his achievement when the spirit has triumphed over the mechanism. When he has reached this point, science will receive from him not only new revelations of nature, but philosophic syntheses of pure thought.

It is my belief that the thing which we should cultivate in our teachers is more the *spirit* than the mechanical skill of the scientist; that is, the *direction* of the *preparation* should be toward the spirit rather than toward the mechanism. For example, when we considered the scientific preparation of teachers to be simply the acquiring of the technique of science, we did not attempt to make these elementary teachers perfect anthropologists, expert experimental psychologists, or masters of infant hygiene; we wished only to *direct them* toward the field of experimental science, teaching them to manage the various instruments with a certain degree of skill. So now, we wish to *direct* the teacher, trying to awaken in him, in connection with his own particular field, the school, that scientific *spirit* which opens the door for him to broader and bigger possibilities. In other words, we wish to awaken in the mind and heart of the educator an *interest in natural phenomena* to such an extent that, loving nature, he shall understand the anxious and expectant attitude of one who has prepared an experiment and who awaits a revelation from it.[3]

The instruments are like the alphabet, and we must know how to manage them if we are to read nature; but as the book, which contains the revelation of the greatest thoughts of an author, uses in the alphabet the means of composing the external symbols or words, so nature, through the mechanism of the experiment, gives us an infinite series of revelations, unfolding for us her secrets.

Now one who has learned to spell mechanically all the words in his spelling-book, would be able to read in the same mechanical way the words in one of Shakespeare's plays, provided the print were sufficiently clear. He who is initiated solely into the making of the bare experiment, is like one who spells out the literal sense of the words in the spelling-book; it is on such a level that we leave the teachers if we limit their preparation to technique alone.

We must, instead, make of them worshippers and interpreters of the spirit of nature. They must be like him who, having learned to spell, finds himself, one day, able to read behind the written symbols the *thought* of Shakespeare, or Goethe, or Dante. As may be seen, the difference is great, and the road long. Our first error was, however, a natural one. The child who has mastered the spelling-book gives the impression of knowing how to read. Indeed, he does read the signs over the shop doors, the names of newspapers, and every word that comes under his eyes. It would be very natural if, entering a library, this child should be deluded into thinking that he knew how to read the *sense* of all the books he saw there. But attempting to do this, he would soon feel that "to know how to read mechanically" is nothing, and that he needs to go back to school. So it is with the teachers whom we have thought to prepare for scientific pedagogy by teaching them anthropometry and psychometry.

But let us put aside the difficulty of preparing scientific masters in the accepted sense of the word. We will not even attempt to outline a programme of such preparation, since this would lead us into a discussion which has no place here. Let us suppose, instead, that we have already prepared teachers through long and patient exercises for the *observation* of *nature*, and that we have led them, for example, to the point attained by those students of natural sciences who rise at night and go into the woods and fields that they may surprise the awakening and the early activities of some family of insects in which they are interested. Here we have the scientist who, though he may be sleepy and tired with walking, is full of watchfulness, who is not aware that he is muddy or dusty, that the mist wets him, or the sun burns him; but is intent only upon not revealing in the least degree his presence, in order that the insects may, hour after hour, carry on peacefully those natural functions which he wishes to observe. Let us suppose these teachers to have reached the standpoint of the scientist who, half blind, still watches through his microscope the spontaneous movements of some particular infusory animalcule. These creatures seem to this scientific watcher, in their manner of avoiding each other and in their way of selecting their food, to possess a dim intelligence. He then disturbs this sluggish life by an electric stimulus, observing how some group themselves about the positive pole, and others about the negative. Experimenting further, with a luminous stimulus, he notices how some run toward the light, while others fly from it. He investigates these and like phenomena; having always in mind this question: whether the fleeing from or running to the stimulus be of the same character as the avoidance of one another or the selection of food—that is, whether such differences are the result of choice and are due to that dim consciousness, rather than to physical attraction or repulsion similar to that of the magnet. And let us suppose that this scientist, finding it to be four o'clock in the afternoon, and that he has not yet lunched, is conscious, with a feeling of pleasure, of the fact that he has been at work in his laboratory instead of in his own home, where they would have called him hours ago, interrupting his interesting observation, in order that he might eat.

Let us imagine, I say, that the teacher has arrived, independently of his scientific training, at such an attitude of interest in the observation of natural phenomena. Very well, but such a preparation is not enough. The master, indeed, is destined in his particular mission not to the observation of insects or of bacteria, but of man. He is not to make a study of man in the manifestations of his daily physical habits as one studies some family of insects, following their movements from the hour of their morning awakening. The master is to study man in the awakening of his intellectual life.

The interest in humanity to which we wish to educate the teacher must be characterised by the intimate relationship between the observer and the individual to be observed; a relationship which does not exist between the student of zoology or botany and that form of nature which he studies. Man cannot love the insect or the chemical reaction which he studies, without sacrificing a part of himself. This self-sacrifice seems to one who looks at it from the standpoint of the world, a veritable renunciation of life itself, almost a martyrdom.

But the love of man for man is a far more tender thing, and so simple that it is universal. To love in this way is not the privilege of any especially prepared intellectual class, but lies within the reach of all men.

To give an idea of this second form of preparation, that of the spirit, let us try to enter into the minds and hearts of those first followers of Christ Jesus as they heard Him speak of a Kingdom not of this world, greater far than any earthly kingdom, no matter how royally conceived. In their simplicity they asked of Him, "Master, tell us who shall be greatest in the Kingdom of Heaven?" To which Christ, caressing the head of a little child who, with reverent, wondering eyes, looked into His face, replied, "Whosoever shall become as one of these little ones, he shall be greatest in the Kingdom of Heaven." Now let us picture among those to whom these words were spoken, an ardent, worshipping soul, who takes them into his heart. With a mixture of respect and love, of sacred curiosity and of a desire to achieve this spiritual greatness, he sets himself to observe every manifestation of this little child. Even such an observer placed in a classroom filled with little children will not be the new educator whom we wish to form. But let us seek to implant in the soul the self-sacrificing spirit of the scientist with the reverent love of the disciple of Christ, and we shall have prepared the *spirit* of the teacher. From the child itself he will learn how to perfect himself as an educator.

Let us consider the attitude of the teacher in the light of another example. Picture to yourself one of our botanists or zoologists experienced in the technique of observation and experimentation; one who has travelled in order to study "certain fungi" in their native environment. This scientist has made his observations in open country and, then, by the aid of his microscope and of all his laboratory appliances, has carried on the later research work in the most minute way possible. He is, in fact, a scientist who understands what it is to study nature, and who is conversant with all the means which modern experimental science offers for this study.

Now let us imagine such a man appointed, by reason of the original work he has done, to a chair of science in some university, with the task before him of doing further original research work with hymenoptera. Let us suppose that, arrived at his post, he is shown a glass-covered case containing a number of beautiful butterflies, mounted by means of pins, their outspread wings motionless. The student will say that this is some child's play, not material for scientific study, that these specimens in the box are more fitly a part of the game which the little boys play, chasing butterflies and catching them in a net. With such material as this the experimental scientist can do nothing.

The situation would be very much the same if we should place a teacher who, according to our conception of the term, is scientifically prepared, in one of the public schools where the children are repressed in the spontaneous expression of their personality till they are almost like dead beings. In such a school the children, like butterflies mounted on pins, are fastened each to his place, the desk, spreading the useless wings of barren and meaningless knowledge which they have acquired.

It is not enough, then, to prepare in our Masters the scientific spirit. We must also make ready the *school* for their observation. The school must permit the *free, natural manifestations* of the *child* if in the school scientific pedagogy is to be born. This is the essential reform.

No one may affirm that such a principle already exists in pedagogy and in the school. It is true that some pedagogues, led by Rousseau, have given voice to impracticable principles and vague aspirations for the liberty of the child, but the true concept of liberty is practically unknown to educators. They often have the same concept of liberty which animates a people in the hour of rebellion from slavery, or perhaps, the conception of *social liberty*, which although it is a more elevated idea is still invariably restricted. "Social liberty" signifies always one more round of Jacob's ladder. In other words it signifies a partial liberation, the liberation of a country, of a class, or of thought.

That concept of liberty which must inspire pedagogy is, instead, universal. The biological sciences of the nineteenth century have shown it to us when they have offered us the means for studying life. If, therefore, the old-time pedagogy foresaw or vaguely expressed the principle of studying the pupil before educating him, and of leaving him free in his spontaneous manifestations, such an intuition, indefinite and barely expressed, was made possible of practical attainment only after the contribution of the experimental sciences during the last century. This is not a case for sophistry or discussion, it is enough that we state our point. He who would say that the principle of liberty informs the pedagogy of today, would make us smile as at a child who, before the box of mounted butterflies, should insist that they were alive and could fly. The principle of slavery still pervades pedagogy, and, therefore, the same principle pervades the school. I need only give one proof—the stationary desks and chairs. Here we have, for example, a striking evidence of the errors of the early materialistic scientific pedagogy which, with mistaken zeal and energy, carried the barren stones of science to the rebuilding of the crumbling walls of the school. The schools were at first furnished with the long, narrow benches upon which the children were crowded together. Then came science and perfected the bench. In this work much attention was paid to the recent contributions of anthropology. The age of the child and the length of his limbs were considered in placing the seat at the right height. The distance between the seat and the desk was calculated with infinite care, in order that the child's back should not become deformed, and, finally, the seats were separated and the width so closely calculated that the child could barely seat himself upon it, while to stretch himself by making any lateral movements was impossible. This was done in order that he might be separated from his neighbour. These desks are constructed in such a way as to render the child visible in all his immobility. One of the ends sought through this separation is the prevention of immoral acts in the schoolroom. What shall we say of such prudence in a state of society where it would be considered scandalous to give voice to principles of sex morality in education, for fear we might thus contaminate innocence? And, yet, here we have science lending itself to this hypocrisy, fabricating machines! Not only this; obliging science goes farther still, perfecting the benches in such a way as to permit to the greatest possible extent the immobility of the child, or, if you wish, to repress every movement of the child.

It is all so arranged that, when the child is well-fitted into his place, the desk and chair themselves force him to assume the position considered to be hygienically comfortable. The seat, the foot-rest, the desks are arranged in such a way that the child can never stand at his work. He is allotted only sufficient space for sitting in an erect position. It is in such ways that schoolroom desks and benches have advanced toward perfection. Every cult of the so-called scientific pedagogy has designed a model scientific desk. Not a few nations have become proud of their "national desk,"—and in the struggle of competition these various machines have been patented.

Undoubtedly there is much that is scientific underlying the construction of these benches. Anthropology has been drawn upon in the measuring of the body and the diagnosis of the age; physiology, in the study of muscular movements; psychology, in regard to perversion of instincts; and, above all, hygiene, in the effort to prevent curvature of the spine. These desks were indeed scientific, following in their construction the anthropological study of the child. We have here, as I have said, an example of the literal application of science to the schools.

I believe that before very long we shall all be struck with great surprise by this attitude. It will seem incomprehensible that the fundamental error of the desk should not have been revealed earlier through the attention given to the study of infant hygiene, anthropology, and sociology, and through the general progress of thought. The marvel is greater when we consider that during the past years there has been stirring in almost every nation a movement toward the protection of the child.

I believe that it will not be many years before the public, scarcely believing the descriptions of these scientific benches, will come to touch with wondering hands the amazing seats that were constructed for the purpose of preventing among our school children curvature of the spine!

The development of these scientific benches means that the pupils were subjected to a régime, which, even though they were born strong and straight, made it possible for them to become humpbacked! The vertebral column, biologically the most primitive, fundamental, and oldest part of the skeleton, the most fixed portion of our body, since the skeleton is the most solid portion of the organism—the vertebral column, which resisted and was strong through the desperate struggles of primitive man when he fought against the desert-lion, when he conquered the mammoth, when he quarried the solid rock and shaped the iron to his uses, bends, and cannot resist, under the yoke of the school.

It is incomprehensible that so-called *science* should have worked to perfect an instrument of slavery in the school without being enlightened by one ray from the movement of social liberation, growing and developing throughout the world. For the age of scientific benches was also the age of the redemption of the working classes from the yoke of unjust labour.

The tendency toward social liberty is most evident, and manifests itself on every hand. The leaders of the people make it their slogan, the labouring masses repeat the cry, scientific and socialistic publications voice the same movement, our journals are full of it. The underfed workman does not ask for a tonic, but for better economic conditions which shall prevent malnutrition. The miner who, through the stooping position maintained during many hours of the day, is subject to inguinal rupture, does not ask for an abdominal support, but demands shorter hours and better working conditions, in order that he may be able to lead a healthy life like other men.

And when, during this same social epoch, we find that the children in our schoolrooms are working amid unhygienic conditions, so poorly adapted to normal development that even the skeleton becomes deformed, our response to this terrible revelation is an orthopedic bench. It is much as if we offered to the miner the abdominal brace, or arsenic to the underfed workman.

Some time ago a woman, believing me to be in sympathy with all scientific innovations concerning the school, showed me with evident satisfaction *a corset or brace for pupils*. She had invented this and felt that it would complete the work of the bench.

Surgery has still other means for the treatment of spinal curvature. I might mention orthopedic instruments, braces, and a method of periodically suspending the child, by the head or shoulders, in such a fashion that the weight of the body stretches and thus straightens the vertebral column. In the school, the orthopedic instrument in the shape of the desk is in great favour today; someone proposes the brace—one step farther and it will be suggested that we give the scholars a systematic course in the suspension method!

All this is the logical consequence of a material application of the methods of science to the decadent school. Evidently the rational method of combating spinal curvature in the pupils is to change the form of their work—so that they shall no longer be obliged to remain for so many hours a day in a harmful position. It is a conquest of liberty which the school needs, not the mechanism of a bench.

Even were the stationary seat helpful to the child's body, it would still be a dangerous and unhygienic feature of the environment, through the difficulty of cleaning the room perfectly when the furniture cannot be moved. The foot-rests, which cannot be removed, accumulate the dirt carried in daily from the street by the many little feet. Today there is a general transformation in the matter of house furnishings. They are made lighter and simpler so that they may be easily moved, dusted, and even washed. But the school seems blind to the transformation of the social environment.

It behooves us to think of what may happen to the *spirit* of the child who is condemned to grow in conditions so artificial that his very bones may become deformed. When we speak of the redemption of the working man, it is always understood that beneath the most apparent form of suffering, such as poverty of the blood, or ruptures, there exists that other wound from which the soul of the man who is subjected to any form of slavery must suffer. It is at this deeper wrong that we aim when we say that the workman must be redeemed through liberty. We know only too well that when a man's very blood has been consumed or his intestines wasted away through his work, his soul must have lain oppressed in darkness, rendered insensible, or, it may be, killed within him. The *moral* degradation of the slave is, above all things, the weight that opposes the progress of humanity—humanity striving to rise and held back by this great burden. The cry of redemption speaks far more clearly for the souls of men than for their bodies.

What shall we say then, when the question before us is that of *educating children?*

We know only too well the sorry spectacle of the teacher who, in the ordinary school-room, must pour certain cut and dried facts into the heads of the scholars. In order to succeed in this barren task, she finds it necessary to discipline her pupils into immobility and to force their attention. Prizes and punishments are ever-ready and efficient aids to the master who must force into a given attitude of mind and body those who are condemned to be his listeners.

It is true that today it is deemed expedient to abolish official whippings and habitual blows, just as the awarding of prizes has become less ceremonious. These partial reforms are another prop approved of by science, and offered to the support of the decadent school. Such prizes and punishments are, if I may be allowed the expression, the *bench* of the soul, the instrument of slavery for the spirit. Here, however, these are not applied to lessen deformities, but to provoke them. The prize and the punishment are incentives toward unnatural or forced effort, and, therefore we certainly cannot speak of the natural development of the child in connection with them. The jockey offers a piece of sugar to his horse before jumping into the saddle, the coachman beats his horse that he may respond to the signs given by the reins; and, yet, neither of these runs so superbly as the free horse of the plains.

And here, in the case of education, shall man place the yoke upon man?

True, we say that social man is natural man yoked to society. But if we give a comprehensive glance to the moral progress of society, we shall see that little by little, the yoke is being made easier, in other words, we shall see that nature, or life, moves gradually toward triumph. The yoke of the slave yields to that of the servant, and the yoke of the servant to that of the workman.

All forms of slavery tend little by little to weaken and disappear, even the sexual slavery of woman. The history of civilisation is a history of conquest and of liberation. We should ask in what stage of civilisation we find ourselves and if, in truth, the good of prizes and of punishments be necessary to our advancement. If we have indeed gone beyond this point, then to apply such a form of education would be to draw the new generation back to a lower level, not to lead them into their true heritage of progress.

Something very like this condition of the school exists in society, in the relation between the government and the great numbers of the men employed in its administrative departments. These clerks work day after day for the general national good, yet they do not feel or see the advantage of their work in any immediate reward. That is, they do not realise that the state carries on its great business through their daily tasks, and that the whole nation is benefited by their work. For them the immediate good is promotion, as passing to a higher class is for the child in school. The man who loses sight of the really big aim of his work is like a child who has been placed in a class below his real standing: like a slave, he is cheated of something which is his right. His dignity as a man is reduced to the limits of the dignity of a machine which must be oiled if it is to be kept going, because it does not have within itself the impulse of life. All those petty things such as the desire for decorations or medals, are but artificial stimuli, lightening for the moment the dark, barren path in which he treads.

In the same way we give prizes to school children. And the fear of not achieving promotion, withholds the clerk from running away, and binds him to his monotonous work, even as the fear of not passing into the next class drives the pupil to his book. The reproof of the superior is in every way similar to the scolding of the teacher. The correction of badly executed clerical work is equivalent to the bad mark placed by the teacher upon the scholar's poor composition. The parallel is almost perfect.

But if the administrative departments are not carried on in a way which would seem suitable to a nation's greatness; if corruption too easily finds a place; it is the result of having extinguished the true greatness of man in the mind of the employee, and of having restricted his vision to those petty, immediate facts, which he has come to look upon as prizes and punishments. The country stands, because the rectitude of the greater number of its employees is such that they resist the corruption of the prizes and punishments, and follow an irresistible current of honesty. Even as life in the social environment triumphs against every cause of poverty and death, and proceeds to new conquests, so the instinct of liberty conquers all obstacles, going from victory to victory.

It is this personal and yet universal force of life, a force often latent within the soul, that sends the world forward.

But he who accomplishes a truly human work, he who does something really great and victorious, is never spurred to his task by those trifling attractions called by the name of "prizes," nor by the fear of those petty ills which we call "punishments." If in a war a great army of giants should fight with no inspiration beyond the desire to win promotion, epaulets, or medals, or through fear of being shot, if these men were to oppose a handful of pygmies who were inflamed by love of country, the victory would go to the latter. When real heroism has died within an army, prizes and punishments cannot do more than finish the work of deterioration, bringing in corruption and cowardice.

All human victories, all human progress, stand upon the inner force.

Thus a young student may become a great doctor if he is spurred to his study by an interest which makes medicine his real vocation. But if he works in the hope of an inheritance, or of making a desirable marriage, or if indeed he is inspired by any material advantage, he will never become a true master or a great doctor, and the world will never make one step forward because of his work. He to whom such stimuli are necessary, had far better never become a physician. Everyone has a special tendency, a special vocation, modest, perhaps, but certainly useful. The system of prizes may turn an individual aside from this vocation, may make him choose a false road, for him a vain one, and forced to follow it, the natural activity of a human being may be warped, lessened, even annihilated.

We repeat always that the world *progresses* and that we must urge men forward to obtain progress. But progress comes from the *new things that are born*, and these, not being foreseen, are not rewarded with prizes: rather, they often carry the leader to martyrdom. God forbid that poems should ever be born of the desire to be crowned in the Capitol! Such a vision need only come into the heart of the poet and the muse will vanish. The poem must spring from the soul of the poet, when he thinks neither of himself nor of the prize. And if he does win the laurel, he will feel the vanity of such a prize. The true reward lies in the revelation through the poem of his own triumphant inner force.

There does exist, however, an external prize for man; when, for example, the orator sees the faces of his listeners change with the emotions he has awakened, he experiences something so great that it can only be likened to the intense joy with which one discovers that he is loved. Our joy is to touch, and conquer souls, and this is the one prize which can bring us a true compensation.

Sometimes there is given to us a moment when we fancy ourselves to be among the great ones of the world. These are moments of happiness given to man that he may continue his existence in peace. It may be through love attained or because of the gift of a son, through a glorious discovery or the publication of a book; in some such moment we feel that there exists no man who is above us. If, in such a moment, someone vested with authority comes forward to offer us a medal or a prize, he is the important destroyer of our real reward—"And who are you?" our vanished illusion shall cry, "Who are you that recalls me to the fact that I am not the first among men? Who stands so far above me that he may give me a prize?" The prize of such a man in such a moment can only be Divine.

As for punishments, the soul of the normal man grows perfect through expanding, and punishment as commonly understood is always a form of *repression*. It may bring results with those inferior natures who grow in evil, but these are very few, and social progress is not affected by them. The penal code threatens us with punishment if we are dishonest within the limits indicated by the laws. But we are not honest through fear of the laws; if we do not rob, if we do not kill, it is because we love peace, because the natural trend of our lives leads us forward, leading us ever farther and more definitely away from the peril of low and evil acts.

Without going into the ethical or metaphysical aspects of the question, we may safely affirm that the delinquent before he transgresses the law, has, *if he knows of the existence of a punishment*, felt the threatening weight of the criminal code upon him. He has defined it, or he has been lured into the crime, deluding himself with the idea that he would be able to avoid the punishment of the law. But there has occurred within his mind, a *struggle between the crime and the punishment*. Whether it be efficacious in hindering crime or not, this penal code is undoubtedly made for a very limited class of individuals; namely, criminals. The enormous majority of citizens are honest without any regard whatever to the threats of the law.

The real punishment of normal man is the loss of the consciousness of that individual power and greatness which are the sources of his inner life. Such a punishment often falls upon men in the fullness of success. A man whom we would consider crowned by happiness and fortune may be suffering from this form of punishment. Far too often man does not see the real punishment which threatens him.

And it is just here that education may help.

Today we hold the pupils in school, restricted by those instruments so degrading to body and spirit, the desk—and material prizes and punishments. Our aim in all this is to reduce them to the discipline of immobility and silence,—to lead them,—where? Far too often toward no definite end.

Often the education of children consists in pouring into their intelligence the intellectual contents of school programmes. And often these programmes have been compiled in the official department of education, and their use is imposed by law upon the teacher and the child.

Ah, before such dense and wilful disregard of the life which is growing within these children, we should hide our heads in shame and cover our guilty faces with our hands!

Sergi says truly: "Today an urgent need imposes itself upon society: the reconstruction of methods in education and instruction, and he who fights for this cause, fights for human regeneration."

Notes

1.   Trevisini, 1892.
2.   Montessori: "L'Antropologia Pedagogica." Vallardi.
3.   See in my treatise on Pedagogical Anthropology the chapter on "The Method Used in Experimental Sciences."

3

My Pedagogic Creed

John Dewey

Article One: What Education Is

I Believe that—all education proceeds by the participation of the individual in the social consciousness of the race. This process begins unconsciously almost at birth, and is continually shaping the individual's powers, saturating his consciousness, forming his habits, training his ideas, and arousing his feelings and emotions. Through this unconscious education, the individual gradually comes to share in the intellectual and moral resources which humanity has succeeded in getting together. He becomes an inheritor of the funded capital of civilization. The most formal and technical education in the world cannot safely depart from this general process. It can only organize it or differentiate it in some particular direction.

- The only true education comes through the stimulation of the child's powers by the demands of the social situations in which he finds himself. Through these demands he is stimulated to act as a member of a unity, to emerge from his original narrowness of action and feeling, and to conceive of himself from the standpoint of the welfare of the group to which he belongs. Through the responses which others make to his own activities he comes to know what these mean in social terms. The value which they have is reflected back into them. For instance, through the response which is made to the child's instinctive babblings the child comes to know what those babblings mean; they are transformed into articulate language, and thus the child is introduced into the consolidated wealth of ideas and emotions which are now summed up in language.
- This educational process has two sides, one psychological and one sociological, and that neither can be subordinated to the other, or neglected, without evil results following. Of these two sides, the psychological is the basis. The child's own instincts and powers furnish the material and give the starting-point for all education. Save as the efforts of the educator connect with some activity which the child is carrying on of his own initiative independent of the educator, education becomes reduced to a pressure from without. It may, indeed, give certain external results, but cannot truly be called educative. Without insight into the psychological structure and activities of the individual, the educative process will, therefore, be haphazard and arbitrary. If it chances to coincide with the child's activity it will get a leverage; if it does not, it will result in friction, or disintegration, or arrest of the child's nature.
- Knowledge of social conditions, of the present state of civilization, is necessary in

order properly to interpret the child's powers. The child has his own instincts and tendencies, but we do not know what these mean until we can translate them into their social equivalents. We must be able to carry them back into a social past and see them as the inheritance of previous race activities. We must also be able to project them into the future to see what their outcome and end will be. In the illustration just used, it is the ability to see in the child's babblings the promise and potency of a future social intercourse and conversation which enables one to deal in the proper way with that instinct.

- The psychological and social sides are organically related, and that education cannot be regarded as a compromise between the two, or a superimposition of one upon the other. We are told that the psychological definition of education is barren and formal—that is gives us only the idea of a development of all the mental powers without giving us any idea of the use to which these powers are put. On the other hand, it is urged that the social definition of education, as getting adjusted to civilization, makes of it a forced and external process, and results in subordinating the freedom of the individual to a preconceived social and political status.

- Each of these objections is true when urged against one side isolated from the other. In order to know what a power really is we must know what its end, use, or function is, and this we cannot know save as we conceive of the individual as active in social relationships. But, on the other hand, the only possible adjustment which we can give to the child under existing conditions is that which arises through putting him in complete possession of all his powers. With the advent of democracy and modern industrial conditions, it is impossible to foretell definitely just what civilization will be twenty years from now. Hence it is impossible to prepare the child for any precise set of conditions. To prepare him for the future life means to give him command of himself; it means so to train him that he will have the full and ready use of all his capacities that his eye and ear and hand may be tools ready to command, that his judgment may be capable of grasping the conditions under which it has to work, and the executive forces be trained to act economically and efficiently. It is impossible to reach this sort of adjustment save as constant regard it had to the individual's own powers, tastes, and interests—that is, as education is continually converted into psychological terms.

In sum, I believe that the individual who is to be educated is a social individual, and that society is an organic union of individuals. If we eliminate the social factor from the child we are left only with an abstraction; if we eliminate the individual factor from society, we are left only with an inert and lifeless mass. Education, therefore, must begin with a psychological insight into the child's capacities, interests, and habits. It must be controlled at every point by reference to these same considerations. These powers, interests, and habits must be continually interpreted—we must know what they mean. They must be translated into terms of their social equivalents—into terms of what they are capable of in the way of social service.

Article Two: What the School Is

I Believe that—the school is primarily a social institution. Education being a social process, the school is simply that form of community life in which all those agencies are concentrated that will be most effective in bringing the child to share in the inherited resources of the race, and to use his own powers for social ends.

- Education, therefore, is a process of living and not a preparation for future living.
- The school must represent present life—life as real and vital to the child as that which he carries on in the home, in the neighborhood, or on the playground.
- That education which does not occur through forms of life, forms that are worth living for their own sake, is always a poor substitute for the genuine reality, and tends to cramp and to deaden.
- The school, as an institution, should simplify existing social life; should reduce it, as it were, to an embryonic form. Existing life is so complex that the child cannot be brought into contact with it without either confusion or distraction; he is either overwhelmed by the multiplicity of activities which are going on, so that he loses his own power of orderly reaction, or he is so stimulated by these various activities that his powers are prematurely called into play and he becomes either unduly specialized or else disintegrated.
- As such simplified social life, the school life should grow gradually out of the home life; that it should take up and continue the activities with which the child is already familiar in the home.
- It should exhibit these activities to the child, and reproduce them in such ways that the child will gradually learn the meaning of them, and be capable of playing his own part in relation to them.
- This is a psychological necessity, because it is the only way of securing continuity in the child's growth, the only way of giving a background of past experience to the new ideas given in school.
- It is also a social necessity because the home is the form of social life in which the child has been nurtured and in connection with which he has had his moral training. It is the business of the school to deepen and extend his sense of the values bound up in his home life.
- Much of present education fails because it neglects this fundamental principle of the school as a form of community life. It conceives the school as a place where certain information is to be given, where certain lessons are to be learned, or where certain habits are to be formed. The value of these is conceived as lying largely in the remote future; the child must do these things for the sake of something else he is to do; they are mere preparations. As a result they do not become a part of the life experience of the child and so are not truly educative.
- The moral education centers upon this conception of the school as a mode of social life, that the best and deepest moral training is precisely that which one gets through having to enter into proper relations with others in a unity of work and thought. The present educational systems, so far as they destroy or neglect this unity, render it difficult or impossible to get any genuine, regular moral training.
- The child should be stimulated and controlled in his work through the life of the community.
- Under existing conditions far too much of the stimulus and control proceeds from the teacher, because of neglect of the idea of the school as a form of social life.
- The teacher's place and work in the school is to be interpreted from this same

basis. The teacher is not in the school to impose certain ideas or to form certain habits in the child, but is there as a member of the community to select the influences which shall affect the child and to assist him in properly responding to these influences.

- The discipline of the school should proceed from the life of the school as a whole and not directly from the teacher.
- The teacher's business is simply to determine, on the basis of larger experience and riper wisdom, how the discipline of life shall come to the child.
- All questions of the grading of the child and his promotion should be determined by reference to the same standard. Examinations are of use only so far as they test the child's fitness for social life and reveal the place in which he can be of the most service and where he can receive the most help.

Article Three: The Subjectmatter of Education

I Believe that—the social life of the child is the basis of concentration, or correlation, in all his training or growth. The social life gives the unconscious unity and the background of all his efforts and of all his attainments.

- The subjectmatter of the school curriculum should mark a gradual differentiation out of the primitive unconscious unity of social life.
- We violate the child's nature and render difficult the best ethical results by introducing the child too abruptly to a number of special studies, of reading, writing, geography, etc., out of relation to this social life.
- The true center of correlation on the school subjects is not science, nor literature, nor history, nor geography, but the child's own social activities.
- Education cannot be unified in the study of science, or so-called nature study, because apart from human activity, nature itself is not a unity; nature in itself is a number of diverse objects in space and time, and to attempt to make it the center of work by itself is to introduce a principle of radiation rather than one of concentration.
- Literature is the reflex expression and interpretation of social experience; that hence it must follow upon and not precede such experience. It, therefore, cannot be made the basis, although it may be made the summary of unification.
- Once more that history is of educative value in so far as it presents phases of social life and growth. It must be controlled by reference to social life. When taken simply as history it is thrown into the distant past and becomes dead and inert. Taken as the record of man's social life and progress it becomes full of meaning. I believe, however, that it cannot be so taken excepting as the child is also introduced directly into social life.
- The primary basis of education is in the child's powers at work along the same general constructive lines as those which have brought civilization into being.
- The only way to make the child conscious of his social heritage is to enable him to perform those fundamental types of activity which make civilization what it is.
- In the so-called expressive or constructive activities as the center of correlation.

- This gives the standard for the place of cooking, sewing, manual training, etc., in the school.
- They are not special studies which are to be introduced over and above a lot of others in the way of relaxation or relief, or as additional accomplishments. I believe rather that they represent, as types, fundamental forms of social activity; and that it is possible and desirable that the child's introduction into the more formal subjects of the curriculum be through the medium of these constructive activities.
- The study of science is educational in so far as it brings out the materials and processes which make social life what it is.
- One of the greatest difficulties in the present teaching of science is that the material is presented in purely objective form, or is treated as a new peculiar kind of experience which the child can add to that which he has already had. In reality, science is of value because it gives the ability to interpret and control the experience already had. It should be introduced, not as so much new subjectmatter, but as showing the factors already involved in previous experience and as furnishing tools by which that experience can be more easily and effectively regulated.
- At present we lose much of the value of literature and language studies because of our elimination of the social element. Language is almost always treated in the books of pedagogy simply as the expression of thought. It is true that language is a logical instrument, but it is fundamentally and primarily a social instrument. Language is the device for communication; it is the tool through which one individual comes to share the ideas and feelings of others. When treated simply as a way of getting individual information, or as a means of showing off what one has learned, it loses its social motive and end.
- There is, therefore, no succession of studies in the ideal school curriculum. If education is life, all life has, from the outset, a scientific aspect, an aspect of art and culture, and an aspect of communication. It cannot, therefore, be true that the proper studies for one grade are mere reading and writing, and that at a later grade, reading, or literature, or science, may be introduced. The progress is not in the succession of studies, but in the development of new attitudes towards, and new interests in, experience.
- Education must be conceived as a continuing reconstruction of experience; that the process and the goal of education are one and the same thing.
- To set up any end outside of education, as furnishing its goal and standard, is to deprive the educational process of much of its meaning, and tends to make us rely upon false and external stimuli in dealing with the child.

Article Four: The Nature of Method

I Believe that—the question of method is ultimately reducible to the question of the order of development of the child's powers and interests. The law for presenting and treating material is the law implicit within the child's own nature. Because this is so I believe the following statements are of supreme importance as determining the spirit in which education is carried on.

- The active side precedes the passive in the development of the child-nature; that expression comes before conscious impression; that the muscular development precedes the sensory; that movements come before conscious sensations; I believe that consciousness is essentially motor or impulsive; that conscious states tend to project themselves in action.

- The neglect of this principle is the cause of a large part of the waste of time and strength in school work. The child is thrown into a passive, receptive, or absorbing attitude. The conditions are such that he is not permitted to follow the law of his nature; the result is friction and waste.
- Ideas (intellectual and rational processes) also result from action and devolve for the sake of the better control of action. What we term reason is primarily the law of order or effective action. To attempt to develop the reasoning powers, the powers of judgment, without reference to the selection and arrangement of means in action, is the fundamental fallacy in our present methods of dealing with this matter. As a result we present the child with arbitrary symbols. Symbols are a necessity in mental development, but they have their place as tools for economizing effort; presented by themselves they are a mass of meaningless and arbitrary ideas imposed from without.
- The image is the great instrument of instruction. What a child gets out of any subject presented to him is simply the images which he himself forms with regard to it.
- If nine-tenths of the energy at present directed towards making the child learn certain things were spent in seeing to it that the child was forming proper images, the work of instruction would be indefinitely facilitated.
- Much of the time and attention now given to the preparation and presentation of lessons might be more wisely and profitably expended in training the child's power of imagery and in seeing to it that he was continually forming definite vivid, and growing images of the various subjects with which he comes in contact in his experience.
- Interests are the signs and symptoms of growing power. I believe that they represent dawning capacities. Accordingly the constant and careful observation of interests is of the utmost importance for the educator.
- These interests are to be observed as showing the state of development which the child has reached.
- They prophesy the stage upon which he is about to enter.
- Only through the continual and sympathetic observation of childhood's interests can the adult enter into the child's life and see what it is ready for, and upon what material it could work most readily and fruitfully.
- These interests are neither to be humored nor repressed. To repress interest is to substitute the adult for the child, and so to weaken intellectual curiosity and alertness, to suppress initiative, and to deaden interest. To humor the interests is to substitute the transient for the permanent. The interest is always the sign of some power below; the important thing is to discover this power. To humor the interest is to fail to penetrate below the surface, and its sure result is to substitute caprice and whim for genuine interest.
- The emotions are the reflex of actions.
- To endeavor to stimulate or arouse the emotions apart from their corresponding activities is to introduce an unhealthy and morbid state of mind.
- If we can only secure right habits of action and thought, with reference to the good, the true, and the beautiful, the emotions will for the most part take care of themselves.

- Next to deadness and dullness, formalism and routine, our education is threatened with no greater evil than sentimentalism.
- This sentimentalism is the necessary result of the attempt to divorce feeling from action.

Article Five: The School and Social Progress

I Believe that—education is the fundamental method of social progress and reform.

- All reforms which rest simply upon the enactment of law, or the threatening of certain penalties, or upon changes in mechanical or outward arrangements, are transitory and futile.
- Education is a regulation of the process of coming to share in the social consciousness; and that the adjustment of individual activity on the basis of this social consciousness is the only sure method of social reconstruction.
- This conception has due regard for both the individualistic and socialistic ideals. It is duly individual because it recognizes the formation of a certain character as the only genuine basis of right living. It is socialistic because it recognizes that this right character is not to be formed by merely individual precept, example, or exhortation, but rather by the influence of a certain form of institutional or community life upon the individual, and that the social organism through the school, as its organ, may determine ethical results.
- In the ideal school we have the reconciliation of the individualistic and the institutional ideals.
- The community's duty to education is, therefore, its paramount moral duty. By law and punishment, by social agitation and discussion, society can regulate and form itself in a more or less haphazard and chance way. But through education society can formulate its own purposes, can organize its own means and resources, and thus shape itself with definiteness and economy in the direction in which it wishes to move.
- When society once recognizes the possibilities in this direction, and the obligations which these possibilities impose, it is impossible to conceive of the resources of time, attention, and money which will be put at the disposal of the education.
- It is the business of everyone interested in education to insist upon the school as the primary and most effective interest of social progress and reform in order that society may be awakened to realize what the school stands for, and arouse to the necessity of endowing the educator with sufficient equipment properly to perform his task.
- Education thus conceived marks the most perfect and intimate union of science and art conceivable in human experience.
- The art of thus giving shape to human powers and adapting them to social service is the supreme art; one calling into its service the best of artists; that no insight, sympathy, tact, executive power, is too great for such service.
- With the growth of psychological service, giving added insight into individual structure and laws of growth; and with growth of social science, adding to our knowledge of the right organization of individuals, all scientific resources can be utilized for the purposes of education.

- When science and art thus join hands the most commanding motive for human action will be reached, the most genuine springs of human conduct aroused, and the best service that human nature is capable of guaranteed.
- The teacher is engaged, not simply in the training of individuals, but in the formation of the proper social life.
- Every teacher should realize the dignity of his calling; that he is a social servant set apart for the maintenance of proper social order and the securing of the right social growth.
- In this way the teacher always is the prophet of the true God and the usherer in of the true kingdom of God.

4

The Public School and the Immigrant Child

Jane Addams

I am always diffident when I come before a professional body of teachers, realizing as I do that it is very easy for those of us who look on to bring indictments against result; and realizing also that one of the most difficult situations you have to meet is the care and instruction of the immigrant child, especially as he is found where I see him, in the midst of crowded city conditions.

And yet in spite of the fact that the public school is the great savior of the immigrant district, and the one agency which inducts the children into the changed conditions of American life, there is a certain indictment which may justly be brought, in that the public school too often separates the child from his parents and widens that old gulf between fathers and sons which is never so cruel and so wide as it is between the immigrants who come to this country and their children who have gone to the public school and feel that they have there learned it all. The parents are thereafter subjected to certain judgment, the judgment of the young which is always harsh and in this instance founded upon the most superficial standard of Americanism. And yet there is a notion of culture which we would define as a knowledge of those things which have been long cherished by men, the things which men have loved because thru generations they have softened and interpreted life, and have endowed it with value and meaning. Could this standard have been given rather than the things which they see about them as the test of so-called success, then we might feel that the public school has given at least the beginnings of culture which the child ought to have. At present the Italian child goes back to its Italian home more or less disturbed and distracted by the contrast between the school and the home. If he throws off the control of the home because it does not represent the things which he has been taught to value he takes the first step toward the Juvenile Court and all the other operations of the law, because he has prematurely asserted himself long before he is ready to take care of his own affairs.

We find in the carefully prepared figures which Mr. Commons and other sociologists have published that while the number of arrests of immigrants is smaller than the arrests of native born Americans, the number of arrests among children of immigrants is twice as large as the number of arrests among the children of native born Americans. It would seem that in spite of the enormous advantages which the public school gives to these children it in some way loosens them from the authority and control of their parents, and tends to send them, without a sufficient rudder and power of self-direction, into the perilous business of living. Can we not say, perhaps, that the schools ought to do more to connect these children with the best things of the past, to make them realize something of the beauty and charm of the language, the history, and the traditions which their parents represent. It is easy to cut them loose from their parents, it requires cultivation to tie them up in sympathy and understanding. The ignorant teacher cuts them off because he himself cannot understand the situation, the cultivated teacher fastens them because his own mind is open to the charm and beauty of that old-country life. In short, it is the business of the school to give to each child the beginnings of a culture so wide and deep and universal that he can interpret his own parents and countrymen by a standard which is worldwide and not provincial. — *Child should be given an encompassing world view*

The second indictment which may be brought is the failure to place the children into proper relation toward the industry which they will later enter. Miss Arnold has told us that children go into industry for a very short time. I believe that the figures of the United States census show the term to be something like six years for the women in industry as against twenty-four years for men, in regard to continuity of service. Yet you cannot disregard the six years of the girls nor the twenty-four years of the boys, because they are the immediate occupation into which they enter after they leave the school—even the girls are bound to go thru that period—that is, the average immigrant girls are—before they enter the second serious business of life and maintain homes of their own. Therefore, if they enter industry unintelligently, without some notion of what it means, they find themselves totally unprepared for their first experience with American life, they are thrown out without the proper guide or clue which the public school might and ought to have given to them. Our industry has become so international, that it ought to be easy to use the materials it offers for immigrant children. The very processes and general principles which industry represents give a chance to prepare these immigrant children in a way which the most elaborated curriculum could not present. Ordinary material does not give the same international suggestion as industrial material does.

Third, I do not believe that the children who have been cut off from their own parents are going to be those who, when they become parents themselves, will know how to hold the family together and to connect it with the state. I should begin to teach the girls to be good mothers by teaching them to be good daughters. Take a girl whose mother has come from South Italy. The mother cannot adjust herself to the changed condition of housekeeping, does not know how to wash and bake here, and do the other things which she has always done well in Italy, because she has suddenly been transported from a village to a tenement house. If that girl studies these household conditions in relation to the past and to the present needs of the family, she is undertaking the very best possible preparation for her future obligations to a household of her own. And to my mind she can undertake it in no better way. Her own children are mythical and far away, but the little brothers and sisters pull upon her affections and her loyalty, and she longs to have their needs recognized in the school so that the school may give her some help. Her mother complains that the baby is sick in America because she cannot milk her own goat; she insists if she had her own goat's milk the baby would be quite well and flourishing, as the children were in Italy. If that girl can be taught that the milk makes the baby ill because it is not clean and be provided with a simple test that she may know when milk is clean, it may take her into the study not only of the milk within the four walls of the tenement house, but into the inspection of the milk of her district. The milk, however, remains good educational material, it makes even more concrete the connection which you would be glad to use between the household and the affairs of the American city. Let her not follow the mother's example of complaining about changed conditions; let her rather make the adjustment for her mother's entire household. We cannot tell what adjustments the girl herself will be called upon to make ten years from now; but we can give her the clue and the aptitude to adjust the family with which she is identified to the constantly changing conditions of city life. Many of us feel that, splendid as the public schools are in their relation to the immigrant child, they do not understand all of the difficulties which surround that child—all of the moral and emotional perplexities which constantly harass him. The children long that the school teacher should know something about the lives their parents lead and should be able to reprove the hooting children who make fun of the Italian mother because she wears a kerchief on her head, not only because they are rude but also because they are stupid. We send young people to Europe to see Italy, but we do not utilize Italy when it lies about the schoolhouse. If the body of teachers in our great cities could take hold of the immigrant colonies, could bring out of them their handicrafts and occupations, their traditions, their folk songs and folk lore, the beautiful stories which every immigrant colony is ready to tell and translate; could get the children to bring these things into school as the material from which culture is made and the material upon which culture is based, they would discover that by comparison that which they give them now is a poor, meretricious and vulgar thing. Give these children a chance to utilize the historic and industrial material which they see about them and they will begin to have a sense of ease in America, a first consciousness of being at home. I believe if these people are welcomed upon the basis of the resources which they represent and the contributions which they bring, it may come to pass that these schools which deal with immigrants will find that they have a wealth of cultural and industrial material which will make the schools in other neighborhoods positively envious. A girl living in a tenement household, helping along this tremendous adjustment, healing over this great moral upheaval which the parents have suffered and which leaves them bleeding and sensitive—such a girl has a richer experience and a finer material than any girl from a more fortunate household can have at the present moment.

I wish I had the power to place before you what it seems to me is the opportunity that the immigrant colonies present to the public school: the most endearing occupation of leading the little child, who will in turn lead his family, and bring them with him into the brotherhood for which they are longing. The immigrant child cannot make this demand upon the school because he does not know how to formulate it; it is for the teacher both to perceive it and to fulfil it.

5

Dare the School Build a New Social Order?

George S. Counts

3

If we may now assume that the child will be imposed upon in some fashion by the various elements in his environment, the real question is not whether imposition will take place, but rather from what source it will come. If we were to answer this question in terms of the past, there could, I think, be but one answer: on all genuinely crucial matters the school follows the wishes of the groups or classes that actually rule society; on minor matters the school is sometimes allowed a certain measure of freedom. But the future may be unlike the past. Or perhaps I should say that teachers, if they could increase sufficiently their stock of courage, intelligence, and vision, might become a social force of some magnitude. About this eventuality I am not over-sanguine, but a society lacking leadership as ours does, might even accept the guidance of teachers. Through powerful organizations they might at least reach the public conscience and come to exercise a larger measure of control over the schools than hitherto. They would then have to assume some responsibility for the more fundamental forms of imposition which, according to my argument, cannot be avoided.

That the teachers should deliberately reach for power and then make the most of their conquest is my firm conviction. To the extent that they are permitted to fashion the curriculum and the procedures of the school they will definitely and positively influence the social attitudes, ideals, and behavior of the coming generation. In doing this they should resort to no subterfuge or false modesty. They should say neither that they are merely teaching the truth nor that they are unwilling to wield power in their own right. The first position is false and the second is a confession of incompetence. It is my observation that the men and women who have affected the course of human events are those who have not hesitated to use the power that has come to them. Representing as they do, not the interests of the moment or of any special class, but rather the common and abiding interests of the people, teachers are under heavy social obligation to protect and further those interests. In this they occupy a relatively unique position in society. Also since the profession should embrace scientists and scholars of the highest rank, as well as teachers working at all levels of the educational system, it has at its disposal, as no other group, the knowledge and wisdom of the ages. It is scarcely thinkable that these men and women would ever act as selfishly or bungle as badly as have the so-called "practical" men of our generation—the politicians, the financiers, the industrialists. If all of these facts are taken into account, instead of shunning power, the profession should rather seek power and then strive to use that power fully and wisely and in the interests of the great masses of the people.

The point should be emphasized that teachers possess no magic secret to power. While their work should give them a certain moral advantage, they must expect to encounter the usual obstacles blocking the road to leadership. They should not be deceived by the pious humbug with which public men commonly flatter the members of the profession. To expect ruling groups or classes to give precedence to teachers on important matters, because of age or sex or sentiment, is to refuse to face realities. It was one of the proverbs of the agrarian order that a spring never rises higher than its source. So the power that teachers exercise in the schools can be no greater than the power they wield in society. Moreover, while organization is necessary, teachers should not think of their problem primarily in terms of organizing and presenting a united front to the world, the flesh, and the devil. In order to be effective they must throw off completely the slave psychology that has dominated the mind of the pedagogue more or less since the days of ancient Greece. They must be prepared to stand on their own feet and win for their ideas the support of the masses of the people. Education as a force for social regeneration must march hand in hand with the living and creative forces of the social order. In their own lives teachers must bridge the gap between school and society and play some part in the fashioning of those great common purposes which should bind the two together.

This brings us to the question of the kind of imposition in which teachers should engage, if they had the power. Our obligations, I think, grow out of the social situation. We live in troublous times; we live in an age of profound change; we live in an age of revolution. Indeed it is highly doubtful whether man ever lived in a more eventful period than the present. In order to match our epoch we would probably have to go back to the fall of the ancient empires or even to that unrecorded age when men first abandoned the natural arts of hunting and fishing and trapping and began to experiment with agriculture and the settled life. Today we are witnessing the rise of a civilization quite without precedent in human history—a civilization founded on science, technology, and machinery, possessing the most extraordinary power, and rapidly making of the entire world a single great society. Because of forces already released, whether in the field of economics, politics, morals, religion, or art, the old molds are being broken. And the peoples of the earth are everywhere seething with strange ideas and passions. If life were peaceful and quiet and undisturbed by great issues, we might with some show of wisdom center our attention on the nature of the child. But with the world as it is, we cannot afford for a single instant to remove our eyes from the social scene or shift our attention from the peculiar needs of the age.

In this new world that is forming, there is one set of issues which is peculiarly fundamental and which is certain to be the center of bitter and prolonged struggle. I refer to those issues which may be styled economic. President Butler has well stated the case: "For a generation and more past," he says, "the center of human interest has been moving from the point which it occupied for some four hundred years to a new point which it bids fair to occupy for a time equally long. The shift in the position of the center of gravity in human interest has been from politics to economics; from considerations that had to do with forms of government, with the establishment and protection of individual liberty, to considerations that have to do with the production, distribution, and consumption of wealth."

Consider the present condition of the nation. Who among us, if he had not been reared amid our institutions, could believe his eyes as he surveys the economic situation, or his ears as he listens to solemn disquisitions by our financial and political leaders on the cause and cure of the depression! Here is a society that manifests the most extraordinary contradictions: a mastery over the forces of nature, surpassing the wildest dreams of antiquity, is accompanied by extreme material insecurity; ~~dire poverty walks hand in hand with the most extravagant living the world has ever known~~; an abundance of goods of all kinds is coupled with privation, misery, and even starvation; an excess of production is seriously offered as the underlying cause of severe physical suffering; ~~breakfastless children march to school past bankrupt shops laden with rich foods gathered from the ends of the earth~~; strong men by the million walk the streets in a futile search for employment and with the exhaustion of hope enter the ranks of the damned; great captains of industry close factories without warning and dismiss the workmen by whose labors they have amassed huge fortunes through the years; automatic machinery increasingly displaces men and threatens society with a growing contingent of the permanently unemployed; racketeers and gangsters with the connivance of public officials fasten themselves on the channels of trade and exact toll at the end of the machine gun; economic parasitism, either within or without the law, is so prevalent that the tradition of honest labor is showing signs of decay; the wages paid to the workers are too meager to enable them to buy back the goods they produce; consumption is subordinated to production and a philosophy of deliberate waste is widely proclaimed as the highest economic wisdom; ~~the science of psychology is employed to fan the flames of desire so that men may be enslaved by their wants and bound to the wheel of production~~; a government board advises the cotton-growers to plow under every third row of cotton in order to bolster up the market; both ethical and aesthetic considerations are commonly overridden by "hard-headed business men" bent on material gain; federal aid to the unemployed is opposed on the ground that it would pauperize the masses when the favored members of society have always lived on a dole; even responsible leaders resort to the practices of the witch doctor and vie with one another in predicting the return of prosperity; an ideal of rugged individualism, evolved in a simple pioneering and agrarian order at a time when free land existed in abundance, ~~is used to justify a system which exploits pitilessly and without thought of the morrow the natural and human resources of the nation and of the world~~. One can only imagine what Jeremiah would say if he could step out of the pages of the Old Testament and cast his eyes over this vast spectacle so full of tragedy and of menace.

The point should be emphasized, however, that the present situation is also freighted with hope and promise. The age is pregnant with possibilities. There lies within our grasp the most humane, the most beautiful, the most majestic civilization ever fashioned by any people. This much at least we know today. We shall probably know more tomorrow. At last men have achieved such a mastery over the forces of nature that wage slavery can follow chattel slavery and take its place among the relics of the past. No longer are there grounds for the contention that the finer fruits of human culture must be nurtured upon the toil and watered by the tears of the masses. The limits to achievement set by nature have been so extended that we are today bound merely by our ideals, by our power of self-discipline, by our ability to devise social arrangements suited to an industrial age. If we are to place any credence whatsoever in the word of our engineers, the full utilization of modern technology at its present level of development should enable us to produce several times as much goods as were ever produced at the very peak of prosperity, and with the working day, the working year, and the working life reduced by half. We hold within our hands the power to usher in an age of plenty, to make secure the lives of all, and to banish poverty forever from the land. The only cause for doubt or pessimism lies in the question of our ability to rise to the stature of the times in which we live.

Our generation has the good or the ill fortune to live in an age when great decisions must be made. The American people, like most of the other peoples of the earth, have come to the parting of the ways; they can no longer trust entirely the inspiration which came to them when the Republic was young; they must decide afresh what they are to do with their talents. Favored above all other nations with the resources of nature and the material instrumentalities of civilization, they stand confused and irresolute before the future. They seem to lack the moral quality necessary to quicken, discipline, and give direction to their matchless energies. In a recent paper Professor Dewey has, in my judgment, correctly diagnosed our troubles: "the schools, like the nation," he says, "are in need of a central purpose which will create new enthusiasm and devotion, and which will unify and guide all intellectual plans."

This suggests, as we have already observed, that the educational problem is not wholly intellectual in nature. Our Progressive schools therefore cannot rest content with giving children an opportunity to study contemporary society in all of its aspects. This of course must be done, but I am convinced that they should go much farther. If the schools are to be really effective, they must become centers for the building, and not merely for the contemplation, of our civilization. This does not mean that we should endeavor to promote particular reforms through the educational system. We should, however, give to our children a vision of the possibilities which lie ahead and endeavor to enlist their loyalties and enthusiasms in the realization of the vision. Also our social institutions and practices, all of them, should be critically examined in the light of such a vision.

4

In *The Epic of America* James Truslow Adams contends that our chief contribution to the heritage of the race lies not in the field of science, or religion, or literature, or art but rather in the creation of what he calls the "American Dream"—a vision of a society in which the lot of the common man will be made easier and his life enriched and ennobled. If this vision has been a moving force in our history, as I believe it has, why should we not set ourselves the task of revitalizing and reconstituting it? This would seem to be the great need of our age, both in the realm of education and in the sphere of public life, because men must have something for which to live. Agnosticism, skepticism, or even experimentalism, unless the last is made flesh through the formulation of some positive social program, constitutes an extremely meager spiritual diet for any people. A small band of intellectuals, a queer breed of men at best, may be satisfied with such a spare ration, particularly if they lead the sheltered life common to their class; but the masses, I am sure, will always demand something more solid and substantial. Ordinary men and women crave a tangible purpose towards which to strive and which lends richness and dignity and meaning to life. I would consequently like to see our profession come to grips with the problem of creating a tradition that has roots in American soil, is in harmony with the spirit of the age, recognizes the facts of industrialism, appeals to the most profound impulses of our people, and takes into account the emergence of a world society.[1]

The ideal foundations on which we must build are easily discernible. Until recently the very word America has been synonymous throughout the world with democracy and symbolic to the oppressed classes of all lands of hope and opportunity. Child of the revolutionary ideas and impulses of the eighteenth century, the American nation became the embodiment of bold social experimentation and a champion of the power of environment to develop the capacities and redeem the souls of common men and women. And as her stature grew, her lengthening shadow reached to the four corners of the earth and everywhere impelled the human will to rebel against ancient wrongs. Here undoubtedly is the finest jewel in our heritage and the thing that is most worthy of preservation. If America should lose her honest devotion to democracy, or if she should lose her revolutionary temper, she will no longer be America. In that day, if it has not already arrived, her spirit will have fled and she will be known merely as the richest and most powerful of the nations. If America is not to be false to the promise of her youth, she must do more than simply perpetuate the democratic ideal of human relationships: she must make an intelligent and determined effort to fulfill it. The democracy of the past was the chance fruit of a strange conjunction of forces on the new continent; the democracy of the future can only be the intended offspring of the union of human reason, purpose, and will. The conscious and deliberate achievement of democracy under novel circumstances is the task of our generation.

Democracy of course should not be identified with political forms and functions—with the federal constitution, the popular election of officials, or the practice of universal suffrage. To think in such terms is to confuse the entire issue, as it has been confused in the minds of the masses for generations. The most genuine expression of democracy in the United States has little to do with our political institutions: it is a sentiment with respect to the moral equality of men: it is an aspiration towards a society in which this sentiment will find complete fulfillment. A society fashioned in harmony with the American democratic tradition would combat all forces tending to produce social distinctions and classes; repress every form of privilege and economic parasitism; manifest a tender regard for the weak, the ignorant, and the unfortunate; place the heavier and more onerous social burdens on the backs of the strong; glory in every triumph of man in his timeless urge to express himself and to make the world more habitable; exalt human labor of hand and brain as the creator of all wealth and culture; provide adequate material and spiritual rewards for every kind of socially useful work; strive for genuine equality of opportunity among all races, sects, and occupations; regard as paramount the abiding interests of the great masses of the people; direct the powers of government to the elevation and the refinement of the life of the common man; transform or destroy all conventions, institutions, and special groups inimical to the underlying principles of democracy; and finally be prepared as a last resort, in either the defense or the realization of this purpose, to follow the method of revolution. Although these ideals have never been realized or perhaps even fully accepted anywhere in the United States and have always had to struggle for existence with contrary forces, they nevertheless have authentic roots in the past. They are the values for which America has stood before the world during most of her history and with which the American people have loved best to associate their country. Their power and authority are clearly revealed in the fact that selfish interests, when grasping for some special privilege, commonly wheedle and sway the masses by repeating the words and kneeling before the emblems of the democratic heritage.

It is becoming increasingly clear, however, that this tradition, if its spirit is to survive, will have to be reconstituted in the light of the great social trends of the age in which we live. Our democratic heritage was largely a product of the frontier, free land, and a simple agrarian order. Today a new and strange and closely integrated industrial economy is rapidly sweeping over the world. Although some of us in our more sentimental moments talk wistfully of retiring into the more tranquil society of the past, we could scarcely induce many of our fellow citizens to accompany us. Even the most hostile critics of industrialism would like to take with them in their retirement a few such fruits of the machine as electricity, telephones, automobiles, modern plumbing, and various labor-saving devices,

must accept industry

or at least be assured of an abundant supply of slaves or docile and inexpensive servants. But all such talk is the most idle chatter. For better or for worse we must take industrial civilization as an enduring fact: already we have become parasitic on its institutions and products. The hands of the clock cannot be turned back.

If we accept industrialism, as we must, we are then compelled to face without equivocation the most profound issue which this new order of society has raised and settle that issue in terms of the genius of our people—the issue of the control of the machine. In whose interests and for what purposes are the vast material riches, the unrivaled industrial equipment, and the science and technology of the nation to be used? In the light of our democratic tradition there can be but one answer to the question: all of these resources must be dedicated to the promotion of the welfare of the great masses of the people. Even the classes in our society that perpetually violate this principle are compelled by the force of public opinion to pay lip-service to it and to defend their actions in its terms. No body of men, however powerful, would dare openly to flout it. Since the opening of the century the great corporations have even found it necessary to establish publicity departments or to employ extremely able men as public relations counselors in order to persuade the populace that regardless of appearances they are lovers of democracy and devoted servants of the people. In this they have been remarkably successful, at least until the coming of the Great Depression. For during the past generation there have been few things in America that could not be bought at a price.

sadly not where the resources are

best for someone/something

If the benefits of industrialism are to accrue fully to the people, this deception must be exposed. If the machine is to serve all, and serve all equally, it cannot be the property of the few. To ask these few to have regard for the common weal, particularly when under the competitive system they are forced always to think first of themselves or perish, is to put too great a strain on human nature. With the present concentration of economic power in the hands of a small class, a condition that is likely to get worse before it gets better, the survival or development of a society that could in any sense be called democratic is unthinkable. The hypocrisy which is so characteristic of our public life today is due primarily to our failure to acknowledge the fairly obvious fact that America is the scene of an irreconcilable conflict between two opposing forces. On the one side is the democratic tradition inherited from the past; on the other is a system of economic arrangements which increasingly partakes of the nature of industrial feudalism. Both of these forces cannot survive: one or the other must give way. Unless the democratic tradition is able to organize and conduct a successful attack on the economic system, its complete destruction is inevitable.

opposing forces

democratic tradition vs

economic arrangements

If democracy is to survive, it must seek a new economic foundation. Our traditional democracy rested upon small-scale production in both agriculture and industry and a rather general diffusion of the rights of property in capital and natural resources. The driving force at the root of this condition, as we have seen, was the frontier and free land. With the closing of the frontier, the exhaustion of free land, the growth of population, and the coming of large-scale production, the basis of ownership was transformed. If property rights are to be diffused in industrial society, natural resources and all important forms of capital will have to be collectively owned. Obviously every citizen cannot hold title to a mine, a factory, a railroad, a department store, or even a thoroughly mechanized farm. This clearly means that, if democracy is to survive in the United States, it must abandon its individualistic affiliations in the sphere of economics. What precise form a democratic society will take in the age of science and the machine, we cannot know with any assurance today. We must, however, insist on two things: first, that technology be released from the fetters and the domination of every type of special privilege; and, second, that the resulting system of production and distribution be made to serve directly the masses of the people. Within these limits, as I see it, our democratic tradition must of necessity evolve and gradually assume an essentially collectivistic pattern. The only conceivable alternative is the abandonment of the last vestige of democracy and the frank adoption of some modern form of feudalism.

wow strong statement here

Note

Chapters 3 and 4, in George S. Counts, *Dare the School Build a New Social Order?* New York: John Day, 1932. Reprinted by permission of Martha L. Counts. Copyright renewed 1959 by George S. Counts.

1. In the remainder of the argument I confine attention entirely to the domestic situation. I do this, not because I regard the question of international relations unimportant, but rather because of limitations of space. All I can say here is that any proper conception of the world society must accept the principle of the moral equality of races and nations.

6

The Rise of Scientific Curriculum-Making and Its Aftermath

Herbert M. Kliebard

When Boyd Bode published *Modern Educational Theories* in 1927, he took on what had already become the entrenched establishment of the curriculum world. With his trenchant criticism of Franklin Bobbitt in the chapter, "Curriculum Construction and Consensus of Opinion" and of W. W. Charters in the succeeding chapter, "Curriculum Making and the Method of Job Analysis," Bode was attacking not only the work of two men who had established themselves as the prototypes of the curriculum specialist, but the very foundations on which curriculum as a field of specialization had been based. Bode probably did not suspect, however, that the notion of careful pre-specification of educational objectives (with variations in terminology and technique) and the notion of activity analysis as the means toward their "discovery" (also with variations in terminology and technique) would become the foundations on which, almost half a century later, many books would be written, Ph.D.s awarded, careers established, and millions of dollars expended. Certainly Bode never dreamed that legislation embodying these principles would be enacted across the United States and that the very ideas he was attacking would become semi-official doctrine in federal and state agencies as well as in many educational institutions.

The Scientific Curriculum Making of Bobbitt and Charters

Bobbitt and Charters lived in auspicious times. Mental discipline as a theoretical basis for the curriculum was almost dead by the early twentieth century. The bright flame of American Herbartianism, which had for a time captured the imagination of the educational world, was flickering. An educational ideology true to the times was needed, and nothing was more appropriate than scientific curriculum making. This doctrine, with its promise of precision and objectivity, had an immediate appeal. Certainly there was no reason why scientific principles applied to education would not meet with the same success as science applied to business in the form of scientific management. The general notion of applied science, as well as the particular model of scientific arrangement, is in fact evident throughout the work of Bobbitt and Charters.

Of the two, Bobbitt was perhaps the first to strike this rich vein. As a young instructor in educational administration at the University of Chicago, he effectively drew the parallel between business techniques and education in a lengthy article in the *Twelfth Yearbook of the National Society for the Study of Education* (Bobbitt 1913). But Bobbitt, unlike other educators who turned to scientific management, was not content merely to apply certain management techniques to education, such as maximum utilization of the school plant; he provided the professional educators in the twentieth century with the concepts and meta-phors—indeed, the very language—that were needed to create an aura of technical expert-ise without which the hegemony of professional educators could not be established. Science was not simply a tool with which to carve out exactitude in educational affairs generally and in the curriculum in particular; it was a means by which one could confer professional status and exclude the uninitiated. Even the term "curriculum specialist" implied a particular set of technical skills unavailable to the untrained. While the notion of science implies a certain aura of exclusiveness, Bobbitt was probably not explicitly aware of such a political use of his technical language. In his two major works, *The Curriculum* (1918) and *How to Make a Curriculum* (1924), as well as in numerous articles on the techniques of curriculum making, he seems simply to have believed that science had the key that idle speculation and even philosophy failed to provide.

Like Bobbitt, W. W. Charters was already a major leader in education by the time Bode's work was published. Charters had written *Methods of Teaching* in 1909 and *Teaching the Common Branches* in 1913, both popular books; but with *Curriculum Construction* in 1923, he established himself in the forefront of curriculum thinking. (In the preface to this book, Charters gives particular thanks to his "former colleague, B. H. Bode" for "his criticism of theoretical principles.") Like Bobbitt also, Charters approached the problems of curric-ulum from the perspective of functional efficiency. Through the method of activity analy-sis (or job analysis, as it was also called), Charters was able to apply professional expertise to the development of curricula in many diverse fields, including secretarial studies, library studies, pharmacy, and especially teacher education (with *The Commonwealth Teacher-Training Study* in 1929). Activity analysis was so universally applicable a technique of curriculum development that Charters was even able to use it to develop a curriculum for being a woman. As with other occupations, one simply had to analyze the particular activities that defined the role and then place these in relationship to the ideals that would control these activities. The training involved in performing the activities well would then become the curriculum (Charters 1921, 1925). Out of the work and thought of Bobbitt and Charters, as well as their contemporaries and disciples, arose a new rationale and a modus operandi for the curriculum field that were to prevail to the present day. So dominant did scientific curriculum making become that Bode's *Modern Educational Theories* stands as one of the few direct assaults on some of its principal tenets and certainly the most important.

Preparing for Adulthood

One of the most basic tenets of scientific curriculum making is a principle enunciated early in Bobbitt's *How to Make a Curriculum*: "Education is primarily for adult life, not for child life. Its fundamental responsibility is to prepare for the fifty years of adulthood, not for the twenty years of childhood and youth" (1924, p. 8). Education, in other words, consists in preparing to become an adult. There is probably no more crucial notion in the entire theory. Without it, there would be no point, for example, in such careful analysis of adult activities and their ultimate transformation into minute and explicit curricular objectives. Moreover, much curriculum policy, such as the strong emphasis on curriculum differentiation with its basis in predicting the probable destination of children as to their adult lives, rests squarely on education as preparation. If education is for what lies ahead, then it becomes of utmost importance to state with reasonable accuracy what that future holds. Bode's criticism is most telling in making the distinction between a prediction by, for example, an astronomer as to the curve of a comet and an educator constructing a future ideal in schooling. Curriculum making, in other words, is a form of utopian thinking, not of crystal-ball gazing. But Dewey, whom Bode cites favorably in this context, had gone even further in attacking the notion of preparation. In "My Pedagogic Creed," Dewey took pains to define education as "a process of living and not a preparation for future living" (1929, p. 292), and he undertook specifically in *Democracy and Education* to point up other deficiencies in the idea. To think of children as merely getting ready for a remote and obscure world, Dewey thought, is to remove them as social members of the community. "They are looked upon as candidates," he said; "they are placed on the waiting list" (1916, p. 63). Furthermore, since children are not directed and stimulated by what is so remote in time, the educator must introduce, on a large scale, extrinsic rewards and punishments. Bode's criticism of education as preparation rests largely on the assumption that it would lead to a social status quo rather than social improvement. While Dewey would no doubt agree, his criticism is more far-reaching and devastating. He considered not only its social significance but its impact on the child and the pedagogical process itself.

A curious sidelight to the importance of education as preparation in scientific curriculum making is Bobbitt's own developing ambivalence toward the idea. In setting forth his curriculum theory in the epic *Twenty-Sixth Yearbook of the National Society for the Study of Education*, Bobbitt says, "Education is not primarily to prepare for life at some future time. Quite the reverse; it purposes to hold high the current living. . . . In a very true sense, life cannot be 'prepared for.' It can only be lived" (1926, p. 43). Later, when asked to write his summary theory of curriculum, Bobbitt declared, "While there are general guiding principles that enable parents and teachers to foresee in advance the long general course that is normally run, yet they cannot foresee or foreknow the specific and concrete details of the course that is to be actualized" (1934, p. 4). In these passages, he sounds more like Kilpatrick than himself. But if Bobbitt was ambivalent, even self-contradictory, on the subject of education as preparation, his disciples and present intellectual heirs are not. If anything is ingrained in curriculum thinking today, it is the notion that it is the job of curriculum planners to anticipate the exact skills, knowledge, and—to use today's most fashionable term—"competencies" that will stand one in good stead at an imagined point in the future. These predictions about what one will need in the future become the bases of curriculum planning.

Specificity of Objectives

A concomitant of the emphasis on preparation is the insistence that the end products of the curriculum be stated with great particularity. Vague Delphic prophecies simply won't do. " 'Ability to care for one's health' . . ." declared Bobbitt, "is too general to be useful. It must be reduced to particularity: ability to manage the ventilation of one's sleeping room, ability to protect one's self against micro-organisms, ability to care for the teeth, and so on" (1924, p. 32). If science is to be identified with exactitude, then scientific curriculum making must demonstrate its elevated status through the precision with which objectives are stated. It is at this point that Bode's criticism is both astute and telling. He points out, for example, that under the guise of scientific objectivity, Bobbitt inserts a submerged ideology. Scientific objectivity, it turns out, becomes a way of preserving the tried and true values of the society as well as making explicit the prevailing practical skills of the contemporary world.

Bode, of course, would not object to a philosophy of education governing curriculum; his objection is that the values of the scientific curriculum makers are disguised and covert. Furthermore, even a cursory examination of Bobbitt's most famous list of objectives would indicate wide latitude in the degree of specificity with which the objectives are stated. Alongside "the ability to keep one's emotional serenity, in the face of circumstances however trying" (1924, p. 25), "an attitude and desire of obedience to the immutable and eternal laws which appear to exist in the nature of things," and "confidence in the beneficence of these laws" (1924, p. 26), we find "ability to read and interpret facts expressed by commonly used types of graphs, diagrams, and statistical tables" (1924, p. 12), as well as "ability to care properly for the feet" (1924, p. 14). Although the injunction to be specific and explicit is unqualified, there seems to be some difficulty in carrying it out simply as a practical matter. In considering the efficient functioning of the human body, for example, we have no guidance as to whether to begin with the leg, the foot, the toe, or the toenail. The same problem would arise if we were dealing with the ability to swing a hammer or the ability to solve quadratic equations. The scientific curriculum makers' allegiance to specificity was allied to Thorndike's conception of the mind as consisting of multitudinous separate and individual functions (1901, p. 249), whereas Bode seems committed to a much broader conception of thought processes as well as a more optimistic view of transfer of training.

Making a Choice

If the practical problem of specificity were somehow resolved, perhaps by extending the list of objectives into the thousands or the hundreds of thousands, another issue would become even more apparent: how would we decide, objectively of course, which objectives to keep and which to leave out? As Bode indicates, one of Bobbitt's solutions was to throw the matter open to a vote or at least to a panel. In his famous Los Angeles study, Bobbitt asserted that his list of objectives "represent[ed] the practically unanimous judgment of some twenty-seven hundred well-trained and experienced adults" (1924, p. 10), a claim about which Bode is clearly skeptical. As Bode points out, the twelve hundred Los Angeles teachers, who were charged with reviewing the list drawn up by the fifteen hundred graduate students at the University of Chicago, were in a dilemma. All of the objectives listed unquestionably represented desirable traits and skills, from "keeping razor in order" (Bobbitt 1922, p. 21) to "ability to tell interesting stories interestingly—and many of them" (p. 26).

The wide agreement, Bode suspects, was probably achieved by a combination of specificity when practical and clearly desirable skills were involved and vagueness or ambiguity when value issues were broached. Inspection of Bobbitt's list of objectives indicates that Bode is essentially correct, thereby accounting in part for the obvious discrepancies in the level of specificity with which the objectives are stated as well as the near unanimity of agreement among twenty-seven hundred adult human beings. State legislators, educators, and the general public frequently find themselves in the same position today when they are asked to give their assent to such educational goals as "self-realization" and "mental health." One can hardly be against them.

A Standard for Living

Although Bode's criticism of the method of consensus is certainly convincing, he considers only indirectly another of Bobbitt's ways of dealing with the seemingly limitless scope of a curriculum defined by the full range of human activity. While the task of the "curriculum discoverer" did involve, according to Bobbitt, a full catalog of the activities of mankind, Bobbitt was careful to indicate that much of what has to be learned is acquired by "undirected experience." *The curriculum of the directed training,*" Bobbitt insisted, "*is to be discovered in the shortcomings of individuals after they have had all that can be given by the undirected training*" (1918, p. 45, original emphasis). Bobbitt's understanding of "shortcomings," actually, is quite similar to the contemporary notion of "needs." A standard is set, a norm; and the curriculum consists of the ways of treating deviations from the standard. Thus the curriculum seems cut down to manageable proportions without resort to the method of consensus. (It is a deceptively simple solution.) The fundamental issue, however, is not whether the list of objectives is derived from this or that method: more basic is the question of whether objectives ought to be prespecified at all. One might argue, therefore, that Bode, in skillfully demolishing the method of consensus, did not quite strike the jugular vein of scientific curriculum making. The central question is whether the curriculum should be a blueprint for what people should be like, not how the blueprint is drawn.

But even if one were to concede prespecification of objectives in such areas as arithmetic, grammar, and spelling, how far could one go in justifying the "social shortcomings" of which Bobbitt speaks (1918, p. 50)? As many of Bobbitt's objectives imply, there was literally no activity of mankind—social, intellectual, or practical—that was not potentially, at least, a curricular objective. Bode correctly identified Herbert Spencer as having anticipated the trend toward specificity in stating objectives, but of at least equal importance is Spencer's role in identifying the scope of the school curriculum with life itself. Spencer, like Bobbitt and Charters, considered the best curriculum to be the one that demonstrated the highest utility. Spencer, it should be remembered, asked the question, "What knowledge is of most worth?," not merely, "What shall the schools teach?" In a subtle way, then, he was reconstructing a basic curriculum question. To the scientific curriculum makers, the two questions were essentially the same; thus by posing their question in this way, scientific curriculum makers were determining the kind of answer that could be given. The answer to the scientific curriculum maker is likely to be phrased in terms of high survival value and functional utility rather than in terms of intellectual virtues. In this sense, the curriculum became the ultimate survival kit for the modern world. For example, in the state of Oregon today, certain districts have instituted requirements for high school graduation of such "survival" skills as listing birth-control methods in order of effectiveness, or demonstrating ability to officiate at two different sports and perform two basic dance steps (*Newsweek*, January 25, 1975, p. 69). Any sense of a distinctive function for the schools is lost.

Limitations of the School

Two serious but often unexamined questions are raised by such a conception of the school curriculum. The first relates to the extent to which the school as one institution of society can as a purely practical matter devote itself to the full range of human activity that man engages in. A second question, perhaps even more fundamental than the first, is whether all activity can be reduced to particular components.

From the days of the *Cardinal Principles* report to the present, the conventional way to begin the process of curriculum development has been to agree on a set of broad goals which in fact represents a categorization of human activity generally. The next step, of course, is to "operationalize" these goals by translating them into numerous minute and specific objectives—in effect, creating a catalog of human activity. Surely if Charters were able to identify the activities that constitute being a secretary or a librarian, it was only a step further to identify all the other activities of mankind. In this way the most urgent of these activities may be identified (e.g., earning a living) and the most pressing social problems addressed (e.g., drug addiction).

The missing ingredient in all this is some attention to the nature of the school. If there is one serious omission in Bode's analysis, it is the failure to recognize the limitations of the institution of schooling. The knowledge that is of the most worth may not be the kind of knowledge that can be transmitted in a school context. The place of the school in the social structure, the makeup of its inhabitants, and the characteristic activities that take place within its boundaries must be considered along with the power of schooling as we know it to produce fundamental and direct changes in human attitudes and behavior. Hence if curriculum makers do not temper the question of what is most important to know with the question of what schools can accomplish, their claims for programs designed to reduce crime, improve human relations, prevent drunken driving, ensure economic independence, or remove sexual inhibitions are unreliable.

Analyzing Human Activity

Furthermore, while it may be true that a limited number of human activities may be anticipated and therefore practiced in advance, the extension of the method of job analysis from the limited realm of routine and replicative behavior into the full universe of human activity represents perhaps the most fundamental fallacy in the whole scientific curriculum-making movement. The source of this assumption, as is the case with other elements of scientific curriculum making, is the example of industry. Just as the global and complex process of building an automobile can be broken down into a series of minute and simple operations, so presumably can the activities of a mother or a teacher. But we do not learn language, for example, by anticipating all of the sentences we will utter in our adult lives and then rehearsing them as part of our preparation to become adults. Instead, we learn or assimilate or perhaps even inherit the governing principles of language that permit us to create or invent sentences that we have never before heard expressed. Similarly, in mathematics we do not scientifically catalog all of the mathematical operations we will perform as adults as a direct rehearsal for the performance of those mathematical operations.

Here Bode's criticism of job analysis as the universal technique of curriculum making is particularly cogent. The analogy between definite operations which imply simply replicative activity and activities that involve, let us say, judgment, simply will not hold. As he puts it, friendliness, courtesy, and honesty "are not reducible to 'definite operations'" (Bode 1927, p. 109). The process of educating a teacher to conduct himself or herself wisely and judiciously in the classroom is not, as current programs of teacher training so often imply, a process of first anticipating the particular situations that will arise in the classroom and then directing the teachers to conduct themselves in a particular way relative to these specific situations. Rather, teacher education can involve the examination, analysis, and adaptation of some broad principles which at some unknown point in the future and in some unanticipated circumstances may provide a guide to keen judgment and wise action.

Scientific Curriculum Making in Teacher Education

Bode's astute criticism of the scientific curriculum makers notwithstanding, it should be clear to anyone familiar with the current state of the art in the curriculum world that the scientific curriculum movement, with few adaptations and modifications, has been triumphant. It is true that behaviorism has provided a few refinements of language in stating objectives, and certain so-called academic subjects such as mathematics and science have perhaps more respectability than in the days of Bobbitt and Charters. But the key ingredients and analogies remain the same. While this modern version of scientific curriculum making is well established in virtually all sectors of the curriculum world, it exists, not surprisingly, in its most virulent form in the area of teacher education. The vogue movements which go under the names of competency-based teacher education (CBTE) and performance-based teacher education (PBTE) are prime examples of what has evolved from the basic principles enunciated by Bobbitt and Charters. Charters himself helped direct a major study begun in 1925 which had all the earmarks of the PBTE (or CBTE) ideology.

The Commonwealth Teacher-Training Study

As is the case with the current programs, the *Commonwealth Teacher-Training Study* was to be based on scientific research into the teaching process as opposed to mere speculation and tradition. As a first step, Charters and Waples "ascertained the traits that characterize excellent teachers" (1929, p. 4). Adapting the consensus approach, the investigators used two methods: analyzing the professional literature and interviewing "expert judges." Working from a list of eighty-three traits, ranging alphabetically from Accuracy through Foresight and Magnetism all the way to Wittiness (pp. 56–61), "translators" were given the task of interpreting statements made in writing or in the interviews. Thus, "knows how to meet people" could become translated into the traits, "adaptability" or "approachability." Reliability among the translators was determined by applying the Spearman prophecy formula. Finally, after some of the original traits of teachers were telescoped, scientifically determined lists were prepared indicating that senior high school teachers should be characterized by twenty-six traits including Good Taste and Propriety, junior high school teachers by Conventionality (morality) and Open-mindedness, and so on.

Next, in an adaptation of the job analysis technique, the investigators collected a master list of 1,001 teacher activities. Perhaps one of these activities is worth quoting in its entirety:

788. Securing cordial relations with superintendent
Maintaining cordial relations with superintendent. This involves being loyal to and respecting the superintendent. Becoming acquainted with superintendent and working in harmony with him. Performing friendly acts for superintendent; remembering superintendent at

Christmas; making designs and drawings for superintendent; making lamp shades for superintendent's wife. (Charters and Waples 1929, p. 423)

Thus, after three years of research by trained investigators and a grant of $42,000 from the Commonwealth Fund, was a blow dealt to fuzzy thinking in teacher education and a major stride taken in the direction of a scientifically determined teacher-education curriculum.

The Contemporary Aftermath

One of the most persistent and puzzling questions in this, the aftermath of the scientific curriculum-making movement, is why we retain, even revere, the techniques and assumptions we have inherited from Bobbitt and Charters, at the same time as we reject, implicitly at least, the actual outcomes of their research. Few people read Bobbitt's famous study, *Curriculum-Making in Los Angeles*, or his magnum opus, *How to Make a Curriculum*, or have even heard of Charters and Waples's *Commonwealth Teacher-Training Study*. If they did read these works, the most likely reaction would be one of amusement. And yet we pursue with sober dedication the techniques on which these works are based. Admittedly, performance-based teacher education may just be a slogan system resting only on a foundation of high-sounding rhetoric and pious promises and covered with a gloss of false novelty; but if it means anything, it surely implies that one can identify the particular components of teaching activity that make for good teachers and that these characteristics (Charters would call them traits) or behaviors (Charters would call them activities) can form the basis of a program of teacher training. Research takes the form of identifying the particular components of teaching that will ensure success. While there seems to be some caution in stating the characteristics and behaviors with the same degree of conviction as Bobbitt and Charters did, an abiding faith in the efficacy of the approach remains. The persistence of this faith in the face of a record of over a half century of failure is a mystery that probably even Bode could not fathom.

Is Teaching a Technology?

At the heart of some of our most fundamental problems in the field of curriculum and of teacher education as well is the question of whether teaching is a technology by which carefully fashioned products in the form of learning or behavior are made. These products would have to be designed with the exactitude and specificity that Bobbitt and Charters called for. Teaching would be the application of standardized means by which predictable results would be achieved, and curriculum development the specification of the end-products and the rules for their efficient manufacture. Teacher education, in turn, would be the process by which persons are transformed into efficient manufacturers. The research evidence that presumably would support such an analogy between the teaching and the manufacturing process, however, has been disappointing to the proponents. For example, a recent thorough examination of the research basis for performance-based teacher education led to the conclusion that eleven process variables previously identified as "promising"—such as "clarity," "variability," and "enthusiasm"—were indeed notably unpromising, leading the authors to conclude that "an empirical basis for performance-based teacher education does not exist" (Heath and Nielson 1974, p. 475). Moreover, pessimism about the ultimate success of the approach was not based simply on flaws in statistical analysis or research design. The more fundamental problem was the framework in which such research was cast—a framework which, by the way, has held sway since the days of Bobbitt, Charters, and the scientific curriculum-making movement.

Bode as Prophet

The point of all this is not simply that Bobbitt, Charters, and their likeminded contemporaries were mistaken in their faith in a given approach; the age in which they lived was one where optimism about the power of science to solve a multitude of human and social problems was near its peak. If they were naive or mistaken, one can hardly blame them. What is almost unforgivable, however, is that the half century since the zenith of their influence has produced little more by way of sophistication and refinement. With few exceptions, Bode's criticism of 1927 would carry as much force today were it directed against the present-day heirs of scientific curriculum making.

Particularly disappointing are the precipitous efforts to convert highly tentative and limited research findings into immediate prescriptions. This may be a function of the large constituency of teachers and school administrators who want immediate and concrete answers to such global questions as What is a good teacher? and What is a good curriculum? Part of the problem, undoubtedly, with the era of the scientific curriculum makers and with ours is the failure to recognize the complexity of the phenomena with which we deal. There is the same confusion between science and desert empiricism, the same naiveté about the nature of the teaching process, the same neglect of conceptual analysis. To be critical of scientific curriculum making, as Bode was, is not to be critical of science or even the importance of scientific inquiry into educational processes: it is to be critical of a simplistic and vulgar scientism. Its persistence is a source of embarrassment.

References

Bobbitt, Franklin. (1913). "Some General Principles of Management Applied to the Problems of City-School Systems." In *The Supervision of City Schools. Twelfth Yearbook of the National Society for the Study of Education*, Part 1, pp. 7–96. Bloomington, Ill.: Public School Publishing Co.
——. (1918). *The Curriculum*. Boston: Houghton Mifflin.
——. (1922). *Curriculum-making in Los Angeles*. Supplementary Educational Monographs, no. 20. Chicago: University of Chicago Press.
——. (1924). *How to Make a Curriculum*. Boston: Houghton Mifflin.
——. (1926). "The Orientation of the Curriculum-maker." In *The Foundations and Technique of Curriculum-construction. Twenty-Sixth Yearbook of the National Society for the Study of Education*, Part 2, pp. 41–55. Bloomington, Ill.: Public School Publishing Co.
——. "A Summary Theory of the Curriculum." *Society for Curriculum Study News Bulletin* 5 (January 12, 1934): 2–4.
Bode, Boyd H. (1927). *Modern Educational Theories*. New York: Macmillan.
Charters, Werrett W. (1909). *Methods of Teaching: Developed from a Functional Standpoint*. Chicago: Row, Peterson & Co.
——. (1913). *Teaching the Common Branches*. Boston: Houghton Mifflin.
——. "The Reorganization of Women's Education." *Educational Review* 62 (October 1921): 224–231.
——. (1923). *Curriculum Construction*. New York: Macmillan.
——. (1925). "Curriculum for Women." In *Proceedings of the High School Conference*. Urbana, Ill.: University of Illinois.

Charters, Werrett W., and Waples, Douglas. (1929). *The Commonwealth Teacher-training Study*. Chicago: University of Chicago Press.

Dewey, John. (1916). *Democracy and Education: An Introduction to the Philosophy of Education*. New York: Macmillan.

———. "My Pedagogic Creed." *Journal of the National Education Association* 18, no. 9 (December 1929): 291–295.

Heath, Robert W., and Nielson, Mark A. "The Research Basis for Performance-based Teacher Education." *Review of Educational Research* 44, no. 4 (Fall 1974): 463–484.

National Education Association Commission on the Reorganization of Secondary Education. (1918). *Cardinal Principles of Secondary Education: A Report*. Washington: Government Printing Office.

Spencer, Herbert. (1860). "What Knowledge Is of Most Worth?" In *Education: Intellectual, Moral and Physical*, pp. 1–96. New York: D. Appleton and Co.

"Survival Test." *Newsweek*, January 25, 1975, p. 69.

Thorndike, E. L., and Woodworth, R. S. "The Influence of Improvement in One Mental Function upon the Efficiency of Other Functions," Part 1. *Psychological Review* 8, no. 3 (May 1901): 247–261.

Part Two

*Curriculum at Education's
Center Stage*

Introduction to Part Two

The readings in this part of the book lead into and reflect the reform efforts of the 1950s and 1960s. As the 1950s wore on concerns arose that the curriculum lacked academic rigor and, as a consequence, academically talented young people were failing to realize their potential. This was especially worrisome to many Americans during a period of cold war in which the services of technological and scientific elites were deemed vital to national security. The popular belief that school programs in the Soviet Union were particularly rigorous only heightened public concern. James Conant (1959), former president of Harvard, was one of a number of well-publicized critics of school programs. Central to his recommendations was the consolidation of small high schools in order to provide greater numbers of advanced, specialized courses for gifted students.

These concerns nourished unprecedented federal and private support for curriculum development projects. The life cycle of these projects alternated between crisis and optimism. Mathematics, science, and foreign language curricula, especially programs for academically talented students, were perceived as directly relevant to national defense, and thus the first to receive attention.

Taking the lead in curriculum change efforts were subject-matter specialists such as physicists and mathematicians as well as a healthy number of psychologists. They had faith that the specialists, armed with specialized knowledge and modern techniques, could set American schools back on track. They set out to construct curriculum materials that would form a foundation for transforming U.S. school programs.

From these heady beginnings, the curriculum reform movement took hold in universities and educational publishing for a decade or so, but the movement was to end in controversy. On the one hand, its political aftermath is symbolized by what eventually came to be an open attack on the National Science Foundation for its role in the development of an elementary social studies curriculum, "Man: A Course of Study." Although this program had been designed to develop concepts through a process of discovery, its content, the nature of humans as a species, came to be seen as a repudiation of mainstream American values (Schaffarzick, 1979). As Jerome Bruner (2006), who headed the MACOS project, observed many years later, "comparing the human condition in different cultures is, alas, too easily interpreted as finding fault with our own" (p. 4). On the other hand, scholarly rather than political controversy came from within academe, symbolized by Joseph Schwab's (this volume, Chapter 12) pronouncement in 1969 that for all practical purposes, the curriculum field had reached a moribund state.

Ralph Tyler's *Basic Principles of Curriculum and Instruction*, which is the first reading in Part Two, is far from the turmoil of the late 1960s. Tyler's slim book, a mere 128 pages cover to cover, was published in 1949. At that time it served as both a precursor to national reform and a culmination of progressive educational thought. In particular, Tyler's rationale reaches back to the work of Franklin Bobbitt and others who sought to bring the field into the modern, scientific age. Their strategy for doing so was to develop curricula using a means-ends model. Tyler specifically organized the process around four questions: What are the purposes of an educational program? What experiences will further these purposes? How shall the program be organized? And, how shall it be evaluated?

These questions represent four design elements, the first of which Tyler gives special emphasis. "All aspects of the educational program," he writes, "are really means to accomplish basic educational purposes" (this volume, Chapter 7). Tyler's book does not venture to suggest specific objectives, but almost half of its pages are devoted to describing sources of information that support the selection of objectives. Three primary sources are discussed early on. The first is the study of learners, including their social and psychological needs. The second source includes studies of contemporary life to help identify "critical knowledge" and aid in the transfer of training. The third source of information includes suggestions from subject matter specialists. Tyler cites the Committee of Ten as an example, but not as an exemplar, of using subject matter specialists to identify educational objectives. This committee was formed in 1892 by the National Education Association, and it was charged with the task of recommending objectives for secondary education. The committee organized its work around particular subjects such as geography, mathematics, and Latin. In this sense, subject matter expertise was foregrounded. From Tyler's perspective, however, the Committee of Ten misunderstood the role of subject matter in general education. For example, Tyler (this volume) observes that the committee's "report in Mathematics outlines objectives for the beginning courses in the training of a mathematician" rather than asking: "What can your subject contribute to the education of young people who are not going to be specialists in your field?"

General education is less in evidence in the next reading by Bruner. In 1959 the National Academy of Sciences organized a special conference on science curriculum change, especially how it pertained to gifted students, at Woods Hole, Massachusetts. Bruner directed the meeting and the attendees were scientists, psychologists interested in learning, and educators. The following year Bruner published an account of the proceedings as *The Process of Education* (1960). It quickly became a bestseller. The principles enunciated in this brief text—at less than 100 pages even shorter than Tyler's *Basic Principles*—were to prove cornerstones of the curriculum reform movement.

Three of the most important of these principles can be glimpsed in the opening paragraphs of the reading on MACOS. First, he proclaims that children will learn more effectively if they discover ideas for themselves rather than the familiar method of being told those ideas. Second, he asserts that children are capable of engaging in authentic intellectual activity from an early age; he rejects the popular notion that children cannot think until instruction has inculcated information to think with. Third, he argues that children should focus on the structure of disciplines, how things are related, rather than on acquisition of mere information. All in all, Bruner contended, skill in discovery and grasp of disciplinary structures made possible significant transfer of training. Rather than commit to memory actual information, of which there was too much and it would soon be dated anyway, children would learn how to learn.

As noted, although MACOS was planned to be an elementary social studies curriculum, it did not fit neatly with how knowledge is conventionally carved up in into school subjects. It drew on anthropology, biology, and linguistics, fields not well represented in elementary school curriculum, and dealt with possibly unfamiliar cultural practices without being judgmental. Thus MACOS's subject matter marked a bold departure from the intellectual habits and content of elementary social studies education in the United States. In effect, as one of Bruner's collaborators (Dow, 1991) put it, MACOS created a "parallel curriculum" which teachers were ill-prepared to implement. Moreover, this new curriculum was more single-mindedly academic, as the reading by Philip Jackson (this volume, Chapter 11) tellingly reveals, than teacher norms and student expectations for "the daily grind" of classrooms.

Both Tyler's rationale and Bruner's innovative curriculum package serve to underscore questions of educational purpose, and doing so sets the stage for the next pair of readings. These readings represent the great objectives debate. By the late 1960s, this debate had come to focus not on whether specific objectives should be used in curriculum planning, but on how objectives should be used, the form they should take, and the functions they should be expected to serve. The dominant camp again worked from a means-ends perspective that required curriculum developers to state clearly the objectives of a program prior to deciding its content or organization. Proponents of this approach, such as W. James Popham and others (e.g., Mager, 1962) argued that pre-specified, clearly stated, and measurable objectives are essential to curriculum planning for at least two reasons. First, educators without such objectives would not know the outcomes they seek to realize, and thus have little basis for deciding how to select or organize classroom activities. Second, without objectives, an evaluator would not know what to look for in determining a program's success or failure. Under the influence of this logic, thousands of American teachers learned to write behavioral objectives in the 1970s using standardized and tightly specified formats.

A dissenting position to the objectives movement is represented by Elliot Eisner's article, "Educational Objectives—Help or Hindrance?" Eisner questioned both the practicality of pre-specified objectives and the underlying assumptions on which they are based. On the practical side, he saw two problems. First, the potential outcomes of instruction are usually so numerous that it would be difficult to anticipate all of these objectives with a high degree of specificity. Second, the objectives-first sequence does not seem to be borne out in practice. That is, while teachers often begin with explicit objectives, they also allow the selection of content and activities to inform and modify objectives as instructional activities unfold in the classroom. To put this another way, Eisner argued that the rationality of teaching is more dynamic, more interactive, and less mechanistic than the proponents of behavioral objectives had assumed. Moreover, Eisner asserts that evaluators have confused objectives with standards. Standards can be applied in a fairly routine manner, but using objectives as criteria for assessment unavoidably entails an element of judgment on the part of the evaluator.

A related criticism was that the objectives movement jumped too quickly from objectives to outcomes, thereby bypassing practice altogether. This concern made Philip Jackson's book, *Life in Classrooms*, particularly distinctive. Jackson did not vault over classrooms, but jumped right into them. In the brief excerpts we have taken from his book, Jackson offers a number of arguments for why the daily routines of practice should be of paramount concern for those interested in school curriculum. These routines are often overshadowed because they are commonplace, repetitive, and ordinary. Herein we find an interesting paradox; for if Jackson is right, practice is ignored for the very reasons that it is so important. Classroom routines have an enduring influence specifically because they are commonplace, repetitive, and ordinary. In addition, Jackson argues that these routines are more than simply ways of delivering subject matter or acquiring academic skills. Rather, "the daily grind" itself teaches a hidden curriculum of unspoken expectations, and these expectations are what most often determine a student's school success or failure. If researchers or evaluators were to examine an educational program solely on the basis of its stated objectives, the hidden curriculum would in all likelihood remain just that—hidden.

The final reading in this section is Joseph Schwab's article, "The Practical: A Language for Curriculum." It is the first of his four articles published between 1970 and 1983 in which Schwab examines a range of issues related to developments within the field and to "the practical arts" of curriculum deliberation. We have included the first of these essays in our collection partly because of its broad scope. It is an essay that can be viewed in several ways: as a critique of the field at large; as an effort to reframe the relationship between theory and practice; and as a call for problem-based, collaborative forms of curriculum development. For its time, the article also reflects a heightened level of self-consciousness about the field's past, present, and future trends.

We also included Schwab's article because its meaning continues to provoke controversy. When he delivered the first paper on "the practical" at the American Educational Research Association in 1969, Schwab raised eyebrows, and his declaring the curriculum field "moribund" was but one of the reasons for the controversy. In recent decades attention has often been focused on his place in curriculum history and his overall contributions to the field. In the 1990s, for instance, Jackson (1992) described Schwab's work as moving away from systematic approaches as conceived in the past, but still offering a version of the dominant perspective that had already been well established in the work of people such as Bobbitt and Tyler. In this view, Schwab was working with variations on the theme. Others, such as William Reid (1993), argued that Schwab's work should be placed in a category by itself, as an alternative to the dominant perspective rather than as a modified version of earlier approaches. The debate about the meanings and significances of Schwab's work has continued into the 21st century: Peter Hlebowitsh's essay (this volume, Chapter 23) gives a recent interpretation of the extent to which Schwab's sense of "the practical" marked continuity or discontinuity with the major traditions of the field.

References

Bruner, J. S. (1960). *The process of education*. Cambridge, MA: Harvard University Press.

Bruner, J. S. (2006). *In search of pedagogy, Volume I*. New York: Routledge.

Conant, J. B. (1959). *The American high school today*. New York: McGraw-Hill.

Dewey, John. (1938). *Experience and Education*. New York: Collier Books.

Dow, P. B. (1991). *Schoolhouse politics*. Cambridge, MA: Harvard University Press.

Jackson, P. W. (1992). Conceptions of curriculum and curriculum specialists. In P. W. Jackson (ed.), Handbook of research on curriculum (pp. 3–40). New York: Macmillan.

Mager, R. F. (1962). *Preparing instructional objectives*. Palo Alto, CA: Fearon.

Reid, W. A. (1993). Does Schwab improve on Tyler? A response to Jackson. *Journal of Curriculum Studies*, 25, 499–510.

Schaffarzick, J. (1979). Federal curriculum reform: A crucible for value conflict. In J. Schaffarzick & G. Sykes (eds.), *Value conflicts and curriculum issues* (pp. 1–24). Berkeley, CA: McCutchan.

7

Basic Principles of Curriculum and Instruction
Ralph W. Tyler

Introduction

This small book[1] attempts to explain a rationale for viewing, analyzing and interpreting the curriculum and instructional program of an educational institution. It is not a textbook, for it does not provide comprehensive guidance and readings for a course. It is not a manual for curriculum construction since it does not describe and outline in detail the steps to be taken by a given school or college that seeks to build a curriculum. This book outlines one way of viewing an instructional program as a functioning instrument of education. The student is encouraged to examine other rationales and to develop his own conception of the elements and relationships involved in an effective curriculum.

The rationale developed here begins with identifying four fundamental questions which must be answered in developing any curriculum and plan of instruction. These are:

1. What educational purposes should the school seek to attain?
2. What educational experiences can be provided that are likely to attain these purposes?
3. How can these educational experiences be effectively organized?
4. How can we determine whether these purposes are being attained?

This book suggests methods for studying these questions. No attempt is made to answer these questions since the answers will vary to some extent from one level of education to another and from one school to another. Instead of answering the questions, an explanation is given of procedures by which these questions can be answered. This constitutes a rationale by which to examine problems of curriculum and instruction.

1. What Educational Purposes should the School Seek to Attain?

Many educational programs do not have clearly defined purposes. In some cases one may ask a teacher of science, of English, of social studies, or of some other subject what objectives are being aimed at and get no satisfactory reply. The teacher may say in effect that he aims to develop a well-educated person and that he is teaching English or social studies or some other subject because it is essential to a well-rounded education. No doubt some excellent educational work is being done by artistic teachers who do not have a clear conception of goals but do have an intuitive sense of what is good teaching, what materials are significant, what topics are worth dealing with and how to present material and develop topics effectively with students. Nevertheless, if an educational program is to be planned and if efforts for continued improvement are to be made, it is very necessary to have some conception of the goals that are being aimed at. These educational objectives become the criteria by which materials are selected, content is outlined, instructional procedures are developed and tests and examinations are prepared. All aspects of the educational program are really means to accomplish basic educational purposes. Hence, if we are to study an educational program systematically and intelligently we must first be sure as to the educational objectives aimed at.

But how are objectives obtained? Since they are consciously willed goals, that is, ends that are desired by the school staff, are they not simply matters of personal preference of individuals or groups? Is there any place for a systematic attack upon the problem of what objectives to seek?

It is certainly true that in the final analysis objectives are matters of choice, and they must therefore be the considered value judgments of those responsible for the school. A comprehensive philosophy of education is necessary to guide in making these judgments. And, in addition, certain kinds of information and knowledge provide a more intelligent basis for applying the philosophy in making decisions about objectives. If these facts are available to those making decisions, the probability is increased that judgments about objectives will be wise and that the school goals will have greater significance and greater validity. For this reason, a large part of the so-called scientific study of the curriculum during the past thirty years has concerned itself with investigations that might provide a more adequate basis for selecting objectives wisely. The technical literature of the curriculum field includes hundreds of studies that collected information useful to curriculum groups in selecting objectives.

Accepting the principle that investigations can be made which will provide information and knowledge useful in deciding about objectives, the question is then raised what sources can be used for getting information that will be helpful in this way. A good deal of controversy goes on between essentialists and progressives, between subject specialists and child psychologists, between this group and that school group over the question of the basic source from which objectives can be derived. The progressive emphasizes the importance of studying the child to find out what kinds of interests he has, what problems he encounters, what purposes he has in mind. The progressive sees this information as providing the basic source for selecting objectives. The essentialist, on the other hand, is impressed by the large body of knowledge collected over many thousands of years, the so-called cultural heritage, and emphasizes this as the primary source for deriving objectives. The essentialist views objectives as essentially the basic learnings selected from the vast cultural heritage of the past.

Many sociologists and others concerned with the pressing problems of contemporary society see in an analysis of contemporary society the basic information from which objectives can be derived. They view the school as the agency for helping young people to deal effectively with the critical problems of contemporary life. If they can determine what these contemporary problems are then the objectives of the school are to provide those knowledges, skills, attitudes, and the like that will help people to deal intelligently with these contemporary problems. On the other hand, the educational philosophers recognize that there are basic values in life, largely transmitted from one generation to another by means of education. They see the school as aiming essentially at the transmission of the basic values derived by comprehensive philosophic study and hence see in educational philosophy the basic source from which objectives can be derived.

The point of view taken in this course is that no single source of information is adequate to provide a basis for wise and comprehensive decisions about the objectives of the school. Each of these sources has certain values to commend it. Each source should be given some consideration in planning any comprehensive curriculum program. Hence, we shall turn to each of the sources in turn to consider briefly what kinds of information can be obtained from the source and how this information may suggest significant educational objectives.

Studies of the Learners Themselves as a Source of Educational Objectives

Education is a process of changing the behavior patterns of people. This is using behavior in the broad sense to include thinking and feeling as well as overt action. When education is viewed in this way, it is clear that educational objectives, then, represent the kinds of changes in behavior that an educational institution seeks to bring about in its students. A study of the learners themselves would seek to identify needed changes in behavior patterns of the students which the educational institution should seek to produce.

An investigation of children in the elementary school in a certain community may reveal dietary deficiency and inadequate physical condition. These facts may suggest objectives in health education and in social studies but they suggest objectives only when viewed in terms of some conception of normal or desirable physical condition. In a society which takes dietary deficiencies for granted, there would be little likelihood of inferring any educational objectives from such data. Correspondingly, studies of adolescence during the depression indicated that a considerable number were greatly perturbed over the possibility that they would be unable to find work upon graduation. This does not automatically suggest the need for vocational guidance or occupational preparation. Studies of the learner suggest educational objectives only when the information about the learner is compared with some desirable standards, some conception of acceptable norms, so that the difference between the present condition of the learner and the acceptable norm can be identified. This difference or gap is what is generally referred to as a need.

There is another sense in which the term "need" is used in the psychological writings of Prescott, Murray, and others. They view a human being as a dynamic organism, an energy system normally in equilibrium between internal forces produced by the energy of the oxidation of food and external conditions. To keep the system in equilibrium it is necessary that certain "needs" be met. That is, certain tensions are produced which result in disequilibrium unless these tensions are relieved. In this sense every organism is continually meeting its needs, that is, reacting in such a way as to relieve these forces that bring about imbalance. In these terms one of the problems of education is to channel the means by which these needs are met so that the resulting behavior is socially acceptable, yet at the same time the needs are met and the organism is not under continuous, unrelieved tensions. Prescott classifies these needs into three types: physical needs such as the need for food, for water, for activity, for sex and the like; social needs such as the need for affection, for belonging, for status or respect from this social group; and integrative needs, the need to relate one's self to something larger and beyond one's self, that is, the need for a philosophy of life. In this sense all children have the same needs and it is the responsibility of the school as with every other social institution to help children to get these needs met in a way which is not only satisfying but provides the kind of behavior patterns that are personally and socially significant. A study of such needs in a given group of children would involve identifying those needs that are not being properly satisfied and an investigation of the role the school can play in helping children to meet these needs. This may often suggest educational objectives in the sense of indicating certain knowledge, attitudes, skills, and the like, the development of which would help children to meet these needs more effectively. These studies may also suggest ways in which the school can help to give motivation and meaning to its activities by providing means for children to meet psychological needs that are not well satisfied outside the school.

Studies of Contemporary Life Outside the School

[margin note: developed after advent of Science + the industrial revolution]

The effort to derive objectives from studies of contemporary life largely grew out of the difficulty of accomplishing all that was laid upon the schools with the greatly increased body of knowledge which developed after the advent of science and the Industrial Revolution. Prior to this time the body of material that was considered academically respectable was sufficiently small so that there was little problem in selecting the elements of most importance from the cultural heritage. With the tremendous increase in knowledge accelerating with each generation after the advent of science, the schools found it no longer possible to include in their program all that was accepted by scholars. Increasingly the question was raised as to the contemporary significance of particular items of knowledge or particular skills and abilities. Herbert Spencer in his essay on *What Knowledge Is of Most Worth?* attempted to deal with this problem in a way that has characterized many of the efforts over the past century. Although this represented the interpretation of informal observations rather than systematic studies, the technique used by Spencer in some respects is very similar to techniques used by investigators today.

When the First World War required the training of a large number of people in the skilled trades, training that must take place in a relatively short period of time, the older and slower apprentice systems were no longer adequate. The idea of job analysis developed and was widely used to work out training programs in World War I which would speed up the training of people for the skilled trades and various types of technology. In essence, job analysis is simply a method of analyzing the activities carried on by a worker in a particular field in order that a training program can be focused upon those critical activities performed by this worker. In essence, most studies of contemporary life have a somewhat similar "logic."

Today there are two commonly used arguments for analyzing contemporary life in order to get suggestions for educational objectives. The first of these arguments is that because contemporary life is so complex and because life is continually changing, it is very necessary to focus educational efforts upon the critical aspects of this complex life and upon those aspects that are of importance today so that we do not waste the time of students in learning things that were important fifty years ago but no longer have significance at the same time that we are neglecting areas of life that are now important and for which the schools provide no preparation.

A second argument for the study of contemporary life grows out of the findings relating to transfer of training. As long as educators believed that it was possible for a student

[margin notes: "Selecting elements from the "cultural heritage"" ; "Very Franklin Bobbitt!" ; "① focus on critical aspects important in the present time"]

to train his mind and the various faculties of the mind in general and that he could use these faculties under whatever conditions might be appropriate, there was less need for analyzing contemporary life to suggest objectives. According to this view the important objectives were to develop the several faculties of the mind and as life developed the student would be able to use this trained mind to meet the conditions that he encountered. Studies of transfer of training, however, indicated that the student was much more likely to apply his learning when he recognized the similarity between the situations encountered in life and the situations in which the learning took place. Furthermore, the student was more likely to perceive the similarity between the life situations and the learning situations when two conditions were met: (1) the life situations and the learning situations were obviously alike in many respects, and (2) the student was given practice in seeking illustrations in his life outside of school for the application of things learned in school. These findings are used to support the value of analyzing contemporary life to identify learning objectives for the school that can easily be related to the conditions and opportunities of contemporary life for use of these kinds of learning.

Using studies of contemporary life as a basis for deriving objectives has sometimes been criticized particularly when it is the sole basis for deriving objectives. One of the most frequent criticisms has been that the identification of contemporary activities does not in itself indicate their desirability. The finding, for example, that large numbers of people are engaged in certain activities does not per se indicate that these activities should be taught to students in the school. Some of these activities may be harmful and in place of being taught in the school some attention might need to be given to their elimination. The second type of criticism is the type made by essentialists who refer to studies of contemporary life as the cult of "presentism." These critics point out that because life is continually changing, preparing students to solve the problems of today will make them unable to deal with the problems they will encounter as adults because the problems will have changed. A third kind of criticism is that made by some progressives who point out that some of the critical problems of contemporary life and some of the common activities engaged in by adults are not in themselves interesting to children nor of concern to children, and to assume that they should become educational objectives for children of a given age neglects the importance of considering the children's interests and children's needs as a basis for deriving objectives.

These criticisms in the main apply to the derivation of objectives solely from studies of contemporary life. When objectives derived from studies of contemporary life are checked against other sources and in terms of an acceptable educational philosophy, the first criticism is removed. When studies of contemporary life are used as a basis for indicating important areas that appear to have continuing importance, and when the studies of contemporary life suggest areas in which students can have opportunity to practice what they learn in school, and also when an effort is made to develop in students an intelligent understanding of the basic principles involved in these matters, the claim that such a procedure involves a worship of "presentism" is largely eliminated. Finally, if studies of contemporary life are used to indicate directions in which educational objectives may aim, while the choice of particular objectives for given children takes into account student interests and needs, these studies of contemporary life can be useful without violating relevant criteria of appropriateness for students of particular age levels. Hence, it is worthwhile to utilize data obtained from studies of contemporary life as one source for suggesting possible educational objectives.

Suggestions About Objectives from Subject Specialists

This is the source of objectives most commonly used in typical schools and colleges. School and college textbooks are usually written by subject specialists and largely reflect their views. Courses of study prepared by school and college groups are usually worked out by subject specialists and represent their conception of objectives that the school should attempt to attain. The reports of the Committee of Ten that appeared at the turn of the century had a most profound effect upon American secondary education for at least twenty-five years. Its reports were prepared by subject specialists and the objectives suggested by them were largely aimed at by thousands of secondary schools.

Many people have criticized the use of subject specialists on the grounds that the objectives they propose are too technical, too specialized, or in other ways are inappropriate for a large number of the school students. Probably the inadequacy of many previous lists of objectives suggested by subject specialists grows out of the fact that these specialists have not been asked the right questions. It seems quite clear that the Committee of Ten thought it was answering the question: What should be the elementary instruction for students who are later to carry on much more advanced work in the field? Hence, the report in History, for example, seems to present objectives for the beginning courses for persons who are training to be historians. Similarly the report in Mathematics outlines objectives for the beginning courses in the training of a mathematician. Apparently each committee viewed its job as outlining the elementary courses with the idea that these students taking these courses would go on for more and more advanced work, culminating in major specialization at the college or university level. This is obviously not the question that subject specialists should generally be asked regarding the secondary school curriculum. The question which they should be asked runs somewhat like this: What can your subject contribute to the education of young people who are not going to be specialists in your field; what can your subject contribute to the layman, the garden variety of citizen? If subject specialists can present answers to this question, they can make an important contribution, because, presumably, they have a considerable knowledge of the specialized field and many of them have had opportunity both to see what this subject has done for them and for those with whom they work. They ought to be able to suggest possible contributions, knowing the field as well as they do, that it might make to others in terms of its discipline, its content, and the like.

Some of the more recent curriculum reports do indicate that subject specialists can make helpful suggestions in answers to this question. The various reports published by the Commission on the Secondary School Curriculum of the Progressive Education Association beginning with "Science in General Education," including "Mathematics in General Education," "Social Studies in General Education," and other titles have been very useful and have thrown some light on the question, "What can this subject contribute to the education of young people who are not to specialize in it?" Other groups have recently prepared somewhat similar reports which also seem promising. Committee reports from the National Council of Mathematics Teachers, the National Council of English Teachers, the National Council of Social Studies Teachers, are cases in point. In general, they recognize much more clearly than did the committee preparing reports for the Committee of Ten that the subject is expected to make contributions to a range of students not considered in the earlier reports. In general, the more recent reports will be found useful as an additional source for suggestions about objectives.

Most of the reports of subject groups do not stop with objectives and many of them do not list objectives specifically. Most of them begin with some outline indicating their conception of the subject field itself and then move on to indicate ways in which it can be used for purposes of general education. Persons working on the curriculum will find it necessary to read the reports in some detail and at many places draw inferences from the statements regarding objectives implied. In general, two kinds of suggestions can be got from the reports as far as objectives are concerned. The first is a list of suggestions regarding the broad functions a particular subject can serve, the second is with regard to particular contributions the subject can make to other large functions which are not primarily functions of the subject concerned.

Let me illustrate these two types of suggestions that can be got from these reports. Recent reports of English groups, for example, have suggested educational functions of English as a study of language. The first function is to develop effective communication including both the communication of meaning and the communication of form. The second type of contribution is to effective expression, including in expression the effort of the individual to make internal adjustments to various types of internal and external pressures. A third function of language is to aid in the clarification of thought as is provided, for example, by the use of basic English as a means of aiding students to see whether they understand ideas clearly enough to translate them into operational words. This last function of clarification of thought is well illustrated by the statement of George Herbert Palmer that when confused he used to write himself clearheaded.

In the realm of literature these English committees see various kinds of contributions in terms of major functions literature can serve. Some emphasize its value in personal exploration. Literature in this sense can provide an opportunity for the individual to explore kinds of life and living far beyond his power immediately to participate in, and also give him a chance to explore vicariously kinds of situations which are too dangerous, too fraught with consequences for him to explore fully in reality. A number of committee reports speak of the general function of literature in providing greater extension to the experience of young people, not limited by geographic opportunities, nor limited in time nor limited in social class or types of occupations or social groups with which they can participate. In this case literature becomes the means of widely extending the horizon of the reader through vicarious experience. Another function of literature is to develop reading interests and habits that are satisfying and significant to the reader. Some English committees stress as an important objective to develop increasing skill in interpreting literary material, not only skill in analyzing the logical development and exposition of ideas but also the whole range of things including human motives which are formulated in written language and can therefore be subject to study and critical interpretation. Finally, some English committees propose that literature serves the function of appreciation, including both an opportunity for significant emotional reactions to literary forms and also opportunities for critical appraisal both of form and content, and a means thereby of developing standards of taste in literature.

These suggestions with regard to possible major functions of language and literature provide large headings under which to consider possible objectives which the school can aim at through language and literature. Such an analysis indicates the pervasive nature of the contribution that language and literature might possibly make to the development of children, adolescents, or adults. They suggest objectives that are more than knowledge, skills, and habits; they involve modes of thinking, or critical interpretation, emotional reactions, interests and the like.

Another illustration of the suggestions of major functions a subject may serve can be obtained from recent reports of science committees. One such report suggests three major functions science can serve for the garden variety of citizen. The first of these is to contribute to the improvement of health, both the individual's health and public health. This includes the development of health practices, of health attitudes, and of health knowledge, including an understanding of the way in which disease is spread and the precautions that can be taken by the community to protect itself from disease and from other aspects of poor health. The second suggested function of science is the use and conservation of natural resources; that is, science can contribute to an understanding of the resources of matter and energy that are available, the ways in which matter and energy can be obtained and utilized so as not greatly to deplete the total reserves, an understanding of the efficiency of various forms of energy transformation, and an understanding of plant and animal resources and the ways in which they can be effectively utilized. The third function of science is to provide a satisfying world-picture, to get clearer understanding of the world as it is viewed by the scientist and man's relation to it, and the place of the world in the larger universe. From these suggested functions of science, again it is possible to infer a good many important objectives in the science field, objectives relating to science, knowledge, attitudes, ability to solve problems, interests and the like.

Recent art reports illustrate another example of suggestions regarding major functions a subject might serve in general education. Some five functions have been proposed in these reports. The first, and in terms of Monroe's writing the most important, is the function of art in extending the range of perception of the student. Through art one is able to see things more clearly, to see them through the eyes of the artist, and thus to get a type of perception he is not likely to obtain in any other way. Both art production and art criticism are likely to extend perception. A second function proposed for art is the clarification of ideas and feelings through providing another medium for communication in addition to verbal media. There are students who find it possible to express themselves and communicate more effectively through art forms than through writing or speaking. For them this is an important educational function of art. A third function is personal integration. This refers to the contribution art has sometimes made to the relieving of tensions through symbolic expression. The making of objects in the studio and shop and expression through dancing and through music have long been known to produce an opportunity for personal expression and personal release from tension that is important in providing for the better integration of some young people. A fourth function is the development of interests and values. It is maintained that aesthetic values are important both as interesting qualities for the student and also as expressing very significant life values in the same category with the highest ultimate values of life. On this basis the contribution art can make in providing satisfaction of these interests and in developing an understanding of and desire to obtain these art values is an important educational function of art. Finally, a fifth function of art is the development of technical competence, a means of acquiring skill in painting or drawing or music, or some other art form which can have meaning and significance to the art student. These art reports are another illustration of material from which a number of significant suggestions regarding educational objectives can be inferred from a statement of functions.

A second type of suggestion that can be got from reports of subject specialists are the particular contributions that a subject can make to other large educational functions, that may not be thought of as unique functions of the subject itself. The Report of the Committee on Science in General Education is an excellent illustration of this type of suggestion. This report is organized in terms of suggested contributions science can make in each of the major areas of human relationships. In personal living, for example, suggestions are made as to ways in which science can help to contribute to personal health, to the need for self assurance, to a satisfying world picture, to a wide range of personal interests, and to aesthetic satisfaction. In the area of personal-social relations, suggestions are made as to ways in which science may help to meet student needs for increasingly mature relationships in home and family life and with adults outside the family, and for successful and increasingly mature relationships with age mates of both sexes. In the area of social-civic relations suggestions are made as to how science may help to meet needs for responsible participation in socially significant activities, and to acquire social recognition. In the area of economic relations suggestions are made as to how science may help to meet needs for emotional assurance of progress toward adult status, to meet the need for guidance in choosing an occupation and for vocational preparation, to meet the need for the wise selection and use of goods and services, and to meet the needs for effective action in solving basic economic problems.

The volume *Science in General Education* then goes on to outline the ways in which science can be taught to encourage reflective thinking and to develop other characteristics of personality such as creative thinking, aesthetic appreciation, tolerance, social sensitivity, self-direction. Critics have questioned the depths of contributions that science might make on a number of these points, but it is clear that these suggestions are useful in indicating possible objectives that a school might wish to aim at, using science or other fields as a means for attaining these objectives. Other subject groups have, in similar fashion, made suggestions regarding specific contributions these subjects might make to areas that are not uniquely the responsibility of these subjects. It is then through the drawing of inferences from reports of this sort regarding both the major functions that specialists think the subject can make and also the more specific contributions that the subject might make to other major functions that one is able to infer objectives from the reports of subject specialists.

I would suggest in order to get some taste of the kind of thing that can be obtained from these reports that you read at least one subject report at the level in which you are interested and jot down your interpretation of the major functions the committee believes that this subject can serve and the more specific contributions it can make to other educational functions. Then, formulate a list of the educational objectives you infer from these statements. This will give you some idea of the kinds of objectives that are likely to be suggested by the reports that are being made by various subject groups.

Note

1. From Ralph W. Tyler, *Basic Principles of Curriculum and Instruction.* Chicago: University Chicago Press, 1949: pp. 1–7, 16–19, 25–33.

8

Man: A Course of Study

Jerome S. Bruner

There is a dilemma in describing a course of study.

One must begin by setting forth the intellectual substance of what is to be taught, else there can be no sense of what challenges and shapes the curiosity of the student. Yet the moment one succumbs to the temptation to "get across" the subject, at that moment the ingredient of pedagogy is in jeopardy. For it is only in a trivial sense that one gives a course to "get something across," merely to impart information. There are better means to that end than teaching. Unless the learner also masters himself, disciplines his taste, and deepens his view of the world, the "something" that is got across is hardly worth the effort of transmission.

The more "elementary" a course and the younger its students, the more serious must be its pedagogical aim of forming the intellectual powers of those whom it serves. It is as important to justify a good mathematics course by the intellectual discipline it provides or the honesty it promotes as by the mathematics it transmits. Indeed, neither can be accomplished without the other.

We begin this article with an account of the substance or structure of a course in "social studies" now in the process of construction. A discussion of pedagogy follows. The aim of the exercise is to write a transitional first draft of the course, a common focus for those of us who have been trying to compose the course, trying to teach parts of it to children in Grade V. If the exercise is finally successful, we shall end with a completed course—with the materials, guides, films, and the other things that must be in the student's hands and on the teacher's shelf. There will be drafts in between. The exercise, we hope, will allow us to be clearer about what we are doing. In the final section we shall consider how we propose to get from a first draft such as this to a course that is ready for teaching.

Structure of the Course

The content of the course is man: his nature as a species, the forces that shaped and continue to shape his humanity. Three questions recur throughout:

What is human about human beings?
How did they get that way?
How can they be made more so?

We seek exercises and materials through which our pupils can learn wherein man is distinctive in his adaptation to the world, and wherein there is discernible continuity between him and his animal forbears. For man represents that crucial point in evolution where adaptation is achieved by the vehicle of culture and only in a minor way by further changes in his morphology. Yet there are chemical tides that run in his blood that are as ancient as the reptiles. We make every effort at the outset to *tell* the children where we hope to travel with them. Yet little of such recounting gets through. It is much more useful, we have found, to pose the three questions directly to the children so that their own views can be brought into the open and so that they can establish some points of view of their own.

In pursuit of our questions we shall explore five matters, each closely associated with the evolution of man as a species, each defining at once the distinctiveness of man and his potentiality for further evolution. The five great humanizing forces are, of course, tool-making, language, social organization, the management of man's prolonged childhood, and man's urge to explain. It has been our first lesson in teaching that no pupil, however eager, can appreciate the relevance of, say, tool-making in human evolution without first grasping the fundamental concept of a tool, or what a language is, or a myth, or social organization. These are not obvious matters. So we are involved in teaching not only the role of tools or language in the emergence of man, but as a necessary precondition for doing so, setting forth the fundamentals of linguistics or the theory of tools. And it is as often the case as not that (as in the case of the "theory of tools") we must solve a formidable intellectual problem ourselves in order to be able to help our pupils do the same.

While one readily singles out these five massive contributors to man's humanization, under no circumstances can they be put into airtight compartments. Human kinship is distinctively different from primate mating patterns precisely because it is classificatory and rests on man's ability to use language. Or, if you will, tool use enhances the division of labor in a society which in turn affects kinship. And language itself is more clearly appreciated by reference to its acquisition in the uniquely human interaction between child and parent. Obviously, the nature of man's world view, whether formulated in myth or in science, depends upon, and is constrained by, the nature of human language. So while each domain can be treated as a separate set of ideas, as we shall see, success in teaching depends upon making it possible for children to have a sense of their interaction.

Language

Teaching the essentials of linguistics to children in the elementary grades has limits, but they are wider than we had expected. There are certain pedagogic precautions to be respected if ten-year-olds are to be captivated by the subject. It must not, to begin with, be presented as a normative subject—as an exercise in how things *should* be written or said. It must, moreover, be disassociated from such traditional "grammar" as the child has encountered. There is nothing so deadening as to have a child handle the "type and order" problem by "recognizing" one category of words as "nouns" and parroting, upon being asked what he means by a noun, that it is a "person, place, or thing." It is not that he is either "right" or "wrong," but rather that he is as remote from the issue as he would be if he attempted to account for grief over the assassination of a President by citing the Constitution on the division of powers. And finally, the discussion needs to remain close to the nature of language in use, its likely origin, and the functions to which it is put.

Whether it is true or not that a ten-year-old has a complete grammatical repertory, he is certainly capable of, and delighted in, recognizing all linguistic features when confronted with instances of them. The chief aid to such recognition is contrast—the opportunity to observe the oppositional features that are so much a feature of human language. What comes hard is to formulate these features conceptually; to go beyond the intuitive grasp of the native speaker to the more self-conscious understanding of the linguist. It is this task—getting children to look at and to ponder the things they can notice in their language long enough to understand them—that is most difficult and it should not be pushed to the point of tedium.

Our section on language includes a consideration of what communication is—by contrasting how humans and animals manage to send and receive messages. The early sessions have proved lively and in the course of them nearly every major issue of linguistics is raised and allowed to go begging. This preliminary exercise has the great virtue that it can be repeated on later occasions, when students have achieved varying levels of sophistication, with the result that they readily recognize how much progress they have made.

The opening session (or sessions, for students often want to continue the arguments over animals and humans) usually indicates which among several openings can be best pursued in later units. The instance which follows is influenced by far too little experience to be considered the general rule, but it is at least one example.

The discussion led naturally to the design features of a language. We designed a language game based on bee language, requiring the children to find hidden objects by using messages in this bee-like language. The children are encouraged to design similar languages and to improve on the design of the language used. They take to this readily and are eager to discuss and make clearer such design features as semanticity, voice-ear link, displacement, and cultural transmission. The game, of course, is a lead into the demonstration of bee language as presented in the von Frisch film (which is not altogether satisfactory). We were struck, however, at how much more interested the children were in talking about their own language than in discussing bee language or von Frisch's analysis of it. It is as if the bee linguistics were interesting as an introduction into the closer analysis of their own language.

Our next objective is to present the powerful ideas of arbitrariness, of productivity, and of duality of patterning, the latter the exclusive property of human language. We have approached arbitrariness by the conventional route of comparing how pictures, diagrams, charades, and words refer to things. There are nice jokes to be used, as in the example given by Hockett of the tiny word *whale* referring to a big thing, while the large word *microorganism* refers to a tiny one. With respect to productivity, we have had considerable initial success with two exercises. The first is with a language containing four types (how, what, when, where) with a limited number of tokens of each type (e.g., by hand, by weapon, by trap, as tokens of the "how" type) and with a highly constrained set of orders each referring to a different kind of food-related activity. By this means we readily establish the idea of *type* and *order* as two basic ideas. They readily grasp the idea of substitutivity of tokens within a type. (Indeed, given the interest in secret codes based on substitution of words or letters for code breaking, they need little instruction on this score.)

Once the ideas of type and order are established, we begin the following amusing exercises to illustrate the interchangeability of language frames. We present:

1	2	3	4	5
The	man	ate	his	lunch
A	lady	wore	my	hat

This	doctor	broke	a	bottle
My	son	drove	our	car

and the children are now asked to provide "matching" examples. They can do so readily. They soon discover that so long as they pick words in the order 1 2 3 4 5, from any place in each column, something "sensible" can be got—even if it is silly or not true like, "My doctor wore a car," or, "A lady ate a bottle," it is at least not "crazy" like, "Man the lunch his ate."

The students need no urging to construct new frames and to insert additional types into frames already set up (like a new first column the tokens of which include, *did, can, has,* etc.). Interesting discoveries are made—such as the relative openness of some positions and the closed nature of others. We hope to devise methods to help the children discover some of the deeper features of grammar, better to grasp what a language is—for example, that one can start with relatively simple sentence frames, "kernel sentences," and transform them progressively into negatives, queries, and passives or any two or even three of these, and that more complex forms can be returned to simpler forms by applying the transformations in reverse.

Finally, a game has been devised (a game involving signaling at sea) to illustrate duality of patterning, that most difficult feature of human language. It involves developing a language initially with a very limited set of building blocks (as with human languages, each of which combines intrinsically meaningless sound elements, phones, into a unique system that renders them into meaningful phonemes, a change in one of which will alter the meaning of a word so that, in English, *rob* and *lob* are different words, but not so in Japanese where /r/ and /l/ are allophones of the same phoneme just as plosive /p/ *(pin)* and non-plosive /p/ *(spin)* are "the same" for us but not for others). Three kinds of word blocks can be arranged in a frame, making twenty-seven possible "words" or lexemes. But there must be rules as to which combinations mean things and which do not. It is very quickly apparent to the children that the blocks as such "mean" nothing, but the frames do—or some do and some do not. We are in progress of going from this point toward other aspects of duality at this time.

It is a natural transition to go from syntax to the question of how language is acquired by young humans and other primates. We shall use the considerable resources provided by recent studies of language acquisition to show the manner in which syntax emerges from certain very elementary forms such as the pivot-plus-open-class and the head-plus-attribute. The idea of "writing a grammar" for any form of speech encountered will also be presented. In addition, the child-adult "expansion-idealization" cycle will be explored as an example of a powerful form of social grouping that is crucial for transmitting the language. For contrast, we hope to examine the problems of language development of Vicki, a chimpanzee raised by a family along with their own child of like age. The subtle problem of "traditional" and "hereditary" transmission is bound to emerge.

Finally, and with the benefit of their newly gained insight into the nature of language, we shall return to the question of the origins of human language and its role in shaping human characteristics. We hope first to cover the newly available materials on the universal characteristics of all human languages—first getting the children to make some informed guesses on the subject. Then we shall consider the role of language in the organization of the early human group and the effectiveness it might add to such group activities as hunting, given its design features and its universals. To go from this point to a consideration of myth and its nature is not a difficult step.

We have examined these matters in some detail here (though not closely enough). Our hope is to give the reader a concrete sense of how far we wish to go. It is plain that the section on language can take as much of a year as one wishes. We are overproducing materials to give us some better idea of what is possible and how to combine what is possible. Some schools may want to devote much time to language, and we hope to make it possible for them to do so. But above all, we hope to provide enough variety so that a teacher can choose an emphasis of his own, whether it be to increase self-consciousness about language or to impart a livelier sense of some distinctively human aspect of human language. In the first stages of our work, the tendency is to concentrate more on "getting the subject right"—in this case linguistics—than on getting the whole course constructed. And just as there is a tension between the requirements of the subject itself and those imposed by the need to teach it to children, so is there a necessary tension between the parts of our course (the five topics) and the whole (the nature and evolution of man). We shall return to this matter in discussing the summer workshop in a later section.

The section on language has required the collaboration of a variety of linguists of different stripe—pure, anthropological, psychological—and of teachers, psychologists, film-makers, artists, and children. At that, it is hardly a quarter done. Gloria Cooper of Harvard has directed the unit, with the aid of David McNeill of Harvard, Mary Henle of the New School, John Mickey of Colorado State, Betsy Dunkman of the Newton Schools, and Florence Jackson of the New York City Schools.

Tool Making

One starts with several truths about children and "tools." They have usually not used many of them, and in general, tools will not be of much interest. This may derive from the deeper truth that, in general, children (like their urban parents) think of tools as set pieces that are to be bought in hardware stores. And finally, children in our technologically mature society usually have little notion of the relation between tools and our way of life. Production takes place in factories where they have never been, its products are packaged to disguise the production process that brought them into being.

The tool unit is still under discussion. What follows are some of the leading ideas that animate the design of the unit.

We begin with a philosophical approach to the nature of tool-using. What is most characteristic of any kind of tool-using is not the tools themselves, but rather the program that guides their use. It is in this broader sense that tools take on their proper meaning as amplifiers of human capacities and implementers of human activity.

Seen as amplifiers, tools can fall into three general classes—amplifiers of sensory capacities, of motor capacities, and of ratiocinative capacities. Within each type there are many subspecies. There are sensory amplifiers like microscopes and ear horns that are "magnifiers," others, like spirit levels and bobs, that are "reference markers," etc. Some implement systems "stretch out" time (slow motion cinematography) and others condense it (time-lapse registration). In the realm of motor amplifiers, some tools provide a basis for binding, some for penetrating, some even for steadying—as when one of our pupils described a draughtsman's compass as a "steadying tool." And, of course, there are the "soft tools" of ratiocination such as mathematics and logic and the "hard tools" they make possible, ranging from the abacus to the high speed digital computer and the automaton.

Once we think of tools as imbedded in a program of use—as implementers of human activity—then it becomes possible to deal with the basic idea of substitutability, an idea as crucial to language as it is to tools. If one cannot find a certain word or phrase, a near equivalent can be substituted in its place. So too with tools: if a skilled carpenter happens not to have brought his chisel to the job, he can usually substitute something else in its place—the edge of a plane blade, a pocket knife, etc. In short, tools are not fixed, and the "functional fixedness" found by so many psychologists studying problem-solving comes finally because so much thinking about tools fixes them to the convention—a hammer is for nails and nothing but nails.

Our ultimate object in teaching about tools is, as noted before, not so much to explicate tools and their significance, but to explore how tools affected man's evolution. The evidence points very strongly to the central part in evolution played by natural selection favoring the user of spontaneous pebble tools over those proto-hominids who depended upon their formidable jaws and dentition. In time, survival depended increasingly on the capacities of the tool-user and tool-maker—not only his opposable forefinger and thumb, but the nervous system to go with them. Within a few hundred thousand years after the first primitive tool-using appears, man's brain size more than doubles. Evolution (or more simply, survival) favored the larger brained creatures capable of adapting by the use of tools, and brain size seems to have been roughly correlated with that capacity. There are many fascinating concomitants to this story. Better weapons meant a shift to carnivorousness. This in turn led to leisure—or at least less food-gathering—which in turn makes possible permanent or semipermanent settlement. Throughout, the changes produced lead to changes in way of life, changes in culture and social organization, changes in what it is possible to do.

All of these matters are now superbly documented in Leaky's excavations in Olduvai Gorge in East Africa. We have consulted with him and he has expressed eagerness to edit four films for us on tool-making and its subsequent effects on the emergence of a new way of life. These are scheduled for the fall of 1965. If we are successful in getting our pupils to speculate about the changes in a society that accompany changes in technology, we will at least have fulfilled one of the original aims of the Social Studies Program: to get across the idea that a technology requires a counterpart in social organization before it can be used effectively by a society.

There happen also to be new materials available on the burgeoning technology of the Magdalenian period when more decorative features appear and tool-makers begin to specialize. We are exploring this work to see whether it too can be used in the same spirit.

A few of the exercises being planned to the "tool section" give some flavor of the pedagogy. One unit calls for the taking of a "census of skills"—the tasks that children know how to perform, along with some effort to examine how they were learned (including tool skills). Another unit consists of trying to design an "all-purpose" tool so that the children can have some notion of the programmatic questions one asks in designing a tool and why specialized use has a role.

There will also be an opportunity (of which more in a later section) for the children to compare "tool play" of an Eskimo boy and Danai boy of New Guinea with the play of immature free-ranging baboons, macaques, and chimpanzees. We are also in process of obtaining films on the technique of manufacture of flint implements and hope also to obtain inexpensive enough materials to have our pupils try their hand at flint knapping and other modes of instrument making, guided possibly by films on the subject by the distinguished French archeologist, Dr Bordes.

There will also be some treatment in the course of tools to make tools as well as of tools that control various forms of natural power. A possible route into this discussion is an overview of the evolution of tool-making generally—from the first "spontaneous" or picked-up tools, to the shaped ones, to those shaped to a pattern, to modern conceptions of man-machine relations as in contemporary systems research. Indeed, if we do follow this approach we shall also explore the design of a game of tool design involving variables such as cost, time, gain, specificity of function, and skill required, with the object of making clear the programmatic nature of tools and the manner in which tools represent a selective extension of human powers.

Social Organization

The section on social organization is still in preliminary planning, save in one respect where work is quite well advanced. The unit has as its objective to make children aware that there is a structure in a society and that this structure is not fixed once and for all. It is an integrated pattern and you cannot change one part of the pattern without other parts of the society changing with it. The way a society arranges itself for carrying out its affairs depends upon a variety of factors ranging from its ecology at one end to the irreversible course of its history and world view at the other.

A first task is to lead children to recognize explicitly certain basic patterns in the society around them, patterns they know well in an implicit, intuitive way—the distinction between kin and others, between face-to-face groups and secondary groups, between reference groups and ones that have corporate being. These, we believe, are distinctions that children easily discover. We should also like the children to grasp the rather abstract fact that within most human groups beyond the immediate family, continuity depends not so much upon specific people, but upon "roles" filled by people—again, as with language and tool-use, there are structures with substitutability.

Such social organization is marked by reciprocity and exchange—cooperation is compensated by protection, service by fee, and so on. There is always giving and getting. There are, moreover, forms of legitimacy and sanction that define the limits of possible behavior in any given role. They are the bounds set by a society and do not depend upon the individual's choice. Law is the classic case, but not the only one. One cannot commit theft legally, but then too one cannot ignore friends with impunity and law has nothing to do with it.

A society, moreover, has a certain world view, a way of defining what is "real," what is "good," what is "possible." To this matter we turn in a later section, mentioning it here only to complete our catalogue of aspirations of ideas we hope to introduce in this part of the course.

We believe that these matters can be presented to children in a fashion that is gripping, close to life, and intellectually honest. The pedagogy is scarcely clear, but we are on the track of some interesting ways of operating. One difficulty with social organization is its ubiquity. Contrast may be our best way of saving social organization from obviousness—by comparing our own forms of social organization with those of baboon troops, of Eskimo, of Bushmen, of prehistoric man as inferred from excavated living floors in Europe and East Africa. But beyond this we are now developing a "family" of games designed to bring social organization into the personal consciousness of the children.

The first of these games, "Hunting," is designed to simulate conditions in an early human group engaged in hunting and is patterned on the life and ecology of the Bushmen of the Kalahari Desert. The elements of the game are Hunters, Prey, Weapons, Habitats, Messages, Predators, and Food. Without going into detail, the game simulates (in the manner of so-called Pentagon games used for increasing the sensitivities of generals) the problem of planning how far one wishes to go in search of various kinds of game, how resources need to be shared by a group to go beyond "varmint" hunting to larger game, how differentiation of labor can come about in weapon-making and weapon-using, how one must decide among different odds in hunting in one terrain or another. Given the form of the game (for which we are principally grateful to Dr Clark Abt), its content can be readily varied to fit the conditions of life of other hunting groups, such as the Eskimo, again with the object of contrast.

What has proved particularly interesting in our early work with the game is that it permits the grouping of a considerable amount of "real" material around it—accounts of the life of the Kalahari Bushmen (of which there is an extraordinarily rich record on film and in both literary and monographic form), their myths and art, the "forbiddingly" desert ecology that is their environment. And so too with the Eskimo; should we go ahead to construct an analogue game for them, for we are in possession of an equally rich documentation on the Netsilik Eskimo of Pelly Bay. Indeed, one of the documentary films made by the ESI Studio in collaboration with the Canadian Film Board and Dr Asen Balikci of the University of Montreal (one of seven half-hour films to be "cut" from our 100,000 feet of film) has already received international acclaim.

Finally, and again by contrast, there now exists a vast store of material on the social organization of higher primates—a considerable portion of which is also in film shot by a crew under Dr Irven DeVore of Harvard for ESI—that serves extremely well to provoke discussion on what is uniquely human about human social organization.

The group now at work on Social Organization consists of Edwin Dethlefsen of Harvard, Richard McCann, on leave from the Newton Schools, and Mrs Linda Braun of the ESI staff.

Child Rearing

This unit has just begun to take shape at the time of writing. It is proceeding on three general themes in the hope of clarifying them by reference to particular materials in the areas of language, of social organization, of tool-making, and of childhood generally. The first general theme is the extent to which and the manner in which the long human childhood (assisted as it is by language) leads to the dominance of sentiment in human life, in contrast to instinctual patterns of gratification and response found to predominate at levels below man. That is to say, affect can now be aroused and controlled by symbols— human beings have an attitude about anger rather than just anger or not anger. The long process of sentiment formation requires both an extended childhood and access to a symbolized culture through language. Without sentiment (or values or the "second signal system" or whatever term one prefers) it is highly unlikely that human society or anything like it would be possible.

A second theme is organized around the human (perhaps primate) tendency toward mastery of skill for its own sake—the tendency of the human being, in his learning of the environment, to go beyond immediate adaptive necessity toward innovation. Recent work on human development has underlined this "push toward effectance," as it has been called. It is present in human play, in the increased variability of human behavior when things get under control. Just as William James commented three-quarters of a century ago that habit was the fly-wheel of society, we can now say that the innovative urge is the accelerator.

The third theme concerns the shaping of the man by the patterning of childhood—that while all humans are intrinsically human, the expression of their humanity is affected by what manner of childhood they have experienced.

The working out of these themes has only begun. One exercise now being tried out is to get children to describe differences between infancy, childhood, and adulthood for different species—using live specimens brought to class (in the case of non-human species) or siblings for humans. For later distribution, of course, the live specimens (and siblings) will be rendered on film. Yet the success of a session, say, with a ten-day-old, stud-tailed macaque suggests that the real thing should be used whenever possible.

Dr Balikci will be cutting a film on Eskimo childhood from the Netsilik footage, and comparable films on baboon and Japanese macaque childhood will also be in preparation. Beyond this there is still little to report. Dr Richard Jones of Brandeis is in charge of the unit, assisted by Miss Catherine Motz, on leave from Germantown Friends School, and Mrs Kathy Sylva and Mrs Phyllis Stein of ESI.

World View

The fifth unit in preparation concerns itself with man's drive to explicate and represent his world. While it concerns itself with myth, with art, with primitive legend, it is only incidentally designed to provide the stories, the images, the religious impulses, and the mythic romance of man's being. It would be more accurate to describe the unit as "beginning philosophy" in both senses of that expression—philosophy at the beginning and, perhaps, philosophy for young beginners.

Central to the unit is the idea that men everywhere are humans, however advanced or "primitive" their civilization. The difference is not one of more or less than human, but of how particular human societies express their human capacities. A remark by the French anthropologist, Levi-Strauss, puts it well.

> Prevalent attempts to explain alleged differences between the so-called primitive mind and scientific thought have resorted to qualitative differences between the working processes of the mind in both cases, while assuming that the entities which they were studying remained very much the same. If our interpretation is correct, we are led toward a completely different view—namely, that the kind of logic in mythical thought is as rigorous as that of modern science, and that the difference lies, not in the quality of the intellectual process, but in the nature of things to which it is applied. This is well in agreement with the situation known to prevail in the field of technology: What makes a steel ax superior to a stone ax is not that the first one is better made than the second. They are equally well made, but steel is quite different from stone. In the same way we may be able to show that the same logical processes operate in myth as in science, and that man has always been thinking equally well; the improvement lies, not in the alleged progress of man's mind, but in the discovery of new areas to which it may apply its unchanged and unchanging powers.

All cultures are created equal. One society—say, that of Eskimos—may have only a few tools, but they are used in a versatile way. The woman's knife does what our scissors do, but it also serves to scrape hides, and to clean and thin them. The man's knife is used for killing and skinning animals, carving wood and bone, cutting snow for building blocks for the igloo, chopping meat into bites. Such simple weapons are "the mother of tools," and by specialization a number of tools derive from them. What is "lost" in variety of tools is won in the versatility of uses; in brief, an Eskimo man and wife have tools for all their tasks and can carry most of these tools about with them at all times.

So too with symbolic systems. The very essence of being human is in the use of symbols. We do not know what the hierarchy of primacy is between speech, song, dance, and drawing; but, whichever came first, as soon as it stood for something else other than the act itself, man was born; as soon as it caught on with another man, culture was born, and as soon as there were two symbols, a system was born. A dance, a song, a painting, and a narrative can all symbolize the same thing. They do so differently. One way of searching for the structure of a world view is to take an important narrative and to see what it ultimately tells. A narrative, or at least a corpus of narratives, may be what philosophy used to be. It may reflect what is believed about the celestial bodies and their relation to man, it may tell how man came into being, how social life was founded, what is believed about death and about life after death, it may codify law and morals. In short, it may give expression to the group's basic tenets on astronomy, theology, sociology, law, education, even esthetics.

In studying symbolic systems, we want the students to understand myths rather than to learn them. We will give them examples from simple cultures for the same reason for which the anthropologist travels into an isolated society. Our hope is to lead the children to understand how man goes about explaining his world, making sense of it and that one kind of explanation is no more human than another.

We have selected for our starting point some hunting societies. An Eskimo society, a Bushman society, and an Australian aboriginal society will certainly suffice to show what the life experience of hunting peoples is. From the scrutiny of the myths of these groups, it is immediately clear that you can tell a society by the narratives it keeps. The ecology, the economy, the social structure, the tasks of men and women, and the fears and anxieties are reflected in the stories, and in a way which the children can handle them. One good example of Eskimo narrative or Eskimo poetry, if skillfully handled in class, can show the child that the problems of an Eskimo are like our problems: to cope with his environment, to cope with his fellow men, and to cope with himself. We hope to show that wherever man lives, he manages not only to survive and to breed, but also to think and to express his thoughts. But we can also let the children enjoy the particulars of a given culture—the sense of an alien ecology, the bush, or ice and snow, and a participant understanding for alien styles.

We introduce an origin myth, things taking their present order, the sun shining over the paths of the Bushmen, and the Bushmen starting to hunt. But we should equip the children with some possible theories to make the discussion profitable, theories not in words, but in ways of reading and understanding a myth. If the narrative is to be called a myth, it should portray conditions radically different from the way things are now. It is possible to devise ways for children to analyze a plot. If done with one story variant only, such an analysis may yield something akin to a phrase-structure grammar; if done with a group of myths, something comparable to a transformational grammar may result. It is intriguing to see how stories change. Children know such things intuitively and can be helped to appreciate them more powerfully.

One last thing: why should such things be taught so early? Why not postpone them until the student can handle the "theory" itself, not only the examples? There is a reason: if such things are new to a twenty-year-old, there is not only a new view to learn, but an old established view to unlearn. We want the children to recognize that man is constantly seeking to bring reason into his world, that he does so with a variety of symbolic tools, and that he does so with a striking and fully rational humanity. The unit on world view is under the direction of Dr Elli Maranda, aided by Mr Pierre Maranda and assisted by Miss Bonnie McLane.

Pedagogy

The most persistent problem in social studies is to rescue the phenomena of social life from familiarity without, at the same time, making it all seem "primitive" and bizarre. Three techniques are particularly useful to us in achieving this end. The first is contrast, of which much has already been said. The second is through the use of "games" that incorporate the formal properties of the phenomena for which the game is an analogue. In this sense, a game is like a mathematical model—an artificialized but often powerful representation of reality. Finally, we use the ancient approach of stimulating self-consciousness about assumptions—going beyond mere admonition to think. We believe there is a learnable strategy for discovering one's unspoken assumptions.

Before considering each of these, a word is in order about a point of view quite different from ours. It holds that one should begin teaching social studies by presenting the familiar world of home, the street, and the neighborhood. It is a thoroughly commendable ideal; its only fault is its failure to recognize how difficult it is for human beings to see generality in what has become familiar. The "friendly postman" is indeed the vicar of federal powers, but to lead the child to the recognition of such powers requires many detours into the realm of what constitutes power, federal or otherwise, and how, for example, constituted power and willfully exercised force differ. We would rather find a way of stirring the curiosity of our children with particulars whose intrinsic drama and human significance are plain—whether close at hand or at a far remove. If we can evoke a feeling for bringing order into what has been studied, the task is well started.

A word first about contrast. We hope to use four principal sources of contrast: man *versus* higher primates, man *versus* prehistoric man, contemporary technological man *versus* "primitive" man, and man *versus* child. We have been gathering materials relevant to each of the contrasts—films, stories, artifacts, readings, pictures, and above all, ideas for pointing up contrasts in the interest of achieving clarity.

Indeed, we often hope to achieve for our pupils a sense of continuity by presenting them first with what seems like contrast and letting them live with it long enough to sense that what before seemed different is, in fact, closely akin to things they understand from their own lives. So it is particularly with our most extensive collection of material, a film record taken through the full cycle of the year of a family of Netsilik Eskimo. The ecology and the externals are full of contrast to daily life in an American or European setting. But there is enough material available to go into depth, to work into the year's cycle of a single family so that our pupils can get a sense of the integrity not only of a family, but of a culture. It is characteristic of Netsilik Eskimo, for example, that they make a few beautifully specialized tools and weapons, such as their fishing lester or spear. But it is also apparent that each man can make do with the stones he finds around him, that the Eskimo is a superbly gifted *bricoleur*. Whenever he needs to do something, improvised tools come from nowhere. A flat stone, a little fish oil, a touch of arctic cotton and he has a lamp. So while the Eskimo film puts modern technological man in sharp contrast, it also serves perhaps even better, to present the inherent, internal logic of any society. Each society has its own approach to technology, to the use of intelligence.

Games go a long way toward getting children involved in understanding language and social organization; they also introduce, as we have already noted, the idea of a theory of these phenomena. We do not know to what extent these games will be successful, but we shall give them a careful try-out. The alleged success of these rather sophisticated games in business management and military affairs is worth extrapolating!

As for stimulating self-consciousness about thinking, we feel that the best approach is through stimulating the art of getting and using information—what is involved in going beyond the information given and what makes it possible to take such leaps. Crutchfield has produced results in this sphere by using nothing more complicated than a series of comic books in which the adventures of a detective, aided by his nephew and niece, are recounted. The theme is using clues cleverly. As children explore the implications of clues encountered, their general reasoning ability increases, and they formulate more and better hypotheses. We plan to design materials in which children have an opportunity to do this sort of thinking with questions related to the course—possibly in connection with pre-historic materials where it will be most relevant. If it turns out to be the case that the clothing that people wore was made from the skins of the ibex, what can they "postdict" about the size of a hunting party and how would they look for data? Professor Leaky informs us that he has some useful material on this subject.

Children should be at least as self-conscious about their strategies of thought as they are about their attempts to commit things to memory. So too the "tools" of thought—what is explanation and "cause." One of those tools is language—perhaps the principal one. We shall try to encourage children to have a look at language in this light.

The most urgent need of all is to give our pupils the experience of what it is to use a theoretical model, with some sense of what is involved in being aware that one is trying out a theory. We shall be using a fair number of rather sophisticated theoretical notions, in intuitively rather than formally stated form, to be sure, but we should like to give children the experience of using alternative models. This is perhaps easiest to do in the study of language, but it can also be done elsewhere.

We shall, of course, try to encourage students to discover on their own. Children surely need to discover generalizations on their own. Yet we want to give them enough opportunity to do so to develop a decent competence at it and a proper confidence in their ability to operate on their own. There is also some need for the children to pause and review in order to recognize the connections within the structure they have learned—the kind of internal discovery that is probably of highest value. The cultivation of such a sense of connectedness is surely the hub of our curriculum effort.

If we are successful, we would hope to achieve five ideals:

1. To give our pupils respect for and confidence in the powers of their own mind.
2. To give them respect, moreover, for the powers of thought concerning the human condition, man's plight, and his social life.
3. To provide them with a set of workable models that make it simpler to analyze the nature of the social world in which they live and the condition in which man finds himself.
4. To impart a sense of respect for the capacities and plight of man as a species, for his origins, for his potential, for his humanity.
5. To leave the student with a sense of the unfinished business of man's evolution.

The Form of the Course

It is one thing to describe the nature of a course in terms of its underlying discipline and its pedagogical aims, and quite another to render these hopes into a workable form for real teachers in real classes. Teachers are sufficiently constrained by their work loads so that it would be vain to hope they might read generally and widely enough in the field to be able to give form to the course in their own terms. The materials to be covered in this particular course, moreover, are so vast in scope as to be forbidding. The materials, in short, have got to be made usable and attractive not only to the highly gifted teacher, but to teachers in general, and to teachers who live with the ordinary fatigue of coping with younger pupils day by day. They cannot be overburdened with reading, nor can the reading be of such an order as to leave them with a feeling of impotence. At the same time, the material presented should be woven loosely enough to permit the teacher to satisfy his interests in forming a final product to be presented to children.

That much said, we can state what we mean by a *unit*, the elements of which the course is made. A unit is a body of materials and exercises that may occupy as much as several days of class time or as little as half a class period. In short, it can be played to the full and consume a considerable amount of the course content, or be taken *en passant*. Indeed, some units will surely be skipped and are intended only for those teachers who have a particular interest in a topic or a particular kind of exercise. There will be more units than can possibly be fitted into a year's course and teachers will be encouraged to put them together in a form that is commodious to their own intent.

In a manner of speaking, a collection of such units constitutes a course of study. But the image is unfortunate, connoting as it does so many beads strung together by some principle of succession. It is our hope that after a certain number of units have been got through, a unit can then be introduced to "recode" what has gone before, to exploit connection. Some units only review and present no new material.

A unit also sits on the teacher's ready shelf, and consists of six constituent elements.

1 Talks to teachers. These consist of lively accounts of the nature of the unit—particularly the nature of its mystery, what about it impels curiosity and wonder. Our experience in preparing these indicates the importance of staying close to the great men in the field, if possible to find a great article that can be presented in somewhat abridged form. The design of a language (taken from Hockett) or the nature of kinship (taken from Radcliffe-Brown) or how a thing should be called (Roger Brown)—these are examples. The genre needs further study and we are exploring the kind of writing required—something that is at once science and poetry. If it should turn out that a student finds "talks to teachers" worth reading, so much the better.

2 Queries and contrasts. In trying out materials to be taught, we have learned certain ways of getting ideas across or getting the students to think out matters on their own. Often these can be embodied in devices—pictures, reading, and diagrams. But sometimes they are best stated as hints to teachers about questions to use and contrasts to invoke.

"How could you improve the human hand?" turns out to be a useful question. So does the question, "What are the different ways something can 'stand for' something else, like a red light 'standing for' *stop?*"

We have already spoken of our tactical fondness for contrasts, and we are coming up with useful ones in our designing. One such is to have students contrast a cry of pain with the words, "It hurts." Another is to compare the usual words from which phonemes may be inferred—hit, hat, hate, hut, hot, etc. Or the difference to be found in the two allo-phones of the phoneme /p/ in the words *spit* and *pit*—the the latter of which will blow out a match held to the lips, the former will not. Yet the two are regarded as the "same letter" or the "same sound" whereas *hot* and *hut* are "different."

3 Devices.   This part of the unit contains the "stuff"—the material for students. Prin-cipal among the devices is, of course, reading material and we are, like others, struggling to get such material prepared. In good season we hope to understand this obscure matter better. Currently, we are operating, much as others have, to find, or cause to be written, material that is interesting, informative, and in a decent style.

But there are many devices beyond reading that are in need of developing for different units. One is the film loop for use with the Technicolor cartridge projectors that we use increasingly. We are putting together four-minute loops constructed from Eskimo and baboon footage, with the intention of *asking* questions or *posing* riddles. Too often, films have a way of producing passivity. Can we devise ones to do the opposite? Why does *Last Year at Marienbad* abrade the curiosity so well?

We are also exploring what can be done with games, as already noted, and with anima-tion and graphics and maps. We shall get help where we can find it within ESI and outside.

4 Model exercises.   From time to time in devising a unit it becomes plain that the problem we face is less in the subject matter and more in the intellectual habits of children in ordinary schools. We have commented on some of these problems already—the dif-ficulty many children and not a few adults have in distinguishing necessary from necessary and sufficient conditions, the tendency of children to be lazy in using information, not exploiting its inferential power to nearly the degree warranted.

Model exercises are designed to overcome such intellectual difficulties. We think they are best kept imbedded in the very materials one is teaching. But it is often helpful to provide the teacher with additional special devices. We intend to use puzzles, conundrums, games—a kind of pedagogical first-aid kit.

5 Documentaries.   These are accounts, or even tape recordings, of ordinary children at work with the materials in the unit. We would like the documentary to be both exemplary and at the same time typical enough to be within reach of a teacher in his own work.

Along with the documentary goes a more analytic description. The analytic docu-mentary is designed to serve dual purposes. The first is to make it plainer both to ourselves and to teachers what in fact are the psychological problems involved in particular kinds of intellectual mastery that we hope to stimulate in children. In this sense, the analytic documentary is a further clarification of our pedagogical objectives. But in another sense, they represent an attempt on our part to accustom teachers to thinking in more general terms about the intellectual life of children. The second objective—call it educational—is to provide teachers with what might be a more useful educational psychology than the kind that is found conventionally in textbooks dedicated to that obscure subject.

It is our hope that as we proceed in our work there will be spin-offs in the form of general research problems that can be worked on by research centers not directly geared to the daily routines of curriculum building and curriculum testing. The work of such cen-ters, as well as research in the regular literature on intellectual development, will constitute a continuing font from which we can draw material for the analytic documentaries.

6 Supplementary materials.   The final section of the unit "kit" consists of such sup-plementary materials as paperbacks (and lists of related paperbacks), additional film and game materials, and such other devices as might attract the attention of either a diligent student or an aspiring teacher. Without question, it will become clearer what is needed by way of supplement once we have gone further into providing what will be our standard fare.

A final word about the unit materials. We hope to issue them in such a form that each year's experience can be added to the previous year's kit. That is to say, we believe that as new experience is gained in teaching the course, new editions of the kits should be made available to all our teachers. We intend to gather the wisdom of teachers who try out the course so that it may be made available later to others, to gather in new materials for teaching, new documentaries, new analyses of the scholarly literature, and fresh attempts through our talks to teachers to lend a still more compelling mystery to those topics that deserve to be taught. Indeed, it is probably obvious by now that the six-sectioned unit kit, stretched from one end of the teacher's shelf to the other, is our proposed substitute for that normally most unhelpful genre, the teacher's manual.

Teacher Training

No plans for teacher training have yet been established, save that we hope within the next two years to bring together for a summer session a group of master teachers to help advise us about proper steps. Our staff now includes several highly gifted and experienced teachers, all now brooding over this very issue.

Try-out and Shaping

The "course," such as it is, will be "taught" to three classes this coming summer (1965) at the Underwood School in Newton. The classes will be fourth, fifth, and sixth grades, with the object of discovering at what level to pitch the material, how to take account of the slow and fast learners, and so on. But teaching is in this case part of a summer workshop effort to get material written, drawn, readied. It will also provide an opportunity to do the kind of intensive interviewing of children to determine what they are making of the material and how their grip may be strengthened.

In short, the summer ahead is a first effort to do an intensive summer workshop on the course.

9

Objectives

W. James Popham

A key feature of any rational planning, educational or otherwise, is the possession of some idea of what is to be accomplished. Educators, of course, characteristically describe these intended accomplishments as their goals or objectives. Some people use the terms "goal" or "objective" interchangeably, as well as such synonyms as "aims," "intents," etc. Other people employ a much more distinctive meaning of the terms, using "goal" to describe a broader description of intent and "objective" to denote a more specific spelling out of the goal. Because there is currently no overwhelmingly preferred usage of these terms, be sure to seek clarification from an educator regarding the manner in which he is using the many terms which may be employed to describe educational goals. In this guidebook, the terms will be employed interchangeably.

Measurability and Clarity

One of the most prominent arenas of educational activity during the 1960's concerned the form in which instructional objectives should be stated. As a consequence of the programmed instruction movement which captured the attention of many educators during the early sixties, we heard more and more about the merits of stating objectives in precise, measurable terms. Programmed instruction enthusiasts pointed out again and again that such objectives were requisite for a proper instructional design. A number of other instructional specialists also began to support the worth of explicitly stated objectives. What was the point of this activity?

For years educators have been specifying their objectives in rather general language such as, "At the end of the year the student will become familiar with important literary insights." There is nothing intrinsically wrong with such an objective, for it probably provides one with a general idea of what is to be done during the year. However, for instructional or evaluation purposes, such an objective is almost useless since it identifies no specific indicator for determining whether or not the objective has been achieved. As a consequence, in recent years an increasing number of educators have urged that in order for objectives to function effectively in instructional and evaluation situations, they must be stated in terms of *measurable learner behavior.* In other words, since educational systems are designed to improve the learner in some way, an educational objective should describe the particular kind of behavior changes which will reflect such improvement. An example of objectives which would satisfy this measurability criterion would be the following: "When given previously unencountered selections from different authors, the student can, by style and other cues, correctly name the writer." The main attribute of a properly stated instructional objective is that it describes what the learner *will do* or is *able to do* at the end of instruction which he could not prior to instruction. Another way of putting it is that a usefully stated objective will invariably be measurable in such a way that an unequivocal determination can be made as to whether the objective has been accomplished.

The major advantages of such objectives is that they promote increased *clarity* regarding educational intents, whereas vague and unmeasurable objectives yield considerable ambiguity and, as a consequence, the possibility of many interpretations not only of what the objective means but, perhaps more importantly, whether it has been accomplished.

During the past several years many books and papers and audiovisual aids have been published[1] which guide the practitioner regarding how instructional objectives should be stated. Some of these guides focus considerable attention on the choice of verb used to describe the hoped-for post-instruction status of the learner. For instance, instead of saying "The learner *will know* the chief battles of the Civil War," the educator is advised to put it this way: "The learner *will list* in writing the chief battles of the Civil War." Note that the only difference is that in the second objective a verb is employed which describes a specific type of action or *behavior* on the part of the learner, in contrast to the verb "know" which can mean many things to many people. In the preferred object-ive a phrase, "in writing," has also been added which ties down the meaning of the objective even more. Since the essential feature of a properly stated objective is that it unambiguously communicates an educational intent, we might also have used such phrases as:

- will recite aloud
- will select from a list
- will write the names of the opposing generals

One can think of different verbs which might be employed to communicate what is intended in an objective. At a very general level there are "internal state" verbs such as "understand." At a more specific level we can think of action verbs such as "identify" or "distinguish." But even these verbs permit some difference in interpretations as to the precise manner in which the learner will identify or distinguish. Even more specific behavioral phrases such as "pointing to" or "reciting aloud" further reduce the ambiguity. In general, the evaluator should employ phrases with sufficient specificity for the task at hand. Usually, that will mean more rather than less specific language.

Because a well formed instructional objective describes the type of learner behavior which is to be produced by the instructional treatment, such statements have often been referred to as *behavioral objectives* or *performance objectives*. The reason why so many educators have recently been advocating such goal statements is that the reduced ambiguity of the objectives yields a significant increase in the clarity needed both for (1) deciding on the *worth* of the objective and (2) determining whether the objective has been *achieved*.

Another important attribute of a well stated instructional objective is that it refers to the *learner's* behavior, not that of the *teacher*. Statements such as "the teacher will introduce the class to the basic elements of set theory" do not qualify as educational objectives, for they merely describe the nature of the educational treatment (in this case provided by the teacher), not what that treatment is to accomplish in terms of modifications in the learner.

An additional element of a usefully formulated instructional objective is that it should refer to the learner's *post-instruction* behavior, not his behavior during instruction. For instance, we might imagine a group of children working furiously on practice problems in a mathematics class. Now it is not on the basis of the learners' skill with these practice problems that the teacher will judge the adequacy of his instruction, but on later problems given as part of an end-of-unit or end-of-course examination. Thus, the type of learner behavior to be described in a properly stated educational objective must definitely occur after the instruction designed to promote it.

The term "post-instruction" should be clarified, however. Certainly we are interested in what is happening to learners during the course of a school year, not merely at its conclusion. Thus, we test or otherwise observe pupils at numerous points during the year. Similarly, we might conceive of a one week or single day instructional period for our treatment. A useful objective, useful in the sense that we can determine whether it has been achieved by the learner, might be promoted by an extremely short instructional period.

Guideline Number 1. The educational evaluator should encourage the use of instructional objectives which provide explicit descriptions of the post-instruction behavior desired of learners.

All, or Nothing at All?

As the evaluator becomes conversant with the advantages of measurable goals he sometimes becomes excessive in his advocacy of such objectives. Educators will ask him, "Must *all* my goals be stated in measurable terms? Aren't there some objectives that I can pursue even if I can't describe precisely how I will measure them?"

For *evaluation purposes*, the response should be that unmeasurable goals are of little or no use. Yet, for instructional purposes a more conciliatory response is warranted. There are undoubtedly some objectives, e.g., promoting a student's appreciation of art, which may currently be unassessable yet are so intrinsically meritorious that they are worth the risk of some instructional investment. Such high-risk high-gain goals might reasonably command a segment of our instructional time, but it is the *proportion* of instruction devoted to the pursuit of such goals which is at issue. Currently, the vast majority of our educational efforts are devoted to the pursuit of such non-measurable aims. We need to alter the proportion so that most of our goals are of a measurable nature, thus permitting us to determine whether they have been accomplished and, consequently, allowing us to get better at achieving them. Some proportion of instructional resources might, on the other hand, because of great potential dividends, be devoted to the pursuit of non-measurable objectives. From an evaluator's point of view, the unmeasurable goals will be of no use, thus he should attempt to reduce the proportion of such non-behavioral goals to a reasonable number. At the same time, of course, we should increase our sophistication in measuring those goals which are important but currently elusive so that in the future we can measure even these.

Guideline Number 2. While recognizing that non-measurable goals will be of limited use for his purposes, the educational evaluator must be aware that instructors may wish to devote a reasonable proportion of their efforts to the pursuit of important but currently unassessable objectives.

Selected and Constructed Learner Responses

When describing the myriad forms of learner behavior which educators might be interested in achieving you will find that the learner is engaging in acts which can be classified under two headings, that is, he is either *selecting* from alternatives or *constructing*. He is *selecting* when he chooses "true" or "false" to describe a statement or when he picks the answer to a multiple choice question. He is *constructing* when he writes an essay, gives an impromptu speech, or performs a free exercise routine in a gymnastics class. In a sense the difference between selected and constructed responses is somewhat similar to the difference between "recognition" and "recall" as used by measurement specialists in connection with customary achievement testing. When the learner is asked to recognize a correct answer from among multiple choice alternatives, he must select the correct response. When he is asked to recall a correct answer, he must construct his own response, presumably based on his recollection of what the correct answer should be. Beyond this difference, however, the selection versus construction distinction can be applied to all types of learner response, noncognitive as well as cognitive, and therefore is more useful.

The distinction between selected and constructed responses becomes important when we realize that with selected response objectives it is relatively simple to determine whether the learner's responses are acceptable, for we merely identify in advance which alternatives are the correct ones. With constructed responses, however, the task is far more difficult since we must identify in advance the criteria by which we will distinguish between acceptable and unacceptable learner responses. To illustrate, if the objective concerns the learner's skill in writing essays, then unless we can specify the standard which all acceptable essays must satisfy, we have an objective which is difficult if not impossible to measure.

The importance of this point cannot be overemphasized, for many educators who zealously proclaim the merits of measurable objectives end up by offering the following type of goal as an example of a well written objective:

> At the conclusion of the course the student will describe the major contributions of each novelist studied during the semester.

The difficulty with such objectives is that the elements needed to render a description satisfactory are not delineated. How will the teacher, in examining the various descriptions prepared by her students, decide which ones are good enough? This should not suggest that such criteria cannot be isolated or described. They definitely can, but it is hard work. Many teachers who rely heavily on constructed response student behavior prefer the work-evading tactic of relying on a "general impression" of the quality of a student's efforts. The unreliability of such general impressions, of course, has been amply documented through the years.

The major point of this discussion is that if an objective is based upon a learner's constructed response, the *criteria of adequacy must be given*, that is, the standards for judging the acceptability of a learner's response must be supplied. The criteria of adequacy should be included in the objective, or at least referred to in the objective. For example, the following objective would be acceptable:

> The learner will deliver a 15 minute extemporaneous speech violating no more than two of the twelve "rules for oral presentation" supplied in class, as judged by a panel of three randomly selected classmates using the standard rating form.

specific

Ideally, the evaluator would prefer a set of crisply stated criteria by which to determine the adequacy of a constructed response. In practice, however, it may be necessary to state such criteria in terms of a group of judges being satisfied. For instance, even without explicating a single criterion, one can frame a satisfactory objective which indicates that a judge (or judges) will consider satisfactory greater proportions of post-instruction learner responses than those which occurred prior to instruction.

An example of this stratagem may prove helpful. Suppose an elementary teacher wants to improve her pupils' abilities to prepare watercolor prints, but has difficulty in describing criteria of adequacy for determining the quality of colors. She might give a particular assignment at the start of instruction, next teach the children, then give an *identical* watercolor assignment after instruction. The two productions of each child are then randomly paired after first having been secretly coded so that the teacher knows which was pre-instruction and which was post-instruction. The pairs are then given to a competent judge who is asked simply to designate which of any pair is better. No criteria at all need be described. The hope, of course, would be that more of the post-instruction watercolors would be judged superior. The objective for such a situation might be phrased like this:

pre + post assignment comparisons

> When compared with pre-instruction watercolor preparations based on an identical assignment, at least 75 per cent of the pupils' post-instruction watercolor productions will be considered superior by an external judge who is not aware of the point at which the watercolors were prepared.

It is important to use an external judge in these situations to avoid bias, conscious or subconscious, on the part of the teacher or, for that matter, anyone involved heavily in the instruction.

? timing It would take + $ to implement

Anytime anyone engaged in educational evaluation encounters a constructed response objective without clearly explicated criteria of adequacy, the deficiency should be remedied or the objective discarded.

Guideline Number 3. The educational evaluator must identify criteria of adequacy when using instructional objectives which require constructed responses from learners.

Content Generality

In the early 1960's any objective which explicitly described the learner's post-instruction behavior was considered to be an acceptable goal statement. Such objectives as the following were frequently found in sets of recommended goals:

The pupil will be able to identify at least three elements in *Beowulf* which are characteristic of the epic form.

Yet, upon examining such objectives it becomes clear that the statement is nothing more than a test item concerning the particular literary work, *Beowulf*. Such objectives, while sufficiently precise, are not very economical to use. To teach a semester or year long course with this type of objectives one might be obliged to have dozens or even hundreds of such statements. At any rate, what most educators wish to accomplish is not so limited in scope, but covers a broad range of learner behaviors, behaviors which hopefully can be employed profitably in many situations. Professor Eva Baker[2] has offered a useful distinction between objectives according to whether they possess content *generality* or *test* item *equivalence*. The former *Beowulf* example, since it dealt with a single test item, possessed test item equivalence and is of limited utility. To possess content generality, that is, to describe a broader range of learner behavior, the objective could be rewritten as follows:

The pupil will be able to identify at least three elements in any epic which are characteristic of that form.

By referring to *any epic*, rather than a particular epic, the objective takes on a more general form, and, as such, can be more parsimoniously employed by educational evaluators. If only to avoid the necessity of dealing with innumerable objectives, educational evaluators should foster the use of content-general objectives and eschew the use of test item equivalent goals.

One of the most vexing problems for those who work with instructional objectives is deciding *just how specific* or *just how general* they should be stated. Although there are no absolute guides here, or even consensus preference, it has become clear that the level of generality for objectives should probably vary from situation to situation. A teacher in the classroom may wish to use extremely explicit objectives. Yet, if the evaluator is attempting to secure reactions from community people regarding their estimates of the worth of certain objectives, then more general statements may be preferable. There are experimental techniques which can be used to cope with the generality level question, but until we have definitive evidence regarding what level works best in given situations, it would be wise for the evaluator to remain flexible on this point.

Guideline Number 4. The educational evaluator should foster the use of measurable objectives which possess content generality rather than test item equivalence.

Proficiency Levels

Once a measurable objective has been formulated, there is another question which should be answered by those framing the objective, namely, *how well* should the learner perform the behavior specified in the objectives. A convenient way of thinking about this question is to consider two kinds of minimal proficiency levels which can be associated with an objective.

First, we are interested in the degree of proficiency which must be displayed by an individual learner. This is called the *student minimal level* and is illustrated by the *italicized* section in the following objective:

The learner will be able to multiply correctly *at least nine out of ten* of any pair of two digit multiplication problems randomly generated by the instructor.

This student minimal level asserts that the learner must perform with at least a 90 per cent proficiency.

A second decision needs to be made with respect to the proportion of the *group of learners who must master the objective*. Does everyone need to achieve the objective? Only half the class? This is established through the *class minimal level* which is illustrated by the *italicized* section of the following objective:

Eighty per cent or more of the learners will be able to multiply correctly at least nine out of ten of any pair of two digit multiplication problems randomly generated by the instructor.

Here we see that for the objective to be achieved at the desired levels of proficiency at least 80 per cent of the learners must perform 90 per cent or better on the multiplication problems. Sometimes this is referred to as an 80–90 proficiency level.

Now the advantage, particularly to the evaluator, of specifying class and student minimal levels *prior to instruction* is that the power of the instructional treatment can then be tested against such standards in producing the hoped-for results. Too often the designers of an instructional system will, after instruction, settle for mediocre levels of proficiency. By pre-setting performance standards those involved in the design and implementation of the instructional treatment are forced to put their pedagogical proficiency on the line.

But it's easier to say how to state minimal proficiency levels than it is to decide just what they should be. Too many educators merely pluck them from the air if they're used at all, e.g., "We want 90–90 levels on all our objectives." Obviously, this would be unthinking, for there are certain objectives which we would hope that *all* of our learners would achieve with 100 per cent proficiency. Examples of these might be in the field of health, rudimentary intellectual skills, etc.

Probably the best we can do now is to seek the wisdom of many people, certainly including those who have experience in the education of the learners with whom we are working. Careful analysis of how well learners have done in the past, coupled with our most insightful appraisal of how well each individual *should* perform with respect to the objective, can yield an approximation of defensible class and student minimal levels.

An important consideration for establishing some proficiency levels is the initial skill of the learner prior to instruction, sometimes referred to as his "entry behavior." For certain instructional situations, e.g., remedial math, learners who commence an instructional sequence with abysmally low entry behaviors might not be expected to perform as well at the close of instruction as other learners who headed into the instruction with an advantage. For other situations, the criterion levels are not so malleable, thus we would expect students in a driver training course to achieve the desired minimal levels irrespective of their entry behavior.

Now it is always possible, of course, to alter performance standards after the instructional treatment has either proven to be ineffectual or more effective than we thought. But this should be done very cautiously, only after pushing the instructional treatment to the limits of its potency.

[Handwritten margin notes: "What proportion of the class must master the objective" · "proportion" · "agree / disagree" · "Best Plan?" · "not a very standardized scheme"]

Guideline Number 5. Prior to the introduction of the instructional treatment educational evaluators should strive to establish minimal proficiency levels for instructional objectives.

The Taxonomies of Educational Objectives

A technique for analyzing objectives which many evaluators find useful stems from the work of Benjamin Bloom and a group of university examiners who in 1956 published a scheme[3] for classifying educational objectives according to the kinds of learner behavior they were attempting to promote. An extension of the classification scheme by David Krathwohl and others appeared in 1964.[4] These two *taxonomies* (classification schemes) of educational objectives first divided instructional goals into three groups or *domains*, the cognitive, affective, and psychomotor. *Cognitive* objectives deal with intellectual learner outcomes such as whether a pupil can analyze sentences into their component parts or can recall the names of the 50 states. *Affective* objectives are concerned with attitudinal, valuing, emotional learner actions such as promoting a pupil's interest in literature or strengthening his esteem for democratic processes. *Psychomotor* objectives describe intended learner outcomes of a largely physical skill nature such as learning to use a typewriter or how to swim the breaststroke.

Each of these three domains has been further subdivided into several levels of learner behaviors which are sought in each domain. For instance, in the cognitive domain we find *knowledge* objectives which, briefly, describe those goals that require the learner to recall information of one sort or another. Another type of objective in the cognitive domain is *analysis* which refers to the learner's ability to subdivide a complex whole into its constituent segments. Within each domain the several levels of objectives are arranged more or less hierarchically so that, for example, analysis objectives are ranked higher than knowledge objectives. Lower levels within a domain are generally considered prerequisite to higher levels.

To the evaluator, the major utility of a taxonomic analysis of the objectives with which he is dealing is that he can detect unsuspected omissions or overemphasis. For example, he might subject a group of objectives under consideration by a school faculty to an analysis according to the taxonomies and discover that there were no affective objectives present or that all of the cognitive objectives were at the lowest levels of the cognitive domain. Once apprised of this situation the school faculty might wish to select the objectives anyway, but at least they have a better idea of the types of goals they are adopting.

Although each of the three domains has been broken down into multiple levels, six for the cognitive, five for the affective and five for the psychomotor,[5] the evaluator may find the use of all of these levels too sophisticated for some of the tasks he must accomplish. Many educators report sufficient utility is gained by using the three major domain headings, i.e., cognitive, affective, and psychomotor, coupled with a rough two-level breakdown in each domain, such as "lowest level" and "higher than lowest level." However, there may be some situations in which a more fine grained analysis is required.[6] Accordingly, brief descriptions of each level in each of the three domains are presented below. An evaluator should, however, regroup the levels into a system of sufficient precision for the task at hand.

hierarchy

Cognitive Domain

— intellectual learner outcomes

The cognitive domain has six levels. They move from knowledge, the lowest level, to evaluation, the highest level.

— Declarative memory

low level

Knowledge. Knowledge involves the recall of specifics or universals, the recall of methods and processes, or the recall of a pattern, structure, or setting. It will be noted that the essential attribute at this level is *recall*. For assessment purposes, a recall situation involves little more than "bringing to mind" appropriate material.

Comprehension. This level represents the lowest form of understanding and refers to a kind of apprehension that indicates that a student knows what is being communicated and can make use of the material or idea without necessarily relating it to other material or seeing it in its fullest implications.

Application. Application involves the use of abstractions in particular or concrete situations. The abstractions used may be in the form of procedures, general ideas, or generalized methods. They may also be ideas, technical principles, or theories that must be remembered and applied to novel situations.

Analysis. Analysis involves the breakdown of a communication into its constituent parts such that the relative hierarchy within that communication is made clear, that the relations between the expressed ideas are made explicit, or both. Such analyses are intended to clarify the communication, to indicate how it is organized and the way in which the communication managed to convey its effects as well as its basis and arrangement.

Synthesis. Synthesis represents the combining of elements and parts so that they form a whole. This operation involves the process of working with pieces, parts, elements, and so on, and arranging them so as to constitute a pattern or structure not clearly present before.

High level

Evaluation. Evaluation requires judgments about the value of material and methods for given purposes. Quantitative and qualitative judgments are made about the extent to which material and methods satisfy criteria. The criteria employed may be those determined by the learner or those given to him.

Affective Domain

— attitudinal valuing emotional learner actions

The affective domain is subdivided into five levels. These levels, in particular, may cause the evaluator much difficulty in classifying objectives. Once more, the five levels may have some value in that they encourage one to think about different forms of objectives, but it is not recommended that the evaluator devote too much time in attempting to classify various objectives within these levels.

Receiving (Attending). The first level of the affective domain is concerned with the learner's sensitivity to the existence of certain phenomena and stimuli, that is, with his willingness to receive or to attend to them. This category is divided into three subdivisions which reflect three different levels of attending to phenomena—namely, awareness of the phenomena, willingness to receive phenomena, and controlled or selected attention to phenomena.

Responding. At this level one is concerned with responses that go beyond merely attending to phenomena. The student is sufficiently motivated that he is not just "willing to attend," but is actively attending.

Valuing. This category reflects the learner's holding of a particular value. The learner displays behavior with sufficient consistency in appropriate situations that he actually is perceived as holding this value.

Organization.   As the learner successively internalizes values, he encounters situations in which more than one value is relevant. This requires the necessity of organizing his values into a system such that certain values exercise greater control.

Characterization by a Value or Value Complex.   At this highest level of the affective taxonomy internalization has taken place in an individual's value hierarchy to the extent that we can actually characterize him as holding a particular value or set of values.

Psychomotor Domain   *— learner outcomes as a largely physical skill nature*

Simpson's psychomotor taxonomy, although not as widely used as the cognitive and affective taxonomies, rounds out our three domain picture. Like the affective taxonomy, this domain consists of five levels.

Perception.   The first step in performing a motor act is the process of becoming aware of objects, qualities or relations by way of the sense organs. It is the main portion of the situation-interpretation-action chain leading to motor activity.

Set.   Set is a preparatory adjustment for a particular kind of action or experience. Three distinct aspects of set have been identified, namely, mental, physical, and emotional.

Guided Response.   This is an early step in the development of a motor skill. The emphasis is upon the abilities that are components of the more complex skill. Guided response is the overt behavioral act of an individual under the guidance of another individual.

Mechanism.   At this level the learner has achieved a certain confidence and degree of skill in the performance of an act. The habitual act is a part of his repertoire of possible responses to stimuli and the demands of situations where the response is appropriate.

Complex Overt Response.   At this level, the individual can perform a motor act that is considered complex because of the movement pattern required. The act can be carried out efficiently and smoothly, that is, with minimum expenditure of energy and time.

Another way in which these taxonomies may be of use to the evaluator is as an aid in generating new objectives. The evaluator may suggest to the educator who is formulating objectives a wider variety of learner behaviors which might be incorporated in the objectives.

Guideline Number 6. The educational evaluator will often find the Taxonomies of Educational Objectives useful both in describing instructional objectives under consideration and in generating new objectives.

Constructing Versus Selecting Objectives

Thus far in the discussion it has been emphasized that the educational evaluator will find the use of measurable instructional objectives invaluable in his work. Recalling that the two major roles of educational evaluation occur in connection with needs assessment and assessing treatment adequacy, the evaluator will find that measurable goals are literally indispensable in properly carrying out either of these two roles. As we continue to examine additional techniques which may be used by evaluators this will become even more evident. Yet, there is a major problem to be faced by the evaluator, namely, where do such measurable goals come from?

Suppose, for example, that an evaluation consultant is called upon by a local school district to help in determining whether a new treatment, in this case a series of new text books, is sufficiently effective. The first thing he does is to ask what objective the treatment is supposed to accomplish. If he discovers that no objectives arise, at least none beyond a few nebulous general goals, what is he to do? Should he refuse to assist the district until they put their objectives in order? Obviously not. Should he prepare the objectives himself? Well, for any extended treatment that requires a tremendous amount of work and, besides, the school staff may not agree with the objectives he constructs. Should he give the school faculty a crash course in how to write objectives, then help them as they spell out their own measurable goals? So far, this seems like the best alternative, but the evaluator had best recognize that most school personnel—teachers through administrators—are already heavily committed to other assignments. Too many evaluators who have used this "help them construct their own objectives" approach will recount frustrating experiences in getting already harassed teachers to write out their own measurable objectives.

A better alternative would seem to be to ask the school faculty to *select* objectives from a set of alternatives rather than to ask them to construct their own. Selecting measurable objectives from a wide ranging set of alternatives represents a task that can reasonably be accomplished by most educators. Asking those same educators to *construct* their own measurable objectives is, generally speaking, an unrealistic request.

During the past few years several agencies have been established to collect large pools of instructional objectives and test measures. In general, these item banks and objectives banks have been assembled to permit educators to employ their resources in activities related to instruction or evaluation. A directory of extant collections of instructional objectives[7] is now available and should be of considerable use to an educational evaluator.

Illustrative of agencies established to collect and distribute educational objectives is the Instructional Objectives Exchange (IOX), founded in 1968. The Exchange has assembled an extensive collection of measurable instructional objectives in grades K-12 in all fields. These objectives were usually contributed to IOX by school districts, Title III projects, curriculum development teams, or individual teachers. Some were developed in the Instructional Objectives Exchange. As soon as a reasonably extensive group of objectives have been assembled in a given field at a given grade range, these are published as an IOX *collection*. Each collection consists of a set of objectives plus one or more measuring devices which may be used to assess the attainment of each objective. The Exchange intends to have at least a half dozen or so test items (broadly defined) for all their objectives so that they can be readily used to constitute pretests, posttests, etc.

By consulting the current listing of IOX objective collections[8] an evaluator can secure a set of alternative objectives from which the educators with whom he is working can select those appropriate for their own instructional situations. It is assumed that only a portion of any collection will be selected. Of course, if all the objectives which are sought are not included in a collection, the local educators can augment those available by writing some of their own. Since this should, in general, be a reasonably small number, the objective construction task should therefore not be too onerous.

Either for needs assessment or assessing treatment adequacy the use of extant objectives collections can prove invaluable. Although we shall be examining the specifics of the process in more detail later, it can be seen how in assessing the current perceptions of students, teachers, and community representatives regarding needed objectives, reactions to a list of possible objectives (selected from extant collections) would represent an economic way to secure such perceptions. Similarly, in assessing the adequacy of a new instructional procedure it should be relatively straightforward to select from an available collection those objectives which the procedure seemed best suited to accomplish. Since in many of the agencies currently distributing objectives a number of test items accompany each objective, it is apparent that it would be relatively simple to assess whether the objective had been accomplished.

To give the reader some idea of the kinds of materials available in these collections, Figure 9.1 includes an example from one of the IOX collections. Although the objectives from other objective pools may be organized somewhat differently, they are essentially comparable. In Figure 9.2 some affective objectives from two recently developed[9] collections, namely, (1) attitude toward school and (2) self-concept, are presented to illustrate the type of non-cognitive goals available in such collections.

Although the objective collections currently available at various locations throughout the country represent an extremely useful resource for the educational evaluator, there may be situations for which an evaluator finds no already prepared objectives available. The most likely alternatives for him to follow have been previously described, and they usually require his heavy involvement in construction of the objectives. Another option, however, is to try to pool the resources of several groups who have similar interests in order to produce a new objective pool. For instance, several of the health professions, notably nursing and dental education, have lately shown considerable interest in establishing objective banks which are specifically designed for their own instructional situations.

As these recently developed objective collections are revised and updated, as different forms of data (e.g., consumer value ratings) are assembled to guide the selector, and as more sophisticated storage and retrieval systems (e.g., computer-based) are established, these objectives/measures banks should provide an increasingly useful set of tools for an educational evaluator.

Objective 87   Collection: Language Arts
                                                                Grades 4–6

Major Category: Mechanics and Conventions
Sub-Category: Capitalization

OBJECTIVE: Given a set of sentences containing uncapitalized proper nouns, the student will identify nouns that should be capitalized.

SAMPLE ITEM: Rewrite all words that should be capitalized in the following sentences.

    1. Some emerald mines in colombia, central america, are more than four hundred years old.

    2. venezuela, colombia, argentina and peru have many oil wells.

    3. brasilia is a large modern city in brazil.

ANSWER: 1. Colombia; Central America

    2. Venezuela; Colombia; Argentina; Peru

    3. Brasilia; Brazil

Figure 9.1 Sample objective and item from an IOX collection.

Attitude Toward School

(Attitude Toward School Subjects) Students will indicate relative preferences for five subject areas (aesthetics—art and music; language arts—spelling, oral participation, listening, writing; mathematics; reading; science), when given sets of three verbal descriptions of classroom activities in specific subject areas and three corresponding pictures, by marking one of the pictures to indicate in which activity they would most like to participate.

(General Attitude) Students will indicate favorable attitudes toward school, in a global sense, by incurring a minimum of absenteeism from school during a specified time period, as observed from teacher or school records.

(Attitude Toward School Subjects) Students will reveal relative preferences for seven subject areas (English, arithmetic, social studies, art, music, physical education, science) by selecting, from among sets of seven "headlines" (each representing one of the subject areas noted above), those that appear most and least interesting to read about.

Self Concept

Given a contrived situation in which the teacher describes several factitiously esteemed students, class members will demonstrate positive self concepts by voluntarily identifying themselves as students who have won the teacher's esteem.

The students will display unconditionally positive self concepts by responding to a 10-item inventory, entitled *Parental Approval Index,* which asks how the child's mother would feel about him as a person if he engaged in certain actions which would normally be expected to yield disapproval of the act.

Students will display an expectation for future success by checking a higher percentage of want ad job requests from the *Choose a Job Inventory* which offer more prestigious, socially approved occupations.

Figure 9.2 Examples of objectives from two IOX collections in the affective domain.

Guideline Number 7. The educational evaluator should consider the possibility of selecting measurable objectives from extant collections of such objectives.

In reviewing the section regarding the uses of instructional objectives by educational evaluators, we have examined (1) the role of measurability as an aid to clarity, (2) selected versus constructed learner responses, (3) content general versus test item equivalent objectives, (4) the proportion of objectives which must be measurable, (5) performance standards, (6) taxonomic analysis of objectives, and (7) selecting objectives from extant collections. For each of those points a guideline was presented which, briefly, suggested a course of action for educational evaluators.

Notes

1. See, for example, Popham, W.J. and Baker, E.L. *Establishing Instructional Goals,* Prentice Hall, Inc., Englewood Cliffs, N.J., 1970, as well as the numerous citations in the selected references section of this guidebook. A series of filmstrip-tape programs distributed by Vimcet Associates, P.O. Box 24714, Los Angeles, California 90024, will also be helpful for training evaluation personnel.
2. Baker, E.L. *Defining Content for Objectives,* Vimcet Associates, Box 24714, Los Angeles, California, 1968.

3. Bloom, Benjamin, et al. *The Taxonomy of Educational Objectives, Handbook I: The Cognitive Domain*, David McKay, New York, 1956.

4. Krathwohl, David, et al. *The Taxonomy of Educational Objectives, Handbook II: The Affective Domain*, David McKay, New York, 1964.

5. Simpson, Elizabeth J. *The Classification of Educational Objectives: Psychomotor Domain*, Research Project No. OE-5-85-104, University of Illinois, Urbana, 1966.

6. It should be noted that in order to make accurate classifications according to the *Taxonomies* it is often necessary to know the nature of the instructional events preceding the point at which the learner's behavior is measured. For example, a given learner behavior might reflect only recall if the topic had been previously treated, but something quite different if not previously encountered in class.

7. The *Directory of Measurable Objectives Sources* at one time could be obtained from the Upper Midwest Regional Educational Laboratory in Minneapolis, Minnesota or in care of Mr. Arthur Olson, Colorado State Department of Education, State Office Building, Denver, Colorado 80203. Objectives and related tests of the Wisconsin Design for Reading Skill Development, an individualized reading system, are also available from National Computer Systems, 4401 West 76th St., Minneapolis, Minnesota 55435.

8. Available from IOX, Box 24095, Los Angeles, California 90024.

9. Support for the development of these affective objective collections was contributed in a cooperative effort of the state level ESEA Title III programs of the following states: Arizona, Colorado, Florida, Hawaii, Idaho, Iowa, Kansas, Massachusetts, Minnesota, Missouri, Montana, North Dakota, Ohio, Rhode Island, South Carolina, Texas and Wisconsin.

10

Educational Objectives—Help or Hindrance?[1]

Elliot W. Eisner

If one were to rank the various beliefs or assumptions in the field of curriculum that are thought most secure, the belief in the need for clarity and specificity in stating educational objectives would surely rank among the highest. Educational objectives, it is argued, need to be clearly specified for at least three reasons: first, because they provide the goals toward which the curriculum is aimed; second, because once clearly stated they facilitate the selection and organization of content; third, because when specified in both behavioral and content terms they make it possible to evaluate the outcomes of the curriculum.

It is difficult to argue with a rational approach to curriculum development—who would choose irrationality? And, if one is to build curriculum in a rational way, the clarity of premise, end or starting point, would appear paramount. But I want to argue in this paper that educational objectives clearly and specifically stated can hamper as well as help the ends of instruction and that an unexamined belief in curriculum as in other domains of human activity can easily become dogma which in fact may hinder the very functions the concept was originally designed to serve.

When and where did beliefs concerning the importance of educational objectives in curriculum development emerge? Who has formulated and argued their importance? What effect has this belief had upon curriculum construction? If we examine the past briefly for data necessary for answering these questions, it appears that the belief in the usefulness of clear and specific educational objectives emerged around the turn of the century with the birth of the scientific movement in education.

Before this movement gained strength, faculty psychologists viewed the brain as consisting of a variety of intellectual faculties. These faculties, they held, could be strengthened if exercised in appropriate ways with particular subject matters. Once strengthened, the faculties could be used in any area of human activity to which they were applicable. Thus, if the important faculties could be identified and if methods of strengthening them developed, the school could concentrate on this task and expect general intellectual excellence as a result.

This general theoretical view of mind had been accepted for several decades by the time Thorndike, Judd, and later Watson began, through their work, to chip away the foundations upon which it rested. Thorndike's work especially demonstrated the specificity of transfer. He argued theoretically that transfer of learning occurred if and only if elements in one situation were identical with elements in the other. His empirical work supported his theoretical views, and the enormous stature he enjoyed in education as well as in psychology influenced educators to approach curriculum development in ways consonant with his views. One of those who was caught up in the scientific movement in education was Franklin Bobbitt, often thought of as the father of curriculum theory. In 1918 Bobbitt published a signal work titled simply, *The Curriculum.*[2] In it he argued that educational theory is not so difficult to construct as commonly held and that curriculum theory is logically derivable from educational theory. Bobbitt wrote in 1918:

> The central theory is simple. Human life, however varied, consists in its performance of specific activities. Education that prepares for life is one that prepares definitely and adequately for these specific activities. However numerous and diverse they may be for any social class, they can be discovered. This requires that one go out into the world of affairs and discover the particulars of which these affairs consist. These will show the abilities, habits, appreciations, and forms of knowledge that men need. These will be the objectives of the curriculum. They will be numerous, definite, and particularized. The curriculum will then be that series of experiences which childhood and youth must have by way of attaining those objectives.[3]

In *The Curriculum*, Bobbitt approached curriculum development scientifically and theoretically: study life carefully to identify needed skills, divide these skills into specific units, organize these units into experiences, and provide these experiences to children. Six years later, in his second book, *How To Make a Curriculum*,[4] Bobbitt operationalized his theoretical assertions and demonstrated how curriculum components—especially educational objectives—were to be formulated. In this book Bobbitt listed nine areas in which educational objectives are to be specified. In these nine areas he listed 160 major educational objectives which run the gamut from "Ability to use language in all ways required for proper and effective participation in community life" to "Ability to entertain one's friends, and to respond to entertainment by one's friends."[5]

Bobbitt was not alone in his belief in the importance of formulating objectives clearly and specifically. Pendleton, for example, listed 1,581 social objectives for English, Guiler listed more than 300 for arithmetic in grades 1–6, and Billings prescribed 888 generalizations which were important for the social studies.

If Thorndike was right, if transfer was limited, it seemed reasonable to encourage the teacher to teach for particular outcomes and to construct curriculums only after specific objectives had been identified.

In retrospect it is not difficult to understand why this movement in curriculum collapsed under its own weight by the early 1930's. Teachers could not manage fifty highly specified objects, let alone hundreds. And, in addition, the new view of the child, not as a complex machine but as a growing organism who ought to participate in planning his own educational program, did not mesh well with the theoretical views held earlier.[6]

But, as we all know, the Progressive movement too began its decline in the forties, and by the middle fifties, as a formal organization at least, it was dead.

By the late forties and during the fifties, curriculum specialists again began to remind us of the importance of specific educational objectives and began to lay down guidelines for their formulation. Rationales for constructing curriculums developed by Ralph Tyler[7] and Virgil Herrick[8] again placed great importance on the specificity of objectives. George Barton[9] identified philosophic domains which could be used to select objectives. Benjamin Bloom and his colleagues[10] operationalized theoretical assertions by building a taxonomy of educational objectives in the cognitive domain; and in 1964, Krathwohl, Bloom, and Masia[11] did the same for the affective domain. Many able people for many years have spent a great deal of time and effort in identifying methods and providing prescriptions for the formulation of educational objectives, so much so that the statement "Educational objectives should be stated in behavioral terms" has been elevated—or lowered—to almost slogan status in curriculum circles. Yet, despite these efforts, teachers seem not to take educational objectives seriously—at least as they are prescribed from above. And when teachers plan curriculum guides, their efforts first to identify over-all educational aims, then specify school objectives, then identify educational objectives for specific subject matters, appear to be more like exercises to be gone through than serious efforts to build tools for curriculum planning. If educational objectives were really useful tools, teachers, I submit, would use them. If they do not, perhaps it is not because there is something wrong with the teachers but because there might be something wrong with the theory.

As I view the situation, there are several limitations to theory in curriculum regarding the functions educational objectives are to perform. These limitations I would like to identify.

Educational objectives are typically derived from curriculum theory, which assumes that it is possible to predict with a fair degree of accuracy what the outcomes of instruction will be. In a general way this is possible. If you set about to teach a student algebra, there is no reason to assume he will learn to construct sonnets instead. Yet, the outcomes of instruction are far more numerous and complex for educational objectives to encompass. The amount, type, and quality of learning that occurs in a classroom, especially when there is interaction among students, are only in small part predictable. The changes in pace, tempo, and goals that experienced teachers employ when necessary and appropriate for maintaining classroom organization are dynamic rather than mechanistic in character. Elementary school teachers, for example, are often sensitive to the changing interests of the children they teach, and frequently attempt to capitalize on these interests, "milking them" as it were for what is educationally valuable.[12] The teacher uses the moment in a situation that is better described as kaleidoscopic than stable. In the very process of teaching and discussing, unexpected opportunities emerge for making a valuable point, for demonstrating an interesting idea, and for teaching a significant concept. The first point I wish to make, therefore, is that the dynamic and complex process of instruction yields outcomes far too numerous to be specified in behavioral and content terms in advance.

A second limitation of theory concerning educational objectives is its failure to recognize the constraints various subject matters place upon objectives. The point here is brief. In some subject areas, such as mathematics, languages, and the sciences, it is possible to specify with great precision the particular operation or behavior the student is to perform after instruction. In other subject areas, especially the arts, such specification is frequently not possible, and when possible may not be desirable. In a class in mathematics or spelling, uniformity in response is desirable, at least insofar as it indicates that students are able to perform a particular operation adequately, that is, in accordance with accepted procedures. Effective instruction in such areas enables students to function with minimum error in these fields. In the arts and in subject matters where, for example, novel or creative responses are desired, the particular behaviors to be developed cannot easily be identified. Here curriculum and instruction should yield behaviors and products which are unpredictable. The end achieved ought to be something of a surprise to both teacher and pupil. While it could be argued that one might formulate an educational objective which specified novelty, originality, or creativeness as the desired outcome, the particular referents for these terms cannot be specified in advance; one must judge after the fact whether the product produced or the behavior displayed belongs in the "novel" class. This is a much different procedure than is determining whether or not a particular word has been spelled correctly or a specific performance, that is, jumping a 3-foot hurdle, has been attained. Thus, the second point is that theory concerning educational objectives has not taken into account the particular relationship that holds between the subject matter being taught and the degree to which educational objectives can be predicted and specified. This, I suppose, is in part due to the fact that few curriculum specialists have high degrees of intimacy with a wide variety of subject matters and thus are unable to alter their general theoretical views to suit the demands that particular subject matters make.

The third point I wish to make deals with the belief that objectives stated in behavioral and content terms can be used as criteria by which to measure the outcomes of curriculum and instruction. Educational objectives provide, it is argued, the standard against which achievement is to be measured. Both taxonomies are built upon this assumption since their primary function is to demonstrate how objectives can be used to frame test items appropriate for evaluation. The assumption that objectives can be used as standards by which to measure achievement fails, I think, to distinguish adequately between the application of a standard and the making of a judgment. Not all—perhaps not even most—outcomes of curriculum and instruction are amenable to measurement. The application of a standard requires that some arbitrary and socially defined quantity be designated by which other qualities can be compared. By virtue of socially defined rules of grammar, syntax, and logic, for example, it is possible to quantitatively compare and measure error in a discursive or mathematical statement. Some fields of activity, especially those which are qualitative in character, have no comparable rules and hence are less amenable to quantitative assessment. It is here that evaluation must be made, not primarily by applying a socially defined standard, but by making a human qualitative judgment. One can specify, for example, that a student shall be expected to know how to extract a square root correctly and in an unambiguous way, through the application of a standard, determine whether this end has been achieved. But it is only in a metaphoric sense that one can measure the extent to which a student has been able to produce an aesthetic object or an expressive narrative. Here standards are unapplicable; here judgment is required. The making of a judgment in distinction to the application of a standard implies that valued qualities are not merely socially defined and arbitrary in character. The judgment by which a critic determines the value of a poem, novel, or play is not achieved merely by applying standards already known to the particular product being judged; it requires that the critic—or teacher—view the product with respect to the unique properties it displays and then, in relation to his experience and sensibilities, judge its value in terms which are incapable of being reduced to quantity or rule.

This point was aptly discussed by John Dewey in his chapter on "Perception and Criticism" in *Art as Experience*.[13] Dewey was concerned with the problem of identifying the means and ends of criticism and has this to say about its proper function:

> The function of criticism is the reeducation of perception of works of art; it is an auxiliary process, a difficult process, of learning to see and hear. The conception that its business is to appraise, to judge in the legal and moral sense, arrests the perception of those who are influenced by the criticism that assumes this task.[14]

Of the distinction that Dewey makes between the application of a standard and the making of a critical judgment, he writes:

> There are three characteristics of a standard. It is a particular physical thing existing under specifiable conditions; it is *not* a value. The yard is a yard-stick, and the meter is a bar deposited in Paris. In the second place, standards are measures of things, of lengths, weights,

capacities. The things measured are not values, although it is of great social value to be able to measure them, since the properties of things in the way of size, volume, weight, are important for commercial exchange. Finally, as standards of measure, standards define things with respect to *quantity*. To be able to measure quantities is a great aid to further judgments, but it is not a mode of judgment. The standard, being an external and public thing, is applied *physically*. The yard-stick is physically laid down upon things to determine their length.[15]

And I would add that what is most educationally valuable is the development of that mode of curiosity, inventiveness, and insight that is capable of being described only in metaphoric or poetic terms. Indeed, the image of the educated man that has been held in highest esteem for the longest period of time in Western civilization is one which is not amenable to standard measurement. Thus, the third point I wish to make is that curriculum theory which views educational objectives as standards by which to measure educational achievement overlooks those modes of achievement incapable of measurement.

The final point I wish to make deals with the function of educational objectives in curriculum construction.

The rational approach to curriculum development not only emphasizes the importance of specificity in the formulation of educational objectives but also implies when not stated explicitly that educational objectives be stated prior to the formulation of curriculum activities. At first view, this seems to be a reasonable way to proceed with curriculum construction: one should know where he is headed before embarking on a trip. Yet, while the procedure of first identifying objectives before proceeding to identify activities is logically defensible, it is not necessarily the most psychologically efficient way to proceed. One can, and teachers often do, identify activities that seem useful, appropriate, or rich in educational opportunities, and from a consideration of what can be done in class, identify the objectives or possible consequences of using these activities. MacDonald argues this point cogently when he writes:

> Let us look, for example, at the problem of objectives. Objectives are viewed as directives in the rational approach. They are identified prior to the instruction or action and used to provide a basis for a screen for appropriate activities.
>
> There is another view, however, which has both scholarly and experiential referents. This view would state that our objectives are only known to us in any complete sense after the completion of our act of instruction. No matter what we thought we were attempting to do, we can only know what we wanted to accomplish after the fact. Objectives by this rationale are heuristic devices which provide initiating consequences which become altered in the flow of instruction.
>
> In the final analysis, it could be argued, the teacher in actuality asks a fundamentally different question from "What am I trying to accomplish?" The teacher asks "What am I going to do?" and out of the doing comes accomplishment.[16]

Theory in curriculum has not adequately distinguished between logical adequacy in determining the relationship of means to ends when examining the curriculum as a *product* and the psychological processes that may usefully be employed in building curriculums. The method of forming creative insights in curriculum development, as in the sciences and arts, is as yet not logically prescribable. The ways in which curriculums can be usefully and efficiently developed constitute an empirical problem; imposing logical requirements upon the process because they are desirable for assessing the product is, to my mind, an error. Thus, the final point I wish to make is that educational objectives need not precede the selection and organization of content. The means through which imaginative curriculums can be built is as open-ended as the means through which scientific and artistic inventions occur. Curriculum theory needs to allow for a variety of processes to be employed in the construction of curriculums.

I have argued in this paper that curriculum theory as it pertains to educational objectives has had four significant limitations. First, it has not sufficiently emphasized the extent to which the prediction of educational outcomes cannot be made with accuracy. Second, it has not discussed the ways in which the subject matter affects precision in stating educational objectives. Third, it has confused the use of educational objectives as a standard for measurement when in some areas it can be used only as a criterion for judgment. Fourth, it has not distinguished between the logical requirement of relating means to ends in the curriculum as a product and the psychological conditions useful for constructing curriculums.

If the arguments I have formulated about the limitations of curriculum theory concerning educational objectives have merit, one might ask: What are their educational consequences? First, it seems to me that they suggest that in large measure the construction of curriculums and the judgment of its consequences are artful tasks. The methods of curriculum development are, in principle if not in practice, no different from the making of art—be it the art of painting or the art of science. The identification of the factors in the potentially useful educational activity and the organization or construction of sequence in curriculum are in principle amenable to an infinite number of combinations. The variable teacher, student, class group, require artful blending for the educationally valuable to result.

Second, I am impressed with Dewey's view of the functions of criticism—to heighten one's perception of the art object—and believe it has implications for curriculum theory. If the child is viewed as an art product and the teacher as a critic, one task of the teacher would be to reveal the qualities of the child to himself and to others. In addition, the teacher as critic would appraise the changes occurring in the child. But because the teacher's task includes more than criticism, he would also be responsible, in part, for the improvement of the work of art. In short, in both the construction of educational means (the curriculum) and the appraisal of its consequences, the teacher would become an artist, for criticism itself when carried to its height is an art. This, it seems to me, is a dimension to which curriculum theory will someday have to speak.

Notes

1. This is a slightly expanded version of a paper presented at the fiftieth annual meeting of the American Educational Research Association, Chicago, February, 1966.
2. Franklin Bobbitt, *The Curriculum* (Boston: Houghton Mifflin Co., 1918).
3. *Ibid.*, p. 42.
4. Franklin Bobbitt, *How To Make a Curriculum* (Boston: Houghton Mifflin Co., 1924).
5. *Ibid.*, pp. 11–29.
6. For a good example of this view of the child and curriculum development, see *The Changing Curriculum, Tenth Yearbook*, Department of Supervisors and Directors of Instruction, National Education Association and Society for Curriculum Study (New York: Appleton-Century Crofts Co., 1937).
7. Ralph W. Tyler, *Basic Principles of Curriculum and Instruction* (Chicago: University of Chicago Press, 1951).
8. Virgil E. Herrick, "The Concept of Curriculum Design," *Toward Improved Curriculum Theory*, (eds.). Virgil E. Herrick and Ralph W. Tyler (Supplementary Educational Monographs, No. 71 [Chicago: University of Chicago Press, 1950]), pp. 37–50.
9. George E. Barton, Jr., "Educational Objectives: Improvement of Curriculum Theory about Their Determination," *ibid.*, pp. 26–35.

10. Benjamin Bloom et al. (ed.), *Taxonomy of Educational Objectives, Handbook I:* The Cognitive Domain (New York: Longmans, Green & Co., 1956).

11. David Krathwohl, Benjamin Bloom, and Bertram Masia, *Taxonomy of Educational Objectives, Handbook II: The Affective Domain* (New York: David McKay, Inc., 1964).

12. For an excellent paper describing educational objectives as they are viewed and used by elementary school teachers, see Philip W. Jackson and Elizabeth Belford, "Educational Objectives and the Joys of Teaching," *School Review*, LXXIII (1965), 267–291.

13. John Dewey, *Art as Experience* (New York: Minton, Balch & Co., 1934).

14. *Ibid.*, p. 324.

15. *Ibid.*, p. 307.

16. James B. MacDonald, "Myths about Instruction," *Educational Leadership*, XXII, No. 7 (May, 1965), 613–614.

11

The Daily Grind

Philip W. Jackson

On a typical weekday morning between September and June some 35 million Americans kiss their loved ones goodbye, pick up their lunch pails and books, and leave to spend their day in that collection of enclosures (totalling about one million) known as elementary school classrooms. This massive exodus from home to school is accomplished with a minimum of fuss and bother. Few tears are shed (except perhaps by the very youngest) and few cheers are raised. The school attendance of children is such a common experience in our society that those of us who watch them go hardly pause to consider what happens to them when they get there. Of course our indifference disappears occasionally. When something goes wrong or when we have been notified of his remarkable achievement, we might ponder, for a moment at least, the meaning of the experience for the child in question, but most of the time we simply note that our Johnny is on his way to school, and now, it is time for our second cup of coffee.

Parents are interested, to be sure, in how *well* Johnny does while there, and when he comes trudging home they may ask him questions about what happened today or, more generally, how things went. But both their questions and his answers typically focus on the highlights of the school experience—its unusual aspects—rather than on the mundane and seemingly trivial events that filled the bulk of his school hours. Parents are interested, in other words, in the spice of school life rather than in its substance.

Teachers, too, are chiefly concerned with only a very narrow aspect of a youngster's school experience. They, too, are likely to focus on specific acts of misbehavior or accomplishment as representing what a particular student did in school today, even though the acts in question occupied but a small fraction of the student's time. Teachers, like parents, seldom ponder the significance of the thousands of fleeting events that combine to form the routine of the classroom.

And the student himself is no less selective. Even if someone bothered to question him about the minutiae of his school day, he would probably be unable to give a complete account of what he had done. For him, too, the day has been reduced in memory into a small number of signal events—"I got 100 on my spelling test," "We went to gym," "We had music." His spontaneous recall of detail is not much greater than that required to answer our conventional questions.

This concentration on the highlights of school life is understandable from the standpoint of human interest. A similar selection process operates when we inquire into or recount other types of daily activity. When we are asked about our trip downtown or our day at the office we rarely bother describing the ride on the bus or the time spent in front of the watercooler. Indeed, we are more likely to report that nothing happened than to catalogue the pedestrian actions that took place between home and return. Unless something interesting occurred there is little purpose in talking about our experience.

Yet from the standpoint of giving shape and meaning to our lives these events about which we rarely speak may be as important as those that hold our listener's attention. Certainly they represent a much larger portion of our experience than do those about which we talk. The daily routine, the "rat race," and the infamous "old grind" may be brightened from time to time by happenings that add color to an otherwise drab existence, but the grayness of our daily lives has an abrasive potency of its own. Anthropologists understand this fact better than do most other social scientists, and their field studies have taught us to appreciate the cultural significance of the humdrum elements of human existence. This is the lesson we must heed as we seek to understand life in elementary classrooms.

I

School is a place where tests are failed and passed, where amusing things happen, where new insights are stumbled upon, and skills acquired. But it is also a place in which people sit, and listen, and wait, and raise their hands, and pass out paper, and stand in line, and sharpen pencils. School is where we encounter both friends and foes, where imagination is unleashed and misunderstanding brought to ground. But it is also a place in which yawns are stifled and initials scratched on desktops, where milk money is collected and recess lines are formed. Both aspects of school life, the celebrated and the unnoticed, are familiar to all of us, but the latter, if only because of its characteristic neglect, seems to deserve more attention than it has received to date from those who are interested in education.

In order to appreciate the significance of trivial classroom events it is necessary to consider the frequency of their occurrence, the standardization of the school environment, and the compulsory quality of daily attendance. We must recognize, in other words, that children are in school for a long time, that the settings in which they perform are highly uniform, and that they are there whether they want to be or not. Each of these three facts, although seemingly obvious, deserves some elaboration, for each contributes to our understanding of how students feel about and cope with their school experience.

The amount of time children spend in school can be described with a fair amount of quantitative precision, although the psychological significance of the numbers involved is another matter entirely. In most states the school year legally comprises 180 days. A full session on each of those days usually lasts about six hours (with a break for lunch), beginning somewhere around nine o'clock in the morning and ending about three o'clock in the afternoon. Thus, if a student never misses a day during the year, he spends a little more than one thousand hours under the care and tutelage of teachers. If he has attended kindergarten and was reasonably regular in his attendance during the grades, he will have logged a little more than seven thousand classroom hours by the time he is ready for junior high school.

The magnitude of 7,000 hours spread over six or seven years of a child's life is difficult to comprehend. On the one hand, when placed beside the total number of hours the child has lived during those years it is not very great—slightly more than one-tenth of his life during the time in question, about one-third of his hours of sleep during that period. On the other hand, aside from sleeping, and perhaps playing, there is no other activity that occupies as much of the child's time as that involved in attending school. Apart from the bedroom (where he has his eyes closed most of the time) there is no single enclosure in which he spends a longer time than he does in the classroom. From the age of six onward he is a more familiar sight to his teacher than to his father, and possibly even to his mother.

wow!

Another way of estimating what all those hours in the classroom mean is to ask how long it would take to accumulate them while engaged in some other familiar and recurring activity. Church attendance provides an interesting comparison. In order to have had as much time in church as a sixth grader has had in classrooms we would have to spend all day at a religious gathering every Sunday for more than 24 years. Or, if we prefer our devotion in smaller doses, we would have to attend a one-hour service every Sunday for 150 years before the inside of a church became as familiar to us as the inside of a school is to a twelve-year-old.

The comparison with church attendance is dramatic, and perhaps overly so. But it does make us stop and think about the possible significance of an otherwise meaningless number. Also, aside from the home and the school there is no physical setting in which people of all ages congregate with as great a regularity as they do in church.

The translation of the child's tenure in class into terms of weekly church attendance serves a further purpose. It sets the stage for considering an important similarity between the two institutions: school and church. The inhabitants of both are surrounded by a stable and highly stylized environment. The fact of prolonged exposure in either setting increases in its meaning as we begin to consider the elements of repetition, redundancy, and ritualistic action that are experienced there.

A classroom, like a church auditorium, is rarely seen as being anything other than that which it is. No one entering either place is likely to think that he is in a living room, or a grocery store, or a train station. Even if he entered at midnight or at some other time when the activities of the people would not give the function away, he would have no difficulty understanding what was *supposed* to go on there. Even devoid of people, a church is a church and a classroom, a classroom.

This is not to say, of course, that all classrooms are identical, anymore than all churches are. Clearly there are differences, and sometimes very extreme ones, between any two settings. One has only to think of the wooden benches and planked floor of the early American classroom as compared with the plastic chairs and tile flooring in today's suburban schools. But the resemblance is still there despite the differences, and, more important, during any particular historical period the differences are not that great. Also, whether the student moves from first to sixth grade on floors of vinyl tile or oiled wood, whether he spends his days in front of a black blackboard or a green one, is not as important as the fact that the environment in which he spends these six or seven years is highly stable.

In their efforts to make their classrooms more homelike, elementary school teachers often spend considerable time fussing with the room's decorations. Bulletin boards are changed, new pictures are hung, and the seating arrangement is altered from circles to rows and back again. But these are surface adjustments at best, resembling the work of the inspired housewife who rearranges the living room furniture and changes the color of the drapes in order to make the room more "interesting." School bulletin boards may be changed but they are never discarded, the seats may be rearranged but thirty of them are there to stay, the teacher's desk may have a new plant on it but there it sits, as ubiquitous as the roll-down maps, the drab olive waste-basket, and the pencil sharpener on the window ledge.

Thoughts on this analogy)

Even the odors of the classroom are fairly standardized. Schools may use different brands of wax and cleaning fluid, but they all seem to contain similar ingredients, a sort of universal smell which creates an aromatic background that permeates the entire building. Added to this, in each classroom, is the slightly acrid scent of chalk dust and the faint hint of fresh wood from the pencil shavings. In some rooms, especially at lunch time, there is the familiar odor of orange peels and peanut butter sandwiches, a blend that mingles in the late afternoon (following recess) with the delicate pungency of children's perspiration. If a person stumbled into a classroom blindfolded, his nose alone, if he used it carefully, would tell him where he was.

All of these sights and smells become so familiar to students and teachers alike that they exist dimly, on the periphery of awareness. Only when the classroom is encountered under somewhat unusual circumstances, does it appear, for a moment, a strange place filled with objects that command our attention. On these rare occasions when, for example, students return to school in the evening, or in the summer when the halls ring with the hammers of workmen, many features of the school environment that have merged into an undifferentiated background for its daily inhabitants suddenly stand out in sharp relief. This experience, which obviously occurs in contexts other than the classroom, can only happen in settings to which the viewer has become uncommonly habituated.

Not only is the classroom a relatively stable physical environment, it also provides a fairly constant social context. Behind the same old desks sit the same old students, in front of the familiar blackboard stands the familiar teacher. There are changes, to be sure—some students come and go during the year and on a few mornings the children are greeted at the door by a strange adult. But in most cases these events are sufficiently uncommon to create a flurry of excitement in the room. Moreover, in most elementary classrooms the social composition is not only stable, it is also physically arranged with considerable regularity. Each student has an assigned seat and, under normal circumstances, that is where he is to be found. The practice of assigning seats makes it possible for the teacher or a student to take attendance at a glance. A quick visual sweep is usually sufficient to determine who is there and who is not. The ease with which this procedure is accomplished reveals more eloquently than do words how accustomed each member of the class is to the presence of every other member.

An additional feature of the social atmosphere of elementary classrooms deserves at least passing comment. There is a social intimacy in schools that is unmatched elsewhere in our society. Buses and movie theaters may be more crowded than classrooms, but people rarely stay in such densely populated settings for extended periods of time and while there, they usually are not expected to concentrate on work or to interact with each other. Even factory workers are not clustered as close together as students in a standard classroom. Indeed, imagine what would happen if a factory the size of a typical elementary school contained three or four hundred adult workers. In all likelihood the unions would not allow it. Only in schools do thirty or more people spend several hours each day literally side by side. Once we leave the classroom we seldom again are required to have contact with so many people for so long a time. This fact will become particularly relevant in a later chapter in which we treat the social demands of life in school.

A final aspect of the constancy experienced by young students involves the ritualistic and cyclic quality of the activities carried on in the classroom. The daily schedule, as an instance, is commonly divided into definite periods during which specific subjects are to be studied or specific activities engaged in. The content of the work surely changes from day to day and from week to week, and in this sense there is considerable variety amid the constancy. But spelling still comes after arithmetic on Tuesday morning, and when the teacher says, "All right class, now take out your spellers," his announcement comes as no surprise to the students. Further, as they search in their desks for their spelling textbooks, the children may not know what new words will be included in the day's assignment, but they have a fairly clear idea of what the next twenty minutes of class time will entail.

Despite the diversity of subject matter content, the identifiable forms of classroom activity are not great in number. The labels: "seatwork," "group discussion," "teacher demonstration," and "question-and-answer period" (which would include work "at the board"), are sufficient to categorize most of the things that happen when class is in session. "Audiovisual display," "testing session," and "games" might be added to the list, but in most elementary classrooms they occur rarely.

Each of these major activities are performed according to rather well-defined rules which the students are expected to understand and obey—for example, no loud talking during seatwork, do not interrupt someone else during discussion, keep your eyes on your own paper during tests, raise your hand if you have a question. Even in the early grades these rules are so well understood by the students (if not completely internalized) that the teacher has only to give very abbreviated signals ("Voices, class," "Hands, please.") when violations are perceived. In many classrooms a weekly time schedule is permanently posted so that everyone can tell at a glance what will happen next.

Thus, when our young student enters school in the morning he is entering an environment with which he has become exceptionally familiar through prolonged exposure. Moreover, it is a fairly stable environment—one in which the physical objects, social relations, and major activities remain much the same from day to day, week to week, and even, in certain respects, from year to year. Life there resembles life in other contexts in some ways, but not all. There is, in other words, a uniqueness to the student's world. School, like church and home, is someplace special. Look where you may, you will not find another place quite like it.

There is an important fact about a student's life that teachers and parents often prefer not to talk about, at least not in front of students. This is the fact that young people have to be in school, whether they want to be or not. In this regard students have something in common with the members of two other of our social institutions that have involuntary attendance: prisons and mental hospitals. The analogy, though dramatic, is not intended to be shocking, and certainly there is no comparison between the unpleasantness of life for inmates of our prisons and mental institutions, on the one hand, and the daily travails of a first or second grader, on the other. Yet the school child, like the incarcerated adult, is, in a sense, a prisoner. He too must come to grips with the inevitability of his experience. He too must develop strategies for dealing with the conflict that frequently arises between his natural desires and interests on the one hand and institutional expectations on the other. Several of these strategies will be discussed in the chapters that follow. Here it is sufficient to note that the thousands of hours spent in the highly stylized environment of the elementary classroom are not, in an ultimate sense, a matter of choice, even though some children might prefer school to play. Many seven-year-olds skip happily to school, and as parents and teachers we are glad they do, but we stand ready to enforce the attendance of those who are more reluctant. And our vigilance does not go unnoticed by children.

In sum, classrooms are special places. The things that happen there and the ways in which they happen combine to make these settings different from all others. This is not to say, of course, that there is no similarity between what goes on in school and the students' experiences elsewhere. Classrooms are indeed like homes and churches and hospital wards in many important respects. But not in all.

The things that make schools different from other places are not only the paraphernalia of learning and teaching and the educational content of the dialogues that take place there, although these are the features that are usually singled out when we try to portray what life in school is really like. It is true that nowhere else do we find blackboards and teachers and textbooks in such abundance and nowhere else is so much time spent on reading, writing, and arithmetic. But these obvious characteristics do not constitute all that is unique about this environment. There are other features, much less obvious though equally omnipresent, that help to make up "the facts of life," as it were, to which students must adapt. From the standpoint of understanding the impact of school life on the student some features of the classroom that are not immediately visible are fully as important as those that are.

The characteristics of school life to which we now turn our attention are not commonly mentioned by students, at least not directly, nor are they apparent to the casual observer. Yet they are as real, in a sense, as the unfinished portrait of Washington that hangs above the cloakroom door. They comprise three facts of life with which even the youngest student must learn to deal and may be introduced by the key words: *crowds, praise,* and *power.*

Learning to live in a classroom involves, among other things, learning to live in a crowd. This simple truth has already been mentioned, but it requires greater elaboration. Most of the things that are done in school are done with others, or at least in the presence of others, and this fact has profound implications for determining the quality of a student's life.

Of equal importance is the fact that schools are basically evaluative settings. The very young student may be temporarily fooled by tests that are presented as games, but it doesn't take long before he begins to see through the subterfuge and comes to realize that school, after all, is a serious business. It is not only what you do there but what others think of what you do that is important. Adaptation to school life requires the student to become used to living under the constant condition of having his words and deeds evaluated by others.

School is also a place in which the division between the weak and the powerful is clearly drawn. This may sound like a harsh way to describe the separation between teachers and students, but it serves to emphasize a fact that is often overlooked, or touched upon gingerly at best. Teachers are indeed more powerful than students, in the sense of having greater responsibility for giving shape to classroom events, and this sharp difference in authority is another feature of school life with which students must learn how to deal.

In three major ways then—as members of crowds, as potential recipients of praise or reproof, and as pawns of institutional authorities—students are confronted with aspects of reality that at least during their childhood years are relatively confined to the hours spent in classrooms. Admittedly, similar conditions are encountered in other environments. Students, when they are not performing as such, must often find themselves lodged within larger groups, serving as targets of praise or reproof, and being bossed around or guided by persons in positions of higher authority. But these kinds of experiences are particularly frequent while school is in session and it is likely during this time that adaptive strategies having relevance for other contexts and other life periods are developed.

In the sections of this chapter to follow, each of the three classroom qualities that have been briefly mentioned will be described in greater detail. Particular emphasis will be given to the manner in which students cope with these aspects of their daily lives. The goal of this discussion, as in the preceding chapters, is to deepen our understanding of the peculiar mark that school life makes on us all. [. . .]

V

As implied in the title of this chapter, the crowds, the praise, and the power that combine to give a distinctive flavor to classroom life collectively form a hidden curriculum which each student (and teacher) must master if he is to make his way satisfactorily through the school. The demands created by these features of classroom life may be contrasted with the academic demands—the "official" curriculum, so to speak—to which educators traditionally have paid the most attention. As might be expected, the two curriculums are related to each other in several important ways.

As has already been suggested in the discussion of praise in the classroom, the reward system of the school is linked to success in both curriculums. Indeed, many of the rewards and punishments that sound as if they are being dispensed on the basis of academic success and failure are really more closely related to the mastery of the hidden curriculum. Consider, as an instance, the common teaching practice of giving a student credit for trying. What do teachers mean when they say a student tries to do his work? They mean, in essence, that he complies with the procedural expectations of the institution. He does his homework (though incorrectly), he raises his hand during class discussion (though he usually comes up with the wrong answer), he keeps his nose in his book during free study period (though he doesn't turn the page very often). He is, in other words, a "model" student, though not necessarily a good one.

It is difficult to imagine any of today's teachers, particularly those in elementary schools, failing a student who tries, even though his mastery of course content is slight. Indeed, even at higher levels of education rewards sometimes go to the meek as well as the mighty. It is certainly possible that many of our valedictorians and presidents of our honor societies owe their success as much to institutional conformity as to intellectual prowess. Although it offends our sensibilities to admit it, no doubt that bright-eyed little girl who stands trembling before the principal on graduation day arrived there at least in part because she typed her weekly themes neatly and handed her homework in on time.

This manner of talking about educational affairs may sound cynical and may be interpreted as a criticism of teachers or as an attempt to subvert the virtues of neatness, punctuality, and courteous conduct in general. But nothing of that kind is intended. The point is simply that in schools, as in prisons, good behavior pays off.

Just as conformity to institutional expectations can lead to praise, so can the lack of it lead to trouble. As a matter of fact, the relationship of the hidden curriculum to student difficulties is even more striking than is its relationship to student success. As an instance, consider the conditions leading to disciplinary action in the classroom. Why do teachers scold students? Because the student has given a wrong answer? Because, try as he might, he fails to grasp the intricacies of long division? Not usually. Rather, students are commonly scolded for coming into the room late or for making too much noise or for not listening to the teacher's directions or for pushing while in line. The teacher's wrath, in other words, is more frequently triggered by violations of institutional regulations and routines than by signs of his students' intellectual deficiencies.

Even when we consider the more serious difficulties that clearly entail academic failure, the demands of the hidden curriculum lurk in the background. When Johnny's parents are called in to school because their son is not doing too well in arithmetic, what explanation is given for their son's poor performance? Typically, blame is placed on motivational deficiencies in Johnny rather than on his intellectual shortcomings. The teacher may even go so far as to say that Johnny is *un*motivated during arithmetic period. But what does this mean? It means, in essence, that Johnny does not even try. And not trying, as we have seen, usually boils down to a failure to comply with institutional expectations, a failure to master the hidden curriculum.

Testmakers describe a person as "test-wise" when he has caught on to the tricks of test construction sufficiently well to answer questions correctly even though he does not know the material on which he is being examined. In the same way one might think of students as becoming "school-wise" or "teacher-wise" when they have discovered how to respond with a minimum amount of pain and discomfort to the demands, both official and unofficial, of classroom life. Schools, like test items, have rules and traditions of their own that can only be mastered through successive exposure. But with schools as with tests all students are not equally adroit. All are asked to respond but not everyone catches on to the rules of the game.

If it is useful to think of there being two curriculums in the classroom, a natural question to ask about the relationship between them is whether their joint mastery calls for compatible or contradictory personal qualities. That is, do the same strengths that contribute to intellectual achievement also contribute to the student's success in conformity to institutional expectations? This question likely has no definite answer, but it is thought-provoking and even a brief consideration of it leads into a thicket of educational and psychological issues.

It is probably safe to predict that general ability, or intelligence, would be an asset in meeting all of the demands of school life, whether academic or institutional. The child's ability to understand causal relationships, as an instance, would seem to be of as much service as he tries to come to grips with the rules and regulations of classroom life as when he grapples with the rudiments of plant chemistry. His verbal fluency can be put to use as easily in "snowing" the teacher as in writing a short story. Thus, to the extent that the demands of classroom life call for rational thought, the student with superior intellectual ability would seem to be at an advantage.

But more than ability is involved in adapting to complex situations. Much also depends upon attitudes, values, and lifestyle—upon all those qualities commonly grouped under the term: *personality*. When the contribution of personality to adaptive strategy is considered, the old adage of "the more, the better," which works so well for general ability, does not suffice. Personal qualities that are beneficial in one setting may be detrimental in another. Indeed, even a single setting may make demands that call upon competing or conflicting tendencies in a person's makeup.

We have already seen that many features of classroom life call for patience, at best, and resignation, at worst. As he learns to live in school our student learns to subjugate his own desires to the will of the teacher and to subdue his own actions in the interest of the common good. He learns to be passive and to acquiesce to the network of rules, regulations, and routines in which he is embedded. He learns to tolerate petty frustrations and accept the plans and policies of higher authorities, even when their rationale is unexplained and their meaning unclear. Like the inhabitants of most other institutions, he learns how to shrug and say, "That's the way the ball bounces."

But the personal qualities that play a role in intellectual mastery are very different from those that characterize the Company Man. Curiosity, as an instance, that most fundamental of all scholarly traits, is of little value in responding to the demands of conformity. The curious person typically engages in a kind of probing, poking, and exploring that is almost antithetical to the attitude of the passive conformist. The scholar must develop the habit of challenging authority and of questioning the value of tradition. He must insist on explanations for things that are unclear. Scholarship requires discipline, to be sure, but this discipline serves the demands of scholarship rather than the wishes and desires of other people. In short, intellectual mastery calls for sublimited forms of aggression rather than for submission to constraints.

This brief discussion likely exaggerates the real differences between the demands of institutional conformity and the demands of scholarship, but it does serve to call attention to points of possible conflict. How incompatible are these two sets of demands? Can both be mastered by the same person? Apparently so. Certainly not all of our student council presidents and valedictorians can be dismissed as weak-willed teacher's pets, as academic Uriah Heeps. Many students clearly manage to maintain their intellectual aggressiveness while at the same time acquiescing to the laws that govern the social traffic of our schools. Apparently it *is* possible, under certain conditions, to breed "docile scholars," even though the expression seems to be a contradiction in terms. Indeed, certain forms of scholarship have been known to flourish in monastic settings, where the demands for institutional conformity are extreme.

Unfortunately, no one seems to know how these balances are maintained, nor even how to establish them in the first place. But even more unfortunate is the fact that few if any school people are giving the matter serious thought. As institutional settings multiply and become for more and more people the areas in which a significant portion of their life is enacted, we will need to know much more than we do at present about how to achieve a reasonable synthesis between the forces that drive a person to seek individual expression and those that drive him to comply with the wishes of others. Presumably what goes on in classrooms contributes significantly to this synthesis. The school is the first major institution, outside the family, in which almost all of us are immersed. From kindergarten onward, the student begins to learn what life is really like in The Company.

The demands of classroom life discussed in this chapter pose problems for students and teachers alike. As we have seen, there are many methods for coping with these demands and for solving the problems they create. Moreover, each major adaptive strategy is subtly transformed and given a unique expression as a result of the idiosyncratic characteristics of the student employing it. Thus, the total picture of adjustment to school becomes infinitely complex as it is manifested in the behavior of individual students.

Yet certain commonalities do exist beneath all the complexity created by the uniqueness of individuals. No matter what the demand or the personal resources of the person facing it there is at least one strategy open to all. This is the strategy of psychological withdrawal, of gradually reducing personal concern and involvement to a point where neither the demand nor one's success or failure in coping with it is sharply felt. In order to better understand student tactics, however, it is important to consider the climate of opinion from which they emerge. Before focusing on what they do in the classroom, we must examine how students feel about school.

12

The Practical: A Language for Curriculum[1]

Joseph J. Schwab

I shall have three points. The first is this: that the field of curriculum is moribund, unable by its present methods and principles to continue its work and desperately in search of new and more effective principles and methods.

The second point: the curriculum field has reached this unhappy state by inveterate and unexamined reliance on theory in an area where theory is partly inappropriate in the first place and where the theories extant, even where appropriate, are inadequate to the tasks which the curriculum field sets them. There are honorable exceptions to this rule but too few (and too little honored) to alter the state of affairs.

The third point, which constitutes my thesis: there will be a renaissance of the field of curriculum, a renewed capacity to contribute to the quality of American education, only if the bulk of curriculum energies are diverted from the theoretic to the practical, to the quasi-practical and to the eclectic. By "eclectic" I mean the arts by which unsystematic, uneasy, but usable focus on a body of problems is effected among diverse theories, each relevant to the problems in a different way. By the "practical" I do *not* mean the curbstone practicality of the mediocre administrator and the man on the street, for whom the practical means the easily achieved, familiar goals which can be reached by familiar means. I refer, rather, to a complex discipline, relatively unfamiliar to the academic and differing radically from the disciplines of the theoretic. It is the discipline concerned with choice and action, in contrast with the theoretic, which is concerned with knowledge. Its methods lead to defensible decisions, where the methods of the theoretic lead to warranted conclusions, and differ radically from the methods and competences entailed in the theoretic. I shall sketch some of the defining aspects of practical discipline at the appropriate time.

A Crisis of Principle

The frustrated state of the field of curriculum is not an idiopathology and not a condition which warrants guilt or shame on the part of its practitioners. All fields of systematic intellectual activity are liable to such crises. They are so because any intellectual discipline must begin its endeavors with untested principles. In its beginnings, its subject matter is relatively unknown, its problems unsolved, indeed unidentified. It does not know what questions to ask, what other knowledge to rest upon, what data to seek or what to make of them once they are elicited. It requires a preliminary and necessarily untested guide to its enquiries. It finds this guide by borrowing, by invention, or by analogy, in the shape of a hazardous commitment to the character of its problems or its subject matter and a commitment to untried canons of evidence and rules of enquiry. What follows these commitments is years of their application, pursuit of the mode of enquiry demanded by the principles to which the field has committed itself. To the majority of practitioners of any field, these years of enquiry appear only as pursuit of knowledge of its subject matter or solution of its problems. They take the guiding principles of the enquiry as givens. These years of enquiry, however, are something more than pursuit of knowledge or solution or problems. They are also tests, reflexive and pragmatic, of the principles which guide the enquiries. They determine whether, in fact, the data demanded by the principles can be elicited and whether, if elicited, they can be made to constitute knowledge adequate to the complexity of the subject matter, or solutions which, in fact, do solve the problems with which the enquiry began.

In the nature of the case, these reflexive tests of the principles of enquiry are, more often than not, partially or wholly negative, for, after all, the commitment to these principles was made before there was well-tested fruit of enquiry by which to guide the commitment. The inadequacies of principles begin to show, in the case of theoretical enquiries, by failures of the subject matter to respond to the questions put to it, by incoherencies and contradictions in data and in conclusions which cannot be resolved, or by clear disparities between the knowledge yielded by the enquiries and the behaviors of the subject matter which the knowledge purports to represent. In the case of practical enquiries, inadequacies begin to show by incapacity to arrive at solutions to the problems, by inability to realize the solutions proposed, by mutual frustrations and cancellings out as solutions are put into effect.

Although these exhaustions and failures of principles may go unnoted by practitioners in the field, at least at the conscious level, what may not be represented in consciousness is nevertheless evidenced by behavior and appears in the literature and the activities of the field as signs of the onset of a crisis of principle. These signs consist of a large increase in the frequency of published paper and colloquia marked by a *flight from the subject of the field*. There are usually six signs of this flight or directions in which the flight occurs.

Signs of Crisis

The first and most important, though often least conspicuous, sign is a flight of the field itself, a translocation of its problems and the solving of them from the nominal practitioners of the field to other men. Thus one crucial frustration of the science of genetics was resolved by a single contribution from an insurance actuary. The recent desuetude of academic physiology has been marked by a conspicuous increase in the frequency of published solutions to physiological problems by medical researchers. In similar fashion, the increasing depletion of psychoanalytic principles and methods in recent years was marked by the onset of contributions to its lore by internists, biochemists, and anthropologists.

A second flight is a flight upward, from discourse about the subject of the field to discourse about the discourse of the field, from *use* of principles and methods to *talk* about them, from grounded conclusions to the construction of models, from theory to metatheory and from metatheory to metametatheory.

A third flight is downward, an attempt by practitioners to return to the subject matter in a state of innocence, shorn not only of current principles but of all principles, in an effort to take a new, a pristine and unmediated look at the subject matter. For example, one conspicuous reaction to the warfare of numerous inadequate principles in experimental psychology has been the resurgence of ethology, which begins as an attempt to return to a pure natural history of behavior, to intensive observation and recording of the behavior of animals undisturbed in their natural habitat, by observers, equally undisturbed by mediating conceptions, attempting to record anything and everything they see before them.

A fourth flight is to the sidelines, to the role of observer, commentator, historian, and critic of the contributions of others to the field.

A fifth sign consists of marked perseveration, a repetition of old and familiar knowledge in new languages which add little or nothing to the old meanings as embodied in the older and familiar language, or repetition of old and familiar formulations by way of criticisms or minor additions and modifications.

The sixth is a marked increase in eristic, contentious, and *ad hominem* debate.

I hasten to remark that these signs of crisis are not all or equally reprehensible. There is little excuse for the increase in contentiousness nor much value in the flight to the sidelines or in perseveration, but the others, in one way or another, can contribute to resolution of the crisis. The flight of the field itself is one of the more fruitful ways by which analogical principles are disclosed, modified, and adapted to the field in crisis. The flight upward, to models and metatheory, if done responsibly, which means with a steady eye on the actual problems and conditions of the field for which the models are ostensibly constructed, becomes, in fact, the proposal and test of possible new principles for the field. The flight backward, to a state of innocence, is at least an effort to break the grip of old habits of thought and thus leave space for needed new ones, though it is clear that in the matter of enquiry, as elsewhere, virginity, once lost, cannot be regained.

In the present context, however, the virtue or vice of these various flights is beside the point. We are concerned with them as signs of collapse of principles in a field, and it is my contention, based on a study not yet complete, that most of these signs may now be seen in the field of curriculum. I shall only suggest, not cite, my evidence.

The Case of Curriculum

With respect to flight of the field itself, there can be little doubt. Of the five substantial high school science curricula, four of them—PSSC, BSCS, Chems and CBA—were instituted and managed by subject-matter specialists; the contribution of educators was small and that of curriculum specialists near vanishing point. Only Harvard Project Physics, at this writing not yet available, appears to be an exception. To one of two elementary science projects, a psychologist appears to have made a substantial contribution but curriculum specialists very little. The other—the Elementary Science Study—appears to have been substantially affected (to its advantage) by educators with one or both feet in curriculum. The efforts of the Commission of Undergraduate Education in the Biological Sciences have been carried on almost entirely by subject-matter specialists. The English Curriculum Study Centers appear to be in much the same state as the high school science curricula: overwhelmingly centered on subject specialists. Educators contribute expertise only in the area of test construction and evaluation, with here and there a contribution by a psychologist. Educators, including curriculum specialists, were massively unprepared to cope with the problem of integrated education and only by little, and late, and by trial and error, put together the halting solutions currently known as Head Start. The problems posed by the current drives toward ethnicity in education find curriculum specialists even more massively oblivious and unprepared. And I so far find myself very much alone with respect to the curriculum problems immanent in the phenomena of student protest and student revolt. (Of the social studies curriculum efforts, I shall say nothing at this time.)

On the second flight—upward—I need hardly comment. The models, the metatheory, and the metametatheory are all over the place. Many of them, moreover, are irresponsible—concerned less with the barriers to continued productivity in the field of curriculum than with exploitation of the exotic and the fashionable among forms and models of theory and metatheory: systems theory, symbolic logic, language analysis. Many others, including responsible ones, are irreversible flights upward or sideways. That is, they are models or metatheories concerned not with the judgment, the reasoned construction, or reconstruction of curriculums but with other matters—for example, how curriculum changes occur or how changes can be managed.

The flight downward, the attempt at return to a pristine, unmediated look at the subject matter, is, for some reason, a missing symptom in the case of curriculum. There are returns—to the classroom, if not to other levels or aspects of curriculum—with a measure of effort to avoid preconceptions (e.g., Smith, Bellack, and studies of communication nets and lines), but the frequency of such studies has not markedly increased. The absence of this symptom may have significance. In general, however, it is characteristic of diseases that the whole syndrome does not appear in all cases. Hence, pending further study and thought, I do not count this negative instance as weakening the diagnosis of a crisis of principle.

The fourth flight—to the sidelines—is again a marked symptom of the field of curriculum. Histories, anthologies, commentaries, criticisms, and proposals of curriculums multiply.

Perseveration is also marked. I recoil from counting the persons and books whose lives are made possible by continuing restatement of the Tyler rationale, of the character and case for behavioral objectives, of the virtues and vices of John Dewey.

The rise in frequency and intensity of the eristic and *ad hominem* is also marked. Thus one author climaxes a series of petulances by the remark that what he takes to be his own forte "has always been rare—and shows up in proper perspective the happy breed of educational reformer who can concoct a brand new, rabble-rousing theory of educational reform while waiting for the water to fill the bathtub."

There is little doubt, in short, that the field of curriculum is in a crisis of principle.

A crisis of principle arises, as I have suggested, when principles are exhausted—when the questions they permit have all been asked and answered—or when the efforts at enquiry instigated by the principles have at last exhibited their inadequacy to the subject matter and the problems which they were designed to attack. My second point is that the latter holds in the case of curriculum: the curriculum movement has been inveterately theoretic, and its theoretic bent has let it down. A brief conspectus of instances will suggest the extent of this theoretic bent and what is meant by "theoretic."

Characteristics of Theory

Consider first the early, allegedly Herbartian efforts (recently revived by Bruner). These efforts took the view that ideas were formed by children out of received notions and experiences of things, and that these ideas functioned thereafter as discriminators and organizers of what was later learned. Given this view, the aim of curriculum was to discriminate the right ideas (by way of analysis of extant bodies of knowledge), determine the order in which they could be learned by children as they developed, and thereafter present these ideas at the right times with clarity, associations, organization, and application. A theory of mind and knowledge thus solves by one mighty coup the problem of what to teach, when and how; and what is fatally theoretic here is not the presence of a theory of mind and a theory of knowledge, though their presence is part of the story, but the dispatch, the sweeping appearance of success, the vast simplicity which grounds this purported solution to the problem of curriculum. And lest we think that this faith in the possibility of successful neatness, dispatch, and sweeping generality is a mark of the past, consider the concern of the National Science Teachers Association only four years ago "with identifying the broad principles that can apply to any and all curriculum development efforts in science," a concern crystallized in just seven "conceptual schemes" held to underlie all science. With less ambitious sweepingness but with the same steadfast concern for a single factor—in this case, supposed fixed structure of knowledge—one finds similar efforts arising from the Association of College Teachers of Education, from historians, even from teachers of literature.

Consider, now, some of the numerous efforts to ground curriculum in derived objectives. One effort seeks the ground of its objectives in social need and finds its social needs in just those facts about its culture which are sought and found under the aegis of a single conception of culture. Another grounds its objectives in the social needs identified by a single theory of history and of political evolution.

A third group of searches for objectives are grounded in theories of personality. The persuasive coherence and plausibility of Freudianism persuaded its followers to aim to supply children with adequate channels of sublimation of surplus libido, appropriate objects and occasions for aggressions, a properly undemanding ego ideal, and an intelligent minimum of taboos. Interpersonal theories direct their adherents to aim for development of abilities to relate to peers, "infeers," and "supeers," in relations nurturant and receiving, adaptive, vying, approving and disapproving. Theories of actualization instruct their adherents to determine the salient potentialities of each child and to see individually to the development of each.

Still other searches for objectives seek their aims in the knowledge needed to "live in the modern world," in the attitudes and habits which minimize dissonance with the prevailing mores of one's community or social class, in the skills required for success in a trade or vocation, in the ability to participate effectively as member of a group. Still others are grounded in some quasi-ethics, some view of the array of goods which are good for man.

Three features of these typical efforts at curriculum making are significant here, each of which has its own lesson to teach us. First, each is grounded in a theory as such. We shall return to this point in a moment. Second, each is grounded in a theory from the social or behavioral sciences: psychology, psychiatry, politics, sociology, history. Even the ethical bases and theories of "mind" are behavioral. To this point, too, we shall return in a moment. Third, they are theories concerning *different* subject matters. One curriculum effort is grounded in concern for the individual, another in concern for groups, others in concern for cultures, communities, societies, minds, or the extant bodies of knowledge.[2]

Need for an Eclectic

The significance of this third feature is patent to the point of embarrassment: no curriculum grounded in but one of these subjects can possibly be adequate, defensible.

A curriculum based on theory about individual personality, which thrusts society, its demands and its structure, far into the background or ignores them entirely, can be nothing but incomplete and doctrinaire, for the individuals in question are in fact members of a society and must meet its demands to some minimum degree since their existence and prosperity as individuals depend on the functioning of their society. In the same way, a curriculum grounded only in a view of social need or social change must be equally doctrinaire and incomplete, for societies do not exist only for their own sakes but for the prosperity of their members as individuals as well. In the same way, learners are not only minds or knowers but bundles of affects, individuals, personalities, earners of livings. They are not only group interactors but possessors of private lives.

It is clear, I submit, that a defensible curriculum or plan of curriculum must be one which somehow takes account of all these subsubjects which pertain to man. It cannot take only one and ignore the others; it cannot even take account of many of them and ignore one. Not only is each of them a constituent and a condition for decent human existence but each interpenetrates the others. That is, the character of human personalities is a determiner of human society and the behavior of human groups. Conversely, the conditions of group behavior and the character of societies determine in some large part the personalities which their members develop, the way their minds work, and what they can learn and use by way of knowledge and competence. These various "things" (individuals, societies, cultures, patterns of enquiry, "structures" of knowledge or of enquiries, apperceptive masses, problem solving), though discriminable as separate subjects of differing modes of enquiry, are nevertheless parts or affectors of one another, or coactors. (Their very separation for purposes of enquiry is what marks the outcomes of such enquiries as "theoretic" and consequently incomplete.) In practice, they constitute one complex, organic agency. Hence, a focus on only one not only ignores the others but vitiates the quality and completeness with which the selected one is viewed.

It is equally clear, however, that there is not, and will not be in the foreseeable future, one theory of this complex whole which is other than a collection of unusable generalities. Nor is it true that the lack of a theory of the whole is due to the narrowness, stubbornness, or merely habitual specialism of social and behavioral scientists. Rather, their specialism and the restricted purview of their theories are functions of their subject, its enormous complexity, its vast capacity for difference and change. Man's competence at the construction of theoretical knowledge is so far most inadequate when applied to the subject of man. There have been efforts to conceive principles of enquiry which would encompass the whole variety and complexity of humanity, but they have fallen far short of adequacy to the subject matter or have demanded the acquisition of data and modes of interpretation of data beyond our capabilities. There *are* continuing efforts to find bridging terms which would relate the principles of enquiry of one subfield of the social sciences to another and thus begin to effect connections among our knowledges of each, but successful bridges are so far few and narrow and permit but a trickle of connection. As far, then, as theoretical knowledge is concerned, we must wrestle as best we can with numerous, largely unconnected, separate theories of these many, artificially discriminated subsubjects of man.

I remarked in the beginning that renewal of the field of curriculum would require diversion of the bulk of its energies from theory to the practical, the quasi-practical, and the eclectic. The state of affairs just described, the existence and the necessarily continuing existence of separate theories of separate subsubjects distributed among the social sciences, constitutes the case for one of these modes, the necessity of an eclectic, of arts by which a usable focus on a common body of problems is effected among theories which lack theoretical connection. The argument can be simply summarized. A curriculum grounded in but one or a few subsubjects of the social sciences is indefensible; contributions from all are required. There is no foreseeable hope of a unified theory in the immediate or middle future, nor of a metatheory which will tell us how to put those subsubjects together or order them in a fixed hierarchy of importance to the problems of curriculum. What remains as a viable alternative is the unsystematic, uneasy, pragmatic, and uncertain unions and connections which can be effected in an eclectic. And I must add, anticipating our discussion of the practical, that *changing* connections and *differing* orderings at different times of these separate theories, will characterize a sound eclectic.

The character of eclectic arts and procedures must be left for discussion on another occasion. Let it suffice for the moment that witness of the high effectiveness of eclectic methods and of their accessibility is borne by at least one field familiar to us all—Western medicine. It has been enormously effective, and the growth of its competence dates from its disavowal of a single doctrine and its turn to eclecticism.

The Place of the Practical

I turn now, from the fact that the theories which ground curriculum plans pertain to different subsubjects of a common field, to the second of the three features which characterize our typical instances of curriculum planning—the fact that the ground of each plan is a theory, a theory as such.

The significance of the existence of theory as such at the base of curricular planning consists of what it is that theory does not and cannot encompass. All theories, even the best of them in the simplest sciences, necessarily neglect some aspects and facets of the facts of the case. A theory covers and formulates the *regularities* among the things and events it subsumes. It abstracts a general or ideal case. It leaves behind the nonuniformities, the particularities, which characterize each concrete instance of the facts subsumed. Moreover, in the process of idealization, theoretical enquiry may often leave out of consideration conspicuous facets of *all* cases because its substantive principles of enquiry or its methods cannot handle them. Thus the constantly accelerating body of classical mechanics was the acceleration of a body in "free" fall, fall in a perfect vacuum, and the general or theoretical rule formulated in classical mechanics is far from describing the fall of actual bodies in actual mediums—the only kinds of fall then known. The force equation of classical dynamics applied to bodies of visible magnitudes ignores friction. The rule that light varies inversely as the square of the distance holds exactly only for an imaginary point source of light. For real light sources of increasing expanse, the so-called law holds more and more approximately, and for very large sources it affords little or no usable information. And what is true of the best of theories in the simplest sciences is true a fortiori in the social sciences. Their subject matters are apparently so much more variable, and clearly so much more complex, that their theories encompass much less of their subjects than do the theories of the physical and biological sciences.

Yet curriculum is brought to bear not on ideal or abstract representatives but on the real thing, on the concrete case in all its completeness and with all its differences from all other concrete cases on which the theoretic abstraction is silent. The materials of a concrete curriculum will not consist merely of portions of "science," of "literature," of "process." On the contrary, their constituents will be particular assertions about selected matters couched in a particular vocabulary, syntax, and rhetoric. They will be particular novels, short stories, or lyric poems, each, for better or for worse, with its own flavor. They will be particular acts upon particular matters in a given sequence. The curriculum will be brought to bear not in some archetypical classroom but in a particular locus in time and space with smells, shadows, seats, and conditions outside its walls which may have much to do with what is achieved inside. Above all, the supposed beneficiary is not the generic child, not even a class or kind of child out of the psychological or sociological literature pertaining to the child. The beneficiaries will consist of very local kinds of children and, within the local kinds, individual children. The same diversity holds with respect to teachers and what they do. The generalities about science, about literature, about children in general, about children or teachers of some specified class or kind, may be true. But they attain this status in virtue of what they leave out, and the omissions affect what remains. A Guernsey cow is not only something more than cow, having specific features omitted from description of the genus; it is also cowy in ways differing from the cowiness of a Texas longhorn. The specific not only adds to the generic; it also modulates it.

These ineluctable characteristics of theory and the consequent ineluctable disparities between real things and their representation in theory constitute one argument for my thesis, that a large bulk of curriculum energies must be diverted from the theoretic, not only to the eclectic but to the practical and the quasi-practical. The argument, again, can be briefly summarized. The stuff of theory is abstract or idealized representations of real things. But curriculum in action treats real things: real acts, real teachers, real children, things richer and different from their theoretical representations. Curriculum will deal badly with its real things if it treats them merely as replicas of their theoretic representations. If, then, theory is to be used well in the determination of curricular practice, it requires a supplement. It requires arts which bring a theory to its application: first, arts which identify the disparities between real things and theoretic representation; second, arts which modify the theory in the course of its application, in the light of the discrepancies; and, third, arts which devise ways of taking account of the many aspects of the real things which the theory does not take into account. These are some of the arts of the practical.

Theories from Social Sciences

The significance of the third feature of our typical instances of curriculum work—that their theories are mainly theories from the social and behavioral sciences—will carry us to the remainder of the argument for the practical. Nearly all theories in all the behavioral sciences are marked by the coexistence of competing theories. There is not one theory of personality but twenty, representing at least six radically different choices of what is relevant and important in human behavior. There is not one theory of groups but several. There is not one theory of learning but half a dozen. All the social and behavioral sciences are marked by "schools," each distinguished by a different choice of principle of enquiry, each of which selects from the intimidating complexities of the subject matter the small fraction of the whole with which it can deal.

The theories which arise from enquiries so directed are, then, radically incomplete, each of them incomplete to the extent that competing theories take hold of different aspects of the subject of enquiry and treat it in a different way. Further, there is perennial invention of new principles which bring to light new facets of the subject matter, new relations among the facets and new ways of treating them. In short, there is every reason to suppose that any one of the extant theories of behavior is a pale and incomplete representation of actual behavior. There is similar reason to suppose that if all the diversities of fact, the different aspects of behavior treated in each theory, were somehow to be brought within the bounds of a single theory, that theory would still fall short of comprehending the whole of human behavior—in two respects. In the first place, it would not comprehend what there may be of human behavior which we do not see by virtue of the restricted light by which we examine behavior. In the second place, such a single theory will necessarily interpret its data in the light of its one set of principles, assigning to these data only one set of significances and establishing among them only one set of relations. It will remain the case, then, that a diversity of theories may tell us more than a single one, even though the "factual" scope of the many and the one are the same.

It follows, then, that such theories are not, and will not be, adequate by themselves to tell us what to do with human beings or how to do it. What they variously suggest and the contrary guidances they afford to choice and action must be mediated and combined by eclectic arts and must be massively supplemented, as well as mediated, by knowledge of some other kind derived from another source.

Some areas of choice and action with respect to human behavior have long since learned this lesson. Government is made possible by a lore of politics derived from immediate experience of the vicissitudes and tangles of legislating and administering. Institution of economic guidances and controls owes as much to unmediated experience of the marketplace as it does to formulas and theories. Even psychotherapy has long since deserted its theories of personality as sole guides to therapy and relies as much or more on the accumulated, explicitly nontheoretic lore accumulated by practitioners, as it does on theory or eclectic combinations of theory. The law has systematized the accumulation of direct experience of actual cases in its machinery for the recording of cases and opinions as precedents which continuously monitor, supplement, and modify the meaning and application of its formal "knowledge," its statutes. It is this recourse to accumulated lore, to experience of actions and their consequences, to action and reaction at the level of the concrete case, which constitutes the heart of the practical. It is high time that curriculum do likewise.

The Practical Arts

The arts of the practical are onerous and complex; hence only a sampling must suffice to indicate the character of this discipline and the changes in educational investigation which would ensue on adoption of the discipline. I shall deal briefly with four aspects of it.

The practical arts begin with the requirement that existing institutions and existing practices be preserved and altered piecemeal, not dismantled and replaced. It is further necessary that changes be so planned and so articulated with what remains unchanged that the functioning of the whole remain coherent and unimpaired. These necessities stem from the very nature of the practical—that it is concerned with the maintenance and improvement of patterns of purposed action, and especially concerned that the effects of the pattern through time shall retain coherence and relevance to one another.

This is well seen in the case of the law. Statutes are repealed or largely rewritten only as a last resort, since to do so creates confusion and diremption between old judgments under the law and judgments to come, confusion which must lead either to weakening of law through disrepute or a painful and costly process of repairing the effects of past judgments so as to bring them into conformity with the new. It is vastly more desirable that changes be instituted in small degrees and in immediate adjustment to the peculiarities of particular new cases which call forth the change.

The consequence, in the case of the law, of these demands of the practical is that the servants of the law must know the law through and through. They must know the statutes themselves, the progression of precedents and interpretations which have effected changes in them, and especially the present state of affairs—the most recent decisions under the law and the calendar of cases which will be most immediately affected by contemplated additions to precedent and interpretation.

The same requirements would hold for a practical program of improvement of education. It, too, would effect its changes in small progressions, in coherence with what remains unchanged, and this would require that we know *what is and has been going on in American schools.*

At present, we do not know. My own incomplete investigations convince me that we have not the faintest reliable knowledge of how literature is taught in the high schools, or what actually goes on in science classrooms. There are a dozen different ways in which the novel can be read. Which ones are used by whom, with whom, and to what effect? What selections from the large accumulation of biological knowledge are made and taught in this school system and that, to what classes and kinds of children, to what effect? To what extent is science taught as verbal formulas, as congeries of unrelated facts, as so-called principles and conceptual structures, as outcomes of enquiry? In what degree and kind of simplification and falsification is scientific enquiry conveyed, if it is conveyed at all?

A count of textbook adoptions will not tell us, for teachers select from textbooks and alter their treatment (often quite properly) and can frustrate and negate the textbook's effort to alter the pattern of instruction. We cannot tell from lists of objectives, since they are usually so vastly ambiguous that almost anything can go on under their aegis or, if they are not ambiguous, reflect pious hopes as much as actual practice. We cannot tell from lists of "principles" and "conceptual structures," since these, in their telegraphic brevity are also ambiguous and say nothing of the shape in which they are taught or the extent.

What is wanted is a totally new and extensive pattern of *empirical* study of classroom action and reaction; a study, not as basis for theoretical concerns about the nature of the teaching or learning process, but as a basis for beginning to know what we are doing, what we are not doing, and to what effect—what changes are needed, which needed changes can be instituted with what costs or economies, and how they can be effected with minimum tearing of the remaining fabric of educational effort.

This is an effort which will require new mechanisms of empirical investigation, new methods of reportage, a new class of educational researchers, and much money. It is an effort without which we will continue largely incapable of making defensible decisions about curricular changes, largely unable to put them into effect and ignorant of what real consequences, if any, our efforts have had.

A very large part of such a study would, I repeat, be direct and empirical study of action and reaction in the classroom itself, not merely the testing of student change. But one of the most interesting and visible alterations of present practice which might be involved is a radical change in our pattern of testing students. The common pattern tries to determine the extent to which *intended* changes have been brought about. This would be altered to an effort to find out what changes have occurred, to determine side effects as well as mainline consequences, since the distinction between these two is always in the eye of the intender and side effects may be as great in magnitude and as fatal or healthful for students as the intended effects.

A second facet of the practical: its actions are undertaken with respect to identified frictions and failures in the machine and inadequacies evidenced in felt shortcomings of its products. This origin of its actions leads to two marked differences in operation from that of theory. Under the control of theory, curricular changes have their origin in new notions of person, group or society, mind or knowledge, which give rise to suggestions of new things curriculum might be or do. This is an origin which, by its nature, takes little or no account of the existing effectiveness of the machine or the consequences to this effectiveness of the institution of novelty. If there is concern for what may be displaced by innovation or for the incoherences which may ensue on the insertion of novelty, the concern is gratuitous. It does not arise from the theoretical considerations which commend the novelty. The practical, on the other hand, because it institutes changes to repair frictions and deficiencies, is commanded to determine the whole array of possible effects of proposed change, to determine what new frictions and deficiencies the proposed change may unintentionally produce.

The other effective difference between theoretical and practical origins of deliberate change is patent. Theory, by being concerned with new things to do, is unconcerned with the successes and failures of present doings. Hence present failures, unless they coincide with what is repaired by the proposed innovations, go unnoticed—as do present successes. The practical, on the other hand, is directly and deliberately concerned with the diagnosis of ills of the curriculum.

These concerns of the practical for frictions and failures of the curricular machine would, again, call for a new and extensive pattern of enquiry. The practical requires curriculum study to seek its problems where its problems lie—in the behaviors, misbehaviors, and nonbehaviors of its students as they begin to evince the effects of the training they did and did not get. This means continuing assessment of students as they leave primary grades for the secondary school, leave secondary school for jobs and colleges. It means sensitive and sophisticated assessment by way of impressions, insights, and reactions of the community which sends its children to the school; employers of students, new echelons of teachers of students; the wives, husbands, and cronies of ex-students; the people with whom ex-students work; the people who work under them. Curriculum study will look into the questions of what games ex-students play; what, if anything, they do about politics and crime in the streets; what they read, if they do; what they watch on television and what they make of what they watch, again, if anything. Such studies would be undertaken, furthermore, not as mass study of products of the American school, taken in toto, but as studies of significantly separable schools and school systems—suburban and inner city, Chicago and Los Angeles, South Bend and Michigan City.

I emphasize sensitive and sophisticated assessment because we are concerned here, as in the laying of background knowledge of what goes in schools, not merely with the degree to which avowed objectives are achieved but also with detecting the failures and frictions of the machine: what it has not done or thought of doing, and what side effects its doings have had. Nor are we concerned with successes and failures only as measured in test situations but also as evidenced in life and work. It is this sort of diagnosis which I have tried to exemplify in a recent treatment of curriculum and student protest.[3]

A third facet of the practical I shall call the anticipatory generation of alternatives. Intimate knowledge of the existing state of affairs, early identification of problem situations, and effective formulation of problems are necessary to effective practical decision but not sufficient. It requires also that there be available to practical deliberation the greatest possible number and fresh diversity of alternative solutions to the problem. The reason for this requirement, in one aspect, is obvious enough: the best choice among poor and shopworn alternatives will still be a poor solution to the problem. Another aspect is less obvious. The problems which arise in an institutional structure which has enjoyed good practical management will be novel problems, arising from changes in the times and circumstances and from the consequences of previous solutions to previous problems. Such problems, with their strong tincture of novelty, cannot be solved by familiar solutions. They cannot be well solved by apparently new solutions arising from old habits of mind and old ways of doing things.

A third aspect of the requirement for anticipatory generation of alternatives is still less obvious. It consists of the fact that practical problems do not present themselves wearing their labels around their necks. Problem situations, to use Dewey's old term, present themselves to consciousness, but the character of the problem, its formulation, does not. This depends on the eye of the beholder. And this eye, unilluminated by possible fresh solutions to problems, new modes of attack, new recognitions of degrees of freedom for change among matters formerly taken to be unalterable, is very likely to miss the novel features of new problems or dismiss them as "impractical." Hence the requirement that the generation of problems be anticipatory and not await the emergence of the problem itself.

To some extent, the *theoretical* bases of curricular change—such items as emphasis on enquiry, on discovery learning, and on structure of the disciplines—contribute to this need but not sufficiently or with the breadth which permits effective deliberation. That is, these theoretic proposals tend to arise in single file, out of connection with other proposals which constitute alternatives, or, more important, constitute desiderata or circumstances which affect the choice or rejection of proposals. Consider, in regard to the problem of the "single file," only one relation between the two recent proposals subsumed under "creativity" and "structure of knowledge." If creativity implies some measure of invention, and "structure of knowledge" implies (as it does in one version) the systematic induction of conceptions as soon as children are ready to grasp them, an issue is joined. To the extent that the latter is timely and well done, scope for the former is curtailed. To the extent that children can be identified as more or less creative, "structure of knowledge" would be brought to bear on different children at different times and in different ways.

A single case, taken from possible academic resources of education, will suggest the new kind of enquiry entailed in the need for anticipatory generation of alternatives. Over the years, critical scholarship has generated, as remarked earlier, a dozen different conceptions of the novel, a dozen or more ways in which the novel can be read, each involving its own emphases and its own arts of recovery of meaning in the act of reading. Novels can be read, for example, as bearers of wisdom, insights into vicissitudes of human life and ways of enduring them. Novels can also be read as moral instructors, as sources of vicarious experience, as occasions for aesthetic experience. They can be read as models of human creativity, as displays of social problems, as political propaganda, as revelations of diversities of manners and morals among different cultures and classes of people, or as symptoms of their age.

Now what, in fact, is the full parade of such possible uses of the novel? What is required by each in the way of competences of reading, discussion, and thought? What are the rewards, the desirable outcomes, which are likely to ensue for students from each kind of reading or combinations of them? For what kinds or classes of students is each desirable? There are further problems demanding anticipatory consideration. If novels are chosen and read as displays of social problems and depictions of social classes, what effect will such instruction in literature have on instruction in the social studies? What will teachers need to know and be able to do in order to enable students to discriminate and appropriately connect the *apercus* of artists, the accounts of historians, and the conclusions of social scientists on such matters? How will the mode of instruction in science (e.g., as verified truths) and in literature (as "deep insights" or artistic constructions or matters of opinion) affect the effects of each?

The same kinds of questions could be addressed to history and to the social studies generally. Yet, nowhere, in the case of literature, have we been able to find cogent and energetic work addressed to them. The journals in the field of English teaching are nearly devoid of treatment of them. College and university courses, in English or education, which address such problems with a modicum of intellectual content are as scarce as hen's teeth. We cannot even find an unbiased conspectus of critical theory more complete than *The Pooh Perplex*, and treatments of problems of the second kind (pertaining to interaction of literature instruction with instruction in other fields) are also invisible.

Under a soundly practical dispensation in curriculum the address of such questions would be a high priority and require recruitment to education of philosophers and subject-matter specialists of a quality and critical sophistication which it has rarely, if ever, sought.

As the last sampling of the practical, consider its method. It falls under neither of the popular platitudes: it is neither deductive nor inductive. It is deliberative. It cannot be inductive because the target of the method is not a generalization or explanation but a decision about action in a concrete situation. It cannot be deductive because it deals with the concrete case, not abstractions from cases, and the concrete case cannot be settled by mere application of a principle. Almost every concrete case falls under two or more principles, and every concrete case will possess some cogent characteristics which are encompassed in no principle. The problem of selecting an appropriate man for an important post is a case in point. It is not a problem of selecting a representative of the appropriate personality type who exhibits the competences officially required for the job. The man we hire is more than a type and a bundle of competences. He is a multitude of probable behaviors which escape the net of personality theories and cognitive scales. He is endowed with prejudices, mannerisms, habits, tics, and relatives. And all of these manifold particulars will affect his work and the work of those who work for him. It is deliberation which operates in such cases to select the appropriate man.

Commitment to Deliberation

Deliberation is complex and arduous. It treats both ends and means and must treat them as mutually determining one another. It must try to identify, with respect to both, what facts may be relevant. It must try to ascertain the relevant facts in the concrete case. It must try to identify the desiderata in the case. It must generate alternative solutions. It must make every effort to trace the branching pathways of consequences which may flow from each alternative and affect desiderata. It must then weigh alternatives and their costs and consequences against one another and choose, not the right alternative, for there is no such thing, but the best one.

I shall mention only one of the new kinds of activity which would ensue on commitment to deliberation. It will require the formation of a new public and new means of communication among its constituent members. Deliberation requires consideration of the widest possible variety of alternatives if it is to be most effective. Each alternative must be viewed in the widest variety of lights. Ramifying consequences must be traced to all parts of the curriculum. The desirability of each alternative must be felt out, "rehearsed," by a representative variety of all those who must live with the consequences of the chosen action. And a similar variety must deal with the identification of problems as well as with their solution.

This will require penetration of the curtains which now separate educational psychologist from philosopher, sociologist from test constructor, historian from administrator; it will require new channels connecting the series from teacher, supervisor, and school administrator at one end to research specialists at the other. Above all, it will require renunciation of the specious privileges and hegemonies by which we maintain the fiction that problems of science curriculum, for example, have no bearing on problems of English literature or the social studies. The aim here is *not* a dissolving of specialization and special responsibilities. Quite the contrary: if the variety of lights we need are to be obtained, the variety of specialized interests, competences, and habits of mind which characterize education must be cherished and nurtured. The aim, rather, is to bring the members of this variety to bear on curriculum problems by communication with one another.

Concretely, this means the establishment of new journals, and education of educators so that they can write for them and read them. The journals will be forums where possible problems of curriculum will be broached from many sources and their possible importance debated from many points of view. They will be the stage for display of anticipatory solutions to problems, from a similar variety of sources. They will constitute deliberative assemblies in which problems and alternative solutions will be argued by representatives of all for the consideration of all and for the shaping of intelligent consensus.

Needless to say, such journals are not alone sufficient. They stand as only one concrete model of the kind of forum which is required. Similar forums, operating viva voce and in the midst of curriculum operation and curriculum change, are required: of the teachers, supervisors, and administrators of a school; of the supervisors and administrators of a school system; of representatives of teachers, supervisors, and curriculum makers in subject areas and across subject areas; of the same representatives and specialists in curriculum, psychology, sociology, administration, and the subject-matter fields.[4]

The education of educators to participate in this deliberative process will be neither easy nor quickly achieved. The education of the present generation of specialist researchers to speak to the schools and to one another will doubtless be hardest of all, and on this hardest problem I have no suggestion to make. But we could begin within two years to initiate the preparation of teachers, supervisors, curriculum makers, and graduate students of education in the uses and arts of deliberation—and we should.

For graduate students, this should mean that their future enquiries in educational psychology, philosophy of education, educational sociology, and so on, will find more effective focus on enduring problems of education, as against the attractions of the current foci of the parent disciplines. It will begin to exhibit to graduate students what their duties are to the future schoolmen whom they will teach. For teachers, curriculum makers, and others close to the classroom, such training is of special importance. It will not only bring immediate experience of the classroom effectively to bear on problems of curriculum but enhance the quality of that experience, for almost every classroom episode is a stream of situations requiring discrimination of deliberative problems and decision thereon.

By means of such journals and such an education, the educational research establishment might at last find a means for channeling its discoveries into sustained improvement of the schools instead of into a procession of ephemeral bandwagons.

Notes

1. Copyright 1969 by Joseph J. Schwab. All rights reserved. A version of this paper was delivered to Section B of the American Educational Research Association, Los Angeles, February 1969. This paper has been prepared as part of a project supported by a grant from the Ford Foundation.
2. It should be clear by now that "theory" as used in this paper does *not* refer only to grand schemes such as the general theory of relativity, kinetic-molecular theory, the Bohr atom, the Freudian construction of a tripartite psyche. The attempt to give an account of human maturation by the discrimination of definite states (e.g., oral, anal, genital), an effort to aggregate human competences into a small number of primary mental abilities—these too are theoretic. So also are efforts to discriminate a few large classes of persons and to attribute to them defining behaviors: e.g., the socially mobile, the culturally deprived, the creative.
3. *College Curriculum and Student Protest* (Chicago: University of Chicago Press, 1969).
4. It will be clear from these remarks that the conception of curricular method proposed here is immanent in the Tyler rationale. This rationale calls for a diversity of talents and insists on the practical and eclectic treatment of a variety of factors. Its effectiveness in practice is vitiated by two circumstances. Its focus on "objectives," with their massive ambiguity and equivocation, provides far too little of the concrete matter required for deliberation and leads only to delusive consensus. Second, those who use it are not trained for the deliberative procedures it requires.

Part Three

Reconceptualizing Curriculum Theory

Introduction to Part Three

As the curriculum reform movement was drawing to a close with the 1960s, Joseph Schwab (see Part Two) famously declared that the curriculum field was "moribund." While the death of the curriculum field turned out to be an exaggeration, he was surely correct that it was ripe for new directions. An important manifestation of change was attention in the 1970s through the 1980s, the times emphasized here in Part Three, to why the preceding ambitious curriculum change efforts had failed to effect reform in the ways envisaged (e.g., McLaughlin, this volume, Chapter 18). Schwab called for an emphasis on deliberation, on the "practical" for "sustained improvement of the schools," and perhaps the 1970s and early 1980s are best characterized as a period of experimentation in the wake of the curriculum reform movement. Looking back, Nel Noddings (2001, pp. 38–39) listed some of the significant experiments: continuous progress programs, modular scheduling, media-centered education, individualized instruction, behavioral objectives, mastery learning, discovery learning, interdisciplinary studies, and learning centers. By the 1970s, as the preceding list implies, experimentation increasingly stressed curricular choice rather than standardization. Students were often provided, for example, with multiple courses, even "mini-courses," which they could elect to meet standard requirements in academic subjects.

Thus one of the themes most important in Part Three is choice, of students having some significant say in what they study or how they study it or both. Choice suggests its alternative, curriculum standardization. Because what schools teach is a political as well as an educational decision, intertwined with issues of choice or standardization are questions of power, as George Counts had so well understood (see Part One). Curriculum scholars in the 1970s returned with greater vigor to issues of power than had been evident since the Great Depression. Power became a complementary theme to choice and standardization for this period. In a sense, then, the period from the late 1960s until the aftermath of the alarmist *A Nation at Risk* (1983) was a competition between the forces of curriculum standardization and curriculum choice. The powers of standardization would win out.

The politics of education and the battles over who controlled what schools teach largely came to be overshadowed by the possibilities unleashed by experimentation. Under the circumstances, innovations may have been insufficiently tested to establish if they "worked." Some innovations, as is evident in the readings, harked back to the centrality John Dewey (this volume, Chapter 3) ascribed to individualization of instruction: "What a child gets out of any subject presented to him is simply the images which he himself forms with regard to it." Unlike the standards movement and its associated testing movement, which secured dominance in U.S. public education in the 1990s, many of the curricular innovations of the 1970s valued the diverse outcomes that resulted from differentiation of standard curricula in the interests of personal relevance. Subsequent insistence by policy-makers on the desirability of a standardized curriculum with uniform outcomes has been widely criticized as a policy, particularly concerning what outcomes should be valued, how it should be implemented, whether it is properly aligned with tests, and so forth. Oddly, however, less attention seems to have been devoted to questioning the premises of standardization with questions such as why uniform outcomes are desirable in the first place and what opportunity costs they entail (see Eisner, 1998). The readings in Part Three could contribute to an ongoing critique of these premises.

The first reading is by Paulo Freire, who had long-time involvement with social movements and adult education, particularly in his native Brazil and other parts of Latin America. By the 1970s his writings were becoming widely read in the United States where he attracted a devoted and enduring set of disciples. Freire's curriculum thought is not easily summarized. Indeed, he was always worried that his ideas would become a recipe-like method to be followed uncritically (Apple, Gandin, & Hypolito, 2001, p. 132). His overarching aim was to teach the oppressed classes to bring about social justice in capitalist societies. He vigorously opposed the transmission model of curriculum, what he referred to as "banking education," because it reinforced the established knowledge already used to oppress the disadvantaged. Rather, he believed "emancipatory" curriculum must grow out of lived experience and their social circumstances. Freire made no clear divide between education and politics:

> The starting point for organizing the program content of education or political action must be the present, existential, concrete situation, reflecting the aspirations of the people. Utilizing certain basic contradictions, we must pose this existential, concrete, present situation to the people as a problem which challenges them and requires a response—not just at the intellectual level, but at the level of action. (This volume, Chapter 13)

Such problem-posing education could be achieved not by anyone "liberating" a social class, but rather through dialogue among educators and the oppressed. In the particular excerpts included here in Part Three, Freire describes what he views as the essential characteristics of such dialogue.

The next reading by Maxine Greene, like Freire's work, openly displays disenchantment with conventional curriculum design. Greene argues that existing school programs are largely irrelevant to the existential desires for meaning and direction salient in the lives of young people. Moreover, such desires could not be addressed by rearrangement of the existing curriculum or its better presentation. Instead, Greene argued that the curriculum must engage students in an "interior journey," adding that:

> Not only may it [an interior journey] result in the effecting of new syntheses within experience; it may result in an awareness of the process of knowing, of believing, of perceiving. It may even result in an understanding of the ways in which meanings have been sedimented in an individual's own personal history. . . . But then there opens up the possibility of presenting curriculum in such a way that it does not impose or enforce. (This volume, Chapter 14)

In the next essay, William Pinar rounds out what might be considered the first set of essays of Part Three in which established approaches to curriculum were found inadequate, incomplete, or both. While maintaining that established approaches to curriculum were "reliant" on each other, Pinar was in the forefront of a new "reconceptualist" movement. He argued that the two other main currents of curriculum thought, perspectives of "traditionalists" and "conceptual-empiricists" (or employers of a "social science" perspective) were inherently incomplete. Two important elements that reconceptualist curriculum theories add, Pinar argued, were their "value-laden perspective" and their "politically emancipatory intent." In large part, however, he distinguishes the movement by what it is not.

According to Pinar, traditionalists, working in the wake of Franklin Bobbitt and Ralph Tyler, were immersed in the assumptions of schools and society as they are—their task is to describe how curriculum improvement could be secured without fundamental alterations in existing institutional and societal arrangements. To do so, Pinar maintained, traditionalists engaged in curriculum theorizing, that "is theoretical only in the questionable sense that it is abstract and usually at variance with what occurs in schools" (this volume, Chapter 15).

Pinar described conceptual-empiricists as curriculum scholars who applied the questions and methods of social science to curricular phenomena. Although he saw this group as an "heir" or successor to the traditionalists, he found their attention to the normative element of their work perfunctory as conceptual-empirical "research in education, in many instances, has become indistinguishable from social science research" (this volume). This concern echoes Montessori's (Part One) apprehension about the specialized interests of trained science versus the social interests of education. For Pinar's part, he seems to have held out hope that the conceptual-empiricists might move toward the reconceptualist position. For instance, he credited the conceptual-empiricist Decker Walker with building on Schwab's call for deliberation rather than remaining preoccupied with "prescriptive curriculum theories" such as the Tyler rationale. Pinar also praised Walker's work because, even though it incorporated traditionalist elements such as "the practical concerns of school people and school curriculum," Walker's use of anthropological research methods placed "his work. . . . closer to some reconceptualists than . . . other mainstream conceptual-empiricists." Pinar, in other words, urged "value-laden," politicized curriculum theorizing, which he thought more likely to occur through anthropological means than in social sciences such as "political science or psychology" (this volume).

Mortimer Adler, the philosopher who contributes the next essay, was interested in curriculum theorizing as a means for promoting what he took for granted as the "best" knowledge and thus the knowledge of most worth. On this point he stood in contrast to the more varied and multifaceted concerns of the preceding four contributors to Part Three who, for all their differences, nonetheless agreed the traditional intellectual foundations of the "best" knowledge were an insufficient basis for sound curriculum theorizing. Adler, on the other hand, was a perennialist, boldly declaring that the best knowledge was unchanging and concerned with the same great questions such as what is the nature of truth and justice. He quoted his one-time associate, Robert Maynard Hutchins (1953), for the central plank of his beliefs: "The best education for the best is the best education for all."

Because in Adler's words, "we are a politically classless society", he believed that all young people in a democracy should study the same curriculum. Adler asserted that this democratic view of schooling has been generally agreed upon in American education, exemplified by thinkers such as Hutchins, Dewey, and Horace Mann. Thus, Adler (and Hutchins) argued the curriculum traditionally preserved for the elite was the best for everyone: "The innermost meaning of social equality is: substantially the same quality of life for all. That calls for the same quality of schooling for all." Although Adler acknowledged the curriculum needed to be taught well and "children in are educable in varying degrees," he still argued that choice in the curriculum would cause "a certain number of students to voluntarily downgrade their own education" (this volume, Chapter 16).

In the next essay, the philosopher of education Nel Noddings roundly disputes Adler's theory of curriculum. To begin with, she disputes that we, except in the most narrow, technical sense, live in a politically classless society. So for Adler to imply that giving everyone the same knowledge appreciably compensates for other inequalities, Noddings thinks is misleading, even dangerous. Moreover, she notes, as Adler must have known but fails to mention, Dewey and Hutchins vigorously disagreed about curriculum. Further, she contests that social equality should be equated with everyone living (or being educated) in the same way. In fact, Noddings contends along with Dewey that equality suggests individual differences should be respected and education build on these legitimate differences.

Noddings allows that Adler's recommendations "follow inexorably" from his assumptions, but she challenges his assumptions. She takes issue, for instance, with Adler's assumption that the "intellectually best" person is the ideal for all persons: "What the schools need to do, instead, is to legitimize multiple models of excellence," with the most important thing being "ethical goodness," which "we need far more urgently than intellectual prowess." Moreover, Noddings rejects Adler's dismissal of divergence from his prescribed subjects in the curriculum as equivalent of "downgrading" of education:

> I am simply pointing out what John Dewey counseled again and again: Any subject freely undertaken as an occupation—as a set of tasks requiring goal-setting, means-ends analysis, choice of appropriate tools and materials, exercise of skills, living through the consequences, and evaluating the results—is educative. . . . It is not the subjects offered that make a curriculum properly a part of education but how those subjects are taught, how they connect to the personal interests and talents of the students who study them, and how skillfully they are laid out against the whole continuum of human experience. (This volume, Chapter 17)

The next reading in Part Three focuses less on the aims and content of curriculum than on its classroom implementation. Milbrey McLaughlin was writing in the aftermath of the curriculum reform movement (see Part Two) that was generally judged to have failed in meeting its objectives. McLaughlin explained that most of the curricular innovations had concentrated on "technological" change. She suggested that "organizational" change in the structure of the institutional setting or the culture of the school might be a more significant factor in effecting educational change. "Innovations in classroom organization such as open education, multiage grouping, integrated day, differentiated staffing, and team teaching," McLaughlin noted by way of illustration, "are not based on a 'model' of classroom organization change to be strictly followed, but a common set of convictions about the nature of learning and the purpose of teaching." Rather than the conventional assumption that implementation consists of "the direct and straightforward application of an educational technology or plan," McLaughlin was suggesting change that matters is associated with "mutual adaptation" or "modification of both the project design and changes in the institutional setting and individual participants during the course of implementation" (this volume, Chapter 18).

If mutual adaptation is the hallmark of successful reform, a "teacher-proof" curriculum would be ineffectual from the start. To state this more broadly, McLaughlin's research is instructive on the nature of meaningful curriculum change. To illustrate, she examined open education projects in two settings. The settings were "similar in almost every aspect—resources, support and interest, target group, background characteristics"—but differed significantly in implementation strategy and implementation outcomes:

> The Eastown open education project had extensive and ongoing staff training, spent a lot of staff time and energy on materials development, arranged for staff to meet regularly, and engaged in regular formative evaluation. This project was also well implemented, ran smoothly, and met its objectives. . . . Implementation in this [the Seaside] project was only pro forma— largely because of the absence of implementation strategies that would allow learning, growth, and development or mutual adaptation to take place. (This volume, Chapter 18)

The next reading, by Michael Apple, again evokes the theme of power common to the earlier Part Three essays on reconceptualism. Perhaps as significantly, however, it presents another view of implementation than the one presented by McLaughlin. Whereas McLaughlin examined curriculum change as potentially beneficial and dependent on teacher "ownership" of the innovation, Apple was looking at what he saw as ominous attempts to impoverish curricula and force acquiescence from teachers. Of course, Apple was writing a decade after McLaughlin, and educational policy-making had turned decidedly more conservative. He contends that teacher discretion over the curriculum, which McLaughlin considered both desirable and inescapable, was diminishing and had come to be deemed undesirable by authorities. Furthermore, McLaughlin tacitly portrays teachers as exercising a good deal of professional autonomy as curricular-instructional gatekeepers (Thornton, 1991) whereas Apple decries teachers having been "de-skilled" as workers by patriarchal, undemocratic policy-makers. Teachers' work, he argued, had intensified while their control over its quality had declined. Certainly much of what Apple described here in the mid 1980s subsequently became in more recent years an even wider discussion on the relationship between teaching and the curriculum.

The final reading in Part Three is instructive because it provides concrete examples of how issues of power are reflected in both social movements and curriculum responses. Rooted in a decade of widespread concern over gender inequities, this reading is excerpted from the 1990s AAUW report, *How Schools Shortchange Girls*. The aim of the report is to promote equity in educational opportunities, and as such it too reflects the concerns over political and personal relevance common to the reconceptualist movement. We have reprinted here the three parts of the report that deal specifically with curriculum. The first part is devoted to the *formal curriculum* reviews, past research and conceptions of equity as they relate to the explicit messages that schools convey. The second part, on the *classroom as curriculum*, which harkens back to Philip Jackson's (Part Two) emphasis on implicit curricula, argues that the attention given students and the ways in which they are asked to learn largely favors boys over girls. The final section is focused on the *evaded curriculum*, or what has also been referred to as the null curriculum (Eisner, 1979; Flinders, Thornton, and Noddings, 1986). This curriculum includes topics ranging from adolescent sexuality and mental health to emotional expression and gender politics. Perhaps these topics have received increased attention in other professional fields over the past decade, but in education they remain controversial, and still largely evaded.

References

Apple, M. W., Gandin, L. A. & Hypolito, A. M. (2001). "Paulo Freire, 1921–1997." In J. Palmer (ed.) *Fifty modern thinkers on education: From Piaget to the present* (pp. 128–133). London: Routledge.

Hutchins, R. M. (1953). *The conflict in education in a democratic society*. New York: Harper.

National Commission on Excellence in Education (1983). *A nation at risk: The imperative for educational reform*. Washington, DC: U.S. Department of Education.

Noddings, N. (2001). Care and coercion in school reform. *Journal of Educational Change*, 2, 35–43.

Thornton, S. J. (1991). Teacher as curricular-instructional gatekeeper in social studies. In J. P. Shaver (ed.), *Handbook of research on social studies teaching and learning* (pp. 237–248). New York: Macmillan.

13

Pedagogy of the Oppressed

Paulo Freire

As we attempt to analyze dialogue as a human phenomenon, we discover something which is the essence of dialogue itself: *the word*. But the word is more than just an instrument which makes dialogue possible; accordingly, we must seek its constitutive elements. Within the word we find two dimensions, reflection and action, in such radical interaction that if one is sacrificed—even in part—the other immediately suffers. There is no true word that is not at the same time a praxis.[1] Thus, to speak a true word is to transform the world.[2]

An unauthentic word, one which is unable to transform reality, results when dichotomy is imposed upon its constitutive elements. When a word is deprived of its dimension of action, reflection automatically suffers as well; and the word is changed into idle chatter, into *verbalism*, into an alienated and alienating "blah." It becomes an empty word, one which cannot denounce the world, for denunciation is impossible without a commitment to transform, and there is no transformation without action.

On the other hand, if action is emphasized exclusively, to the detriment of reflection, the word is converted into *activism*. The latter—action for action's sake—negates the true praxis and makes dialogue impossible. Either dichotomy, by creating unauthentic forms of existence, creates also unauthentic forms of thought, which reinforce the original dichotomy.

Human existence cannot be silent, nor can it be nourished by false words, but only by true words, with which men transform the world. To exist, humanly, is to *name* the world, to change it. Once named, the world in its turn reappears to the namers as a problem and requires of them a new *naming*. Men are not built in silence,[3] but in word, in work, in action-reflection.

But while to say the true word—which is work, which is praxis—is to transform the world, saying that word is not the privilege of some few men, but the right of every man. Consequently, no one can say a true word alone—nor can he say it *for* another, in a prescriptive act which robs others of their words.

Dialogue is the encounter between men, mediated by the world, in order to name the world. Hence, dialogue cannot occur between those who want to name the world and those who do not wish this naming—between those who deny other men the right to speak their word and those whose right to speak has been denied them. Those who have been denied their primordial right to speak their word must first reclaim this right and prevent the continuation of this dehumanizing aggression.

If it is in speaking their word that men, by naming the world, transform it, dialogue imposes itself as the way by which men achieve significance as men. Dialogue is thus an existential necessity. And since dialogue is the encounter in which the united reflection and action of the dialoguers are addressed to the world which is to be transformed and humanized, this dialogue cannot be reduced to the act of one person's "depositing" ideas in another, nor can it become a simple exchange of ideas to be "consumed" by the discussants. Nor yet is it a hostile, polemical argument between men who are committed neither to the naming of the world, nor to the search for truth, but rather to the imposition of their own truth. Because dialogue is an encounter among men who name the world, it must not be a situation where some men name on behalf of others. It is an act of creation; it must not serve as a crafty instrument for the domination of one man by another. The domination implicit in dialogue is that of the world by the dialoguers; it is conquest of the world for the liberation of men.

Dialogue cannot exist, however, in the absence of a profound love for the world and for men. The naming of the world, which is an act of creation and re-creation, is not possible if it is not infused with love.[4] Love is at the same time the foundation of dialogue and dialogue itself. It is thus necessarily the task of responsible Subjects and cannot exist in a relation of domination. Domination reveals the pathology of love: sadism in the dominator and masochism in the dominated. Because love is an act of courage, not of fear, love is commitment to other men. No matter where the oppressed are found, the act of love is commitment to their cause—the cause of liberation. And this commitment, because it is loving, is dialogical. As an act of bravery, love cannot be sentimental; as an act of freedom, it must not serve as a pretext for manipulation. It must generate other acts of freedom; otherwise, it is not love. Only by abolishing the situation of oppression is it possible to restore the love which that situation made impossible. If I do not love the world—if I do not love life—if I do not love men—I cannot enter into dialogue.

On the other hand, dialogue cannot exist without humility. The naming of the world, through which men constantly re-create that world, cannot be an act of arrogance. Dialogue, as the encounter of men addressed to the common task of learning and acting, is broken if the parties (or one of them) lack humility. How can I dialogue if I always project ignorance onto others and never perceive my own? How can I dialogue if I regard myself as a case apart from other men—mere "its" in whom I cannot recognize other "I"s? How can I dialogue if I consider myself a member of the in-group of "pure" men, the owners of truth and knowledge, for whom all non-members are "these people" or "the great unwashed?" How can I dialogue if I start from the premise that naming the world is the task of an elite and that the presence of the people in history is a sign of deterioration, thus to be avoided? How can I dialogue if I am closed to—and even offended by—the contribution of others? How can I dialogue if I am afraid of being displaced, the mere possibility causing me torment and weakness? Self-sufficiency is incompatible with dialogue. Men who lack humility (or have lost it) cannot come to the people, cannot be their partners in naming the world. Someone who cannot acknowledge himself to be as mortal as everyone else still has a long way to go before he can reach the point of encounter. At the point of encounter there are neither utter ignoramuses nor perfect sages; there are only men who are attempting, together, to learn more than they now know.

Dialogue further requires an intense faith in man, faith in his power to make and remake, to create and re-create, faith in his vocation to be more fully human (which is not the privilege of an elite, but the birthright of all men). Faith in man is an *a priori* requirement for dialogue; the "dialogical man" believes in other men even before he meets them face to face. His faith, however, is not naïve. The "dialogical man" is critical and knows that although it is within the power of men to create and transform, in a concrete situation of alienation men may be impaired in the use of that power. Far from destroying his faith in man, however, this possibility strikes him as a challenge to which he must respond. He is convinced that the power to create and transform, even when thwarted in concrete situations, tends to be reborn. And that rebirth can occur—not gratuitously, but in and through the struggle for liberation—in the supersedence of slave labor by emancipated labor which gives zest to life. Without this faith in man, dialogue is a farce which inevitably degenerates into paternalistic manipulation.

Founding itself upon love, humility, and faith, dialogue becomes a horizontal relationship of which mutual trust between the dialoguers is the logical consequence. It would be a contradiction in terms if dialogue—loving, humble, and full of faith—did not produce this climate of mutual trust, which leads the dialoguers into ever closer partnership in the naming of the world. Conversely, such trust is obviously absent in the anti-dialogics of the banking method of education. Whereas faith in man is an *a priori* requirement for dialogue, trust is established by dialogue. Should it founder, it will be seen that the preconditions were lacking. False love, false humility, and feeble faith in man cannot create trust. Trust is contingent on the evidence which one party provides the others of his true, concrete intentions; it cannot exist if that party's words do not coincide with his actions. To say one thing and do another—to take one's own word lightly—cannot inspire trust. To glorify democracy and to silence the people is a farce; to discourse on humanism and to negate man is a lie.

Nor yet can dialogue exist without hope. Hope is rooted in men's incompletion, from which they move out in constant search—a search which can be carried out only in communion with other men. Hopelessness is a form of silence, of denying the world and fleeing from it. The dehumanization resulting from an unjust order is not a cause for despair but for hope, leading to the incessant pursuit of the humanity denied by injustice. Hope, however, does not consist in crossing one's arms and waiting. As long as I fight, I am moved by hope; and if I fight with hope, then I can wait. As the encounter of men seeking to be more fully human, dialogue cannot be carried on in a climate of hopelessness. If the dialoguers expect nothing to come of their efforts, their encounter will be empty and sterile, bureaucratic and tedious.

Finally, true dialogue cannot exist unless the dialoguers engage in critical thinking—thinking which discerns an indivisible solidarity between the world and men and admits of no dichotomy between them—thinking which perceives reality as process, as transformation, rather than as a static entity—thinking which does not separate itself from action, but constantly immerses itself in temporality without fear of the risks involved. Critical thinking contrasts with naïve thinking, which sees "historical time as a weight, a stratification of the acquisitions and experiences of the past,"[5] from which the present should emerge normalized and "well-behaved." For the naïve thinker, the important thing is accommodation to this normalized "today." For the critic, the important thing is the continuing transformation of reality, in behalf of the continuing humanization of men. In the words of Pierre Furter:

> The goal will no longer be to eliminate the risks of temporality by clutching to guaranteed space, but rather to temporalize space.... The universe is revealed to me not as space, imposing a massive presence to which I can but adapt, but as a scope, a domain which takes shape as I act upon it.[6]

For naïve thinking, the goal is precisely to hold fast to this guaranteed space and adjust to it. By thus denying temporality, it denies itself as well.

Only dialogue, which requires critical thinking, is also capable of generating critical thinking. Without dialogue there is no communication, and without communication there can be no true education. Education which is able to resolve the contradiction between teacher and student takes place in a situation in which both address their act of cognition to the object by which they are mediated. Thus, the dialogical character of education as the practice of freedom does not begin when the teacher-student meets with the students-teachers in a pedagogical situation, but rather when the former first asks himself *what* he will dialogue with the latter *about*. And preoccupation with the content of dialogue is really preoccupation with the program content of education.

For the anti-dialogical banking educator, the question of content simply concerns the program about which he will discourse to his students; and he answers his own question, by organizing his own program. For the dialogical, problem-posing teacher-student, the program content of education is neither a gift nor an imposition—bits of information to be deposited in the students—but rather the organized, systematized, and developed "re-presentation" to individuals of the things about which they want to know more.[7]

Authentic education is not carried on by "A" *for* "B" or by "A" *about* "B," but rather by "A" *with* "B," mediated by the world—a world which impresses and challenges both parties, giving rise to views or opinions about it. These views, impregnated with anxieties, doubts, hopes, or hopelessness, imply significant themes on the basis of which the program content of education can be built. In its desire to create an ideal model of the "good man," a naïvely conceived humanism often overlooks the concrete, existential, present situation of real men. Authentic humanism, in Pierre Furter's words, "consists in permitting the emergence of the awareness of our full humanity, as a condition and as an obligation, as a situation and as a project."[8] We simply cannot go to the laborers—urban or peasant[9]—in the banking style, to give them "knowledge" or to impose upon them the model of the "good man" contained in a program whose content we have ourselves organized. Many political and educational plans have failed because their authors designed them according to their own personal views of reality, never once taking into account (except as mere objects of their action) the *men-in-a-situation* to whom their program was ostensibly directed.

For the truly humanist educator and the authentic revolutionary, the object of action is the reality to be transformed by them together with other men—not other men themselves. The oppressors are the ones who act upon men to indoctrinate them and adjust them to a reality which must remain untouched. Unfortunately, however, in their desire to obtain the support of the people for revolutionary action, revolutionary leaders often fall for the banking line of planning program content from the top down. They approach the peasant or urban masses with projects which may correspond to their own view of the world, but not to that of the people.[10] They forget that their fundamental objective is to fight alongside the people for the recovery of the people's stolen humanity, not to "win the people over" to their side. Such a phrase does not belong in the vocabulary of revolutionary leaders, but in that of the oppressor. The revolutionary's role is to liberate, and be liberated, with the people—not to win them over.

In their political activity, the dominant elites utilize the banking concept to encourage passivity in the oppressed, corresponding with the latter's "submerged" state of consciousness, and take advantage of that passivity to "fill" that consciousness with slogans which create even more fear of freedom. This practice is incompatible with a truly liberating course of action, which, by presenting the oppressors' slogans as a problem, helps the oppressed to "eject" those slogans from within themselves. After all, the task of the humanists is surely not that of pitting their slogans against the slogans of the oppressors, with the oppressed as the testing ground, "housing" the slogans of first one group and then the other. On the contrary, the task of the humanists is to see that the oppressed become aware of the fact that as dual beings, "housing" the oppressors within themselves, they cannot be truly human.

This task implies that revolutionary leaders do not go to the people in order to bring them a message of "salvation," but in order to come to know through dialogue with them both their *objective situation* and their *awareness* of that situation—the various levels of perception of themselves and of the world in which and with which they exist. One cannot expect positive results from an educational or political action program which fails to respect the particular view of the world held by the people. Such a program constitutes cultural invasion,[11] good intentions notwithstanding.

The starting point for organizing the program content of education or political action must be the present, existential, concrete situation, reflecting the aspirations of the people. Utilizing certain basic contradictions, we must pose this existential, concrete, present situation to the people as a problem which challenges them and requires a response—not just at the intellectual level, but at the level of action.[12]

We must never merely discourse on the present situation, must never provide the people with programs which have little or nothing to do with their own preoccupations, doubts, hopes, and fears—programs which at times in fact increase the fears of the oppressed consciousness. It is not our role to speak to the people about our own view of the world, not to attempt to impose that view on them, but rather to dialogue with the people about their view and ours. We must realize that their view of the world, manifested variously in their action, reflects their *situation* in the world. Educational and political action which is not critically aware of this situation runs the risk either of "banking" or of preaching in the desert.

Often, educators and politicians speak and are not understood because their language is not attuned to the concrete situation of the men they address. Accordingly, their talk is just alienated and alienating rhetoric. The language of the educator or the politician (and it seems more and more clear that the latter must also become an educator, in the broadest sense of the word), like the language of the people, cannot exist without thought; and neither language nor thought can exist without a structure to which they refer. In order to communicate effectively, educator and politician must understand the structural conditions in which the thought and language of the people are dialectically framed.

It is to the reality which mediates men, and to the perception of that reality held by educators and people, that we must go to find the program content of education. The investigation of what I have termed the people's "thematic universe"[13]—the complex of their "generative themes"—inaugurates the dialogue of education as the practice of freedom. The methodology of that investigation must likewise be dialogical, affording the opportunity both to discover generative themes and to stimulate people's awareness in regard to these themes. Consistent with the liberating purpose of dialogical education, the object of the investigation is not men (as if men were anatomical fragments), but rather the thought-language with which men refer to reality, the levels at which they perceive that reality, and their view of the world, in which their generative themes are found.

Equally appropriate for the methodology of thematic investigation and for problem-posing education is this effort to present significant dimensions of an individual's contextual reality, the analysis of which will make it possible for him to recognize the interaction of the various components. Meanwhile, the significant dimensions, which in their turn are constituted of parts in interaction, should be perceived as dimensions of total reality. In this way, a critical analysis of a significant existential dimension makes possible a new, critical attitude towards the limit-situations. The perception and comprehension of reality are rectified and acquire new depth. When carried out with a methodology of *conscientização* the investigation of the generative theme contained in the minimum thematic universe (the generative themes in interaction) thus introduces or begins to introduce men to a critical form of thinking about their world.

In the event, however, that men perceive reality as dense, impenetrable, and enveloping, it is indispensable to proceed with the investigation by means of abstraction. This method does not involve reducing the concrete to the abstract (which would signify the negation of its dialectical nature), but rather maintaining both elements as opposites which interrelate dialectically in the act of reflection. This dialectical movement of thought is exemplified perfectly in the analysis of a concrete, existential, "coded" situation.[14] Its "decoding" requires moving from the abstract to the concrete; this requires moving from the part to the whole and then returning to the parts; this in turn requires that the Subject recognize himself in the object (the coded concrete existential situation) and recognize the object as a situation in which he finds himself, together with other Subjects. If the decoding is well done, this movement of flux and reflux from the abstract to the concrete which occurs in the analysis of a coded situation leads to the supersedence of the abstraction *by* the critical perception of the concrete, which has already ceased to be a dense, impenetrable reality.

When an individual is presented with a coded existential situation (a sketch or photograph which leads by abstraction to the concreteness of existential reality), his tendency is to "split" that coded situation. In the process of decoding, this separation corresponds to the stage we call the "description of the situation," and facilitates the discovery of the interaction among the parts of the disjoined whole. This whole (the coded situation), which previously had been only diffusely apprehended, begins to acquire meaning as thought flows back to it from the various dimensions. Since, however, the coding is the representation of an existential situation, the decoder tends to take the step from the representation to the very concrete situation in which and with which he finds himself. It is thus possible to explain conceptually why individuals begin to behave differently with regard to objective reality, once that reality has ceased to look like a blind alley and has taken on its true aspect: a challenge which men must meet.

In all the stages of decoding, men exteriorize their view of the world. And in the way they think about and face the world—fatalistically, dynamically, or statically—their generative themes may be found. A group which does not concretely express a generative thematics—a fact which might appear to imply the nonexistence of themes—is, on the contrary, suggesting a very dramatic theme: *the theme of silence*. The theme of silence suggests a structure of mutism in face of the overwhelming force of the limit-situations.

I must re-emphasize that the generative theme cannot be found in men, divorced from reality; nor yet in reality, divorced from men; much less in "no man's land." It can only be apprehended in the men-world relationship. To investigate the generative theme is to investigate man's thinking about reality and man's action upon reality, which is his praxis. For precisely this reason, the methodology proposed requires that the investigators and the people (who would normally be considered objects of that investigation) should act as *co-investigators*. The more active an attitude men take in regard to the exploration of their thematics, the more they deepen their critical awareness of reality and, in spelling out those thematics, take possession of that reality.

Some may think it inadvisable to include the people as investigators in the search for their own meaningful thematics: that their intrusive influence (N.B., the "intrusion" of those who are most interested—or ought to be—in their own education) will "adulterate" the findings and thereby sacrifice the objectivity of the investigation. This view mistakenly presupposes that themes exist, in their original objective purity, outside men—as if themes were *things*. Actually, themes exist in men in their relations with the world, with reference to concrete facts. The same objective fact could evoke different complexes of generative themes in different epochal sub-units. There is, therefore, a relation between the given objective fact, the perception men have of this fact, and the generative themes.

A meaningful thematics is expressed by men, and a given moment of expression will differ from an earlier moment, if men have changed their perception of the objective facts to which the themes refer. From the investigator's point of view, the important thing is to detect the starting point at which men visualize the "given" and to verify whether or not during the process of investigation any transformation has occurred in their way of perceiving reality. (Objective reality, of course, remains unchanged. If the perception of that reality changes in the course of the investigation, that fact does not impair the validity of the investigation.)

We must realize that the aspirations, the motives, and the objectives implicit in the meaningful thematics are *human* aspirations, motives, and objectives. They do not exist "out there" somewhere, as static entities; *they are occurring*. They are as historical as men themselves; consequently, they cannot be apprehended apart from men. To apprehend these themes and to understand them is to understand both the men who embody them and the reality to which they refer. But—precisely because it is not possible to understand these themes apart from men—it is necessary that the men concerned understand them as well. Thematic investigation thus becomes a common striving towards awareness of reality and towards self-awareness, which makes this investigation a starting point for the educational process or for cultural action of a liberating character.

The real danger of the investigation is not that the supposed objects of the investigation, discovering themselves to be co-investigators, might "adulterate" the analytical results. On the contrary, the danger lies in the risk of shifting the focus of the investigation from the meaningful themes to the people themselves, thereby treating the people as objects of the investigation. Since this investigation is to serve as a basis for developing an educational program in which teacher-student and students-teachers combine their cognitions of the same object, the investigation itself must likewise be based on reciprocity of action.

Thematic investigation, which occurs in the realm of the human, cannot be reduced to a mechanical act. As a process of search, of knowledge, and thus of creation, it requires the investigators to discover the interpenetration of problems, in the linking of meaningful themes. The investigation will be most educational when it is most critical, and most critical when it avoids the narrow outlines of partial or "focalized" views of reality, and sticks to the comprehension of *total* reality. Thus, the process of searching for the meaningful thematics should include a concern for the links between themes, a concern to pose these themes as problems, and a concern for their historical-cultural context.

Just as the educator may not elaborate a program to present *to* the people, neither may the investigator elaborate "itineraries" for researching the thematic universe, starting from points which *he* has predetermined. Both education and the investigation designed to support it must be "sympathetic" activities, in the etymological sense of the word. That is, they must consist of communication and of the common experience of a reality perceived in the complexity of its constant "becoming."

The investigator who, in the name of scientific objectivity, transforms the organic into something inorganic, what is becoming into what is, life into death, is a man who fears change. He sees in change (which he does not deny, but neither does he desire) not a sign of life, but a sign of death and decay. He does want to study change—but in order to stop it, not in order to stimulate or deepen it. However, in seeing change as a sign of death and in making people the passive objects of investigation in order to arrive at rigid models, he betrays his own character as a killer of life.

Notes

1. Action ⎫
    Reflection ⎬ word = work = praxis
    ⎭
    Sacrifice of action = verbalism
    Sacrifice of reflection = activism
2. Some of these reflections emerged as a result of conversations with Professor Ernani Maria Fiori.
3. I obviously do not refer to the silence of profound meditation, in which men only apparently leave the world, withdrawing from it in order to consider it in its totality, and thus remaining with it. But this type of retreat is only authentic when the meditator is "bathed" in reality; not when the retreat signifies contempt for the world and flight from it, in a type of "historical schizophrenia."
4. I am more and more convinced that true revolutionaries must perceive the revolution, because of its creative and liberating nature, as an act of love. For me, the revolution, which is not possible without a theory of revolution— and therefore science—is not irreconcilable with love. On the contrary: the revolution is made by men to achieve their humanization. What, indeed, is the deeper motive which moves men to become revolutionaries, but the dehumanization of man? The distortion imposed on the word "love" by the capitalist world cannot prevent the revolution from being essentially loving in character, nor can it prevent the revolutionaries from affirming their love of life. Guevara (while admitting the "risk of seeming ridiculous") was not afraid to affirm it: "Let me say, with the risk of appearing ridiculous, that the true revolutionary is guided by strong feelings of love. It is impossible to think of an authentic revolutionary without this quality." *Venceremos—The Speeches and Writings of Che Guevara*, edited by John Gerassi (New York, 1969), p.398.
5. From the letter of a friend.
6. Pierre Furter, *Educação e Vida* (Rio, 1966), pp. 26–27.
7. In a long conversation with Malraux, Mao-Tse-Tung declared, "You know I've proclaimed for a long time: we must teach the masses clearly what we have received from them confusedly." André Malraux, *Anti-Memoirs* (New York, 1968), pp. 361–362. This affirmation contains an entire dialogical theory of how to construct the program content of education, which cannot be elaborated according to what the *educator* thinks best for *his* students.
8. Furter, *op. cit.*, p. 165.
9. The latter, usually submerged in a colonial context, are almost umbilically linked to the world of nature, in relation to which they feel themselves to be component parts rather than shapers.
10. "Our cultural workers must serve the people with great enthusiasm and devotion, and they must link themselves with the masses, not divorce themselves from the masses. In order to do so, they must act in accordance with the needs and wishes of the masses. All work done for the masses must start from their needs and not from the desire of any individual, however well-intentioned. It often happens that objectively the masses need a certain change, but subjectively they are not yet conscious of the need, not yet willing or determined to make the change. In such cases, we should wait patiently. We should not make the change until, through our work, most of the masses have become conscious of the need and are willing and determined to carry it out. Otherwise we shall isolate ourselves from the masses. . . . There are two principles here: one is the actual needs of the masses rather than what we fancy they need, and the other is the wishes of the masses, who must make up their own minds instead of our making up their minds for them." From the *Selected Works of Mao-Tse-Tung*, Vol. III. "The United Front in Cultural Work" (October 30, 1944) (Peking, 1967), pp. 186–187.
11. This point will be analyzed in detail in Chapter 4.
12. It is as self-contradictory for true humanists to use the banking method as it would be for rightists to engage in problem-posing education. (The latter are always consistent—they never use a problem-posing pedagogy.)
13. The expression "meaningful thematics" is used with the same connotation.
14. The coding of an existential situation is the representation of that situation, showing some of its constituent elements in interaction. Decoding is the critical analysis of the coded situation.

14

Curriculum and Consciousness

Maxine Greene

Curriculum, from the learner's standpoint, ordinarily represents little more than an arrangement of subjects, a structure of socially prescribed knowledge, or a complex system of meanings which may or may not fall within his grasp. Rarely does it signify possibility for him as an existing person, mainly concerned with making sense of his own life-world. Rarely does it promise occasions for ordering the materials of that world, for imposing "configurations"[1] by means of experiences and perspectives made available for personally conducted cognitive action. Sartre says that "knowing is a moment of praxis," opening into "what has not yet been."[2] Preoccupied with priorities, purposes, programs of "intended learning"[3] and intended (or unintended) manipulation, we pay too little attention to the individual in quest of his own future, bent on surpassing what is merely "given," on breaking through the everyday. We are still too prone to dichotomize: to think of "disciplines" or "public traditions" or "accumulated wisdom" or "common culture" (individualization despite) as objectively existent, external to the knower—there to be discovered, mastered, learned.

Quite aware that this may evoke Dewey's argument in *The Child and the Curriculum*, aware of how times have changed since 1902, I have gone in search of contemporary analogies to shed light on what I mean. ("Solution comes," Dewey wrote, "only by getting away from the meaning of terms that is already fixed upon and coming to see the conditions from another point of view, and hence in a fresh light."[4]) My other point of view is that of literary criticism, or more properly philosophy of criticism, which attempts to explicate the modes of explanation, description, interpretation, and evaluation involved in particular critical approaches. There is presently an emerging philosophic controversy between two such approaches, one associated with England and the United States, the other with the Continent, primarily France and Switzerland; and it is in the differences in orientation that I have found some clues.

These differences are, it will be evident, closely connected to those separating what is known as analytic or language philosophy from existentialism and phenomenology. The dominant tendency in British and American literary criticism has been to conceive literary works as objects or artifacts, best understood in relative isolation from the writer's personal biography and undistorted by associations brought to the work from the reader's own daily life. The new critics on the Continent have been called "critics of consciousness."[5] They are breaking with the notion that a literary work can be dealt with objectively, divorced from experience. In fact, they treat each work as a manifestation of an individual writer's experience, a gradual growth of consciousness into expression. This is in sharp contrast to such a view as T.S. Eliot's emphasizing the autonomy and the "impersonality" of literary art. "We can only say," he wrote in an introduction to *The Sacred Wood*, "that a poem, in some sense, has its own life; that its parts form something quite different from a body of neatly ordered biographical data; that the feeling, or emotion, or vision resulting from the poem is something different from the feeling or emotion or vision in the mind of the poet."[6] Those who take this approach or an approach to a work of art as "a self-enclosed isolated structure"[7] are likely to prescribe that purely aesthetic values are to be found in literature, the values associated with "significant form"[8] or, at most, with the contemplation of an "intrinsically interesting possible."[9] M.H. Abrams has called this an "austere dedication to the poem *per se*,"[10] for all the enlightening analysis and explication it has produced. "But it threatens also to commit us," he wrote, "to the concept of a poem as a language game, or as a floating Laputa, insulated from life and essential human concerns in a way that accords poorly with our experience in reading a great work of literature."

For the critic of consciousness, literature is viewed as a genesis, a conscious effort on the part of an individual artist to understand his own experience by framing it in language. The reader who encounters the work must recreate it in terms of *his* consciousness. In order to penetrate it, to experience it existentially and empathetically, he must try to place himself within the "interior space"[11] of the writer's mind as it is slowly revealed in the course of his work. Clearly, the reader requires a variety of cues if he is to situate himself in this way; and these are ostensibly provided by the expressions and attitudes he finds in the book, devices which he must accept as orientations and indications—"norms," perhaps, to govern his recreation. *His* subjectivity is the substance of the literary object; but, if he is to perceive the identity emerging through the enactments of the book, he must subordinate his own personality as he brackets out his everyday, "natural" world.[12] His objective in doing so, however, is not to analyze or explicate or evaluate; it is to extract the experience made manifest by means of the work. Sartre says this more concretely:

> Reading seems, in fact, to be the synthesis of perception and creation. . . . The object is essential because it is strictly transcendent, because it imposes its own structures, and because one must wait for it and observe it; but the subject is also essential because it is required not only to disclose the object (that is, to make *there be* an object) but also that this object might *be* (that is, to produce it). In a word, the reader is conscious of disclosing in creating, of creating by disclosing. . . . If he is inattentive, tired, stupid, or thoughtless most of the relations will escape him. He will never manage to "catch on" to the object (in the sense in which we see that fire "catches" or "doesn't catch"). He will draw some phrases out of the shadow, but they will appear as random strokes. If he is at his best, he will project beyond the words a synthetic form, each phrase of which will be no more than a partial function: the "theme," the "subject," or the "meaning."[13]

There must be, he is suggesting, continual reconstructions if a work of literature is to become meaningful. The structures involved are generated over a period of time, depending upon the perceptiveness and attentiveness of the reader. The reader, however, does not simply regenerate what the artist intended. His imagination can move him beyond the artist's traces, "to project beyond the words a synthetic form," to constitute a new totality. The autonomy of the art object is sacrificed in this orientation; the reader, conscious of lending his own life to the book, discovers deeper and more complex levels than the level of "significant form." (Sartre says, for instance, that "Raskolnikov's waiting is *my* waiting, which I lend him. Without this impatience of the reader he would remain only a collection of signs. His hatred of the police magistrate who questions him is my hatred which has been solicited and wheedled out of me by signs, and the police magistrate himself would not exist without the hatred I have for him via Raskolnikov."[14])

Disclosure, Reconstruction, Generation

The reader, using his imagination, must move within his own subjectivity and break with the common sense world he normally takes for granted. If he could not suspend his ordinary ways of perceiving, if he could not allow for the possibility that the horizons of daily life are not inalterable, he would not be able to engage with literature at all. As Dewey put it: "There is work done on the part of the percipient as there is on the part of the artist. The one who is too lazy, idle, or indurated in convention to perform this work will not see or hear. His 'appreciation' will be a mixture of scraps of learning with conformity to norms of conventional admiration and with a confused, even if genuine, emotional excitation."[15] The "work" with which we are here concerned is one of disclosure, reconstruction, generation. It is a work which culminates in a bringing something into being by the reader—in a "going beyond" what he has been.[16]

Although I am going to claim that learning, to be meaningful, must involve such a "going beyond," I am not going to claim that it must also be in the imaginative mode. Nor am I going to assert that, in order to surpass the "given," the individual is required to move into and remain within a sealed subjectivity. What I find suggestive in the criticism of consciousness is the stress on the gradual disclosure of structures by the reader. The process is, as I have said, governed by certain cues or norms perceived in the course of reading. These demand, if they are to be perceived, what Jean Piaget has called a "continual 'decentering' without which [the individual subject] cannot become free from his intellectual egocentricity."[17]

The difference between Piaget and those interested in consciousness is, of course, considerable. For one thing, he counts himself among those who prefer not to characterize the subject in terms of its "lived experience." For another thing, he says categorically that "the 'lived' can only have a very minor role in the construction of cognitive structures, for these do not belong to the subject's *consciousness* but to his operational *behavior*, which is something quite different."[18] I am not convinced that they are as different as he conceives them to be. Moreover, I think his differentiation between the "individual subject" and what he calls "the epistemic subject, that cognitive nucleus which is common to all subjects at the same level,"[19] is useful and may well shed light on the problem of curriculum, viewed from the vantage point of consciousness. Piaget is aware that his stress on the "epistemic subject" looks as if he were subsuming the individual under some impersonal abstraction;[20] but his discussion is not far removed from those of Sartre and the critics of consciousness, particularly when they talk of the subject entering into a process of generating structures whose being (like the structures Piaget has in mind) consists in their "coming to be."

Merleau-Ponty, as concerned as Piaget with the achievement of rationality, believes that there is a primary reality which must be taken into account if the growth of "intellectual consciousness" is to be understood. This primary reality is a perceived life-world; and the structures of the "perceptual consciousness"[21] through which the child first comes in contact with his environment underlie all the higher level structures which develop later in his life. In the prereflective, infantile stage of life he is obviously incapable of generating cognitive structures. The stage is characterized by what Merleau-Ponty calls "egocentrism" because the "me" is part of an anonymous collectivity, unaware of itself, capable of living "as easily in others as it does in itself."[22] Nevertheless, even then, before meanings and configurations are imposed, there is an original world, a natural and social world in which the child is involved corporeally and affectively. Perceiving that world, he effects certain relations within his experience. He organizes and "informs" it before he is capable of logical and predicative thought. This means for Merleau-Ponty that consciousness exists primordially—the ground of all knowledge and rationality.

The growing child assimilates a language system and becomes habituated to using language as "an open system of expression" which is capable of expressing "an indeterminate number of cognitions or ideas to come."[23] His acts of naming and expression take place, however, around a core of primary meaning found in "the silence of primary consciousness." This silence may be understood as the fundamental awareness of being present in the world. It resembles what Paulo Freire calls "background awareness"[24] of an existential situation, a situation actually lived before the codifications which make new perceptions possible. Talking about the effort to help peasants perceive their own reality differently (to enable them, in other words, to learn), Freire says they must somehow make explicit their "real consciousness" of their worlds, or what they experienced while living through situations they later learn to codify.

The point is that the world is constituted for the child (by means of the behavior called perception) prior to the "construction of cognitive structures." This does not imply that he lives his life primarily in that world. He moves outward into diverse realms of experience in his search for meaning. When he confronts and engages with the apparently independent structures associated with rationality, the so-called cognitive structures, it is likely that he does so as an "epistemic subject," bracketing out for the time his subjectivity, even his presence to himself.[25] But the awareness remains in the background; the original perceptual reality continues as the ground of rationality, the base from which the leap to the theoretical is taken.

Merleau-Ponty, recognizing that psychologists treat consciousness as "an object to be studied," writes that it is simply not accessible to mere factual observation:

> The psychologist always tends to make consciousness into just such an object of observation. But all the factual truths to which psychology has access can be applied to the concrete subject only after a philosophical correction. Psychology, like physics and the other sciences of nature, uses the method of induction, which starts from facts and then assembles them. But it is very evident that this induction will remain blind if we do not know in some other way, and indeed from the inside of consciousness itself, what this induction is dealing with.[26]

Induction must be combined "with the reflective knowledge that we can obtain from ourselves as conscious objects." This is not a recommendation that the individual engage in introspection. Consciousness, being intentional, throws itself outward *towards* the world. It is always consciousness of something—a phenomenon, another person, an object in the world: Reflecting upon himself as a conscious object, the individual—the learner, perhaps—reflects upon his relation to the world, his manner of comporting himself with respect to it, the changing perspectives through which the world presents itself to him. Merleau-Ponty talks about the need continually to rediscover "my actual presence to myself, the fact of my consciousness which is in the last resort what the word and the concept of consciousness mean."[27] This means remaining in contact with one's own perceptions, one's own experiences, and striving to constitute their meanings. It means achieving a state of what Schutz calls "*wide-awakeness* . . . a plane of consciousness of highest tension originating in an attitude of full attention to life and its requirements."[28] Like Sartre, Schutz emphasizes the importance of attentiveness for arriving at new perceptions, for carrying out cognitive projects. All this seems to me to be highly suggestive for a conception of a learner who is "open to the world,"[29] eager, indeed *condemned* to give meaning to it—and, in the process of doing so, recreating or generating the materials of a curriculum in terms of his own consciousness.

Some Alternative Views

There are, of course, alternative views of consequence for education today. R.S. Peters, agreeing with his philosophic precursors that consciousness is the hallmark of mind and always "related in its different modes to objects," asserts that the "objects of consciousness are first and foremost objects in a public world that are marked out and differentiated by a public language into which the individual is initiated."[30] (It should be said that Peters is, *par excellence*, the exponent of an "objective" or "analytic" approach to curriculum, closely related to the objective approach to literary criticism.) He grants that the individual "represents a unique and unrepeatable viewpoint on this public world"; but his primary stress is placed upon the way in which the learning of language is linked to the discovery of that separately existing world of "objects in space and time." Consciousness, for Peters, cannot be explained except in connection with the demarcations of the public world which meaning makes possible. It becomes contingent upon initiation into public traditions, into (it turns out) the academic disciplines. Since such an initiation is required if modes of consciousness are to be effectively differentiated, the mind must finally be understood as a "product" of such initiation. The individual must be enabled to achieve a state of mind characterized by "a mastery of and care for the worthwhile things that have been transmitted, which are viewed in some kind of cognitive perspective."[31]

Philip H. Phenix argues similarly that "the curriculum should consist entirely of knowledge which comes from the disciplines, for the reason that the disciplines reveal knowledge in its teachable forms."[32] He, however, pays more heed to what he calls "the experience of reflective self-consciousness,"[33] which he associates specifically with "concrete existence in direct personal encounter."[34] The meanings arising out of such an encounter are expressed, for him, in existential philosophy, religion, psychology, and certain dimensions of imaginative literature. They are, thus, to be considered as one of the six "realms of meaning" through mastery of which man is enabled to achieve self-transcendence. Self-transcendence, for Phenix, involves a duality which enables the learner to feel himself to be agent and knower, and at once to identify with what he comes to know. Self-transcendence is the ground of meaning; but it culminates in the engendering of a range of "essential meanings," the achievement of a hierarchy in which all fundamental patterns of meaning are related and through which human existence can be fulfilled. The inner life of generic man is clearly encompassed by this scheme; but what is excluded, I believe, is what has been called the "subjectivity of the actor," the *individual* actor ineluctably present to himself. What is excluded is the feeling of separateness, of strangeness when such a person is confronted with the articulated curriculum intended to counteract meaninglessness. Schutz writes:

> When a stranger comes to the town, he has to learn to orientate in it and to know it. Nothing is self-explanatory for him and he has to ask an expert . . . to learn how to get from one point to another. He may, of course, refer to a map of the town, but even to use the map successfully he must know the meaning of the signs on the map, the exact point within the town where he stands and its correlative on the map, and at least one more point in order correctly to relate the signs on the map to the real objects in the city.[35]

The prestructured curriculum resembles such a map; the learner, the stranger just arrived in town. For the cartographer, the town is an "object of his science," a science which has developed standards of operation and rules for the correct drawing of maps. In the case of the curriculum-maker, the public tradition or the natural order of things is "the object" of his design activities. Here too there are standards of operation: the subject matter organized into disciplines must be communicable; it must be appropriate to whatever are conceived as educational aims. Phenix has written that education should be understood as "a guided recapitulation of the processes of inquiry which gave rise to the fruitful bodies of organized knowledge comprising the disciplines."[36] Using the metaphor of the map, we might say that this is like asking a newcomer in search of direction to recapitulate the complex processes by which the cartographer made his map. The map may represent a fairly complete charting of the town; and it may ultimately be extremely useful for the individual to be able to take a cartographer's perspective. When that individual first arrives, however, his peculiar plight ought not to be overlooked: his "background aware-ness" of being alive in an unstable world; his reasons for consulting the map; the interests he is pursuing as he attempts to orient himself when he can no longer proceed by rule of thumb. He himself may recognize that he will have to come to understand the signs on the map if he is to make use of it. Certainly he will have to decipher the relationship between those signs and "real objects in the city." But his initial concern will be con-ditioned by the "objects" he wants to bring into visibility, by the landmarks he needs to identify if he is to proceed on his way.

Learning—A Mode of Orientation

Turning from newcomer to learner (contemporary learner, in our particular world), I am suggesting that his focal concern is with ordering the materials of his own life-world when dislocations occur, when what was once familiar abruptly appears strange. This may come about on an occasion when "future shock" is experienced, as it so frequently is today. Anyone who has lived through a campus disruption, a teachers' strike, a guerilla theatre production, a sit-in (or a be-in, or a feel-in) knows full well what Alvin Toffler means when he writes about the acceleration of change. "We no longer 'feel' life as men did in the past," he says. "And this is the ultimate difference, the distinction that separates the truly con-temporary man from all others. For this acceleration lies behind the impermanence—the transience—that penetrates and tinctures our consciousness, radically affecting the way we relate to other people, to things, to the entire universe of ideas, art and values."[37] Obviously, this does not happen in everyone's life; but it is far more likely to occur than ever before in history, if it is indeed the case that change has speeded up and that forces are being released which we have not yet learned to control. My point is that the con-temporary learner is more likely than his predecessors to experience moments of strange-ness, moments when the recipes he has inherited for the solution of typical problems no longer seem to work. If Merleau-Ponty is right and the search for rationality is indeed grounded in a primary or perceptual consciousness, the individual may be fundamentally aware that the structures of "reality" are contingent upon the perspective taken and that most achieved orders are therefore precarious.

The stage sets are always likely to collapse.[38] Someone is always likely to ask unexpect-edly, as in Pinter's *The Dumb Waiter*, "Who cleans up after we're gone?"[39] Someone is equally likely to cry out, "You seem to have no conception of where we stand! You won't find the answer written down for you in the bowl of a compass—I can tell you that."[40] Disorder, in other words, is continually breaking in; meaninglessness is recurrently overcoming landscapes which once were demarcated, meaningful. It is at moments like these that the individual reaches out to reconstitute meaning, to close the gaps, to make sense once again. It is at moments like these that he will be moved to pore over maps, to disclose or generate structures of knowledge which may provide him unifying perspectives and thus enable him to restore order once again. His learning, I am saying, is a mode of orientation—or reorientation in a place suddenly become unfamiliar. And "place" is a metaphor, in this context, for a domain of consciousness, intending, forever thrusting outward, "open to the world." The curriculum, the structures of knowledge, must be presented to such a consciousness as possibility. Like the work of literature in Sartre's viewing, it requires a subject if it is to be disclosed; it can only *be* disclosed if the learner, himself engaged in generating the structures, lends the curriculum his life. If the curriculum, on the other hand, is seen as external to the search for meaning, it becomes an alien and an alienating edifice, a kind of "Crystal Palace" of ideas.[41]

There is, then, a kind of resemblance between the ways in which a learner confronts socially prescribed knowledge and the ways in which a stranger looks at a map when he is trying to determine where he is in relation to where he wants to go. In Kafka's novel, *Amerika,* I find a peculiarly suggestive description of the predicament of someone who is at once a stranger and a potential learner (although, it eventually turns out, he never succeeds in being taught). He is Karl Rossmann, who has been "packed off to America" by his parents and who likes to stand on a balcony at his Uncle Jacob's house in New York and look down on the busy street:

> From morning to evening and far into the dreaming night that street was a channel for the constant stream of traffic which, seen from above, looked like an inextricable confusion, for ever newly improvised, of foreshortened human figures and the roofs of all kinds of vehicles, sending into the upper air another confusion, more riotous and complicated, of noises, dusts and smells, all of it enveloped and penetrated by a flood of light which the multitudinous objects in the street scattered, carried off and again busily brought back, with an effect as palpable to the dazzled eye as if a glass roof stretched over the street were being violently smashed into fragments at every moment.[42]

Karl's uncle tells him that the indulgence of idly gazing at the busy life of the city might be permissible if Karl were traveling for pleasure; "but for one who intended to remain in the States it was sheer ruination." He is going to have to make judgments which will shape his future life; he will have, in effect, to be reborn. This being so, it is not enough for him to treat the unfamiliar landscape as something to admire and wonder at (as if it were a cubist construction or a kaleidoscope). Karl's habitual interpretations (learned far away in Prague) do not suffice to clarify what he sees. If he is to learn, he must identify what is questionable, try to break through what is obscure. Action is required of him, not mere gazing; *praxis*, not mere reverie.

If he is to undertake action, however, he must do so against the background of his original perceptions, with a clear sense of being present to himself. He must do so, too, against the background of his European experience, of the experience of rejection, of being "packed off" for reasons never quite understood. Only with that sort of awareness will he be capable of the attentiveness and commitment needed to engage with the world and make it meaningful. Only with the ability to be reflective about what he is doing will he be brave enough to incorporate his past into the present, to link the present to a future. All this will demand a conscious appropriation of new perspectives on his experience and a continual reordering of that experience as new horizons of the "Amerika" become visible, as new problems arise. The point is that Karl Rossmann, an immigrant in an already structured and charted world, must be conscious enough of himself to strive towards rationality; only if he achieves rationality will he avoid humiliations and survive.

As Kafka tells it, he never does attain that rationality; and so he is continually manipulated by forces without and within. He never learns, for example, that there can be no justice if there is no good will, even though he repeatedly and sometimes eloquently asks for justice from the authorities—always to no avail. The ship captains and pursers, the business men, the head waiters and porters all function according to official codes of discipline which are beyond his comprehension. He has been plunged into a public world with its own intricate prescriptions, idiosyncratic structures, and hierarchies; but he has no way of appropriating it or of constituting meanings. Throughout most of the novel, he clings to his symbolic box (with the photograph of his parents, the memorabilia of childhood and home). The box may be egocentrism; it may signify his incapacity to embark upon the "decentering" required if he is to begin generating for himself the structures of what surrounds.

In his case (and, I would say, in the case of many other people) the "decentering" that is necessary is not solely a cognitive affair, as Piaget insists it is. Merleau-Ponty speaks of a "lived decentering,"[43] exemplified by a child's learning" "to relativise the notions of the youngest and the eldest" (to learn, e.g., to become the eldest in relation to the newborn child) or by his learning to think in terms of reciprocity. This happens, as it would have to happen to Karl, through actions undertaken within the "vital order," not merely through intellectual categorization. It does not exclude the possibility that a phenomenon analogous to Piaget's "epistemic subject" emerges, although there appears to be no reason (except, perhaps, from the viewpoint of empirical psychology) for separating it off from the "individual subject." (In fact, the apparent difference between Piaget and those who talk of "lived experience" may turn upon a definition of "consciousness." Piaget, as has been noted,[44] distinguishes between "consciousness" and "operational behavior," as if consciousness did *not* involve a turning outward to things, a continuing reflection upon situationality, a generation of cognitive structures.) In any case, every individual who consciously seeks out meaning is involved in asking questions which demand essentially epistemic responses.[45] These responses, even if incomplete, are knowledge claims; and, as more and more questions are asked, there is an increasing "sedimentation" of meanings which result from the interpretation of past experiences looked at from the vantage point of the present. Meanings do not inhere in the experiences that emerge; they have to be constituted, and they can only be constituted through cognitive action.

Returning to Karl Rossmann and his inability to take such action, I have been suggesting that he *cannot* make his own "primary consciousness" background so long as he clings to his box; nor can he actively interpret his past experience. He cannot (to stretch Piaget's point somewhat) become or will himself to be an "epistemic subject." He is, as Freire puts it, submerged in a "dense, enveloping reality or a tormenting blind alley" and will be unless he can "perceive it as an objective-problematic situation."[46] Only then will he be able to intervene in his own reality with attentiveness, with awareness—to act upon his situation and make sense.

It would help if the looming structures which are so incomprehensible to Karl were somehow rendered cognitively available to him. Karl might then (with the help of a teacher willing to engage in dialogue with him, to help him pose his problems) reach out to question in terms of what he feels is thematically relevant or "worth questioning."[47] Because the stock of knowledge he carries with him does not suffice for a definition of situations in which porters manhandle him and women degrade him, in which he is penalized for every spontaneous action, he cannot easily refer to previous situations for clues. In order to cope with this, he needs to single out a single relevant element at first (from all the elements in what is happening) to transmute into a theme for his "knowing consciousness." There is the cruel treatment meted out to him, for example, by the Head Porter who feels it his duty "to attend to things that other people neglect." (He adds that, since he is in charge of all the doors of the hotel [including the "doorless exits"], he is "in a sense placed over everyone," and everyone has to obey him absolutely. If it were not for his repairing the omissions of the Head Waiter in the name of the hotel management, he believes, "such a great organization would be unthinkable."[48]) The porter's violence against Karl might well become the relevant element, the origin of a theme.

Making Connections

"What makes the theme to be a theme." Schutz writes, "is determined by motivationally relevant interest-situations and spheres of problems. The theme which thus has become relevant has now, however, become a problem to which a solution, practical, theoretical, or emotional, must be given."[49] The problem for Karl, like relevant problems facing any individual, is connected with and a consequence of a great number of other perplexities, other dislocations in his life. If he had not been so badly exploited by authority figures in times past, if he were not so childishly given to blind trust in adults, if he were not so likely to follow impulse at inappropriate moments, he would never have been assaulted by the Head Porter. At this point, however, once the specific problem (the assault) has been determined to be thematically relevant for him, it can be detached from the motivational context out of which it derived. The mesh-work of related perplexities remains, however, as an outer horizon, waiting to be explored or questioned when necessary. The thematically relevant element can then be made interesting in its own right and worth questioning. In the foreground, as it were, the focus of concern, it can be defined against the background of the total situation. The situation is not in any sense obliterated or forgotten. It is *there*, at the fringe of Karl's attention while the focal problem is being solved; but it is, to an extent, "bracketed out." With this bracketing out and this foreground focusing, Karl may be for the first time in a condition of wide-awakeness, ready to pay active attention to what has become so questionable and so troubling, ready to take the kind of action which will move him ahead into a future as it gives him perspective on his past.

The action he might take involves more than what is understood as problem-solving. He has, after all, had some rudimentary knowledge of the Head Porter's role, a knowledge conditioned by certain typifications effected in the prepredicative days of early childhood. At that point in time, he did not articulate his experience in terms of sense data or even in terms of individual figures standing out against a background. He saw typical structures according to particular zones of relevancy. This means that he probably saw his father, or the man who was father, not only as bearded face next to his mother, not only as large figure in the doorway, but as over-bearing, threatening, incomprehensible Authority who was "placed over everyone" and had the right to inflict pain. Enabled, years later, to confront something thematically relevant, the boy may be solicited to recognize his present knowledge of the porter as the sediment of previous mental processes.[50] The knowledge of the porter, therefore, has a history beginning in primordial perceptions; and the boy may succeed in moving back from what is seemingly "given" through the diverse mental processes which constituted the porter over time. Doing so, he will be exploring both the inner and outer horizons of the problem, making connections within the field of his consciousness, interpreting his own past as it bears on his present, reflecting upon his own knowing.

And that is not all. Having made such connections between the relevant theme and other dimensions of his experience, he may be ready to solve his problem; he may even feel that the problem is solved. This, however, puts him into position to move out of his own inner time (in which all acts are somehow continuous and bound together) into the intersubjective world where he can function as an epistemic subject. Having engaged in a reflexive consideration of the activity of his own consciousness, he can now shift his attention back to the life-world which had been rendered so unrecognizable by the Head Porter's assault. Here too, meanings must be constituted; the "great organization" must be understood, so that Karl can orient himself once again in the everyday. Bracketing out his subjectivity for the time, he may find many ways of engaging as a theoretical inquirer with the problem of authority in hotels and the multiple socioeconomic problems connected with that. He will voluntarily become, when inquiring in this way, a partial self, an inquirer deliberately acting a role in a community of inquirers. I am suggesting that he could not do so as effectively or as authentically if he had not first synthesized the materials within his inner time, constituted meaning in his world.

The analogy to the curriculum question, I hope, is clear. Treating Karl as a potential learner, I have considered the hotels and the other structured organizations in his world as analogous to the structures of prescribed knowledge—or to the curriculum. I have suggested that the individual, in our case the student, will only be in a position to learn when he is committed to act upon his world. If he is content to admire it or simply accept it as given, if he is incapable of breaking with egocentrism, he will remain alienated from himself and his own possibilities; he will wander lost and victimized upon the road; he will be unable to learn. He may be conditioned; he may be trained. He may even have some rote memory of certain elements of the curriculum; but no matter how well devised is that curriculum, no matter how well adapted to the stages of his growth, learning (as disclosure, as generating structures, as engendering meanings, as achieving mastery) will not occur.

At once, I have tried to say that unease and disorder are increasingly endemic in contemporary life, and that more and more persons are finding the recipes they habitually use inadequate for sense-making in a changing world. This puts them, more and more frequently, in the position of strangers or immigrants trying to orient themselves in an unfamiliar town. The desire, indeed the *need*, for orientation is equivalent to the desire to constitute meanings, all sorts of meanings, in the many dimensions of existence. But this desire, I have suggested, is not satisfied by the authoritative confrontation of student with knowledge structures (no matter how "teachable" the forms in which the knowledge is revealed). It is surely not satisfied when the instructional situation is conceived to be, as G.K. Plochmann has written, one in which the teacher is endeavoring "with respect to his subject matter, to bring the understanding of the learner in equality with his own understanding."[51] Described in that fashion, with "learner" conceived generically and the "system" to be taught conceived as preexistent and objectively real, the instructional situation seems to me to be one that alienates because of the way it ignores both existential predicament and primordial consciousness. Like the approach to literary criticism Abrams describes, the view appears to commit us to a concept of curriculum "as a floating Laputa, insulated from life and essential human concerns. . . ."[52]

[Handwritten margin annotations:]
Connecting present w/ past
meaning in your own world 1st
interactions
Cannot ignore primordial consciousness or existential predicament

The cries of "irrelevance" are still too audible for us to content ourselves with this. So are the complaints about depersonalization, processing, and compulsory socialization into a corporate, inhuman world. Michael Novak, expressing some of this, writes that what our institutions "decide is real is enforced as real." He calls parents, teachers, and psychiatrists (like policemen and soldiers) "the enforcers of reality"; then he goes on to say:

> When a young person is being initiated into society, existing norms determine what is to be considered real and what is to be annihilated by silence and disregard. The good, docile student accepts the norms; the recalcitrant student may lack the intelligence—or have too much; may lack maturity—or insist upon being his own man.[53]

I have responses like this in mind when I consult the phenomenologists for an approach to curriculum in the present day. For one thing, they remind us of what it means for an individual to be present to himself; for another, they suggest to us the origins of significant quests for meaning, origins which ought to be held in mind by those willing to enable students to be themselves.

If the existence of a primordial consciousness is taken seriously, it will be recognized that awareness begins perspectively, that our experience is always incomplete. It is true that we have what Merleau-Ponty calls a "prejudice" in favor of a world of solid, determinate objects, quite independent of our perceptions. Consciousness does, however, have the capacity to return to the precognitive, the primordial, by "bracketing out" objects as customarily seen. The individual can release himself into his own inner time and rediscover the ways in which objects arise, the ways in which experience develops. In discussing the possibility of Karl Rossmann exploring his own past, I have tried to show what this sort of interior journey can mean. Not only may it result in the effecting of new syntheses within experience; it may result in an awareness of the process of knowing, of believing, of perceiving. It may even result in an understanding of the ways in which meanings have been sedimented in an individual's own personal history. I can think of no more potent mode of combatting those conceived to be "enforcers of the real," including the curriculum designers.

But then there opens up the possibility of presenting curriculum in such a way that is does not impose or enforce. If the student is enabled to recognize that reason and order may represent the culminating step in his constitution of a world, if he can be enabled to see that what Schutz calls the attainment of a "reciprocity of perspectives"[54] signifies the achievement of rationality, he may realize what it is to generate the structures of the disciplines on his own initiative, against his own "background awareness." Moreover, he may realize that he is projecting beyond his present horizons each time he shifts his attention and takes another perspective on his world. "To say there exists rationality," writes Merleau-Ponty, "is to say that perspectives blend, perceptions confirm each other, a meaning emerges."[55] He points out that we witness at every moment "the miracles of related experiences, and yet nobody knows better than we do how this miracle is worked, for we are ourselves this network of relationships." Curriculum can offer the possibility for students to be the makers of such networks. The problem for their teachers is to stimulate an awareness of the questionable, to aid in the identification of the thematically relevant, to beckon beyond the everyday.

> I am a psychological and historical structure, and have received, with existence, a manner of existence, a style. All my actions and thoughts stand in a relationship to this structure, and even a philosopher's thought is merely a way of making explicit his hold on the world, and what he

is. The fact remains that I am free, not in spite of, or on the hither side of these motivations, but by means of them. For this significant life, this certain significance of nature and history which I am, does not limit my access to the world, but on the contrary is my means of entering into communication with it. It is by being unrestrictedly and unreservedly what I am at present that I have a chance of moving forward; it is by living my time that I am able to understand other times, by plunging into the present and the world by taking on deliberately what I am fortuitously, by willing what I will and doing what I do, that I can go further.[56]

To plunge in; to choose; to disclose; to move: this is the road, it seems to me, to mastery.

Notes

1. Maurice Merleau-Ponty, *The Primary of Perception*. James M. Edie, (ed.) Evanston, Ill.: Northwestern University Press, 1964, p. 99.
2. Jean Paul Sartre, *Search for a Method*. New York: Alfred A. Knopf, 1963, p. 92.
3. Ryland W. Crary, *Humanizing the School Curriculum: Development and Theory*. New York: Alfred A. Knopf, 1969, p. 13.
4. John Dewey, "The Child and the Curriculum." Martin S. Dworking, (ed.) *Dewey on Education*. New York: Teachers College Bureau of Publications, 1959, p. 91.
5. Sarah Lawall, *Critics of Consciousness*. Cambridge, Mass.: Harvard University Press, 1968.
6. T.S. Eliot, *The Sacred Wood*. New York: Barnes & Noble University Paperbacks, 1960, p. x.
7. Dorothy Walsh. "The Cognitive Content of Art." Francis J. Coleman, (ed.) *Aesthetics*. New York: McGraw-Hill, 1968, p. 297.
8. Clive Bell, *Art*. London: Chatto & Windus, 1914.
9. Walsh, *op. cit.*
10. M.H. Abrams, "Belief and the Suspension of Belief." M.H. Abrams, (ed.) *Literature and Belief*. New York: Columbia University Press, 1957, p. 9.
11. Maurice Blanchot. *L'Espace littéraire*. Paris: Gallimard, 1955.
12. See, e.g., Alfred Schutz, "Some Leading Concepts of Phenomenology." Maurice Natanson, (ed.) *Collected Papers I*. The Hague: Martinus Nijhoff, 1967, pp. 104–105.
13. Jean Paul Sartre. *Literature and Existentialism*. 3rd ed. New York: The Citadel Press, 1965, p. 43.
14. *Ibid*. p. 15.
15. John Dewey. *Art as Experience*. New York: Minton, Balch & Company, 1934, p. 54.
16. Sartre. *Search for a Method. op. cit.*, p. 91.
17. Jean Piaget. *Structuralism*. New York: Basic Books, 1970, p. 139.
18. *Ibid.*, p. 68.
19. *Ibid.*, p. 139.
20. *Ibid.*
21. Maurice Merleau-Ponty. *Phenomenology of Perception*. London: Routledge Kegan Paul Ltd., 1962.
22. Merleau-Ponty. *The Primacy of Perception, op. cit.*, p. 119.
23. *Ibid.*, p. 99.
24. Paulo Freire. *Pedagogy of the Oppressed*. New York: Herder and Herder, 1970, p. 108.
25. Schutz. "On Multiple Realities." *op. cit.*, p. 248.
26. Merleau-Ponty. *The Primacy of Perception, op. cit.*, p. 58.
27. Merleau-Ponty. *Phenomenology of Perception, op. cit.*, p. xvii.
28. Schutz. "On Multiple Realities." *op. cit.*
29. Merleau-Ponty, *op. cit.*, p. xv.
30. R.S. Peters. *Ethics and Education*. London: George Allen and Unwin, 1966, p. 50.
31. R.S. Peters. *Ethics and Education*. Glenview, Ill.: Scott Foresman and Co., 1967, p. 12.
32. Philip H. Phenix, "The Uses of the Disciplines as Curriculum Content." Donald Vandenberg, (ed.) *Theory of Knowledge and Problems of Education*. Urbana, Ill.: University of Illinois Press, 1969, p. 195.
33. Philip H. Phenix. *Realms of Meaning*. New York: McGraw-Hill, 1964, p. 25.
34. *Ibid.*
35. Schutz. "Problem of Rationality in the Social World." Natanson, (ed.) *Collected Papers II*. The Hague: Martinus Nijhoff, 1967, p. 66.
36. Phenix, "Disciplines as Curriculum Content," *op. cit.*, p. 195.
37. Alvin Toffler. *Future Shock*. New York: Random House, 1970, p. 18.

38. Albert Camus. *The Myth of Sisyphus*. New York: Alfred A. Knopf, 1955, p. 72.
39. Harold Pinter. *The Dumb Waiter*. New York: Grove Press, 1961, p. 103.
40. Tom Stoppard. *Rosencrantz and Guildenstern are Dead*. New York: Grove Press, 1967, pp. 58–59.
41. Cf. Fyodor Dostoevsky. *Notes from Underground*, in *The Short Novels of Dostoevsky*. New York: Dial Press, 1945. "You believe in a palace of crystal that can never be destroyed . . . a palace at which one will not be able to put out one's tongue or make a long nose on the sly." p. 152.
42. Franz Kafka. *Amerika*. Garden City, N.Y.: Doubleday Anchor Books, 1946, p. 38.
43. Merleau-Ponty. *The Primacy of Perception, op. cit.*, p. 110.
44. Piaget, *op. cit.*
45. Richard M. Zaner. *The Way of Phenomenology*. New York: Pegasus Books, 1970, p. 27.
46. Freire, *op. cit.*, p. 100.
47. Schutz. "The Life-World." Natanson, (ed.) *Collected Papers, III*. The Hague: Martinus Nijhoff, 1967, p. 125.
48. Kafka, *op. cit.*, p. 201.
49. Schutz. "The Life-World." *op. cit.*, p. 124.
50. Schutz, "Leading Concepts of Phenomenology," *op. cit.*, p. 111.
51. G.K. Plochmann. "On the Organic Logic of Teaching and Learning." Vandenberg, *op. cit.*, p. 244.
52. Cf. footnote 10.
53. Michael Novak. *The Experience of Nothingness*. New York: Harper & Row, 1970, p. 94.
54. Schutz. "Symbols, Reality, and Society." *Collected Papers I, op. cit.*, p. 315.
55. Merleau-Ponty, *Phenomenology of Perception, op. cit.*, p. xix.
56. *Ibid.*, pp. 455–56.

15

The Reconceptualization of Curriculum Studies

William F. Pinar

What some observers have designated a "movement" is visible in the field of curriculum studies in the United States. Some have termed it "reconceptualism," others "the new curriculum theory." Both terms suggest more thematic unity among the curriculum writing characterized as the "reconceptualization" than, upon close examination, appears to exist. Nonetheless, some thematic similarities are discernible, though insufficient in number to warrant a characterization like "ideology" or composite, agreed-upon point of view. What can be said, without dispute, is that by the summer of 1978, there will have been six conferences and five books[1] in the past six years which are indications of a socio-intellectual phenomenon in this field, and a phenomenon which clearly functions to reconceptualize the field of curriculum studies. Thus, while the writing published to date may be somewhat varied thematically, it is unitary in its significance for the field. If this process of transformation continues at its present rate, the field of curriculum studies will be profoundly different in 20 years time than it has been during the first 50 years of its existence.

What is this reconceptualization? The answer, at this point, is a slippery one, and to gain even an inchoate grip, one looks to the field as it is. This will indicate, in part, what is not. To a considerable extent, the reconceptualization is a reaction to what the field has been, and what it is seen to be at the present time.

Traditionalists

Most curricularists at work in 1977 can be characterized as *traditionalists*. Their work continues to make use of the "conventional wisdom" of the field, epitomized still by the work of Tyler. More important in identifying traditionalists than the allusion to Tyler is citing the *raison d'être* for traditional curriculum work. Above all, the reason for curriculum writing, indeed curriculum work generally, is captured in the phrase "service to practitioners." Curriculum work tends to be field-based and curriculum writing tends to have school teachers in mind. In short, traditional curriculum work is focused on the schools. Further, professors of curriculum have tended to be former school people. In fact, school service of some sort, ordinarily classroom teaching, is still viewed as a prerequisite for a teaching post in the field in a college or university. To an extent not obvious in certain of the other subfields of education (for instance, philosophy and psychology of education, recently in administration and the "helping services"), curricularists are former school people whose intellectual and subcultural ties tend to be with school practitioners. They tend to be less interested in basic research, in theory development, in related developments in allied fields, than in a set of perceived realities of classrooms and school settings generally.

There is, of course, an historical basis for traditional curriculum work. Cremin suggests that it was after superintendent Newlon's work in curriculum revision, in the early 1920s in Denver, that the need for a curriculum specialist became clear.[2] It is plausible to imagine school administrators like Newlon asking teachers who demonstrated an interest in curriculum and its development to leave classroom teaching and enter an administrative office from which they would attend full-time to matters curricular. There were no departments of curriculum in colleges of education in the 1920s; Newlon and other administrators could go nowhere else but to the classroom for curriculum personnel. When the training of curriculum personnel began at the university level in the 1930s, it surfaced in departments of administration and secondary education, indicating further the field's origin in and loyalty to the practical concerns of school personnel. This affiliation, more tenuous and complex at the present time than it was in the 1920s and 1930s, is evident in the programmes of the largest professional association of curricularists in the United States, the Association for Supervision and Curriculum Development. The programmes of ASCD annual meetings indicate a considerable and growing presence of school personnel. Further, the workshops and papers listed, the authors of which are university teachers, tend to have an explicit thematic focus on whatever school concerns are *au courant*.

There is another sense in which traditionalists carry forward the tradition of the field. The curriculum field's birth in the 1920s was understandably shaped by the intellectual character of that period. Above all it was a time of an emerging scientism when so-called scientific techniques from business and industry were finding their way into educational theory and practice. The early curricularist came to employ what Kliebard has termed the "bureaucratic model."[3] This model is characterized by its ameliorative orientation, ahistorical posture, and an allegiance to behaviourism and to what Macdonald has termed a "technological rationality." The curriculum worker is dedicated to the "improvement" of schools. He honours this dedication by accepting the curriculum structure as it is. "Curriculum change" is measured by comparing resulting behaviours with original objectives. Even humanistic educators tend to accept many of these premises, as they introduce, perhaps, "values clarification" into the school curriculum. Accepting the curriculum structure as it is, and working to improve it, is what is meant by the "technician's mentality." In a capsule way, it can be likened to adjusting an automobile engine part in order to make it function more effectively. This is also technological rationality, and its manifestations in school practice run the gamut from "competency-based teacher education" to "modular scheduling." The emphasis is on design, change (behaviourally observable), and improvement.

What has tended to be regarded as curriculum theory in the traditional sense, most notably Tyler's rationale,[4] is theoretical only in the questionable sense that it is abstract and usually at variance with what occurs in schools. Its intent is clearly to guide, to be of assistance to those in institutional positions who are concerned with curriculum. Of course, this is a broad concern. Most teachers share it, at least in terms of daily lesson planning. But as well as an element of teaching, curriculum is traditionally thought to include considerations such as evaluation, supervision, and also curriculum development and implementation. The boundaries of the field are fuzzy.

Thematically there is no unity. From Tyler to Taba and Saylor and Alexander to the current expression of this genre in Daniel and Laurel Tanner's book, Neil's and Zais' writing (all of which attempt an overview of considerations imagined pertinent to a curriculum worker) to the humanistic movement (for instance the work of such individuals as Fantini, Jordan, Simon, Weinstein) is a broad thematic territory.[5] What makes this work one territory is its fundamental interest in working with school people, with revising the curricula of schools. Traditional writing tends to be journalistic, necessarily so, in order that it can be readily accessible to a readership seeking quick answers to pressing, practical problems. The publications of the Association for Supervision and Curriculum Development also exemplify, to a considerable extent, this writing. ASCD is the traditionalists' professional organization. Relatively speaking, there exists a close relationship between traditional curricularists and school personnel.

Conceptual-Empiricists

A relationship between school personnel and the other two groups of curricularists—*conceptual-empiricists* and *reconceptualists*—also exists. But the nature of this relationship differs from the alliance historically characteristic of the field. This difference becomes clearer as we examine, momentarily, a second group of curricularists, a group which, until reconceptualists appeared, seemed to be the only heir to the field.

I use the word heir advisedly, for the traditional curriculum field has been declared terminally ill or already deceased by several influential observers, among them Schwab and Huebner. What has caused, in the past 15 to 20 years, the demise of the field? A comprehensive answer to this important question is inappropriate in the present context. What can be pointed to is two-fold. First, the leadership of the so-called curriculum reform movement of the 1960s was outside the field. This bypass was a crippling blow to its professional status. If those whose work was curriculum development and implementation were called on primarily as consultants and only rarely at that, then clearly their claim to specialized knowledge and expertise was questionable. Second, the economic situation of the past six years has meant a drying up of funds for in-service work and for curriculum proposals generally. A field whose professional status was irreparably damaged now lost the material basis necessary for its functioning. How could curricularists work with school people without money or time for in-service workshops? How could curriculum proposals be implemented without requisite funds?

With the traditional, practical justification of the field attenuated—even teacher-training efforts have slowed dramatically—new justifications appeared. Curriculum and other education subfields have become increasingly vulnerable to criticisms regarding scholarly standards by colleagues in so-called cognate fields. Particularly the influence of colleagues in the social sciences is evident, paralleling the political ascendency of these disciplines in the university generally. In fact, research in education, in many instances, has become indistinguishable from social science research. The appearance and proliferation of conceptual-empiricists in the curriculum field is a specific instance of this general phenomenon. There remains, of course, the notion that research has implications for classroom practice, but it is usually claimed that many years of extensive research are necessary before significant implications can be obtained.

This development has gone so far that, examining the work done by a faculty in a typical American college of education, one has little sense of education as a field with its own identity. One discovers researchers whose primary identity is with the cognate field. Such individuals view themselves as primarily psychologists, philosophers, or sociologists with "research interests" in schools and education-related matters. By 1978, it is accurate to note that the education field has lost whatever (and it was never complete of course) intellectual autonomy it possessed in earlier years, and now is nearly tantamount to a colony of superior, imperialistic powers.

The view that education is not a discipline in itself but an area to be studied by the disciplines is evident in the work of those of curricularists I have called conceptual-empiricists. The work of this group can be so characterized, employing conceptual and empirical in the sense social scientists typically employ them. This work is concerned with developing hypotheses to be tested, and testing them in methodological ways characteristic of mainstream social science. This work is reported, ordinarily, at meetings of the American Educational Research Association. Just as the Association for Supervision and Curriculum Development is the traditionalists' organization, AERA tends to be the organization of conceptual-empiricists. (In relatively small numbers traditionalists and reconceptualists also read papers at AERA annual meetings.)

An illustrative piece of conceptual work from this second group of curricularists was published in the AERA-sponsored *Review of Educational Research*. It is George Posner's (with Kenneth Strike) "A categorization scheme for principles of sequencing content." A prefatory paragraph indicates that his view is a social scientist's one, reliant upon hypothesis-making, data collection, and interpretation.

> We have very little information, based on hard data, regarding the consequences of alternative content sequences and will need a good deal more research effort before we are able to satisfactorily suggest how content *should* be sequenced. Our intention here is to consider the question, What are the alternatives?[7]

The article is a conceptual one, concerned with what the authors view as logically defensible content sequencing alternatives, and it is empirical in its allegiance to the view of empirical research, one yielding "hard data," typical of social science at the present time.

In a recently published essay, Decker F. Walker, another visible conceptual-empiricist, moves away somewhat from strict social science as exemplified in Posner's work.[8] His essay, or case study as he terms it, is more anthropological in its methodological form, demonstrating a type of curriculum research which Walker's co-editor Reid endorses.[9] Anthropology, it should be noted, while regarded as not as "pure" a social science as political science or psychology, is nonetheless generally categorized as a social science.

Taking his cue from Schwab, Walker argues that prescriptive curriculum theories, (partly because they do not reflect the actual process of curriculum change), are not useful. Rather than focus on why curriculum developers did not follow the Tyler rationale, Walker concentrates on how, in fact, the developers did proceed. In his study he finds little use for terms like objectives and important use for terms such as platform and deliberation. He concludes that curricularists probably ought to abandon the attempt to make actual curriculum development mirror prescriptive theories, accept "deliberation" as a core aspect of the development process, and apply the intellectual resources of the field toward improving the quality of deliberation and employing it more effectively.

This work I find significant to the field in two ways. First it deals another hard blow to the Tyler rationale and its influence. Second, Walker is moving away from social science. His work remains social science, but it is closer to the work of some reconceptualists than it is to that of Posner, and other mainstream conceptual-empiricists. Walker retains the traditional focus upon the practical concerns of school people and school curriculum, and no doubt he has and will spend a portion of his professional time on actual curriculum projects. Further, his methods seem more nearly those of the ethnomethodologist whose approaches do not easily fit the picture of conventional theories of the middle range, as projected by individuals such as the sociologist Robert Merton, who has influenced so many conceptual-empirical studies in the field of sociology. Walker appears to be moving outside mainstream conceptual-empiricism.

Also in the Reid and Walker book is work by another visible conceptual-empiricist, Ian Westbury. With his co-author Lynn McKinney, Westbury studies the Gary, Indiana school system during the period 1940–1970.[10] Like Walker's study of the art project, McKinney and Westbury's study would seem to be outside mainstream conceptual-empiricism, even close to work characteristic of the humanities. The structure of the study, however, indicates its allegiance to social science, thus warranting its categorization as conceptual-empirical. The work is an historical study done in the service of generalization, work that has interest in the particular (the Gary district) as it contributes to understanding of the general. The "general" in this instance is the phenomenon of stability and change, which the authors "now believe are the two primary functions of the administrative structure which surround the schools."[11] Finally what the study demonstrates is "that a concern for goals without a concomitant concern for organizational matters addresses only a small part of the problem of conceiving new designs for schools."[12] This use of the specific to illustrate a general, ahistorical "law" is, of course, a fundamental procedure of mainstream social science.

Reconceptualists

This concern for generalization is not abandoned in the work of the third group of curricularists, the reconceptualists. For example, at the fourth conference at the University of Wisconsin-Milwaukee, Professor Apple reported the results of a study he and a colleague conducted in a kindergarten, substantiating claims he has made before regarding the socio-political functions of classroom behaviour.[13] His case study is distinguishable from the work of a typical conceptual-empiricist in two significant respects: (1) his acknowledged "value-laden" perspective, and (2) a perspective with a politically emancipatory intent. That is, in contrast to the canon of traditional social science, which prescribes data collection, hypothesis substantiation or disconfirmation in the disinterested service of building a body of knowledge, a reconceptualist tends to see research as an inescapably political as well as intellectual act. As such, it works to suppress, or to liberate, not only those who conduct the research, and those upon whom it is conducted, but as well those outside the academic subculture. Mainstream social science research, while on the surface seemingly apolitical in nature and consequence, if examined more carefully can be seen as contributing to the maintenance of the contemporary social-political order, or contributing to its dissolution. Apple and Marxists and neo-Marxists go further and accept a teleological view of historical movement, allying themselves with the lower classes, whose final emergence from oppression is seen to be inevitable. A number of reconceptualists, while not Marxists, nonetheless accept some variation of this teleological historical view. And many of these, at least from a distance, would seem to be "leftists" of some sort. Nearly all accept that a political dimension is inherent in any intellectual activity.

This political emphasis distinguishes the work of Apple, Burton, Mann, Molnar, some of the work of Huebner and Macdonald, from the work of traditionalists and conceptual-empiricists.[14] It is true that Reid and Walker in their *Case Studies in Curriculum Change* acknowledge that curriculum development is political, but the point is never developed, and never connected with a view of history and the contemporary social order. The focus of Walker's case study and of other case studies in the book is limited to literal curriculum change, without historicizing this change, indicating its relationship to contemporary historical movement generally. In the 1975 ASCD year-book, on the other hand, which is edited by Macdonald and Zaret, with essays also by Apple, Burton, Huebner, and Mann, this sitting of curriculum issues in the broad intellectual-historical currents of twentieth-century life is constant.[15] Macdonald speaks, for instance, of technological rationality, an intellectual mode comparable in its pervasiveness and taken-for-grantedness to the ascendency of technology in human culture at large.[16] Such individuals would argue that comprehension of curriculum issues is possible only when they are situated historically.

The 1975 ASCD year-book speaks to school people. It is not that reconceptualists do not speak to this constituency of the curriculum field. But there is a conscious abandonment of the "technician's mentality." There are no prescriptions or traditional rationales. What this year-book offers, instead, is heightened awareness of the complexity and historical significance of curriculum issues. Because the difficulties these reconceptualists identify are related to difficulties in the culture at large, they are not "problems" that can be "solved." That concept created by technological rationality, is itself problematic. Thus, what is necessary, in part, is fundamental structural change in the culture. Such an aspiration cannot be realized by "plugging into" the extant order. That is why an elective or two on Marx in high-school social studies classes, or the teaching of autobiographical reflection in English classes, bring indifference and often alarm to most reconceptualists. That "plugging into," "co-opting" it was termed in the 1960s during the student protests, accepts the social order as it is. What is necessary is a fundamental reconceptualization of what curriculum is, how it functions, and how it might function in emancipatory ways. It is this commitment to a comprehensive critique and theory development that distinguishes the reconceptualist phenomenon.

To understand more fully the efforts of the individuals involved in inquiry of this kind requires some understanding of metatheory and philosophy of science. Without such grounding, it is difficult, if not impossible, for curricularists to see clearly their work in the context of the growth of knowledge in general. Max van Manen's paper at the 1976 Wisconsin conference was a significant effort to analyse various structures of theoretic knowledge as they related to dominant modes of inquiry in the field of curriculum.[17] His work builds on basic analyses undertaken by philosophers of science such as Radnitzky and Feyerabend.[18] More work needs to be done along this line.

The reconceptualization, it must be noted, is fundamentally an intellectual phenomenon, not an interpersonal-affiliative one. Reconceptualists have no organized group, such as ASCD or AERA. Individuals at work, while sharing certain themes and motives, do not tend to share any common interpersonal affiliation. (In this one respect their work parallels that of the so-called romantic critics of the 1960s. But here any such comparison stops.) Conferences have been held yearly; the most recent on the campus of Rochester Institute of Technology, Rochester, New York. A journal and a press emphasizing this work are scheduled to appear by 1979.

Conclusion

As an interpreter of metatheories, Richard Bernstein recently analysed, in detail, individuals at work in four areas—empirical research, philosophical analysis, phenomenology and critical theory of society.[19] (The first category corresponds to conceptual-empirical, the third and fourth to reconceptualist work.) He ends his study with this conviction:

> In the final analysis we are not confronted with exclusive choices: either empirical or interpretative theory or critical theory. Rather there is an internal dialectic in the restructing of social political theory: when we work through any one of these movements we discover the others are implicated.[20]

This is so in the field of curriculum studies also. We are not faced with an exclusive choice: either the traditional wisdom of the field, or conceptual-empiricism, or the reconceptualization. Each is reliant upon the other. For the field to become vital and significant to American education it must nurture each "moment," its "internal dialectic." And it must strive for synthesis, for a series of perspectives on curriculum that are at once empirical, interpretative, critical, emancipatory.

But such nurturance and synthesis do not characterize, on the whole, the field today. Some of the issues raised by the British sociologist David Silverman are germane here.[21] As a prologue to more adequate social science theorizing, Silverman proposes that we learn how to read Castaneda's account of his apprenticeship to Don Juan in order that we may come to know the kinds of questions that need to be asked. He is convinced that mainstream conceptual-empiricists, regardless of field, do not now know what questions to ask, and are, indeed, intolerant of reconceptualizations that differ from their own. This intolerance is discernible in the American curriculum field. To some extent it can be found in each group of curricularists.

I am convinced that this intolerance among curricularists for work differing from one's own must be suspended to some extent if significant intellectual movement in the field is to occur. Becoming open to another genre of work does not mean loss of one's capacity for critical reflection. Nor does it mean, necessarily, loss of intellectual identity. One may remain a traditionalist while sympathetically studying the work of a reconceptualist. One's own point of view may well be enriched. Further, an intellectual climate may become established in which could develop syntheses of current perspectives, regenerating the field, and making more likely that its contribution to American education be an important one.

Acknowledgment

This is a revised version of a paper presented at the Annual Meeting of the American Educational Research Association in New York in April, 1977.

Notes

1. Conferences have been held at the University of Rochester (1973), Xavier University of Cincinnati (1974), the University of Virginia (1975), the University of Wisconsin at Milwaukee (1976), Kent State University (1977), and the Rochester Institute of Technology (1978). Books include:

Pinar, W. (Ed) *Heightened Consciousness, Cultural Revolution and Curriculum Theory* (McCutchan Publishing Corp., Berkeley, CA, 1974);

IDEM, *Curriculum Theorizing: The Reconceptualists* (McCutchan Publishing Corp., Berkeley, CA, 1975); Pinar, W., and Grumet, M. R. *Toward a Poor Curriculum* (Kendall/Hunt Publishing Co., Dubuque, IA, 1976).

At a 1976 conference held at the State University of New York at Geneseo; Professors Apple, Greene, Kliebard and Huebner read papers. Each of these persons has been associated with the reconceptualists although the chairmen of this meeting, Professors DeMarte and Rosarie, did not see this seminar as being in the tradition of the others. The papers from this seminar were published in *Curriculum Inquiry*, Vol. 6, No. 4 (1977).

2. Cremin, L. "Curriculum-making in the United States." In Pinar, W. (ed.), *Curriculum Theorizing*, pp. 19–35.

3. Kliebard, H. M. "Persistent curriculum issues in historical perspective," and "Bureaucracy and curriculum theory." In Pinar, W. (ed.) *Curriculum Theorizing*, pp. 39–69.

4. Tyler, R. W., *Basic Principles of Curriculum and Instruction* (University of Chicago Press, Chicago, 1950).

5. Taba, H. *Curriculum Development: Theory and Practice* (Harcourt, Brace and World, New York, 1962);

Saylor, G., and Alexander, W. *Curriculum Planning for Modern Schools* (Holt, Rinehart and Winston, New York, 1966);

Tanner, D., and Tanner, L. N. *Curriculum Development: Theory into Practice* (MacMillan, New York, 1975);

Neil, J. D. *Curriculum: A Comprehensive Introduction* (Little, Brown and Co., Boston, 1977);

Zais, R. S. *Curriculum: Principles and Foundations* (Thomas Y. Browell, New York, 1976);

Weinstein, G., and Fantini, M. D. *Toward Humanistic Education: A Curriculum of Affect* (Praeger Publishers, New York, 1971);

Simon, S., et al. *Values Clarification* (Hart, New York, 1972);

Jordan, D. "The ANISA Model." Paper presented to conference on curriculum at the University of Virginia, 1975 (available from Charles W. Beegle, Curry Memorial School of Education, University of Virginia, Charlottesville, VA 22903, USA).

6. Schwab, J. J. *The Practical: A Language for Curriculum* (National Education Association, Washington, D.C., 1970);

Huebner, D. "The moribund curriculum field: Its wake and our work." *Curriculum Inquiry*, Vol. 6, No. 2 (1976).

7. Posner, G. J. and Strike, K. A. "A categorization scheme for principles of sequencing content." *Review of Educational Research*, Vol. 46, No. 4 (1976).

8. Walker, D. F. "Curriculum development in an art project." In Reid, W. A., and Walker, D. F. (eds.) *Case Studies in Curriculum Change* (Routledge and Kegan Paul, London, 1975).

9. Reid, W. A. "The changing curriculum: theory and practice." In Reid and Walker, op. cit.

10. McKinney, W. L., and Westbury, I. "Stability and change; the public schools of Gary, Indiana, 1940–70." In Reid and Walker, op. cit.

11. Ibid., p. 44.

12. Ibid., p. 50.

13. Apple, M. W., and King, N. "What do schools teach?" Paper presented at the University of Wisconsin and Milwaukee Conference.

14. For discussion of this point see my prefatory remarks in *Curriculum Theorizing* (Note 1). See also: Klohr, P. R. "The State of the Field." Paper presented at the Xavier University Conference on Curriculum; Miller, J. L. "Duality: Perspectives on the reconceptualization." Paper presented to University of Virginia Conference;

Macdonald, J. B. "Curriculum Theory as intentional activity." Paper presented to University of Virginia Conference (see Note 5);

Macdonald, J. B. "Curriculum Theory and human interests." In Pinar, W. (ed.) *Curriculum Theorizing*;

Benham, B. J. "Curriculum Theory in the 1970s: the reconceptualist movement." Texas Technical University, 1976, unpublished paper.

15. Zaret, E., and Macdonald, J. B. *Schools in Search of Meaning* (Association for Supervision and Curriculum Development, Washington, D.C., 1975).

16. Macdonald, J. B. "The quality of everyday life in schools." In Zaret and Macdonald, op. cit.

17. Van Manen, M. "Linking ways of knowing with ways of being practical." *Curriculum Inquiry*, Vol. 6, No. 3 (1977).

18. Radnitzky, G. *Contemporary Schools of Metascience* (Henry Regnery Co., Chicago, 1973); Feyerbend P. K. "Against method; outline of an anarchist theory of knowledge." In *Minnesota Studies in the Philosophy of Science*, Vol. 4 (University of Minnesota Press, Minneapolis, 1970).

19. Bernstein, R. J. *The Restructuring of Social and Political Theory* (Harcourt, Brace, Jovanovich, New York, 1976).

20. Ibid., 235.

21. Silverman, D. *Reading Castaneda: A Prologue to the Social Sciences* (Routledge and Kegan Paul, London, 1975).

16

The Paideia Proposal

Mortimer J. Adler

Democracy and Education

We are on the verge of a new era in our national life. The long-needed educational reform for which this country is at last ready will be a turning point toward that new era.

Democracy has come into its own for the first time in this century. Not until this century have we undertaken to give twelve years of schooling to all our children. Not until this century have we conferred the high office of enfranchised citizenship on all our people, regardless of sex, race, or ethnic origin.

The two—universal suffrage and universal schooling—are inextricably bound together. The one without the other is a perilous delusion. Suffrage without schooling produces mobocracy, not democracy—not rule of law, not constitutional government by the people as well as for them.

The great American educator, John Dewey, recognized this early in this century. In *Democracy and Education*, written in 1916, he first tied these two words together and let each shine light upon the other.

A revolutionary message of that book was that a democratic society must provide equal educational opportunity not only by giving to all its children the same quantity of public education—the same number of years in school—but also by making sure to give to all of them, all with no exceptions, the same quality of education.

The ideal Dewey set before us is a challenge we have failed to meet. It is a challenge so difficult that it is understandable, perhaps excusable, that we have so far failed. But we cannot continue to fail without disastrous consequences for all of us. For the proper working of our political institutions, for the efficiency of our industries and businesses, for the salvation of our economy, for the vitality of our culture, and for the ultimate good of our citizens as individuals, and especially our future citizens—our children—we must succeed.

We are all sufferers from our continued failure to fulfill the educational obligations of a democracy. We are all the victims of a school system that has only gone halfway along the road to realize the promise of democracy.

At the beginning of this century, fewer than 10 percent of those of an age eligible for high school entered such schools. Today, almost 100 percent of our children enter, but not all complete such secondary schooling; many drop out for many reasons, some of them understandable.

It has taken us the better part of eighty years to go halfway toward the goal our society must achieve if it is to be a true democracy. The halfway mark was reached when we finally managed to provide twelve years of basic public schooling for all our children. At that point, we were closer to the goal that Horace Mann set for us more than a century ago when he said: "Education is the gateway to equality."

But the democratic promise of equal educational opportunity, half fulfilled, is worse than a promise broken. It is an ideal betrayed. Equality of educational opportunity is not, in fact, provided if it means no more than taking all the children into the public schools for the same number of hours, days, and years. If once there they are divided into the sheep and the goats, into those destined solely for toil and those destined for economic and political leadership and for a quality of life to which all should have access, then the democratic purpose has been undermined by an inadequate system of public schooling.

It fails because it has achieved only the same quantity of public schooling, not the same quality. This failure is a downright violation of our democratic principles.

We are politically a classless society. Our citizenry as a whole is our ruling class. We should, therefore, be an educationally classless society.

We should have a one-track system of schooling, not a system with two or more tracks, only one of which goes straight ahead while the others shunt the young off onto sidetracks not headed toward the goals our society opens to all. The innermost meaning of social equality is: *substantially the same quality of life for all.* That calls for: *the same quality of schooling for all.*

We may take some satisfaction, perhaps, in the fact that we have won half the battle—the quantitative half. But we deserve the full development of the country's human potential. We should, therefore, be vexed that we have not yet gone further. We should be impatient to get on with it, in and through the schools.

Progress toward the fulfillment of democracy by means of our educational system should and can be accelerated. It need not and must not take another century to achieve uniform quality for all in our public schools.

There are signs on all sides that tell us the people want that move forward now. The time is ripe. Parents, teachers, leaders of government, labor unions, corporations—above all, the young themselves—have uttered passionate complaints about the declining quality of public schooling.

There is no acceptable reason why trying to promote equality should have led to a lessening or loss of quality. Two decades after John Dewey, another great American educator, Robert Maynard Hutchins, as much committed to democracy as Dewey was before him, stated the fundamental principle we must now follow in our effort to achieve a true equality of educational conditions. "The best education for the best," he said, "is the best education for all."

The shape of the best education for the best is not unknown to us. But we have been slow to learn how to provide it. Nor have we always been honest in our commitment to democracy and its promise of equality. A part of our population—and much too large a part—has harbored the opinion that many of the nation's children are not fully educable. Trainable for one or another job, perhaps, but not educable for the duties of self-governing citizenship and for the enjoyment of things of the mind and spirit that are essential to a good human life.

We must end that hypocrisy in our national life. We cannot say out of one side of our mouth that we are for democracy and all its free institutions including, preeminently, political and civil liberty for all; and out of the other side of our mouth, say that only some of the children—fewer than half—are educable for full citizenship and a full human life.

With the exception of a few suffering from irremediable brain damage, every child is educable up to his or her capacity. Educable—not just trainable for jobs! As John Dewey said almost a century ago, vocational training, training for particular jobs, is not the education of free men and women.

True, children are educable in varying degrees, but the variation in degree must be of the same kind and quality of education. If "the best education for the best is the best education for all," the failure to carry out that principle is the failure on the part of society—a failure of parents, of teachers, of administrators—not a failure on the part of the children.

There are no unteachable children. There are only schools and teachers and parents who fail to teach them.

The Same Course of Study for all

To give the same quality of schooling to all requires a program of study that is both liberal and general, and that is, in several, crucial, overarching respects, one and the same for every child. All sidetracks, specialized courses, or elective choices must be eliminated. Allowing them will always lead a certain number of students to voluntarily downgrade their own education.

Elective choices are appropriate only in a curriculum that is intended for different avenues of specialization or different forms of preparation for the professions or technical careers. Electives and specialization are entirely proper at the level of advanced schooling—in our colleges, universities, and technical schools. They are wholly inappropriate at the level of basic schooling.

The course of study to be followed in the twelve years of basic schooling should, therefore, be completely required, with only one exception. That exception is the choice of a second language. In addition to competence in the use of English as everyone's primary language, basic schooling should confer a certain degree of facility in the use of a second language. That second language should be open to elective choice.

The diagram depicts in three columns three distinct modes of teaching and learning, rising in successive gradations of complexity and difficulty from the first to the twelfth year. All three modes are essential to the overall course of study.

These three columns are interconnected, as the diagram indicates. The different modes of learning on the part of the students and the different modes of teaching on the part of the teaching staff correspond to three different ways in which the mind can be improved—(1) by the acquisition of organized knowledge; (2) by the development of intellectual skills; and (3) by the enlargement of understanding, insight, and aesthetic appreciation.

In addition to the three main Columns of Learning, the required course of study also includes a group of auxiliary subjects, of which one is physical education and care of the body. This runs through all twelve years. Of the other two auxiliary subjects, instruction in a variety of manual arts occupies a number of years, but not all twelve; and the third consists of an introduction to the world of work and its range of occupations and careers. It is given in the last two of the twelve years.

	COLUMN ONE	*COLUMN TWO*	*COLUMN THREE*
Goals	ACQUISITION OF ORGANIZED KNOWLEDGE	DEVELOPMENT OF INTELLECTUAL SKILLS—SKILLS OF LEARNING	ENLARGED UNDERSTANDING OF IDEAS AND VALUES
	by means of	by means of	by means of
Means	DIDACTIC INSTRUCTION LECTURES AND RESPONSES TEXTBOOKS AND OTHER AIDS	COACHING, EXERCISES, AND SUPERVISED PRACTICE	MAIEUTIC OR SOCRATIC QUESTIONING AND ACTIVE PARTICIPATION
	in three areas of subject-matter	in the operations of	in the
Areas of Operations and Activities	LANGUAGE, LITERATURE, AND THE FINE ARTS, MATHEMATICS AND NATURAL SCIENCE, HISTORY, GEOGRAPHY, AND SOCIAL STUDIES	READING, WRITING, SPEAKING, LISTENING CALCULATING, PROBLEM-SOLVING, OBSERVING MEASURING, ESTIMATING EXERCISING CRITICAL JUDGMENT	DISCUSSION OF BOOKS (NOT TEXTBOOKS) AND OTHER WORKS OF ART AND INVOLVEMENT IN ARTISTIC ACTIVITIES e.g., MUSIC, DRAMA, VISUAL ARTS

THE THREE COLUMNS DO NOT CORRESPOND TO SEPARATE COURSES, NOR IS ONE KIND OF TEACHING AND LEARNING NECESSARILY CONFINED TO ANY ONE CLASS.

17

The False Promise of the Paideia: A Critical Review of *The Paideia Proposal*

Nel Noddings

The Paideia Proposal is offered as an educational prescription for all of America's children. It is based on two major premises: that "the shape of the best education for the best is not unknown to us" (p. 7) and that "the best education for the best . . . is the best education for all" (p. 6). Surely no humane and decent person finds it easy to counsel against a proposal that promises to provide the "same quality of schooling to all," and thereby to educate all of our children to their fullest potential. Hard as it is, however, I believe that we should reject the recommendations in *The Paideia Proposal*. I will argue that "equality of quality" in education cannot be achieved by forcing all students to take exactly the same course of study, nor can the ideal of a democratic, classless society be actualized by establishing only one model of excellence.

The *Paideia*'s recommendations fall into two major categories: content and method. Those on method will be discussed at the end of this essay. The recommendations on content are encapsulated in this paragraph from the *Paideia*:

> The course of study to be followed in the twelve years of basic schooling should, therefore, be completely required, with only one exception. That exception is the choice of a second language. (Adler 1982, p. 21)

There is little use in arguing directly against the *Paideia*'s recommendations, because they follow inexorably from Mortimer Adler's two basic assumptions. But both of Adler's premises may be called into question as well as his strategy of persuasion: linking John Dewey and Robert Hutchins together as though no disagreement separated the two should cause thoughtful educators considerable uneasiness. I will start by examining that strategy, and then I will examine each of Adler's premises in turn.

1

The Paideia Proposal is dedicated to Horace Mann, John Dewey, and Robert Hutchins, "who would have been our leaders were they alive today." This is a lovely dedication, but Adler fails to mention that, if Dewey and Hutchins were alive today, they would almost certainly be engaged in the continuing battle of method and principle that they so vigorously mounted during their actual lifetimes. Mr. Hutchins would be an eloquent and outspoken advocate of the *Paideia*: Mr. Dewey would be a softer spoken but rigorously thoughtful opponent of the program. To suggest, even tacitly, that the *Paideia* fulfills the dreams and recommendations of both John Dewey and Robert Hutchins does a monumental disservice to John Dewey. The man and his educational thought deserve better. Further, Adler is thoroughly informed on the differences I shall point out, and one wonders why he chose to omit their discussion. Perhaps he believes that it is high time for reconciliation between Hutchins and Dewey and that this reconciliation holds promise for real improvement in the system of public education that both men loved (in some ideal form) and that is now so terribly beset with problems. Granted this generous motive, he still cannot responsibly attempt to effect reconciliation by assimilating a worthy opponent to the position of his adversary without even mentioning the problems that opponent would encounter in considering such a reconciliation.

Dewey and Hutchins are linked in Adler's arguments through their manifest interests in democracy and "equality of quality" in education. But their views on both concepts differed radically. Adler refers to Dewey's *Democracy and Education* when he says:

> A revolutionary message of that book was that a democratic society must provide equal opportunity not only by giving to all its children the same quantity of public education—the same number of years in school—but also by making sure to give to all of them, all with no exceptions, the same quality of education. (*Paideia*, p. 4)

Now, it is clear that Dewey did advocate a substantial "equality of quality" in education for all children. But his ideas on this were very different from those of Hutchins. In *The School and Society*, Dewey (1899, p. 3) said:

> What the best and wisest parent wants for his own child, that must the community want for all its children. Any other ideal for our schools is narrow and unlovely; acted upon, it destroys our democracy.

Clearly, we have to ask what Dewey meant when he referred to "the best and wisest parent." It is crystal clear at the outset, however, that he meant by "best" something very different from the "best" of Hutchins in the initial premises cited by Adler. Yet Adler throws them together in the same paragraph as though both were advocates of the program under construction. He says:

> There is no acceptable reason why trying to promote equality should have led to a lessening or loss of quality. Two decades after John Dewey, another great American educator, Robert Maynard Hutchins, as much committed to democracy as Dewey was before him, stated the fundamental principle we must follow in our effort to achieve a true equality of educational conditions. "The best education for the best," he said, "is the best education for all." (*Paideia*, p. 6)

Dewey would certainly challenge this premise if "best" is interpreted as "intellectually best"—as it surely is in the writings of Hutchins and Adler. Further, Dewey *did* challenge both premises in direct rebuttal of Hutchins. In a series of 1937 articles in *The Social Frontier*, Dewey (1937a, b) criticized the program of higher education that Hutchins proposed in *The Higher Learning in America*. Dewey made it clear in the ensuing exchange of views that, while he accepted and admired some of Hutchins' analysis, he rejected the proposed remedy. He said:

> The essence of the remedy . . . is emancipation of higher learning from . . . practicality, and its devotion to the cultivation of intellectuality for its own sake. (Dewey 1937a, p. 103)

Dewey's objections to the remedies suggested in *The Higher Learning* centered on two matters that he thought were at the heart of Hutchins' ideas: belief in "the existence of fixed and eternal authoritative principles" and the separation of "higher learning from contemporary social life." It is not an exaggeration to say that Dewey's voluminous writings over a lifetime of effort attacked these ideas again and again from a wide variety of perspectives. The separation of learning from contemporary social life was, indeed, a favorite target of his criticism. Exactly the same objections may be brought against the *Paideia*: It elevates intellectual life above that which it should serve (the social communion of human beings), and it assumes an essential sameness in human beings and values that suggests, logically, a sameness in education.

It would be fun (and instructive, too) to follow the Dewey-Hutchins debate further, but I cannot do that here. Suffice it to say that these two great educators did not really communicate with each other. Hutchins, indeed, began his rejoinder to Dewey by saying that he could not "in any real sense" respond to Dewey for

> Mr. Dewey has stated my position in such a way as to lead me to think that I cannot write, and has stated his own in such a way as to make me suspect that I cannot read.
>
> (Hutchins 1937, p. 137)

This sort of wit was a favorite gambit of Hutchins. He did not engage in *dialogue* with Dewey and continually side-stepped Dewey's most telling points, preferring to display verbal pyrotechnics and to persuade through rhetoric. The same charade is now being replayed. Adler offers us a tightly argued program based on rhetorical premises, themselves entirely unsupported by logical argumentation. Accept his premises and he has you, because he does not make errors in the logic of *developing* his program. What is sad is that so many educators are listening to Adler without a murmur of logical protest. He is right about one thing—and, paradoxically, it is working for him—the education of educators is not all that it should be.

2

Let me raise a murmur of logical protest. Put aside for the moment the premise that makes claims about the "shape of the best education," and let's concentrate on the other. The best education for the best is the best education for all.

The word "best" is used three times here. All three uses invite scrutiny, but the second deserves special attention. It is used elliptically as a noun. If we insist that the ellipsis be filled and that "best" be used as an adjective, what noun will it modify? It is clear that "best" is not meant to modify such nouns as "life" or "effort" or "performance" or the like. Both Hutchins and Adler are talking about *people* when they refer to "the best." Now what noun shall we insert: people? students? minds? It is eminently clear that Hutchins meant to refer to an *intellectually best* when he used the word and that an accurate filling in of the ellipsis would be, "The best education for the intellectually best students is the best education for all." Further, because the two premises have influenced each other historically, "intellectually best" has been narrowed to "academically best" in the traditional sense. Adler wants all children to receive an education that is, in content at least, the education designed for our academically best students.

Why should we consider doing this? Are the academically best the only group that should provide a model for school learning? Is the mission of the school to provide training or "education" only for the mind? Or are there many models of excellence that must be recognized in both society and school? In my own secondary schooling, I participated in a program very like the one Adler outlines. I loved it. I was completely captivated by Caesar's Gallic Wars, geometry, trigonometric identities, and even Cicero's essay on old age. It was not until years later that I learned about the utter misery most of my classmates endured in the "same" environment. Mr. Adler, to his great credit, would try to alleviate that misery by better classroom teaching and individual coaching, but he is mistaken in what he believes would be effected. No special effort or even genius in teaching would have brought most of my classmates into fair competition with me. Whatever they did, however they improved, I would have done more of it and at a higher level. It is not that I was "better" than they. I was *interested* in the sort of material the school wanted me to learn. Now one might claim a special benefit in this side effect: the academically able would be pushed through increased competition to surpass themselves. But then they would be engaged in academics (if they remained engaged) for largely the wrong reasons and with loss of the joy that accompanies doing what one has chosen out of love to do. We should consider the *Paideia*'s proposals, then, if we want this sort of effect.

Giving all of our children the *same* education, especially when that "sameness" is defined in a model of intellectual excellence, cannot equalize the quality of education. When parents and their children want the sort of education prescribed in the *Paideia*, it seems right to accommodate them, but to impose a plan such as this on all children in the name of equality is wrong. It proceeds in part from the stated assumption that we are "politically a classless society" and that we should, therefore, be an "educationally classless society." Mr. Adler has the cart before the horse. We are *not*, in any but the most technical sense, a classless society and to impose a uniform and compulsory form of education on all children is likely to aggravate an already unhealthy condition. When children must all study the same material and strive to meet the same standards, it becomes infinitely easier to sort and grade them like so many apples on a conveyor belt. Some children will be in the top quartile and some will be in the bottom quartile. Are we to say, then, that they all had an "equal chance" and that the "classes" thus established are, at least, objectivly and fairly established?

To put the horse properly before the cart, we would have to ask what education might do to help the society arrive at the classless ideal it has stated for itself. Many theorists insist that the schools can do very little to change the society: As institutions *of* the society, they are instruments for the reproduction of society as it is. We can certainly take a more hopeful view than this, but whatever view we take must be realistic at the outset. People in our society perform a huge variety of tasks, have hundreds of different interests, hold a variety of precious values. We do not offer equality when we ask them to model themselves after the traditional profile of an "intellectual best." What the schools need to do, instead, is to legitimize multiple models of excellence, e.g., mechanical, artistic, physical, productive, academic, and caretaking. Standing over all these should be the ethical, for what we need far more urgently than intellectual prowess is ethical goodness.

Many thoughtful planners shrink from the notion of "multiple models" of excellence because they believe the schools are already asked to accomplish too much. John Gardner, for example, in his influential *Excellence* (1961), lauded excellence in all its forms at the level of societal activity, but he charged the school with the task of promoting only academic excellence. It seems entirely right in a society such as ours to value "excellent plumbers above mediocre philosophers," but must we not also value the budding plumber—the youngster who will be a craftsman—while he or she is still a student? Gardner argued that the schools cannot do everything and that they are best organized to achieve *academic* excellence. The weakest part of his argument was revealed when he admitted that some youngsters (probably many) would not do well in a program so oriented. They would have to understand, he said, that the failure they had experienced in school was only *one form* of failure and that they might still achieve excellence in other enterprises. But I ask you this: How is a youngster who has been at the bottom of the heap for twelve years going "to understand" that his or her failure so far is only "one form" of failure? Surely, if we value plumbing, and farming, and dancing, and writing, and repairing electronic devices at the societal level, we can find ways of valuing the talents that lead to these occupations during school years. We really *have* to do this if our talk of equality is to be anything more than *mere* talk.

To be reasonable, however, we do have to consider Gardner's concern that demands on the schools have so proliferated that they cannot achieve any sort of excellence. I suggest that it is not subject and activity demands that have overburdened our schools but, rather, demands to solve the problems of a society unwilling to bear its burdens where they should properly be shouldered. A society unwilling to rid itself of racial prejudice asks the *schools* to achieve desegregation. A society unwilling to talk with its children about love, delight, and commitment asks the *schools* to teach sex education. A society unwilling to recognize the forms of excellence that Mr. Gardner identifies asks the *schools* to teach everyone algebra. The greatest burden of the schools, as a result, is trying to find some way to teach to adequately intelligent students things that they do not want to learn.

Acting on the *Paideia* would not produce a "classless education." The *Paideia* selects a form of education traditionally associated with an academically privileged class— "education for the best"—and prescribes it for all children, regardless of home influences, individual interests, special talents, or any realistic hope that all can participate in the sort of professional life that such an education has traditionally aspired to. Even if we were to deny the existence of classes in our current society, we would inevitably produce them under the *Paideia*. In this system, *everyone* is to be judged by the standards usually applied to the academically talented. I object to this. I object as a teacher, as a parent, and as a thoughtful human being. There is more to life, more to excellence, more to success, and more to devotion than can be captured in a single intellectual model of excellence.

To provide an equal quality of education for all our children requires, first, that we hold the variety of their talents and legitimate interests to be equally valuable. This does not mean that schools should provide no common learnings. Of course the schools should teach all children to read, write, and compute. But the schools should also teach all children how to operate the technical machinery and gadgets that fill our homes and offices; to care responsibly for living things; to develop their bodies for lifelong physical grace; to obtain and convey information; to use their hands in making and finishing things; to develop their receptive capacities in the arts; to develop a commitment to service in some capacity. This sounds like an impossible list—and it is almost certainly incomplete. But the beautiful truth is that when we take all of the valuable aspects of life into consideration and when we respect all of our children's legitimate interests in our educational planning, it becomes *easier* to teach the basic skills. They become obviously necessary to the satisfaction of real problems and actual tasks. The answer is not to spend more and more time on "basics" but to revitalize the basics in a broad scheme of general education that is laid out boldly along the entire continuum of human experience.

Now, I can imagine at least some of the advocates of *Paideia* saying: But that is exactly what we mean to do; that is what education for the best has traditionally done! It provides a broad, general education that aims to liberate the human mind; it conduces to the "examined life." It . . . "Whoa up!" I'd have to say. You are still talking about an essentially abstract and bookish sort of education. Consider this: Is it not at least possible that academic talent is *per se* a somewhat specialized talent? If it is, and I believe there is evidence to support the contention, then so long as our schooling is highly "intellectualized," we have a specialized curriculum no matter how many traditional subjects we force people to take in the name of breadth. Such a program can hardly meet the criteria for "equality of quality."

3

Now, consider the second premise. Adler claims that "the shape of the best education for the best is not unknown to us." If he means by this that we know what has been provided for an intellectually and socially privileged class in the past, the claim seems reasonable. The force of his argument would then be, "Let us now give all our children what we have given these privileged few in the past." But is the traditional "education for the best" really the "best" even for our academically most able students? On what grounds is it so judged? The *Paideia* aims at an education that will enable all children to earn a living in an intelligent and responsible fashion, to function as intelligent and responsible citizens, and to make both of these things serve the purpose of leading intelligent and responsible lives—to enjoy as fully as possible all the goods that make a human life as good as it can be (p. 18).

"To achieve these three goals," Adler writes (p. 18):

> basic schooling must have for all a quality that can be best defined, *positively*, by saying that it must be general and liberal; and *negatively*, by saying that it must be nonspecialized and non-vocational.

There are at least two difficulties here. One has to do with the word "vocational" and its uses. Another is the meaning of "nonspecialized." I have already argued that the sort of abstract and bookish education recommended by the *Paideia* is itself—in spite of its internal breadth—a specialized curriculum. It is designed for those whose further education will be academic, and there is little evidence that it will promote continued learning across other fields of endeavor. One could design a "mechanical-technical" education every bit as broad (internally) as the *Paideia*'s "liberal" education (thus avoiding the rapid obsolescence of skills), and most of us would still consider it too highly specialized to be used exclusively and for all our children. One can imagine, however, several such beautifully designed curricula, equally valuable, each characterized by internal breadth, offered on equal levels and freely chosen by well-informed students. This sort of plan might realistically avoid premature specialization. Further, the freedom of choice provided seems appropriate preparation for democratic life.

In its own effort to prepare children "equally" for participation in "democracy," the *Paideia* sacrifices a first principle of democracy: In the pursuit of eventual freedom, it denies students any freedom whatsoever in the choice of their own studies.

The one-track system of public schooling that *The Paideia Proposal* advocates has the same objectives for all without exception (p. 15).

Further:

> All sidetracks, specialized courses, or elective choices must be eliminated. Allowing them
> will always lead a certain number of students to voluntarily downgrade their own education
> (p. 21).

Think what we are suggesting in making or accepting such a recommendation. Why
should electives in cooking, photography, or science fiction constitute a "downgrading" of
education? Is James Beard a failure? Is Edward Steichen? Is Ray Bradbury? Now I am not
arguing for premature specialization. I am simply pointing out what John Dewey coun-
seled again and again: Any subject freely undertaken as an occupation—as a set of tasks
requiring goal-setting, means-ends analysis, choice of appropriate tools and materials,
exercise of skills, living through the consequences, and evaluating the results—is educative.
Cooking can be approached with high intelligence and elegant cultural interests or it can
deteriorate to baking brownies and cleaning ovens: similarly, mathematics can be taught
so as to require deep reflective and intuitive thinking or it can be taught as a mindless
bag of tricks. It is not the subjects offered that make a curriculum properly a part of
education but how those subjects are taught, how they connect to the personal interests
and talents of the students who study them, and how skillfully they are laid out against the
whole continuum of human experience.

We see in this discussion another area of great disagreement between John Dewey
and the perennialists, and this involves the difficulty I mentioned concerning the word
"vocational." It is true, as Adler points out, that Dewey argued against something called
"vocational education." But Dewey was arguing against a narrow form of specialization
that tended to downgrade the participants *as persons*. He was arguing against a form of
schooling, not education at all, that labels some children fit only to do Vocation X, where
X itself may be held in disdain. More importantly, however, he wanted all children to
experience education *through* occupations or vocations more broadly construed. He said:

> A vocation signifies any form of continuous activity which renders service to others and
> engages personal powers in behalf of the accomplishment of results. (Dewey 1916, p. 319)

Dewey insisted that education could be conducted through occupations or vocations in
the important sense we are considering here. He insisted upon the organic connection
between education and personal experience and, thus, between education and contemporary social life. Students do not have to study exactly the same subject matter nor need they
be deprived of choice in order to be truly educated. Dewey spoke favorably of Plato's
fundamental principle of tailoring education to the abilities of students, but he drew back
from the hierarchical evaluation connected with this form of education, saying:

> His [Plato's] error was not in qualitative principle, but in his limited conception of the scope of
> vocations socially needed: a limitation of vision which reacted to obscure his perception of the
> infinite variety of capacities found in different individuals. (Ibid. 1916, p. 309)

Dewey wanted us to avoid two equally pernicious ideas in education: first, that education must consist of a set of prespecified material to be transmitted to everyone regardless
of personal interest: second, that education should consist of a hierarchically ordered
set of curricula—the "highest" given to the "best," the "lowest" to the "least." To provide
"equality of quality" in education for all our children requires that we start with equal

respect for their talents and aspirations and that we help them to choose wisely within the domain of their interests.

My main aim in this section has been to cast doubt on Mr. Adler's claim that "the shape of the best education for the best is not unknown to us." On the contrary. I believe that far more reflection and responsible experimentation are required before we can support such a claim.

4

I promised at the beginning of this essay to say something about the recommendations the *Paideia* makes concerning methods of instruction. Three modes of teaching are pre-scribed, and they are all useful. Each mode of teaching is connected to a mode of learning: for the acquisition of organized knowledge, didactic instruction is recommended; for the development of intellectual skills, coaching is to be employed; and for the enlargement of understanding, insight, and aesthetic appreciation, "maieutic" or Socratic methods are to be used. All three methods, properly implemented, are sound and useful, and education would take a giant step forward if teachers were skilled in each of them.

But the methods as they are described are somewhat warped by the prescribed subject matter. There is no mention of the enormous skill required of teachers in setting the environment so that children will formulate purposes and thus *seek* to acquire segments of organized knowledge. Nor is the choice of coach or the relation between coach and student mentioned. These are oversights that I need not belabor. The attitude of which I complain pervades the *Paideia*: Students are treated as "minds" to be filled equally with the same quality material. Nowhere is there proper consideration of the *persons* who are, in their essential freedom and infinite diversity, central and instrumental in their own education.

References

Mortimer J. Adler. (1982). *The Paideia Proposal*. New York: Macmillan Publishing Co., Inc.

John Dewey. (1915). *The School and Society*. Chicago: The University of Chicago Press.

John Dewey. (1916). *Democracy and Education*. New York: The Free Press.

John Dewey. "President Hutchins' Proposals to Remake Higher Education," *The Social Frontier* 3 (1937a): 103–104.

John Dewey. "The Higher Learning in America," *The Social Frontier* 3 (1937b): 167–169.

John Gardner. (1961). *Excellence: Can We Be Equal and Excellent Too?* New York: Harper.

Robert Maynard Hutchins. "Grammar, Rhetoric, and Mr. Dewey," *The Social Frontier* 3 (1937): 137–139.

18

Implementation as Mutual Adaptation: Change in Classroom Organization

Milbrey Wallin McLaughlin

Most observers believe that the educational innovations undertaken as part of the curriculum reform movement of the 1950s and early 1960s, as well as the innovations that comprised the initiatives of the "Education Decade," generally have failed to meet their objectives.[1] One explanation for these disappointments focuses on the type of innovations undertaken and points out that until recently few educators have elected to initiate innovations that require change in the traditional roles, behavior, and structures that exist within the school organization or the classroom. Instead, most innovative efforts have focused primarily on technological change, not organizational change. Many argue that without changes in the structure of the institutional setting, or the culture of the school, new practices are simply "more of the same" and are unlikely to lead to much significant change in what happens to students.

Since 1970, however, a number of educators have begun to express interest in practices that redefine the assumptions about children and learning that underlie traditional methods—new classroom practices that attempt to change the ways that students, teachers, parents, and administrators relate to each other. Encouraged and stimulated by the work of such writers as Joseph Featherstone, Charles Silberman, and William Glasser, some local schoolmen have undertaken innovations in classroom organization such as open education, multiage grouping, integrated day, differentiated staffing, and team teaching. These practices are not based on a "model" of classroom organization change to be strictly followed, but on a common set of convictions about the nature of learning and the purpose of teaching. These philosophical similarities, which can be traced to the work of the Swiss psychologist Piaget, are based on a belief that humanistic, individualized, and child-centered education requires more than incremental or marginal change in classroom organization, educational technology, or teacher behavior.

Because classroom organization projects require teachers to work out their own styles and classroom techniques within a broad philosophical framework, innovations of this type cannot be specified or packaged in advance. Thus, the very nature of these projects requires that implementation be a *mutually adaptive process* between the user and the institutional setting—that specific project goals and methods be made concrete over time by the participants themselves.

Classroom organization projects were among the local innovations examined as part of Rand's Change-Agent Study.[2] Of the 293 projects surveyed, eighty-five could be classified as classroom organization projects; five of our thirty field sites were undertaking innovation of this nature. The findings of the change-agent study suggest that the experience of these projects should be examined in some detail. At the most general level, the change study concluded that implementation—rather than educational treatment, level of resources, or type of federal funding strategy—dominates the innovative process and its outcomes. The study found that the mere adoption of a "better" practice did not automatically or invariably lead to "better" student outcomes. Initially similar technologies undergo unique alterations during the process of implementation and thus their outcomes cannot be predicted on the basis of treatment alone. Further, the process of implementation that is inherent in classroom organization projects was found to describe effective implementation generally. Specifically, the change-agent study concluded that *successful implementation is characterized by a process of mutual adaptation.*

Contrary to the assumptions underlying many change strategies and federal change policies, we found that implementation did not merely involve the direct and straightforward application of an educational technology or plan. Implementation was a dynamic organizational process that was shaped over time by interactions between project goals and methods, and the institutional setting. As such, it was neither automatic nor certain. Three different interactions characterized this highly variable process.

One, *mutual adaptation*, described successfully implemented projects. It involved modification of both the project design and changes in the institutional setting and individual participants during the course of implementation.

A second implementation process, *cooptation*, signified adaptation of the project design, but no change on the part of participants or the institutional setting. When implementation of this nature occurred, project strategies were simply modified to conform in a pro forma fashion to the traditional practices the innovation was expected to replace—either because of resistance to change or inadequate help for implementers.

The third implementation process, *nonimplementation*, described the experience of projects that either broke down during the course of implementation or were simply ignored by project participants.

Where implementation was successful, and where significant change in participant attitudes, skills and behavior occurred, implementation was characterized by a process of mutual adaptation in which project goals and methods were modified to suit the needs and interests of participants and in which participants changed to meet the requirements of the project. This finding was true even for highly technological and initially well specified projects: unless adaptations were made in the original plans or technologies, implementation tended to be superficial or symbolic and significant change in participants did not occur.

Classroom organization projects provided particularly clear illustration of the conditions and strategies that support mutual adaptation and thus successful implementation. They are especially relevant to understanding the operational implications of this change-agent study finding for policy and practice not only because mutual adaptation is intrinsic to change in classroom organization, but also because the question of institutional receptivity does not cloud the view of effective implementation strategies afforded by these projects.

The receptivity of the institutional setting to a proposed innovation varied greatly among the projects we examined—from active support to indifference to hostility. The amount of interest, commitment, and support evidenced by principal actors had a major influence on the prospects for successful project implementation. In particular, the attitudes and interest of central administrators in effect provided a "signal" to project participants as to how seriously they should take project goals and how hard they should work to achieve them. Unless participants perceived that change-agent projects represented a school and district educational priority, teachers were often unwilling to put in the extra time and emotional investment necessary for successful implementation. Similarly, the attitudes of teachers were critical. Unless teachers were motivated by professional concerns (as opposed to more tangible incentives such as extra pay or credit on the district salary scale, for example), they did not expend the extra time and energy requisite to the usually painful process of implementing an innovation.

Classroom organization projects were almost always characterized by high levels of commitment and support for their initiation, both at the district and at the building level. This is not surprising when we consider the risk and difficulty associated with these projects; it is unlikely that a district would elect to undertake a project of this nature unless they believed strongly in the educational approach and were committed to attempting the changes necessary to implement it.

In fact, classroom organization projects possess none of the features traditionally thought to encourage local decision makers to adopt a given innovation:

1. Ease of explanation and communication to others.
2. Possibility of a trial on a partial or limited basis.
3. Ease of use.
4. Congruence with existing values.
5. Obvious superiority over practices that existed previously.[3]

Innovations that focus on classroom organization are at odds with all five of these criteria. First, since there is no specific "model" to be followed, it is difficult to tell people how these approaches operate. Advocates can only offer general advice and communicate the philosophy or attitudes that underlie innovation in classroom organization and activities.

Second, although open classroom or team-teaching strategies can be implemented slowly, and can be installed in just one or two classrooms in a school, it is generally not possible to be "just a little bit" open or just a "sometime" part of a team-teaching situation. The method is based on fundamental changes which are hard to accomplish piecemeal.

Third, change in classroom organization is inherently very complex. Innovations of this nature require the learning of new attitudes, roles and behavior on the part of teachers and administrators—changes far more difficult to bring about than the learning of a new skill or gaining familiarity with a new educational technology. Classroom organization changes also typically require new arrangements of classroom space, the provision of new instructional materials, and usually new school scheduling and reporting practices.

Fourth, strategies of open education or team teaching are a radical departure from the traditional or standard practices of a school, district, or teacher. Change in classroom organization means changing deeply held attitudes and customary behavior. These projects, by attempting to change organizational structure and goals, attempt to affect the fundamental nature of the organization and are therefore basically incongruent with existing values.

Fifth, although proponents argue that humanistic, child-centered education represents a big advance, the objective evidence is ambiguous. Most evaluations of informal classrooms conclude that participating children do better on affective measures, but there is little evidence of significant cognitive differences that could confidently be attributed to open classrooms themselves. An administrator contemplating a change in classroom organization is confronted with a complicated innovation that shows no clear advantage over existing practices—at least in the ways that often matter most to school boards, voters, and anxious parents.

Thus, given the complex, unspecified, and inherently difficult nature of these projects, they were rarely initiated without the active support and commitment of district officials and participants. Consequently, the insufficient institutional support that negatively influenced implementation in other projects and so made it difficult to obtain a clear picture of the strategic factors affecting project implementation (i.e., did disappointing implementation result from a lack of enthusiasm or from inadequate training?) generally was not a problem for classroom organization projects. Variance in the implementation outcome of classroom organization projects, consequently, can be attributed in large measure to the project's particular implementation strategy.

For classroom organization projects, as for other change-agent projects, *institutional receptivity was a necessary but not a sufficient condition for successful implementation.* Unless project implementation strategies were chosen that allowed institutional support to be engaged and mutual adaptation to occur, project implementation foundered. A project's particular implementation strategy is the result of many local choices about how best to implement project goals and methods. What seems to be the most effective thing to do? What is possible given project constraints? What process fits best with local needs and conditions? Decisions about the type and amount of training, the planning necessary, and project participants are examples of such choices. They effectively define how a proposed innovation is put into practice. Implementation strategies are distinguishable from project treatment. That is, the educational method chosen for a project (i.e., team teaching, diagnostic/prescriptive reading) is different from the strategies selected for implementing the method. No two reading projects, for example, employ quite the same process or strategy for achieving their almost identical goals.

Implementation Strategy

Each project employs its own combination of strategies that effectively defines its *implementation strategy.* Thus, in addition to identifying especially effective component strategies, it is meaningful to examine how and why the various individual strategies interact with each other to form a "successful" implementation strategy and to promote mutual adaptation. The experience of classroom organization projects suggests at least three specific strategies that are particularly critical and that work together to form an adaptive implementation strategy: local materials development; ongoing and concrete staff training; iterative, on-line planning combined with regular and frequent staff meetings.

Local Material Development

In almost all of the classroom organization projects, the staff spent a substantial amount of time developing materials to use in the project classrooms. These materials either were developed from scratch or put together from bits of commercially-developed materials. Although these activities were sometimes undertaken because the staff felt they couldn't locate appropriate commercial materials, the real contribution lay not so much in "better pedagogical products" but in providing the staff with a sense of involvement and an opportunity to "learn-by-doing." Working together to develop materials for the project gave the staff a sense of pride in its own accomplishments, a sense of "ownership" in the project. It also broke down the traditional isolation of the classroom teacher and provided a sense of "professionalism" and cooperation not usually available in the school setting. But even more important, materials development provided an opportunity for users to think through the concepts which underlay the project, in practical, operational terms—an opportunity to engage in experience-based learning. Although such "reinvention of the wheel" may not appear efficient in the short run, it appears to be a critical part of the individual learning and development necessary for significant change.

Staff Training

All the classroom organization projects we visited included both formal and informal, pre-service and in-service staff training. For example, one project's formal training took place in a two-week summer session before the project began; its informal development activities had been extensive, providing for almost constant interaction among project staff. Almost all of these projects provided preservice training that included observations in operating classrooms. One open classroom project staff even participated in a trip to observe British infant schools. All projects also conducted regular workshops throughout the first three years of project implementation.

One-shot training, or training heavily concentrated at the beginning of the project, was not effective. Although such training designs have the virtues of efficiency and lower cost, they ignore the critical fact that project implementors cannot know what it is they need to know until project operations are well underway. This is generally true for all innovative efforts, but particularly salient in the case of amorphous classroom organization projects. There is just so much that a would-be implementor can be taught or can understand until problems have arisen in the course of project implementation, and solutions must be devised. Training programs that attempt to be comprehensive and cover all contingencies at the outset are bound to miss their mark and also to be less than meaningful to project participants.

Project staffs agreed that staff development and training activities were a critical part of successful implementation. They also agreed that some kinds of training activities were more useful than others. With few exceptions, visits by outside consultants and other outside "experts" were not considered particularly helpful. Teachers in all the change-agent projects we examined complained that most visiting consultants could not relate to the particular problems they were experiencing in their classrooms, or that their advice was too abstract to be helpful. Where outside experts were considered useful, their participation was concrete and involved working closely with project teachers in their classrooms or in "hands-on" workshops. However, it was unusual for outside consultants to have either the time or the inclination to provide assistance in other than a lecture format. Such expert delivery of "truth and knowledge," however, was seldom meaningful to participants, and foreclosed more powerful learning opportunities.

The sessions participants thought most useful were regular meetings of the project staff with local resource personnel in which ideas were shared, problems discussed, and support given. Materials development often provided the focus for these concrete, how-to-do-it training sessions. Visits to other schools implementing similar projects were also considered helpful; the teachers felt that seeing a similar program in operation for just a few hours was worth much more than several days of consultants delivering talks on philosophy.

Some commentators on the outcomes of planned change contend that where innovations fail, particularly innovations in classroom organization, they fail because their planners overlooked the "resocialization" of teachers. Even willing teachers have to go through such a *learning (and unlearning) process* in order to develop new attitudes, behaviors, and skills for a radically new role. Concrete, inquiry-based training activities scheduled regularly over the course of project implementation provide a means for this developmental process to occur.

Adaptive Planning and Staff Meetings

Because of their lack of prior specification, almost all classroom organization projects engaged in adaptive or on-line planning. Planning of this nature is a continuous process that establishes channels of communication and solicits input from a representative group of project participants. It provides a forum for reassessing project goals and activities, monitoring project activities, and modifying practices in light of institutional and project demands. Planning of this nature has a firm base in project and institutional reality; thus issues can be identified and solutions determined before problems become crises. Just as one-shot training activities can neither anticipate the information needs of implementors over time nor be comprehensible to trainees in the absence of direct experience with particular problems, neither can highly structured planning activities that attempt extensive prior specification of operational procedures and objectives effectively address all contingencies in advance or foresee intervening local conditions. Often problems arise and events occur during the course of implementation that are unexpected and unpredictable. As a result, project plans drawn up at one point in time may or may not be relevant to project operations at a later date. Planning activities that are ongoing, adaptive, and congruent with the nature of the project and the changing institutional setting are better able to respond to these factors.

Frequent and regular staff meetings were often used as a way to carry out project planning on a continuous basis. Projects that made a point of scheduling staff meetings on a frequent and regular basis had fewer serious implementation problems and greater staff cohesiveness. Staff meetings not only provided a vehicle for articulating and working out problems, but they also gave staff a chance to communicate project information, share ideas, and provide each other with encouragement and support.

Finding time for these meetings or planning activities was a problem that some districts were able to solve and others were not. One classroom organization project, for example, arranged time off one afternoon a week for meetings. Project participants almost universally singled out these meetings as one of the most important factors contributing to project success. Such time to share ideas and problems was, in the view of all classroom organization respondents, especially important in the rough and exhausting first year of the project. Where meetings were infrequent or irregular, morale was noticeably lower and reports of friction within the project were higher.

Past research on implementation is almost unanimous in citing "unanticipated events" and "lack of feedback networks" as serious problems during project implementation.[4] Routinized and frequent staff meetings combined with ongoing, iterative planning can serve to institutionalize an effective project feedback structure, as well as provide mechanisms that can deal with the unanticipated events that are certain to occur.

Two Open Classroom Projects[5]

The critical role that such elements of an adaptive implementation strategy play in project implementation and outcomes is best illustrated by describing the experiences of two open classroom projects that were similar in almost every respect—resources, support and interest, target group background characteristics—but differed significantly in implementation strategy and in implementation outcome. The Eastown open education project had extensive and ongoing staff training, spent a lot of staff time and energy on materials development, arranged for staff to meet regularly, and engaged in regular formative evaluation. This project was also well implemented, ran smoothly, and met its objectives. In fact, this project received validation as a national exemplary project in its second year—a year before it was theoretically eligible.

The very similar Seaside project, in contrast, did not employ such an implementation strategy. Because of late funding notification, there was little time for advance planning or preservice training; project teachers were asked to implement a concept that they supported but that few had actually seen in operation. The planning that was done subsequently was mainly administrative in nature. The in-service training was spotty and was offered almost totally by "outside experts." The Seaside project did no materials development but instead tried to convert traditional materials to the goals of open education. This project has not only been less successful than hoped, but in our judgment, its central percepts and objectives are yet to be fully implemented. Teacher classroom behavior exhibits only a very superficial understanding of the rhetoric of open education; our observations led to the conclusion that teachers have yet to understand the practical implications of the tenets of open education, and have made only symbolic use of the more standard methods. For example, in many of the classrooms we visited, although the teacher had set up interest centers, these centers had not been changed in six or seven months. Thus they failed to serve their purpose of providing a continually changing menu of material for students. Teachers in the Seaside project had dutifully rearranged their classroom furniture and acquired rugs—as befits the open classroom—but even in this changed physical space, they continued to conduct their classes in a traditional manner. A student teacher commented that many of the teachers in this school conducted their class in the small groups or individualized manner appropriate to this educational philosophy only on visitors' day. In our judgment, many of the teachers in the school honestly wanted to implement open education, and many sincerely believed that they had accomplished that goal. But, in our view, implementation in this project was only *pro forma*—largely because of the absence of implementation strategies that would allow learning, growth, and development or mutual adaptation to take place.

Summary

In summary, overcoming the challenges and problems inherent to innovations in classroom organization contributes positively and significantly to their effective implementation. The amorphous yet highly complex nature of classroom organization projects tends to *require* or *dictate* an adaptive implementation strategy that permits goals and methods to be reassessed, refined and made explicit during the course of implementation, and that fosters "learning-by-doing."

The adaptive implementation strategies defined by effectively implemented local projects were comprised of three common and critical components—local materials development; concrete, ongoing training; on-line or adaptive planning and regular, frequent staff meetings. These elements worked together in concert to promote effective implementation. Where any one component was missing or weak, other elements of the overall implementation strategy were less effective than they might be. A most important characteristic these component strategies hold in common is their support of individual learning and development—development most appropriate to the user and to the institutional setting. The experience of classroom organization projects underlines the fact that the process of mutual adaptation is fundamentally a learning process.

General Implications

It is useful to consider the implications of the classroom organization projects and the general change-agent study findings in the context of the ongoing debate about the "implementation problem."

The change-agent study is not the first research to point to the primary importance of implementation in determining special project outcomes.[6] A number of researchers and theoreticians have come to recognize what many practitioners have been saying all along: Educational technology is not self-winding. Adoption of a promising educational technology is only the beginning of a variable, uncertain, and inherently local process. It is the unpredictability and inconsistency of this process that have generated what has come to be called the "implementation problem."

There is general agreement that a major component of the "implementation problem" has to do with inadequate operational specificity.[7] There is debate concerning *who* should make project operations more specific, *how* it can be done, and *when* specificity should be introduced.

One approach prescribes more specificity prior to local initiation. Adherents of this solution ask that project planners and developers spell out concrete and detailed steps or procedures that they believe will lead to successful project implementation. It is hoped that increased prior operational specificity will minimize the necessity for individual users to make decisions or choices about appropriate project strategies or resources as the project is implemented. This essentially technological approach to the "implementation problem"— exemplified at the extreme by "teacher-proof" packages—aims at standardizing project implementation across project sites. It is expected that user adherence to such standardized and well-specified implementation procedures will reduce local variability as project plans are translated into practice and so lead to predictable and consistent project outcomes, regardless of the institutional setting in which the project is implemented.

A second approach takes an organizational rather than a technological perspective and focuses primarily on the development of the user, rather than on the prior development of the educational treatment or product. This approach assumes that local variability is not only inevitable, but a good thing if a proposed innovation is to result in significant and sustained change in the local setting. This approach also assumes that the individual learning requisite to successful implementation can only occur through user involvement and direct experience in working through project percepts. Instead of providing packages which foreclose the necessity for individuals to make decisions and choices during the course of project implementation, proponents of this perspective maintain that implementation strategies should be devised that give users the skills, information, and learning opportunities necessary to make these choices effectively. This approach assumes that specificity of project methods and goals should evolve over time in response to local conditions and individual needs. This second solution to the "implementation problem," in short, assumes that mutual adaptation is the key to effective implementation.

The findings of the change-agent study strongly support this second perspective and its general approach to the "implementation problem." We found that *all* successfully implemented projects in our study went through a process of mutual adaptation to some extent. Even fairly straightforward, essentially technological projects were either adapted in some way to the institutional setting—or they were only superficially implemented and were not expected to remain in place after the withdrawal of federal funds. Where attempts were made to take short cuts in this process—out of concern for efficiency, for example—such efforts to speed up project implementation usually led to project breakdown or to only *pro forma* installation of project methods.

Viewed in the context of the debate over the "implementation problem," these findings have a number of implications for change-agent policies and practice. At the most general level, they suggest that adaptation, rather than standardization, is a more realistic and fruitful objective for policy makers and practitioners hoping to bring about significant change in local educational practice. Such an objective would imply change-agent policies that focused on implementation, not simply on adoption—policies that were concerned primarily with the development of users and support of adaptive implementation strategies. Specifically, the classroom organization projects suggest answers to the strategic issues of "who, how, and when" innovative efforts should be made operationally explicit, and how user development can be promoted.

Furthermore, the classroom organization projects, as well as other innovative efforts examined as part of the change-agent study, imply that the would-be innovator also must be willing to learn and be motivated by professional concerns and interests if development is to take place. Thus, change-agent policies would be well advised not only to address the user needs that are part of the implementation process *per se*, but also to consider the developmental needs of local educational personnel that are requisite to the initial interest and support necessary for change-agent efforts. It is not surprising that teachers or administrators who have not been outside their district for a number of years are less eager to change—or confident in their abilities to do so—than planners would hope. Internships and training grants for administrators, or travel money and released time for teachers to participate in innovative practices in other districts, are examples of strategies that may enable educational personnel to expand their horizons and generate enthusiasm for change.

The findings of the change-agent study and the experience of the classroom organization projects also have implications for the dissemination and expansion of "successful" change-agent projects. They suggest, for example, that an effective dissemination strategy should have more to do with people who could provide concrete "hands-on" assistance than with the transcription and transferral of specific successful project operations. It is somewhat ironic that staff of the "developer-demonstrator" projects who last year pointed to the central importance of local materials development are, in their dissemination year, packaging their project strategies and materials without a backward glance. Indeed, the change-agent findings concerning the importance of mutual adaptation and "learning by doing" raise a number of critical questions for educational planners and disseminators. For example, to what extent can this developmental process be telescoped as project accomplishments are replicated in a new setting? What kinds of "learning" or advice can be transferred? If adaptation is characteristic of effective implementation and significant change, what constitutes the "core" or essential ingredients of a successful project?

District administrators hoping to expand successful project operations face similar issues. Our findings suggest that—even within the same district—replication and expansion of "success" will require that new adopters replicate, in large measure, the developmental process of the original site. While there are, of course, general "lessons" that original participants can transfer to would-be innovators, there is much that the new user will have to learn himself.

In summary, the experience of classroom organization projects together with the general change-agent study findings suggest that adaptation should be seen as an appropriate goal for practice and policy—not an undesirable aberration. These findings suggest a shift in change-agent policies from a primary focus on the *delivery system* to an emphasis on the *deliverer*. An important lesson that can be derived from the change-agent study is that unless the developmental needs of the users are addressed, and unless project methods are modified to suit the needs of the user and the institutional setting, the promises of new technologies are likely to be unfulfilled. Although the implementation strategy that classroom organization projects suggest will be effective represent "reinvention of the wheel" to a great extent—an unpalatable prospect for program developers, fiscal planners, and impatient educational policy makers—the experience of these projects counsels us that a most important aspect of significant change is not so much the "wheel" or the educational technology but the process of "reinvention" or individual development. Though new education technologies are undoubtedly important to improved practices, they cannot be effective unless they are thoroughly understood and integrated by the user. The evidence we have seen strongly suggests that the developmental process mutual adaptation is the best way to ensure that change efforts are not superficial, trivial, or transitory.

Notes

1. This essay is a revision of a paper presented at the March 1975 American Educational Research Association meeting in Washington, D.C. It is based on the data collected for The Rand Corporation study of federal programs supporting educational change. However, the interpretation and speculations offered in this paper are my sole responsibility and do not necessarily represent the views of The Rand Corporation, or the study's sponsor, the United States Office of Education, or my colleague Paul Berman, who has been so helpful in formulating this paper.

2. The conceptual model, methodology, and results of the first year of the Rand Change-Agent Study are reported in four volumes: Paul Berman and Milbrey Wallin McLaughlin. *Federal Programs Supporting Educational Change, Vol. I: A Model of Educational Change.* Santa Monica, Calif.: Rand Corporation, R-1589/1-HEW, April 1975; Paul Berman and Edward W. Pauly, *Federal Programs Supporting Educational Change, Vol. II: Factors Affecting Change Agent Projects.* Santa Monica, Calif.: Rand Corporation, R-1589/2-HEW, April 1975; Peter W. Greenwood, Dale Mann, and Milbrey Wallin McLaughlin. *Federal Programs Supporting Educational Change, Vol. III: The Process of Change.* Santa Monica, Calif.: Rand Corporation, R-1589/3-HEW, April 1975; and Paul Berman and Milbrey Wallin McLaughlin. *Federal Programs Supporting Educational Change, Vol. IV: The Findings in Review.* Santa Monica, Calif.: Rand Corporation, R-1589/4-HEW, April 1975. Four technical appendices to Volume III describe in detail the federal program management approach, state education agency participation, and case studies for each of the programs in the study.

3. E. Rogers and F. Shoemaker. *Communication of Innovation.* New York, N.Y.: Free Press, 1962.

4. See for example, W. W. Charters et al. *Contrasts in the Process of Planning Change of the School's Institutional Organization, Program 20.* Eugene, Ore.: Center for the Advanced Study of Educational Administration, 1973; O. Carlson et al. *Change Processes in the Public Schools.* Eugene, Ore.: Center for the Advanced Study of Educational Administration, 1971; M. Fullan and A. Pomfret. *Review of Research on Curriculum Implementation.* Toronto, Ont.: The Ontario Institute for Studies in Education, April 1975; M. Shipman. *Inside a Curriculum Project.* London, Eng.: Methuen, 1974; N.C. Gross et al. *Implementing Organizational Innovations.* New York, N.Y.:

Basic Books, 1971; and L.M. Smith and P.M. Keith. *Anatomy of Educational Innovations: An Organizational Analysis of an Elementary School.* New York, N.Y.: John Wiley, 1971.

5. Project and site names are fictitious.

6. See especially the analysis of this debate in Fullan and Pomfret, *op. cit.* See also E.C. Hargrove. *The Missing Link: The Study of the Implementation of Social Policy.* Washington, D.C.: The Urban Institute, 1975, paper 797–1; and W. Williams, "Implementation Analysis and Assessment," Public Policy Paper No.8, Institute of Governmental Research, University of Washington, February 1975.

7. See Fullan and Pomfret, *op. cit.*

19

Controlling the Work of Teachers

Michael W. Apple

1986 from Book "Teacher + Texts"

Proletarianization: Class and Gender

An examination of changes in class composition over the past two decades points out something quite dramatically. The process of proletarianization has had a large and consistent effect. There has been a systematic tendency for those positions with relatively little control over their labor process to expand during this time period. At the same time, there was a decline in positions with high levels of autonomy.[1]

This should not surprise us. In fact, it would be unusual if this did not occur, especially now. In a time of general stagnation and of crises in accumulation and legitimation, we should expect that there will also be attempts to further rationalize managerial structures and increase the pressure to proletarianize the labor process. This pressure is not inconsequential to educators, both in regard to the kinds of positions students will find available (or not available) after completing (or not completing) schooling, and also in regard to the very conditions of working within education itself. The labor of what might be called "semi-autonomous employees" will certainly feel the impact of this. Given the fiscal crisis of the state, this impact will be felt more directly among state employees such as teachers as well. One should expect to see a rapid growth of plans and pressures for the rationalization of administration and labor within the state itself.[2] This is one of the times when one's expectations will not be disappointed.

In earlier work, I argued that teachers have been involved in a long but now steadily increasing restructuring of their jobs. I claimed that they were more and more faced with the prospect of being de-skilled because of the encroachment of technical control procedures into the curriculum in schools. The integration together of management systems, reductive behaviorally based curricula, pre-specified teaching "competencies" and procedures and student responses, and pre- and post-testing, was leading to a loss of control and a separation of conception from execution. In sum, the labor process of teaching was becoming susceptible to processes similar to those that led to the proletarianization of many other blue-, pink-, and white-collar jobs. I suggested that this restructuring of teaching had important implications given the contradictory class location of teachers.[3]

When I say that teachers have a contradictory class location, I am *not* implying that they are by definition within the middle classes, or that they are in an ambiguous position somehow "between" classes. Instead, along with Wright, I am saying that it is wise to think of them as located simultaneously in two classes. They thus share the interests of both the petty bourgeoisie and the working class.[4] Hence, when there is a fiscal crisis in which many teachers are faced with worsening working conditions, layoffs, and even months without being paid—as has been the case in a number of urban areas in the United States—and when their labor is restructured so that they lose control, it is possible that these contradictory interests will move closer to those of other workers and people of color who have historically been faced with the use of similar procedures by capital and the state.[5]

Yet, teachers are not only classed actors. They are gendered actors as well—something that is too often neglected by investigators. This is a significant omission. A striking conclusion is evident from the analyses of proletarianization. In every occupational category, *women* are more apt to be proletarianized than men. This could be because of sexist practices of recruitment and promotion, the general tendency to care less about the conditions under which women labor, the way capital has historically colonized patriarchal relations, the historical relation between teaching and domesticity, and so on. Whatever the reason, it is clear that a given position may be more or less proletarianized depending on its relationship to the sexual division of labor.[6]

In the United States, it is estimated that over 90 percent of women's (paid) work falls into four basic categories: (1) employment in "peripheral" manufacturing industries and retail trades, and considerably now in the expanding but low-paid service sector of the economy; (2) clerical work; (3) health and education; and (4) domestic service. Most women in, say, the United States and the United Kingdom are concentrated in either the lowest-paid positions in these areas or at the bottom of the middle-pay grades when there has been some mobility.[7] One commentator puts it both bluntly and honestly: "The evidence of discrimination against women in the labour market is considerable and reading it is a wearing experience."[8]

This pattern is, of course, largely reproduced within education. Even given the years of struggle by progressive women and men, the figures—most of which will be quite familiar to many of you—are depressing. While the overwhelming majority of school teachers are women (a figure that becomes even higher in the primary and elementary schools), many more men are heads or principals of primary and elementary schools, despite the proportion of women teachers.[9] As the vertical segregation of the workforce increased, this proportion actually increased in inequality. In the United States in 1928, women accounted for 55 percent of the elementary school principalships. Today, with nearly 90 percent of the teaching force in elementary schools being women, they account for only 20 percent of principals.[10] This pattern has strong historical roots—roots that cannot be separated from the larger structures of class and patriarchy outside the school.

In this chapter, I shall want to claim that unless we see the connections between these two dynamics—class and gender—we cannot understand the history of and current attempts at rationalizing education or the roots and effects of proletarianization on teaching itself. Not all teaching can be unpacked by examining it as a labor process or as a class phenomenon, though as I have tried to demonstrate in some of my previous work much of it is made clearer when we integrate it into theories of and changes in class position and the labor process. Neither can all of teaching be understood as totally related to patriarchy, though why it is structured the way it is is due in very large part to the history of male dominance and gender struggles,[11] a history I shall discuss in considerably more detail in the next chapter. The two dynamics of class and gender (with race, of course) are not reducible to each other, but intertwine, work off, and codetermine the terrain on which each operates. It is at the intersection of these two dynamics that one can begin to unravel some of the reasons why procedures for rationalizing the work of teachers have evolved. As we shall see, the ultimate effects of these procedures, with the loss of control that accom-

[handwritten: Capital — any produced thing that can enhance a person's power to perform commercially useful work]

panies them, can bear in important ways on how we think about the "reform" of teaching and curriculum and the state's role in it.

Academic Knowledge and Curricular Control

[handwritten margin: an important relationship]

So far I have made a number of general claims about the relationship between proletarianization and patriarchy in the constitution of teaching. I want to go on to suggest ways we can begin to see this relationship in operation. Some sense of the state's role in sponsoring changes in curricular and teaching practice in the recent past is essential here.

The fact that schools have tended to be largely organized around male leadership and female teachers is simply that—a social fact—unless one realizes that this means that educational authority relations have been formally patriarchal. As in the home and the office, male dominance is there; but teachers—like wives, mothers, clerical workers, and other women engaged in paid and unpaid labor—have carved out spheres of power and control in their long struggle to gain some autonomy. This autonomy only becomes a problem for capital and the state when what education is for needs revision.

[handwritten margin: autonomy of teachers & problem for reform]

To take one example outside of education: in offices clerical work is in the process of being radically transformed with the introduction of word-processing technologies, video display terminals, and so on. Traditional forms of control—ones usually based on the dominance of the male boss—are being altered. Technical control, where one's work is de-skilled and intensified by the "impersonal" machinery in the office, has made significant inroads. While certainly not eliminating patriarchal domination, it has in fact provided a major shift in the terrain on which it operates. Capital has found more efficient modes of control than overt patriarchal authority.[12]

[handwritten margin: ? mean by Capital]

Similar changes have occurred in schools. In a time when the needs of industry for technical knowledge and technically trained personnel intersect with the growth in power of the new petty bourgeoisie (those people in technical and middle management positions) and the reassertion of academic dominance in the curriculum, pressures for curricular reform can become quite intense. Patience over traditional forms of control will lessen.

Patriarchal relations of power, therefore, organized around the male principal's relations to a largely female teaching staff, will not necessarily be progressive for capital or the state. While they once served certain educational and ideological ends, they are less efficient than what has been required recently. Gender relations must be partly subverted to create a more efficient institution. Techniques of control drawn from industry will tend to replace older styles which depended more on a sexual division of power and labor within the school itself.

[handwritten margin: > A's call for more math + science. Here no fear. imp. quote]

Perhaps an example will document the long and continuing history of these altered relationships. In the United States, for instance, during the late 1950s and the 1960s, there was rather strong pressure from academics, capital, and the state to reinstitute academic disciplinary knowledge as the most "legitimate" content for schools. In the areas of mathematics and science especially, it was feared that "real" knowledge was not being taught. A good deal of effort was given to producing curricular programs that were systematic, based on rigorous academic foundations, and, in the elementary school material in particular, were teacher-proof. Everything a teacher was to deal with was provided and prespecified. The cost of the development of such programs was socialized by the state (i.e., subsidized by tax dollars). The chance of their being adopted by local school districts was heightened by the National Defense Education Act, which reimbursed school districts for a large portion of the purchase cost. That is, if a school system purchased new material of this type and the technology which supported it, the relative cost was minimal. The bulk of the expense was repaid by the state. Hence, it would have seemed irrational not to buy the material—irrational in two ways: (1) the chance of getting new curricula at low cost is clearly a rational management decision within industrial logic, and (2) given its imprimatur of science and efficiency, the material itself seemed rational.

All of this is no doubt familiar to anyone who lived through the early years of this movement, and who sees the later, somewhat less powerful, effects it had in, say, England and elsewhere. Yet this is not only the history of increasing state sponsorship of and state intervention in teaching and curriculum development and adoption. *It is the history of the state, in concert with capital and a largely male academic body of consultants and developers, intervening at the level of practice into the work of a largely female workforce.* That is, ideologies of gender, of sex-appropriate knowledge, need to be seen as having possibly played a significant part here. The loss of control and rationalization of one's work forms part of a state/class/gender "couplet" that works its way out in the following ways. Mathematics and science teaching are seen as abysmal. "We" need rapid change in our economic responsiveness and in "our" emerging ideological and economic struggle with the Soviet Union.[13] Teachers (who just happen to be almost all women at the elementary level) aren't sophisticated enough. Former ways of curricular and teaching control are neither powerful nor efficient enough for this situation. Provide both teacher-proof materials and financial incentives to make certain that these sets of curricula actually reach the classroom.

One must integrate an analysis of the state, changes in the labor process of state employees, and the politics of patriarchy to comprehend the dynamics of this history of curriculum. It is not a random fact that one of the most massive attempts at rationalizing curricula and teaching had as its target a group of teachers who were largely women. I believe that one cannot separate out the fact of a sexual division of labor and the vision of who has what kinds of competence from the state's attempts to revamp and make more "productive" its educational apparatus. In so doing, by seeing these structurally generated relationships, we can begin to open up a door to understanding part of the reasons behind what happened to these curriculum materials when they were in fact introduced.

As numerous studies have shown, when the material was introduced into many schools, it was not unusual for the "new" math and "new" science to be taught in much the same manner as the old math and old science. It was altered so that it fitted into both the existing regularities of the institution and the prior practices that had proven successful in teaching.[14] It is probably wise to see this as not only the result of a slow-to-change bureaucracy or a group of consistently conservative administrators and teachers. Rather, I think it may be just as helpful to think of this more structurally in labor process and gender terms. The supposed immobility of the institution, its lack of significant change in the face of the initial onslaught of such material, is at least partly tied to the resistances of a female workforce against external incursions into the practices they had evolved over years of labor. It is in fact more than a little similar to the history of ways in which other women employees in the state and industry have reacted to past attempts at altering traditional modes of control of their own labor.[15]

A Note on the State

The points I have just made about the resistances of the people who actually work in the institutions, about women teachers confronted by external control, may seem straightforward. However, these basic arguments have very important implications not only about how we think about the history of curriculum reform and control, but more importantly about how many educators and political theorists have pictured the larger issue of the state's role in supporting capital. In the historical example I gave, state intervention on the side of capital and for "defense" is in opposition to other positions within the state itself. The day-to-day interests of one occupational position (teachers) contradict the larger interests of the state in efficient production.[16] Because of instances such as this, it is probably inappropriate to see the state as a homogeneous entity, standing above day-to-day conflicts.

Since schools *are* state apparatuses, we should expect them to be under intense pressure to act in certain ways, especially in times of both fiscal and ideological crises. Even so, this does not mean that people employed in them are passive followers of policies laid down from above. As Roger Dale has noted:

> Teachers are not merely "state functionaries" but do have some degree of autonomy, and [this] autonomy will not necessarily be used to further the proclaimed ends of the state apparatus. Rather than those who work there fitting themselves to the requirements of the institutions, there are a number of very important ways in which the institution has to take account of the interests of the employees and fit itself to them. It is here, for instance, that we may begin to look for the sources of the alleged inertia of educational systems and schools, that is to say what appears as inertia is not some immutable characteristic of bureaucracies but is due to various groups within them having more immediate interests than the pursuit of the organization's goals.[17]

Thus, the "mere" fact that the state wishes to find "more efficient" ways to organize teaching does not guarantee that this will be acted upon by teachers who have a long history of work practices and self-organization once the doors to their rooms are closed. As we shall see in a moment, however, the fact that it is primarily women employees who have faced these forms of rationalization has meant that the actual outcomes of these attempts to retain control of one's pedagogic work can lead to rather contradictory ideological results.

Legitimating Intervention

While these initial attempts at rationalizing teaching and curricula did not always produce the results that were anticipated by their academic, industrial, and governmental proponents, they did other things that were, and are, of considerable import. The situation is actually quite similar to the effects of the use of Tayloristic management strategies in industry. As a management technology for de-skilling workers and separating conception from execution, Taylorism was less than fully successful. It often generated slowdowns and strikes, exacerbated tensions, and created new forms of overt and covert resistance. Yet, its ultimate effect was to legitimate a particular ideology of management and control both to the public and to employers and workers.[18] Even though it did not succeed as a set of techniques, it ushered in and finally brought acceptance of a larger body of ideological practices to de-skill pink-, white-, and blue-collar workers and to rationalize and intensify their labor.

This too was one of the lasting consequences of these earlier curriculum "reform" movements. While they also did not completely transform the practice of teaching, while patriarchal relations of authority which paradoxically "gave" teachers some measure of freedom were not totally replaced by more efficient forms of organizing and controlling their day-to-day activity, they legitimated both new forms of control and greater state intervention using industrial and technical models and brought about a new generation of more sophisticated attempts at overcoming teacher "resistance." Thus, this new generation of techniques that are being instituted in so many states in the United States and elsewhere currently—from systematic integration of testing, behavioral goals and curriculum, competency-based instruction and prepackaged curricula, to management by objectives, and so forth—has not sprung out of nowhere, but, like the history of Taylorism, has grown out of the failures, partial successes, and resistances that accompanied the earlier approaches to control. As I have claimed, this is not only the history of the control of state employees to bring about efficient teaching, but a rearticulation of the dynamics of patriarchy and class in one site, the school.

Intensification and Teaching

In the first half of this chapter, we paid particular attention to the historical dynamics operating in the schools. I would like now to focus on more current outgrowths of this earlier history of rationalization and control.

The earlier attempts by state bureaucrats, industry, and others to gain greater control of day-to-day classroom operation and its "output" did not die. They have had more than a decade to grow, experiment, and become more sophisticated. While gender will be less visible in the current strategies (in much the same way that the growth of management strategies in industry slowly covered the real basis of power in factories and offices), as we shall see it will be present in important ways once we go beneath the surface to look at changes in the labor process of teaching, how some teachers respond to current strategies, and how they interpret their own work.

Since in previous work I have focused on a number of elements through which curricula and teaching are controlled—on the aspects of de-skilling and re-skilling of labor, and on the separation of conception from execution in teachers' work—here I shall want to concentrate more on something which accompanies these historically evolving processes: what I shall call *intensification*. First, let me discuss this process rather generally.

Intensification "represents one of the most tangible ways in which the work privileges of educational workers are eroded." It has many symptoms, from the trivial to the more complex—ranging from being allowed no time at all even to go to the bathroom, have a cup of coffee or relax, to having a total absence of time to keep up with one's field. We can see intensification most visibly in mental labor in the chronic sense of work overload that has escalated over time.[19]

This has had a number of notable effects outside of education. In the newspaper industry, for example, because of financial pressures and the increased need for efficiency in operation, reporters have had their story quotas raised substantially. The possibility of doing non-routine investigative reporting, hence, is lessened considerably. This has had the effects of increasing their dependence "on prescheduled, preformulated events" in which they rely more and more on bureaucratic rules and surface accounts of news provided by official spokespersons.[20]

Intensification also acts to destroy the sociability of non-manual workers. Leisure and self-direction tend to be lost. Community tends to be redefined around the needs of the labor process. And, since both time and interaction are at a premium, the risk of isolation grows.[21]

Intensification by itself "does not necessarily reduce the range of skills applied or possessed by educated workers." It may, in fact, cause them to "cut corners" by eliminating what seems to be inconsequential to the task at hand. This has occurred with doctors, for instance; many examinations now concentrate only on what seems critical. The chronic work overload has also caused some non-manual workers to learn or relearn skills. The financial crisis has led to shortages of personnel in a number of areas. Thus, a more diverse array of jobs must be done that used to be covered by other people—people who simply do not exist within the institution any more.[22]

While this leads to a broader range of skills having to be learned or relearned, it can lead to something mentioned earlier—the loss of time to keep up with one's field. That is, what might be called "skill diversification" has a contradiction built into it. It is also part of a dynamic of intellectual de-skilling[23] in which mental workers are cut off from their own fields and again must rely even more heavily on ideas and processes provided by "experts."

While these effects are important, one of the most significant impacts of intensification may be in reducing the *quality*, not the quantity, of service provided to people. While, traditionally, "human service professionals" have equated doing good work with the interests of their clients or students, intensification tends to contradict the traditional interest in work well done, in both a quality product and process.[24]

As I shall document, a number of these aspects of intensification are increasingly found in teaching, especially in those schools which are dominated by behaviorally prespecified curricula, repeated testing, and strict and reductive accountability systems. (The fact that these kinds of curricula, tests, and systems are now more and more being mandated should make us even more cautious.) To make this clear, I want to draw on some data from recent research on the effects of these procedures on the structure of teachers' work.

I have argued here and elsewhere that there has been a rapid growth in curricular "systems" in the United States—one that is now spreading to other countries.[25] These curricula have goals, strategies, tests, textbooks, worksheets, appropriate student response, etc., integrated together. In schools where this is taken seriously,[26] what impact has this been having? We have evidence from a number of ethnographic studies of the labor process of teaching to be able to begin to point to what is going on. For example, in one school where the curriculum was heavily based on a sequential list of behaviorally defined competencies and objectives, multiple worksheets on skills which the students were to complete, with pre-tests to measure "readiness" and "skill level" and post-tests to measure "achievement" that were given often and regularly, the intensification of teacher work is quite visible.

In this school, such curricular practice required that teachers spend a large portion of their time evaluating student "mastery" of each of the various objectives and recording the results of these multiple evaluations for later discussions with parents or decisions on whether or not the student could "go on" to another set of skill-based worksheets. The recording and evaluation made it imperative that a significant amount of time be spent on administrative arrangements for giving tests, and then grading them, organizing lessons (which were quite often standardized or pre-packaged), and so on. One also found teachers busy with these tasks before and after school and, very often, during their lunch hour. Teachers began to come in at 7:15 in the morning and leave at 4:30 in the afternoon. Two hours' more work at home each night was not unusual, as well.[27]

Just as I noted in my general discussion of the effects of intensification, here too getting done became the norm. There is so much to do that simply accomplishing what is specified requires nearly all of one's efforts. "The challenge of the work day (or week) was to accomplish the required number of objectives." As one teacher put it, "I just want to get this done. I don't have time to be creative or imaginative."[28] We should not blame the teacher here. In mathematics, for example, teachers typically had to spend nearly half of the allotted time correcting and recording the worksheets the students completed each day.[29] The situation seemed to continually push the workload of these teachers up. Thus, even though they tended to complain at times about the long hours, the intensification, the time spent on technical tasks such as grading and record-keeping, the amount of time spent doing these things grew inexorably.[30]

Few of the teachers were passive in the face of this, and I shall return to this point shortly. Even though the elements of curricular control were effective in structuring major aspects of their practice, teachers often responded in a variety of ways. They subtly changed the pre-specified objectives because they couldn't see their relevance. They tried to resist the intensification as well: first by trying to find some space during the day for doing slower-paced activities; and second by actually calling a halt temporarily to the frequent pre- and post-tests, worksheets and the like and merely having "relaxed discussions with students on topics of their own choosing."[31]

This, of course, is quite contradictory. While these examples document the active role of teachers in attempting to win back some time, to resist the loss of control of their own work, and to slow down the pace at which students and they were to proceed, the way this is done is not necessarily very powerful. In these instances, time was fought for simply to relax, if only for a few minutes. The process of control, the increasing technicization and intensification of the teaching act, the proletarianization of their work—all of this was an absent presence. It was misrecognized as a symbol of their increased *professionalism*.

Profession and Gender

We cannot understand why teachers interpreted what was happening to them as the professionalization of their jobs unless we see how the ideology of professionalism works as part of both a class and gender dynamic in education. For example, while reliance on "experts" to create curricular and teaching goals and procedures grew in this kind of situation, a wider range of technical skills had to be mastered by these teachers. Becoming adept at grading all those tests and worksheets quickly, deciding on which specific skill group to put a student in, learning how to "efficiently manage" the many different groups based on the tests, and more, all became important skills. As responsibility for designing one's own curricula and one's own teaching decreased, responsibility over technical and management concerns came to the fore.

Professionalism and increased responsibility tend to go hand in hand here. The situation is more than a little paradoxical. There is so much responsibility placed on teachers for technical decisions that they actually work harder. They feel that since they constantly make decisions based on the outcomes of these multiple pre- and post-tests, the longer hours are evidence of their enlarged professional status. Perhaps a quote will be helpful here.

> One reason the work is harder is we have a lot of responsibility in decision-making. There's no reason not to work hard, because you want to be darn sure that those decisions you made are something that might be helpful . . . So you work hard to be successful at these decisions so you look like a good decision maker.[32]

It is here that the concept of professionalism seemed to have one of its major impacts. Since the teachers thought of themselves as being more professional to the extent that they employed technical criteria and tests, they also basically accepted the longer hours and the intensification of their work that accompanied the program. To do a "good job," you needed to be as "rational" as possible.[33]

We should not scoff at these preceptions on the part of the teachers. First, the very notion of professionalization has been important not only to teachers in general but to women in particular. It has provided a contradictory yet powerful barrier against interference by the state; and just as critically, in the struggle over male dominance, it has been part of a complex attempt to win equal treatment, pay, and control over the day-to-day work of a largely female labor force.[34]

Second, while we need to remember that professionalism as a social goal grew at the same time and was justified by the "project and practice of the market professions during the liberal phase of capitalism,"[35] the strategy of professionalism has historically been used to set up "effective defenses against proletarianization."[36] Given what I said earlier about the strong relationship between the sexual division of labor and proletarianization, it would be not only ahistorical but perhaps even a bit sexist as well wholly to blame teachers for employing a professional strategy.

Hence, the emphasis on increasing professionalism by learning new management skills and so on today and its partial acceptance by elementary school teachers can best be understood not only as an attempt by state bureaucrats to de-skill and re-skill teachers, but as part of a much larger historical dynamic in which gender politics have played a significant role.

Yet the acceptance of certain aspects of intensification is not only due to the history of how professionalism has worked in class and gender struggles. It is heightened by a number of internal factors as well. For example, in the school to which I referred earlier, while a number of teachers believed that the rigorous specification of objectives and teaching procedures actually helped free them to become more creative, it was clear that subtle pressures existed to meet the priorities established by the specified objectives. Even though in some subject areas they had a choice of how they were to meet the objectives, the objectives themselves usually remained unchallenged. The perceived interests of parents and their establishment of routines helped assure this. Here is one teacher's assessment of how this occurs.

> Occasionally you're looking at the end of the book at what the unit is going to be, these are the goals that you have to obtain, that the children are going to be tested on. That may affect your teaching in some way in that you may by-pass other learning experiences simply to obtain the goal. These goals are going home to parents. It's a terrible thing to do but parents like to see 90's and 100's rather than 60's on skills.[37]

In discussing the use of the skills program, another teacher points out the other element besides parents that was mentioned: "It's got a manual and you follow the manual and the kids know the directions and it gets to be routine."[38] Coupled with perceived parental pressure and the sheer power of routine is something else: the employment practices surrounding teaching. In many schools, one of the main criteria for the hiring of teachers is their agreement with the overall curricular, pedagogic, and evaluative framework which organizes the day-to-day practice. Such was the case in this study. Beyond this, however, even though some investigators have found that people who tend to react negatively to these pre-packaged, standardized, and systematized curricular forms often leave teaching,[39] given the depressed market for new teachers in many areas that have severe fiscal problems and the conscious decision by some school districts to hire fewer teachers and increase class size, fewer jobs are available right now. The option of leaving or even protesting seems romantic, though current teacher shortages may change this.

Gendered Resistance

At this point in my argument it would be wise to return to a claim I made earlier. Teachers have not stood by and accepted all this. In fact, our perception that they have been and are passive in the face of these pressures may reflect our own tacit beliefs in the relative passivity of women workers. This would be an unfortunate characterization. Historically, for example, as I shall demonstrate in the following chapter, in England and the United States the picture of women teachers as non-militant and middle-class in orientation is not wholly accurate. There have been periods of exceptional militancy and clear political commitment.[40] However, militancy and political commitment are but one set of ways in which control is contested. It is also fought for on the job itself in subtle and even "unconscious" (one might say "cultural") ways—ways which will be contradictory, as we shall now see. Once again, gender will become of prime importance.

In my own interviews with teachers it has become clear that many of them feel rather uncomfortable with their role as "managers." Many others are less than happy with the emphasis on programs which they often feel "lock us into a rigid system." Here the resistance to rationalization and the loss of historically important forms of self-control of one's labor has very contradictory outcomes, partly as a result of sexual divisions in society. Thus, a teacher using a curricular program in reading and language arts that is very highly structured and test-based states:

> While it's really important for the children to learn these skills, right now it's more important for them to learn to feel good about themselves. That's my role, getting them to feel good. That's more important than tests right now.

Another primary grade teacher, confronted by a rationalized curriculum program where students move from classroom to classroom for "skill groups," put it this way:

> Kids are too young to travel between classrooms all the time. They need someone there that they can always go to, who's close to them. Anyway, subjects are less important than their feelings.

In these quotes, discomfort with the administrative design is certainly evident. There is a clear sense that something is being lost. Yet the discomfort with the process is coded around the traditional distinctions that organize the sexual division of labor both within the family and in the larger society. The *woman's* sphere is that of providing emotional security, caring for feelings, and so on.

Do not misconstrue my points here. Teachers should care for the feelings and emotional security of their students. However, while these teachers rightly fight on a cultural level against what they perceive to be the ill-effects of their loss of control and both the division and the intensification of their labor, they do so at the expense of reinstituting categories that partly reproduce other divisions that have historically grown out of patriarchal relations.[41]

This raises a significant point: much of the recent literature on the role of the school in the reproduction of class, sex, and race domination has directed our attention to the existence of resistances. This realization was not inconsequential and was certainly needed to enable us to go further than the overly deterministic models of explanation that had been employed to unpack what schools do. However, at the same time, this literature has run the risk of romanticizing such resistances. The fact that they exist does not guarantee that they will necessarily be progressive at each and every moment. Only by uncovering the contradictions within and between the dynamics of the labor process *and* gender can we begin to see what effects such resistances may actually have.[42]

Labor, Gender, and Teaching

I have paid particular attention here to the effects of the restructuring of teachers' work in the school. I have claimed that we simply cannot understand what is happening to teaching and curriculum without placing it in a framework which integrates class (and its accompanying process of proletarianization) and gender together. The impact of de-skilling and intensification occurs on a terrain and in an institution that is populated primarily by women teachers and male administrators—a fact that needs to be recognized as being historically articulated with both the social and sexual divisions of labor, knowledge, and power in our society.

Yet, since elementary school teachers are primarily women, we must also look beyond the school to get a fuller comprehension of the impact of these changes and the responses of teachers to them. We need to remember something in this regard: women teachers often work in *two* sites—the school and then the home. Given the modification of patriarchal relations and the intensification of labor in teaching, what impact might this have outside the school? If so much time is spent on technical tasks at school and at home, is it possible that less time may be available for domestic labor in the home? Other people in the family may have to take up the slack, thereby partly challenging the sexual division of household labor. On the other hand, the intensification of teachers' work, and the work overload that may result from it, may have exactly the opposite effect. It may increase the exploitation of unpaid work in the home by merely adding more to do without initially altering conditions in the family. In either case, such conditions will lead to changes, tensions, and conflicts outside of the sphere where women engage in paid work.[43] It is worth thinking very carefully about the effects that working in one site will have on the other. The fact that this dual exploitation exists is quite consequential in another way. It opens up possible new avenues for political intervention by socialist feminists, I believe. By showing the relationship between the home and the job and the intensification growing in both, this may provide for a way of demonstrating the ties between both of these spheres and between class and gender.

Thinking about such issues has actually provided the organizing framework for my analysis. The key to my investigation in this chapter has been reflecting about changes in *how* work is organized over time and, just as significantly, *who* is doing the work. A clearer sense of both of these—how and who—can enable us to see similarities and differences between the world of work in our factories and offices and that of semi-autonomous state employees such as teachers.

What does this mean? Historically the major struggles labor engaged in at the beginning of the use of systematic management concerned resistance to speed-ups.[44] That is, the intensification of production, the pressure to produce more work in a given period, led to all kinds of interesting responses. Craft workers, for example, often simply refused to do more. Pressure was put on co-workers who went too fast (or too slow). Breaks were extended. Tools and machines suddenly developed "problems."

Teachers—given their contradictory class location, their relationship to the history of patriarchal control and the sexual division of labor, and the actual conditions of their work—will find it difficult to respond in the same way. They are usually isolated during their work, and perhaps more so now given the intensification of their labor. Further, machinery and tools in the usual sense of these terms are not visible.[45] And just as importantly, the perception of oneself as professional means that the pressures of intensification and the loss of control will be coded and dealt with in ways that are specific to that workplace and its own history. The ultimate effects will be very contradictory.

In essence, therefore, I am arguing that—while similar labor processes may be working through institutions within industry and the state which have a major impact on women's paid work—these processes will be responded to differently by different classes and class segments. The ideology of professional discretion will lead to a partial acceptance of, say, intensification by teachers on one level, and will generate a different kind of resistance— one specific to the actual work circumstances in which they have historically found themselves. The fact that these changes in the labor process of teaching occur on a terrain that has been a site of patriarchal relations plays a major part here.

My arguments here are not to be construed as some form of "deficit theory." Women have won and will continue to win important victories, as I will demonstrate in the following chapter. Their action on a cultural level, though not overtly politicized, will not always lead to the results I have shown here. Rather, my points concern the inherently *contradictory* nature of teachers' responses. These responses are victories and losses at one and the same time. The important question is how the elements of good sense embodied in these teachers' lived culture can be reorganized in specifically feminist ways—ways that maintain the utter importance of caring and human relationships without at the same time reproducing other elements on that patriarchal terrain.

I do not want to suggest that once you have realized the place of teaching in the sexual division of labor, you have thoroughly understood de-skilling and re-skilling, intensification and loss of control, or the countervailing pressures of professionalism and proletarianization in teachers' work. Obviously, this is a very complex issue in which the internal histories of bureaucracies, the larger role of the state in a time of economic and ideological crisis,[46] and the local political economy and power relations of each school play a part. What I do want to argue quite strongly, however, is the utter import of gendered labor as a constitutive aspect of the way management and the state have approached teaching and curricular control. Gendered labor is the absent presence behind all of our work. How it became such an absent presence is the topic of the next chapter.

Notes

1. Erik Olin Wright and Joachim Singelmann, "The Proletarianization of Work in American Capitalism," University of Wisconsin-Madison Institute for Research on Poverty, Discussion Paper No. 647–81, 1981, p. 38.
2. *Ibid.*, p. 43. See also Michael W. Apple, "State, Bureaucracy and Curriculum Control," *Curriculum Inquiry* 11 (Winter 1981), 379–388. For a discussion that rejects part of the argument about proletarianization, see Michael Kelly, *White Collar Proletariat* (Boston and London: Routledge & Kegan Paul, 1980).

3. De-skilling, technical control and proletarianization are both technical and political concepts. They signify a complex historical process in which the control of labor has altered—one in which the skills employees have developed over many years on the job are broken down into atomistic units, redefined, and then appropriated by management to enhance both efficiency and control of the labor process. In the process, workers' control over timing, over defining appropriate ways to do a task, and over criteria that establish acceptable performance are all slowly taken on as the prerogatives of management personnel who are usually divorced from the actual place in which the work is carried out. De-skilling, then, often leads to the atrophy of valuable skills that workers possessed, since there is no longer any "need" for them in the redefined labor process. The loss of control or proletarianization of a job is hence part of a larger dynamic in the separation of conception from execution and the continuing attempts by management in the state and industry to rationalize as many aspects of one's labor as possible. I have discussed this in considerably more detail in Michael W. Apple, *Education and Power* (Boston and London: Routledge & Kegan Paul, 1982). See also Richard Edwards, *Contested Terrain* (New York: Basic Books, 1979), and Michael Burawoy, *Manufacturing Consent* (Chicago: University of Chicago Press, 1979).

4. Erik Olin Wright, "Class and Occupation," *Theory and Society* 9 (No. 2, 1980), 182–183.

5. Apple, *Education and Power*.

6. Wright, "Class and Occupation," 188. Clearly race plays an important part here too. See Michael Reich, *Racial Inequality* (Princeton: Princeton University Press, 1981), and Mario Barrera, *Race and Class in the Southwest: A Theory of Racial Inequality* (Notre Dame: Notre Dame University Press, 1979).

7. Janet Holland, "Women's Occupational Choice: The Impact of Sexual Divisions in Society," Stockholm Institute of Education, Department of Educational Research, Reports on Education and Psychology, 1980, p. 7.

8. *Ibid.*, p. 27.

9. *Ibid.*, p. 45.

10. Gail Kelly and Ann Nihlen, "Schooling and the Reproduction of Patriarchy," in Michael W. Apple (ed.), *Cultural and Economic Reproduction in Education: Essays on Class, Ideology and the State* (Boston and London: Routledge & Kegan Paul, 1982), pp. 167–168. One cannot fully understand the history of the relationship between women and teaching without tracing out the complex connections among the family, domesticity, child care, and the policies of and employment within the state. See especially, Miriam David, *The State, the Family and Education* (Boston and London: Routledge & Kegan Paul, 1980).

11. For an interesting history of the relationship among class, gender and teaching, see June Purvis, "Women and Teaching in the Nineteenth Century," in Roger Dale, Geoff Esland, Ross Fergusson, and Madeleine MacDonald (eds.), *Education and the State, Vol. 2: Politics, Patriarchy and Practice* (Barcombe, Sussex: Falmer Press, 1981), pp. 359–375. I am wary of using a concept such as patriarchy, since its very status is problematic. As Rowbotham notes, "Patriarchy suggests a fatalistic submission which allows no space for the complexities of women's defiance" (quoted in Tricia Davis, "Stand by Your Men? Feminism and Socialism in the Eighties,") in George Bridges and Rosalind Brunt (eds.), *Silver Linings: Some Strategies for the Eighties* (London: Lawrence & Wishart, 1981), p.14. A history of women's day-to-day struggles falsifies any such theory of "fatalistic submission."

12. Jane Barker and Hazel Downing, "Word Processing and the Transformation of the Patriarchal Relations of Control in the Office," in Dale, Esland, Fergusson and MacDonald (eds.), *Education and the State, Vol. 2*, pp. 229–256. See also the discussion of de-skilling in Edwards, *Contested Terrain*.

13. For an analysis of how such language has been employed by the state, see Michael W. Apple, "Common Curriculum and State Control," *Discourse* 2 (No. 4, 1982), 1–10, and James Donald, "Green Paper: Noise of a Crisis," *Screen Education* 30 (Spring 1979), 13–49.

14. See, for example, Seymour Sarason, *The Culture of the School and the Problem of Change* (Boston: Allyn & Bacon, 1971).

15. Apple, *Education and Power*, and Susan Porter Benson, "The Clerking Sisterhood: Rationalization and the Work Culture of Sales Women in American Department Stores," Radical America 12 (March/April 1978), 41–55.

16. Roger Dale's discussion of contradictions between elements within the state is very interesting in this regard. See Roger Dale, "The State and Education: Some Theoretical Approaches," in *The State and Politics of Education* (Milton Keynes: The Open University Press, E353, Block 1, Part 2, Units 3–4, 1981), and Roger Dale, "Education and the Capitalist State: Contributions and Contradictions," in Apple (ed.), *Cultural and Economic Reproduction in Education*, pp. 127–161.

17. Dale, "The State and Education," p. 13.

18. I have examined this in greater detail in Apple, *Education and Power*. See as well Edwards, *Contested Terrain*, and Daniel Clawson, *Bureaucracy and the Labor Process* (New York: Monthly Review Press, 1980).

19. Magali Larson, "Proletarianization and Educated Labor," *Theory and Society* 9 (No. 2, 1980), 166.

20. *Ibid.*, 167.

21. *Ibid.* Larson points out that these problems related to intensification are often central grievances even among doctors.

22. *Ibid.*, 168.

23. *Ibid.*, 169.

24. *Ibid.*, 167.

25. Apple, *Education and Power*. See also Carol Buswell, "Pedagogic Change and Social Change," *British Journal of Sociology of Education* 1 (No. 3, 1980), 293–306.

26. The question of just how seriously schools take this, the variability of their response, is not unimportant. As Popkewitz, Tabachnick and Wehlage demonstrate in their interesting ethnographic study of school reform, not all schools use materials of this sort alike. See Thomas Popkewitz, B. Robert Tabachnick, and Gary Wehlage, *The Myth of Educational Reform* (Madison: University of Wisconsin Press, 1982).

27. This section of my analysis is based largely on research carried out by Andrew Gitlin. See Andrew Gitlin, "Understanding the Work of Teachers," unpublished Ph.D. dissertation, University of Wisconsin, Madison, 1980.

28. *Ibid.*, 208.

29. *Ibid.*

30. *Ibid.*, 197.

31. *Ibid.*, 237.

32. *Ibid.*, 125.

33. *Ibid.*, 197.

34. This is similar to the use of liberal discourse by popular classes to struggle for personal rights against established property rights over the past one hundred years. See Herbert Gintis, "Communication and Politics," *Socialist Review* 10 (March/June 1980), 189–232. The process is partly paradoxical, however. Attempts to professionalize do give women a weapon against some aspects of patriarchal relations; yet, there is a clear connection between being counted as a profession and being populated largely by men. In fact, one of the things that are very visible historically is the relationship between the sexual division of labor and professionalization. There has been a decided tendency for full professional status to be granted only when an activity is "dominated by men—in both management and the ranks." Jeff Hearn, "Notes on Patriarchy: Professionalization and the Semi-Professions," *Sociology* 16 (May 1982), 195.

35. Magali Larson, "Monopolies of Competence and Bourgeois Ideology," in Dale, Esland, Fergusson, and MacDonald (eds.), *Education and the State, Vol. 2,* p. 332.

36. Larson, "Proletarianization and Educated Labor," p. 152. Historically, class as well as gender dynamics have been quite important here, and recent research documents this clearly. As Barry Bergen has shown in his recent study of the growth of the relationship between class and gender in the professionalization of elementary school teaching in England, a large portion of elementary school teachers were both women and of the working class. As he puts it:

> Teaching, except at the university level, was not highly regarded by the middle class to begin with, and teaching in the elementary schools was the lowest rung on the teaching ladder. The middle class did not view elementary teaching as a means of upward mobility. But the elementary school teachers seemed to view themselves as having risen above the working class, if not having reached the middle class. . . . Clearly, the varied attempts of elementary teachers to professionalize constitute an attempt to raise their class position from an interstitial one between the working class and middle class to the solidly middle class position of a profession.

> See Barry H. Bergen, "Only a Schoolmaster: Gender, Class, and the Effort to Professionalize Elementary Teaching in England, 1870–1910," *History of Education Quarterly* 22 (Spring 1982), 10.

37. Gitlin, "Understanding the Work of Teachers," p. 128.

38. *Ibid.*

39. Martin Lawn and Jenny Ozga, "Teachers: Professionalism, Class and Proletarianization," unpublished paper, The Open University, Milton Keynes, 1981, p. 15 in mimeo.

40. Jenny Ozga, "The Politics of the Teaching Profession," in *The Politics of Schools and Teaching* (Milton Keynes: The Open University Press, E353, Block 6, Units 14–15, 1981), p. 24.

41. We need to be very careful here, of course. Certainly, not all teachers will respond in this way. That some will not points to the partial and important fracturing of dominant gender and class ideologies in ways that signal significant alterations in the consciousness of teachers. Whether these alterations are always progressive is an interesting question. Also, as Connell has shown, such "feminine" approaches are often important counterbalances to masculinist forms of authority in schools. See R. W. Connell, *Teachers' Work* (Boston and London: George Allen & Unwin, 1985).

42. See Henry Giroux, "Theories of Reproduction and Resistance in the New Sociology of Education: A Critical Analysis," *Harvard Educational Review* 53 (August 1983), 257–293, even though he is not specifically interested in gender relations.

43. While I have focused here on the possible impacts in the school and the home on women teachers, a similar analysis needs to be done on men. We need to ask how masculinist ideologies work through male teachers and administrators. Furthermore, what changes, conflicts, and tensions will evolve, say, in the patriarchal authority structures of the home given the intensification of men's labor? I would like to thank Sandra Acker for raising this

critically important point. For an analysis of changes in women's labor in the home, see Susan Strasser, *Never Done: A History of American Housework* (New York: Pantheon, 1982).

44. Clawson, *Bureaucracy and the Labor Process*, pp. 152–153.

45. In addition, Connell makes the interesting point that since teachers' work has no identifiable object that it "produces," it can be intensified nearly indefinitely. See Connell, *Teachers' Work*, p. 86.

46. Apple, *Education and Power*, and Manuel Castells, *The Economic Crisis and American Society* (Princeton: Princeton University Press, 1980).

1992

educational Foundation Report wash D.C

20

How Schools Shortchange Girls: Three Perspectives on Curriculum

American Association of University Women (AAUW)

The Formal Curriculum

Corriculum as a tool (Philip Jackson)

The formal curriculum is the central message-giving instrument of the school. It creates images of self and the world for all students. The curriculum can strengthen or decrease student motivation for engagement, effort, growth, and development through the messages it delivers to students about themselves and the world.

Grades

Students spend more hours of the day in academic classes than in any other activity. The chief subject areas today are basically the same as they were at the turn of the century, albeit with some changes in name: English (or language arts), history (or social studies), mathematics, science, foreign (or second) language, arts, and physical education. Accreditation of students for further education or employment depends more on grades given for curricular work in these areas than on any other formal measure.

changing lenses

Despite the importance of curriculum, its actual content received scant attention in national reports on education and education restructuring in the late 1980s.[1] These reports found student achievement unsatisfactory, but very few questioned whether curriculum content might in fact be counterproductive to student achievement. The reports suggest that levels of literacy, numeracy, and commitment to life-long learning are not satisfactory for either girls or boys in our society. Improving the situation for girls can also improve it for boys, for when one looks carefully at girls' dilemmas, boys' dilemmas are seen from new perspectives.

Yet in 138 articles on educational reform that appeared in nine prominent educational journals between 1983 and 1987, less than 1 percent of the text addressed sex equity. Only one article discussed curriculum and instruction as they relate to sex equity.[2] A 1990 survey commissioned by the National Education Association revealed that even among programs sponsored by organizations and institutions concerned with equity in education, only three national professional development programs for teachers focused on gender and race in English and social studies curriculum content.[3]

Research on Curriculum

Since the early 1970s, many studies have surveyed instructional materials for sex bias.[4] Published in 1975, *Dick and Jane As Victims: Sex Stereotyping in Children's Readers* set a pattern for line-by-line examination of the messages about girls and boys delivered by texts, examples, illustrations, and thematic organization of material in everything from basal readers to science textbooks.[5] In 1971 a study of thirteen popular U.S. history textbooks revealed that material on women comprised no more than 1 percent of any text, and that women's lives were trivialized, distorted, or omitted altogether.[6] Studies from the late 1980s reveal that although sexism has decreased in some elementary school texts and basal readers, the problems persist, especially at the secondary school level, in terms of what is considered important enough to study.[7]

A 1989 study of book-length works taught in high school English courses reports that, in a national sample of public, independent, and Catholic schools, the ten books assigned most frequently included only one written by a woman and none by members of minority groups.[8] This research, which used studies from 1963 and 1907 as a base line, concludes that "the lists of most frequently required books and authors are dominated by white males, with little change in overall balance from similar lists 25 or 80 years ago."[9]

During the late 1970s and '80s, experiments with more inclusive school curricula were aided by the rapid development of scholarly work and courses in black studies, ethnic studies, and women's studies in colleges and universities. Publications of the Council on Interracial Books for Children (founded in 1966), The Feminist Press (founded in 1970), and the federally funded Women's Educational Equity Program (started in 1974) inspired many teachers to develop more inclusive reading lists and assignments that draw on students' lives.

What effects did the revised curricula have on students? A 1980 review of research on how books influence children cited twenty-three studies that demonstrated that books do transmit values to young readers, that multicultural readings produce markedly more favorable attitudes toward nondominant groups than do all-white curricula, that academic achievement for all students was positively correlated with use of nonsexist and multicultural curriculum materials, and that sex-role stereotyping was reduced in those students whose curriculum portrayed females and males in nonstereotypical roles.[10]

During the 1980s, federal support for research and action on sex equity and race equity dropped sharply.[11] But many individual teachers, librarians, authors, and local or state school authorities continued a variety of efforts to lessen stereotyping and omission, or expand and democratize the curriculum.[12]

Virtually all textbook publishers now have guidelines for nonsexist language. Unfortunately, not all insist that authors follow them.[13] Change in textbooks is observable but not striking. Research on high school social studies texts reveals that while women are more often included, they are likely to be the usual "famous women," or women in protest movements. Rarely is there dual and balanced treatment of women and men, and seldom are women's perspectives and cultures presented on their own terms.[14]

Researchers at a 1990 conference reported that even texts designed to fit within the current California guidelines on gender and race equity for textbook adoption showed subtle language bias, neglect of scholarship on women, omission of women as developers of history and initiators of events, and absence of women from accounts of technological developments.[15] An informal survey of twenty U.S. history textbooks compiled each year from 1984 to 1989 found a gradual but steady shift away from an overwhelming emphasis on laws, wars, and control over territory and public policy, toward an emphasis on people's daily lives in many kinds of circumstances.[16]

The books, however, continued to maintain the abstract, disengaged tone that was characteristic of the earlier texts. The recommended assignments still relied heavily on debate techniques in which students were asked to develop an argument defending a single point of view. Few assignments offered students an opportunity to reflect on a genuine variety of perspectives or to consider feelings as well as actions.[17]

Conceptualizations of Equity in the Curriculum

Side by side with research on gender and the curriculum came various ways of conceptualizing and categorizing what is meant by gender and race equity in curriculum content. Recognizing elements of bias was an important first step. Building on earlier efforts, including work by Martha Matthews and Shirley McCune at the National Foundation for the Improvement of Education, leaders of workshops sponsored by the National Council of Teachers of Foreign Languages in 1984 listed six common forms of sex bias in instructional materials: *exclusion* of girls, *stereotyping* of members of both sexes, *subordination or degradation* of girls, *isolation* of materials on women, *superficiality* of attention to contemporary issues or social problems, and *cultural inaccuracy*, through which most of the people active in a culture are excluded from view.[18] The Coalition of Women in German has monitored textbooks using this checklist for several years and reports significant changes in texts.[19]

In 1990, after a review of more than 100 sex- and race-equity programs identified further markers of bias in the classroom, the National Education Association developed a checklist specifying eleven kinds of sex bias. The "overt and subtle behaviors" it listed include: double standards for males and females, condescension, tokenism, denial of achieved status or authority, backlash against women who succeed in improving their status, and divide-and-conquer strategies that praise individuals as better than others in their ethnic or gender group.[20]

Unfortunately, checklists on bias, prejudice, and discrimination can sometimes hurt the very groups they are meant to help by assigning them the status of "victims." In a provocative essay, "Curriculum As Window and Mirror," Emily Style compares the curriculum to an architectural structure that schools build around students.[21] Ideally, the curriculum provides each student with both windows out onto the experiences of others and mirrors of her or his own reality and validity. But for most students, the present curriculum provides many windows and few mirrors.

Teachers themselves may recall few mirrors. For the last eleven years, teachers joining a large faculty-development project have been asked, "What did you study about women in high school?" More than half initially respond, "Nothing." Some recall a heroine, one or two historical figures, a few goddesses or saints. Marie Curie is the only female scientist who has been mentioned in ten years of this survey.[22] Many women as well as men are surprised at their answers, and surprised to realize how little they themselves are teaching about women and girls. Questions about cultural diversity draw similar responses. Virtually all teachers polled recall feeling a distance between their own lives and what was portrayed in the formal curriculum.

Curriculum researcher Gretchen Wilbur states that gender-fair curriculum has six attributes. It acknowledges and affirms *variation*, i.e., similarities and differences among and within groups of people. It is *inclusive*, allowing both females and males to find and identify positively with messages about themselves. It is *accurate*, presenting information that is data-based, verifiable, and able to withstand critical analysis. It is *affirmative*, acknowledging and valuing the worth of individuals and groups. It is *representative*, balancing multiple perspectives. And, finally, it is *integrated*, weaving together the experiences, needs, and interests of both males and females.[23]

Wilbur maintains that so far no major curriculum-reform efforts have used explicitly gender-fair approaches. For example, the National Council of Teachers of Mathematics has developed new mathematics standards that shift the emphasis of curriculum from computational skills to mastery of concepts and processes.[24] The new standards advocate (1) conceptual orientation, (2) active involvement physically and mentally, (3) thinking, reasoning, and problem solving, (4) application, (5) broad range of content, and (6) use of calculators.[25] Wilbur states that, if implemented effectively, this approach will fulfill three out of the six criteria for gender-fair content: variation, accuracy, and representation. However, there is no assurance that the curriculum will be inclusive, affirming, or integrated.

Currently, science-curriculum-reform efforts under Project 2061 of the American Association for the Advancement of Science describe equity as the central organizing principle; however, the materials produced to date send contradictory messages. For example, while acknowledging that scientific discoveries have been made around the world, the new science materials refer specifically to only European scientific history and the usual "great men." So far, women are no more visible in Project 2061 than in standard science-curriculum materials.[26]

Wilbur categorizes many attempts to design gender-fair courses as *pullout* curricula, which target a "problem" population (for example, pregnant teenagers or persons with disabilities), or *fragmented* curricula, which add units on "women's issues" to the main curriculum. Such approaches, she maintains, fall short of genuinely gender-fair integration of women into central course content.

These and other kinds of corrective programs have been noted by other educators. James Banks identifies four ways in which ethnic content has been integrated into the curriculum since the 1960s. He describes these ways, or "levels," as follows.

Level 1: The Contributions Approach	Focuses on heroes, holidays, and discrete cultural elements.
Level 2: The Additive Approach	Content, concepts, themes, and perspectives are added to the curriculum without changing its structure.
Level 3: The Transformation Approach	The structure of the curriculum is changed to enable students to view concepts, issues, events, and themes from the perspectives of diverse ethnic and cultural groups.
Level 4: The Social Action Approach	Students make decisions on important social issues and take actions to help solve them.[27]

In another typology, Peggy McIntosh identifies five interactive phases of curricular and personal change that she observed in educators trying to teach more inclusively than they were themselves taught.[28] The following analysis, which uses history as an example, applies to all subject areas. McIntosh describes Phase I as "Womanless and All-White History." Phase II is "Exceptional Women and Persons of Color in History," but only considered from the conventional perspective of, for instance, military, political, or publicly acknowledged leaders. Phase III she terms the "Issues Curriculum," treating "Women and People of Color as Problems, Anomalies, Absences, or Victims in History." Phases I, II, and III have a vertical axis of "either/or thinking" that views winning and losing as the only alternatives. An important conceptual and emotional shift occurs in Phase IV, which she labels "Women's Lives or the Lives of People of Color *As* History." In Phase IV we see, for the first time, the cyclical nature of daily life, the making and mending of the social fabric, which was projected onto "lowercaste" people. Phase IV features lateral and plural thinking, sees "vertical" thinking as simply one version of thinking, and encourages all students to "make textbooks of their lives."[29] This phase, when interactively explored with the other phases, makes possible the eventual reconstruction of Phase V, "History Redefined and Reconstructed to Include Us All."

Many school subjects, as presently taught, fall within the general descriptions of Phases I and II. In the upper grades especially, the curriculum narrows and definitions of knowing take on gender-specific and culture-specific qualities associated with Anglo-European male values.[30] For example, current events and civics curricula, which take up topics from the news media, tend to focus, like their sources, on news as controversy and conflict. Much of the daily texture of life is ignored in most current-events classes.[31]

Debate clubs, usually located at the boundary of the formal curriculum as an extracurricular activity, take for granted the
definition of the citizen in debate clu
psychologist Carol Gilligan names "th
bilities) than to "the ethos of care"
connections and avoid damage).[32]

Over the last forty years, most educa
the curriculum serve a useful purpose.
alternatives is difficult. They are view
especially in preparation for standardiz
individual subject areas. Increasingly,
testing agencies themselves are ackno
ability not only to describe concepts
discipline-based courses, while providi
do this.

Changing the curriculum in any s
resistance. A recent study commissione
several key barriers to gender equit
reluctance to be singled out as having cultural or gender experience that does not fit the assumed norms; parents' suspicions about unfamiliar curricula; teachers' lack of training on multicultural and gender-neutral goals and techniques; unwillingness to commit funds for teachers to participate in curriculum-change efforts.[33]

School systems often lack in-service funds and energy to provide new opportunities for teachers. Tracy Kidder's noted study of a year in the life of a fourth-grade teacher, *Among Schoolchildren*, notes that the teacher uses twenty-year-old curriculum guides.[34]

Arthur Applebee, author of the noted *Study of Book-Length Works Taught in High School English Courses*, says that twenty years of consciousness raising and resource development have not changed the basic curriculum because teachers have not had the time and support to familiarize themselves with new materials. He recommends preservice course work in schools of education, in-service workshops, and departmental discussion groups to give teachers enough familiarity with alternative materials so that they will be comfortable in finding their own ways to introduce new works into their classes.[35] The restructuring of schools should acknowledge that curricular design and revision are central—not peripheral—to teachers' work with students.

The Multicultural Debate

Age old Ques.

The most important impediment to gender-fair and multicultural curricula may be inherited views of what education is and whom it should serve. For example, when it became clear that New York's schools were not serving the population well, New York Commissioner of Education Thomas Sobol created a committee for the review and development of Social Studies curricula in the schools. The committee's report is a clear commitment to curricular principles of democracy, diversity, economic and social justice, globalism, ecological balance, ethics and values, and the individual and society.[36] It recommends that curriculum and teaching methods be more inclusive and respectful of diversity. The report has created a furor in the New York media, reflecting the larger debate going on throughout the country. Critics have called Ethnic Studies and Women's Studies "political," as if a curriculum that leaves women out altogether is not also "political." Multicultural work has been termed "divisive" without recognizing that an exclusively white male curriculum is divisive when it ignores the contributions others make to society. Critics who insist that students must focus on our "common heritage" appear to overlook the experiences of Native Americans as well as the immigrant history of the rest of the population, which makes diversity one of the key elements of the "common" heritage of the United States.

In a democracy, schools must address the educational needs of all students. Each student should find herself or himself reflected in the curriculum. When this happens, students learn and grow.

relates back to Jane Addams

Girls, Self-Esteem, and the Curriculum

Researchers have puzzled over the drop in girls' self-esteem as they go through school, even though they do as well as boys on many standardized measures and get better grades. Teacher trainer Cathy Nelson attributes this drop in self-esteem to the negative messages delivered to girls by school curricula.[37] Students sit in classes that, day in and day out, deliver the message that women's lives count for less than men's. Historian Linda Kerbez suggests a plausible connection between falling self-esteem and curricular omission and bias. "Lowered self-esteem is a perfectly reasonable conclusion if one has been subtly instructed that what people like oneself have done in the world has not been important and is not worth studying."[38] There is no social science research to document cause and effect in this matter, but educators must take more responsibility for understanding that the curriculum is the central message-giving instrument of the school.

The Classroom as Curriculum

ideaf dialogue here

Students can learn as much from what they experience in school as they can from the formal content of classroom assignments. Classroom interactions, both with the teacher and other students, are critical components of education. These interactions shape a school. They determine in large measure whether or not a school becomes a community: a place where girls and boys can learn to value themselves and others, where both the rights and the responsibilities of citizens are fostered.

back to Bobbit p 15

Teacher-Student Interactions

Whether one looks at preschool classrooms or university lecture halls, at female teachers or male teachers, research spanning the past twenty years consistently reveals that males receive more teacher attention than do females.[1] In preschool classrooms boys receive more instructional time, more hugs, and more teacher attention.[2] The pattern persists through elementary school and high school. One reason is that boys demand more attention. Researchers David and Myra Sadker have studied these patterns for many years. They report that boys in one study of elementary and middle school students called out answers eight times more often than girls did. When boys called out, the typical teacher reaction was to listen to the comment. When girls called out, they were usually corrected with comments such as, "Please raise your hand if you want to speak."[3]

It is not only the attention demanded by male students that explains their greater involvement in teacher-student exchanges. Studies have found that even when boys do not volunteer, the teacher is more likely to solicit their responses.[4]

The issue is broader than the inequitable distribution of teacher *contacts* with male and female students; it also includes the inequitable *content* of teacher comments. Teacher remarks can be vague and superficial or precise and penetrating. Helpful teacher comments provide students with insights into the strengths and weaknesses of their answers. Careful and comprehensive teacher reactions not only affect student learning, they can also influence student self-esteem.[5]

The Sadkers conducted a three-year study of more than 100 fourth-, sixth- and eighth-grade classrooms. They identified four types of teacher comments: praise, acceptance, re-mediation, and criticism.

They found that while males received more of all four types of teacher comments, the difference favoring boys was greatest in the more useful teacher reactions of praise, criticism, and remediation. When teachers took the time and made the effort to specifically evaluate a student's performance, the student receiving the comment was more likely to be male.[6] These findings are echoed in other investigations, indicating that boys receive more precise teacher comments than females in terms of both scholarship and conduct.[7]

The differences in teacher evaluations of male and female students have been cited by some researchers as a cause of "learned helplessness," or lack of academic perseverance, in females. Initially investigated in animal experiments, "learned helplessness" refers to a lack of perseverance, a debilitating loss of self-confidence.[8] This concept has been used to explain why girls sometimes abandon while boys persistently pursue academic challenges for which both groups are equally qualified.[9]

One school of thought links learned helplessness with attribution theory. While girls are more likely to attribute their success to luck, boys are more likely to attribute their success to ability. As a result of these different causal attributions, boys are more likely to feel mastery and control over academic challenges, while girls are more likely to feel powerless in academic situations.[10]

Studies also reveal that competent females have higher expectations of failure and lower self-confidence when encountering new academic situations than do males with similar abilities.[11] The result is that female students are more likely to abandon academic tasks.[12]

However, research also indicates that the concepts of learned helplessness and other motivation constructs are complex. Psychologist Jacquelynne Eccles and her colleagues have found that there is a high degree of variation within each individual in terms of motivational constructs as one goes across subject areas. New evidence indicates that it is too soon to state a definitive connection between a specific teacher behavior and a particular student outcome.[13] Further research on the effects of teacher behavior and student performance and motivation is needed.

The majority of studies on teacher-student interaction do not differentiate among subject areas. However, there is some indication that the teaching of certain subjects may encourage gender-biased teacher behavior while others may foster more equitable interactions. Sex differences in attributing success to luck versus effort are more likely in subject areas where teacher responses are less frequent and where single precise student responses are less common.[14]

Two recent studies find teacher-student interactions in science classes particularly biased in favor of boys.[15] Some mathematics classes have less biased patterns of interaction overall when compared to science classes, but there is evidence that despite the more equitable overall pattern, a few male students in each mathematics class receive particular attention to the exclusion of all other students, male and female.[16]

Research on teacher-student interaction patterns has rarely looked at the interaction of gender with race, ethnicity, and/or social class. The limited data available indicate that while males receive more teacher attention than females, white boys receive more attention than boys from various racial and ethnic minority groups.[17]

Evidence also suggests that the attention minority students receive from teachers may be different in nature from that given to white children. In elementary school, black boys tend to have fewer interactions overall with teachers than other students and yet they are the recipients of four to ten times the amount of qualified praise ("That's good, but . . .") as other students.[18] Black boys tend to be perceived less favorably by their teachers and seen as less able than other students.[19] The data are more complex for girls. Black girls have less interaction with teachers than white girls, but they attempt to initiate interaction much more often than white girls or than boys of either race. Research indicates that teachers may unconsciously rebuff these black girls, who eventually turn to peers for interaction, often becoming the class enforcer or go-between for other students.[20] Black females also receive less reinforcement from teachers than do other students, although their academic performance is often better than boys.[21]

In fact, when black girls do as well as white boys in school, teachers attribute their success to hard work but assume that the white boys are not working up to their full potential.[22] This, coupled with the evidence that blacks are more often reinforced for their social behavior while whites are likely to be reinforced for their academic accomplishments, may contribute to low academic self-esteem in black girls.[23] Researchers have found that black females value their academic achievements less than black males in spite of their better performance.[24] Another study found that black boys have a higher science self-concept than black girls although there were no differences in achievement.[25]

The Design of Classroom Activities

Research studies reveal a tendency beginning at the preschool level for schools to choose classroom activities that will appeal to boys' interests and to select presentation formats in which boys excel or are encouraged more than are girls.[26] For example, when researchers looked at lecture versus laboratory classes, they found that in lecture classes teachers asked males academically related questions about 80 percent more often than they questioned females; the patterns were mixed in laboratory classes.[27] However, in science courses, lecture classes remain more common than laboratory classes.

Research indicates that if pupils begin working on an activity with little introduction from the teacher, everyone has access to the same experience. Discussion that follows after all students have completed an activity encourages more participation by girls.[28] In an extensive multistate study, researchers found that in geometry classes where the structure was changed so that students read the book and did problems *first* and *then* had classroom discussion of the topic, girls outperformed boys in two of five tests and scored equally in the other three. Girls in the experimental class reversed the general trend of boys' dominance on applications, coordinates, and proof taking, while they remained on par with boys on visualizations in three dimensions and transformations. In traditional classes where topics were introduced by lecture first and then students read the book and did the problems, small gender differences favoring boys remained.[29]

Successful Teaching Strategies

There are a number of teaching strategies that can promote more gender-equitable learning environments. Research indicates that science teachers who are successful in encouraging girls share several strategies.[30] These included using more than one textbook, eliminating sexist language, and showing fairness in their treatment and expectations of both girls and boys.

Other research indicates that classrooms where there are no gender differences in math are "girl friendly," with less social comparison and competition and an atmosphere students find warmer and fairer.[31]

In their 1986 study, *Women's Ways of Knowing*, Belenky, Clinchy, Goldberger, and Tarule point out that for many girls and women, successful learning takes place in an atmosphere that enables students to empathetically enter into the subject they are studying, an approach the authors term "connected knowing." The authors suggest that an acceptance of each individual's personal experiences and perspectives facilitates students' learning. They argue for classrooms that emphasize collaboration and provide space for exploring diversity of opinion.[32]

Few classrooms foster "connected learning," nor are the majority of classrooms designed to encourage cooperative behaviors and collaborative efforts. The need to evaluate, rank, and judge students can undermine collaborative approaches. One recent study that sampled third-, fifth-, and seventh-grade students found that successful students reported fewer cooperative attitudes than did unsuccessful students. In this study the effects of gender varied as a function of grade level. Third-grade girls were more cooperative than their male peers, but by fifth grade the gender difference had disappeared.[33] Other studies do not report this grade level-gender interaction, but rather indicate that girls tend to be more cooperative than boys but that cooperative attitudes decline for all students as they mature.[34]

Some educators view the arrival of new classroom organizational structures as a harbinger of more effective and more equitable learning environments. "Cooperative learning" has been viewed as one of these potentially more successful educational strategies. Cooperative learning is designed to eliminate the negative effects of classroom competition while promoting a cooperative spirit and increasing heterogeneous and cross-race relationships. Smaller cooperative work groups are designed to promote group cohesion and interdependence, and mobilize these positive feelings to achieve academic objectives.[35] Progress and academic performance are evaluated on a group as well as an individual basis; the group must work together efficiently or all its members will pay a price.[36] A number of positive results have been attributed to cooperative learning groups, including increasing cross-race friendships, boosting academic achievement, mainstreaming students with disabilities, and developing mutual student concerns.[37]

However, positive cross-sex relationships may be more difficult to achieve than cross-race friendships or positive relationships among students with and without disabilities. First, as reported earlier in this report, there is a high degree of sex-segregation and same-sex friendships in elementary and middle school years.[38] Researchers have found that the majority of elementary students preferred single-sex work groups.[39] Second, different communication patterns of males and females can be an obstacle to effective cross-gender relationships. Females are more indirect in speech, relying often on questioning, while more direct males are more likely to make declarative statements or even to interrupt.[40] Research indicates that boys in small groups are more likely to receive requested help from girls; girls' requests, on the other hand, are more likely to be ignored by the boys.[41] In fact, the male sex may be seen as a status position within the group. As a result, male students may choose to show their social dominance by not readily talking with females.[42]

Not only are the challenges to cross-gender cooperation significant, but cooperative learning as currently implemented may not be powerful enough to overcome these obstacles. Some research indicates that the infrequent use of small, unstructured work groups is not effective in reducing gender stereotypes, and, in fact, increases stereotyping. Groups often provide boys with leadership opportunities that increase their self-esteem. Females are often seen as followers and are less likely to want to work in mixed-sex groups in the future.[43] Another study indicates a decrease in female achievement when females are placed in mixed-sex groups.[44] Other research on cooperative education programs have reported more positive results.[45] However, it is clear that merely providing an occasional group learning experience is not the answer to sex and gender differences in classrooms.

Problems in Student Interactions

The ways students treat each other during school hours is an aspect of the informal learning process, with significant negative implications for girls. There is mounting evidence that boys do not treat girls well. Reports of student sexual harassment—the unwelcome verbal or physical conduct of a sexual nature imposed by one individual on another—among junior high school and high school peers are increasing. In the majority of cases a boy is harassing a girl.[46]

Incidents of sexual harassment reveal as much about power and authority as they do about sexuality; the person being harassed usually is less powerful than the person doing the harassing. Sexual harassment is prohibited under Title IX, yet sex-biased peer interactions appear to be permitted in schools, if not always approved. Rather than viewing sexual harassment as serious misconduct, school authorities too often treat it as a joke.

When boys line up to "rate" girls as they enter a room, when boys treat girls so badly that they are reluctant to enroll in courses where they may be the only female, when boys feel it is good fun to embarrass girls to the point of tears, it is no joke. Yet these types of behaviors are often viewed by school personnel as harmless instances of "boys being boys."

The clear message to both girls and boys is that girls are not worthy of respect and that appropriate behavior for boys includes exerting power over girls—or over other, weaker boys. Being accused of being in any way like a woman is one of the worst insults a boy can receive. As one researcher recently observed:

> "It is just before dismissal time and a group of very active fourth-graders are having trouble standing calmly in line as they wait to go to their bus. Suddenly one of the boys grabs another's hat, runs to the end of the line, and involves a number of his buddies in a game of keep-away. The boy whose hat was taken leaps from his place in line, trying to intercept it from the others, who, as they toss it back and forth out of his reach, taunt him by yelling, ' "You woman! You're a woman!" ' When the teacher on bus duty notices, she tells the boys that they all have warnings for not waiting in line properly. The boys resume an orderly stance but continue to mutter names—'Woman!' 'Am not.' 'Yes, you are.'—under their breath."
>
> (Margaret Stubbs, October 1990)

Harassment related to sexual orientation or sexual preference has received even less attention as an equity issue than heterosexual sexual harassment.[47] Yet, examples of name calling that imply homophobia, such as "sissy," "queer," "gay," "lesbo," are common among students at all levels of schooling. The fourth-grade boys who teased a peer by calling him a "woman" were not only giving voice to the sex-role stereotype that women are weaker than and therefore inferior to men; they were also challenging their peer's "masculinity" by ascribing feminine characteristics to him in a derogatory manner. Such attacks often prevent girls, and sometimes boys, from participating in activities and courses that are traditionally viewed as appropriate for the opposite sex.

When schools ignore sexist, racist, homophobic, and violent interactions between students, they are giving tacit approval to such behaviors. Environments where students do not feel accepted are not environments where effective learning can take place.

Implications

Teachers are not always aware of the ways in which they interact with students. Videotaping actual classrooms so that teachers can see themselves in action can help them to develop their own strategies for fostering gender-equitable education. The use of equitable teaching strategies should be one of the criteria by which teaching performance is evaluated.

Research studies indicate that girls often learn and perform better in same-sex work groups than they do in mixed-sex groupings. Additional research is needed, however, to better understand the specific dynamics of these interactions, particularly the circumstances under which single-sex groupings are most beneficial. Single-sex classes are illegal under Title IX, but usually single-sex work groups within coed classes are not. Teachers should be encouraged to "try out" many different classroom groupings, not only in mathematics and science classes but across a wide range of subject matter. It is critical that they carefully observe the impact of various groupings and write up and report their findings.

The Evaded Curriculum

The evaded curriculum is the term coined in this report for matters central to the lives of students and teachers but touched upon only briefly, if at all, in most schools. These matters include the functioning of bodies, the expression and valuing of feelings and the dynamics of power. In both formal course work and in the informal exchanges among teachers and students, serious consideration of these areas is avoided. When avoidance is not possible—as in the case of required health or sex-education courses—the material is often presented in a cursory fashion. Students are offered a set of facts devoid of references to the complex personal and moral dilemmas they face in understanding and making decisions about critical facets of their lives.

Youth is traditionally seen as a time of healthy bodies and carefree minds, but as numerous studies, reports, and television documentaries have outlined recently, young people in the United States are falling prey to what are being called the "new morbidities." These new morbidities are not necessarily caused by viruses or bacteria but rather by societal conditions that can lead young people into eating disorders, substance abuse, early sexual activity, unintended pregnancy, sexually transmitted diseases (including AIDS), and suicide.

Not only are many young people engaging in risky behaviors, frequently with lifetime consequences, but they are taking part in constellations of behaviors that are interrelated.[1] Young people who drink, for example, are far more likely than others to engage in unprotected sex or be involved in car accidents. Girls who are doing badly in school are five times as likely as others to become teen parents.[2] It is estimated that about one-quarter of all adolescents engage in multiple problem behaviors, often with devastating consequences.[3]

While the exact demographic makeup of the highest risk groups is not known, data on separate risk behaviors indicate that there are more young males than females at high risk. When the different patterns of risk behavior are considered, however, it becomes clear that in some areas girls are at higher risk than their male classmates.

The health and well-being of young people are related to their ability to complete school.[4] It is obvious that girls who use drugs or liquor, suffer from depression, become pregnant, or give birth as teenagers cannot take full advantage of the educational programs presented them.

Substance Use

The initial use of harmful substances is occurring at younger ages than ever before. A recent survey showed that among the 1987 high school class, significant numbers of students first tried alcohol and drugs during elementary and middle school. Two out of three students using cigarettes began smoking before the ninth grade, and one out of four first used marijuana before the ninth grade. One out of twenty students who used cocaine used it before entering ninth grade.[5]

Differences between male and female patterns of reported drug use have declined over the past two decades to the point where researchers no longer consider the sex of an adolescent a good predictor of drug use.[6] One report states that "girls are more like boys in use of substances during adolescence than at any time later in life."[7] There are some sex differences in use patterns, however. Girls are more likely to use stimulants and over-the-counter weight-reduction pills, while boys are slightly more likely to report higher levels of illicit-drug use and episodes of binge drinking.[8] White high school students are more than twice as likely as black students to smoke cigarettes, and more white females are frequent smokers than students from any other sex/race group.[9]

Sexual Activity/Contraceptive Use

Initiation of sexual activity is also occurring at younger ages. Recent reports state that at least 28 percent of adolescents are sexually active by their fourteenth birthday; the average age at the initiation of sexual activity for this group is 12.[10] A recent survey from the Alan Guttmacher Institute indicates that 38 percent of girls between the ages of fifteen and seventeen are sexually active—a 15 percent increase since 1973.[11] There has been a dramatic increase in the numbers of sexually active teenage girls who are white or from higher-income families, reducing previous racial and income differences.[12]

Contraceptive use for adolescents remains erratic, and age is a significant factor, with younger adolescents using contraception far less frequently. Reasons adolescents give for not using contraception include (1) inadequate knowledge (both boys and girls state that they are not at risk of becoming involved in a pregnancy if they have unprotected sex), (2) lack of access to birth control, and (3) not liking to plan to have sex.[13]

Before age fifteen, only 31 percent of sexually active girls report using contraceptives. By age fifteen, only 58 percent report contraceptive use; but by age nineteen, 91 percent report that they use contraceptives.[14] Meanwhile, there is some preliminary evidence that condom use is increasing; among seventeen- to nineteen-year-old males in metropolitan areas, reports of condom use at last intercourse more than doubled in the last decade— from 21 percent in 1979 to 58 percent in 1988.[15] Because of increased condom use, the proportion of teens using contraception at first intercourse rose from half to two-thirds between 1982 and 1988.[16] Unprotected sexual intercourse can result in too-early child-bearing, discussed in detail earlier in this report. It can also result in sexually transmitted diseases (STDs).

Sexually Transmitted Diseases

Syphilis rates are equal for boys and girls, but more adolescent females than males contract gonorrhea.[17]

More than 1 million teens each year suffer from chlamydia infections, the most common STD among adolescents. Researchers speculate that teenage girls suffer high rates of STDs because the female reproductive system is particularly vulnerable during the early teen years.[18]

Nearly 715 teenagers age thirteen to nineteen have diagnosed cases of AIDS.[19] The number with HIV infection, which normally precedes AIDS, is much higher. The HIV infection rate for teenage girls is comparable to, and in some cases higher than, that for boys. While among adults, male AIDS cases are nine times more prevalent than female cases, the pattern of HIV infection among adolescents is very different. A 1989 study in the District of Columbia reports the HIV infection rate at 4.7 per 1,000 for girls, almost three times the 1.7 rate for boys.[20]

Other researchers who have been following the incidence of AIDS nationally state that teenage girls between thirteen and nineteen represent 24.9 percent of reported cases among females.[21] Women make up the fastest-growing group of persons with AIDS in the United States. The Centers for Disease Control (CDS) acknowledges that the number of reported cases is probably underestimated by 40 percent and the undercounting of women is probably more severe than for other groups because many of their symptoms are not listed in the CDC surveillance definition.[22]

Idea that school system hurting women/girls as both students + teachers

Furthermore, there are differences in how AIDS is transmitted between men and women. Many more women (32.7 percent) than men (2.3 percent) become infected through a heterosexual contact; more women than men also contact AIDS through intravenous drug use.[23]

Body Image/Eating Disorders

Girls are much less satisfied with their bodies than are boys and report eating disorders at far higher rates. For example, more girls than boys report food bingeing and chronic dieting. They are also more likely to report vomiting to control their weight.[24] Severe cases of bulimia (binge eating followed by forced vomiting) and anorexia nervosa (the refusal to maintain an adequate body weight) can cause death.

Depression

An important longitudinal research study recently noted evidence of increasingly early onset and high prevalence of depression in late adolescence, with slightly more girls than boys scoring in the high range of depressive symptomology. One of the most striking findings of the study is that severely depressed girls had higher rates of substance abuse than did similarly depressed boys. Significant gender differences were found in school performance measures among the most depressed students. Grade point averages were lower for girls, and 40 percent more girls failed a grade than boys.[25]

? related to curriculum

Suicide

Adolescent girls are four to five times more likely than boys to attempt suicide (although boys are more likely to die because they choose more lethal methods, for example guns rather than sleeping pills).

heartbreaking

A recent survey of eighth- and tenth-graders found girls are twice as likely as boys to report feeling sad and hopeless. This is consistent with clinical literature, which shows that females have higher rates of depression than males, both during adolescence and adulthood.[26]

Cohesive families, neighborhoods with adequate resources, caring adults, and quality schools all help protect teens.[27] But because the dangers they face result from a complex web of interactive social conditions and behaviors, there can be no single solution. For any program to succeed in reducing risks to teens, policymakers at every level must recognize that the needs and circumstances of girls and young women often differ from those of boys and young men.

like teachers can't care if no time!

The Functioning of Healthy Bodies

In spite of reports indicating strong public support for sex education in the schools and an increase in the number of sex-education programs offered, sex education is neither widespread nor comprehensive.[28] Few schools include sex education in the early grades, and most middle and junior high schools offer short programs of ten hours or less. It has been estimated that fewer than 10 percent of all students take comprehensive sex-education courses, i.e., courses of more than forty hours or courses designed as components within a K-12 developmental-health or sex-education program.[29]

For most teachers, knowledge of human sexuality is largely a matter of personal history rather than informed study.[30] Such knowledge is often based on traditional male-defined views of human sexuality, including unexamined gender-role-stereotyped beliefs about sexual behavior. Knowledge about sexual development is usually limited, regardless of whether the teacher is male or female.

The content of sex-education classes varies from locale to locale, in part because program planners must address local sensitivities.[31] One of the few carefully controlled field studies on sexuality- and contraceptive-education programs recently compared the impact of a special sex-education class on thirteen- to nineteen-year-old males and females.[32] The findings indicate that publicly funded sexuality- and contraceptive-education programs as brief as eight to twelve hours appear to help participants increase their knowledge, initiate effective contraceptive use, and improve the consistent use of effective contraceptive methods by both girls and boys.

The experimental intervention appears to have been most helpful for males with prior sexual experience, improving the consistency of their use of effective methods of contraception. Females without prior sexual experience seemed to respond better to traditional sex-education programs; researchers hypothesize that the girls may have been uncomfortable with the structured, interactive, and confrontational aspects of the experimental program. The study also found that prior experience with sex education was an important predictor of contraceptive efficiency, suggesting that formal sexuality education may be an incremental learning process whose efforts may not be evident on short-term follow-up.

The absence of adequate instruction and discussion about menstruation and contraception is only a piece of the problem. The alarming increases in STDs and HIV infection among adolescents, the increase in childbearing among young teens and the increase in eating disorders make the lack of comprehensive courses on sexuality, health, and the human body unacceptable. An understanding of one's body is central to an understanding of self. The association of sexuality and health instruction exclusively with danger and disease belies the human experience of the body as a source of pleasure, joy, and comfort. Schools must take a broader, more comprehensive approach to education about growth and sexuality. An awareness that relationships with others and the development of intimacy involve both the body and the mind should be critical components of these courses.

The Expression and Valuing of Feelings

By insisting [on a dichotomy] between feelings and emotions on the one hand and logic and rationality on the other, schools [shortchange] all students. Classrooms must become places where girls and boys can express feelings and discuss personal experiences. The lessons we learn best are those that answer our own questions. Students must have an opportunity to explore the world as they see it and pose problem that they consider important. From Sylvia Ashton Warner to AAUW teacher awardee Judy Logan, good teachers have always known this and have reflected it in their teaching. The schools must find ways to facilitate these processes.

When this is done, issues that may not always be considered "appropriate" will undoubtedly arise. They should. Child abuse is a brutal fact of too many young lives. Children must have a "safe place" to acknowledge their pain and vulnerability and receive help and support. While girls and boys are more or less equally subjected to most forms of physical and emotional abuse, girls confront sexual abuse at four times the rate of boys.

We need to help all children, particularly girls, to know and believe that their bodies are their own to control and use as they feel appropriate—and not objects to be appropriated by others.[34] This, of course, is particularly difficult in a culture that uses the female body to advertise everything from toilet cleanser to truck tires and where the approved female roles remain service-oriented. The so-called "womanly" values of caring for and connecting with others are not ones that women wish to lose, but they are values that must be buttressed by a sense of self and a faith in one's own competence.

In July 1991, *Newsweek* ran a story titled "Girls Who Go Too Far," about the newly aggressive pursuit of boyfriends by some young teens.[35] The comments of the girls themselves illustrate their dilemma in having grown up to believe that a man is an essential part of every woman's life, that only male attention can give them a sense of themselves, and that the culturally accepted way to achieve a goal is to resort to aggressive, even violent, behavior.

Rather than highlighting aggressive behavior among girls, we must address the degree to which violence against women is an increasingly accepted aspect of our culture. School curricula must help girls to understand the extent to which their lives are constrained by fear of rape, the possibility of battering, and the availability of pornography. Boys must be helped to understand that violence damages both the victim and the perpetrator, and that violence against women is not in a somehow-more-acceptable category than other violent acts. The energies and passions so routinely expressed in violence toward others in our culture must be rechanneled and redirected if our society is to fulfill its promise.

A strong line of feminist research and thinking, including the work of Jane Rowan Martin, Jean Baker Miller, Carol Gilligan, Nel Noddings, and Mary Belenky and her colleagues, addresses the strengths girls and women can bring to communities through the sense of connection with and concern for others that is more often encouraged and "permitted" in their lives than it is in boys'.[36] Others, such as Alfie Kohn, have written extensively about the need for schools that can help students learn and grow as part of a "prosocial" community.[37] A democracy cannot survive without citizens capable of seeing beyond immediate self-interest to the needs of the larger group.

When asked to describe their ideal school, one group of young women responded:

> "School would be fun. Our teachers would be excited and lively, not bored. They would act caring and take time to understand how students feel. . . . Boys would treat us with respect. . . . If they run by and grab your tits, they would get into trouble".[38]

Care, concern, and respect—simple things, but obviously not the norm in many of our nation's classrooms. These young women are not naive. Their full statement recognizes the need to pay teachers well and includes a commitment to "learn by listening and consuming everything" as well as a discussion of parental roles.[39] What they envision is needed by their male classmates and their teachers as well; it is what we as a nation must provide.

Gender and Power

Data presented earlier in this report reveal the extent to which girls and boys are treated differently in school classrooms and corridors. These data themselves should be a topic of discussion. They indicate power differentials that are perhaps the most evaded of all topics in our schools. Students are all too aware of "gender politics." In a recent survey, students in Michigan were asked, "Are there any policies, practices, including the behavior of teachers in classrooms, that have the effect of treating students differently based on their sex?" One hundred percent of the middle school and 82 percent of the high school students responding said "yes."[40]

Gender politics is a subject that many in our schools may prefer to ignore, but if we do not begin to discuss more openly the ways in which ascribed power, whether on the basis of race, sex, class, sexual orientation, or religion, affects individual lives, we will not be truly preparing our students for citizenship in a democracy.

Notes

The Formal Curriculum

1. We analyze these reports in Part One. None examines curriculum content in depth. Recently, however,the leaders of more than thirty-three national subject-matter groups met to form an organization devoted to putting curricular issues at the top of the education-reform agenda. This effort promises to call attention to the central position of curriculum in schooling. "Alliance Formed to Push Curriculum to Front of Reform Agenda," *Education Week*, September 4, 1991, p. 14.

2. M. Sadker, D. Sadker, and S. Steindam, "Gender Equity and Education Reform," *Educational Leadership* 46, no. 6 (1989):44–47. See also M. Tetreault and P. Schmuck, "Equity, Education Reform, and Gender," *Issues in Education* 3, no. 1 (198):45–67.

3. K. Bogart, *Solutions That Work: Identification and Elimination of Barriers to the Participation of Female and Minority Students in Academic Educational Programs*, 3 vols. and User's Manual (Washington, D.C.: National Education Association, forthcoming, 1992). The three ongoing national faculty-development programs that focus on creation of gender-fair curriculum in K-12 classes in humanities and social studies are the National Women's History Project, Windsor, CA; the Harvard Graduate School of Education, Summer Institutes on "American History: The Female Experience"; and the multidisciplinary National SEED Project (Seeking Educational Equity and Diversity) of the Wellesley College Center for Research on Women. The Educational Materials and Service Center of Edmonds, WA, and the GESA Program (Gender Expectations and Student Achievement) of the Graymill Foundation, Earlham, IA, offer equity training that bears indirectly on course content.

4. For general reviews of curriculum research, see P. Arlow and C. Froschl, "Textbook Analysis," in F. Howe, (ed.) *High School Feminist Studies* (Old Westbury, NY: The Feminist Press, 1976), pp. xi–xxviii; K. Scott and C. Schau, "Sex Equity and Sex Bias in Instructional Materials," and P. Blackwell and L. Russo, "Sex Equity Strategies in the Content Areas," in S. Klein, (ed.) *Handbook for Achieving Sex Equity Through Education* (Baltimore, MD: Johns Hopkins University Press, 1985), pp. 218–260; M. Hulme, "Mirror, Mirror on the Wall: Biased Reflections in Textbooks and Instructional Materials," in A. Carelli, (ed.) *Sex Equity in Education: Readings and Strategies* (Springfield, IL: Charles C. Thomas, 1988), pp. 187–208.

5. *Dick and Jane As Victims: Sex Stereotyping in Children's Readers* (Princeton, NJ: Women on Words and Images, 1975); *Help Wanted: Sexism in Career Education Materials* (Princeton, NJ: Women on Words and Images, 1976) and *Sexism in Foreign Language Texts* (Princeton, NJ: Women on Words and Images, 1976). See also L. Weitzman and D. Rizzo, *Biased Textbooks and Images of Males and Females in Elementary School Textbooks* (Washington, D.C.: Resource Center on Sex Roles in Education, 1976); G. Britton and M. Lumpkin, *A Consumer's Guide to Sex, Race, and Career Bias in Public School Textbooks* (Corvallis, OR: Britton Associates, 1977).

6. J. Trecker, "Women in U.S. History High School Textbooks," *Social Education* 35, no. 3 (1971):249–260, 338.

7. O. Davis et al. "A Review of U.S. History Textbooks," *The Education Digest* 52, no. 3 (November 1986):50–53; M. Hitchcock and G. Tompkins, "Basal Readers: Are They Still Sexist?" *The Reading Teacher* 41, no. 3 (December 1987):288–292; M. Tetreault, "Integrating Women's History: The Case of United States History High School Textbooks," *The History Teacher* 19 (February 1986):211–262; M. Tetreault, "The Journey from Male-Defined to

Gender-Balanced Education," *Theory into Practice* 25, no. 4 (Autumn 1986):227–234; A. Nilsen, "Three Decades of Sexism in School Science Materials," *School Library Journal* 34, no. 1 (September 1987):117–122; E. Hall, "One Week for Women? The Structure of Inclusion of Gender Issues in Introductory Textbooks," *Teaching Sociology* 16, no. 4 (October 1988):431–442; P. Purcell and L. Stewart, "Dick and Jane in 1989," *Sex Roles* 22, nos. 3 and 4 (February 1990):177–185.

8. A. Applebee, *A Study of Book-Length Works Taught in High School English Courses* (Albany, NY: Center for the Learning and Teaching of Literature, State University of New York School of Education, 1989).

9. Ibid., p. 18.

10. P. Campbell and J. Wirtenberg, "How Books Influence Children: What the Research Shows," *Interracial Books for Children Bulletin* 11, no. 6 (1980):3–6.

11. At its highest level of support in 1980, the Office of Education spent only 2 percent of its budget on sex equity. Subsequently, however, the Reagan administration attempted unsuccessfully to reduce to "zero budget" the two largest programs supporting race and sex equity, the Title IV programs of the Civil Rights Act and the Women's Educational Equity Act. The sense that race equity and sex equity programs figured in a federal agenda diminished. This disinvestment is reflected by the absence of sex, gender, and cultural awareness in most of the national reports of the late 1980s. See K. Levy, *What's Left of Federal Funding for Sex Equity in Education and Social Science Research?* (Tempe, AZ: Arizona State University Publications Office, 1985).

12. Initiatives have included classroom innovations by thousands of individual teachers, conferences, and summer institutes for teachers at the University of Arizona, University of New Hampshire, Dana Hall School, and Ohio State University. The National Coalition for Sex Equity in Education (NCSEE) developed an active network of equity professionals. Further efforts have also included the forming of women's caucuses in professional organizations; workshops and materials from the National Women's History Project; dissemination of syllabi and bibliographies; new journals including *Feminist Teacher*; special focus sections of journals, for example, *English Journal* 77, no. 6 (October 1988), 78, no. 6 (October 1989); inservice activities sponsored by local school boards and districts; and aid from ten federal Equity Assistance Centers. Despite decreased funding, the Women's Education Equity Act Program continues to fund projects and to support the dissemination of materials via the WEEA Publishing Center at the Educational Development Center in Newton, MA.

13. Scott and Schau, "Sex Equity and Sex Bias," p. 226. See also the discussion by B. Wright in "The Feminist Transformation of Foreign Language Teaching," in M. Burkhard and E. Waldstein, (eds.) *Women in German Yearbook 1* (Lanham, MD: University Press of America, 1985), pp. 95–97. Wright lists thirteen publishing houses that issued guidelines between 1972 and 1981 on avoiding or eliminating sex stereotypes. She discusses problems of non-compliance, as well as the limits of strategies for elimination of simple sex stereotyping in the face of larger problems such as overwhelmingly masculine and/or elite perspectives in texts as a whole.

14. M. Tetreault, "Integrating Women's History: The Case of U.S. History High School Textbooks," *The History Teacher* 19 (February 1986):211–262; "Women in the Curriculum," *Comment on Conferences and Research on Women* (February 1986):1–2; "Rethinking Women, Gender, and the Social Studies," *Social Education* 51 (March 1987):171–178.

15. Newsletter of the Special Interest Group on Gender and Social Justice, National Council for Social Studies, December 1990.

16. Surveys were taken in the Andrew W. Mellon, Geraldine Rockefeller Dodge, Kentucky and National SEED Project Seminars for College and School Teachers, sponsored by the Wellesley College Center for Research on Women. Twenty U.S. History textbooks were analyzed each year with regard to the representation of women as authors/ editors and subjects in text and illustrations and the representation of domains of life outside of war, law, policy, government, and management of public affairs.

17. Homework assignments and study questions given in textbooks most frequently depend on the type of knowing which the authors of *Women's Ways of Knowing* identify as "separated," in which the mode is detached or distant from the subject. Girls and women, in a study of students in six schools and colleges, preferred a mode of knowing that the investigators named "connected," which involves empathetic identification with the subject. The investigators call for more "connected teaching," in which the capacity for identification is seen as an aspect of knowing and of learning about course content. M. Belenky et al. *Women's Ways of Knowing* (New York: Basic Books, 1986), pp. 100–130, 214–229.

18. See B. Wright, "What's in a Noun? A Feminist Perspective on Foreign Language Instruction," *Women's Studies Quarterly* 12, no. 3 (Fall 1984):2–6; B. Schmitz, "Guidelines for Reviewing Foreign Language Textbooks for Sex Bias," *Women's Studies Quarterly* 12, no. 3 (Fall 1984):7–9.

19. L. Pinkle, "Language Learning from a Feminist Perspective: Selected College-Level Grammar Textbooks," *Women's Studies Quarterly* 12, no. 3 (Fall 1984):10–13. Since 1985, *The Women in German Yearbook* (Lanham, MD: University Press of America) has published periodic reviews of research on instructional materials for German courses, including high school texts. The most recent review was published in the Spring 1991 issue: "Frauen/Unterricht: Feminist Reviews of Teaching Materials," L. French, K. Von Ankum, and M. Webster, (eds.).

20. Bogart, *Solutions That Work*, vol. 3, pp. 107–108.

21. E. Style, "Curriculum As Window and Mirror," in *Listening for All Voices: Gender Balancing the School Curriculum* (Summit, NJ: Oak Knoll School, 1988), pp. 6–12.

22. Surveys were taken in the Andrew W. Mellon, Geraldine Rockefeller Dodge, Kentucky, and National SEED Project Seminars for college and school teachers, sponsored by the Wellesley College Center for Research on Women.

23. G. Wilbur, "Gender-fair Curriculum," research report prepared for Wellesley College Center for Research on Women, August, 1991.

24. National Council of Teachers of Mathematics, *Curriculum and Evaluation Standards for School Mathematics* (Reston, VA: National Council of Teachers of Mathematics, 1989).

25. Ibid., p. 17.

26. F. Rutherford and A. Ahlgren, *Science for All Americans* (New York: Oxford University Press, 1989), pp. 204–214.

27. J. Banks, "Integrating the Curriculum with Ethnic Content: Approaches and Guidelines," in J. Banks and C. Banks, (eds.) *Multicultural Education: Issues and Perspectives* (Boston, MA: Allyn and Bacon, 1989), pp. 192–207.

28. P. McIntosh, *Interactive Phases of Curricular Re-Vision: A Feminist Perspective*, Working Paper No. 124 (Wellesley, MA: Wellesley College Center for Research on Women, 1983). For further typologies in phase theory, see M. Schuster and S. Van Dyne, (eds.) *Women's Place in the Academy: Transforming the Liberal Arts* (Totawa, NJ. Rowman and Allanheld, 1985); and M. Tetreault, "Feminist Phase Theory: An Experience-Derived Evaluation Model," *Journal of Higher Education* 56 (July–August 1985); and "Integrating Content about Women and Gender into the Curriculum," in Banks and Banks, (eds.) *Multicultural Education*, pp. 124–144. See also *Comment on Conferences and Research on Women* 15, no. 2, Claremont, CA (February 1986): 1–4.

29. E. Style, *Multicultural Education and Me: The Philosophy and the Process, Putting Product in Its Place* (Madison, WI: Teacher Corps Associates, University of Wisconsin, 1982), p. 11.

30. "Stages of Curriculum Transformation," in M. Schuster and S. Van Dyne, (eds.) *Women's Place in the Academy: Transforming the Liberal Arts Curriculum* (Totawa, NJ: Rowman & Allanheld Publishers, 1985), pp. 13–29; M. Tetreault, "Women in U.S. History—Beyond a Patriarchal Perspective," *Interracial Books for Children Bulletin* 11 (1980):F-10; McIntosh, *Interactive Phases of Curricular Re-Vision*. See also M. Belenky et al. *Women's Ways of Knowing* (New York: Basic Books, Inc., 1986); C. Gilligan, *In a Different Voice* (Cambridge, MA: Harvard University Press, 1982); E. Minnich, *Transforming Knowledge* (Philadelphia, PA: Temple University Press; 1990).

31. P. McIntosh, *Interactive Phases of Curricular and Personal Re-Vision With Regard to Race*, Working Paper No. 219 (Wellesley, MA: Wellesley College Center for Research on Women, 1990), p. 6.

32. Gilligan, *In a Different Voice*.

33. Bogart, *Solutions That Work*, vol. 1, pp. 97–98.

34. T. Kidder, *Among Schoolchildren* (New York: Avon Books, 1989), p. 27.

35. A. Applebee, *A Study of Book-Length Works*, p. 18. For an example of a product that came out of a school-based departmental discussion, see *New Voices for the English Classroom* C. Peter, (ed.) (Providence, RI: Lincoln School, 1986). For similar strategies, see E. Style, *Multicultural Education and Me*, and the school-based, teacher-led seminars established through the National SEED Project on Inclusive Curriculum, Wellesley College Center for Research on Women.

36. State of New York, Education Department, *One Nation, Many Peoples: A Declaration of Cultural Interdependence, The Report of the New York State Social Studies Review and Development Committee, June 1991*, pp. 18–126. See also memos of July 12 and 15 from Commissioner T. Sobol to the Board of Regents.

37. C. Nelson, "Gender and the Social Studies: Training Preservice Secondary Social Studies Teachers" (Ph.D. diss., University of Minnesota, 1990), pp. 8, 38–39.

38. J. Kerber, " 'Opinionative Assurance': The Challenge of Women's History," address to the Organization of History Teachers, American Historical Association, New York, NY, 28 December 1990, p. 11.

The Classroom as Curriculum

1. See for example, J. Brophy and T. Good, *Teacher-Student Relationships: Causes and Consequences* (New York: Holt, Rinehart, and Winston, 1974); M. Jones, "Gender Bias in Classroom Interactions," *Contemporary Education* 60 (Summer 1989):216–222; M. Lockheed, *Final Report: A Study of Sex Equity in Classroom Interaction* (Washington, D.C.: National Institute of Education, 1984); M. Lockheed and A. Harris, *Classroom Interaction and Opportunities for Cross-Sex Peer Learning in Science*, paper presented at the Annual Meeting of the American Educational Research Association, New York, April 1989; M. Sadker and D. Sadker, "Sexism in the Classroom: From Grade School to Graduate School," *Phi Delta Kappan* 68 (1986):512; R. Spaulding, *Achievement, Creativity and Self-Concept Correlates of Teacher-Pupil Transactions in Elementary School* Cooperative Research Project No. 1352 (Washington, D.C.: U.S. Department of Health Education and Welfare, 1963).

2. L. Serbin et al. "A Comparison of Teacher Responses to the Pre-Academic and Problem Behavior of Boys and Girls," *Child Development* 44 (1973):796–804; M. Ebbeck, "Equity for Boys and Girls: Some Important Issues," *Early Child Development and Care* 18 (1984):119–131.

3. D. Sadker, M. Sadker, and D. Thomas, "Sex Equity and Special Education," *The Pointer* 26 (1981):33–38.

4. D. Sadker and M. Sadker, "Is the OK Classroom OK?," *Phi Delta Kappan* 55 (1985):358–367.

5. J. Brophy, "Teacher Praise: A Functional Analysis," *Review of Educational Research* 51 (1981):5–32; A. Gardner, C. Mason, and M. Matyas, "Equity, Excellence and 'Just Plain Good Teaching!' " *The American Biology Teacher* 51 (1989):72–77.

6. M. Sadker and D. Sadker, *Year 3: Final Report, Promoting Effectiveness in Classroom Instruction* (Washington, D.C.: National Institute of Education, 1984).

7. D. Baker, "Sex Differences in Classroom Interactions in Secondary Science," *Journal of Classroom Interaction* 22 (1986):212–218; J. Becker, "Differential Treatment of Females and Males in Mathematics Classes," *Journal for Research in Mathematics Education* 12 (1981):40–53; L. Berk and N. Lewis, "Sex Role and Social Behavior in Four School Environments," *Elementary School Journal* 3 (1977):205–221; L. Morse and H. Handley, "Listening to Adolescents: Gender Differences in Science Classroom Interaction," in *Gender Influences in Classroom Interaction*, L. Wilkerson and C. Marrett, (eds.) (Orlando, FL: Academic Press, 1985), pp. 37–56.

8. M. Seligman and S. Maier, "Failure to Escape Traumatic Shock," *Journal of Experimental Psychology* 74 (1967):1–9.

9. C. Dweck and N. Repucci, "Learned Helplessness and Reinforcement Responsibility in Children," *Journal of Personality and Social Psychology* 25 (1973):109–116; C. Dweck and T. Goetz, "Attributions and Learned Helplessness," in *New Directions in Attributions Research*, J. Harvey, W. Ickes, and R. Kidd, (eds.) (Hillsdale, NJ: Erlbaum, 1978).

10. See for example, K. Deaux, "Sex; A Perspective on the Attribution Process," in *New Directions in Attribution Research*; C. Dweck and E. Bush, "Sex Differences in Learned Helplessness: I. Differential Debilitation with Peer and Adult Evaluators," *Developmental Psychology* 12 (1976):147–156; C. Dweck, T. Goetz, and N. Strauss, "Sex Differences in Learned Helplessness: IV. An Experimental and Naturalistic Study of Failure Generalization and Its Mediators," *Journal of Personality and Social Psychology* 38 (1980):441–452; L. Reyes, *Mathematics Classroom Processes*, paper presented at the Fifth International Congress on Mathematical Education, Adelaide, Australia, August 1984; P. Wolleat et al. "Sex Differences in High School Students' Causal Attributions of Performance in Mathematics," *Journal for Research in Mathematics Education* 11 (1980):356–366; D. Phillips, "The Illusion of Incompetence among Academically Competent Children," *Child Development* 55 (1984): 2000–2016; E. Fennema et al. "Teachers' Attributions and Belief about Girls, Boys, and Mathematics," *Educational Studies in Mathematics* 21 (1990):55–69.

11. E. Maccoby and C. Jacklin, *The Psychology of Sex Differences* (Stanford, CA: Stanford University Press, 1974); E. Lenney, "Women's Self-Confidence in Achievement Settings," *Psychological Bulletin* 84 (1977):1–13; J. Parsons and D. Ruble, "The Development of Achievement-Related Expectancies," *Child Development* 48 (1977):1075–1079; Dweck, Goetz, and Strauss, "Sex Differences in Learned Helplessness IV"; J. Goetz, "Children's Sex Role Knowledge and Behavior. An Ethnographic Study of First Graders in the Rural South," *Theory and Research in Social Education* 8 (1981):31–54.

12. W. Shepard and D. Hess, "Attitudes in Four Age Groups Toward Sex Role Division in Adult Occupations and Activities," *Journal of Vocational Behavior* 6 (1975):27–39; C. Dweck and E. Elliot, "Achievement Motivation," in *Handbook of Child Psychology*, vol. 4, P. Mussen and E. Hetherington, (eds.) (New York: Wiley, 1983); R. Felson, "The Effect of Self-Appraisals of Ability on Academic Performance," *Journal of Personality and Social Psychology* 47 (1984):944–952; M. Stewart and C. Corbin, "Feedback Dependence among Low Confidence Preadolescent Boys and Girls," *Research Quarterly for Exercise and Sport* 59 (1988):160–164.

13. J. Eccles-Parsons et al. "Sex Differences in Attributions and Learned Helplessness," *Sex Roles* 8 (1982):421–432; J. Eccles-Parsons, C. Kaczala, and J. Meece, "Socialization of Achievement Attitudes and Beliefs: Classroom Influences," *Child Development* 53 (1982):322–339; J. Eccles, "Expectancies, Values and Academic Behaviors," in *Achievement and Achievement Motives*, J. Spence, (ed.) (San Francisco, CA: W.H. Freeman and Co., 1983); J. Eccles, *Understanding Motivation: Achievement Beliefs, Gender-Roles and Changing Educational Environments*, address before American Psychological Association, New York, 1987.

14. B. Licht, S. Stader, and C. Swenson, "Children's Achievement Related Beliefs: Effects of Academic Area, Sex, and Achievement Level," *Journal of Educational Research* 82 (1989):253–260.

15. J. Kahle, "Why Girls Don't Know," in *What Research Says to the Science Teacher—the Process of Knowing*, M. Rowe, (ed.) (Washington; DC: National Science Testing Association, 1990), pp. 55–67; V. Lee, "Sexism in Single-Sex and Co-educational Secondary School Classrooms," paper presented at the annual meeting of the American Sociological Association, Cincinnati, OH, August 8, 1991.

16. J. Eccles, "Bringing Young Women to Math and Science," in *Gender and Thought: Psychological Perspectives*, M. Crawford and M. Gentry, (eds.) (New York: Springer-Verlag, 1989), pp. 36–58; Licht et al., "Children's Achievement Related Beliefs."

17. Sadker and Sadker, *Year 3*; L. Grant, "Race-Gender Status, Classroom Interaction and Children's Socialization in Elementary School," in *Gender Influences in Classroom Interaction*, L. Wilkinson and C. Marrett, (eds.) (Orlando, FL: Academic Press, 1985), pp. 57–75.

18. Grant, "Race-Gender Status," p. 66.

19. C. Cornbleth and W. Korth, "Teacher Perceptions and Teacher-Student Interaction in Integrated Classrooms," *Journal of Experimental Education* 48 (Summer 1980):259–263; B. Hare, *Black Girls: A Comparative Analysis of Self-Perception and Achievement by Race, Sex and Socioeconomic Background*, Report No. 271 (Baltimore, MD: John Hopkins University, Center for Social Organization of Schools, [1979]).

20. S. Damico and E. Scott, "Behavior Differences Between Black and White Females in Desegregated Schools," *Equity and Excellence* 23 (1987):63–66; Grant, "Race-Gender Status." See also J. Irvine, "Teacher-Student Interactions: Effects of Student Race, Sex, and Grade Level," *Journal of Educational Psychology* 78 (1986):14–21.

21. Damico and Scott, "Behavior Differences"; Hare, "Black Girls: A Comparative Analysis."

22. Damico and Scott, "Behavior Differences;" L. Grant, "Black Females 'Place' in Integrated Classrooms," *Sociology of Education* 57 (1984):98–111.

23. Damico and Scott, "Behavior Differences."

24. D. Scott-Jones and M. Clark, "The School Experience of Black Girls: The Interaction of Gender, Race and Socioeconomic Status," *Phi Delta Kappan* 67 (March 1986):20–526.

25. V. Washington and J. Newman, "Setting Our Own Agenda: Exploring the Meaning of Gender Disparities Among Blacks in Higher Education," *Journal of Negro Education* 60 (1991):19–35.

26. E. Fennema and P. Peterson, "Effective Teaching for Girls and Boys: The Same or Different?" in *Talks to Teachers*, D. Berliner and B. Rosenshine, (eds.) (New York: Random House, 1987), pp. 111–125; J. Stallings, "School Classroom and Home Influences on Women's Decisions to Enroll in Advanced Mathematics Courses," in *Women and Mathematics: Balancing the Equation*, S. Chipman, L. Brush, and D. Wilson, (eds.) (Hillsdale, NJ: Erlbaum, 1985), pp. 199–224; S. Greenberg, "Educational Equity in Early Education Environments," in *Handbook for Achieving Sex Equity Through Education*, S. Klein, (ed.) (Baltimore, MD: Johns Hopkins University Press, 1985), pp. 457–469.

27. D. Baker, "Sex Differences in Classroom Interactions in Secondary Science," *Journal of Classroom Interaction* 22 (1986):212–218.

28. D. Jorde and A. Lea, "The Primary Science Project in Norway," in *Proceedings of Growth GSAT Conference*, J. Kahle, J. Daniels, and J. Harding, (eds.) (West Lafayette, IN: Purdue University, 1987), pp. 66–72.

29. P. Flores, "How Dick and Jane Perform Differently in Geometry: Test Results on Reasoning, Visualization and Affective Factors," paper presented at American Educational Research Association Meeting, Boston, MA, April 1990.

30. J. Kahle, *Factors Affecting the Retention of Girls in Science Courses, and Careers: Case Studies of Selected Secondary Schools* (Reston, VA: The National Association of Biology Teachers, October 1983).

31. Eccles, "Bringing Young Women to Math and Science."

32. M. Belenky et al. *Women's Ways of Knowing—The Development of Self, Body, and Mind* (New York: Basic Books, Inc., 1986).

33. G. Engelhard and J. Monsaas, "Academic Performance, Gender and the Cooperative Attitudes of Third, Fifth and Seventh Graders," *Journal of Research and Development in Education* 22 (1989):13–17.

34. A. Ahlgren and D. Johnson, "Sex Differences in Cooperative and Competitive Attitudes from 2nd Through the 12th Grades," *Development Psychology* 15 (1979):45–49; B. Herndon and M. Carpenter, "Sex Differences in Cooperative and Competitive Attitudes in a Northeastern School," *Psychological Reports* 50 (1982):768–770; L. Owens and R. Straton, "The Development of Co-operative Competitive and Individualized Learning Preference Scale for Students," *Journal of Educational Psychology* 50 (1980):147–161.

35. S. Sharon et al. (eds.) *Cooperation in Education* (Provo, UT: Brigham Young University Press, 1980); S. Bossert, *Task Structure and Social Relationships* (Cambridge, MA: Harvard University Press, 1979); W. Shrum, N. Cheek, and S. Hunter, "Friendship in the School: Gender and Racial Homophily," *Sociology of Education* 61 (1988):227–239.

36. E. Aronson, *The Jigsaw Classroom* (Beverly Hills, CA: Sage, 1978); D. DeVries and K. Edwards, "Student Teams and Learning Games: Their Effects on Cross-Race and Cross-Sex Interaction," *Journal of Educational Psychology* 66 (1974):741–749; P. Okebukola, "Cooperative Learning and Students' Attitude to Laboratory Work," *Social Science and Mathematics* 86 (1986):582–590; R. Slavin, "How Student Learning Teams Can Integrate the Desegregated Classroom," *Integrated Education* 15 (1977):56–58.

37. N. Blaney et al. "Interdependence in the Classroom: A Field Study," *Journal of Educational Psychology* 69 (1977):121–128; D. Devries and K. Edwards, "Student Teams and Learning Games: Their Effects on Cross-Race and Cross-Sex Interaction," *Journal of Educational Psychology* 66 (1974):741–749; Sharon et al., *Cooperation in Education*; R. Slavin, "Cooperative Learning," *Review of Educational Research* 50 (1980):315–342; R. Slavin, "Cooperative Learning and Desegregation," in W. Hawley, (ed.) *Effective School Desegregation* (Berkeley, CA: Sage, 1981); R. Weigle, P. Wiser, and S. Cook, "The Impact of Cooperative Learning Experiences on Cross-Ethnic Relations and Attitude," *Journal of Social Issues* 3 (1975):219–244.

38. M. Hallinan, *The Evolution of Children's Friendship Cliques* (ERIC Document Reproduction Service No. ED 161556, 1977); R. Best, *We've All Got Scars: What Boys and Girls Learn in Elementary School* (Bloomington, IN: University Press, 1983); J. Eccles-Parsons, "Sex Differences in Mathematics Participation," in M. Steinkamp and M. Maehr, (eds.) *Women in Science* (Greenwich, CT: JAI Press, 1984); M. Hallinan and N. Tumma, "Classroom Effects on Change in Children," *Sociology of Education* 51 (1978):170–282.

39. M. Lockheed, K. Finklestein, and A. Harris, *Curriculum and Research for Equity: Model Data Package* (Princeton, NJ: Educational Testing Service, 1979).

40. B. Eakins and R. Eakins, "Sex Roles, Interruptions, and Silences in Conversation," in B. Thorne and N. Henley, (eds.) *Sex Differences in Human Communication* (Boston, MA: Houghton Mifflin, 1978); N. Henley and B. Thorne, "Women Speak and Men Speak: Sex Differences and Sexism in Communications, Verbal and Nonverbal," in A. Sargent, (ed.) *Beyond Sex Roles* (St. Paul, MN: West Publishing Company, 1977); R. Lakoff, *Languages and Women's Place* (New York: Harper Colophone Books, 1976); D. Tannen, *You Just Don't Understand: Women and Men in Conversation* (New York: William Morrow, 1990).

41. L. Wilkinson, J. Lindow, and C. Chiang, "Sex Differences and Sex Segregation in Students' Small-Group Communication," in L. Wilkinson and C. Marret, (eds.) *Gender Influences in Classroom Interaction* (Orlando, FL: Academic Press, 1985), pp. 185–207.

42. J. Berger, T. Conner, and M. Fisek, (eds.) *Expectation States Theory: A Theoretical Research Program* (Cambridge, MA: Winthrop, 1974); M. Lockheed and A. Harris, "Cross-Sex Collaborative Learning in Elementary Classrooms," *American Educational Research Journal*, 21 (1984):275–294.

43. Lockheed and Harris, "Cross-Sex Collaborative Learning."

44. C. Weisfeld et al. "The Spelling Bee: A Naturalistic Study of Female Inhibitions in Mixed-Sex Competitions," *Adolescence* 18 (1983):695–708.

45. For example, M. Lockheed and A. Harris, "Classroom Interaction and Opportunity for Cross-Sex Peer Learning in Science," *Journal of Early Adolescence* (1982):135–143.

46. S. Strauss, "Sexual Harassment in the School; Legal Implications for Principals," *National Association of Secondary School Principles Bulletin* (1988):93–97; N. Stein, "Survey on Sexual Harassment," *Vocational Options in Creating Equity*, VI (Boston, MA: Department of Education, 1990), p. 1.

47. D. Grayson, "Emerging Equity Issues Related to Homosexuality," *Peabody Journal of Education* 64 (1989):132–145.

The Evaded Curriculum

1. R. Jessor, "Risk Behavior in Adolescence: A Psychosocial Framework for Understanding and Action," paper prepared for Cornell University Medical College Conference "Adolescents at Risk: Medical and Social Perspectives," Cornell University, February 1991; J. Dryfoos, *Youth at Risk: Prevalence and Prevention* (Oxford: Oxford University Press, 1990).

2. *Preventing Adolescent Pregnancy: What Schools Can Do* (Washington, D.C.: Children's Defense Fund, 1986).

3. Dryfoos, *Youth at Risk*, p. 107.

4. J. Earle and V. Roach, "Female Dropouts: A New Perspective," in *Women's Educational Equity Act Publishing Center Digest* (Newton, MA: Education Development Center, 1988); M. Fine, *Framing Dropouts* (Albany, NY: State University of New York Press, 1991).

5. J. Gans and D. Blyth, *America's Adolescents: How Healthy Are They?* (Chicago, IL: American Medical Association, 1990), p. 28.

6. H. Adger, "Problems of Alcohol and Other Drug Use and Abuse in Adolescence," paper prepared for Cornell University Medical College Conference "Adolescents at Risk: Medical and Social Perspectives," Cornell University, February 1991.

7. *Facts and Reflections on Girls and Substance Use* (New York: Girls Clubs of America, Inc., 1988), p. 9.

8. Adger, "Problems of Alcohol."

9. U.S. Centers for Disease Control, Youth Risk Behavior Survey, quoted in Ellen Flax, "White Students Twice as Likely as Blacks to Smoke, Study Finds," *Education Week* 11 (September 1991):10.

10. D. Scott-Jones and A. White, "Correlates of Sexual Activity in Early Adolescence," *Journal of Early Adolescence* 10 (May 1990):221–38; Dryfoos, *Youth at Risk*, chart p. 67.

11. D. Forrest and S. Singh, "The Sexual and Reproductive Behavior of American Women," *Family Planning Perspectives* 22 (1990):208, Table 4.

12. C. Irwin and M. Shafer, "Adolescent Sexuality: The Problem of a Negative Outcome of a Normative Behavior," paper prepared for the Cornell University Medical College Conference "Adolescents at Risk: Medical and Social Perspectives," Cornell University, February 1991.

13. M. Sullivan, *The Male Role in Teenage Pregnancy and Parenting: New Directions for Public Policy* (New York: Vera Institute of Justice, 1990), p. 21.

14. Irwin and Shafer, "Adolescent Sexuality."

15. Children's Defense Fund, unpublished paper, Washington, D.C., 1991.

16. K. Moore, *Facts at a Glance* (Washington, D.C.: Child Trends, 1988). See also K. Moore, "Trends in Teenage Childbearing in the U.S.: 1970–1988" (Los Alamitos, CA: TEC Networks, March 1991).

17. Irwin and Shafer, "Adolescent Sexuality."

18. Ibid.

19. Quoted over the phone by the National AIDS Clearing House from U.S. Centers for Disease Control, *U.S. AIDS Cases Reported in July 1991*, 1991.

20. L. D'Angelo et al. "HIV Infection in Adolescents: Can We Predict Who Is at Risk?" poster presentation at the Fifth International Conference on AIDS, June 1989.

21. M. Wolfe, "Women and HIV/AIDS Education," paper prepared for the NEA Health Information Network, Atlanta, 1991. .

22. Ibid.

23. Ibid.

24. *The State of Adolescent Health in Minnesota*, Minnesota Youth Health Survey (Minneapolis: Adolescent Health Database Project, February 1989).

25. H. Reinherz, A. Frost, and B. Pakiz, *Changing Faces: Correlates of Depressive Symptoms in Late Adolescence* (Boston: Simmons College School of Social Work, 1990).

26. Gans and Blyth, *America's Adolescents*, p. 11.

27. D. Hawkins, "Risk Focussed Prevention," speech to the Coordinating Council on Juvenile Justice and Delinquency Prevention, 1990; Jessor, "Risk Behavior"; J. Gibbs, *Not Schools Alone* (Sacramento, CA: California Department of Education, 1990); E. Werner, "Vulnerability and Resiliency: The Children of Kauai," paper presented at a conference on Vulnerability and Resiliency in Children and Families, Baltimore, March 1991.

28. U.S. National Research Council, Panel on Adolescent Pregnancy and Childbearing, C. Hayes, (ed.) *Risking the Future: Adolescent Sexuality, Pregnancy, and Childbearing* (Washington, D.C.: National Academy, 1987).

29. Hayes, *Risking the Future*; D. Kirby, *Sexuality Education: An Evaluation of Programs and Their Effects* (Santa Cruz: Network Publications, 1984); J. Leo, "Sex and Schools," *Time* (November 1986):54–60.

30. M. Stubbs, *Sex Education and Sex Stereotypes: Theory and Practice*, Working Paper No. 198 (Wellesley, MA: Wellesley College Center for Research on Women, ERIC Document Service No. 306–655, 1989), p. 7.

31. Ibid., p. 8; M. Rotheram-Borus et al. "Reducing HIV Sexual Risk Behaviors among Runaway Adolescents," *Journal of the American Medical Association* 266 (4 September 1991): 1237–1241.

32. M. Eisen, G. Zellman, and A. McAlister, "Evaluating the Impact of a Theory-Based Sexuality and Contraceptive Education Program," *Family Planning Perspectives* 22 (November/December 1990):261–271; M. Rotheram-Borus et al. "Reducing HIV Sexual Risk Behaviors."

33. S. Ashton-Warner, *Teacher* (New York: Simon and Schuster, 1963); J. Logan, *Teaching Stories*, paper presented at the American Association of University Women Fellowship, Washington, D.C., 1991.

34. For some disabled girls and women, issues surrounding control and ownership of their own bodies are particularly problematic. For a full discussion of many of these issues see M. Fine and A. Asch, (eds.) *Women with Disabilities: Essays In Psychology, Culture, and Politics* (Philadelphia, PA: Temple University Press, 1988).

35. Emily Yoffe; "Girls Who Go Too Far," *Newsweek*, 22 July 1991, pp. 58–59.

36. J. Martin, *Reclaiming a Conversation: The Ideal of the Educated Woman* (New Haven, CT: Yale University Press, 1985); J. Miller, *Toward a New Psychology of Women* (Boston, MA: Beacon Press, 1976); C. Gilligan, N. Lyons, and T. Hammer, (eds.) *Making Connections: The Relational Worlds of Adolescent Girls at the Emma Willard School* (Troy, NY: Emma Willard School, 1989); C. Gilligan et al., (eds.) *Mapping the Moral Domain: A Contribution of Women's Thinking to Psychological Theory and Education* (Cambridge, MA: Harvard University Press, 1988); N. Noddings and P. Shore, *Awakening the Inner Eye: Intuition in Education* (New York: Teachers College Press, 1984); N. Noddings, *Caring: A Feminine Approach to Ethics and Moral Education* (Berkeley, CA: University of California Press, 1984); C. Witherell and N. Noddings, *Stories Lives Tell: Narrative and Dialogue in Education* (New York: Teachers College Press, 1991); M. Belenkey et al., *Women's Ways of Knowing: The Development of Self, Voice, and Mind* (New York: Basic Books, 1986); see also P. Elbow, *Writing without Teachers* (London: Oxford University Press, 1973).

37. A. Kohn, "Caring Kids: The Role of the School," *Phi Delta Kappan* 72 (March 1991):496–506; A. Kohn, "Responding to Others: The Child Development Project," *The Brighter Side of Human Nature* (New York: Basic Books, 1990).

38. As quoted in *In Their Own Voices: Young Women Talk about Dropping Out*, Project on Equal Education Rights (New York: National Organization for Women Legal Defense and Education Fund, 1988), p. 12.

39. Ibid.

40. State of Michigan, Department of Education, Office of Sex Equity in Education, "The Influence of Gender Role Socialization on Student Perceptions," June 1990.

Part Four

*After a Century of Curriculum
Thought: Change and Continuity*

Introduction to Part Four

Our purpose in this last section of the *Reader* is to sample the contemporary field of curriculum studies. Partly our intent is to introduce a range of topics. Still, focusing on recent scholarship is a tricky business. A challenge that we did not face in summarizing the previous readings is that here in the final section we lack the advantage of hindsight. As scholarship ages, its significance seems to emerge almost like the images in a developing photograph. But with contemporary work we are still guessing. What makes a given line of inquiry a part of the curriculum field? Or does it more properly belong to some other specialization? And if scholarship is included in the broad category of curriculum studies, how central is it to the field? When do particular studies represent the influence of other fields, and when do they represent contributions? What counts as pioneering work, or work that is likely to make a difference in the next generation of curriculum scholarship?

In selecting and organizing the following articles, we have not always had firm or clear answers to these important questions. Rather, we have done our best to steer a general course by acknowledging both change and continuity in the field's contemporary landscape. All of the following articles are conceptually linked (in various ways) to the traditions represented in earlier sections of the *Reader*. This continuity is what gives the readings a family resemblance common to curriculum scholarship *per se*. At the same time, many of the readings either cross into other fields or signal new directions for previous work. On both counts, we looked for scholarship that did not simply follow the beaten path.

The inseparability of change and continuity is important for practical reasons. If we were concerned only with change such as the field's responsiveness to political headlines, the following scholarship would represent little more than a survey of last season's curricular fashions. Veteran scholars know that today's hot topics in the educational press may well be tomorrow's forgotten curiosities. But if we were to take the other extreme, concerned solely with continuity, our selection would include just those authors who are undisputed "curriculum" scholars and only those reading that focus on developments internal to the field. To do so is to close the field by talking just with those in our particular "discourse." To put this another way, a preoccupation with who we are risks diverting attention from broader educational trends, and it does seem that the field on occasion has been caught unaware as the day-to-day realities of school practice marched over the horizon and out of sight.

We hope our selections avoid both the extremes of faddism and intellectual stasis. As with a number of readings later in this section, the first reading illustrates vital connections between the field and current national issues. The reading, "HIV/AIDS Education: Toward a Collaborative Curriculum," is a chapter from Jonathan Silin's book, *Sex, Death, and the Education of Children.* Most of the chapter is based on the author's work with classroom teachers as they examine how curricula convey both information and cultural myths about HIV/AIDS. In Silin's view, recognizing HIV/AIDS as a social construction is important because the embeddedness of this disease in social norms and cultural beliefs is what creates special challenges for teachers and curriculum developers. These norms and beliefs range from conceptions of childhood to questions of teacher authority. In framing these issues, Silin acknowledges his debt to earlier curriculum thinkers, including John Dewey, the field's critical theorists, and those who have approached curriculum from a phenomenological perspective. Silin also argues that, for better and worse, other past curriculum traditions have significantly influenced practices in contemporary schools.

The next reading, William Doll Jr.'s excerpt from his book *A Post-Modern Perspective on Curriculum*, illustrates the connections between past and present curriculum thought in another way. Doll argues that our role as scholars is to bring the curriculum field into our post-modern era. On the one hand, the need to update curriculum thought, to move it forward with the times, signals a break from the past, and especially a break from modernism. On the other hand, breaking from tradition is itself something of a tradition in the field. To group Doll with the likes of Bobbitt and Tyler hardly seems appropriate. But regardless of how we categorize this author, Doll's alternative to the Tyler rationale opens up intriguing questions around the criteria he labels:

Richness—a curriculum's depth of meaning;
Recursion—the complex structures that support critical reflection;
Relations—the intersecting of curriculum and cultures, and
Rigor—a commitment to exploration.

Whereas Doll seeks to supplant tradition, the third reading, Peter Hlebowitsh's "Generational Ideas in Curriculum: A Historical Triangulation," is less ready to lay tradition to rest. He sees the ideas of Bobbitt and Tyler (both this volume) stretching down to the present in the still-discussed work of Schwab. Hlebowitsh closely examines just what has and what has not changed in the curriculum field. As noted in Part Two, questions persist about Schwab's iconoclastic pronouncement that the field was moribund: Was he calling for burying the field or resurrecting it? Scholars have discerned signs of both. Hlebowitsh takes the position that, for all his iconoclasm, Schwab's championing of deliberation about the practical was a continuation of the Bobbitt-Tyler tradition, albeit in an enhanced way that did more to include classroom teachers.

Whatever merit deliberation by teachers might hold, by the time *A Nation at Risk* (1983) was published policymakers were again looking to top-down reform. The next article, by Wayne Au, is titled "High-Stakes Testing and Curricular Control: A Qualitative Metasynthesis." It serves to introduce the broader trends related to testing, the standards movement, and school accountability as tools to coerce reform. For example, by the opening years of the 21st century, *No Child Left Behind* mandated testing and it was widely assumed that the curriculum would increasingly conform to what was tested: teachers would teach to the test. That is the curriculum would narrow, thus reducing opportunities, for example, for curricular enrichment and individualization of instruction.

Through his analysis of 49 qualitative studies, Au concludes that generally the curriculum is narrowed by high-stakes testing with, for example, instructional emphasis on fragmented pieces of knowledge that are expected to appear on the test. He also concludes, however, that in a significant minority of cases high-stakes testing is associated with enriching curriculum through ways such as integration of knowledge. Thus the general effects of high-stakes testing need to be qualified in much the same way that research by Susan Stodolsky (1999) qualified the old saw that teachers teach by following the textbook: "Too little attention has been given," Stodolsky warned, "to the nature of the books in relation to their use" (p. 145).

The next chapter, by Christine Sleeter and Jamy Stillman, looks at curriculum control in California via content standards in reading/language arts and social studies. Adopting Basil Bernstein's constructs on how curriculum is classified (i.e. how knowledge boundaries and hierarchies are established) and framed (i.e. the degree to which teachers and students have authority to use the curriculum to their own ends and in their own ways), they discern that content standards have been about far more than the declared aim of improving learning through standardizing subject matter. They charge that the standards have been used, for example, to "sanitize" (c.f. Silin, this volume, Chapter 21) ethnic conflict, value competence in English but not the first languages of English Language Learners, and, as Apple (this volume, Chapter 19) puts it, control the work of teachers. Given the breadth of their topic, Sleeter and Stillman inevitably must deal in generalizations about curriculum design, some of which readers might well question. Nevertheless, the weight of evidence clearly suggests their thesis cannot easily be dismissed.

While standards-based accountability has placed renewed emphasis, at least in the United States, on reading and mathematics, the next reading by Leslie Siskin focuses on how high school subjects "outside the core" have responded to this trend. Siskin's report is part of a larger study that examined how the standards movement has played out across various subjects, locations, and different types of schools. Siskin looks specifically at music. Like other subjects, music is uniquely positioned in the hierarchy of secondary school curricula and in how it garners resources. Music also differs from many subjects in its assessment strategies and in traditions. To explore how these concerns shape responses to high-stakes accountability, Siskin examines schools in Kentucky. This state is unlike most others in deciding to include music as a tested subject. With this decision, as Siskin notes, music teachers faced a number of practical challenges, not the least of which was finding agreement on what knowledge and skills across the wide scope of this subject would be appropriate for all students and thus what knowledge and skills should be required for a student to graduate.

In the next reading Elliot Eisner contends that we should know more about schools than simply how well their students score on a standardized test. Eisner has been a consistent voice deploring recent reforms for setting the educational bar too low and devaluing rather than capitalizing on individual differences. He asks us to think more deeply about what schools might accomplish by imagining a temporary halt to all testing. Without the scores, what questions would we ask to determine the quality of any given school? Some of Eisner's own questions include: What forms of thinking do school experiences invite? Are these experiences connected to life outside of school, and do they encourage multiple forms of literacy? Will these experiences help students form their own purposes, work cooperatively, cultivate their personal talents, and take an active part in assessing their own achievements? Eisner admits that these are difficult questions to answer, but he also contends that such questions are at the heart of coming to value diversity in our schools.

The next three readings take up this theme of valuing diversity and the challenges this presents for curriculum design and implementation. The first reading is by Angela Valenzuela. She examines how dominant English-speaking culture affects schooling for children of Mexican descent. Valenzuela studied a large, comprehensive inner-city high school in Houston where virtually all the students are Mexican (45 percent immigrant and 55 percent U.S. born). Eighty-one percent of the teachers are non-Latino and 19 percent Latino.

Her thesis is that a process of "de-Mexicanization" was taking place, by which schools "subtract" cultural resources from students. Thus, although schooling is supposed to be "additive," for many of the students she observed the opposite happened. She sees two main reasons for this plight. First, students' culture and language, which are "consequential to their achievement and orientations toward school," are devalued by the school and education system more generally. Second, the school and the system see the students as unresponsive or even hostile to well-intentioned efforts to educate them. Regardless of the students' nativity, Valenzuela argues, education is understood in Mexican culture as more than just book knowledge but also "to live responsibly in the world as a caring human being, respectful of the individuality and dignity of others" (this volume). Valenzuela finds this view of education to fit closely with Nel Noddings' theory of care. For Noddings *authentic caring* is premised on *relation*, in this case between students and teachers or administrators. Thus, while the teachers charged that students don't *care about* their schoolwork, such caring is unlikely to happen until these students' expectations of being *cared for* are met.

The third reading in this group is authored by Elaine Chan who describes a study conducted in Canada. While the location differs, the themes in her article hold more than a passing similarity to the aforementioned studies conducted in California and Texas. Chan studied two teachers at a school in Toronto neighborhood with a diverse population, many of whom were immigrants. The teachers tried to acknowledge the ethnic, linguistic, and religious diversity of their students and the community in their curriculum and teaching practices.

Chan's report focuses on the "complications and challenges" that arise in organizing a 4-day field trip for an outdoor education activity, which school personnel saw as holding strong educational potential. The two teachers soon found, however, that a number of parents did not wish their children to go on the trip. The reasons varied but all were related in one way or another to diversity of views and needs among the school's varied constituents. For example, one parent was opposed to the field trip because the student was needed at home as a caregiver for a younger sibling, another parent did not believe girls should go on such a trip, and so on. Chan underscores how diversity has layers of meaning affecting school communities that go beyond multicultural content or culturally-sensitive pedagogy. It is no simple task, apparently, to respect diversities that may have contradictory tenets. Indeed, Chan ponders the questions: "What does it mean for a school community to be "accepting" of diversity?" (this volume, Chapter 29).

In the next reading, Stephen Thornton looks at another aspect of diversity: the heteronormativity of curriculum. Thornton argues that although gay issues are a visible part of public life in the contemporary U.S., they are avoided in schools and especially absent in social studies curricula. Not only can this absence be damning in itself, but it entirely dismisses the question of how sexual orientation should be represented, on what terms, and from whose perspective. Avoiding these questions leave students in the hands of what Thornton calls "the hidden curriculum everyone sees." This is a curriculum that stigmatizes any deviance from heterosexual experience, which Thornton notes "is surely one of the most successful exercises in social training that schools perform" (this volume, Chapter 30).

The next three readings do not so much leave diversity as a theme but insert it in what many consider the fundamental issue of the times, globalization. In the first of these articles, David Geoffrey Smith takes a postmodern perspective on globalization. He suggests the term is understood in 3 primary ways: as radical neo-liberalism or free-market ideology, as how people around the world are accommodating to or resisting globalization, and as global dialogue about sustainable human futures. His most direct relevance to this *Reader* is his view of proper educational responses to the third sense of globalization. To this end, he suggests curricular emphases on, for example, peace. He also dwells, like Valenzuela, on the central place of relationship in teaching, which he sees as ever more important in a globalizing world where young people may feel disconnected from their roots.

The next reading by Peggy McIntosh looks at what gender means in education for citizenship in a globalizing world. Citizenship and education about it, she notes, has traditionally been gendered, with its very definition being centered fundamentally in male experience rather than a human experience. With vivid autobiographical detail McIntosh lays out what curriculum, and the essentials of teacher education to support it, for citizenship in a globalizing world might look like if women's experience was given equal weight with men's experience.

The next reading by C. A. Bowers is concerned with globalization and its impact on ecological sustainability. Bowers work is rooted in the sociology of knowledge and his longstanding concern for how language tacitly reproduces ways of thinking developed in the past to suit modern, industrial societies. These ways of thinking support the free-market ideology that has been detrimental to both environmental and cultural sustainability. As a counter to this ideology and its related preoccupation with unbridled consumerism, Bowers focuses on using forms of cultural inquiry to teach about the commons. He uses the term "commons" to identify the diverse cultural resources that are openly shared by a wide range of cultural groups. The cultural commons include education itself, but also knowledge of food preparation and storage, the arts, ceremonies and narratives, physical landscapes, built environments, and certain aspects of technology. Bowers argues that teachers should have two aims in teaching about these topics. First, they should strive to show how the commons offers an alternative to individual interests and our contemporary lifestyles that consume such high levels of energy and expand the harmful impact of humans on the environment. The second aim is to help students understand how the commons are increasingly being enclosed by those who are determined to use them as marketing opportunities.

The final reading is a chapter on educational aims from Nel Noddings' book, *Happiness and Education*. It is an apt closing piece for the *Reader* as she notes how school reform has increasingly lurched forward with scant debate on whether the movement is in the right direction, let alone "right direction" for whom? No educational question, she reminds us, is more basic than purpose. Are the purposes of schooling limited to individual and national economic advancement, as the language of school reform in recent decades tacitly or not so tacitly suggests?

Noddings surveys the purposes of aims-talk in the work of past educational thinkers and suggests its relevance to the contemporary situation. To underscore the absence of aims-talk in current policy trends, Noddings makes a distinction among educational *objectives*, which typically reference the sequence in which content is taught; *goals*, which reference reasons for teaching particular students a given subject; and *aims*, which refer to who benefits and how. Noddings also argues that while aims are especially important to consider in analyzing present policies, aims more generally do not serve us in mechanical or deterministic ways. Rather, Noddings urges us to consider that aims may be to education what freedom is to democracy. Their relationship is dependent, but not one we can take for granted.

Reference

Stodolsky, S. S. (1999). Is teaching really by the book? In M. J. Early & K. J. Rehage (eds.), *Issues in curriculum* (pp. 141–168). Chicago: National Society for the Study of Education.

21

HIV/AIDS Education: Toward a Collaborative Curriculum

Jonathan Silin

AIDS radically calls into question the pleasures and dangers of teaching.
(Cindy Patton, *Inventing AIDS*)

AIDS makes no sense. However, the continuing proliferation of HIV/AIDS curricula speaks to our very real desire to claim epistemological rationality and epidemiological certainty in a world plagued by a new and as yet incurable disease. In defining HIV/AIDS as a biomedical event that can be addressed only by those trained in science and health education, we attempt to make it safe, contained within a specific discipline, so that it will not contaminate other areas of study. When the topic of HIV/AIDS is sanitized, teachers and students are protected from the truly unhealthy aspects of society that might otherwise be revealed; the status quo is ensured.

But diseases are constituted through dynamic interactions of biomedical, economic, psychosocial, and political factors. The existential realities of otherness, the politics of distancing, and our search for certainty suggest key elements in the social construction of HIV/AIDS. Understanding the meanings of a given illness involves far more than simply identifying a causal agent and a medical remedy. Just as efforts at prevention cannot be limited to the presentation of risk-reduction strategies, in the hope that exposure to a few facts and rehearsal of skills will lead to lasting changes in behavior, so coming to terms with the social ramifications of HIV/AIDS cannot be achieved through a limited focus on scientific knowledge. Effective prevention involves individual struggles with the meaning of sex and drugs, and a successful societal response calls for recognition of the multiple factors shaping the disease process.

HIV/AIDS presents a complex set of challenges for the curriculum maker. At first, school administrators perceived HIV/AIDS primarily as a policy problem requiring the attention of legal and public health experts to assess the feasibility of excluding students and staff with HIV. But as the crisis over the presence of people with HIV/AIDS in the schools abated, and awareness that HIV/AIDS was not confined to marginal risk groups grew, educators turned toward their pedagogical function. The process was hastened as more and more states mandated K–12 AIDS education.

Early curricular materials reflected simplified interpretations of the disease; they focused on prevention for adolescents and claimed to offer only "facts." But the assertion of objectivity is in itself a form of bias, carrying the implication that it is possible to separate fact from value, object from subject, the word from the world. It is this mindset that was exemplified by a New York City public school official who, in response to a film made to be shown in the city high schools, remarked, "There was a segment that was too long, simply to the effect that you should be nice to homosexuals. The attitude was not a problem, but this is not an attitude film. This is supposed to be an *educational* film" (*CDC AIDS Weekly*, 1986, p. 9). In the scene referred to, a heterosexual man recounts his first reactions to learning that his brother is gay and has AIDS.

If we acknowledge that attitudes and values play a role in shaping individual behaviors and the allocation of material resources in society, it is hard to understand how exclusion of these very factors can lead to a serious discussion of the problem at hand. The denial of subjectivity within the curriculum only falsifies experience and alienates students from their own possibilities. This is not to say that subjectively held opinions must be accepted uncritically but rather that they can become the text for examining the social determination of "private" ideas. Students can learn to question the sources of their knowledge and its reliability and to identify alternative reference points. HIV/AIDS provides an opportunity to practice the critical thinking skills valued so highly by educators today. It is an issue that most graphically illustrates the paradoxes and contradictions of our society.

In this chapter I seek to understand the fundamental inadequacies of our past efforts to talk with children about HIV/AIDS and to create new possibilities for such dialogues. Beginning with younger children and moving on to adolescents, I draw on my work with teachers, administrators, children, and parents in many public and private schools across New York State. These schools were located in a diverse cross-section of racial, ethnic, religious, and economic communities and reflected very different commitments to HIV/AIDS education.

Listening to Young Children

As an early childhood educator, I was trained to listen to and observe young children. Raised and educated in a Deweyan tradition, I understand curriculum as a negotiated process, an outgrowth of the interests of the child and the community. While teachers come to the classroom with an agenda based on knowledge of the community, their art rests in helping children move outward from more narrowly based concerns toward the world of larger ideas. At its best, education enables children to see the way that the concepts and skills offered by their teachers, and eventually encoded in the formal disciplines, amplify their powers of understanding and control. The role of teachers is to help their students make sense of the world. Imposing predetermined, formal curriculum on children without reference to their lived experience can leave them alienated from the possibilities of school-based learning.

When I was a doctoral student, encounters with Marxist and critical theorists made me conscious of the manner in which schooling functions to maintain and reproduce unequal distributions of economic and cultural capital (Apple, 1979; Bowles & Gintis, 1976). Recognizing that the most mundane classroom activities, such as recess, might be described as moments of ideological hegemony, I also began to think about the internal contradictions within any system that allow for reflection and transformation. But it is the phenomenologically oriented educationists (Barritt, Beekman, Bleeker, & Mulderij, 1985; van Manen, 1990) who are most mindful of the limitations of scientistically imposed frames of reference and of the need to ground our work in the world of childhood. They urge us to return to the children themselves to uncover what it is that seems to matter, to grasp how they make sense of experience. To accept such a challenge is to abandon the safety of science that allows us to know children from the privileged position of distanced adults. It is to risk the uncertainty of an engagement that threatens the boundaries between knower and known.

When called on to assist schools with curriculum formulation, I began by asking teachers what the children were saying about AIDS. This obviously reflected my commitment as a progressive educator as well as my experiences learning from people with HIV infection. The teachers' responses clearly indicated that HIV/AIDS had entered their classrooms through the voices of their students, regardless of age or formal instruction. Ironically, many of these opportunities occurred in elementary classrooms—that is, precisely those classrooms in which the prospect of HIV/AIDS education seemed most daunting. Sometimes these voices had been heard at unexpected moments, sometimes on more predictable occasions. Almost always, teachers had felt unprepared to take advantage of the moment to begin a dialogue that could lead to more structured learning.

Interestingly, teachers often had to work hard even to remember these incidents. Emblematic of this forgetfulness were the responses of teachers in a seminar I conducted in a semirural community on eastern Long Island. My inquiry as to what they had observed about their students' knowledge of HIV/AIDS was greeted with a painfully long silence. I began to wonder if I had arrived in the only area in New York State that had not been touched by the disease. Then a first-grade teacher tentatively raised her hand. She described the pandemonium that had broken out in her classroom that very morning when the principal announced, over the school intercom, that AIDS would be the subject of the afternoon staff meeting. Children started accusing each other of having AIDS and warning the teacher not to attend the meeting for fear she might contract HIV from the guest speaker. Given permission by the principal's announcement, the children had released their suppressed concerns. And then a third-grade teacher confirmed that for the past several months AIDS had been the reigning epithet on the playground during recess. It was the label of choice when a group of children wanted to ostracize someone. Games of tag were predicated on avoiding a child who was supposedly HIV-infected.

To these children the mere mention of AIDS provoked excited responses. Whether motivated by specific fears and anxieties, or simply the emotional resonance of the word in our culture, their behaviors accurately mimicked the responses of the majority of adults. To know in more detail what AIDS means to children would require the kind of probing by teachers that leads to a negotiated curriculum, a curriculum in which dialogue is respected and teachers learn with and from their students. For the moment, however, it should be noted that isolation and fear of contagion are being played out without interruption. Educators must recognize their complicity in discrimination by permitting children to use HIV/AIDS, if only in their games, as a means to exclude someone from the social arena. Like gender, race, ethnicity, and disability, HIV/AIDS is an issue of equity.

But children also reveal their awareness of HIV/AIDS in moments that are less incendiary and more focused. In an urban setting, for example, a teacher reported her consternation on a recent class trip upon hearing one child anxiously admonish a friend not to sit down in the subway for fear of contracting AIDS from the seat. The teacher admitted that it was only her concern for the children's safety in the moving train that prompted her to contradict this advice, which had been delivered in the most serious tone. A colleague at the same meeting described overhearing one little boy warning another not to pick up a stick in the park. The warning was based on the child's knowledge that people who use drugs frequented the area at night and his belief that they are the source of HIV infection.

There are few formal studies of young children's knowledge. Farquhar (1990b) documents the practical difficulties in conducting research when we would prefer to protect children than provoke their curiosity. Although Schvaneveldt, Lindauer, and Young (1990) indicate that preschool children know very little about HIV/AIDS, this should not be taken as an indication that they know nothing at all or that AIDS education is irrelevant to their lives. As the anecdotes reported here suggest, HIV/AIDS can be a specter that haunts their movement in the world. For young children, and for many adults as well, fear needs to be replaced by understanding, misinformation by facts. HIV is part of daily life and should be treated as such in schools. To be meaningful, HIV/AIDS information should not be delayed till fourth-grade science curriculum or sixth-grade health class, where it may seem too abstract, removed from students' lived experience. Containing HIV/AIDS within the confines of the highly rational curriculum may offer adults a sense of protection but only at the price of placing their students at increased risk. If we avoid engaging with children about HIV/AIDS, even to counter false information about transmission, we foster the belief that HIV/AIDS is a mystery, a taboo subject that teachers cannot or will not address.

What teachers think about childhood also influences how or even if they will approach HIV/AIDS with their students. For some, children inhabit a very different world from adults. Despite what they may be exposed to at home, on the street, or in the media, they require educational settings where the flow of information is carefully controlled. In contrast, others suggest that what happens to children outside of school should become the object of classroom study. The school is a safe place to make sense of complex and confusing realities. Teachers who believe in this approach are more likely to provide opportunities for critical social issues to become part of the curriculum. For example, I observed a teacher of 6- and 7-year-olds open a class meeting with the simple questions, "What do people use drugs for?" Information and misinformation poured forth from the children. They debated the ethical implications of the use of steroids by Olympic athletes (a subject very much in the news at the time), tried to understand how people actually snort cocaine (believing that it is placed on the outside of the nose), and struggled with why people do things to themselves that they know are harmful. The children saw drugs, rather than infected blood, as the source of HIV infection, and they clearly equated AIDS with death. They proved themselves to be curious, knowledgeable, and capable of thoughtful reflection. Their mistakes were surprisingly rational, the questions they raised worthy of any adult's attention.

In other classrooms the subject of HIV/AIDS may come up in a more oblique manner. A second-grade teacher reported, for example, that her AIDS curriculum began with the failure of two baby rabbits to thrive. Sitting near the cage with a small group of concerned children, one girl began to wonder out loud if perhaps they might have AIDS. The teacher told the children that, while she did not know very much about HIV/AIDS, she did not think it was a disease of animals. Picking up on their concern, the teacher sought more information from the health teacher, whom she also recruited to talk directly with the children. In the kindergarten classroom down the hall, the children had built a block city with a large hospital at its center. In questioning them one day about the ambulance speeding toward its entrance, the teacher was informed that it was carrying a person with AIDS who was very, very sick and going to die. For her, this was the moment to explore what the children really knew about AIDS, part of a larger commitment to understand her students and to bring greater definition to their worlds.

Farquhar (1990b), observing 8- and 10-year-olds, confirms that children's HIV/AIDS knowledge is variable in the extreme. Researchers using developmental frameworks suggest that knowledge is primarily age-dependent. However, Farquhar offers two insights that broaden our appreciation of children's social learning. First, students' emergent understanding of HIV/AIDS is closely associated with knowledge of related topics like sexual behavior or drug use. For example, an 8-year-old's belief that you could "catch AIDS . . . when you go to bed in the same bed" is not surprising given that the child describes "sex" as going to bed with somebody. Similarly, the statement by another child that "smoking causes AIDS" should be understood in the context of her knowledge that cigarettes contain nicotine, nicotine is a drug, and drugs are somehow implicated in HIV transmission. Second, Farquhar notes that many beliefs reflect the myths and stereotypes held by adults and promoted by the media. As they struggle to construct their own meaning, children's knowledge often mirrors that of the adults who surround them.

Even while those committed to conserving the past try to limit the role of the school, the majority are asking it to address an increasingly broad social agenda. Under pressure to do more and to do it better, in a world that offers fewer and fewer support systems for children, there is always the danger of reductionism. Schools reduce complicated social problems to simplified fragments of information, adopt pedagogic strategies that focus on measurable, behavioral outcomes, and define the child as a "learner," as the sum of his or her cognitive competencies. Many teachers see the curriculum in place as the biggest obstacle to effective education, for they recognize that issues such as HIV/AIDS cannot be segmented into discrete, 40-minute units.

The Curriculum in Place

Attending to children suggests the informal ways that HIV/AIDS enters the school and the daily openings teachers have for beginning a dialogue that can lead to a more formal learning plan. Unfortunately, most teachers learn about HIV/AIDS through the demands of a highly rationalized curriculum and without time for reflection. It is not surprising that they react with anger and frustration. Teachers need to be supported as curriculum makers who can respond to their students' immediate concerns while cognizant of the larger bodies of knowledge with which they may be connected. This approach is not compatible with the top-down imposition of lesson plans that are far removed from the children's lived experiences.

The New York State *AIDS Instructional Guide* (New York State Education Department, 1987) is one example of the technocratic mindset that undermines the role of teachers as decision makers. Although designed to be a "guide" and carefully labeled as such, it is worth considering in detail, since many districts adopted it *in toto* as the curriculum in order to save time and avoid controversy. This is an interesting political document, with its community review panels to assure decency, its denial of the sexual realities of teenagers' lives, and its careful attention to parents' rights to withdraw their children from lessons dealing with HIV prevention. To educators, however, this guide may appear as a far more curious pedagogical document because of the way that it parcels out information across the grades.

The *AIDS Instructional Guide* presents a total of 37 lesson plans clustered by grade levels. The K–3 lessons deal with health in general. They barely mention HIV/AIDS at all, though teachers are told that some children may fear contracting the disease and that their questions should be addressed "honestly and simply." Somewhat less than half of the grade 4–6 lessons deal with HIV/AIDS. They describe communicable diseases, the immune system, how HIV is not transmitted, and how to prevent AIDS by abstaining from drug use. Only in the grade 7–8 lessons, a majority of which directly address HIV/AIDS, is there discussion of the sexual transmission of HIV and the possibility of prevention through sexual abstinence. Then, in a country where the median age of first intercourse is 16, and where a third of males and 20% of females have intercourse by 15—and of those currently sexually active, less than half report using condoms—teachers are instructed to emphasize the 13 ways that abstinence makes us free (*Chronic Disease and Health . . .*, 1990).

On the grade 9–12 level, the social and economic consequences of HIV/AIDS are confined to a single lesson featuring a debate on mandatory HIV-antibody testing. Although certain lessons are geared to elicit sympathy for people with HIV/AIDS and thus attempt to curb potential discrimination, never does the guide address the homophobia, racism, and addictophobia underlying much of the HIV/AIDS hysteria that the curriculum is ostensibly trying to dispel. This superficial approach to "humanizing" the disease belies the extensive introductory comments about the importance of pluralism and democratic values. It also denies the fundamental reality of HIV infection in our country—that it has disproportionately affected groups of people who have been marginalized and subjected to various forms of physical and psychological violence (Fraser, 1989). Convincing students to listen to any messages about HIV/AIDS and to understand personal vulnerability cannot be accomplished without interrupting the "us-versus-them" mentality that pervades our social thinking.

There are two assumptions underlying this curriculum guide that bear careful scrutiny. The first is that children's minds are compartmentalized, able to deal with HIV/AIDS information in a logical, sequential order. It assumes, for example, that children can discuss how HIV is *not* transmitted while holding in abeyance for several lessons and/or years how it is transmitted—and how to prevent its spread. No attempt is made to assess what knowledge children come to school with or the kinds of questions their personal experiences may have generated. The child is read as a *tabula rasa* with respect to HIV/AIDS. The New York State Planners appear to have been attending more to the logical order in which they wanted to present a specific body of information than to the psychological order that may reflect children's questions and interests. It seems only fair to ask for the voices of the children in the curriculum—the voices heard on the playground, on the subway, and in the block area. But who is listening? Who has the time?

The second assumption is that HIV/AIDS is a medical phenomenon to be located within the confines of the health curriculum. If we accept that there are economic, political, and social as well as biomedical strands in the Gordian knot that is HIV/AIDS, then an effective educational response does not reside in the province of the health teacher alone. A successful response is a collaborative one involving teachers from all the disciplines, administrators, and parents. In order for students to understand the disease, they must understand the cultural context in which it is occurring. For it is this context that defines how individuals and society at large respond to people with HIV and assign resources to prevention, research, and care.

From this perspective it is easy to see how HIV/AIDS lends itself as a subject for current events and social studies classes. HIV/AIDS raises many questions about access to health care and its costs, the ethics of confidentiality, diseases of poverty, availability of new drugs, and conduct of scientific research. Sloane and Sloane (1990) report on the integration of HIV/AIDS in a class on the history of the United States since 1877, which already includes discussion of the living conditions of North American cities in the late nineteenth century and the incredible toll of epidemic diseases, such as yellow fever, scarlet fever, influenza, and consumption. Here the modern-day epidemic can help students understand the fears and responses of earlier generations and offer the opportunity to clarify the differences between airborne diseases and HIV/AIDS.

There is also a growing body of novels, plays, and poetry emerging in response to this disease, and they provide further opportunities to introduce HIV/AIDS into language arts and English classes (Klein, 1989; Murphy & Poirier, 1993; Nelson, 1992; Pastore, 1992; Preston, 1989). More and more artists and musicians are also turning their attention to the issue, as well might our students in their own work (Klusacek & Morrison, 1992; J. Miller, 1992). The curriculum should reflect the richness of all these imaginative reconstructions, as they offer alternative routes to understanding the impact of HIV/AIDS (Brunner, 1992; Engler, 1988).

In effect, I want to argue that students would be best served if the assumptions underlying the curriculum in place were inverted. First, rather than creating elaborate instructional guides based on a formal ordering of facts, it would be far more helpful to ground the curriculum in the issues that children themselves find challenging, a principle upheld by progressive educators from Dewey to Friere. Second, our very definition of the disease needs to be reexamined in such a way as to permit its multiple ramifications to emerge across the disciplines. This is not to deny the importance of messages about prevention but to underscore the less visible interconnectedness of our social institutions. Successful prevention efforts at all age levels do not seek to abstract and control specific behaviors but rather to help people examine sexual and drug-using practices in the context of their total lives.

The Teacher's Perspective

My own research on pedagogical authority in early childhood (Silin, 1982) revealed that teachers think of themselves as objective professionals acting in the best interests of children. By legitimating this self-definition in their knowledge of child development, teachers could speak authoritatively about other people's children while suggesting a space for family prerogatives with respect to the inculcation of values. Interviews with primary school teachers illustrate the commitment to keeping personal attitudes and beliefs out of the classroom (Farquhar, 1990a). One teacher commented:

> It would be very wrong of me to put my personal interpretation, the standards I use for living my life, to tell them "this is how you should live." . . . It is not the place of the school to criticize in that way, or the teacher to criticize or to imply that one way is right and another way is wrong. (p. 12)

Teachers want to believe that the primary school is simply a purveyor of objective knowledge, that "we present a neutral sort of attitude to facts" (p. 12).

My work on HIV/AIDS curricula with teachers, however, suggests that personal values, prejudices, and preconceptions play a critical role in determining what information they do and do not provide. When people first began to take the facts about HIV transmission seriously, they had to explore previously unrecognized moments of vulnerability in their own lives. The middle-aged woman whose husband had just been through major surgery needed to calculate the odds that he might have received a unit of infected blood; the young male teacher needed to assess his resistance to carrying a condom on his weekend date; and the mother of a grown daughter who shared an apartment with two gay men needed to come to terms with her anxieties about casual contact as a source of HIV infection. Although everyone is better informed today than in 1985, when I began working with teachers on HIV/AIDS curricula, immersion in this issue inevitably leads to rethinking potential risk. When this does not happen, the lack of personal relevance can in some cases lead to a lack of interest. As one of Farquhar's (1990a) interviewees commented:

> This is a big turn-off. It's a big bore for me, because I know I've got nothing to worry about. I've led a monogamous life, I know I'm clear, and I'll always be clear, and I'm not going to come into touch with it. I'm not going to get caught up in drugs, I'm not going to go injecting myself. The blood contamination is the only one that could get me. (p. 12)

In a sense HIV/AIDS happens all at once. Coming to learn about HIV/AIDS in the context of their professional lives, most teachers recognize that this disease has meanings that extend far beyond the clinic, office or hospital room, meanings that will seep into conversations with their own children, affect attitudes toward friends and family, and change lifelong behaviors. It has meaning that even challenges their sense of safety in the workplace. This is the all-at-onceness of HIV/AIDS, a disease that not only destroys an individual's immune system but also breaks down the artificial barriers that we construct between professional and personal lives.

Successful preservice and inservice education depends on the provision of adequate time for teachers to express their feelings about HIV/AIDS and their reactions to talking with children about HIV-related issues (Basch, 1989; Sanders & Farquhar, 1991). For only after these feelings have been acknowledged and discussed can teachers attend to the task at hand. In describing the introduction of an anti-bias curriculum, for example, Derman-Sparks and the A.B.C. Task Force (1989) provide a model for staff development about HIV/AIDS. They emphasize group consciousness-raising for teachers as the first step in creating new curricula on social issues. This process is one that respects the teacher as an adult learner, providing an opportunity to understand the subject matter in more than a superficial manner. A reading of the anti-bias curriculum also suggests that teachers who have placed equity issues high on their own agendas will have less difficulty integrating HIV/AIDS into the ongoing curriculum; these teachers have already created environments in which human differences are discussed and valued. HIV/AIDS education must proceed out of a meaningful context, so students can recognize the familiar and understandable as well as the new and unexpected in this issue.

Institutional Constraints

Talk of staff development, consciousness-raising groups, and adults as learners is not to deny the real constraints under which teachers work. Ironically, the press for school reform initiated by the publication of *A Nation at Risk* in 1984 has resulted in increased demands for required courses, quantitative measurement, and universal standards. The introduction of HIV/AIDS education has meant that teachers must squeeze an additional topic into their already overcrowded, overorganized days. It becomes another requirement that impinges on what little discretionary time remains to them. Even as leaders of industry and labor are calling for greater teacher autonomy to increase school effectiveness, and experiments in teacher-based school governance proliferate, state mandates for HIV/AIDS education allocate few resources for staff development (Kenney, Guardado, & Brown, 1989). If teachers are to engage in the decision-making activities that would define them as professionals, then they must be given the opportunity to develop the knowledge appropriate to such responsibilities (Wirth, 1989).

Thus for teachers, the introduction of HIV/AIDS into the curriculum has also meant preoccupation with negotiating school bureaucracies and calculating the risks of foment-ing change. In most school districts where I have worked, teachers are in agreement about institutionally imposed limitations on what may be said. However, they are often in dis-agreement as to what their individual responses should be. Three solutions to this dilemma are common.

The first solution accepts the limits but recognizes that there are ways to work around them. The second solution, more cynical and despairing, resists any participation in what are perceived to be duplicitous practices. For teachers advocating the first solution, com-promise is essential in order to get critical information to their students. For teachers adopting the second solution, however, the main compromise—that they may respond to questions as raised by students but not initiate certain "hot" topics—is unacceptable. Placing teachers in a position where they rely on student questions, and then refer students back to their parents or to after-school counseling sessions, can undermine the teacher's authority. Unfortunately, the legitimate anger expressed over the moral bind in which they are placed is too often projected onto the subject of HIV/AIDS itself rather than directed at creating a changed educational context.

A third solution to institutionally imposed limits is premised on the teacher's sense of privacy and control when the classroom door is closed; these teachers feel that they are free to say what they want when they are alone with students. Grumet (1988), exploring the experiences of women teachers as well as the histories of women writers and artists, sug-gests the self-defeating nature of this strategy. Describing the importance of private spaces for the development of ideas, she also points to the incipient dangers of isolation and privatization that can result when the doors to these rooms are never opened. The poten-tial for community change can be fostered or thwarted by our willingness to make public that which has been nurtured in private.

But the institutions in which we live and work are often far more permeable than we imagine (Sarason, 1982). If teachers are to be successful change agents—and HIV/AIDS always involves change—then professional education programs must prepare them for their extra-classroom roles. Knowledge of institutional power structures, budget making, and community relations is as appropriate for the classroom teacher as for the administra-tor. All school personnel need to understand that institutions are often less monolithic and more heterogeneous when looked at closely with specific ends in view. Internal contradic-tions provide openings for change. Frequently it is our own perception of hegemony that is the biggest block to creating effective local strategies. Finally, while for some adults the reluctance to talk with children about HIV/AIDS reflects their own lack of knowledge, for others it is part of a consciously held belief system about the nature of childhood. For example, Robin Alexander (1984), in a study of British primary and junior schools, found teachers committed to the idea of childhood as a time of innocence. Although the "pri-mary ideology" recognizes that children are capable of unacceptable behavior, it also deems them free of any malicious intent. Ideas about original sin once promoted by religious reformers have been abandoned, replaced by images of moral purity. In an observational study of three schools, R. King (1978) confirms teachers' determination to protect young children from harsh and corrupting realities of the adult world. In America, California kindergarten teachers have opposed any discussion of HIV/AIDS in their class-rooms because they want to protect children from any unpleasant and, in their view, irrelevant subjects.

When *Young Children*, the Journal of the National Association for the Education of Young Children (NAEYC), published its first HIV/AIDS article, entitled "What We Should and Should Not Tell Our Children About AIDS," it emphasized that the role of the teacher was to soothe the potentially frightened child and avoid presenting unnecessary information (Skeen & Hudson, 1987). Two years later an article on substance abuse prevention in the same journal reinforced a similar philosophy. Misleadingly titled "Drug Abuse Prevention Begins in Early Childhood (And is much more than a matter of instructing young children about drugs!)," it deals solely with the need for parent education and calls for an analysis of parenting styles that promote positive self-images among young children (Oyemade & Washington, 1989). There is little recognition in either article that children may be all too aware of the social problems that exist in their communities. While teachers are constantly reminded to structure environments that are psychologically supportive of personal growth, never is it suggested that they take the lead in providing information about HIV/AIDS or drugs. Nor are they encouraged to help students sort through the multiple meanings they may have already assigned to them. The message is that as long as we follow developmentally appropriate practices, little must change in the way we think about children's lives.

Preparing Classroom Teachers to Talk about HIV/AIDS

To accept that children live in a world where they come to learn about HIV/AIDS, drugs, poverty, and homelessness at a far earlier age than most of us would prefer does not mean we are participating in the denial of childhood. But it does mean we need to create classrooms in which children feel comfortable exploring these issues. Teacher educators can foster this process in two critical ways. First, they can highlight for their students the tension between what we have learned about the social construction of childhood, the embeddedness of our ideas in specific historical contexts, and what we may believe to be optimal conditions for children's growth (James & Prout, 1990a). Wanting the newcomer to feel at home in the world, we each struggle with the degree to which we see childhood as a separate life period requiring specialized protections and professionalized care, and the degree to which we see it as a time for full participation in the ongoing life of the community. The work of those who look at how the social environment is changing the experience of childhood—from the growth of electronic information sources, parental pressure for achievement, and the increasing isolation of children in age-segregated institutions, to the pervasive violence in young people's lives—would be especially helpful with this project (Elkind, 1981b; Garbarino, 1992; Polakow, 1982; Postman, 1982).

Second, given the stressful lives of contemporary children, it is important for teacher educators to emphasize their competencies as well as their developmental deficiencies, a theme I pursue at greater length elsewhere. Here I would mention the use of the anthropological or sociological lens (Felsman, 1989; Glauser, 1990) to focus on the strengths and healthy adaptation rather than weaknesses or pathology of children living in difficult circumstances. I also refer to our increasing knowledge of young children's narrative skills, their use of and understanding of abstract concepts, binary oppositions, metaphor, and humor (Egan, 1988; Sutton-Smith, 1988). Like Robert Coles (1989), we need to listen to the moral energy coursing through the stories of older children living in poverty, as they question and reflect upon their experiences. These stories can tell us how children resist despair, claim dignity in dehumanizing situations, and create redemptive moments out of sorrow.

A Question of Authority

Preparing classroom teachers to integrate HIV/AIDS into the curriculum is a complex process not just because it raises personal concerns for individuals or because it may force them to address new subjects such as sex and death. It is complex because it provokes inquiry into basic philosophical issues about the nature of pedagogy, the meaning of childhood, and the role of the teacher as change agent. An incident in the spring of 1986 crystallized for me the underlying theme of this inquiry and much of the teacher discourse on HIV/AIDS. At that time I was asked to talk to a group of angry parents and teachers who were attempting to exclude a 5-year-old girl with AIDS from their school. Within a few minutes of my opening remarks about the severity of the HIV/AIDS problem in the community, I was interrupted by an angry, bearded man in his mid-30s who announced himself to be a teacher, an historian of science, and a parent in the school. Citing the newness of the disease and the constant flow of information from the medical world, he began to question the credentials of the panelists—a physician, a public health official, a school administrator, a parent leader, and myself—one by one. At that moment of attack, rather than becoming defensive as many of the others did, I began to relax. As a former teacher, I recognized a familiar issue emerging, the issue of authority. This irate father was challenging not only the specific information we offered but, more significantly, our fundamental right to influence his children. The shadow of the school–family struggle for the child was lengthening to include HIV/AIDS.

Although this scene took place at the height of HIV/AIDS hysteria, it exemplifies a critical and ongoing theme in the HIV/AIDS discourse: the challenge that the disease poses to traditional concepts of authority. For many, authority implies certainty, the right to guide others based on full knowledge of the outcomes of the recommended actions. But HIV/AIDS is not about absolutes. It is defined by a series of changing practices, bodies of knowledge, and contexts. AIDS educators and policy makers are skilled at juxtaposing theoretical possibilities against actual probabilities, an unsatisfying dialectic for those who feel personally threatened and seek safety through guarantees. Yet physicians and other officials who assert certainty lose credibility as well. For in their attempt to reassure, they fail to acknowledge the reality of indeterminacy, an acknowledgment that would allow them to form a sympathetic alliance with an anxious audience. The ethical and practical implications of HIV/AIDS test our tolerance for uncertainty as well as our commitment to live the democratic principles that speak to inclusive rather than exclusive modes of behavior.

While the father described in this incident was particularly direct in his attempt to discredit our authority, or perhaps more accurately, even the possibility of the existence of authoritative knowledge about HIV/AIDS, he was raising the same question that emerged in countless sessions with teachers at that time. Teachers were faced with a dual quandary. They saw themselves as possibly in danger, not only because they were acceding to policies based on calculated risks, but also because they were being asked to initiate HIV/AIDS instruction without feeling confident about the information they would be transmitting. Obviously, HIV/AIDS also meant talking about sex, drugs, and death, often taboo subjects that are not easily packaged into highly rationalized lessons. Without certainty, lacking definitive research or a legitimated history to support current assertions, teachers wondered what stance to adopt with regard to the subject. They wondered how not to place their own authority in jeopardy with students. When teachers believe their ability to influence students rests in the control of information, the lack of that control can lead to a lethal silence.

Teachers now recognize that their failure to respond to many teachable moments reflects a lack of confidence in their own HIV/AIDS knowledge. A subtle but more positive shift in attitudes has occurred when professionals refer to their ignorance rather than to lack of scientific proof. The reservations are less about the validity of scientific knowledge than about their familiarity with it. Yet there is something fundamentally askew when teachers are unwilling to admit to students that they do not know the answers to their questions and use this as a rationale for pretending that the subject does not exist. While the obvious remedy to this situation is to provide all teachers with a good basic education about HIV/AIDS so that they feel competent, a long-range response must also be pursued by encouraging teachers and those who work with them to examine the sources of their authority. For HIV/AIDS is not the only difficult issue teachers face in the classroom where the willingness to model the role of learner takes precedence over the traditional role of knower.

Collaboration in Health and Education

The high degree of control and standardization in American public schools that under-mines the initiative of teachers has been amply documented by historians and sociologists of education (Apple, 1982; Tyack, 1974). Frequently denied the choices that would express their pedagogic expertise, teachers are reluctant to take on subjects like sex, illness, and death that leave them in undefined territory where previous understandings of authority may seem less relevant. In such territory, student-teacher distinctions based on the owner-ship of knowledge may break down in the face of the greater commonalities that we all share regardless of age.

The breakdown of hierarchical authority that may ensue when certainty becomes doubtful has been actively sought by people with HIV/AIDS and their advocates and is a development educators might watch carefully. As individuals confront radical care and treatment decisions, the authority of institutions and private practitioners has come under increasing scrutiny. People with HIV/AIDS often have more information about new drugs or treatments than their health care provider; at other times, the provider may have to acknowledge that little is known about how a drug works or even if it is effective. A collaborative model of health care in which the patient is a full participant seems only appropriate given these circumstances. Such a collaborative model has implications for all professionals who may have once defined their right to practice by the exclusive control of a particular body of knowledge and skills.

As more and more people with HIV/AIDS strive to become involved in the decisions affecting their care, they set an agenda for themselves that does not sound so very different from one that good teachers may set for their students—or indeed that teachers as a group may have for their own development. This is an agenda of increasing independence, autonomy, and self-reliance. Illich (1976), in a book written just prior to the emergence of HIV/AIDS, makes an illuminating distinction between medical and health care, associat-ing the former with the highly rationalized scientific management of illness offered by experts in institutional settings, and the latter with the sociopolitical process that enables people to make life-affirming choices on a daily basis. To Illich, medical care is only a part of a larger set of contextual issues that facilitate or inhibit health. This is not to deny the critical role of technology and professional care but to question how reliance on them affects our sense of dignity and agency.

It would seem that teachers express a similar set of concerns, not only when they *expert* question the ultimate meanings of the <u>technocratic curriculum</u> but also when they assess *control* the administrative structures that frustrate their ability to decide how and what they will *undermines* teach. For the belief in expert control undermines teachers who are asked only to imple-*teachers* ment curricula designed by others, undermines students forced to learn in classrooms in which they are not active participants, and undermines sick people made passive observers of the healing process (Rosenberg, 1987). Collaboration, in education as in health care, may appear risky because it means that experts relinquish some of their control. But it is also a recognition that not all knowledge is about control. While there needs to be space for mastery, there also needs to be a role for understanding and acceptance, for emancipation and liberation.

Is there Safety in Safer Sex?

The interests of early childhood and elementary classroom teachers in becoming knowl-edgeable and establishing a rationale for HIV/AIDS education with younger children are different from those of teachers working with adolescents. In junior and senior high schools, health teachers are trained to talk about sex and sexuality, though permitted to do so with varying degrees of freedom. <u>It is now assumed that HIV/AIDS education is relevant to all students who are potentially sexually active. This has not always been the case.</u>

It is understandable that adults were at first reluctant to admit the presence of a com-plex, wily virus such as HIV in a chameleon-like population that itself often appears to have no other goal than to test the limits of human possibility. During the earliest years of the epidemic, this reluctance to view teenagers as vulnerable to HIV infection was reinforced by the dominant risk-group vocabulary, which suggested that the virus would be contained within specific populations. The social and political marginalization of gay men and injection drug users allowed many to discount their experiences. <u>Today</u>, although there continues to be widespread denial of the existence of gay-identified youth in our classrooms (Rofes, 1989), there is a greater acceptance of the fact that any teenager may *still today 2012?* experiment with behaviors or accede to peer pressure in such a way as to place him- or her-self at risk for contracting HIV. Indeed, it is these very attributes that are most frequently cited as the reasons for making HIV education so daunting.

Whether motivated by irrational fear or realistic assessment of the problem, a strong national consensus exists in favor of HIV/AIDS education for young people (Center for Population Options, 1989). Although compliance may be inconsistent and resistance from the religious right fierce (Gallagher, 1993), over half of the states have mandated HIV/AIDS education in their schools and most others strongly recommend it. Only 13 states have established complete programs including published curricula, training or certifica-tion requirements, and inservice education for staff (Kenney et al., 1989). The absence of resources for staff development is especially notable given recent calls for greater teacher autonomy to increase school effectiveness and the adoption of experiments in teacher-based school governance. <u>In many of the nation's largest school districts, education about HIV has begun to take precedence over education about sexuality.</u> While the majority of schools address both topics, the transitional and often confusing nature of the moment is evidenced by the number of sites that offer HIV/AIDS education but not sexuality education, and others where the situation is reversed.

HIV-related curricula tend to have a strong prevention focus. Not surprisingly, the prevention method of choice is clearly abstinence. Of the 27 state-approved curricula, only 8 address abstinence and strategies appropriate for sexually active students in a balanced manner and provide comprehensive information about the epidemic. Indeed, the subject of safer sex is one of the least likely to be discussed with students. While teachers blame their own discomfort with this topic on parental and administrative constraints, lack of appropriate materials, and the embarrassment with which students approach discussions of sexuality, they report little difficulty teaching abstinence and sexual decision making (Kerr, Allensworth, & Gayle, 1989). This suggests that the latter topic is not so much about learning to make choices from a world of possibilities as about deciding to say "no" to sex, based on a predetermined set of behavioral rules. That decision making has become a code phrase for a "just say no" message is underlined by teachers' responses to survey questions. There is almost universal commitment to programs that enable students to examine and develop their own values; yet three-quarters of the same teachers believe that students should be explicitly taught not to have sex (Forrest & Silverman, 1989). The values clarification discussion becomes the critical vehicle for persuading students to own the adult perspective.

Despite media and school-based efforts, teenagers remain woefully ignorant about HIV and ill disposed toward people with AIDS (Brooks-Gunn, Boyer, & Hein, 1988; Hingson & Strunin, 1989). This is of increased concern for African-American and Latino communities whose youth represent 34 percent and 18 percent respectively of adolescents with AIDS but who, in comparison with their white peers, are less knowledgeable about HIV and the effectiveness of condoms for prevention (DiClemente, Boyer, & Morales, 1988). Overall, AIDS is the sixth leading cause of death among those aged 15 to 24 (*Chronic Disease and Health . . .*, 1990). While adolescents are only 2 percent of total AIDS cases, for the past six years the number of cases among 13- to 19-year-olds has doubled every 14 months, the same rate of expansion seen among gay males in the first years of the epidemic. Other studies indicate that 7 percent of homeless and runaway youth and 1 percent of all teenagers in high-incidence cities like New York and Miami may have already contracted HIV (Society for Adolescent Medicine, 1994). Most disturbingly, over one-fifth of people with AIDS are in their 20s. Because the average latency period between initial infection with HIV and the onset of CDC-defined AIDS is 10 years or more, it can be inferred that many of these people contracted the virus as teenagers.

State-approved HIV/AIDS curricula usually give priority to information about healthful lifestyles, communicable diseases, and HIV transmission and prevention. But many pose constraints to the discussion of subjects that might be interpreted as facilitating sexual activity—contraception, safer sex, and sexuality—even though studies indicate that sex education leads not to more sex but to more responsible sex, including the postponement of first intercourse, safer practices, and fewer unwanted pregnancies (Altman, 1993a).

Unfortunately, evidence also suggests a lack of practical efficacy in our efforts; only 8 percent of males and 2 percent of females reported condom use after exposure to AIDS education. Among homosexual/bisexual males, those who reported using condoms increased from 2 percent to 19 percent after AIDS education (Bell, 1991). Studies (New York City Board of Education, 1990) conducted two years after implementation of specific curricula point to little or no change in actual knowledge. When asked, students report that they learn about HIV/AIDS primarily from the media and interpersonal sources—for example, friends and parents ("What High School Students Want . . .," 1990). Schools are listed third, and teachers are described as ill informed, reluctant to talk about disease and sexual activity, and uninterested in HIV/AIDS education. Students themselves request more extensive and intensive education, beginning earlier, and including presentations by people with HIV/AIDS, targeted information about prevention, condom availability, and discussion of the psychosocial impact of the disease.

The Life-Skills Approach

In order to create more effective programs, some curriculum makers (Basch, 1989; Keeling, 1989) have focused on what they perceive as a critical gap between information and/or self-perception and behavioral change. Mickler (1993), studying AIDS-preventive behavior among college adolescents, found that knowledge of AIDS was not predictive or strongly related to safer sex practices. Others (Koopman, Rotheram-Borus, Henderson, Bradley, & Hunter, 1990), working with adolescent runaways and self-identified gay males, reported that both groups had moderately positive beliefs about their self-efficacy and self-control in sexual situations. Yet in focus groups they were unable to role-play safer behaviors, such as asking about their partners' sexual history or asking their partners to use a condom. More significantly, although three-quarters had engaged in sexual activity in the previous three months, with a mean of 2.7 partners, all reported infrequent condom use.

Increasingly, HIV/sexuality education curricula emphasize an ill-defined cluster of behaviors variously labeled as coping, problem solving, or life skills. Depending on the commitment of the particular curriculum, it is claimed that these skills will enable teenagers to remain abstinent until marriage, delay intercourse until an unspecified time in the future, or negotiate safer sex practices as necessary. Through active participation in role-playing, brainstorming sessions, and games, students are taught resistance or refusal skills so that they will not succumb to pressures from peers. These skills are often reduced to a set of sharp retorts that permit students to say "no" to sexual activity without losing face among their friends. In some instances a few lessons are added to more traditional, direct-instruction curricula, while in others, information is interwoven into a consistently interactive format (Brick, 1989).

But as progressive educators have asserted since the last century (Dewey, 1900/1956), students learn most effectively when in the midst of meaningful activities. Programs that abstract social skills provide neither the motivation nor intentionality required for substantive learning. A curriculum that attempts, in a few brief lessons, to teach students how to make critical decisions cannot make up for years of education that have denied them the right to become autonomous, self-determining learners. Friday afternoon "magic circles" to build self-esteem or Monday morning rehearsals of refusal skills divert our attention from the realities of contemporary children, who too seldom have the opportunity to make meaningful choices, follow through on them, and reflect on their consequences.

Skill-based approaches are built on the understanding that the lack of a positive self-image is the biggest factor preventing teenagers from making healthy decisions. Nationally distributed curricula such as "Project Charlie" (Charest, Gwinn, Reinisch, Terrien, & Strawbridge, 1987) and "Growing Healthy" (National Center for Health Education, 1985) are being described as panaceas to a wide variety of problems, including high school dropout rates, lowered academic performance, widespread alcohol and substance abuse, and teenage pregnancy. As in similar programs designed to improve adult productivity in the workplace, the focus on changes in self-perception and interpersonal skills masks material barriers to real equity and autonomy (Steinberg, 1990; L. Williams, 1990).

Self-esteem has become a popular buzzword for efforts to promote better psychological adjustment to the political status quo.

The seemingly humanistic techniques of self-empowerment models often become a means to reproduce a hegemonic ideology, instantiating subtle but powerful forms of social control (Young, 1990). This occurs, for example, when the press to insure safer sex, whether condom use for gay men or abstinence for teenagers, impels facilitators to assume responsibility *for* group members rather than *toward* them. The most sympathetic educators may fail to exercise pedagogical tact when confronting HIV/AIDS. Programs are coercive to the degree that they compromise the participants' abilities to draw their own conclusions from experiences that take place within a context that specifically proclaims the importance of individual choice. Experiential learning becomes a means to an end rather than an open exploration of possibility, including the potential rejection of safer sex practices.

Both individual behavior change and self-empowerment models are based on the instrumentalist assumption that behavior can be isolated, analyzed, and understood apart from the socioeconomic context in which it occurs—an assumption that negates the necessity of addressing issues of the differential distribution of economic and cultural capital. Brandt (1987) comments:

> These assumptions with which we still live regarding health-related behavior rest upon an essentially naive, simplistic view of human nature. If anything has become clear in the course of the twentieth century it is that behavior is subject to complex forces, internal psychologies, and external pressures all not subject to immediate modifications, or, arguably, to modifications at all. (p. 202)

The historical record not only documents the past failure of narrow approaches to the control of sexually transmitted diseases but also the degree to which they are constructed upon a set of moralistic judgments about the nature of sexual activity (Fee & Fox, 1988).

In a democratic society that is respectful of pluralism and accepting of different rates and ways of learning, the public health goal of zero transmission, 100% risk reduction, is not only counterproductive but politically unacceptable (Bell, 1991). Compromise is inevitable in societies where absolute control over citizens' (mis)behaviors is given up in the interests of the responsible exercise of individual freedom. It is as inappropriate to employ coercive measures as it is to gauge the success of HIV/AIDS education by gross measures of behavioral change.

The Collective-Action Approach

While much is to be learned from the cognitive social learning theory (e.g., active engagement of students, multiple levels of learning, and variable strategies) underlying skill-based programs (Flora & Thoresen, 1988), its limitations are highlighted by a triphasic map of health education including individual behavioral change, self-empowerment, and collective action models (French & Adams, 1986; Homans & Aggleton, 1988). The underlying assumption of the first two approaches, also referred to as direct-instruction or experientially based programs, is that increased information about HIV risk behaviors reduces infections (Eckland, 1989). The linear reasoning embedded in these approaches, along with questions of long-term effectiveness and ethics, is exposed when they are juxtaposed against a collective-action model of health education. In addition to addressing the need for information and communicative skills, the collective-action approach encourages organizing to transform the social and political forces that shape and give meaning to individual behavior.

When the connection between health status and poverty, employment, income, and social class is fully recognized, then socioeconomic factors appear to have greater significance for health than do individual behaviors ("Demand side," 1993; Hubbard, 1993). These factors are best addressed through collective action in the political process. While this position is consistent with radical definitions of health and illness (Illich, 1976), it threatens the official governmental position on disease causation, as summarized by the Presidential Commission on the Human Immunodeficiency Virus Epidemic (1988), which is that "the heaviest burden of illness in the technically advanced countries today is related to individual behavior, especially the long-term patterns of behavior often referred to as 'life-style' " (p. 89). Paradoxically, it is this attempt to define critical social issues as private and personal rather than as public and political that heightens the very bigotry that the Presidential Commission seeks to dispel.

In fact, safer sex organizing began as a grass roots political movement within the gay community (Patton, 1990). Its greatest successes occurred in the first years of the epidemic prior to the professionalization and bureaucratization of HIV prevention. Some continue to understand that health education, community building, and political resistance are inextricably linked. Cranston (1992), for example, proposes HIV/AIDS education among gay and lesbian youth based on Paulo Freire's concept of the community of conscience. Consistent with a collective action model, this is HIV prevention that leads to political engagement because it values and fosters respect for gay histories, identities, and futures. Others (Gasch, Poulson, Fullilove, & Fullilove, 1991) understand the disproportional impact of HIV/AIDS on African-American populations as part of a more generalized pattern of excessive risk and mortality. They stress the role of the social and material environment in conditioning health-related behaviors. Poor African-American communities are best served by developing an analysis that will enable their members to work toward means connecting individual behavior to larger social changes.

Assessing the impact of a curriculum requires an exploration of the knowledge assumptions on which it is based. This assessment is critical to dispelling the myths about sexual identity and behavior that prevent effective HIV/AIDS education. Limiting the terrain of HIV/AIDS education to that of a "solvable" social question involving risk-reduction strategies has led to correspondingly limited answers focusing on either behavioral or attitudinal changes (Diorio, 1985). Valued knowledge is construed in the former case as the sum of facts and skills and in the latter as the ability to understand the intentions of others through improved communication abilities. However, HIV/AIDS is not only a question of individual behaviors and social norms. It is also a question of material conditions and resources, and structural inequities based on race, class, gender and sexual identities.

Sex, HIV, and the Permeable Curriculum

AIDS is a disease of contradictions. It is a disease that is not a disease, a biological reality that has had a greater impact on sociopolitical practices than on medical care, an illness of hiddenness that has led to irreversible changes in public discourse. Unfortunately, HIV infection has also become a disease of adolescence, a period characterized in our society by its own unique logic—moments of sudden growth and regression, of open search and certain definition, of personal power and extreme susceptibility to the influence of others. An additional conundrum now presents itself: Safer sex alone will not make us safe from the effects of HIV.

The complexity of HIV/AIDS mandates a multifaceted approach. Reconceptualizing HIV/AIDS education means abandoning the instrumentalist assumptions of information- and skill-based programs that have led many to theorize the problem of HIV/AIDS education as one of bridging a gap between knowledge and behavior. Preventing the transmission of HIV involves not only learning about condoms, spermicides, and negotiating sex; it also means developing tools of political analysis, a commitment to social change, and an ethic of caring and responsibility. In short, we must shift our attention from HIV prevention narrowly defined as a means of behavioral control to a broader focus that would more accurately reflect our students' life worlds. HIV/AIDS education should further the goal of preparing students to become active participants in a democratic society. But what are the elements of such an approach?

First, HIV/AIDS education needs to begin with the youngest children and permeate the curriculum in order to break down the taboos with which it is associated and to make the subject a more comfortable one for discussion (Quackenbush & Villarreal, 1988). Our efforts should be informed by an appreciation of the development levels and experiential bases of different groups of students. We must ask whether the curriculum ensures equal access to HIV/AIDS information for all students. Access means that students not only have the opportunity to hear information but that it is presented in a language and style easily understood by specific target groups (Nettles & Scott-Jones, 1989). At the same time, as with other subject areas, we must be concerned with unwarranted differences in curriculum predicated on the race, class, gender, or sexual orientation of our students (Apple & Weiss, 1983; Willis, 1977).

Effective sexuality education itself, education that empowers students by building their sense of entitlement and decreasing their vulnerability, is based on our willingness to listen to and work with experiences students bring with them. This requires giving up presuppositions about the nature of sexuality and the outcomes of our efforts in favor of a socio-historical appreciation of the ways in which sexual meanings are constructed and changed (D'Emilio & Freedman, 1988; Rubin, 1984). Safer sex can be less about the limitations imposed by HIV and the inculcation of specific behaviors and more about exploring multiple zones of bodily pleasures and the transformation of culturally determined constraints (Patton, 1985). In a time of HIV/AIDS, a discursive analysis becomes essential to re-imagining sexual practices in life-affirming, sex-positive ways.

Our goal should be to replace isolated lessons calculated to build self-esteem and social skills with an ongoing discourse of desire that problematizes violence and victimization (Fine, 1988). If the experiences of our students are valorized, they will be better able to understand the sources of pleasure and danger in their own lives. This process begins when students find a safe place in which to tell their stories. To accept these narratives is not only to foster respect for individual differences but also to reveal their distance from officially given versions of human sexuality, a distance that is clearly identified by recent studies of the high school curriculum (Trudell, 1992; Ward & Taylor, 1992). At the same time it is impossible to ignore externally imposed constraints to liberation, for even the best-intended pedagogic efforts may have little impact without increased life options for poorer students and easy access to birth control materials, health clinics, and substance-abuse treatment for everyone.

The permeable curriculum requires balancing our concerns about individual responsibility for transmitting HIV with an analysis of the changing social context in which it thrives. At a personal level, the curriculum causes students to reflect on their own behaviors as they affect the transmission of HIV and the lives of those who already carry the virus. At a social level, the curriculum provokes critical consciousness, fostering responsive and responsible citizens. Students should be asking questions about the societal responses to HIV/AIDS and learning to see themselves as citizens who can make decisions that will give direction to that response in the future. They need access to all kinds of citizens, especially those living with HIV, who model active responses to the disease (Navarre, 1987).

And what does the permeable curriculum say about people with HIV infection—gays, injection drug users, and others? Fear-based appeals have never been successful in preventing the spread of sexually transmitted diseases (Mickler, 1993). Greater familiarity with HIV, not less, is needed in order to break down the distancing mechanisms that allow us to feel that we can remain untouched. Images of diversity remind us that people with HIV/AIDS are a part of all our lives. Although some have real anxiety about what they perceive as a disintegration of culture and an erosion of values in the modern world, HIV/AIDS is not an appropriate metaphor for these concerns. The permeable curriculum is about caring for others and inclusion, not about isolation and exclusion.

Just as effective sexuality education is based on an entire school experience that encourages decision making, problem solving, and self-worth, successful HIV/AIDS education is built on a continuing appreciation of equity and pluralism in society. It cannot be assumed that an absence of negative comment signifies a lack of bias or commitment to social justice (Croteau & Morgan, 1989; Vance, 1984). Educators must take an active role in bringing the full spectrum of human differences to the classroom, acknowledging the ways that these have become sources of conflict and domination as well as the ways that they enrich and form the basis of participatory democracy. A curriculum that is permeable to the impact of students, one through which they can learn the skills of responsible citizenship, lays the groundwork for all AIDS education. For the history of HIV constantly reminds us not only of individual suffering and pain but also of the power and creativity that reside in a collective response.

Although HIV/AIDS may challenge our prior ideas about pedagogical authority, it also offers us an opportunity to examine new models that more accurately reflect who we understand ourselves to be and what we would like our students to become. From HIV/AIDS we learn about the limits of science and the importance of human vision, the frailty of the body and the strength of the spirit, the need to nurture the imagination even as we direct our attention to rational cognitive structures. In the end, the HIV/AIDS curriculum can be more about life than about death, more about health than about illness, more about the body politic than the body physical.

References

Alexander, R. J. (1984). *Primary teaching*. London: Holt, Rinehart & Winston.

Altman, L. (1993a, June 15). Conference ends with little hope for AIDS cure. *The New York Times*, p. C1, 3.

Apple, M. W. (1979). *Ideology and curriculum*. London: Routledge & Kegan Paul.

Apple, M. W. (Ed.). (1982). *Cultural and economic reproduction in education*. Boston: Routledge & Kegan Paul.

Apple, M. W., & Weiss, L. (eds.). (1983). *Ideology and practice in schooling*. Philadelphia: Temple University Press.

Barritt, L., Beekman, T., Bleeker, H., & Mulderij, K. (1985). *Researching educational practice*. Grand Forks: University of North Dakota Press.

Basch, C. E. (1989). Preventing AIDS through education: Concepts, strategies, and research priorities. *Journal of School Health, 59,* 296–300.

Bell, N. Z. (1991). Ethical issues in AIDS education. In F. G. Reimer (ed.), *AIDS and ethics* (pp. 128–154). New York: Columbia University Press.

Bowles, S., & Gintis, H. (1976). *Schooling in capitalist America.* New York: Basic Books.

Brandt, A. M. (1987). *No magic bullet: A social history of venereal disease in the United States since 1800.* New York: Oxford University Press.

Brick, P. (1989). *Teaching safer sex.* Hackensack, NJ: Planned Parenthood of Bergen County.

Brooks-Gunn, J., Boyer, C. B., & Heim, K. (1988). Preventing HIV infection and AIDS in children and adolescents: Behavioral research and intervention strategies. *American Psychologist, 43,* 958–965.

Brunner, D. D. (1992). Discussing sexuality in the language arts classroom: Alternative meaning making and meaning making as an alternative. In J. T. Sears (ed.), *Sexuality and the curriculum* (pp. 226–242). New York: Teachers College Press.

CDC AIDS Weekly. (December 15, 1986). p. 9.

Center for Population Options (1989). *Adolescents, AIDS and HIV: A community wide responsibility.* [Available from Center for Population Options, 1012 14th Street, N. W., Washington, D.C.]

Charest, P., Gwinn, T., Reinisch, N., Terrien, J., & Strawbridge, C. (1987). *Project Charlie.* [Available from Storefront/ Youth Action, 4570 West 77th Street, Edina, MN 55435.]

Chronic disease and health promotion reprints from the mmwr: 1990 youth risk behavior surveillance system. (1990). [Available from U.S. Department of Health and Human Services, Centers for Disease Control, Atlanta, GA 30333.]

Coles, R. (1989). Moral·energy in the lives of impoverished children. In T. F. Duggan & R. Coles (eds.), *The child in our times: Studies in the development of resiliency* (pp. 45–55). New York: Brunner/Mazel.

Cranston, K. (1992). HIV education for gay, lesbian, and bisexual youth: Personal risk, personal power, and the community of conscience. In K. Harbeck (ed.), *Coming out of the classroom closet* (pp. 247–259). New York: Haworth.

Croteau, J. M., & Morgan, S. (1989). Combating homophobia in AIDS education. *Journal of Counseling & Development, 68,* 86–91.

The demand side of the health care crisis. (1993). *Harvard Magazine, 95*(4), 30–32.

D'Emilio, J., & Freedman, E. B. (1988). *Intimate matters: A history of sexuality in America.* New York: Harper & Row.

Derman-Sparks, L., & the A.B.C. Task Force (1989). *Anti-bias curriculum: Tools for empowering young children.* Washington, D.C.: National Association for the Education of Young Children.

Dewey, J. (1956). *The child and the curriculum/The school and society.* Chicago: University of Chicago Press. (Original works published 1902 and 1900).

DiClemente, R. J., Boyer, C. B., & Morales, E. D. (1988). Minorities and AIDS: Knowledge, attitudes and misconceptions among black and Latino adolescents. *American Journal of Public Health, 78,* 55–57.

Dioro, J. (1985). Contraception, copulation, domination, and the theoretical barrenness of sex education literature. *Educational Theory, 35,* 239–255.

Eckland, J. D. (1989). Policy choices for AIDS education in the public schools. *Education Evaluation and Policy Analysis, 11,* 377–387.

Egan, K. (1988). Education and the mental life of young children. In L. Williams & D. Fromberg (eds.), *The proceedings of "Defining the field of early childhood education: An invitational symposium"* (pp. 41–77). New York: Teachers College, Columbia University.

Elkind, D. (1981b). *The hurried child: Growing up too fast, too soon.* Reading, MA: Addison-Wesley.

Engler, R. K. (1988, October). *Safe sex and dangerous poems: AIDS, literature and the gay and lesbian community college student.* Paper presented at the Annual National Literature Conference, Chicago.

Farquhar, C. (1990a). *Answering children's questions about HIV/AIDS in the primary school: Are teachers prepared?* Unpublished manuscript, University of London, Institute of Education, Thomas Coram Research Unit, London.

Farquhar, C. (1990b). *What do primary school children know about AIDS?* (Working Paper No. 1). London: University of London, Institute of Education, Thomas Coram Research Unit.

Fee, E., & Fox, D. M. (1988). *AIDS: The burdens of history.* Berkeley: University of California Press.

Felsman, J. K. (1989). Risk and resiliency in childhood: The lives of street children. In T. F. Duggan & R. Coles (eds.), *The child in our times: Studies in the development of resiliency* (pp. 56–80). New York: Brunner/Mazel.

Fine, M. (1988). Sexuality, schooling, and adolescent females: The missing discourse of desire. *Harvard Educational Review, 58*(1), 29–53.

Flora, J. A., & Thoresen, C. E. (1988). Reducing the risk of AIDS in adolescents. *American Psychologist, 43,* 965–971.

Forrest, J. D., & Silverman, J. (1989). What public school teachers teach about preventing pregnancy, AIDS and sexually transmitted diseases. *Family Planning Perspectives, 21*(2), 65–72.

Fraser, K. (1989). *Someone at school has AIDS.* Alexandria, VA: National Association of State Boards of Education.

French, J., & Adams, L. (1986). From analysis to synthesis. *Health Education Journal, 45*(2), 71–74.

Gallagher, J. (1993, June 15). Why Johnny can't be safe. *The Advocate, 631,* 46–47.

Garbarino, T. (1992). *Children in danger.* San Francicso: Jossey-Bass.

Gasch, H., Poulson, M., Fullilove, R., & Fullilove, M. (1991). Shaping AIDS education and prevention programs for African Americans amidst community decline. *Journal of Negro Education, 60*(1), 85–96.

Glauser, B. (1990). Street children: Deconstructing a construct. In A. James & A. Prout (eds.), *Constructing and reconstructing childhood* (pp. 138–156). New York: Falmer Press.

Grumet, M. (1988). *Bitter milk.* Amherst: University of Massachusetts Press.

Hingson, R., & Strunin, L. (1989). *Summary of results: Boston schools baseline surveys, Spring 1988, 1989.* Unpublished manuscript, Boston University, School of Public Health.

Homans, H., & Aggleton, P. (1988). Health education, HIV infection and AIDS. In P. Aggleton & H. Homans (eds.), *Social aspects of AIDS* (pp. 154–176). London: Falmer Press.

Hubbard, R. (1993, Spring). Viewpoint. *The AIDS Report* [The Harvard AIDS Institute], pp. 13–14.

Illich, I. (1976). *Medical nemesis: The expropriation of health.* New York: Pantheon.

James, A., & Prout, A. (1990a). *Constructing and reconstructing childhood: Contemporary issues in the sociological study of childhood.* New York: Falmer.

Keeling, R. P. (Ed.). (1989). *AIDS on the college campus.* Rockville, MD: American College Health Association.

Kenney, A. M., Guardado, S., & Brown, L. (1989). Sex education and AIDS education in the schools: What states and large school districts are doing. *Family Planning Perspectives, 21*(2), 56–64.

Kerr, D. L., Allensworth, D. D., & Gayle, J. A. (1989). The ASHA national HIV education needs assessment of health and education professionals. *Journal of School Health, 59,* 301–305.

King, R. (1978). *All things bright and beautiful: A sociological study of infants' classrooms.* Chichester: Wiley.

Klein, M. (1989). *Poets for life: Seventy-six poets respond to AIDS.* New York: Crown.

Klusacek, A., & Morrison, K. (1992). *Leap in the dark: AIDS, art & contemporary cultures.* Montreal: Véhicule Press.

Koopman, C., Rotheram-Borus, M., Henderson, R., Bradley, J., & Hunter, J. (1990). Assessment of knowledge of AIDS and beliefs about prevention among adolescents. *AIDS Education and Prevention, 2*(1), 58–70.

Mickler, S. E. (1993). Perceptions of vulnerability: Impact on AIDS-preventive behavior among college adolescents. *AIDS Education and Prevention, 5*(1), 43–53.

Miller, J. (ed.). (1992). *Fluid exchanges: Artists and critics in the AIDS crisis.* Toronto: University of Toronto Press.

Murphy, T.F., & Poirier, S. (eds.). (1993). *Writing AIDS: Gay literature, language and analysis.* New York: Columbia University Press.

National Center for Health Education. (1985). *Growing healthy.* (Available from the National Center for Health Education, 30 East 29th Street, New York, NY 10016.)

Navarre, M. (1987). Fighting the victim label. *October, 43,* 143–147.

Nelson, E. S. (1992). *AIDS: The literary response.* New York: Twayne Publishers.

Nettles, S. M., & Scott-Jones, D. (1989). The role of sexuality and sex equity in the education of minority adolescents. *Peabody Journal of Education, 64*(4), 183–198.

New York State Education Department (1987). *AIDS Instructional Guide.* Albany, NY: Author.

Oyemade, U. J., & Washington, V. (1989). Drug abuse prevention begins in early childhood. *Young Children, 44*(5), 6–12.

Pastore, J. (1992). *Confronting AIDS through literature.* Champaign: University of Illinois Press.

Patton, C. (1985). *Sex and germs: The politics of AIDS.* Boston: South End Press.

Patton, C. (1990). *Inventing AIDS.* New York: Routledge.

Polakow, V. (1982). *The erosion of childhood.* Chicago: University of Chicago Press.

Postman, N. (1982). *The disappearance of childhood.* New York: Delacorte.

Presidential Commission on the Human Immunodeficiency Virus Epidemic. (1988). *Report of the Presidential Commission on the Human Immunodeficiency Virus Epidemic.* Washington, D.C.: U.S. Government Printing Office.

Preston, J. (1989). *Dispatches.* Boston: Alyson Press.

Quackenbush, M., Villarreal, S. (1988). *"Does AIDS hurt?" Educating young children about AIDS.* Santa Cruz, CA: Network Publications.

Rofes, E. (1989). Opening up the classroom closet: Responding to the educational needs of gay and lesbian youth. *Harvard Educational Review, 59*(4), 444–452.

Rosenberg, C. E. (1987). *The care of strangers: The rise of America's hospital system.* New York: Basic Books.

Rubin, G. (1984). Thinking sex: Notes for a radical theory of the politics of sexuality. In C. S. Vance (ed.), *Pleasure and danger: Exploring female sexuality* (pp. 267–320). Boston: Routledge & Kegan Paul.

Sarason, S. B. (1982). *The culture of the school and the problem of change.* Boston: Allyn & Bacon.

Schvaneveldt, J. D., Lindauer, S., & Young, M. H. (1990). Children's understanding of AIDS: A developmental viewpoint. *Family Relations, 38,* 330–335.

Silin, J. (1982). *Protection and control: Early childhood teachers talk about authority.* Unpublished doctoral dissertation, Teachers College, Columbia University, New York.

Skeen, P., & Hudson, D. (1987). What we should and should not tell our children about AIDS. *Young Children, 42*(4), 65–71.

Sloane, D. C., & Sloane, B. C. (1990). AIDS in schools: A comprehensive initiative. *McGill Journal of Education*, *25*(2), 205–227.

Society for Adolescent Medicine. (1994). HIV infection and AIDS in adolescents: A position paper for the Society for Adolescent Medicine. *Journal of Adolescent Health*, *15*(5), 427–434.

Steinberg, C. (1990, February 18). How "magic circles" build self-esteem. *The New York Times*, sec. 12, p. 1.

Sutton-Smith, B. (1988). Radicalizing childhood: The multivocal mind. In L. Williams & D. Fromberg (eds.), *The proceedings of "Defining the field of early childhood education: An invitational symposium"* (pp. 77–153). New York: Teachers College, Columbia University.

Trudell, B. K. (1992). Inside a ninth-grade sexuality classroom: The process of knowledge construction. In J. T. Sears (ed.), *Sexuality and the curriculum* (pp. 203–226). New York: Teachers College Press.

Tyack, D. (1974). *The one best system.* Cambridge, MA: Harvard University Press.

Vance, C. S. (1984). Pleasure and danger: Toward a politics of sexuality. In C. S. Vance (ed.), *Pleasure and danger: Exploring female sexuality* (pp. 1–27). Boston: Routledge & Kegan Paul.

van Manen, M. (1990). *Researching lived experience: Human science for an action sensitive pedagogy.* Albany: State University of New York Press.

Ward, J. V., & Taylor, J. M. (1992). Sexuality education for immigrant and minority students: Developing culturally appropriate curriculum. In J. T. Sears (ed.), *Sexuality and the curriculum* (pp. 183–203). New York: Teachers College Press.

What high school students want from an HIV education program and how it can be delivered effectively: A report to the Bureau of School Health Education Services, New York State Education Department. (1990). (Available from MAGI Educational Services, Inc., Larchmont, NY.)

Williams, L. (1990, March 28) Using self-esteem to fix society's ills. *The New York Times*, pp. C1, 10.

Willis, P. (1977). Learning to labour. Westmead, UK: Saxon House.

Wirth, A. G. (1989). The violation of people at work in schools. *Teachers College Record*, *90*(4), 535–549.

Young, R. (1990). *A critical theory of education.* New York: Teachers College Press.

22

The Four R's—An Alternative to the Tyler Rationale
William E. Doll Jr.

The three R's of "Readin', 'Ritin', and 'Rithmetic" were late nineteenth- and early twentieth-century creations, geared to the needs of a developing industrial society. Reading was the functional reading of sales slips and bills of lading, combined with the inspirational stories of Horatio Alger and the moral aphorisms of McGuffey. Writing was literally penmanship, with the Palmer method introducing a ledger-oriented style in the first grade. Such cursive training had to begin early, for by the fifth grade half of those who had entered as first graders had left. Arithmetic, not mathematics, was essentially column addition and subtraction, with algorithmic multiplication and division coming in the later elementary years. Again, the emphasis was on store clerk functionalism, keeping the sales slips and ledgers accurate and neat. Problem solving was introduced as early as the second grade, but it was heavily, if not exclusively, associated with buying in an urban store.

Born in the early 1930s, I had my early elementary school training in these three R's. My word-lists for reading and spelling prepared me for the urban, industrial society my parents and I inhabited. The Palmer method was begun in the first grade, with an itinerant teacher brought in weekly to instruct us in the big O's and C's so distinctive of its style—flowing but clear. From Miss Wiley, Miss James, and Miss Thatcher—the maiden ladies who taught grades one, two, and three—I learned to keep my ten's column digits out of my hundred's column or my unit's column, and *always* beginning with the right column to "bring down" a single digit and to "carry" into the next column any digits left over. Miss Newcomb in the fourth grade made a small modification to this "consonant" method—namely, that with decimals it was the decimal points which needed to form a vertical, unbroken phalanx. Zeros were added to the right of the decimal point to keep the right column, the hundredths (often considered as pennies), in line.

Mr. Bartlett, our corner grocer, was not as good as my triumvirate of maiden teachers at keeping his columns straight. Further, he began his addition with the left, not the right column. When questioned he stated that he wished to make no mistakes with the dollars or dimes and this method assured him greater accuracy with those important columns. Worse, he grouped digits together either in his head or with small notations in combinations equal to ten. This method intrigued me. I passed on my newfound wisdom to Miss Thatcher (married women were not allowed to teach school). She, however, dismissed Mr. Bartlett's methods as heresy. In retrospect, I think Mr. Bartlett was more industrially oriented than Miss Thatcher and maybe even a better pedagogue. In dealing with my own elementary school classes, I have found that much columnar addition—at least of any practical type—has a better "feel" when it is done left to right, thus allowing intuition and estimation to come into play. Further, doing simple columnar work by grouping numerals into combinations of ten not only produces more accurate and quicker answers but also encourages structural and situational thinking—for example, doing 101–49 as 102–50, or maybe as 100–50 with two added on. Such "chaotic ordering" has been a hallmark of my students' *modus operandi* for many years now—before I read Whitehead or heard of postmodernism; it has generally served them well (Doll, 1977, 1989).

At first glance one does not see a connection between the Tyler rationale and the three R's. However, a pre-set functionalism underlies both. While Tyler's frame expands and broadens industrial functionalism beyond the sales slips and ledgers of the three R's, the assumption of pre-set goals still exists. In this frame, *goals* do not emerge—as Cvitanovi? suggests they should—by "playing with" experiences; rather, goals are pre-determined as are the *experiences* and *methods* for developing those experiences. All are firmly in place before any interaction with students occurs. *Evaluations* are designed to correlate the experiences only with the pre-set goals, not to explore what the students generate personally after reflecting on the experiences. In fact, as was pointed out earlier in the chapter, framing evaluation in terms of generation, reflection, transformation is virtually oxymoronic from a modernist perspective.

So what would serve as criteria for a curriculum designed to foster a post-modern view? What criteria might we use to evaluate the quality of a post-modern curriculum—a curriculum generated not predefined, indeterminate yet bounded, exploring the "fascinating imaginative realm born of God's laughter," and made up of an ever-increasing network of "local universalities?" I suggest the four R's of Richness, Recursion, Relations and Rigor might serve this purpose.

Richness. This term refers to a curriculum's depth, to its layers of meaning, to its multiple possibilities or interpretations. In order for students and teachers to transform and be transformed, a curriculum needs to have the "right amount" of *indeterminacy, anomaly, inefficiency, chaos, disequilibrium, dissipation, lived experience*—to use words and phrases already described. Just what is the "right amount" for the curriculum to be provocatively generative without losing form or shape cannot be laid out in advance. This issue is one to be continually negotiated among students, teachers, and texts (the latter having long histories and basic assumptions that cannot be neglected). But the issue of the curriculum needing disturbing qualities is not to be negotiated; these qualities form the problematics of life itself and are the essence of a rich and transforming curriculum. Another way to state this is to say that the *problematics, perturbations, possibilities* inherent in a curriculum are what give the curriculum not only its richness but also its sense of being, its *dasein*.

The main academic disciplines taught in schools have their own historical contexts, fundamental concepts, and final vocabularies. Hence, each will interpret richness in its own way. Language—including reading, writing, literature, and oral communication—develops its richness by focusing heavily (but not exclusively) on the interpretation of metaphors, myths, narratives. Saying this places language within a hermeneutic frame; it is to see language as integrated with culture, as one of the determinants of culture.

Mathematics—a subject in which computational arithmetic plays but a small part—takes its form of richness from "playing with patterns." Obviously, this can be done *par excellence* with computers—tools that any mathematically rich curriculum should possess—but computers are not a *sine qua non*. Patterns may be seen, developed; played with in simple number combinations (as with the Fibonnaci series) or with geometry of both a Euclidean and fractal sort. Breaking a square into right triangles is an example of the former; the Sierpinski triangle is an example of the latter. At all levels, from kindergarten through graduate school, mathematics can be dealt with meaningfully as "playing with patterns." *Can't "prove"*

Science—including the biological and the physical—can be seen as intuiting, developing, probing, "proving" hypotheses concerning the world in which we live. This moves science beyond the collection of "facts"—with the assumption these facts are objective bits of reality—into the realm of manipulating, creating, working with facts or information in an imaginative and (thermo)dynamic manner. This view of science is obviously more Whiteheadian than Newtonian, more oriented toward Prigogine than Laplace. The social sciences—those multiple disciplines of anthropology, economics, history, psychology, and sociology—take their concept of richness from dialoguing about, or negotiating passages between, various (often competing) interpretations of societal issues. Here, probably more than in any other discipline, assumptions are questioned. It is these assumed givens that form the foundations of society's mores, norms, standards; and in a democratic society it is imperative these givens be open to dialogue. *assumptions must be open to dialogue*

Obviously these disciplines, their languages, and histories are not mutually exclusive. The concept of developing richness through dialogue, interpretations, hypothesis generation and proving, and pattern playing can apply to all we do in curriculum. Again, such ideas sound strange to those imbued with a modernist perspective, which helps explain why we need to transcend this perspective to a post-modernist one.

Recursion. From recur, to happen again,[1] recursion usually is associated with the mathematical operation of iteration. In iteration a formula is "run" over and over, with the output of one equation being the input for the next. In $y = 3x + 1$, a y of 4 (if the $x = 1$) becomes the next x, and the new y of 13 becomes the next x, and so on. In such iterations, there is both stability and change; the formula stays the same, the variables change (in an orderly but often nonpredictable manner). As was explained earlier, some interesting complex patterns develop with particular formulae and particular x, y variables.

However, when Bruner (1986) states that "any formal theory of mind is helpless without recursion" (p. 97)—and asserts the importance of recursion for epistemology and pedagogy—he refers less to mathematics and more to the human capacity of having thoughts loop back on themselves. Such looping, thoughts on thoughts, distinguishes human consciousness; it is the way we make meaning. As Bruner says: *thoughts looping back*

> Much of the process of education consists of being able to distance oneself in some way from what one knows by being able to reflect on one's own knowledge. (p. 127)

also imp. for memory

This is also the way one produces a sense of self, through reflective interaction with the environment, with others, with a culture. As I pointed out earlier, such "recursive reflection" lies at the heart of a transformative curriculum; it is *the process* which Dewey, Piaget, Whitehead all advocate. In the 1960s Bruner made a beginning at defining a recursive curriculum with his "spiral curriculum" (1960) and his elementary school social studies program, "Man: A Course of Study" (1966). However, in our then-modernist mode both of these were mis-seen, attaining only popular approval and notoriety. Their power never became evident; the former got lost in the question of calculus for first graders, the latter in the issue of Bruner's patriotism.

In a curriculum that honors, values, uses recursion, there is no fixed beginning or ending. As Dewey has pointed out, every ending is a new beginning, every beginning emerges from a prior ending. Curriculum segments, parts, sequences are arbitrary chunks that, instead of being seen as isolated units, are seen as opportunities for reflection. In *No fixed beginning or end* *like it* such a frame, every test, paper, journal entry can be seen not merely as the completion of one project but also as the beginning of another—to explore, discuss, inquire into both ourselves as meaning makers and into the text in question. This curriculum will, of course, be open not closed; like post-modernism itself, it is Janus-faced, eclectic, interpretive.

Recursion and repetition differ in that neither one, in any way, reflects the other. Repetition, a strong element in the modernist mode, is designed to improve set performance. Its frame is closed. Recursion aims at developing competence—the ability to organize, combine, inquire, use something heuristically. Its frame is open. The functional difference between repetition and recursion lies in the role reflection plays in each. In repetition, reflection plays a negative role; it breaks the process. There is a certain automaticity to repetition that keeps the same process going—over and over and over, as in flash card arithmetic drills or in ball machine tennis drills. In recursion, reflection plays a positive role; for thoughts to leap back on themselves, as in Dewey's secondary experience reflecting back on primary experience, or in Piaget's reflexive intelligence reflecting back on practical intelligence, it is necessary, as Bruner has said, to step back from one's doings, to "distance oneself in some way" from one's own thoughts.[2] Thus, in recursion it is a necessity to have others—peers, teachers—look at, critique, respond to what one has done. Dialogue becomes the *sine qua non* of recursion: Without reflection—engendered by dialogue—recursion becomes shallow not transformative; it is not reflective recursion, it is only repetition.

Relations. The concept of relations is important to a post-modern, transformative curriculum in two ways: in a pedagogical way and in a cultural way. The former might, naturally, be called pedagogical relations, referring to those within the curriculum—the matrix or network which gives it richness. The latter might, just as naturally, be called cultural relations, referring to those cultural or cosmological relations which lie outside the curriculum but form a large matrix within which the curriculum is embedded. Both relations are important; each complements the other.

In focusing on *pedagogical relations*, one focuses on the connections within a curriculum's structure which give the curriculum its depth as this is developed by recursion. Here the twin processes of doing and reflecting-on-doing are important, and through these processes the curriculum becomes richer with the passage of time. As Prigogine is fond of saying, time in a Newtonian frame is *reversible and unimportant*; in the dissipative structure frames he studies, it is *irreversible and important* (1988; with Stengers, 1984, Ch. 7). If the universe is already set, time does no more than give one the chance to "see" more of that universe. "Mastery learning" assumes this frame—the student is to take the time necessary to master the material presented to a certain, predetermined level of repetitious proficiency (Torshen, 1977). In a universe of and in process, time takes on a different, qualitative dimension; it acquires a transformative aspect, since development of one sort or another is always occurring. Conditions, situations, relations are always changing; the present does not recreate the past (though it is certainly influenced by the past) nor does the present determine the future (though it is an influencer). So, too, the curriculum frame operating at the beginning of the course is unavoidably different from the curriculum frame operating at the end of the course. The issue is not difference but degree or quality of difference—whether the difference is a difference that makes a difference.

Recognizing the contingency of relations, and hoping that these relations will be positively and communally developed during the course of a semester, I organize my undergraduate and graduate university courses to enhance this development. Among the devices I use, one is to provide a syllabus that lists common readings for only two-thirds of the course; for the last third various groups choose their readings from a selected list. Class time is devoted not to summarizing these various readings but to interconnecting them to both the common readings and to each other. The quality of discussion improves as the semester *develops*; so, too, papers written early in the semester improve dramatically when rewritten and reframed after utilizing the insights gained. Sometimes the change is transformative.

In junior high classes, where I have often used a set text, I build time-oriented relationships by asking students to reframe the material presented, to choose from or reframe chapter questions, and to deal with the textual material on both a "what-if" (imaginary) basis and a "relate-it-to-yourself" (real) basis. In dealing with elementary school grades, I follow the same general procedures but use far more manipulative materials, story telling, projects, and dramatic presentations. The textbook, throughout all this, is seen as something to revise, not as something to follow. It is the base from which transformation occurs. Curriculum in a post-modern frame needs to be created (self-organized) by the classroom community, not by textbook authors.

It should be obvious in all these personal anecdotes that, in building a curriculum matrix with a rich set of relationships, I have been strongly influenced by Whitehead's (1929/1967) dictum to "not teach too many subjects" but to "teach thoroughly" what I do teach, and to let the main ideas "be thrown into every combination possible" (p. 2).

The concept of *cultural relations* grows out of a hermeneutic cosmology—one which emphasizes narration and dialogue as key vehicles in interpretation. Narration brings forward the concepts of history (through story), language (through oral telling), and place (through a story's locality). Dialogue interrelates these three to provide us with a sense of culture that is local in origin but global in interconnections. Thus, all our interpretations relate to local culture and interconnect with other cultures and their interpretations via a global matrix. Discourse (narration and dialogue) operates, then, within such a double-tiered cultural frame; it does this far more so than within the foundationalist, abstract, and privileged frame modernism posited. Discourse now becomes what Jim Cheney (1989) calls "contextualist" (p. 123)—bound always by the localness of ourselves, our histories, our language, our place, but also expanding into an ever-broadening global and ecological network. It is this double-tiered or dual-focused nature that makes cultural relations so complex.

Recognizing the contextualist nature of discourse helps us realize that the constructs of those participating frame all conversations, all acts of teaching. As teachers we cannot, do not, transmit information directly; rather, we perform the teaching act when we help others negotiate passages between their constructs and ours, between ours and others'. This is why Dewey says teaching is an interactive process with learning a *by-product* of that interaction.

Modernism has not adopted such an interrelational view; it has taken as one of its hallmarks movement beyond the local and contextual to the universal and abstract. Instead of the narrational, it has aimed for, indeed created, the *meta*narrational, the *grand écrit* Lyotard attacks. Teachers, fitting unconsciously into this paradigm—as we all do— have unwittingly carried on their discourses with students by speaking *ex cathedra*. Too often, teacher explanations have resounded with the authority of God; too rarely have meaningful, interactive, participating dialogues been held.

C.A. Bowers (1987; with Flinders, 1990) has tied the concept of cultural relationships to the ecological crises we face today. In doing this he draws our attention to modernism's overly strong sense of individualism. Individualism has tended to pit humanity against nature (civilization is defined as society improving on nature) and to believe that progress occurs through competition, not cooperation. This is one of modernism's myths founded on beliefs like Bacon's that we should *subject Nature to the hand of man*. This statement would be abhorrent, even sacrilegious, to pre-modern or tribal cultures such as the North American Indian.

But this belief in competition and the virtue of controlling the natural is part of our present day pedagogy and cosmology. Bowers, Griffin, and Oliver (also Lydon, 1992) are among the few curricularists who encourage us to rethink our concept of relations, who see that *cultural relationships* extend beyond our personal selves to include the ecosystem—indeed the cosmos in which we live. Only now, in the past decade or so, are we beginning to develop a cosmic and interrelational consciousness. The challenge of such recognition is twofold: on the one hand, to honor the localness of our perceptions and, on the other hand, to realize that our local perspectives integrate into a larger cultural, ecological, cosmic matrix. Our progress and our existence—as individuals, as communities, as a race, as a species, as a life form—depend on our ability to bring these two perspectives into complementary harmony.

Rigor. In some ways the most important of the four criteria, rigor keeps a transformative curriculum from falling into either "rampant relativism" or sentimental solipsism. In presenting transformation as an alternative to our current measurement frame, it is easy to see transformation as no more than anti-measurement or nonmeasurement. Here, transformation becomes not a true alternative but yet another variation on the very thing it tries to replace. This certainly happened in the progressive and open education movements. Dewey wrestled with the problem in the progressive education movement and wrote "Need for a Philosophy of Education" to explain why progressive education needed to be more than anti-traditional, why progressive education had to have its own foundation and frame. In contrasting his view of progressive education—developmental and transformative—with either the received progressive view (which he considered too romantic) or the established traditional view (which he considered too rigid), he said:

> This alternative is not just a middle course or compromise between the two procedures. It is something radically different from either. Existing likes and powers are to be treated as possibilities. (1934/1964, p. 8)

In such a transformative frame, with its emphasis on indeterminacy, shifting relationships, and spontaneous self-organization, rigor wears a very different set of clothes than it did in the modernist frame. Rigor began, at least in the scholastic sense, with the Jesuits' Q.E.D.—"Quod Erat Demonstrandum" (thus it is demonstrated)—from the deductive power of their Aristotlean-based logic. Descartes objected to this logic, replacing it with his own "clear and distinct" ideas—those which no reasonable person could doubt, those he received from God, but also ones he "saw" with his mind's eye. Rigor thus moved from Aristotlean-Euclidean logic to deeply felt perceptions and conceptions. The English empiricists wanted to move rigor yet again, away from subjective states, no matter how personally appealing, to the objective and observable. Here rigor entered a world that could be measured and manipulated. Our present twentieth-century concept of rigor has elements of all these strains—scholastic logic, scientific observation, and mathematical precision.

To think of rigor without these qualities is to call for a virtual redefinition of the concept. Rigor in a post-modern frame requires just this. It draws on qualities foreign to a modernist frame—interpretation and indeterminacy, to mention but two. In dealing with indeterminacy, one can never be certain one "has it right"—not even to the 95th or 99th percentile of probability. One must continually be exploring, looking for new combinations, interpretations, patterns. This is why, in his scientific methodology, Dewey (1933/1971) listed the fourth stage as "the mental elaboration of an idea" (p. 107), "developing the relations of ideas to one another" (p. 113), and "playing with concepts" (p. 182). Here we find echoes and presagings of statements made by Whitehead, Kuhn, Bruner—not to close too early or finally on the rightness of an idea, to throw all ideas into various combinations. Here rigor means purposely looking for different alternatives, relations, connections. Michel Serres does this well, as shown in his wolf and sheep essay, drawing together LaFontaine's fable and Descartes' right method.

In dealing with interpretation rigorously, one needs to be aware that all valuations depend on (often hidden) assumptions. As frames differ so do the problems, procedures, and valued results. Rigor here means the conscious attempt to ferret out these assumptions, ones we or others hold dear, as well as negotiating passages between these assumptions, so the dialogue may be meaningful and transformative. As Iser points out, dialogue between reader and text is a two-way process, each has a voice, and in this dialogue there is a combining of determinacy and indeterminacy. Indeterminacy here does not mean arbitrariness; rather, it "allows [for] a spectrum of actualization" (1978, p. 24)—better yet, it allows for a range of possibilities from which actualizations appear. Which actualization does appear for development depends on the interaction process itself, on mixing indeterminacy with determinacy.

So, too, rigor may be defined in terms of mixing—indeterminacy with interpretation. The quality of interpretation, its own richness, depends on how fully and well we develop the various alternatives indeterminacy presents. In this new frame for rigor—combining the complexity of indeterminacy with the hermeneutics of interpretation—it seems necessary to establish a community, one critical yet supportive. Such a community is, I believe, what Dewey thought a school should be.

Notes

1. It is interesting to note that *recursion* (as well as *recur*) is derived from the Latin *recurrere* (to run back). In this way recursion is allied with *currere* (to run), the root word for curriculum.
2. As I've said already, it is this distancing of oneself from one's actions and thoughts that is missing in Schön's concept of reflection.

References

Bowers, C.A. (1987). *Elements of a post-liberal theory of education*. New York: Teachers College Press.

Bowers, C.A., & Flinders, D. J. (1980). *Responsive teaching*. New York: Teachers College Press.

Bruner, J. (1960). *The process of education*. Cambridge, MA: Harvard University Press.

——— . (1986). *Actual minds, possible worlds*. Cambridge, MA: Harvard University Press.

Cheney, J. (1989). Post-Modern environmental ethics: Ethics as bioregional narrative. *Environmental Ethics, 11* (Summer), 117–134.

Dewey, J. (1964). Need for a philosophy of education. In R. D. Archambault (ed.), *John Dewey on education: Selected writings* (pp. 3–14). New York: Random House. (Original work published 1934.)

——— . (1971). *How we think*. Chicago: Henry Regnery. (Original work published 1933.)

Doll, W. E., Jr. (1977). The role of contrast in the development of competence. In Alex Molner & John Zahorik (eds.), *Curriculum theory* (pp. 50–63). Washington, D.C.: Association for Supervision and Curriculum Development.

—— . (1989). Complexity in the classroom. *Educational Leadership, 47*, 65–70.

Iser, W. (1978). *The act of reading.* Baltimore: Johns Hopkins University Press.

Lydon, A. (1992). Cosmology and curriculum. Unpublished dissertation, Louisiana State University.

Prigogine, I. (1988). The rediscovery of time. In Richard F. Kitchener (ed.), *The world view of contemporary physics: Does it need a new metaphysics?* (pp. 125–143). Albany: SUNY Press.

Prigogine, I., & Stengers, I. (1984). *Order out of chaos: Man's new dialogue with nature.* New York: Bantam Books.

Torshen, K. (1977). *The mastery approach to competency-based education.* New York: Academic Press.

Whitehead, A. N. (1967). *The aims of education.* New York: Free Press. (Original work published 1929.)

23

Generational Ideas in Curriculum: An Historical Triangulation

Peter S. Hlebowitsh

The formalization of curriculum development as a practice in the American public schools can be traced to the defining principles embodied in the work of John Franklin Bobbitt and to the wider social efficiency tradition that he helped to express. Bobbitt's (1918) idea of circumscribing the school around predetermined activities and actualizing the curriculum in a way that served a functionalist view of society has had a lasting effect on public schooling. The basic nature of his ideas could be found in later advocacy for competency-based instruction, and even in recent support for curriculum mapping strategies and test-driven curricula anchored in hyperspecified curriculum standards.

Not surprisingly, some curriculum scholars continue to see the curriculum field as a historical creature (a miscreant, even) still burdened by the ideas and principles inherited from its social efficiency derivations. Pinar and others (1995), for instance, see these vestiges in what they view as the field's continued obsession with only procedural and prescriptive matters in the school experience, and in its accompanying failure to generate new theoretical lines of understanding. They have little hesitancy in proposing that the curriculum field's main problems still reside at the historical door of the field, believing that the orientation of curriculum studies has been stuck in a simplistic management-style interplay between forming curriculum objectives and telling teachers how to carry them out. And they are confident enough in this view to proclaim the need for the field to repudiate its history and to reconceptualize itself along broader theoretical and less school-bound lines.

Such claims, of course, are reliant on understanding what I call the generational inheritance of the field. By generational, I mean the main ideas and principles that have endured and evolved over at least two generations of curriculum work—ideas and principles that have given the field some coherence and sense of identification. If the historical record documents the persistence of social efficiency traditions in the generational ideas of the field, as others have claimed, then we are likely to see and ultimately approach our present-day problems in a way that differs from an interpretation that does not carry the weight of a social efficiency history. Thus, our handling of generational ideas becomes a matter of certain present-day importance.

One promising line of inquiry in this regard can be explored in the generational lines of the curriculum field defined and delineated in the works of John Franklin Bobbitt, Ralph Tyler, and Joseph Schwab. All three were education professors on faculty at the University of Chicago. Each used a different point of departure when traveling through the field of curriculum studies. Bobbitt worked in the field of educational administration, Tyler in policy and evaluation, and Schwab in philosophy. Each was also well known and well represented in the literature, and together their work encompasses a landscape of thinking about the curriculum that tells us much about the field itself.

But what makes this triangulation of curriculum thinkers especially helpful is the distinct and unusual way that it holds together. Besides the University of Chicago connection, our group of three is typically cast in an analytical web that puts Tyler in kinship with Bobbitt, and that puts Schwab, by virtue of his declaration of moribundity against the field, in separation from Tyler (and Tyler's presumed progenitors). Tyler is viewed, in a manner of speaking, as the inheritor of the kingdom, while Schwab is the revolutionary, seeking an overthrow and the installation of a whole new worldview. Even mainstream curriculum thinkers are taken by this implication, including Eisner (1984), whose own review of Schwab's practical papers led to him to ask, "What are we to make of a man who tells us, if we read him as I think he wishes to be read, that we have for eighty years been barking up the wrong tree?" (p. 208).

The Triangulation

The pivotal point in the triangulation is Ralph Tyler, who was a student at the University of Chicago during Bobbitt's tenure there and who is typically cited as among Bobbitt's intellectual progeny. He is especially important to the reconceptualist critique because he is viewed as the good son who modernized social efficiency schemes by continuing to put a premium on the normative, and by detailing a new instrumentality for curriculum development conceived around behavioral objectives and testing mechanisms. Reconceptualists, notably Pinar, believed that Tyler's rationale was the quintessential social efficiency achievement—not much more than a management device designed to stifle teacher creativity and to close the discretionary space for teacher judgment in the classroom. In this sense, Bobbitt's generational principles are viewed as succeeding seamlessly into a second generation of curriculum development commandeered and modernized by Tyler.

For those taken by this criticism against Tyler, hope nevertheless arrives, and not from afar, but from within the very intellectual home of Bobbitt and Tyler. In 1969, Joseph Schwab made his entrance, offering a trenchant criticism of the curriculum field, punctuated with a proclamation that curriculum studies, his newly adopted area of intellectual inquiry, is moribund—dead at its theoretic roots and otherwise stunted in its practice.

Schwab, however, was not content simply to criticize. He went quite a bit further and designed an alternative view that spoke directly to questions of curriculum practice: what curriculum scholars should actually do. In this way, Schwab, who was hired by Tyler at the University of Chicago, clearly tried to represent a new promise for the field.

For many, Schwab embodied an important separation, or break, from Tyler and Bobbitt. He was, in many ways, a scholar with a new orientation and even a new vocabulary. How could one, in fact, see him any other way? After all, wasn't his frustration with the field and his confidence in declaring it moribund a clear indictment of Bobbitt and Tyler? And isn't it obvious that Schwab's analytical focus had little regard for the generational principles first forged by Bobbitt? In Schwab, for instance, one will not find any talk about matching objectives to experiences, and certainly no talk about key Tylerian traditions, such as formulating evaluative mechanisms aligned to core school purposes. Schwab undoubtedly gave us a new theoretical configuration for thinking about the curriculum, and was ultimately embraced by a good share of the curriculum community as an important departure from Tyler—a radical break, some might say, of almost paradigmatic proportions.

So, one version of the triangulation between Bobbitt, Tyler, and Schwab shows us how the field has walked away from Tyler (and his social efficiency ancestors) and toward Schwab, with the implication being that Schwab's voice stood as a separation from the historic curriculum field. This is, of course, a preferred version among those satisfied with the evidence that builds a separation between Tyler and Schwab, and among those who are inclined to see little discernible lines of separation between Bobbitt and Tyler. *It is not a version I accept.*

I am not the first to have my hand at analyzing these historical lines. In a 1992 essay, Philip Jackson put it to the reader directly, asking if Tyler's ideas posed any improvement over Bobbitt's ideas and if Schwab's ideas posed any improvement over Tyler's. The focus on improvement was itself revealing, because by aiming to find some new contribution in the work of the three, Jackson's essay settled onto common ground—which is to say, the ground of curriculum development. As Jackson observed, all three (Bobbitt, Tyler, and Schwab) sought to "help practitioners who wanted to improve the curriculum of the school in which they work" (p. 30). To ask the question of improvement implied a basis for marking (comparing and contrasting) the nature of the improvement. In this way, Jackson took an epistemological position that allowed him to argue that the three voices were following a line common enough for us to be confident in noting scales of improvement. Tellingly, Jackson had no issue with comparability and never once found himself saying that the perspectives were so radically different that they could not be managed along a common analytical ground.

Interestingly, Tyler and Schwab apparently felt the same way. Tyler (1984), for his part, claimed that Schwab's analytical focus gave him new clarity on his past curriculum development projects, noting especially that it clarified factors in his experience as director of the evaluation staff of the Eight-Year Study. Tyler even observed that he had done as Schwab might have advised, putting together some deliberative groups that included "persons with the variety of characteristics outlined by Schwab" (p. 98). And Schwab (1969), far from seeing himself as a separation from Tyler, noted in his first practical essay "that the conception of curricular method" he proposed was "immanent in the Tyler rationale" (p. 320). In fact, one of Schwab's complaints about the rationale had to do with its commitment to the use of objectives in the curriculum. Schwab, however, did not cite a social efficiency criticism against objectives. Far from seeing objectives as hopeless impositions on teachers, Schwab feared that they ultimately failed to offer *enough* concrete direction for the school. Yet Schwab, it should be said, is certainly not obvious in the work of Tyler. And if Schwab's views were immanent in the Tyler rationale, as Schwab himself maintained, we might begin to also say that Schwab produced an analytical extension to Tyler that, in the final analysis, was less of a departure from Tyler than an improvement on Tyler.

In 1993, William Reid found the Tyler/Schwab connection to be important enough to offer a response to Jackson, in an essay that made direct reference to Jackson's original query: "Does Schwab Improve on Tyler?" So now, for a second time, we took on a question that, by virtue of being asked, said so much about the curriculum field. But Reid flipped the analytical switch, first by articulating a frustration with Jackson's focus on the point of improvement, which he correctly noted implied commonality, and then by directing his attention to the question of difference between Schwab and Tyler. Reid's conclusions naturally diverged from Jackson's account, but the paradox of Reid's work is that the case of commonality between Tyler and Schwab became stronger because of it.

Reid sees Schwab as different enough from Tyler (as prizing a process of curriculum development completely overlooked by Tyler) that even comparability between the two is an issue. Moreover, Reid does not accept the separation drawn by Jackson between Tyler's vision-oriented view of curriculum and Schwab's problem-centered view (a distinction we will explore later), and he certainly does not accept Jackson's implication that Tyler's more dominant position in the field is more useful for curriculum thinkers. But are the differences between the two so dramatic? Or are they precisely the kind of differences that fit together nicely into a broader and more holistic puzzle?

Both Tyler and Schwab, as will be discussed, advanced curriculum approaches that gave meaning and operation to idealistic visions, but that did not predesign or hardwire any social vision from within. They went about this in different ways, and it is in these different ways that Reid is convinced that the two are not compatible, nor even of the same tradition. Schwab put down his analytical stakes in the soil of a deliberative problem-solving or decision-making process. Tyler, on the other hand, viewed this process as implied in his more procedural approach.

But is this as much a difference as it is two sides of the same coin? Do these two approaches clash in the real world of schools, or do they (or can they) work together? Schwab was probably saying something important when he observed that his work was immanent in the Tyler rationale. The statement probably meant that Schwab saw Tyler as standing quite separate from Bobbitt's legacy (think of Bobbitt's idealistic curriculum approach), and quite close to the kind of hard-knuckled school-based action that Schwab valorized in his essays. Obviously, Schwab didn't focus on what concerned Tyler. Why should he? He focused on what Tyler missed, and Tyler did miss something important. The result can only be interpreted as representing an improvement on Tyler. Because the Tyler rationale was never revised, we could only guess whether Tyler might have made any attempt to synthesize insights from Schwab. But a kind of synchronicity can be observed between the work of Tyler and the work of Schwab.

Generational Ideas in Curriculum

If curriculum development is a generational idea, we could say that Bobbitt stands as its patriarch. Bobbitt is significant because he helped to formalize and legitimize curriculum development as an academic field of inquiry. His 1924 book, *How to Build a Curriculum*, is an unabashed testament to his atheoretical orientation. Bobbitt was not a philosopher and didn't take much interest in theory, seeing his work instead along strictly practical lines—what Jackson (1992) referred to as "advice giving."

Here is a generational line in the field of curriculum that ties Bobbitt to Tyler for sure, but it also implicates Schwab. Although Schwab was clearly a theoretician par excellence, certainly in a way that Bobbitt and Tyler were not, Schwab's work is markedly advice-giving in its implications. In *The Practical: Translation Into Curriculum*, Schwab (1973) itemized the kinds of participants needed in the deliberative process (their titles, the education they require, and the roles they fulfill), the size of the planning group, and "the five bodies of experience that must be represented in a group undertaking curriculum revision" (p. 365). He also argued for the centrality of the commonplaces in the process of curriculum revision.

Reid (1993) assessed Schwab's advice-giving capacity as "falling short," largely because of the complexity of his language and the nuances of his ideas. But Schwab himself made it clear that to be a scholar in the field of curriculum studies meant to work the ground of local practice. One should recall that Schwab's (1969) main complaint about the curriculum field was its "inveterate, unexamined and mistaken reliance on theory" (p. 287). Schwab did not want the field to be atheoretical, but he did want it to recognize itself along the lines of its practice and the practical skills needed to help improve school learning environments. His four landmark essays written over the course of four years all contained the word "practical" in the title. His fourth essay was subtitled "Something for Curriculum Professors to Do." A concern for practice does not necessarily translate into advice, but in Schwab, it certainly comes close to the mark of advice-giving.

Another generational principle emerging from the work of Bobbitt has to do with the attention he placed on the local management of the school. Bobbitt was circumspect about forming activities in the school experience that were relevant to the life of the local community. He took this very seriously, so much so that one could find very detailed job analysis reports that he and his students conducted in city school districts, including Los Angeles (Bobbitt, 1922) and San Antonio (Bobbitt, 1915). In fact, Bobbitt was so attached to the idea of linking specific activity to the present local condition that other progressives accused him of designing a curriculum doomed to become an anachronism. Bode (1927), for instance, contended that Bobbitt's job analysis represented little more than training for adjustment to existing social conditions. In a democracy, Bode observed, society is best served when education proceeds from the level of general training, in areas such as problem-solving and communication skills. The school needs to be responsive to local conditions, Bode explained, but it cannot be trapped by them. Because specific activities change over time, the idea of specificity in the curriculum runs the risk of promoting outdated training that would likely not have much currency beyond the present.

Tyler, of course, also had a high regard for the local, starting his career as an advice-giver to faculty at the Ohio State University, offering them ideas on how to design evaluation devices attuned to their course purposes, and later playing a front and center role in the Eight-Year Study, where he first formulated his famous rationale. Tyler undoubtedly embraced the local authority of the school, making it clear even in his rationale that the formation of school purposes needs to be screened through local community values and concerns, as well as local knowledge of the learner.

But Tyler must have read Bode's criticism of Bobbitt, because his advice for local schools contained an important difference from Bobbitt.[1] Where Bobbitt concerned himself with the development of specific activities that he believed contributed to the adjustment of the individual to society, Tyler's focus was diametrically opposed to the specificity that Bobbitt sought. Tyler made repeated efforts to draw attention to the need for the school to retain a strong sense of generalizability in its design of purposes, thus keeping the school experience open to important changes and leaving more discretionary space for teacher judgment. This was Tyler's way of operationalizing Dewey's conception of present-as-future, meaning that Tyler wanted to use the curriculum to cultivate general skills and values that had currency beyond the present (problem-solving skills, communication skills, inquiry skills, study skills, appreciation toward learning, and so forth). Bobbitt's focus on the specific activities of the present could only secure a better present, not necessarily a better future. In this way, Tyler extended Bobbitt's idea, improved on it, and showed the way to a generational idea that still honors the local management of schools.

Schwab inherited the generational idea of local authority and embraced it as a key ingredient in his thinking. Schwab, in fact, sanctified the local ground of school decision-making in a way that went beyond even Bobbitt or Tyler, emphasizing the need for the curriculum to be moved by a participatory and communal process. He made it clear that decisions made away from the classroom and the school could not capture local conditions, and tended instead to rely on theory for guidance, something that theory was not equipped to provide. Abstractions about the curriculum were to be avoided largely because, as Schwab (1969) put it, "real acts, real teachers, real children are richer than and different from their theoretical representations" (p. 310). To Schwab, teachers, children, and curriculum decisions were essentially "unreal" in theory. However, it should be remembered that Schwab came to this conclusion only after his involvement in the National Science Foundation (NSF)-sponsored Biological Sciences Curriculum Study (BSCS) curriculum, a science education curriculum designed by scientists far removed from local school conditions, and far removed from any understanding of the nature of the learner. BSCS was a national curriculum project exported to the local schools, designed by participants not only outside of the local community, but also outside of the institution of precollege schooling altogether. Schwab (1983) might have acknowledged this when he made a reference to the fact that he was opposed to a centralized command curriculum "decided in Moscow and telegraphed to the provinces" (p. 240)—a reference perhaps to the Washingtonian (NSF) curriculum prescriptions of which he was a part. But the point is that when Schwab was wrong about the curriculum, he was outside of a generational principle established by Bobbitt and Tyler, and when was right and most prized for his writing about the curriculum, he settled into a generational principle that clearly ties him to Bobbitt and Tyler. One could also argue that Schwab indeed provided some improvement on this legacy by highlighting a feature of local thinking (the deliberative process) that was never contemplated by Bobbitt and Tyler.

Another generational principle founded by Bobbitt had to do with tying the work of the curricularist to the procedural features of the curriculum. To be a curriculum worker to Bobbitt meant to help atomize or to particularize the activities of the curriculum. To Tyler, the action of the curriculum moved along a continuum, starting not (as Bobbitt preferred) with activities, but with purposes, and moving along to the formation of learning experiences, and finally, to the fashioning of an evaluative strategy allegiant to the purposes. The issue of evaluation is critical because Tyler conveyed a message that no one else had previously understood. Tyler showed us that evaluation, a term that he claims to have originally coined in the context of schooling, need not be a prefashioned pencil-and-paper-testing affair, but could instead be approached as an evidence collection process requiring creative and innovative thinking about finding ways to demonstrate whether certain core purposes in the curriculum have been fulfilled. One cannot find much talk of evaluation from Bobbitt, but plenty from Tyler. In fact, Tyler could be (and should be) considered the father of portfolio assessment, although no one seems to want to give him credit for this. So, we have a generational line of thought that targets curriculum processes (a sense of what is meant to organize a curriculum) between Bobbitt and Tyler, which ultimately shows signs of improvement and change. The very idea of testing and evaluation was changed by Tyler because of its residency in the curriculum process.

So, where does Schwab fit here? Clearly, he does not have as much concern for the elements of curriculum development that we see in Tyler and Bobbitt. But Schwab's work is ultimately tested against the effects that it has on the curriculum development process. Schwab is, in effect, saying that what we teach, and how we teach it, is undeniably important, but that the best way of nurturing such processes is to look to the participants in the curriculum. Schwab (1973) injected himself into the processes of the curriculum by putting his stock into the participants of the curriculum and the vital processes of the deliberative engagement.

At one point, Schwab even designed the elements of a problem-solving team that could undertake the act of curriculum revision. He outlined the responsibilities of the members on the team but didn't get into the business of advising a *particular* problem-solving method, although he did outline what he called the commonplaces of the curriculum (the main sources of evidence for deliberative engagements). These commonplaces involve four elements: teachers, subject matters, students, and milieu. Schwab's notion of deliberation in the curriculum speaks to who teaches, what gets taught, who gets taught, and the cultural climate in which it is taught.

Tyler, of course, adumbrated his curriculum questions with what he called screens, insisting that all curriculum procedures be filtered through three screens: a regard for the nature of the learner, for the values of society and community, and for the contributions of specialized subject matter. One can see the isomorphism between three of the commonplaces (students, subject matter, and milieu) and Tyler's three screens. Schwab added the teacher (the key participant) to the conceptual framework, again showing Schwab's proclivity to put analytical focus on the actual participants in the curriculum design project.

Tyler's work clearly did not analytically reach into the act of deliberation. Tyler's original rationale, for instance, was formed in response to a call for help and guidance from the participating teachers in the experimental schools of the Eight-Year Study. The rationale came to the teachers in the context of the practical problems associated with managing expressly experimental schools. Tyler gave the teachers guidance via the rationale, but failed to offer much to them in the way of deliberative engagements that might have helped with the interpretation and use of the guiding principles of the rationale. Little attention went in the direction of the deliberative body. Tyler's inattention to this matter was emblematic of a wider prejudice in the field.

The problem was pervasive enough that, in later years, the curriculum field would identify something known as the implementation problem, which was a direct reference to the fact that curriculum knowledge simply was not making its way into the implementation of the school, or into the working consciousness of school leaders, including teachers. Schwab, of course, had an answer to this problem because of the investment he made in attempting to localize decision-making so that teachers might have ownership in what and how they teach. Today, much of what Schwab taught us is ignored at our cost. For instance, many still believe that a focus on an institutional matter, such as reducing class size, will necessarily yield positive effects for children, without thinking that, in the absence of deliberation, teachers might continue to teach—reduced class size or not—as they always taught. The effect, of course, is that nothing necessarily positive comes from the reduction.

Schwab, as indicated earlier, is simply not the idealist or vision-builder that we clearly see in Bobbitt, and less intensively, in Tyler. Schwab embraced the idea of principle more than the idea of planning, and hence is more inclined to advance problem-solving rather than vision-building as the main end of curriculum development. Contrast this to Bobbitt, whose work was embodied in the idea of using the school curriculum as a grand society-building plan—a desire to socialize children into their social stations for the purpose of keeping the social harmony. Tyler almost straddles the line between Bobbitt and Schwab. He did indeed focus on the construction of purpose as the main engine for the operation of the curriculum, but he did so without imposing the kind of worldview implied in Bobbitt. At the same time, Tyler was also not neutral or strictly procedural about the school experience either. He did make a case for the three screens (learner, society, and subject matter) and the exercise of a philosophy. But like Schwab (and unlike Bobbitt), Tyler did not exercise any particular vision in the development of the school experience. In fact, it should be recalled once more that Tyler was criticized on this count by Schwab

(1969) himself, who judged Tyler's commitment to curriculum objectives as largely bringing forth ambiguity and equivocation in the curriculum, a point repeated in Kliebard's (1970) well-known criticism of the rationale. In fact, I've heard it said often that part of the problem with the Tyler rationale is that any low or narrow-minded cultural tradition could find a helpful curriculum procedure in the rationale. It seems that the lesson against using the curriculum as a hegemonic cultural device, as an instrument for the installation of a predesigned social plan, was learned well by Tyler and embraced equally by Schwab.

The Bells Toll

But how could we put Schwab into the same line of thinking as Tyler when he is precisely the person who tolled the bells, as it were, whose declaration of moribundity must have targeted so much of what Tyler stood for? The primary implication of what Schwab said was, after all, similar to the main implication of the later reconceptualist critique, which is that curriculum professors can no longer do what they've been doing in order for their field to thrive, and that a change (even maybe a reconceptualization) needs to occur to resurrect the profession.

What exactly *was* Schwab saying when he declared the field moribund? His was not a specific attack on any line of thinking in the field (he mentioned no names), but an attack on what Schwab believed to be a settled tradition in the field. Was this tradition a generational idea that moved from Bobbitt's hand to Tyler's?

The declaration of moribundity in the curriculum, as Schwab originally pronounced it, had to do with a perceived overzealous commitment in the field to the prescriptive powers of theory. According to Schwab (1969), the role of theory had achieved an exaggerated status in the context of the practical, leading to the pursuit of overreaching principles and procedures of curriculum development. The problem was in the way that these theoretical formulations overwhelmed and overlooked the emergent quality of the situational or practical context. Schwab believed that curriculum theory had to be diverted from the kind of theoretical pursuits that led to the formulations of universal rules and other invariant instructional elements (such as fixed taxonomies and plug-in teaching models). Such pursuits, he claimed, although guided by the banner of "theory into practice," were actually ill-fitting to practice.

> Theory, by its very character, does not and cannot take account of all the matters which are crucial to questions of what, who, and how to teach; that is, theories cannot be applied, as principles, to the solutions of problems concerning what to do for real individuals, small groups, or real institutions located in time and space—the subjects and clients of schooling and schools. (Schwab, 1969, p. 287)

Schwab called for a more careful consideration of the practical in the interests of understanding and honoring situational and local conditions. Theory could not act alone in the schooling context; it had to be supplemented by practical arts that kept the real or concrete in focus.

> If, then, theory is to be used well in the determination of curricular practice, it requires a supplement. It requires arts which bring a theory to its application; first, arts which identify the disparities between real thing and theoretic representation; second, arts which modify the theory in the course of its application, in light of the discrepancies; and, third, arts which

devise ways for taking account of the many aspects of the real thing which the theory does not take into account. (Schwab, 1969, p. 310)

Is there an indictment of Tyler somewhere in this? Certainly Tyler's work had become an instrument for many of the universal instructional models that prevailed in the school, including dubious interpretations of the rationale that reduced it to a purely instructional affair. The role of behavioral objectives, which Tyler highlighted in his rationale, had also wreaked its share of damage as various performance-based or competency-based curricula had found their ways into schools, promising mastery rates of achievement. But Tyler was as much a critic of these actions as Schwab.

A better place to go to answer the question of whether Tyler stands indicted by Schwab is to the six signs of crisis that Schwab identified in the curriculum field in 1969.[2] If we could accuse Tyler of helping to fortify any of the signs of crisis detailed by Schwab (1969), we could simultaneously say something about a separation, or even the grander notion of reconceptualization. The six signs are (1) "a translocation of its problems and the solving of them from the practitioners of the field to other men" (p. 301); (2) "a flight from use of principles and methods to talk about them" (p. 301); (3) "an attempt by practitioners to return to the subject matter in a state of innocence, shorn not only of current principles but of all principles" (p. 301); (4) "a flight to the sidelines, to the role of observer, commentator, historian and critic of the contributions of others to the field" (p. 301); (5) "a repetition of old and familiar knowledge in new languages which adds little or nothing to the old meanings as embodied in the older and familiar language" (p. 301); and (6) "a marked increase in eristic, contentious and ad hominem debate" (p. 302). Let us take each and see if we can show that Schwab was indicting (directly or otherwise) the generational lines of thinking brought to us by Tyler and Bobbitt.

The translocation of the field's "problems from the practitioners of the field to other men" might be construed as an argument against Tyler, depending on what we mean by the problems of the field. If we take it to mean problems in the school curriculum, some scholars might claim that Tyler's rationale represents exactly the type of curriculum thinking that has allowed so much of today's school curriculum to be influenced by outside forces, most notably test makers. Certainly, Educational Testing Service (ETS) and Iowa Testing Programs (ITP) have more influence on the school curriculum today than any curriculum professors do. But Tyler's rationale never offered a word of support for a test-driven curriculum. And Tyler, who was an expert in educational measurement, made it very clear that tests entail only some part of the evaluation process, and that the design or form of all evaluation should follow the function or the purposes of the school. The effect of translocating authority away from curriculum practitioners through the use of the Tyler rationale was, if real, unintended and certainly unwanted. The fact of the matter is that Schwab's fears about translocating the solving of the field's problems "to other men" is not a very compelling fear from the standpoint of Tyler's or Bobbitt's influence. In fact, the primary criticism emerging from reconceptualist thinking against Tyler constructs him as a hegemonist, far from anyone who might produce or otherwise accept any translocation of authority.

Schwab (1969) also saw crisis in "a flight from the use and principles of methods to talk about them" and its variants, "a retreat to the role of observer, commentator, historian and critic of the contributions of others to the field," as well as "a marked increase in contentious and ad hominem debate" (pp. 301–302). Bobbitt and Tyler really were not "critics" at all, and they certainly did not qualify as theoretical thinkers. They were largely curriculum developers who were in and of the schools. One will not find either of them in the middle of any weighty epistemological debates. Tyler, in fact, never even offered a response to Kliebard's (1970) popular and still widely received criticism of his rationale. He did what Schwab must have admired: he openly said that he would not respond to criticism of the rationale that did not offer a practical alternative. Tyler did involve himself in some national educational policy concerns, but this too was practical advice-giving work, which included giving counsel to several U.S. presidents and helping to construct and formulate national testing programs, such as the National Assessment of Educational Progress (NAEP).

Similarly, Schwab's (1969) third reference to crisis, which he described as "an attempt by practitioners to return to the subject matter in a state of innocence, shorn not only of current principles but of all principles" (p. 301), has no target in Tyler or Bobbitt. Being shorn of all principles implies a failure to build on earlier ideas and precedential work. Tyler's work, as discussed, is embedded in generational ideas that live by precedent and sustained attention, a condition that flies in the face of Schwab's violation. Tyler surely improved on Bobbitt and Schwab arguably improved on Tyler, and the overall effect is an evolving framework of thinking about the school curriculum that is time-proven and avoids careless reinvention.

Finally, the idea of "repeating old and familiar knowledge in new languages which adds little or nothing to the old meanings" (Schwab, 1969, p. 301) is a sign of crisis that Tyler's critics are keen to level against him. Tyler, they say, is old wine, produced and aged from the social efficiency vineyards, in a new bottle. But as I indicated earlier, the differences between Tyler and Bobbitt are equal to their commonalties. To look past these vital differences is to completely misunderstand Tyler. Much of the old knowledge is still there, as it should be, but as demonstrated, new meanings and new insights prevail too.

Conclusions

The history of the curriculum field has had its share of dark episodes, but it has nevertheless given us a heritage of thought and insight that speaks directly to school improvements. These generational lines of insight, some of which are rooted in social efficiency, are the basic building blocks of the field. They are at the core of all who have been thinking about the school curriculum. The turbulence caused by Schwab's criticism of field, far from supporting an argument for some iconoclastic separation from the generational lines, could more accurately have been interpreted as an endorsement (with improvements) of the generational field of curriculum development. The focus on the development of the school experience, the belief in the local management of the school, the tendency to approach the curriculum without a priori ideological commitments, and the references to key sources for decision-making (society, students, and subject matter) were generational ideas that Schwab used to the benefit of his own essays. Schwab's "new look" at the curriculum inherited these insights and then went an important step further by showing us the way toward a more participatory process in curriculum decision-making that kept the school close to the hands of the people and the practitioners, and that produced better teacher ownership of and investment in school reform.

Schwab, in this sense, was as much a tool of continuity in the field as he was an innovator. The six signs of crisis he outlined very much imply a return to many of the first principles we find in Tyler's work. To avoid a crisis, Schwab says, we (curriculum professors) should work in schools rather than talk about them; we should take charge of the school rather than allow others do it; we should build on past knowledge and not reinvent the wheel; we should focus more on the practical than the theoretical and avoid the entanglements of ad hominem debate. Tyler and Bobbitt would agree because this undeniably describes the kind of orientation toward the school curriculum that they favored and nurtured throughout their professional careers.

Notes

1. This break from Bobbitt makes sense in other ways too. Tyler's critics often forget that one of Tyler's mentors at the University of Chicago was Charles Judd, a psychologist whose research focused on the role of generalization in the transfer of learning.
2. William Wraga first saw the value of using the six signs as a way to evaluate the present-day conditions of the curriculum field. Recently we used them to demonstrate what needs to be done to bring new synthesis and understanding to the divisions in the curriculum field; see Wraga, W., and P. S. Hlebowitsh. 2003. Toward a renaissance in curriculum theory and development in the USA. *Journal of Curriculum Studies* 35 (4): 425–437.

References

Bobbitt, J. F. (1915). *San Antonio public school system.* San Antonio, TX: San Antonio School Board.

——— . (1918). *The curriculum.* New York: Arno Press.

——— . (1922). *Curriculum-making in Los Angeles.* Chicago: University of Chicago Press.

——— . (1924). *How to make a curriculum.* Boston: Houghton-Mifflin.

Bode, B. (1927). *Modern educational theories.* New York: Macmillan.

Eisner, E. (1984). No easy answers: Joseph Schwab's contributions to curriculum. *Curriculum Inquiry* 14 (2): 201–210.

Jackson, P. W. (1992). Conceptions of curriculum and curriculum specialists. In *Handbook of research on curriculum,* (ed.) Philip W. Jackson, 3–40. New York: Macmillan.

Kliebard, H. (1970). Reappraisal: The Tyler Rationale. *School Review* 78 (2): 259–272.

Pinar, W. et al. (1995). *Understanding curriculum.* New York: Peter Lang.

Reid, W. A. (1993). Does Schwab improve on Tyler? *Journal of Curriculum Studies* 25 (6): 499–510.

Schwab, J. J. (1969). The practical: A language for curriculum. *School Review* 78 (1): 1–23. Reprinted in *Science, curriculum and liberal education,* (eds.) Ian Westbury and Neil Wilkof, 287–321. Chicago: University of Chicago Press, 1978.

——— . (1971). The practical: Arts of eclectic. *School Review* 79 (August): 493–542. Reprinted in *Science, curriculum and liberal education,* (eds.) Ian Westbury and Neil Wilkof, 322–364. Chicago: University of Chicago Press, 1978.

——— . (1973). The practical 3: Translation into curriculum. *School Review* 81 (August): 501–522. Reprinted in *Science, curriculum and liberal education,* (eds.) Ian Westbury and Neil Wilkof, 365–383. Chicago: University of Chicago Press, 1978.

——— . (1983). The practical 4: Something for curriculum professors to do. *Curriculum Inquiry* 13 (Fall): 239–256.

Tyler, R. W. (1984). Dialogue II. Personal reflections on the Practical 4. *Curriculum Inquiry* 14 (1): 97–102.

24

High-Stakes Testing and Curriculum Control: A Qualitative Metasynthesis

Wayne Au

With the advent of federally mandated high-stakes testing since the No Child Left Behind Act of 2001, many important questions have been raised regarding the implementation of this policy tool at the classroom level. In this article, I focus on one such question: What, if any, is the effect of high-stakes testing on curriculum? To answer this question, I begin by exploring the meanings of two key terms, "curriculum" and "high-stakes testing," and by offering a brief review of some of the literature regarding the relationship between the two. Then, using the method of qualitative metasynthesis, I undertake a comparative study of 49 qualitative studies of high-stakes testing to better understand testing's impact on curriculum.

Curriculum

There exists a wide range of definitions of the term "curriculum" (Beauchamp, 1982; Jackson, 1996; Kliebard, 1989). Historically, the word has its roots in the Latin word *currere*, which means a course to be run (Eisner, 1994), and was first used at the University of Glasgow in the 17th century to describe "a formal course of study that the students completed" (Harden, 2001, p. 335). This definition is perhaps the simplest and easiest for most to recognize because it is evident in the way schools are generally organized around a course of predetermined, required subject matter classes that students must pass to graduate. Thus most scholars and educators would at least recognize that curriculum encompasses a body of content knowledge to be learned in some way, shape, or form.

However, to stop at the level of content obscures other crucial aspects of curriculum because subject matter content within schools implies not only *selection* but also *transmission* of knowledge. As McEwan and Bull (1991) state,

> Subject matter is always an expression of a desire to communicate ideas to others. . . . Differences within the form and content of various expressions of subject matter reflect an understanding of differences in the backgrounds of potential audiences and the circumstances of the subject matter's formulation. (p. 331)

Indeed, all content is pedagogical. It implies the communication of ideas to an audience and does so through the structuring of knowledge (Segall, 2004a, 2004b). The concept of curriculum, therefore, also implicates the structure of knowledge embedded in curricular *form*—the form of how knowledge is organized and presented within a curriculum (Apple,

1995), as well as pedagogy—the intended form of communication of selected content. Thus the trilogy of (a) subject matter content knowledge, (b) structure or form of curricular knowledge, and (c) pedagogy are three defining aspects of "curriculum." This basic conception of curriculum is what I use for the present analysis.

High-Stakes Testing

A test is high-stakes when its results are used to make important decisions that affect students, teachers, administrators, communities, schools, and districts (Madaus, 1988). In very specific terms, high-stakes tests are a part of a *policy design* (Schneider & Ingram, 1997) that "links the score on one set of standardized tests to grade promotion, high school graduation and, in some cases, teacher and principal salaries and tenure decisions" (Orfield & Wald, 2000, p. 38). As part of the accountability movement, stakes are also deemed high because the results of tests, as well as the ranking and categorization of schools, teachers, and children that extend from those results, are reported to the public (McNeil, 2000).

The Research Debate

The question of whether high-stakes testing affects curriculum has been highly contested in the field of educational research. For instance, at a time when high-stakes testing policies were inconsistently implemented across individual states, Airasian (1987) and Madaus (1988) offered some of the earliest assertions that the tests would control classroom practice. M. L. Smith (1991) followed with one of the few early empirical studies, finding that high-stakes tests promote "multiple choice teaching." More recent research on high-stakes testing is more conflicted. Some research finds that high-stakes tests merely represent one limited factor, among others, influencing classroom practice (see, e.g., Cimbricz, 2002; Firestone, Mayrowetz, & Fairman, 1998; Grant, 2003), have little to no influence on what teachers do in the classroom (see, e.g., Gradwell, 2006; van Hover, 2006), or lead to improved learning experiences and positive educational outcomes (see, e.g., Braun, 2004; Williamson, Bondy, Langley, & Mayne, 2005). Other research challenges these claims, however, finding that high-stakes testing undermines education because it narrows curriculum, limits the ability of teachers to meet the sociocultural needs of their students, and corrupts systems of educational measurement (see, e.g., Amrein & Berliner, 2002a, 2002b; Lipman, 2004; McNeil, 2000; McNeil & Valenzuela, 2001; Nichols & Berliner, 2005, 2007; Watanabe, 2007). Given the wide range of research evidence, and given the ubiquity of high-stakes testing in education in the United States, the purpose of this study is to develop a broader, more complex understanding of the ways that these tests influence curriculum at the classroom level.

Method

For the purposes of this study I have chosen to analyze examples of qualitative research because of their focus on human interaction and attention to the day-to-day functioning of schools and classrooms (Valenzuela, Prieto, & Hamilton, 2007). To review the body of evidence reported in qualitative studies, I draw on the methodology of qualitative metasynthesis (DeWitt-Brinks & Rhodes, 1992; Noblit & Hare, 1988; Sandelowski, Docherty, & Emden, 1997; Thorne, Jensen, Kearney, Noblit, & Sandelowski, 2004), also referred to as qualitative meta-analysis (McCormick, Rodney, & Varcoe, 2003). Qualitative metasynthesis is part of a tradition of metaresearch that involves synthesizing the results of qualitative studies to gain a better understanding of the general nature of given phenomenon (DeWitt-Brinks & Rhodes, 1992; Thorne et al., 2004).

In this study I make use of a specific form of qualitative metasynthesis known as template analysis (Crabtree & Miller, 1999; King, 1998, 2006). In this form of thematic meta-analysis, textual data are coded using a template of codes designed by the researcher. These codes are often hierarchical in nature, starting with broad themes and moving toward more narrow or specific ones. In this case the textual data used are from the collection of qualitative studies gathered by the researcher. In template analysis the coding template is developed in two stages based on themes that arise from the body of textual data. In the first stage the researcher begins by developing an initial template based on a combination of a priori codes and an initial reading and coding of a subset of the textual data. In the second stage, the initial template is then applied to the whole data set, and codes are added to the template as new themes arise. This leads to the creation of the final template. The final template is then used to interpret the textual data set as a whole, and the findings are presented in some form (King, 1998, 2006).

Data Collection

The data set consists of 49 qualitative studies. These studies were gathered from a search completed in June of 2006 using the Educational Resources Information Center (ERIC), Academic Search, and Education Full Text databases, as well as the library book database at the University of Wisconsin, Madison. Initially, the search terms "high-stakes testing" and "state-mandated testing" were used to identify potential studies for use in my qualitative metasynthesis. This rather large initial pool was then narrowed to studies (a) based on original, scholarly research, (b) using qualitative methods, (c) taking place in the United States, and (d) specifically addressing the relationship between high-stakes tests and either curriculum or instruction, or both. Because this study focuses on the relationship between high-stakes testing and curriculum at the K-12 classroom level, the sample excludes studies that examine the relationship between high-stakes testing and retention, studies that focus on the role of high-stakes testing and access to teacher education programs (e.g., Praxis II), studies that focus on the tests themselves (e.g., discourse analyses of the actual test content), and policy studies that use qualitative methods to compare pressures between states. In addition, because of their ambiguous and complicated positions in school hierarchies, studies that focus on student teachers are also excluded.

Based on the self-identification of the researchers, the data gathered and analyzed from the 49 studies used in the qualitative metasynthesis performed here include at least 740 "teachers" identified as participants; 845 "educators" or "teachers and administrators" (not broken out into "teachers" alone) identified as participants; 96 schools identified as the focus of study; 38 districts identified as the level of focus of study; and covers at least 19 states (Arizona, Colorado, Florida, Illinois, Kansas, Kentucky, Maine, Maryland, Massachusetts, Michigan, Minnesota, New York, North Carolina, Ohio, Oregon, Texas, Vermont, Virginia, and Washington). In addition, of the 49 qualitative studies used in this metasynthesis, 15 focus on elementary education, 23 focus on secondary education, and 11 are K-12 analyses. Alternatively, while several of the included studies (23) are more general in focus, 14 are history/social studies-specific (3 elementary and 11 secondary), 9 are English/language arts-specific (1 elementary and 8 secondary), and 3 are math/science-specific. (See Table 24.1 for a complete listing of the studies analyzed here.)

Table 24.1 Qualitative Metasynthesis Studies and Codes

Article	*Codes[a]*
Agee, 2004	SAC, PCT, KCF
Anagnostopolous, 2003a	SAC, SAE, PCT, KCF
Anagnostopolous, 2003b	SAC, PCT, KCF
Barton, 2005	SAE, KCI
Bol, 2004	PCT, KCF
Bolgatz, 2006	KCI
Booher-Jennings, 2005	PCT
Brimijoin, 2005	SAC, PCT
Clarke et al., 2003	SAC, SAE, PCT, PCS, KCI
Costigan, 2002	PCT
Debray, Parson, & Avila, 2003	SAC
Fickel, 2006	SAE, PCT, KCI
Firestone, Mayrowetz, & Fairman, 1998	SAC, PCT, KCF
Gerwin & Visone, 2006	SAC, PCT, KCF
Gradwell, 2006	No changes[b]
Grant, 2003	No changes[b]
Grant et al., 2002	SAC, PCT, KCF
Groves, 2002	SAC, PCT
Hillocks, 2002	SAC, KCF
Landman, 2000	SAC, PCT, KCF
Libresco, 2005	SAE, PCS, KCI
Lipman, 2002	SAC, PCT, KCF
Lomax et al., 1995	SAC, PCT, KCF
Luna & Turner, 2001	SAC, SAE, PCT, KCF
McNeil, 2000	SAC, PCT, KCF
McNeil & Valenzuela, 2001	SAC, PCT, KCF
Murillo & Flores, 2002	SAC
Passman, 2001	SAC, PCT, KCF
Perreault, 2000	SAC, PCT
Renter et al., 2006	SAC
Rex, 2003	SAC, PCT
Rex & Nelson, 2004	SAE, PCS, KCI
Salinas, 2006	SAE, SAC
Segall, 2003	SAE, SAC, PCT, KCF, KCI
Siskin, 2003	SAC
Sloan, 2005	SAC, PCT, KCF
Smagorinsky, Lakly, & Johnson, 2002	SAC, PCT, KCF
Smith, A. M., 2006	SAE, SAC, PCT, KCF
Taylor et al., 2001	SAC, PCT, KCF
Valenzuela, 2000	SAC, PCT, KCF
van Hover, 2006	SAC, KCF
van Hover & Heinecke, 2005	PCT, KCF
Vogler, 2003	SAC, SAE
Williamson et al., 2005	PCT
Wolf & Wolf, 2002	SAE, PCS, KCI
Wollman-Bonilla, 2004	SAE, PCS, KCI

(Continued Overleaf)

Table 24.1 Continued

Article	Codes[a]
Wright & Choi, 2005	SAC
Yeh, 2005	SAE, PCS, KCI
Zancanella, 1992	SAC, PCT, KCF

a See Table 24.2 and the text discussion of it for explanations of the codes.
b These two studies reported no curricular changes in response to high-stakes testing.

Data Analysis

For this study I tracked the citation information, research sites, scope, and methods of inquiry of the 49 qualitative studies, including the dominant themes in each study's findings. I then coded dominant themes using the above definition of curriculum as the framework for my initial template of analysis. Thus my thematic coding began with three broad categories: Subject Matter Content, Pedagogy, and Structure of Knowledge. Consistent with the template analysis methodological framework, the full elaboration of my coding template evolved during the course of the research. For instance, it has been widely asserted over the past 20-plus years that high-stakes tests cause a narrowing or contraction of nontested subject areas. I was aware of research substantiating this assertion prior to beginning the template analysis and thus assumed that I would need to code the studies that reported the theme of contraction of subject matter content. Based on my previous understandings and on an initial analysis of qualitative studies, I produced an initial template of codes. However, after I undertook the template analysis, for instance, in addition to finding the theme of narrowing/contraction of curriculum to align with high-stakes tests, I also encountered the theme of subject matter content expansion. This finding required the addition of a new thematic code. As I read and reread the 49 qualitative studies, I added thematic codes as the patterns emerged and used them to develop the final template of codes for metasynthesis.

The thematic codes in Table 24.2 can be explained as follows. The first set of thematic codes seeks to track whether teachers, as individual actors at the classroom level, aligned their classroom content to the high-stakes tests. If they did, the thematic codes then mark the nature of this alignment—either subject matter content expansion or subject matter content contraction. In looking for subject matter contraction, I studied the research findings for occurrences of teachers and schools reducing the amount of instructional time

Table 24.2 Qualitative Metasynthesis Code Template

Curriculum	Code
Content	SAC—Subject matter content alignment, contraction
	SAE—Subject matter content alignment, expansion
Knowledge form	KCF—Form of knowledge changed, fractured
	KCI—Form of knowledge changed, integrated
Pedagogy	PCT—Pedagogic change to teacher-centered
	PCS—Pedagogic change to student-centered

and course offerings in either tested or nontested subject areas. An example of findings being coded for content matter expansion can be found in the research of Renter and colleagues (Renter et al., 2006), who found that schools were reducing the amount of instruction in science and social studies because those subjects were not a focus of the high-stakes tests. Conversely, in looking for subject matter expansion, I analyzed the data for reports of teachers and schools increasing the teaching of either tested or nontested subjects in response to high-stakes tests. Vogler (2003) is an example of a study that was coded for test-related content expansion because he found that social studies teachers in his study added language arts/literacy instruction to their social studies curriculum in response to high-stakes tests, which tested for writing but not for social studies content knowledge.

The second set of thematic codes tracked whether the high-stakes tests affected curricular knowledge forms. This theme was perhaps the most elusive of the three because it required that I follow how teachers organized the knowledge in their classrooms in relation to high-stakes testing. If a study reported that there was a shift in how teachers structured the knowledge they taught, I then coded for whether classroom knowledge forms became more fragmented and isolated into discrete, test-driven bits or became more expansive, inclusive in integrated wholes. As an instance of a study being coded for knowledge fragmentation, one study in this metasynthesis found that math and science were increasingly being taught as a collection of procedures and facts, as opposed to being taught as conceptual, thematic, and higher-order mathematic and scientific thinking (Lomax, West, Harmon, Viator, & Madaus, 1995). Such test-influenced instruction thus essentially fragmented the content knowledge into individuated and isolated procedures and facts for use on the high-stakes test. Other examples can be found where researchers reported that subjects such as social studies were broken up into collections of historical data (see, e.g., Grant et al., 2002) or subjects such as writing were reduced to the production of formulaic and procedural five-paragraph essays (see, e.g., Hillocks, 2002). Conversely, more integrated knowledge forms were coded in studies that found, for instance, some teachers focusing on more conceptual, higher-order thinking that sought to develop more holistic understanding of mathematics (see, e.g., Firestone et al., 1998) or studies that found language arts teachers focusing more conceptually on the process of writing as opposed to step-by-step procedural essay writing (see, e.g., Hillocks, 2002).

Third, I looked at the theme of teachers' pedagogy in response to high-stakes tests. If a study reported that teachers changed their instructional practice because of the testing, then I coded for the theme of teacher-centered instructional strategies or the theme of student-centered instructional strategies. In tracking these themes, I analyzed the studies' findings for evidence of teachers' increasing their use of direct instruction or increasing their use of more interactive pedagogies in response to the tests. For instance, in their research into high-stakes-testing-related social studies instruction, Gerwin and Visone (2006) found that teachers in their study showed dramatic increases in the amount of teacher-centered, fact-driven instruction in subjects included in state-mandated tests. Studies such as this were coded as demonstrating increased teacher-centered pedagogy. Studies reporting teachers' increasing the amount of student-centered, constructivist instruction in response to high-stakes tests, for example, some studies of language arts classrooms where teachers increased their use of interactional and student-led activities (see Wollman-Bonilla, 2004), were coded accordingly.

Once coding was completed, I analyzed the codes for patterns and anomalies on three levels. First, looking at the data as a whole collection, I tracked the predominant themes in terms of individual codes, essentially asking, what do these studies tell us about the overall effects of high-stakes testing on curriculum in terms of content, form, and pedagogy? Within this first level of analysis, I then sought to find relationships between the trends at the level of the single codes and other contextual variables found within the research, looking for overlaps between grade levels and subject areas and the trends found among individual themes.

At the second level I analyzed theme pairings. This involved tracking the number of times that particular codes appeared in corresponding pairs to determine if any relationships existed between changes in content, knowledge structures, and pedagogy. At this level of analysis, I also tracked whether the pairings corresponded to particular grade levels or subject areas.

Finally, at the third level, I analyzed theme triplets, seeking any potential connections between all three areas of content, pedagogy, and knowledge form in relation to the effects of high-stakes testing on classroom practice.

In addition to these three levels of analysis, I looked at the anomalies or weaker thematic relationships. Some studies simply came up with singular findings that did not match or support the trends and patterns of the larger metasynthesis; some groups of studies (such as are found within the social studies) were more conflicted in their findings.

Study Reliability

Reliability is a known issue within template analysis (King, 1998, 2006; Pawson, Greenhalgh, Harvey, & Walshe, 2005), and I have used two strategies to ensure the reliability of the findings of this study. First, to empirically determine the interrater reliability of my own coding, two colleagues independently coded findings of a sample subset of 10 studies. The findings of these coders were then checked against my own, resulting in the following interrater reliability percentages: subject matter content contraction, 86.7 percent; subject matter content expansion, 83.3 percent; knowledge fragmentation, 93.3 percent; knowledge integration, 96.7 percent; teacher-centered pedagogy, 90 percent; student-centered pedagogy, 86.7 percent. The overall interrater reliability for this study was 89.4 percent.

Second, reliability in template analysis is also improved when researchers are explicitly reflexive about both the process of their research and their positioning in relation to their study (King, 1998, 2006; Pawson et al., 2005). Thus it is important to explain my research orientation. I approach this study from within the critical realist tradition, which holds that a real world exists objectively outside human perception, that this world is to varying extents knowable through human cognition, and that this world is in fact changeable relative to our knowledge of it. Furthermore, critical realism recognizes human subjectivity in the understanding of the externally existing world, and as such views knowledge as a social process and as fallible. In these ways, critical realism simultaneously rejects both positivist objectivist *and* relativist subjectivist theories of knowledge in favor of an epistemology that in essence synthesizes aspects of both—an objectively existing world and a socially mediated understanding of that world (Benton & Craib, 2001; Bhaskar, 1989). Consequently, my use of template analysis combined with critical realism makes this study a form of realist review (Pawson et al., 2005).

My critical realist positioning also influences this study in that the use of the word "critical" points to a particular set of political commitments on the part of the researcher. Critical realists seek to understand the world to change it for the better, seek to reflexively understand social mechanisms to promote social equality (Benton & Craib, 2001; Bhaskar, 1989). A similar political commitment underlies the impetus for this study, because I, as a social justice educator, scholar, and activist, have sought to understand the relationship between education and power (see, e.g., Au, 2005, 2006; Au & Apple, 2004). As such, I am interested in the relationship between high-stakes testing and inequalities associated with race and socioeconomic status (see, e.g., Hunter & Bartee, 2003; Kim & Sunderman, 2005; Sirin, 2005). However, although ultimately inseparable from my overall research agenda, for the purposes of this study I have attempted to put my political commitments aside in favor of a focused empirical analysis of how high-stakes testing affects curriculum. Thus, although these effects may have implications for educational equality and social justice, I have made a conscious choice here to bracket those implications as beyond the scope of this specific study and analysis.

Study Limits

Before presenting the findings, it is important to recognize that this study has a specific focus and is therefore limited in at least two particular ways. First, in this metasynthesis I inquire into the frequency and types of curricular change induced by high-stakes testing. Consequently, my inquiry excludes instances where high-stakes testing does not affect the curriculum. As this study's findings will show, the body of research analyzed here focuses predominantly on test-related events, as opposed to test-related nonevents. In this regard, even though a handful of studies included here specifically focus on a lack of test-related instructional changes (see, e.g., Bolgatz, 2006; Gradwell, 2006; Grant, 2003), the findings of this qualitative metasynthesis are inherently skewed toward what the researchers in the majority of these studies chose to focus on in their research: class-room-level changes due to high-stakes tests.

A second way in which the findings of this qualitative metasynthesis are limited relates to the time periods reported on. The studies analyzed here report inconsistently on how curriculum changes in response to high-stakes testing relative to time. Thus some studies focus on periods of curricular change in the months, weeks, or days leading up to high-stakes tests, and others focus on test-related curricular change more generally. Consequently, it was difficult to ascertain whether high-stakes testing was affecting the curriculum all year or simply in time periods immediately preceding the tests. I would argue, however, that these two limits do not take away from the power of the findings presented here. Rather, the limits simply refine the focus of this qualitative metasynthesis, which provides a snapshot and general depiction of the types and frequency of changes made to curricula in high-stakes testing environments.

Findings

As Table 24.3 indicates, the findings of this study suggest that there is a significant relationship between the implementation of high-stakes testing and changes in the content of a curriculum, the structure of knowledge contained within the content, and the types of pedagogy associated with communication of that content. These changes represent three types of control that high-stakes tests exert on curriculum: content control, formal control, and pedagogic control.

Table 24.3 Summary Findings: Effects of High-Stakes Testing on Curriculum

Curricular Change	Number of Studies, N = 49	Percentage of Total	Exemplar of Dominant Theme
Subject matter	41	83.7%	A Colorado teacher: "Our district has told us to
Contraction	34	69.4%	focus on reading, writing, and mathematics.
Expansion	14	28.6%	Therefore, science and social studies . . . don't get taught." Taylor et al., 2001, p. 30
Knowledge form	34	69.4%	A Massachusetts teacher: "You know, we're not really
Fractured	24	49%	teaching them how to write. We're teaching them
Integrated	10	20.4%	how to follow a format. . . . It's like . . . they're doing paint-by-numbers." Luna & Turner, 2001, p. 83
Pedagogy	38	77.6%	A Kansas teacher: ". . . I don't get to do as many fun
Teacher-centered	32	65.3%	activities, like cooperative learning activities or
Student-centered	6	12.3%	projects. . . . [T]his year I've done a lot more direct teaching than being able to do student-led learning. . . ." Clarke et al., 2003, p. 50

Note: Individual code totals do not necessarily equal the total for any one category because some studies exhibit multiple, even contradictory, codes; for example, subject alignment contraction and subject alignment expansion may appear in the same study.

Content Control

The dominant theme found in the qualitative research regarding high-stakes testing and curriculum is that of content alignment. More than 80% of the studies contained the theme of curricular content change, whether by contraction or expansion. Furthermore, as Table 24.3 shows, in an overwhelming number of the qualitative studies, participants reported instances of the narrowing of curriculum, or curricular contraction to tested subjects. This phenomenon was the most prominent way in which "teaching to the test" manifested in curricula, as nontested subjects were increasingly excluded from curricular content. A more detailed analysis finds that the narrowing of curricular content was strongest among participants in the studies that focused on secondary education, with the most narrowing found in studies of social studies and language arts classrooms. In addition, in another expression of curricular alignment, a significant minority of studies reported some form of content expansion as a result of high-stakes testing, with most of these coming from studies focusing on secondary education and social studies classrooms. As the above evidence suggests, whether in the form of content contraction or content expansion, high-stakes testing leverages a significant amount *content control* over curriculum.

Formal Control

Table 24.3 also indicates that, in a significant number of the qualitative studies, participants reported changes to the form that curricular knowledge took in response to high-stakes testing. The dominant theme in this category suggests that there is a relationship between high-stakes testing and teachers' increasing the fragmentation of knowledge. Such fragmentation manifested in the teaching of content in small, individuated, and isolated test-size pieces, as well as teaching in direct relation to the tests rather than in relation to other subject matter knowledge. However, it is important to note that, as shown in Table 24.3, a minority of studies found that high-stakes testing had led to the increased integration of knowledge in the classroom. Thus, within the body of qualitative research, a dominant theme is that, whether leading to fragmentation or integration of knowledge, high-stakes testing affects curricular form, that is, it leverages *formal control* over the curriculum.

Pedagogic Control

A third dominant theme that appears in the qualitative research is pedagogic change. As shown in Table 3, a significant number of participants in qualitative studies reported that their pedagogy changed in response to high-stakes tests and that a significant majority of the changes included an increase in teacher-centered instruction associated with lecturing and the direct transmission of test-related facts. In addition, as Table 24.3 indicates, a small but important number of studies exhibited the theme of increased student-centered instruction as an effect of high-stakes testing. Further analysis shows that, in this metasynthesis, a cluster of test-related, teacher-centered pedagogy exists surrounding instruction in both language arts and social studies classrooms. Whether in the form of increased teacher-centered instruction or increased student-centered instruction, the evidence suggests that high-stakes testing exerts significant *pedagogic control* over curriculum.

Theme Pairings

An analysis of theme pairings generally mirrors the above findings but also provides a more nuanced outline of potentially significant relationships between dominant themes.

As Table 24.4 indicates, the most prominent theme pairing suggests that there is a relationship between the narrowing of curriculum and an increase in teacher-centered instruction as teachers respond to pressures created by high-stakes testing environments. The next highest occurrence of theme pairing suggests that increased teacher-centered pedagogy and increased fragmentation of knowledge forms are likely to coincide in response to high-stakes testing. The third most frequent theme pairing suggests a relationship

Table 24.4 Summary of Selected Theme Pairings

Theme Pairing	Occurrence
Content contraction/teacher-centered pedagogy	26/37 (70.3%)
Teacher-centered pedagogy/knowledge fragmentation	23/35 (65.7%)
Content contraction/knowledge fragmentation	22/34 (64.7%)
Content expansion/knowledge integration	9/34 (26.5%)
Student-centered pedagogy/knowledge integration	6/35 (17.1%)
Content contraction/content expansion	7/43 (16.3%)
Content expansion/teacher-centered pedagogy	6/37 (16.2%)
Content expansion/student-centered pedagogy	6/37 (16.2%)

between curricular content narrowing and the fragmentation of knowledge forms, which are likely to occur together in response to high-stakes testing.

The findings further suggest that there are weaker but significant relationships between the expansion of subject matter and an increase of a more integrated structure of knowledge in response to high-stakes testing, as well as a contraction or narrowing of curricular content and a simultaneous content expansion. Three other significant theme pairings appear in the study, two of which are seemingly contradictory to the dominant trends outlined above. As Table 24.4 shows, theme pairing of curricular expansion and an increase in teacher-centered pedagogy in response to high-stakes testing was also found. Other findings showed increases in student-centered pedagogy paired with an increase in the integration of knowledge in response to high-stakes testing.

Theme Triplets

A total of 28 studies in this qualitative metasynthesis produced codes within each area of curriculum identified here. I now turn to the final level of analysis, examining these theme triplets to determine if there are any potential relationships between all three thematic areas. Overwhelmingly, the prevalent theme triplet in the qualitative research was the combination of contracting curricular content, fragmentation of the structure of knowledge, and increasing teacher-centered pedagogy in response to high-stakes testing. This theme triplet appears 21 times (75%) among the 28 studies that produced themes in all three areas, suggesting a relationship between the themes in response to high-stakes testing. The second most frequently occurring theme triplet, that of curricular content expansion, increasing integration of knowledge, and increasing student-centered instruction, appears 6 times (21.4%) in the study. This triplet is indeed the exact opposite of the dominant triplet.

Discussion

Despite some researchers' claims to the contrary, the findings of this study suggest that high-stakes tests encourage curricular alignment to the tests themselves. This alignment tends to take the form of a curricular content narrowing to tested subjects, to the detriment or exclusion of nontested subjects. The findings of this study further suggest that the structure of the knowledge itself is also changed to meet the test-based norms: Content is increasingly taught in isolated pieces and often learned only within the context of the tests themselves. Finally, in tandem with both content contraction and the fragmentation of knowledge, pedagogy is also implicated, as teachers increasingly turn to teacher-centered instruction to cover the breadth of test-required information and procedures. Thus I have identified three different, interrelated types of curricular control associated with high-stakes testing: *content, formal,* and *pedagogic.* The control over knowledge content and the form the knowledge takes are related to and associated with control of pedagogy as well.

As I noted in Tables 24.3 and 24.4, however, several less frequently occurring themes seemed to contradict the predominant findings of this study. The data suggest that in a small number of cases, high-stakes testing was associated with an increase in student-centered instruction, content integration, and subject matter expansion. For instance, there are seven simultaneous occurrences of the themes of content contraction and content expansion related to high-stakes tests, most of which come from secondary social studies and language arts (see, e.g., Anagnostopolous, 2003b; Luna & Turner, 2001; Segall, 2003; A. M. Smith, 2006; Vogler, 2003). In these cases, teachers are both adding some content to meet the demands of the tests and contracting content in other areas. In addition, because the stakes of state-mandated social studies testing vary greatly from state to state (Grant & Horn, 2006), the findings indicate that high-stakes-test-induced curricular expansion has taken place in social studies classrooms as teachers integrate reading-test-related literacy skills into their own social studies curricula (see, e.g., Vogler, 2003). Indeed, this phenomenon of expanding curricular content due to the integration of test-required literacy skills or test-specific content accounts for the majority of the instances of curricular expansion (see, e.g., Barton, 2005; Clarke et al., 2003; Libresco, 2005; Rex & Nelson, 2004; Wolf & Wolf, 2002; Wollman-Bonilla, 2004; Yeh, 2005).

There appears to be a similar relationship regarding the small numbers of increases in student-centered pedagogies relative to high-stakes testing. Almost all occurrences of the theme of increases in student-centered pedagogy occur with instances of subject matter expansion. These cases revolve around teachers whose test-based instruction involves the development of critical literacy skills (see, e.g., Clarke et al., 2003; Libresco, 2005; Rex & Nelson, 2004; Wolf & Wolf, 2002; Wollman-Bonilla, 2004; Yeh, 2005). For instance, New York State's history exam involves a mix of multiple-choice questions and a document-based essay question (DBQ; Grant, 2003). Social studies teachers, in preparing students for DBQs, have the charge of teaching a specific critical literacy skill set instead of being forced to focus solely on a rigidly imposed collection of historical facts (see, e.g., Bolgatz, 2006; Clarke et al., 2003; Grant, 2003; Libresco, 2005). It is likely that teachers in these studies thus find the potential for increased flexibility in the content and pedagogy they use to teach social studies in their respective high-stakes environments. Furthermore, because social studies instruction figures prominently in the above contradictory findings, and because the only two studies to argue that testing does not influence any aspect of curriculum also focus on this subject area (Gradwell, 2006; Grant, 2003), it is also possible that social studies represents a special case in relation to high-stakes testing and curricular control (Au, in press).

The above discussion indicates a likely relationship between the construction of the high-stakes tests themselves and the curricular changes induced by the tests. Research supports the existence of such a relationship. As Yeh (2005) finds, teachers in Minnesota report that their pedagogy is not negatively affected by high-stakes tests because they feel the tests there are well designed and do not promote drill and rote memorization. Another example comes from Hillocks (2002), who analyzes the teaching of writing in relation to the writing examinations delivered in Texas, Illinois, New York, Oregon, and Kentucky. One of Hillocks's main findings is that states with poorly designed systems of writing assessment promote a technical, mechanical, five-paragraph essay form, and that teachers' pedagogy adapts to that form in those states. The findings of these studies suggest that test construction matters in terms of teachers' curricular responses to high-stakes tests (see also Clarke et al., 2003).

Conclusion

In this study, using a form of qualitative metasynthesis called template analysis, I have reviewed the findings of 49 qualitative studies addressing the impact of high-stakes testing on curriculum. As Tables 3 and 4 indicate, the evidence presented here strongly suggests that as teachers negotiate high-stakes testing educational environments, the tests have the predominant effect of narrowing curricular content to those subjects included in the tests, resulting in the increased fragmentation of knowledge forms into bits and pieces learned for the sake of the tests themselves, and compelling teachers to use more lecture-based, teacher-centered pedagogies. Another significant finding of this study is that, in a minority of cases, high-stakes tests have led to increases in student-centered pedagogy and increases in content knowledge integration. Combined, these findings indicate that high-stakes testing exerts significant amounts of control over the content, knowledge forms, and pedagogies at the classroom level.

The curricular control found in this study further suggests that high-stakes testing represents the tightening of the loose coupling between policymakers' intentions and the institutional environments created by their policies (Burch, 2007). This conclusion should not be surprising to educational researchers and practitioners because systems of educational accountability built on high-stakes, standardized tests are in fact intended to increase external control over what happens in schools and classrooms. As Moe (2003) explains, the rationale behind systems of high-stakes accountability is quite clear:

> The movement for school accountability is essentially a movement for more effective top-down control of the schools. The idea is that, if public authorities want to promote student achievement, they need to adopt organizational control mechanisms—tests, school report cards, rewards and sanctions, and the like—designed to get district officials, principals, teachers, and students to change their behavior.... Virtually all organizations need to engage in top-down control, because the people at the top have goals they want the people at the bottom to pursue, and something has to be done to bring about the desired behaviors.
> The public school system is just like other organizations in this respect. (p. 81)

The intentions of promoters of high-stakes test-based educational reforms are thus apparent in the policy designs, which are purposefully constructed to negate "asymmetries" between classroom practice and the policy goals of those with political and bureaucratic power (Wöþmann, 2003).

Given the central findings of this study, however, a crucial question is raised: Are test-driven curriculum and teacher-centered instruction good or bad for teachers, students, schools, communities, and education in general? Considering the body of research connecting high-stakes testing with increased drop-out rates and lower achievement for working-class students and students of color (see, e.g., Amrein & Berliner, 2002b; Groves, 2002; Madaus & Clarke, 2001; Marchant & Paulson, 2005; Nichols, Glass, & Berliner, 2005), the findings of this study point to the need for further analysis of how curricular control may or may not contribute to educational inequality.

Note

I would like to thank Diana Hess, Simone Schweber, Keita Takayama, Ross Collin, Eduardo Cavieres, Quentin Wheeler-Bell, the three anonymous *ER* reviewers, and *ER* editor Gregory Camilli for their invaluable feedback on this article.

References

References marked with an asterisk indicate studies included in the metasynthesis.

*Agee, J. (2004). Negotiating a teaching identity: An African American teacher's struggle to teach in test-driven contexts. *Teachers College Record, 106*(4), 747–774.

Airasian, P. W. (1987). State mandated testing and educational reform: Context and consequences. *American Journal of Education, 95*(3), 393–412.

Amrein, A. L., & Berliner, D. C. (2002a, December). *An analysis of some unintended and negative consequences of high-stakes testing.* Tempe, AZ: Educational Policy Studies Laboratory, Arizona State University. Retrieved February 12, 2006, from http://www.asu.edu/educ/epsl/EPRU/epru_2002_Research_Writing.htm

Amrein, A. L., & Berliner, D. C. (2002b). High-stakes testing, uncertainty, and student learning. *Education Policy Analysis Archives, 10*(18). Retrieved September 27, 2005, from http://epaa.asu.edu/epaa/v10n18

*Anagnostopolous, D. (2003a). The new accountability, student failure, and teachers' work in urban high schools. *Educational Policy, 17*(3), 291–316.

*Anagnostopolous, D. (2003b). Testing and student engagement with literature in urban classrooms: A multi-layered perspective. *Research in the Teaching of English, 38*(2), 177–212.

Apple, M. W. (1995). *Education and power* (2nd ed.). New York: Routledge.

Au, W. (2005). Power, identity, and the third rail. In P. C. Miller (ed.), *Narratives from the classroom: An introduction to teaching* (pp. 65–85). Thousand Oaks, CA: Sage.

Au, W. (2006, November). Against economic determinism: Revisiting the roots of neo-Marxism in critical educational theory. *Journal for Critical Education Policy Studies, 4*(2). Retrieved December 12, 2006, from http://www.jceps.com/?pageID=article&articleID=66

Au, W. (in press). Social studies, social justice: W(h)ither the social studies in high-stakes testing? *Teacher Education Quarterly.*

Au, W., & Apple, M. W. (2004). Interrupting globalization as an educational practice. *Educational Policy, 18*(5), 784–793.

*Barton, K. C. (2005). "I'm not saying these are going to be easy": Wise practice in an urban elementary school. In E. A. Yeager & O. L. Davis Jr. (eds.), *Wise social studies teaching in an age of high-stakes testing* (pp. 11–31). Greenwich, CT: Information Age Publishing.

Beauchamp, G. A. (1982). Curriculum theory: Meaning, development, and use. *Theory Into Practice, 21*(1), 23–27.

Benton, T., & Craib, I. (2001). *Philosophy of social science: The philosophical foundations of social thought.* New York: Palgrave.

Bhaskar, R. (1989). *Reclaiming reality: A critical introduction to contemporary philosophy* (2nd ed.). New York: Verso.

*Bol, L. (2004). Teachers' assessment practices in a high-stakes testing environment. *Teacher Education and Practice, 17*(2), 162–181.

*Bolgatz, J. (2006). Using primary documents with fourth-grade students: Talking about racism while preparing for state-level tests. In S. G. Grant (ed.), *Measuring history: Cases of state-level testing across the United States* (pp. 133–156). Greenwich, CT: Information Age Publishing.

*Booher-Jennings, J. (2005). Below the bubble: "Educational triage" and the Texas accountability system. *American Educational Research Journal, 42*(2), 231–268.

Braun, H. (2004). Reconsidering the impact of high-stakes testing. *Education Policy Analysis Archives, 12*(1). Retrieved March 29, 2006, from http://epaa.asu.edu/epaa/v12n1

*Brimijoin, K. (2005). Differentiation and high-stakes testing: An oxymoron? *Theory Into Practice, 44*(3), 254–261.

Burch, P. E. (2007). Educational policy and practice from the perspective of institutional theory: Crafting a wider lens. *Educational Researcher, 36*(2), 84–95.

Cimbricz, S. (2002). State testing and teachers' thinking and practice. *Education Policy Analysis Archives, 10*(2). Retrieved September 4, 2006, from http://epaa.asu.edu/epaa/v10n2.html

*Clarke, M., Shore, A., Rhoades, K., Abrams, L. M., Miao, J., & Li, J. (2003, January). *Perceived effects of state-mandated testing programs on teaching and learning: Findings from interviews with educators in low-, medium-, and high-stakes states.* Boston: National Board on Educational Testing and Public Policy, Lynch School of Education, Boston College. Retrieved March 20, 2006, from http://www.bc.edu/research/nbetpp/reports.html

*Costigan, A. T., III. (2002). Teaching the culture of high stakes testing: Listening to new teachers. *Action in Teacher Education, 23*(4), 28–34.

Crabtree, B. F., & Miller, W. L. (1999). Using codes and code manuals: A template organizing style of interpretation. In B. F. Crabtree & W. L. Miller (eds.), *Doing qualitative research* 2nd ed., (pp. 163–178). Thousand Oaks, CA: Sage.

*Debray, E., Parson, G., & Avila, S. (2003). Internal alignment and external pressure. In M. Carnoy, R. Elmore, & L. S. Siskin (eds.), *The new accountability: High schools and high-stakes testing* (pp. 55–85). New York: RoutledgeFalmer.

DeWitt-Brinks, D., & Rhodes, S. C. (1992, May 20–25). *Listening instruction: A qualitative meta-analysis of twenty-four selected studies.* Paper presented at the annual meeting of the International Communication Association, Miami, FL.

Eisner, E. W. (1994). *The educational imagination: On the design and evaluation of school programs* (3rd ed.). New York: Macmillan.

*Fickel, L. H. (2006). Paradox of practice: Expanding and contracting curriculum in a high-stakes climate. In S. G. Grant (ed.), *Measuring history: Cases of state-level testing across the United States* (pp. 75–103). Greenwich, CT: Information Age Publishing.

*Firestone, W. A., Mayrowetz, D., & Fairman, J. (1998). Performance-based assessment and instructional change: The effects of testing in Maine and Maryland. *Educational Evaluation and Policy Analysis, 20*(2), 94–113.

*Gerwin, D., & Visone, F. (2006). The freedom to teach: Contrasting history teaching in elective and state-tested course. *Social Education, 34*(2), 259–282.

*Gradwell, J. M. (2006). Teaching in spite of, rather than because of, the test: A case of ambitious history teaching in New York State. In S. G. Grant (ed.), *Measuring history: Cases of state-level testing across the United States* (pp. 157–176). Greenwich, CT: Information Age Publishing.

*Grant, S. G. (2003). *History lessons: Teaching, learning, and testing in U.S. high school classrooms*. Mahwah, NJ: Lawrence Erlbaum.

*Grant, S. G., Gradwell, J. M., Lauricella, A. M., Derme-Insinna, A., Pullano, L., & Tzetzo, K. (2002). When increasing stakes need not mean increasing standards: The case of the New York state global history and geography exam. *Theory and Research in Social Education, 30*(4), 488–515.

Grant, S. G., & Horn, C. L. (2006). The state of state-level history tests. In S. G. Grant (ed.), *Measuring history: Cases of state-level testing across the United States* (pp. 9–27). Greenwich, CT: Information Age Publishing.

*Groves, P. (2002). "Doesn't it feel morbid here?" High-stakes testing and the widening of the equity gap. *Educational Foundations, 16*(2), 15–31.

Harden, R. M. (2001). The learning environment and the curriculum. *Medical Teacher, 23*(4), 335–336.

*Hillocks, G., Jr. (2002). *The testing trap: How state writing assessments control learning*. New York: Teachers College Press.

Hunter, R. C., & Bartee, R. (2003). The achievement gap: Issues of competition, class, and race. *Education and Urban Society, 35*(2), 151–160.

Jackson, P. W. (1996). Conceptions of curriculum and curriculum specialists. In P. W. Jackson (ed.), *Handbook of research on curriculum: A project of the American Educational Research Association* (pp. 3–40). New York: Simon & Schuster Macmillan.

Kim, J. S., & Sunderman, G. L. (2005). Measuring academic proficiency under the No Child Left Behind Act: Implications for educational equity. *Educational Researcher, 34*(8), 3–13.

King, N. (1998) Template analysis. In G. Symon & C. Cassell (eds.), *Qualitative methods and analysis in organizational research: A practical guide* (pp. 118–134). London: Sage.

King, N. (2006, October 23). *What is template analysis?* University of Huddersfield School of Human and Health Sciences. Retrieved April 27, 2007, from http://www.hud.ac.uk/hhs/research/template_analysis/whatis.htm

Kliebard, H. M. (1989). Problems of definition in curriculum. *Journal of Curriculum and Supervision, 5*(1), 1–5.

*Landman, J. (2000, January 7). *A state-mandated curriculum, a high-stakes test: One Massachusetts high school history department's response to a very new policy context*. Doctoral qualifying paper, Harvard Graduate School of Education, Cambridge, MA. (ERIC Document Reproduction Service No. ED440915)

*Libresco, A. S. (2005). How she stopped worrying and learned to love the test . . . sort of. In E. A. Yeager & O. L. Davis Jr. (eds.), *Wise social studies teaching in an age of high-stakes testing* (pp. 33–49). Greenwich, CT: Information Age Publishing.

*Lipman, P. (2002). Making the global city, making inequality: The political economy and cultural politics of Chicago school policy. *American Educational Research Journal, 39*(2), 379–419.

Lipman, P. (2004). *High stakes education: Inequality, globalization, and urban school reform*. New York: RoutledgeFalmer.

*Lomax, R. G., West, M. M., Harmon, M. C., Viator, K. A., & Madaus, G. F. (1995). The impact of mandated standardized testing on minority students. *Journal of Negro Education, 64*(2), 171–185.

*Luna, C., & Turner, C. L. (2001). The impact of the MCAS: Teachers talk about high-stakes testing. *English Journal, 91*(1), 79–87.

Madaus, G. F. (1988). The influence of testing on the curriculum. In L. N. Tanner (ed.), *Critical issues in curriculum: Eighty-seventh year-book of the national society for the study of education* (pp. 83–121). Chicago: University of Chicago Press.

Madaus, G. F., & Clarke, M. (2001). The adverse impact of high-stakes testing on minority students: Evidence from one hundred years of test data. In G. Orfield & M. L. Kornhaber (eds.), *Raising standards or raising barriers? Inequality and high-stakes testing in public education* (pp. 85–106). New York: Century Foundation Press.

Marchant, G. J., & Paulson, S. E. (2005, January 21). The relationship of high school graduation exams to graduation rates and SAT scores. *Education Policy Analysis Archives, 13*(6). Retrieved February 8, 2006, from http://epaa.asu.edu/epaa/v13n6/

McCormick, J., Rodney, P., & Varcoe, C. (2003). Reinterpretations across studies: An approach to meta-analysis. *Qualitative Health Research, 13*(7), 933–944.

McEwan, H., & Bull, B. (1991). The pedagogic nature of subject matter knowledge. *American Educational Research Journal, 28*(2), 316–334.

*McNeil, L. M. (2000). *Contradictions of school reform: Educational costs of standardized testing.* New York: Routledge.

*McNeil, L. M., & Valenzuela, A. (2001). The harmful impact of the TAAS system of testing in Texas: Beneath the accountability rhetoric. In G. Orfield & M. L. Kornhaber (eds.), *Raising standards or raising barriers? Inequality and high-stakes testing in public education* (pp. 127–150). New York: Century Foundation Press.

Moe, T. M. (2003). Politics, control, and the future of school accountability. In P. E. Peterson & M. R. West (eds.), *No child left behind? The politics and practice of school accountability* (pp. 80–106). Washington, DC: Brookings Institution Press.

*Murillo E. G., Jr., & Flores, S. Y. (2002). Reform by shame: Managing the stigma of labels in high-stakes testing. *Educational Foundations, 16*(2), 93–108.

Nichols, S. L., & Berliner, D. C. (2005, March). *The inevitable corruption of indicators and educators through high-stakes testing* (No. EPSL-0503-101-EPRU). Tempe; AZ: Education Policy Studies Laboratory, Arizona State University. Retrieved September 27, 2005, from http://www.asu.edu/educ/epsl/EPRU/documents/EPSL-0503-101-EPRU-exec.pdf

Nichols, S. L., & Berliner, D. C. (2007). *Collateral damage: How high-stakes testing corrupts America's schools.* Cambridge, MA: Harvard Education Press.

Nichols, S. L., Glass, G. V., & Berliner, D. C. (2005, September). *High-stakes testing and student achievement: Problems for the No Child Left Behind Act* (No. EPSL-0509-105-EPRU). Tempe, AZ: Education Policy Studies Laboratory, Arizona State University. Retrieved September 27, 2005, from http://www.asu.edu/educ/epsl/EPRU/documents/EPSL-0509-105-EPRU.pdf

Noblit, G. W., & Hare, R. D. (1988). *Meta-ethnography: Synthesizing qualitative studies* (Vol. 11). Newbury Park, CA: Sage.

Orfield, G., & Wald, J. (2000). Testing, testing: The high-stakes testing mania hurts poor and minority students the most. *Nation, 270*(22), 38–40.

*Passman, R. (2001). Experiences with student-centered teaching and learning in high-stakes assessment environments. *Education, 122*(1), 189–199.

Pawson, R. Greenhalgh, T., Harvey, G., & Walshe, K. (2005). Realist review: A new method of systematic review designed for complex policy interventions. *Journal of Health Services Research & Policy, 10*(1), 21–84.

*Perreault, G. (2000). The classroom impact of high-stress testing. *Education, 120*(4), 705–710.

*Renter, D. S., Scott, C., Kober, N., Chudowsky, N., Joftus, S., & Zabala, D. (2006, March 28). *From the capital to the classroom: Year 4 of the No Child Left Behind Act.* Washington, DC: Center on Education Policy. Retrieved March 28, 2006, from http://www.cep-dc.org

*Rex, L. A. (2003). Loss of the creature: The obscuring of inclusivity in classroom discourse. *Communication Education, 52*(1), 30–46.

*Rex, L. A., & Nelson, M. C. (2004). How teachers' professional identities position high-stakes preparation in their classrooms. *Teachers College Record, 106*(6), 1288–1331.

*Salinas, C. (2006). Teaching in a high-stakes testing setting: What becomes of teacher knowledge. In S. G. Grant (ed.), *Measuring history: Cases of state-level testing across the United States* (pp. 177–193). Greenwich, CT: Information Age Publishing.

Sandelowski, M., Docherty, S., & Emden, C. (1997). Qualitative meta-synthesis: Issues and techniques. *Research in Nursing & Health, 20*(4), 365–371.

Schneider, A. L., & Ingram, H. (1997). *Policy design for democracy.* Lawrence: University of Kansas.

*Segall, A. (2003). Teachers' perceptions of the impact of state-mandated standardized testing: The Michigan Educational Assessment Program (MEAP) as a case study of consequences. *Theory and Research in Social Education, 31*(3), 287–325.

Segall, A. (2004a). Blurring the lines between content and pedagogy. *Social Education, 68*(7), 479–482.

Segall, A. (2004b). Revisiting pedagogical content knowledge: The pedagogy of content/the content of pedagogy. *Teaching and Teacher Education, 20,* 489–504.

Sirin, S. R. (2005). Socioeconomic status and student achievement: A meta-analytic review of research. *Review of Educational Research, 75*(3), 417–453.

*Siskin, L. S. (2003). Outside the core: Accountability in tested and untested subjects. In M. Carnoy, R. Elmore, & L. S. Siskin (eds.), *The new accountability: High schools and high-stakes testing* (pp. 87–98). New York: RoutledgeFalmer.

*Sloan, K. (2005). Playing to the logic of the Texas accountability system: How focusing on "ratings"—not children—undermines quality and equity. In A. Valenzuela (ed.), *Leaving children behind: How "Texas-style" accountability fails Latino youth* (pp. 153–178). Albany: State University of New York.

*Smagorinsky, P., Lakly, A., & Johnson, T. S. (2002). Acquiescence, accommodation, and resistance in learning to teach within a prescribed curriculum. *English Education, 34*(3), 187–213.

*Smith, A. M. (2006). Negotiating control and protecting the private: History teachers and the Virginia standards of learning. In S. G. Grant (ed.), *Measuring history: Cases of state-level testing across the United States* (pp. 221–247). Greenwich, CT: Information Age Publishing.

Smith, M. L. (1991). Put to the test: The effects of external testing on teachers. *Educational Researcher, 20*(5), 8–11.

*Taylor, G., Shepard, L., Kinner, F., & Rosenthal, J. (2001, September). *A survey of teachers' perspectives on high-stakes testing in Colorado: What gets taught, what gets lost.* Boulder, CO: CRESST/CREDE/University of Colorado at Boulder. Retrieved February 24, 2006, from http://education.colorado.edu/epic/COStdRprts/COstdrpreptitle.asp

Thorne, S. E., Jensen, L., Kearney, M. H., Noblit, G. W., & Sandelowski, M. (2004). Qualitative metasynthesis: Reflections on methodological orientation and ideological agenda. *Qualitative Health Research, 14*(10), 1342–1365.

*Valenzuela, A. (2000). The significance of the TAAS test for Mexican immigrant and Mexican American adolescents: A case study. *Hispanic Journal of Behavioral Sciences, 22*(4), 524–539.

Valenzuela, A., Prieto, L., & Hamilton, M. P. (2007). No Child Left Behind and minority youth: What the qualitative evidence suggests. *Anthropology & Education Quarterly, 38*(1), 1–8.

*van Hover, S. D. (2006). Teaching history in the old dominion: The impact of Virginia's accountability reform on seven secondary beginning history teachers. In S. G. Grant (ed.), *Measuring history: Cases of state-level testing across the United States* (pp. 195–219). Greenwich, CT: Information Age Publishing.

*van Hover, S. D., & Heinecke, W. (2005). The impact of accountability reform on the " 'wise practice" of secondary history teachers: The Virginia experience. In E. A. Yeager & O. L. Davis Jr. (eds.), *Wise social studies teaching in an age of high-stakes testing* (pp. 89–105). Greenwich, CT: Information Age Publishing.

*Vogler, K. E. (2003). An integrated curriculum using state standards in a high-stakes testing environment. *Middle School Journal, 34*(4), 10.

Watanabe, M. (2007). Displaced teacher and state priorities in a high-stakes accountability context. *Educational Policy, 21*(2), 311–368.

*Williamson, P., Bondy, E., Langley, L., & Mayne, D. (2005). Meeting the challenge of high-stakes testing while remaining child-centered: The representations of two urban teachers. *Childhood Education, 81*(4), 190–195.

Wöþmann, L. (2003). Central exit exams and student achievement: International evidence. In P. E. Peterson & M. R. West (eds.), *No child left behind? The politics and practice of school accountability* (pp. 292–324). Washington, DC: Brookings Institution Press.

*Wolf, S. A., & Wolf, K. P. (2002). Teaching *true* and *to* the test in writing. *Language Arts, 79*(3), 240.

*Wollman-Bonilla, J. E. (2004). Principled teaching to(wards) the test? Persuasive writing in two classrooms. *Language Arts, 81*(6), 502–511.

*Wright, W. E., & Choi, D. (2005, December). *Voices from the classroom: A statewide survey of experienced third-grade English Language Learner teachers on the impact of language and high-stakes testing policies in Arizona.* Tempe, AZ: Educational Policy Studies Laboratory, Arizona State University. Retrieved February 12, 2006, from http://www.asu.edu/educ/epsl/EPRU/epru_2005_Research_Writing.htm

*Yeh, S. S. (2005, October 28). Limiting the unintended consequences of high-stakes testing. *Education Policy Analysis Archives, 13*(43). Retrieved February 8, 2006, from http://epaa.asu.edu/epaa/v13n43/

*Zancanella, D. (1992). The influence of state-mandated testing on teachers of literature. *Educational Evaluation and Policy Analysis, 14*(3), 283–295.

25

Standardizing Knowledge in a Multicultural Society

Christine Sleeter and Jamy Stillman

Introduction

> Curriculum in any time and place becomes the site of a battleground where the fight is over whose values and beliefs will achieve the legitimation and the respect that acceptance into the national discourse provides. (Kliebard, 1995, p. 250–251)

Across the United States, in an attempt to raise standards for student learning, states have developed curriculum standards that specify what students are to learn. Raising standards has become synonymous with standardizing curriculum. This study critically examines two sets of current curriculum standards document in California. There, very detailed curriculum standards were developed during the 1990s in history-social science, reading/language arts, mathematics, natural science, and visual and performing arts. In 2001, state legislation created a seamless web specifying not only subject matter content in every discipline for K-12, but also disciplinary subject matter university coursework for teacher preparation. Standards for teacher credentialing were also aligned to K-12 content standards, making the main role of teacher education preparation to teach state-adopted curriculum. The purpose of this article is to examine standards in two disciplines in order to explore their connection with broader power relationships.

Theoretical Framework

For over a century, curriculum in the United States has periodically surfaced as a lightening rod for debate about what schools should do, and more broadly, about basic values and beliefs about how young people should view society, and what adults expect of them as they enter the adult world. Like Kliebard (1995), Bernstein and Solomon (1999) argued that in any society, groups struggle for the means to control consciousness of people, and that education develops the consciousness of children and youth: "The pedagogic device, the condition for the materializing of symbolic control, is the object of a struggle for domination, for the group who appropriates the device has access to a ruler and distributor of consciousness, identity, and desire" (p. 268).

To examine the legitimation of power and control in two disciplines in California, we used Bernstein's (1975) theory of codes of power in curriculum. Bernstein suggested that codes of power can be uncovered by examining how curriculum is classified and framed.

Classification refers to the degree to which curriculum contents are separated and bounded—for example, the strength of boundaries among disciplines, or between school knowledge and everyday knowledge. "Where classification is strong, contents are well insulated from each other by strong boundaries" (p. 88). Bernstein distinguished between two basic types of curriculum in relationship to classification: a collection code curriculum, and an integrated code curriculum. A *collection code* reflects strong classification; the stronger the classification, the more hierarchical the structure of knowledge, the more status academic knowledge has over everyday knowledge, and the greater degree to which teaching moves sequentially from basic facts toward the deep structure of a given discipline. An *integrated code* curriculum is weakly classified, boundaries are blurred, and knowledge is viewed much less hierarchically. Curriculum tends to be organized around themes and emphasizes the knowledge construction process rather than accumulation of disciplinary facts and concepts. Bernstein suggested that movements away from collection to integrated code curricula may reflect broader social movements that attempt to "alter power structures and principles of control" (p. 111). Conversely, movements that attempt to reestablish collection code curricula may reflect broader movements to reestablish traditional power hierarchies.

Frame refers to "the degree of control teacher and pupil possess over the selection, organization, pacing and timing of the knowledge transmitted and received in the pedagogical relationship" (Bernstein, 1975, p. 89). Under strong framing, teachers and students learn to work within a set of received knowledge; under weak framing, they are encouraged to use their own sense-making process. Curriculum that has strong framing offers little decision-making power to teachers or students; curriculum that has weak framing encourages classroom decision-making. "Framing regulates the form of socialization into the category system, that is, into the positional structure, and into the form of the power relationships which constitute, maintain and reproduce the structure" (p. 179). In other words, teachers and students learn their place in hierarchical power relationships through the degree of power they have over selecting, organizing, and teaching or learning curriculum.

These codes are constructed and play out within structural relationships, which include relationships among teachers (grade level, subject area), between teachers and administrators, and among students (particularly how students are grouped in school). Ultimately, Bernstein was interested in how young people are inducted into a stratified and segmented society. Because he viewed education as a primary regulator of society, he saw classification and framing as tools for examining how regulation is imposed and, at times, disrupted.

The standards movement in the United States followed a period in which power relations in the broader society had been disrupted. The civil rights movement had spawned various movements to redistribute power, which in education took forms such as school desegregation, multicultural education, and bilingual education. To what extent can the standards movement be understood as an attempt to restore earlier power relations? Bernstein's framework enables us to examine this question as it is reflected in curriculum documents. Below, we develop and situate the standards movement in an historic context, then report our analysis of a set of content standards documents.

From Civil Rights to Standardization

Beginning with the civil rights movement in the 1960s, the ethnic studies movement, the women's movement, and other democratically based equity movements challenged collection code curricula that had defined academic knowledge of Europeans and European Americans as superior to other knowledge systems. When schools were initially desegregated, parents and community leaders of color began to demand that the curriculum reflect their communities, and that teachers expect the same level of academic learning of their children as they did of white children (Gay, 1995; Weinberg, 1977). Historically disenfranchised communities argued that textbooks and other sources of curriculum were too often culturally irrelevant to students of color, and inaccessible to students of non-English language backgrounds. Particularly on college campuses, youth demanded ethnic studies courses that related to their own experiences. Ethnic studies and women's studies scholarship burgeoned; faculty hired to teach such courses found themselves needing to unearth subjugated knowledge to construct new curricula (Gay).

By the 1980s, models and approaches to multicultural and bilingual curriculum had been created; they tended to follow integrated curriculum codes and weakened framing in that many of the models emphasized teachers' and students' power over the knowledge construction process. For example, Watkins's (1993) six black curriculum frameworks and Tetreault's (1989) phases of the integration of women into curriculum dislodged classifications within traditional academic knowledge. Ladson-Billings's (1994) and Gay's (1995) research on culturally relevant pedagogy, along with bilingual education research, demonstrated how essential it is for all students, and especially second-language learners to build their academic skills on everyday life experiences and family-based knowledge (e.g., Cummins, 1996; Gutierrez et al., 2002; Ruíz, 1995; Tharp et al., 2000). Bilingual education research demonstrated that primary language literacy among English learners supports second language acquisition, and that fluency in multiple languages is superior to fluency in only one (e.g., Cummins, 1996; Dicker, 1996; Hakuta, 1986; Thomas & Collier, 1999).

More general conceptions of language learning and language arts instruction also shifted. In particular, more holistic and integrated approaches to reading and writing instruction emerged and began to challenge traditional pedagogical models of language arts instruction (Emig, 1971, 1982; Goodman & Goodman, 1979; Graves, 1982; Gutierrez, 2001). Scholarship that argued for a more social and cultural notion of language learning followed (e.g., Heath, 1983), and influenced the development of and research about language arts instructional models that showed effectiveness for culturally and linguistically diverse children. In particular, researchers came to considerable consensus about the most helpful instructional principles and processes, emphasizing the importance of contextualized rather than skill-driven instruction, and the connections between language, thinking, values, culture, and identity (Center for Research on Education, Diversity and Excellence, 2002; Gibbons, 2002; Wink & Putney, 2002).

Social science was also a subject of debates. One view was that the main purpose of social studies is to prepare citizens. That view conflicted with the more traditional view of social science as discipline based, with curriculum drawing from discipline-specific content. Yet a third view defined social science as a process of reflective inquiry (Brophy & VanSledright, 1997); for example, Wineberg (2001) suggested teaching students to think historically and to analyze historical texts as artifacts of human production in specific contexts, rather than delivering historian-constructed interpretations of the past.

The mid-1980s ushered in the standards movement, which viewed the main purpose of schooling as bolstering the U.S. economy and its national sovereignty and security (Coles, 2000; Engels, 2000). Its genesis is often traced to the publication of *A Nation at Risk* in 1983 (National Commission on Excellence in Education). Subsequent reform reports expressed concerns of the business community: that technological advances and global restructuring were transforming the nature of production and work, and that the United States would need to develop many, many more workers for demands of this new economy. These new workers would need to master "technological visualization; abstract reasoning, mathematical, scientific, and computer expertise; knowledge of specific technologies and production techniques; individual initiative; and so forth" (Berliner & Biddle, 1995, p. 141). On the heels of these reform reports came a barrage of highly visible conservative critiques of multiculturalism and bilingual education (e.g., Bloom, 1989; Ravitch, 1990; Schlesinger, 1992), which targeted curricular changes and policies that had been instituted in schools and universities. They charged that multiculturalism was damaging education and social cohesion, and that multicultural and bilingual curricula were intellectually weak, addressing minority student achievement in damaging ways by appealing mainly to self-esteem rather than hard work and intellectual challenge.

The reform reports and the conservative critiques of multiculturalism depicted schools, and U.S. society generally, as being in a state of crisis. In response; beginning in the 1980s, states began to construct disciplinary content standards. By the mid-1990s, most states had content standards in place and were designing or beginning to implement statewide systems of testing based on them. No Child Left Behind, passed by Congress and signed into law in 2001, mandates that states receiving federal funding implement accountability systems, with annual testing in reading and math.

The specificity, user-friendliness, and prescriptiveness of content standards vary from state to state. In some states, they are highly detailed and specific, leaving fairly little room for local decision-making, while in others, they are very broad and general. For example, in their analysis of 14 states' language arts standards documents, Wixson and Dutro (1999) compared the structure of standards in Texas and California, both of which serve diverse students. While California's language arts standards comprise three volumes, only one of which explicitly addresses how to teach English language learners (ELLs), Texas includes both standards and instructional guidelines in one accessible and user-friendly document that integrates strategies throughout for tailoring instruction to ELLs.

Within the standards movement, the general paradigm shifted from integrated code curricula to collection code curricula, and from weak framing to strong framing, using science to justify certain pedagogies. State and federal governments define science to mean studies that claim to be value-neutral and rely heavily on quantitative methods. Reading and language arts particularly were affected by the seminal "scientific" study supporting phonics instruction, commonly called The Foorman Study (Foorman et al., 1998) and sponsored by the National Institute of Child Health and Human Development (NICHD).[1] Across the country, "alignment" has become a watchword as schools and school districts have worked to align their curriculum with state standards and state testing.

Standardizing Curriculum in California

California has a highly diverse student population. In academic year 2002–2003, students in California public schools were 45 percent Hispanic, 34 percent non-Hispanic White, 8 percent Black, 8 percent Asian, 3 percent Filipino 1 percent American Indian/Alaskan Native, and 1 percent Pacific Islander (Educational Demographics Office, 2004). Over 25 percent of the students came to school speaking a first language other than English. One out of every four students was an ELL, and one in three elementary school students was considered to have limited English proficiency (Gándara et al., 2003).

California is often cited as having led the nation's standards movement by drafting curriculum frameworks in the early 1980s, which became the cornerstone of its standards-based reform program. For all content areas, the State Board of Education, appointed by the governor, makes curriculum decisions. Subject-matter decisions are made by committees that report to the Curriculum Commission. Members of the Curriculum Commission are appointed by the State Board of Education, the governor, and the Speaker of the House of the Assembly. Commission recommendations go to the State Board of Education, which then flow down to the colleges and the counties, then to districts, then to schools. In other words, the decision-making structure is decidedly top-down.

Content standards guide adoption of textbooks for grades one through eight by the State Board of Education and construction of state achievement tests. The Public School Accountability Act of 1999 established a system of achievement testing based on curriculum standards, and on rewarding high-performing schools and sanctioning low-performing schools. The 2002 Master Plan for Education, which outlines recommendations for education from preschool through university, makes frequent reference throughout to aligning curriculum and teacher preparation to the state's content frameworks and standards.

Our main question, then, is this: Given the historic context of struggles over curriculum, how has the standards movement reconfigured codes of power as manifest in curriculum, and in whose interests?

The Standards Documents

We conducted a content analysis of the following California frameworks and standards.

- *History-Social Framework and Standards for California Public Schools* (California Department of Education, 2001)
- *English-Language Arts Content Standards for California Public Schools* (California Department of Education, 1997)
- *Reading/Language Arts Framework for California Public Schools* (California Department of Education, 1999b)
- *English Language Development Standards* (California Department of Education, 1999a)

Content standards in both disciplines were initially adopted in 1987. The *History-Social Science Framework and Standards* document, which was readopted three times with only minor updates, describes what should be taught in the social studies curriculum in considerable detail for every grade except ninth. (For ninth grade, there are suggested units, but local decision-making over curriculum is allowed.) Its initial adoption was highly controversial and was contested vigorously by numerous educators, community groups, and scholars, particularly African American scholars. The main objection was that it had been written primarily by European American scholars working within a European American perspective that conceptualizes everyone within an immigrant paradigm. In so doing, it ignores perspectives that arise from nonimmigrant historical experiences, such as those of Native Americans and African Americans (see Cornbleth & Waugh, 1995; King, 1992). These concerns were never addressed. In fact, the preface to the newest edition says that "a consensus existed in the field for the framework" (p. viii). Ultimately, several school districts (notably San Francisco, Oakland, and Hayward) rejected the adopted texts or recommended that they be used only with substantial alternatives.

In 1997, California adopted a new set of reading/language arts standards and frameworks to replace those adopted in 1987. These new documents embody a distinctly different theoretical orientation from those issued previously by shifting away from a constructivist, literature-based approach to reading instruction to a direct instruction approach. This shift is evident throughout all three of the reading/language arts documents that we analyzed, mainly in the authors' tendencies to make theoretical claims reminiscent of the previous framework, and then offer content standards and practical guidelines from the direct instruction approach.

Introductions to the documents in both disciplines address California's diverse students, especially the increasing number of students who are not proficient in English. The authors make clear their dedication to the academic success of such students and their perception that the content frameworks and standards are based upon consensus about what California's students need to know. What does an analysis of how curriculum is classified and framed reveal?

Methodology

We used two main processes to analyze these documents. First, we read them for themes, keeping systematic notes on each theme. For the reading/language arts documents, we read for themes reflecting a sociocultural perspective (operationalized through terms such as contextualization, scaffolding, primary language instruction, bilingual, and bicultural) and a skill-based perspective (operationalized through terms such as decode, phonics, phonemic awareness, and phoneme). For the history-social science document, we read for themes reflecting multicultural content (such as depiction of African American history, depiction of women, depiction of European immigration) and pedagogical approaches (such as interdisciplinarity, use of student-generated historical analysis, use of expert-generated historical analysis)

Second, we counted words and items in each document that reflected patterns related to our thematic analysis. We counted the demographic characteristics of people named for study in the history-social science document, but not the reading/language arts documents, which did not name people for study. There, we counted terms representing pedagogical approaches, and references to ELLs.

Results of Analysis

Below, we describe how curriculum is classified and framed, according to Bernstein's analytical framework.

Classification

Our analysis of classification addresses how knowledge boundaries and hierarchies are established. The boundaries we identified include those between disciplines and languages. We also noted distinct patterns in sequencing and structuring knowledge in each discipline.

The standards solidify disciplinary boundaries. Separate disciplinary committees prepared the standards, and even though the covers of the documents are similar, their overall internal structure is not. The English-language arts standards for every grade level are organized into four areas: reading, writing, written, and oral English language conventions, and listening and speaking. Standards and substandards are then organized into each of these four areas. In history-social science, the standards and substandards are organized mainly according to theme, time period, and geographic location, which differ from one grade level to the next. For example, second grade is organized around the theme of "people who make a difference"; it includes five standards that have up to four substandards. Eighth grade is organized chronologically around U.S. history; 12 standards each have between three and nine substandards. That each discipline's standards are organized according to a different internal logic would tend to discourage constructing interdisciplinary curriculum.

The English-Language Arts Content Standards (ELA) mandates *what* all students must learn. The *Reading/Language Arts Framework* details *how* and *in what order* teachers must introduce language arts material. These two documents separate what students must learn from pedagogy and instructional decision-making.

The three reading/language arts documents solidify language boundaries and the primacy of English. The English Language Development Standards (ELD) are mapped against the English-Language Arts Content Standards to help California's ELLs to " 'catch up' to the state's monolingual English speakers" (California Department of Education, 1997, p. 1). The ELA standards are named 130 times as *the* instructional objectives of the ELD standards. Learning in English is given clear primacy over learning reading, writing, and other language arts skills in any other language. The documents ignore language arts proficiencies that students might have in a language other than English. For example, while the introduction to the ELD standards document acknowledges research supporting the value of primary language literacy, the standards themselves encourage teachers to tap students' primary language knowledge only with reference to students' familiarity with English phonemes.

The standards set up a complex structure of knowledge for each discipline. In both, knowledge derived from students' experience is subordinated to school knowledge. For example, the ELA standards refer to students' familiar experiences and interests primarily with reference to their selection of topics in which to practice oral presentation. Otherwise, there is little reference to students' interests and experiences. The history-social science standards refer to students' community and local area in the primary grades, but from fourth grade onward, detail content to learn without reference to students' lived experiences. In the remainder of this section, we examine how disciplinary knowledge is constructed within each of the two disciplines.

Language arts is hierarchically structured into a learning sequence, leading toward classification of students based on mastery of that sequence. Students are to learn skills first, and build meaning on skills. This emphasis on sequence is premised on the assumption that "a comprehensive program ensures that students master foundational skills as a gateway to using all forms of language as tools for thinking, learning and communicating" (California Department of Education, 1999b, p. 4). The authors emphasize their commitment to a *balanced* literacy program, but also state that "balanced does not mean that all skills and standards receive equal emphasis at a given point in time. Rather, it implies that the overall emphasis accorded to a skill or standard is determined by its priority or importance relative to students' language and literacy levels and needs" (p. 4). Further, the standards embrace balance mainly when addressing the learning needs of native English speakers. They relegate students who are still learning English to a "back-to-basics" program until they master foundational skills.

This is not to preclude a well-trained teacher from delivering high-quality reading/language arts instruction to ELLs. Nonetheless, following the standards' sequencing with fidelity may lead teachers who have received little or no training in this area to a very imbalanced program, particularly for ELLs. The *Reading/Language Arts Framework* contends that "simplified texts should be used only with students with weak proficiency in English," and that "students who use the simplified text need intensive English language instruction to enable them to catch up with their peers" (California Department of Education, 1999b, p. 76). In other words, California's reading/language arts standards enable balanced instruction more for students who read English at or above grade level than for others.

All three reading/language arts documents are heavily weighted toward phonics instruction and construct literacy largely as word analysis, particularly in the early grades. The words "phonemes," "phonics," and "phonemic awareness" are mentioned 200 times in these documents collectively. They are mentioned only 22 times in the 84-page ELA document (14 of which are in the glossary), but 66 times in the 93-page ELD document (only two of which are in the glossary). Further, the ELD standards emphasize it from kindergarten through the 12th grade, while in the ELA standards, most references to phonics-driven instruction appropriately diminish after the fourth grade. Thus, the ELD standards treat phonics mastery as a gatekeeper for English learners through the 12th grade.

As a result, language minority students may be precluded from engaging in literary analysis and other intellectual activities that would prepare them for admission to higher education institutions. And although the standards at times suggest to teachers that optimal student learning happens when skill instruction is embedded in authentic texts, discrete skill instruction is consistently separated from comprehension or literary analysis by requiring that activities such as literature-based instruction be introduced only *after* students demonstrate their discrete skill mastery.

Literature is further separated from skills instruction by being developed in yet a fourth document. Each time the authors of the reading/language arts documents suggest using literature, they advise teachers to refer to the state-sponsored list, *Recommended Literature: Kindergarten Through Grade Twelve* (California Department of Education, 1996). None of the titles is integrated into the standards documents.

The *History-Social Science Framework and Standards* document gives clear primacy to history as "a story well told" (California Department of Education, 2001, p. 4). The story around which the standards are structured develops over about 10 grade levels. Its central idea is that, as an immigrant society, the United States has always been multicultural; students need to "understand the special role of the United States in world history as a nation of immigrants" (p. 21). At the same time, "its institutions were founded on the Judeo-Christian heritage, the ideals of the Enlightenment, and English traditions of self-government" (p. 64). Its unfinished story tells "the historic struggle to extend to all Americans the constitutional guarantees of equality and freedom" (p. 21). Much of its content revolves around the political system of the United States as outlined in the Constitution, and is developed primarily through the conceptual tools of chronology and geography, as its introduction states.

The dominant storyline revolves around European and European Americans, particularly men. For example, we counted representation of people. Of the 96 Americans named for study, 82 percent were male and 18 percent were female. They were 77 percent white, 18 percent African American, 4 percent Native American, 1 percent Latino, and 0 percent Asian American. Authors of the history-social science framework recommend integrating children's literature with history (a break in the otherwise strong classification system) and gave specific suggestions. We tallied the racial and gender composition of the 88 authors of recommended children's literature. Fifty-seven percent were male, and 35 percent were female; we were unable to identify the gender of 8 percent. Sixty-two percent were European or European American, 19 percent were African or African American, 1 percent (one author) was Native American, 7 percent were Asian or Asian American, and none was Latino or South American; we were unable to identify the background of 10 percent. We saw a noticeable effort to include stories about diverse European ethnic groups, including Swedish, Irish, and Russian immigrants.

Because history-social science was constructed mainly as a story of immigration, stories of conquest were filtered through that paradigm using the tools of timelines and maps. Students first study European colonialism briefly in fourth grade in the context of California history. In fifth grade, they meet European explorers largely through map study, and then they study English settlements in North America. In seventh grade, they examine different world regions, concluding with a unit on "the Age of Exploration to the Enlightenment." European exploration and conquest are mentioned, but political ideals of the Enlightenment receive at least as much attention. This is important because it casts colonialism not as the taking of land, life, and sovereignty, but rather as the spread of reason, ideas, and liberty. In eighth grade, students encounter "the extension of the United States beyond its borders" (California Department of Education, 2001, p. 106), but relationships between the United States and Puerto Rico, the Philippines, or islands in the Pacific and Caribbean are not mentioned. In tenth grade, there is some review of "the worldwide expansion that was fueled by the industrial nations' demand for natural resources and markets and by their nationalist aspirations," presented as map study in which students survey colonial possessions of several European nations and the United States (California Department of Education, 2001, p. 126). Thus, it is possible to graduate from high school with only a fuzzy idea of European and United States histories of conquest and exploitation.

The conquests of northern Mexico and indigenous peoples are marginalized and sanitized. In third grade, students briefly study indigenous people of the past, then move on. In fourth grade, when studying the history of California, they briefly study American Indian nations in California's past. In fifth grade, students begin to study U.S. history, starting with a unit devoted to pre-Columbian indigenous people. After that unit, indigenous people appear only sporadically, and in relationship to the story of the westward movement of European Americans. Students study the conquest of Mexico in fourth, fifth, and eighth grades, but do so mainly as map study and timelines. Given that California used to be part of Mexico, and became a part of the United States through conquest, this casting of history negates family knowledge of many students of Mexican and indigenous descent.

To summarize, the documents set up strong classification, solidifying a collection code. With the exception of the history-social science framework's recommendation to connect history with children's literature, the disciplines are treated as distinctly separate, each having its own internal and hierarchical structure of knowledge. Reading/language arts is conceptualized as an accretion of skills acquired sequentially and in English. As a result, ELLs may well have less access to higher-order thinking than native English speakers, because thinking and literary analysis in a student's first language do not count. History-social science is constructed as a detailed story, sequenced over several grade levels, and organized around historically dominant groups' perspectives, experiences, and ways of seeing the world. The high degree of detail in both disciplines and the differing organizational systems that structure them would discourage interdisciplinary teaching or development of other integrated code curricula. Further, the privileging of English and use of English proficiency as a gatekeeper and the privileging of a European American immigration story as the backbone for academic content in the social sciences establish knowledge of white English speakers as dominant.

Framing

Framing refers to the degree to which teachers and students have authority to bring their own questions, points of view, organization, and pacing to the curriculum. We found reading/language arts to be more strongly framed than history-social science.

Compliance with the standards is enforced mainly through testing and textbooks. This alignment is more direct in reading/language arts than in history-social science. Each year, all public school students in grades 2–11 are required by state law to take standardized tests, which focus heavily on reading. For grades K-3, schools can choose between only two reading series, both of which are heavily skills based and scripted. Teachers at higher grade levels have a little more choice; for example, fourth-grade teachers can select from six reading texts, and eighth-grade teachers can select from among eight texts.

Although some of California's few remaining bilingual education programs are permitted to administer standardized tests in languages other than English, these tests merely supplement English standardized tests and are not used, as the English tests are, to determine class placement, grade promotion, or a school's ranking on the scale used to determine a school's funding and state intervention efforts. Because California's Public School Accountability Act uses English tests as the *only* outcome measures in its school ranking system, it is increasingly difficult for teachers to stray from the reading/language arts standards even if their own professional experience leads them to believe that doing so would benefit their students.

Compliance with the history-social science content standards is enforced at the elementary level mainly through the state's textbook adoption process. Elementary students are not yet tested on mastery of this content. However, at grades 8, 10, and 11, social studies is part of the state's standardized testing program; the eighth-grade test is designed to cover the curriculum for grades six through eight. Secondary teachers have more latitude than elementary teachers to choose texts, but are held accountable through student testing.

Both disciplines are strongly framed through the degree to which content and skills are minutely specified, and through use of disciplinary expertise and science to support the standards. The reading/language arts documents mask ideological debates about literacy by using rhetoric of science. For example, the introduction to the *Reading/Language Arts Framework* document states, "reading/language arts and related disciplines are the beneficiaries of an abundance of converging research that produces a professional knowledge base related to fostering and sustaining competence in the language arts, particularly beginning reading" (California Department of Education, 1999b, p. 3). The authors name a study sponsored by the National Research Council (1998) as "most important" because of its claim that "there is [now] a convergence of evidence to guide instruction in the language arts" (p. 3). All three documents rely heavily on this research to substantiate their emphasis on phonics instruction and phonemic awareness, but there is a notable absence of references to studies that support alternative approaches to reading instruction, particularly sociocultural approaches that may be more effective than phonics-driven methods, especially for diverse students.

We examined the documents for the extent to which they frame how teaching is to occur, particularly given the diverse students teachers have. Content in reading/language arts is highly prescribed. At several points in the ELD and ELA documents, the authors mention the "special needs" of ELLs and suggest that teachers modify their instruction to better meet them. Paradoxically, neither document suggests how to do this. In fact, neither document mentions the terms "scaffold," "specially designed academic instruction in English (SDAIE)," or "contextualize," all of which are commonly used in literature that details effective ways of teaching second-language acquisition.

The *Reading/Language Arts Framework*, on the other hand, mentions the word "scaffold" many times in the section entitled "Universal Access." This section, featured throughout the document, is broken down into three subsections in an effort to address the needs of (1) students with reading difficulties or disabilities, (2) ELLs, and (3) advanced learners. A universal access section is offered at each of the early grade levels, but it is included less frequently at the higher grades. At each grade level, only a few standards are mentioned and discussed in detail; teachers are then given suggestions for adapting the standards to meet their students' needs. For example, project extension guidelines are offered for advanced learners, and scaffolding interventions are offered for English learners. To the extent that the universal access section suggests that teachers tailor their instruction to their students, it could be seen as weakening the framing of curriculum by inviting teacher judgment. At the same time, we found the 300-plus-page *Reading/Language Arts Framework* so unwieldy, it was difficult to imagine a teacher finding the time or wherewithal to study these suggestions. Overall, the three reading documents language arts taken together specify so many skills (English-Language Arts Content Standards for California Public Schools, Reading/Language Arts Framework for California Public Schools, and English Language Development Standards) to teach and the order in which they are to be introduced, that one could see drill on the standards as the best way to get through everything.

In addition, the universal access section of the *Reading/Language Arts Framework* emphasizes using students' scores ("standard deviations") on the language arts portion of the state's standardized test to "diagnose" students' gaps in learning. Accordingly, teachers are then urged to integrate test preparation into their intervention efforts (California Department of Education, 1999b, pp. 226–229). Closely tying the standards documents to standardized tests raises questions about the degree to which teachers have the latitude to implement the standards as they deem most effective, particularly for special needs students such as ELLs and learning disabled students.

The language arts' emphasis on sequencing similarly strengthens the framing of the language arts curriculum, particularly for English learners and their teachers. For example, the *Reading/Language Arts Framework* suggests that when students demonstrate persistent difficulty in mastering the language arts standards for their grade level, teachers should be "differentiating curriculum and instruction, using grouping strategies effectively, and implementing other strategies" in order to meet the needs of these students (California Department of Education, 1999b, p. 226). In principle, this would allow for a weaker framing of the curriculum by affording teachers the chance to exercise their own professional judgment about instructional delivery. Yet, the *Framework* also encourages teachers to deliver instruction for special needs students that is even more sequential than for other students (p. 229). This sequential format, which reads like a list of skills and instructional activities, would most easily be aligned with a scripted skill-driven program, leaving little room for modification.

The *History-Social Science Framework and Standards* encourages higher-order thinking and active teaching processes throughout the grade levels. The document acknowledges that historians construct history, and that students should become aware of debates among them. For instance, a standard for 11th grade requires that students "evaluate major debates among historians concerning alternative interpretations of the past" (California Department of Education, 2001, p. 142). And occasionally the *History-Social Science Framework* mentions how historians work and that they often disagree with each other. But the main learning process that the *History-Social Science Framework* authorizes is consumption of an interpretation of the past prepared by someone else, rather than learning to construct an interpretation using the tools of historical thinking. The standards are largely content driven, spelling out conclusions that students should reach. For example, the term "analyze" is used repeatedly to describe what students should do: "At the same time students should analyze periodic waves of hostility toward newcomers and recognize that the nation has in different eras restricted immigration on the basis of racial, ethnic, or cultural grounds." (p. 10). But the authors have already constructed a general analysis for students; their task is to comprehend analysis rather than learn to construct an original analysis based on historic data. The authors recommend using a variety of teaching strategies such as debates, simulations, role-play, narratives, and video so that students will become engaged in learning the material. It is possible for teachers to alter how they construct their history or social studies curriculum, but because the curriculum as a whole is packed, it is simply easier for teachers to follow what they are given.

California's new teacher credential standards also strengthen the framing of the curriculum. As discussed elsewhere (Sleeter, 2003), the teacher credential standards explicitly define teacher education as preparation to deliver the state's academic content standards. The phrase "state-adopted academic content standards" appears 34 times in California's new Professional Teacher Preparation document, and 26 times in its Professional Teacher Induction Program document. By contrast, the phrases "culturally relevant," "multicultural," and "justice" appear in neither one. Disciplinary content preparation for teachers is also tied to the content standards; disciplinary programs must be approved by the state as being aligned to the content standards for certification programs to be authorized. In this way, what teachers learn in the university should match with what is in the standards, lessening the possibility that teachers will bring to the classroom ideas that conflict.

To summarize, the state standards strongly frame curriculum in both reading/language arts and history-social science. In the reading/language arts documents, the emphasis on sequence, the prescriptive nature, and the strict compliance enforced by high-stakes standardized testing ensures that a back-to-basics reading/language arts curriculum will be implemented across the state, and will be the most strictly enforced with special needs children. In addition, the dearth of instructional strategies for teachers of English learners and the inaccessibility of guidelines that are included discourage straying from or expanding upon the curriculum, even in the interest of meeting the needs of individual students. Further, because of the theoretical contradictions present throughout all three reading/language arts documents, a teacher may be given the impression that he or she can implement a literature-based and linguistically responsive reading/language arts program, but then be limited from doing so simply because of a lack of available instructional time, and/or state and district pressure to "teach to the test." The *History-Social Science Frame-work and Standards* are content driven, although filled with suggestions for student activities. Teachers have more latitude for deciding how to teach history and social studies than reading, but the curriculum is so packed and backed up by state-adopted texts that it is an effort to not follow the standards.

Discussion and Implications

Given the context of California and the historic context of struggles over curriculum, how has the content standards movement reconfigured codes of power, and in whose interests?

Our analysis of the way that the standards classify curriculum shows that they reassert disciplinary boundaries and boundaries between traditional academic knowledge in English versus knowledge in languages other than English, as well as knowledge from home and community. In both reading/language arts and history-social science, the content standards specify a structure of knowledge and sequence for teaching it. In reading/language arts, the structure builds higher-order thinking on discrete skills, and in so doing, makes higher-order thinking more accessible to English-speaking students with average or above average reading skills than to everyone else. Further, the reading/language arts documents consistently refer to California's non-white, non-English speaking students as "these students" and "they" instead of one of "us." History-social science is structured largely as a story of European immigration and the construction of a nation around Judeo-Christian values and European political institutions. Implicitly, in an attempt to reduce the significance of the growing demographic diversity of California students, the content standards set up a we/they perspective in which "we" are of European, Judeo-Christian heritage and English-speaking, and "they" are not. Ideologically, the curriculum in both disciplines rests most comfortably on historically dominant groups' perspectives, language, and ways of seeing the world.

Framing examines the place that teachers and students are expected to take within this structure, and the degree of latitude they have for defining that place. Our analysis of the standards shows that, particularly in reading/language arts, teachers and students are expected to follow the state's prescription. Compliance is enforced mainly through statewide standardized testing in English, and through the textbook adoption process. Compliance is also enforced through the sheer prescriptiveness of a packed curriculum, particularly at the elementary level. Further, compliance in the way that reading/language arts is taught is to be enforced mainly in schools that score low on standardized tests, and with students designated as having special needs.

Although the content standards in both disciplines rest within a specific ideology, they are presented as if there were no serious ideological debates to consider. Both present a detailed curriculum outline, and both give enough verbal recognition to cultural, racial, and linguistic diversity that teachers without a deep understanding of diverse intellectual funds of knowledge, diverse ideological perspectives, and effective pedagogy for diverse students might see the standards as fully inclusive. The use of disciplinary "experts" as curriculum document writers and the use of "scientific" research about reading encourage compliance. Although the documents occasionally suggest use of project- and literature-based teaching, the prescriptiveness of the standards, limited availability of instructional time, and adoption of a mandatory scripted reading program steer teachers toward a back-to-basics curriculum. In the top-down curriculum-making structure of California, teachers and students have little recognized power.

This standards-based curriculum planning process hearkens back to that described by Cubberley almost a century ago, when he characterized schools as "factories in which the raw products (children) are to be shaped and fashioned into products to meet the various demands of life" (cited in Beyer & Liston, 1996, p. 19). Like a century ago, curriculum is being organized scientifically for efficiency, deriving learning objectives from social and economic needs and casting teachers as managers of the process of producing student achievement scores. But both sets of standards, and particularly those in reading/language arts, deflect attention from their ideological underpinnings by virtue of being situated within a testing movement. Rather than asking whose knowledge, language, and points of view are most worth teaching children, teachers and administrators are pressed to ask how well children are scoring on standardized measures of achievement.

Our analysis suggests that California's curriculum standards fit within a political movement to reconfigure power relations among racial, ethnic, language, and social class groupings. This is not simply about trying to improve student learning, but more important, about reasserting who has a right to define what schools are for, whose knowledge has most legitimacy, and how the next generation should think about the social order and their place within it.

Note

1. This use of science may explain why the current standards go largely unquestioned (Shannon, 2001). A growing body of research is beginning to demonstrate that *The Foorman Study* was flawed and even deliberately manipulated to attain particular results (Coles, 2000; Taylor, 1998), and that subsequent advocacy of phonological reading strategies has been overstated (Swanson et al., 2003).

References

Berliner, D. C., and B. J. Biddle. (1995). *The manufactured crisis.* Cambridge, MA: Perseus Books.

Bernstein, B. (1975). *Class, codes and control.* (Rev. ed.) London: Routledge and Kegan Paul.

Bernstein, B., and J. Solomon. (1999). Pedagogy, identity, and the construction of a theory of symbolic control: Basil Bernstein questioned by Joseph Solomon. *British Journal of Sociology of Education* 20 (2): 265–280.

Beyer, L., and D. Liston. (1996). *Curriculum in conflict.* New York: Teachers College Press.

Bloom, A. C. (1989). *The closing of the American mind.* New York: Simon & Schuster.

Brophy, J., and B. VanSledright. (1997). *Teaching and learning history in elementary schools.* New York: Teachers College Press.

California Department of Education. (1996). *Recommended literature: Kindergarten through grade twelve.* Sacramento, CA: Author. Available at http://www.cde.ca.gov/ci/literature.

——. (1997). *English-language arts content standards for California public schools.* Sacramento, CA: Author.

——. (1999a). *English language development standards.* Sacramento, CA: Author.

——. (1999b). *Reading/language arts framework for California public schools.* Sacramento, CA: Author.

——. (2001). *History-social science framework and standards for California public schools.* Sacramento, CA: Author.

Center for Research on Education, Diversity, and Excellence. (2002). *Research evidence: Five standards for effective pedagogy and student outcomes.* Technical Report No. Gl, March 2002. University of California, Santa Cruz. Available at http://crede.ucsc.edu/pdf/evidence_gl.pdf.

Coles, G. (2000). *Misreading reading: The bad science that hurts children.* Portsmouth, NH: Heinemann.

Cornbleth, C., and Waugh, D. (1995). *The great speckled bird: Multicultural politics and education decision-making.* New York: St. Martin's Press.

Cummins, J. (1996). *Negotiating identities: Education for empowerment in a diverse society.* Ontario, CA: California Association for Bilingual Education.

Dicker, S. (1996). *Languages in America: A pluralist view.* Clevedon, UK: Multilingual Matters.

Educational Demographics Office. (2004). *Enrollment in California public schools by ethnic designation, 1981–82 through 2002–03.* Sacramento: California Department of Education. Available at http://goldmine.cde.ca.gov/demographics/reports/index.html.

Emig, J. (1971). *The composing process of twelfth graders.* NCTE Research Report No. 13. Urbana, IL: National Council of Teachers of English.

——. (1982). Inquiry paradigms and writing. *College Composition and Communication* 33: 64–75.

Engels, M. (2000). *The struggle for the control of public education: Market ideology vs. democratic values.* Philadelphia: Temple University Press.

Foorman, B. R., Francis, D. J., Fletcher, J. M. and Scatschneider, C. (1998). The role of instruction in learning to read: Preventing reading failure in at-risk children. *Journal of Educational Psychology* 90: 37–55.

Gándara, P., Rumberger, R., Maxwell-Jolly, J., and Callahan, R. (2003). English learners in California schools: Unequal resources, unequal outcomes. *Education Policy Analysis Archives* 11, no. 36. Available at http://epaa.asu.edu/epaa/v11n36/.

Gay, G. (1995). Curriculum theory and multicultural education. In J. A. Banks and C. A. M. Banks (eds.), *Handbook of research on multicultural education,* 25–43. New York: Macmillan.

Gibbons, P. (2002). *Scaffolding language, scaffolding learning: Teaching second language learners in the mainstream classroom.* Portsmouth, NH: Heinemann.

Goodman, K., and Goodman, Y. (1979). Learning to read is natural. In L. Resnick and P. Weaver (eds.), *Theory and practice of early reading,* vol. 1, 137–154. Hillsdale, NJ: Erlbaum.

Graves, D. (1982). How do writers develop? *Language Arts* 59 (2): 173–79.

Gutierrez, K. (2001). So what's new in the English language arts: Challenging policies and practices, ¿y que? *Language Arts Journal* 78 (6): 564–69.

Gutierrez, K., Asato, J., Swantos, M., and Gotanda, N. (2002). Backlash pedagogy: Language and culture and the politics of reform. *The Review of Education, Pedagogy, and Cultural Studies* 24 (4): 335–51.

Hakuta, K. (1986). *Mirror of language: The debate on bilingualism.* New York: Basic Books.

Heath, S. B. (1983). *Ways with words: Language, life, and work in communities and classrooms.* Cambridge, UK: Cambridge University Press.

King, J. E. (1992). Diaspora literacy and consciousness in the struggle against mis-education in the black community. *Journal of Negro Education* 61 (3): 317–340.

Kliebard, H. M. (1995). *The struggle for the American curriculum.* 2nd ed. New York: Routledge.

Ladson-Billings, G. (1994). *The dreamkeepers.* New York: Jossey-Bass.

National Commission on Excellence in Education. (1983). *A nation at risk.* Washington, DC: U.S. Government Printing Office.

National Research Council. (1998). *Preventing reading difficulties in young children.* Washington, DC: National Academy Press.

Ravitch, D. (1990). Diversity and democracy: Multicultural education in America. *American Educator* 14 (1): 16–20, 46–68.

Ruiz, N. T. (1995). The social construction of ability and disability: Optimal and at-risk lessons in a bilingual special education classroom. *Journal of Learning Disabilities* 28: 491–502.

Schlesinger, A. M., Jr. (1992). *The disuniting of America.* New York: Norton.

Shannon, P. (2001). What's my name? A politics of literacy in the latter half of the 20th century in America. In P. Shannon (ed.), *Becoming political, too: New readings and writings on the politics of literacy education,* 112–141. Portsmouth, NH: Heinemann.

Sleeter, C. E. (2003). Reform and control: An analysis of SB 2042. *Teacher Education Quarterly* 30(1): 19–30.

Taylor, D. (1998). *Beginning to read and the spin doctors of science: The political campaign to change America's mind about how children learn to read.* Urbana, IL: National Council of Teachers of English.

Tetreault, M. K. T. (1989). Integrating content about women and gender into the curriculum. In J. A. Banks and C. A. M. Banks (eds.), *Multicultural education: Issues and perspectives,* 124–144. Boston: Allyn & Bacon.

Tharp, R., Estrada, P., Dalton, S. S., and Yamauchi, L. A. (2000). *Teaching transformed: Achieving excellence, fairness, inclusion and harmony.* Boulder, CO: Westview Press.

Thomas, W., and Collier, V. (1999). *School effectiveness for language minority students.* Washington, DC: National Clearinghouse for Bilingual Education, George Washington University.

Watkins, W. H. (1993). Black curriculum orientations: A preliminary inquiry. *Harvard Educational Review* 65 (3): 321–338.

Weinberg, M. (1977). *A chance to learn: The history of race and education in the United States.* Cambridge, UK: Cambridge University Press.

Wineberg, S. (2001). *Historical thinking and other unnatural Acts.* Philadelphia: Temple University Press.

Wink, J., and Putney, L. (2002). *A vision of Vygotsky.* Boston: Allyn & Bacon.

Wixson, K. K., and Dutro, E. (1999). Standards for primary-grade reading: An analysis of state frameworks. *The Elementary School Journal* 100 (2): 89–100.

26

Outside the Core: Accountability in Tested and Untested Subjects

Leslie Santee Siskin

Standards-based accountability policies entered the public schooling system at the end of the twentieth century as a major reform effort, one that has the potential to dramatically change the face and function of the comprehensive high school. For the past hundred years, the pattern of high school change has mainly been one of enrollment growth. In the middle of that period, the Conant Report (1959) posed the primary challenge to high school organization: could high schools accommodate the "horde of heterogeneous students that has descended on our secondary schools" (p. 602)? To do so, high schools would grow not only in size but in structure, offering a widely differentiated array of courses aimed at the "heterogeneous" tastes and talents of diverse students, and organizing teachers and content into discrete departments.

Conant argued that high schools would also have to develop differentiated expectations. Some courses would "maintain high standards" for those of high ability, while others, by necessity, would have "another standard." Just what those standards would be, however, were not specified by reformers nor standardized by policy makers. Instead, they were quietly and locally negotiated—classroom-by-classroom, track-by-track, subject-by-subject. The American high school grew, as Powell, Farrar, and Cohen (1985) vividly described it, into a version of a "shopping mall" with something for everyone, where "some [students] shop at Sears, others at Woolworth's or Bloomingdale's" (p. 8)—but where not every neighborhood was likely to attract a Bloomingdale's.

It is against that pattern of practice that current reformers press, arguing for high standards that will be the same for all schools, and for all students within a school. But when policies directed at the whole school hit the high school, they collide with that differentiated structure, refracting at different angles through different departments, bending and even reconstituting different subjects. Through establishing standards, choosing which subjects (and what content) will be tested, and then attaching stakes to achievement scores on those tests, the states materialize what kinds of knowledge count, and how much. In some cases, policy makers explicitly quantify how much.

Kentucky, which includes music (or at least humanities) among the tested subjects, counts performance in that area as worth 7.13 percent of the school's total score. Performance in English, on the other hand, counts for 14.25 percent directly. But, recognized as a basic skill needed for performance in other subject areas, English is understood to count much more. An English teacher in Kentucky talked of how the state standards have made teaching her subject more central to the work of the whole school: "Now, it's not just up to the English teachers. It's up to everybody in the school." Those subjects outside the core, less central to achieving a good score, are likely to see their value go down. As the pressure for schools to perform on accountability tests rises, and resources are reallocated to provide extra time to students in the tested areas, teachers in untested subjects wonder what will become of their subjects, and whether their jobs are at stake under high-stakes accountability policies.

To understand how high schools are responding to new state accountability policies (or why they are not), we need to take account of the internal differentiation which characterizes the comprehensive high school. We need to examine the ways in which different subjects and departments receive and respond to the call for common standards and standardized tests. To understand the kinds of changes that are taking place under this policy shift, we also need to look to evidence at the level of the subject and the department. Even large changes taking place at this level may be lost if data are aggregated or averaged to the level of the school.

Drawing on interview data gathered over two years of fieldwork though the CPRE project on accountability and the high school, this essay examines the case of one subject "outside the core"—music. To do so, I adapt, to the level of subject departments, a framework that has emerged out of our analyses of school-level responses to accountability. That framework suggests that to understand school response we need to consider three distinct but interrelated factors: the initial position of the school, relative to the policy; the internal conditions already present—the organizational structures, internal accountability systems, and collective expectations; and then, within that context, the strategic choices and actions of those within it.

In applying this framework to subject departments, we distinguish between the *subject* as a knowledge category that extends across schools and the *department* as an organizational sub-unit within a school. Thus, we need to analyze:

- The initial position of the *subject* relative to the policy;
- The internal conditions of the *department*—the structure, internal accountability system, and collective expectations; and then
- The strategic choices and actions of those within them.

Initial Position

Even before the accountability reform kicks in, some subjects start out positioned favorably within the schooling system. They have high status and high levels of agreement on what the subject is, what should be taught, and even, in some subjects, how the subject should be taught (Goodson 1993; Siskin 1994). Math, for example, commands a relatively high status position, and is considered to have a relatively tight paradigm (agreement and coherence about what counts as knowledge). As one math teacher explained, "every math teacher" across the country knows what should be known in algebra II: "Algebra II, you have to do certain things, and every math teacher knows that when you're done with Algebra II you know these things."

Moreover, math content is considered highly stable, and the sequencing of what topics are to be covered is firmly established—so much so that past reforms have found it almost impossible to dislodge (Leinhart and Smith 1985; Siskin 1994; Stodolsky 1993). When high stakes accountability has encountered a subject that begins from this position, the problem has not been figuring out what should be on the test, but rather how to get students into the sequence so they get to algebra II and "know these things" before they take the test.

English may also be part of the academic core but it does not command the same status or demonstrate the same tightness in its paradigm, stability in its curriculum, or solidified sequence. Coming to consensus on what things a student should know at the end of tenth grade English, and therefore what the state can reasonably expect its testing to assess, is a different problem.

Music, as a subject, occupies a position that, as one Massachusetts teacher explained to me, "has pretty high status; it's somewhat elite, but also . . . marginalized." Music is not typically considered a core subject, or a top contender for the lists of "what every high school student should know and be able to do" that are central to accountability policy. One science teacher in New York, for example, argued that there should be high standards and testing for (almost) all students—but only in some subjects: "For the majority? Yes, there should be, certainly, the English standards, and the social studies standards, and the math standards. I actually disagree on the science standards for some, and I'm a science teacher." He did note, however, that there should be some standards in science for everyone, since "everybody should know how their body works, so they can make informed medical decisions." But the possibility of standards for everyone in the arts does not even enter the conversation.

Among music teachers, however, the contention is widely made that they do have standards, and that they have had them since long before the terminology of standards-based accountability came into vogue: "We tend, I think—and I'm speaking generally—I think as musicians, we've always tended to be sort of standards-based without knowing it." In almost all the interviews, teachers talked of how they have "always" had standards, "for a long time," or "for centuries." A Vermont teacher described the lineage of a discipline with a well-established history of shared standards: "I think we've always had a standard. My joke in front of the staff and the audiences here in [Garrison] has been that standards for us were established over five hundred years ago. Bach in the 1600s developed the equal temperament, and that's how we've been tuning our pianos ever since. Pythagoras came up with the original scale that we use. So we can go a long ways back for the standards."

For these teachers, it's not simply that there are standardized instruments and scales, but that there are widely shared standards about what should be taught in music, and even about what the order is for learning the essentials. A Kentucky teacher explained that "you can't skip levels. I guess it's sort of like math." A Vermont colleague concurred that "for a long, long, time music has always been taught sequentially." Teachers can be quite precise about just what it is that students need to know to meet these standards: "They need to know note value . . . Quarter note, eighth note, sixteenth note. They need to know note value. They need to know the letter names of notes, lines, and spaces. They need to know rhythm, be able to identify rhythm . . . Name it; perform it. They need to be able to sing, that's a category. You need to be able to sing alone and in a group. . . . You should be able to know music terminology, basic music terminology . . . Dynamics . . . Degrees of loud and soft . . . Vivace, which means lively, fast . . . Allegro, which is also a form of fast. It's not as fast as vivace . . . Be able to recognize grande, or dolce."

Mixed in with the lists of standards for what students need to be able to "recognize" or to "know" are the verbs for what they need to be able to *do*—to sing, to "perform." For, as teachers across the schools and states consistently point out, music as a subject has "for centuries" been not only standards-based, but performance-based. Ultimately, it is the performance of their students that counts: "I realize I've got to teach these students how to play their instruments. Bottom line."

Especially in group-performance oriented subjects, such as band or orchestra, the essential importance of having shared standards becomes immediately and concretely apparent. After all, explained one teacher, "to tie it all together consistently, we're all using the same evaluation pieces. So I know when the flutes come in to join the band rehearsal, they've had the same material as the clarinets and the trumpets." One of the remarkable aspects of music in this area is that the need to "tie it all together" so that students can "join" in for a group performance operates not only within the school, but also across schools. Several teachers describe preparing students to go out to regional and state-level performances where they may perform all together in a larger orchestra, or compete against other groups performing the same piece. The need to have everyone on the same page—to know and to be able to perform the same material in concert—transmits and reinforces the establishment of common standards throughout the musical community.

That focus on performance to a commonly shared standard, on the skills students need to be able to "tie it all together" to perform a musical piece, has put music teachers ahead of their colleagues in shifting to standards-based accountability. As three music teachers told us:

> One thing that we always found interesting was that music and fine arts are performance-based. We have products. We have outcomes. And they tried to take what we do and move us out of the performance area so they could put us back in. And instead of looking at what we have done through the centuries . . . a lot of the other areas have not bought in to this idea that we are where they want to be.

> We didn't have to change the way we taught. We didn't have to change the curriculum. We didn't have to change anything. It's like, now everyone is catching up with what music has been doing all along, which is really interesting. We've been performance-based all along. How we grade is how you perform.

> I think the folks who have been in the arts have been on the front edge of this for many, many years . . . And when I've gone to different classes and so forth, on how to use rubrics and things, we've had instructors that have said, "you folks in the arts always seem to be so far ahead. You already know what it is you want to assess, you know what you want for results." And so for me, the biggest thing is learning this new language of "how do we want to assess kids?" And once we came up with a rubric, it was pretty easy to just go ahead.

State rubrics and standards seem "pretty easy" in part because they don't introduce accountability into the field. Instead, music teachers have long seen themselves as accountable to their communities for the performance of their students—not on tests, but in the public arena. As two teachers told us:

> If I teach the [state] standards, well, maybe they'll be able to think about music better, which is good. But when we're at a basketball game, and when they're playing a song and it sounds awful, everybody's going to say, well, that's a bad band director.

> [That's what my] role as a teacher is, and that's to have these students play when I'm no longer around. And they can't do that unless they learn certain skills. And that's what I'm accountable to. The community has had a great deal of pride, even though it's a very small school . . . concerts are always well attended here, basketball games, football games.

And unlike the state accountability system, in this kind of arena, the stakes can be very high, and attach directly to individual teachers:

So, yeah, the theory behind having the test, those questions—the theory behind the [state] standards, [the district] standards, is great. But the real practical aspect is, I've got to get those kids to learn how to play these instruments. If I don't do that, the band will sound awful; therefore my job can be on the line.

The subject of music thus provides a certain anchoring in a culturally valued and long established discipline, one where standards are widely shared, where the work is highly performance-based, and where that performance is embedded in a system of public accountability which predates, and may even compete with, new state accountability policies. But to understand why this teacher's job would be "on the line" and why that would be so consequential, we also need to look to the conditions of music as a department within the current organization of the high school.

Internal Conditions of the Department

In the complex organization of the comprehensive high school, teachers are likely to identify themselves, not only as subject specialists, but as members of a particular department that provides them with the primary social, political, and intellectual context for their work (Siskin 1994). These departments, especially in large high schools, can be like different worlds, where English teachers may never have met their science colleagues, and have little or no structured opportunity to see themselves as part of the same collective professional community, to develop shared expectations about student work, or about what teaching should be (Siskin 1991). The distances between departments and the "two worlds phenomenon" tend to be even more pronounced between teachers in the "core" academic departments and those in the "special" subjects like vocational education or the arts (Little 1993; see also Goodson 1993; Siskin 1994).

In this study music teachers also described feeling like they were in a different world from their academic colleagues: "Nothing against the school, but it seems that we're kind of in a world of our own. The choral department, the band, and the orchestra." Even when there was an effort to have the whole faculty focus on state tests, teachers had a hard time "relating" to the work of their distant colleagues: "There has [been discussion of how the school is doing]. And the way I work, it's hard for me to relate to things, or students, or student bodies that I don't know about. Or if they're talking math, or English, you know, there's no point of reference for me personally."

Another teacher we asked about school discussions of state tests (in Vermont, where music is not tested) believed that such discussions probably were taking place, but ". . . not that I'm aware of. I'm sure it takes place within the academic communities who are mandated to reaching [those scores]. And since we're not, we kind of fall by the wayside and in the cracks, and don't really . . . aren't really part of that circle."

The distance between the "two worlds" is not simply one of physical or social geography, but often takes the form of material difference. Some departments have more status and more resources; some, like music, may derive cultural status from their discipline, but little material resource or political support for their organizational status. Resources, even the basic resource of *having* a job, can be hard to come by. A music teacher in Vermont noted that "we have three music teachers in our district." Not in the school, but in the entire district. Another, in New York, explained that: "Music positions are not very easy to come by. Most of the teachers who have music or art positions, they hold on to them for life because the chances of them finding another job are pretty much zero. It's not easy to find a music opening."

Moreover, the positions that music teachers do find are in many cases quite different from the jobs of their colleagues in other subjects. Across the schools we studied, these three teachers described positions that cross school boundaries:

> I'm here every day, last block, but I also go to four elementary schools, and a middle school.

> Well, this year, they started this vertical teaming, and I'm actually assigned to elementary now. So, since we have set up here on a block schedule and you have A days and B days, on my B days, I go twice a day to the elementary and I teach there.

> This is my home school, and then I have eight elementary schools.

The assignment to nine different schools mentioned by this teacher may be an extreme case, but part time assignments across multiple buildings are not unusual. As the nine-school teacher also told us, that can make organizational accountability a complex and difficult issue: "To figure out with all the principals, whose schedule you are on, who you're responsible to, and that kind of thing . . . Every principal thinks you work for them, and each school has a different music program, so you've got to go in and figure out what they want, what's expected of you, what you can expect from them. Trying to figure out who, indeed, you do answer to, and who, indeed, you don't answer to." Each school may have a different music program (although in our sample, one school does not have a music program or music teacher), but each school does not have a different music department.

Instead, when it comes to departmental status, music is often in the position of the transient stepchild, put into the arts family in one school, for example, or into the English department in another. But while that might make bureaucratic sense, given the small numbers of music teachers, it creates a "problem" when departments are expected to be the site for substantive conversation about working toward standards: "The principal has told us to take a couple of hours in our department meetings to talk about the standards and how to use them. The problem is, they're always putting me with foreign language and arts teachers. And I guess they kind of group us all together in the arts." As that teacher continued, the "best thing" the school could do would be to have "all the band directors from across the county get together, and we could talk about the standards, and we could wrestle with them." Wrestling with English teachers, or foreign language teachers, however, doesn't seem to help. Nor can many of these music teachers turn to their department heads for substantive support. When we asked one teacher, in Kentucky, about department support, he replied that the person he would go to is another music teacher—but not his chair: "But again, being with the arts and humanities, we answer to, actually, a French teacher. Well, not answer to, but that is our department chair."

What it means to "answer to" a chair in such a multidisciplinary department illustrates one weakness of internal school accountability systems with regard to subjects like music. For when asked if he has been evaluated in this workplace, this same teacher replied, "I have not. Well, not to my knowledge." And when he described what he thought that evaluation would look like, it seemed unlikely that it would actually inform his practice: "I mean, you probably know; in any workplace that they seem to pick out the least important things, and make the most of them. For the most part."

At the one school in our study that does have a strong, single-subject music department, there are other reasons why teachers still feel outside the core—in this case literally, since they are housed in a separate building. Even at this physical distance, however, they view themselves as part of the school community and as an essential part of school pride—at least as long as they keep doing well in regional, state, and even national competitions. They turn to that other public accountability system—external to the school but integral to the field of music—for meaningful evaluation, for professional support, and even for fiscal resources.

As a department, as a sub-unit of the school, music does have a claim to a share of the school budget. As one teacher there explained, the school does honor that claim, but the amount is minimal: "the school gives up $2,800 a year . . . I don't do anything but buy a computer or a piece of equipment with that." Music is an expensive subject, especially when students need, not only equipment, but funding to travel to the essential competitions or stage performances at home that will bring public support: instruments, costumes, sets and scenery—costs that this teacher estimates at over $400 for a student in chorus, over $700 for one in band: "Then we find a way to earn it. Then we do a show, and we have 2,000 seats in the auditorium. We do $10 a seat. We pack the house several times. Do the math. We clear $40,000 a show. Our budget is just under half a million dollars every year. And it all comes from fundraising and performances." Although music teachers often describe feeling "outside the circle" of the school's departmental system, it is not clear that they really want to move into it, or that they feel themselves accountable to it. The principal doesn't have time to evaluate them, the department chair is not in their field, but they do have strong ties to, shared expectations with, and accountability mechanisms developed among the other music teachers in their district, region, and professional community. Like other teachers in the arts studied by Sikes, Measor, and Wood (1985), these teachers see (or hear) themselves as active participants in their field, not just as subject teachers but as practitioners and performers of music: music teachers are musicians in a way that physics teachers are not physicists.

To Test or Not to Test

Music teachers are concerned about being pushed further outside the technical core of schooling by standards-based accountability actions of the state and by the predictable responses of their schools. From the vantage point of the Kentucky music department, teachers relate how, as a department and as a subject group, they received and responded to the shift in policy. They responded early, with direct action, and with unanticipated results.

Once it seemed clear that the state of Kentucky was moving to a new testing system, and that testing would be the new measure of school success, music teachers recognized the shift as a direct threat to their survival. Jobs might be lost altogether, or music turned into more of a "dumping ground" to relieve the "real" teachers of the discipline problems that interfered with their academic work: "For so long, music teachers were thought of [as if] the only reason we existed was to give the real teacher an off period. And we're still dealing with that issue, and it's tacky . . . but it's a real issue all across this country. Music teachers are not real teachers. But we are." Under this new wave of accountability policy, to be real is to be tested. So these music teachers, and others across the state, joined together to orchestrate a movement to have their subject count.

While music might be weak in terms of departmental status, as a subject it has significant strengths. Teachers were able to unite their forces through powerful cross-institutional professional connections (music teachers across our states are remarkable in the number and intensity of references to subject associations), to invoke national standards (widely shared), to mobilize parents who saw in the subject knowledge to be valued in and of itself, for its connections to adult life after school, or for its ability to connect students, who might otherwise be disengaged from high school (and any high school or district official can testify to the latent power of band parents). They were able to successfully lobby to have music on the agendas of state accountability policy makers.

They were not, however, able to convince policy makers that all high school students should know and be able to demonstrate the kinds of standards embodied in the national standards for music—and it is almost impossible to imagine a policy system that could agree that every student in the state should really be able to read, compose, and perform to any meaningful standard. So what Kentucky adopted was a required standard for the humanities, including music, but including it along with other arts.

There are two profound and problematic consequences of this compromise. First, music as a tested subject had to become something new, something that all students could be expected to do (although many students had never been music students) and that could be "done" on a paper and pencil test. That entails a major shift within the subject, one that many music teachers see as both a transformation and a lowering of the centuries-old standards of the discipline: "It makes it real difficult when we're in performance mode with all the competitions and performances coming up . . . when we're doing so much performance, it's a little difficult to have them talking about the rhythms and the Brandenberg concertos, as opposed to getting out there playing."

Second, the act created a new subject—humanities—that no teacher had ever taught and no student had ever taken: "Some of it is music, some of it is art. Some of it deals with historical-type things as far as art, how it's related, and dance. There's some dance. And what I found phenomenal about the dance part, is there are only select schools that teach dance. And the PE teachers are supposed to teach dance . . . I haven't seen any of those teachers teach that in the ten years I've been teaching."

Across Kentucky, teachers scrambled to construct new curricula, to identify places in the existing curriculum where the required knowledge might fit, and to compose a new subject—one that crosses both disciplinary and departmental boundaries:

> My first year, we had no one teaching humanities . . . and basically we rotated the kids [the juniors] two weeks before they were to take the test. So we had all the juniors lumped together, and we divided them, thirty each, divided them amongst five different majors [PE, dance, history, art, and music]. So we divided those kids between all five of us, because some of those kids had never had music. In all the years they had been in school, they'd never had music. Meaning if there was a music question on the test, they would never understand what a treble clef was . . . so that's how we did it the first year I was here. We split them into groups of thirty and rotated them every thirty minutes. Then we filled them with as much knowledge as we could fill them with.

That kind of new subject, in which established disciplines are truncated into two-week bursts, decontextualized and disconnected from the performance standards that have long characterized the field, changes not only the knowledge of the subject but the nature of teaching. One music teacher noted the irony in that now "we're embracing the fact that we're going to become reading and writing teachers who also teach music."

The example of music dramatically illuminates one of the major problems confronting high-stakes accountability at the high school level. Once we move beyond (or arrive at) required standards for reading and writing, is there actually agreement on what all high school students should know and be able to do to earn a high school diploma? Are high standards possible across all subjects? Will we expect all students to achieve high standards in chemistry or to "know how their body works, so they can make informed medical decisions"? To perform the *Gloria Vivaldi* or to correctly label the kind of dance illustrated by a picture of dancers in poodle skirts and flat tops? In transforming subjects into something all students need to be able to demonstrate on a test, do we inadvertently lower performance standards, weaken existing professional accountability systems, or lose knowledge outside the core altogether?

The knowledge that standards are supposed to measure—to ensure that the next generation receives it intact—is being altered by the act of measuring itself. In an irony that Heisenberg would have appreciated, accountability policies may well be held accountable for changing the very disciplines they were devised to perpetuate.

References

De Brabander, C. J. (1993). Subject conceptions of teachers and school culture. In F. K. Kievet and R. Vandenberghe (eds.), *School culture, school improvement, and teacher development*, 77–107. Leiden: DSWO Press.

Goodson, I. F. (1993). *School subjects and curriculum change*. (3rd ed.) London: Falmer Press.

Kliebard, H. (1986). *The struggle for the American curriculum, 1893–1958*. London: Routledge and Kegan Paul.

Leinhart, G., and Smith, D. A. (1985). Expertise in mathematics: Subject matter knowledge. *Journal of Educational Psychology* 77: 247–271.

Little, J. W. (1993). Professional community in comprehensive high schools: The two worlds of academic and vocational teachers. In J. W. Little and M. W. McLaughlin (eds.), *Teachers' work: Individuals, colleagues, and contexts*, 137–163. New York: Teachers College Press.

McNeil, L. M. (2000). *Contradictions of school reform*. New York: Routledge.

Powell, A. G., Farrar, E., and Cohen, D. K. (1985). *The shopping mall high school: Winners and losers in the educational marketplace*. Boston: Houghton Mifflin.

Sikes, P., Measor, L., and Woods, P. (eds.) (1985). *Teacher careers: Crises and continuities*. London: Falmer Press.

Siskin, L. S. (1991). Departments as different worlds: Subject subcultures in secondary schools. *Educational Administration Quarterly* 27: 134–160.

Siskin, L. S. (1994). *Realms of knowledge: Academic departments in secondary schools*. London and New York: Falmer Press.

Stodolsky, S. S. (1993). A framework for subject matter comparisons in high schools. *Teaching and Teacher Education* 9: 333–346.

Young, M. F. D. (ed.) (1971). *Knowledge and control*. London: Collier-Macmillan.

27

What Does it Mean to Say a School is Doing Well?

Elliot W. Eisner

Driven by discontent with the performance of our schools, we are, once again, in the midst of education reform, as we were in 1983 with *A Nation at Risk*, in 1987 with *America 2000*, and a few years later with *Goals 2000*. Each of these reform efforts was intended to rationalize the practice and performance of our schools. Each was designed to work out and install a system of measurable goals and evaluation practices that would ensure that our nation would be first in science and mathematics by the year 2000, that all our children would come to school ready to learn, and that each school would be drug-free, safe, and nonviolent.[1]

The formulation of standards and the measurement of performance were intended to tidy up a messy system and to make teachers and school administrators truly accountable. The aim was then, and is today, to systematize and standardize so that the public will know which schools are performing well and which are not. There were to be then, and there are today, payments and penalties for performance.

America is one of the few nations in which responsibility for schools is not under the aegis of a national ministry of education. Although we have a federal agency, the U.S. Department of Education, the 10th Amendment to the U.S. Constitution indicates that those responsibilities that the Constitution does not assign explicitly to the federal government belong to the states (or to the people). And since the Constitution makes no mention of education, it is a responsibility of the states.

As a result, we have 50 departments of education, one for each state, overseeing some 16,000 school districts that serve 52 million students in more than 100,000 schools. In addition, each school district has latitude for shaping education policy. Given the complexity of the way education is organized in the U.S., it is understandable that from one perspective the view looks pretty messy and not altogether rational. Furthermore, more than a few believe that we have a national problem in American education and that national problems require national solutions. The use of highly rationalized procedures for improving schools is a part of the solution.

I mention the concept of rationalization because I am trying to describe the ethos being created in our schools. I am trying to reveal a world view that shapes our conception of education and the direction we take for making our schools better.

Rationalization as a concept has a number of features. First, it depends on a clear specification of intended outcomes.[2] That is what standards and rubrics are supposed to do. We are supposed to know what the outcomes of educational practice are to be, and rubrics are to exemplify those outcomes. Standards are more general statements intended to proclaim our values. One argument for the use of standards and rubrics is that they are necessary if we are to function rationally. As the saying goes, if you don't know where you're headed, you will not know where you have arrived. In fact, it's more than knowing where you're headed; it's also knowing the precise destination. Thus the specification of intended outcomes has become one of the primary practices in the process of rationalizing school reform efforts. Holding people accountable for the results is another.

Second, rationalization typically uses measurement as a means through which the quality of a product or performance is assessed and represented. Measurement, of course, is *one* way to describe the world. Measurement has to do with determining matters of magnitude, and it deals with matters of magnitude through the specification of units. In the United States, the unit for weight is pounds. In Sweden or the Netherlands, it is kilograms. It's kilometers in Europe; it's miles in the United States. It really doesn't matter what unit you use, as long as everyone agrees what the unit is.[3]

Quantification is believed to be a way to increase objectivity, secure rigor, and advance precision in assessment. For describing some features of the world, including the educational world, it is indispensable. But it is not good for everything, and the limitations of quantification are increasingly being recognized. For example, although initial discussions about standards emphasized the need for them to be *measurable*, as standards have become increasingly general and ideological, measurability has become less salient.

Third, the rationalization of practice is predicated on the ability to control and predict. We assume that we can know the specific effects of our interventions, an assumption that is questionable.

Fourth, rationalization downplays interactions. Interactions take into account not simply the conditions that are to be introduced in classrooms or schools but also the kinds of personal qualities, expectations, orientations, ideas, and temperaments that interact with those conditions. Philosophical constructivists have pointed out that what something means comes both from the features of the phenomenon to be addressed and from the way those features are interpreted or experienced by individuals.[4] Such idiosyncratic considerations always complicate assessment. They complicate efforts to rationalize education as well. Prediction is not easy when what the outcome is going to be is a function not only of what is introduced in the situation but also of what a student makes of what has been introduced.

Fifth, rationalization promotes comparison, and comparison requires what is called "commensurability." Commensurability is possible only if you know what the programs were in which the youngsters participated in the schools being compared. If youngsters are in schools that have different curricula or that allocate differing amounts of time to different areas of the curriculum, comparing the outcomes of those schools without taking into account their differences is extremely questionable. Making comparisons between the math performance of youngsters in Japan and those in the United States without taking into account cultural differences, different allocations of time for instruction, or different approaches to teaching makes it impossible to account for differences in student performance or to consider the side effects or opportunity costs associated with different programs in different cultures. The same principle holds in comparing student performance across school districts in the U.S.

Sixth, rationalization relies upon extrinsic incentives to motivate action; that's what vouchers are intended to do. Schools are likened to businesses, and the survival of the fittest is the principle that determines which ones survive. If schools don't produce effective results on tests, they go out of business.

In California and in some other parts of the country, principals and superintendents are often paid a bonus if their students perform well on standardized tests: payment by results. And, of course, such a reward system has consequences for a school's priorities. Are test scores the criteria that we want to use to reward professional performance?

The features that I have just described are a legacy of the Enlightenment. We believe our rational abilities can be used to discover the regularities of the universe and, once we've found them, to implement, as my colleague David Tyack titled his book, "the one best system."[5] We have a faith in our ability to discover what the U.S. Department of Education once described as "what works." The result is an approach to reform that leaves little room for surprise, for imagination, for improvisation, or for the cultivation of productive idiosyncrasy. Our reform efforts are closer in spirit to the ideas of René Descartes and August Compte than to those of William Blake. They are efforts that use league tables to compare schools and that regard test scores as valid proxies for the quality of education our children receive.[6] And they constitute an approach to reform that has given us three major educationally feckless reform efforts in the past 20 years. Are we going to have another?

What are the consequences of the approach to reform that we have taken and what should we pay attention to in order to tell when a school is doing well? First, one of the consequences of our approach to reform is that the curriculum gets narrowed as school district policies make it clear that what is to be tested is what is to be taught. Tests come to define our priorities. And now we have legitimated those priorities by talking about "core subjects." The introduction of the concept of core subjects explicitly marginalizes subjects that are not part of the core. One of the areas that we marginalize is the arts, an area that when well taught offers substantial benefits to students. Our idea of core subjects is related to our assessment practices and the tests we use to determine whether or not schools are doing well.

Because those of us in education take test scores seriously, the public is reinforced in its view that test scores are good proxies for the quality of education a school provides. Yet what test scores predict best are other test scores. If we are going to use proxies that have predictive validity, we need proxies that predict performances that matter outside the context of school. The function of schooling is not to enable students to do better in school. The function of schooling is to enable students to do better in life. What students learn in school ought to exceed in relevance the limits of the school's program.

As we focus on standards, rubrics, and measurement, the deeper problems of schooling go unattended. What are some of the deeper problems of schooling? One has to do with the quality of conversation in classrooms. We need to provide opportunities for youngsters and adolescents to engage in challenging kinds of conversation, and we need to help them learn how to do so. Such conversation is all too rare in schools. I use "conversation" seriously, for challenging conversation is an intellectual affair. It has to do with thinking about what people have said and responding reflectively, analytically, and imaginatively to that process. The practice of conversation is almost a lost art. We turn to talk shows to experience what we cannot do very well or very often.

The deeper problems of schooling have to do with teacher isolation and the fact that teachers don't often have access to other people who know what they're doing when they teach and who can help them do it better.[7] Although there are many issues that need attention in schooling, we search for the silver bullet and believe that, if we get our standards straight and our rubrics right and make our tests tough enough, we will have an improved school system. I am not so sure.

The message that we send to students is that what really matters in their education are their test scores. As a result, students in high-stakes testing programs find ways to cut corners—and so do some teachers. We read increasingly often not only about students who are cheating but also about teachers who are unfairly helping students get higher scores on the tests.[8] It's a pressure that undermines the kind of experience that students ought to have in schools.

Perhaps the major consequence of the approach we have taken to rationalize our schools is that it ineluctably colors the school climate. It promotes an orientation to practice that emphasizes extrinsically defined attainment targets that have a specified quantitative value. This, in turn, leads students to want to know just what it is they need to do to earn a particular grade. Even at Stanford, I sometimes get requests from graduate students who want to know precisely, or as precisely as I can put it, what they need to do in order to get an A in the class.

Now from one angle such a request sounds reasonable. After all, it is a means/ends approach to educational planning. Students are, it can be said, rationally planning their education. But such planning has very little to do with intellectual life, where risk-taking, exploration, uncertainty, and speculation are what it's about. And if you create a culture of schooling in which a narrow means/ends orientation is promoted, that culture can undermine the development of intellectual dispositions. By intellectual dispositions I mean a curiosity and interest in engaging and challenging ideas.

What the field has not provided is an efficient alternative to the testing procedures we now use. And for good reason. The good reason is that there are no efficient alternatives. Educationally useful evaluation takes time, it's labor intensive and complex, and it's subtle, particularly if evaluation is used not simply to score children or adults but to provide information to improve the process of teaching and learning.

The price one pays for providing many ways for students to demonstrate what has been learned is a reduction of commensurability. Commensurability decreases when attention to individuality increases. John Dewey commented about comparisons in a book that he wrote in 1934 when he was 76 years old. The book is *Art as Experience*. He observed that nothing is more odious than comparisons in the arts.[9] What he was getting at was that attention to or appreciation of an art form requires attention to and appreciation of its distinctive features. It was individuality that Dewey was emphasizing, and it is the description of individuality we would do well to think about in our assessment practices. We should be trying to discover where a youngster is, where his or her strengths are, where additional work is warranted. Commensurability is possible when everybody is on the same track, when there are common assessment practices, and when there is a common curriculum. But when students work on different kinds of problems, and when there is concern with the development of an individual's thumbprint, so to speak, commensurability is an inappropriate aim.

What have been the consequences of the rationalized approach to education reform that we have embraced? Only this: in our desire to improve our schools, education has become a casualty. That is, in the process of rationalization, education—always a delicate, complex, and subtle process having to do with both cultural transmission and self-actualization—has become a commodity. Education has evolved from a form of human development serving personal and civic needs into a product our nation produces to compete in a global economy. Schools have become places to mass produce this product.

Let us assume that we impose a moratorium on standardized testing for a five-year period. What might we pay attention to in schools in order to say that a school is doing well? If it is not higher test scores that we are looking for, what is it? Let me suggest the kind of data we might seek by raising some questions that might guide our search.

What kinds of problems and activities do students engage in? What kind of thinking do these activities invite? Are students encouraged to wonder and to raise questions about what they have studied? Perhaps we should be less concerned with whether they can answer our questions than with whether they can ask their own. The most significant intellectual achievement is not so much in problem solving, but in question posing. What if we took that idea seriously and concluded units of study by looking for the sorts of questions that youngsters are able to raise as a result of being immersed in a domain of study? What would that practice teach youngsters about inquiry?

What is the intellectual significance of the ideas that youngsters encounter? (I have a maxim that I work with: If it's not worth teaching, it's not worth teaching well.) Are the ideas they encounter important? Are they ideas that have legs? Do they go someplace?

Are students introduced to multiple perspectives? Are they asked to provide multiple perspectives on an issue or a set of ideas? The implications of such an expectation for curriculum development are extraordinary. To develop such an ability and habit of mind, we would need to invent activities that encourage students to practice, refine, and develop certain modes of thought. Taking multiple perspectives is just one such mode.

In 1950 the American psychologist J.P. Guilford developed what he called "the structure of intellect," in which 130 different kinds of cognitive processes were identified.[10] What if we used that kind of structure to promote various forms of thinking? My point is that the activities in which youngsters participate in classes are the means through which their thinking is promoted. When youngsters have no reason to raise questions, the processes that enable them to learn how to discover intellectual problems go undeveloped.

The ability to raise telling questions is not an automatic consequence of maturation. Do you know what's the biggest problem that Stanford students have in the course of their doctoral work? It is not getting good grades in courses; they all get good grades in courses. Their biggest obstacle is in framing a dissertation problem. We can do something about that before students get to the doctoral level. In a school that is doing well, opportunities for the kind of thinking that yields good questions would be promoted.

What connections are students helped to make between what they study in class and the world outside of school? A major aim of education has to do with what psychologists refer to as "transfer of learning." Can students apply what they have learned or what they have learned how to learn? Can they engage in the kind of learning they will need in order to deal with problems and issues outside of the classroom? If what students are learning is simply used as a means to increase their scores on the next test, we may win the battle and lose the war. In such a context, school learning becomes a hurdle to jump over. We need to determine whether students can use what they have learned. But even being able to use what has been learned is no indication that it will be used. There is a difference between what a student can do and what a student will do.

The really important dependent variables in education are not located in classrooms. Nor are they located in schools. The really important dependent variables are located outside schools. Our assessment practices haven't even begun to scratch that surface. It's what students do with what they learn when they can do what they want to do that is the real measure of educational achievement.

What opportunities do youngsters have to become literate in the use of different representational forms? By representational forms, I mean the various symbol systems through which humans shape experience and give it meaning.[11] Different forms of human meaning are expressed in different forms of representation. The kinds of meaning one secures from poetry are not the kinds of meaning one secures from propositional signs. The kinds of meanings expressed in music are not the meanings experienced in the visual arts. To be able to secure any of those meanings, you have to know how to "read" them. Seeing is a reading. Hearing is a reading. They are processes of interpreting and *construing* meaning from the material encountered; reading text is not only a process of decoding, it is also a process of encoding. We *make* sense of what we read.

What opportunities do students have to formulate their own purposes and to design ways to achieve them? Can a school provide the conditions for youngsters, as they mature, to have increased opportunity to set their own goals and to design ways to realize them? Plato once defined a slave as someone who executes the purposes of another. I would say that, in a free democratic state, at least a part of the role of education is to help youngsters learn how to define their own purposes.

What opportunities do students have to work cooperatively to address problems that they believe to be important? Can we design schools so that we create communities of learners who know how to work with one another? Can we design schools and classrooms in which cooperating with others is part of what it means to be a student?

Do students have the opportunity to serve the community in ways that are not limited to their own personal interests? Can we define a part of the school's role as establishing or helping students establish projects in which they do something beyond their own self-interest? I want to know that in order to know how well a school is doing.

To what extent are students given the opportunity to work in depth in domains that relate to their aptitudes? Is personal talent cultivated? Can we arrange the time for youngsters to work together on the basis of interest rather than on the basis of age grading? Youngsters who are interested in ceramics might work in depth in ceramics; those interested in science might work in depth in science. To make these possibilities a reality, we would need, of course, to address the practical problems of allocating time and responsibility. But without a conception of what is important, we will never even ask questions about allocating time. A vision of what is educationally important must come first.

Do students participate in the assessment of their own work? If so, how? It is important for teachers to understand what students themselves think of their own work. Can we design assessment practices in which students can help us?

To what degree are students genuinely engaged in what they do in school? Do they find satisfaction in the intellectual journey? How many students come to school early and how many would like to stay late? The motives for such choices have to do with the "locus of satisfactions." Satisfactions generate reasons for doing something. Basically, there are three reasons for doing anything. One reason for doing something is that you like what it feels like and you like who you are when you do it. Sex, play, and art fall into this category. They are intrinsically satisfying activities.

A second reason for doing something is not because you like doing it, but because you like the results of having done it. You might like a clean kitchen, but you might not enjoy cleaning your kitchen. The process is not a source of enjoyment, but the outcome is.

A third reason for doing something is not because you like the process or even the outcome, but because you like the rewards. You like the grades you earn. You like the paycheck you receive. That's what Hannah Arendt described as labor.[12] There is too much labor in our schools—and not enough work. Work is effort from which you derive satisfaction. We ought to be paying attention to the joy of the journey. This is easy to say but difficult and challenging to do. Nevertheless, we ought to keep our minds focused on it as a goal.

Are teachers given the time to observe and work with one another? To what degree is professional discourse an important aspect of what being a teacher means in the school? Is the school a resource, a center for the teacher's own development? Is the school a center for teacher education?

The center for teacher education is not the university; it is the school in which the teacher works. Professional growth should be promoted during the 25 years that a teacher works in a school—not just during the year and a half that he or she spends in a teacher education program. Can we create schools that take the professional development of teachers seriously? And what would they look like? Schools will not be better for students than they are for the professionals who work in them.

All of us who teach develop repertoires. We all have routines. We all get by. We get by without serious problems, but getting by is not good enough. We need to get better. And to get better, we have to think about school in ways that address teachers' real needs. And when I say, "addressing teachers' real needs," I don't mean sending them out every 6,000 miles to get "inserviced" by a stranger.

Are parents helped to understand what their child has accomplished in class? Do they come to understand the educational import of what is going on? Very often children's artwork is displayed in the school, with the only information provided being the student's name, the grade, and the teacher's name, all in the lower right-hand corner. Then the best student work is posted more formally. What we do, in effect, is use a gallery model of exhibition. We take the best work, and we display it. What we need to create is an educationally interpretive exhibition that explains to viewers what problems the youngsters were addressing and how they resolved them.[13] This can be done by looking at prior work and comparing it with present work—that is, by looking at what students have accomplished over time. I am talking about interpretation. I am talking about getting people to focus not so much on what the grade is, but on what process led to the outcome.

What is my point? All my arguments have had to do with creating an educationally informed community. We need to ask better questions.

Can we widen what parents and others believe to be important in judging the quality of our schools? Can we widen and diversify what they think matters? Can those of us who teach think about public education not only as the education of the public in the schools (i.e., our students), but also as the education of the public outside of our schools (i.e., parents and community members)? Can a more substantial and complex understanding of what constitutes good schooling contribute to better, more enlightened support for our schools?

Can a more informed conception of what constitutes quality in education lead to greater equity for students and ultimately for the culture? Educational equity is much more than just allowing students to cross the threshold of the school. It has to do with what students find after they do so. We ought to be providing environments that enable each youngster in our schools to find a place in the educational sun. But when we narrow the program so that there is only a limited array of areas in which assessment occurs and performance is honored, youngsters whose aptitudes and interests lie elsewhere are going to be marginalized in our schools. The more we diversify those opportunities, the more equity we are going to have because we are going to provide wider opportunities for youngsters to find what it is that they are good at.

And that leads me to the observation that, in our push for attaining standards, we have tended to focus on outcomes that are standard for all youngsters. We want youngsters to arrive at the same place at about the same time. I would argue that really good schools increase variance in student performance. Really good schools increase the variance *and* raise the mean. The reason I say that is because, when youngsters can play to their strengths, those whose aptitudes are in, say, mathematics are going to go faster and further in that area than youngsters whose aptitudes are in some other field. But in those other fields, those youngsters would go faster and further than those whose aptitudes are in math. Merely by conceiving of a system of educational organization that regards productive variance as something to be valued and pursued, we undermine the expectation that everybody should be moving in lockstep through a series of 10-month years in a standardized system and coming out at pretty much the same place by age 18.

Part of our press toward standardization has to do with what is inherent in our age-graded school system. Age-graded systems work on the assumption that children remain more alike than different over time and that we should be teaching within the general expectations for any particular grade. Yet, if you examine reading performance, for example, the average range of reading ability in an ordinary classroom approximates the grade level. Thus at the second grade, there is a two-year spread; at the third grade, a three-year range; at the fourth grade, a four-year range. Consider how various the picture would be if performance in four or five different fields of study were examined. Children become more different as they get older, and we ought to be promoting those differences and at the same time working to escalate the mean.

Does more enlightened grasp of what matters in schools put us in a better position to improve them? I hope so. What I have argued here is intended to divert our focus away from what we normally use to make judgments about the quality of schools and redirect it instead toward the processes, conditions, and culture that are closer to the heart of education. I am unabashedly endorsing the promotion of improvisation, surprise, and diversity of outcomes as educational virtues that we ought to try to realize through our teaching.

The point of the questions I have raised is to provide something better than the blinkered vision of school quality that now gets front-page coverage in our newspapers. Perhaps this vision serves best those in positions of privilege. Perhaps our society needs losers so it can have winners. Whatever the case, I believe that those of us who wish to exercise leadership in education must do more than simply accept the inadequate criteria that are now used to determine how well our schools are doing.

We need a fresh and humane vision of what schools might become because what our schools become has everything to do with what our children and our culture will become. I have suggested some of the features and some of the questions that I believe matter educationally. We need reform efforts that are better than those we now have. The vision of education implicit in what I have described here is just a beginning.

Notes

1. The document that most directly expresses this view is National Commission on Excellence in Education, *A Nation at Risk: The Imperative for Educational Reform* (Washington, D.C.: U.S. Government Printing Office, 1983).

2. Donald Schon describes the process of rationalization of behavior as "technical rationality." See Donald Schon, *The Reflective Practitioner: How Professionals Think in Action* (New York: Basic Books, 1983). Nor is this the first time technically rational approaches to planning and assessment have dominated schooling. The efficiency movement in American schools—from about 1913 to about 1930—is one example. The behavioral objectives and accountability movements of the 1960s and 1970s are two more.

3. For a discussion of issues pertaining to the quantification and use of standards, see Elliot W. Eisner, "Standards for American Schools: Help or Hindrance?," *Phi Delta Kappan*, June 1995, pp. 758–764.

4. One of the foremost philosophical constructivists is John Dewey. The concept of interaction was a central notion

in his philosophy of mind and in his conception of the educational process. For a succinct view of his ideas pertaining to education, see John Dewey, *Experience and Education* (New York: Macmillan, 1938).

5. David Tyack, *The One Best System* (Cambridge, Mass.: Harvard University Press, 1974).

6. League tables not only affect the priorities of the school, they are a major influence on real estate values. The value of houses is influenced significantly by perceptions of the quality of the schools in a neighborhood, and test scores are the indices used to determine such quality.

7. For a full discussion of the processes of observation and disclosure as they pertain to teaching and its improvement, see my book *The Enlightened Eye: Qualitative Inquiry and the Enhancement of Educational Practice* (New York: Macmillan, 1991).

8. For an insightful and lucid discussion of the pressures secondary school students experience in the high-stakes environment that we have created in schools, see Denise Pope, "Doing School" (Doctoral dissertation, Stanford University, 1998).

9. John Dewey, *Art as Experience* (New York: Minton, Balch and Company, 1934), especially chap. 13.

10. J.P. Guilford, *The Nature of Human Intelligence* (New York: McGraw-Hill, 1967).

11. Elliot W. Eisner, "Forms of Understanding and the Future of Educational Research," *Educational Researcher*, October 1993, pp. 5–11. Also see my book *Cognition and Curriculum Reconsidered* (New York: Teachers College Press, 1994).

12. Hannah Arendt, *The Human Condition* (Chicago: University of Chicago Press, 1958).

13. For a discussion and illustration of what I call educationally interpretive exhibitions, see Elliot W. Eisner et al. *The Educationally Interpretive Exhibition: Rethinking the Display of Student Art* (Reston, Va.: National Art Education Association, 1997).

28

Subtractive Schooling, Caring Relations, and Social Capital in the Schooling of U.S.-Mexican Youth

Angela Valenzuela

Schools subtract resources from youth in two major ways. The first involves a process of "de-Mexicanization," or subtracting students' culture and language, which is consequential to their achievement and orientations toward school. The second involves the role of caring between teachers and students in the educational process. De-Mexicanization erodes students' social capital (Coleman 1988, 1990; also see Stanton-Salazar, 1997), by making it difficult for constructive social ties to develop between immigrant and U.S.-born youth. By *social capital*, I mean the social ties that connect students to each other, as well as the levels of resources (like academic skills and knowledge) that characterize their friendship groups. This dynamic is of special consequence to regular-track, U.S.-born Mexican youth, who often lack a well-defined and effective achievement orientation.

Regarding caring, teachers expect students to *care about* school in a technical fashion before they *care for* them, while students expect teachers to *care for* them before they *care about* school. By dismissing students' definition of education—an orientation thoroughly grounded in Mexican culture and advanced by caring theorists (e.g., Noddings, 1984, 1992)—schooling subtracts resources from youth.

After describing the study I undertook at Seguín High School,[1] I explain how I derived the concept of "subtractive schooling." This description incorporates my concerns about current theorizing (especially see Portes, 1995) that narrowly casts achievement differences between immigrant and U.S.-born youth as evidence of "downward assimilation." I then elaborate on how culture and caring relations are involved in the process of subtractive schooling. Throughout, I draw selectively on both quantitative and qualitative evidence that lends support to my thesis.

The Seguín High School Study

Seguín High is a large, comprehensive, inner-city high school located in the Houston Independent School District. Its 3,000-plus student body is virtually all Mexican and generationally diverse (45 percent immigrant and 55 percent U.S. born).[2] Teachers, on the other hand, are predominantly non-Latino. Currently, 81 percent are non-Latino, and 19 percent are Latino (mostly Mexican American).

Seguín's failure and dropout rates are very high. In 1992 a full quarter of the freshman class repeated the grade for at least a second time, and a significant portion of these were repeating the ninth grade a third and fourth time. An average of 300 students skip daily. Between 1,200 and 1,500 students enter the 9th grade each year and only 400 to 500 students graduate in any given year. Low expectations are virtually built into this school: Were students to progress normally from one grade to the next, there would be no space to house them. As things stand, Seguín's 3,000-plus student body is crammed into a physical facility capable of housing no more than 2,600. Because of the school's high failure and dropout rates, the freshman class makes up more than half of the school population.

An ethnic brand of politics that has focused on problems in the school has made for a contentious relationship between Seguín and its surrounding community. Although local community activists have historically supported numerous causes, including legal challenges against segregation during the early 1970s, a massive student walkout in October 1989, and a number of school reforms such as site-based management, little has changed to significantly alter its underachieving profile. Seguín is locked in inertia. Steeped in a logic of technical rationality, schooling centers on questions of how best to administer the curriculum rather than on why, as presently organized, it tends to block the educational mobility of huge segments of its student body. Excepting those located in the privileged rungs of the curriculum—that is, honors classes, the magnet school program, and the upper levels of the Career and Technology Education (CTE) vocational program[3]—the academic trajectories of the vast majority are highly circumscribed. Because as a group, 9th graders are especially "at risk," I tried to talk to as many of them as possible and to incorporate their voices and experiences into this ethnographic account.

Although my study makes use of quantitative data, the key modes of data collection are based on participant observation and open-ended interviews with individuals and with groups of students. Group interviews enabled me not only to tap into peer-group culture but also to investigate the social, cultural, and linguistic divisions that I observed among teenagers at Seguín. Before elaborating my framework, I will first address relevant survey findings that pertain to parental education, schooling orientations, and generational differences in achievement.[4]

First, students' parental education levels are very low, hovering around nine years of schooling completed for third-generation students.[5] Though higher than the average for parents of first-generation respondents (i.e., six years of schooling), a "high" of nine for the U.S.-born population means that parents have little educational "advantage" to confer to their children (Lareau 1989). That is, most parents have either no high school experience or a negative one to pass on to their progeny. Rather than aberrant, this finding is consistent with Chapa (1988), who found that third-generation Mexican Americans in the state of Texas complete an average of 9.3 years of education and that the dropout rate is 56 percent.[6]

These data indicate that with such low average attainment levels, the major responsibility for education falls on the school by default. School officials, however, tend not to see it this way. They tend to blame the students, their parents, their culture, and their community for their educational failure. This tendency on the part of teachers and administrators to blame children, parents, and community has been amply observed in ethnographies of minority youth in urban schools (Fine, 1991; Peshkin, 1991; Yeo, 1997; McQuillan, 1998).

Complicating matters—and reinforcing many teachers' and other school officials' opinion that students "don't care" about school—is that a significant proportion of students, mostly U.S. born, have become adept at breaking school rules. For example, they skip class and attend all three lunch periods knowing that the numbers are on their side and that they are unlikely to get processed even if they get spotted by school officials. A common scenario is the presence of several administrators in the school cafeteria alongside scores of students whom they know are skipping class. The sheer amount of time, paperwork, and effort that would be required to process every offender discourages massive action. In short, violations of school policies are so common that they outstrip the administration's capacity of address them, making Seguín a capricious environment that minimizes many students' sense of control, on the one hand, and their respect toward authority, on the other. Despite the fact that certain types of students, discussed shortly, consistently succeed, the prevailing view is that students "don't care."

Another finding from survey data corroborated in the ethnographic account is that immigrant youth experience school significantly more positively than do their U.S.-born peers. That is, they see teachers as more caring and accessible than do their U.S.-born counterparts, and they rate the school climate in more positive terms as well. They are also much less likely to evade school rules and policies. These students' attitudes contrast markedly with those of their second- and third-generation counterparts, whose responses in turn are not significantly different from one another. Particularly striking is how generational status—and not gender or curriculum track placement—influences orientations toward schooling.

Because of its relevance, I interject at this point how ethnographic evidence additionally reveals that immigrant, more than U.S.-born, youth belong to informal peer groups that exhibit an esprit-de-corps, proschool ethos. Immigrants' collective achievement strategies, when combined with the academic competence their prior schooling provides, directly affect their level of achievement. Academic competence thus functions as a human-capital variable that, when marshaled in the context of the peer group, *becomes* a social-capital variable (Coleman, 1988, 1990). This process is especially evident among females in Seguín's immigrant student population (see Valenzuela, 1999). In contrast, and borrowing from Putnam (1993, 1995), regular-track, U.S.-born youth are "socially decapitalized." Through a protracted, institutionally mediated process of de-Mexicanization that results in a de-identification from the Spanish language, Mexico, and things Mexican, they lose an organic connection to those among them who are academically oriented. U.S.-born youth are no less solidaristic; their social ties are simply devoid of academically productive social capital.

Finally, quantitative evidence points to significantly higher academic achievement among immigrants than among U.S.-born youth located in the regular track. Though not controlling for curriculum track placement, other scholars have observed this tendency among Mexican and Central American students (Buriel, 1984; Buriel & Cardoza, 1988; Matute-Bianchi, 1991; Ogbu, 1991; Suárez-Orozco, 1991; Vigil & Long, 1981). This finding has been primarily interpreted from an individual assimilationist perspective rather than from a critical analysis of assimilating institutions.

Invoking a generational analysis of change, classic assimilation theory (Gordon, 1964) suggests that achievement should improve generationally if assimilation worked for Mexicans in the way that it has worked for European-origin immigrant groups in the United States. Though unintended, this generational model encourages a construction of U.S.-born youth as "deficient" and as fundamentally lacking in the drive and enthusiasm possessed by their immigrant counterparts. Drawing on several works that examine the phenomenon of oppositionality among minority youth (Fordham & Ogbu, 1986; Matute-Bianchi, 1991; Ogbu, 1991), Portes and Zhou (1993, 1994) conclude that U.S.-born minority youth are members of "adversarial cultures" (or "reactive sub-cultures"). They convey the imagery of a downward achievement spiral that accompanies the assimilation process, culminating, often by the second generation, in a devaluation of education as a key route to mobility. Sorely lacking in their account is an understanding of the myriad ways in which powerful institutions such as schools are implicated in both the curtailment of students' educational mobility and, consequently, in the very development of the alleged "adversarial culture" about which Portes and Zhou express concern.

My data show that institutionalized curricular tracking is a good place to begin assessing the academic well-being of the would-be socially ascendant. That is, the previously observed pattern of higher immigrant achievement vis-à-vis U.S.-born underachievement is *only* evident among youth within the regular, noncollege-bound track. In other words, as one would expect, location in the college-bound track erases these differences. At Seguín, however, the vast majority of youth are located in the regular academic track. Only between 10 and 14 percent of the entire student body is ever located in either honors courses, the magnet school program, or the upper-levels of the Career and Technology Education (CTE) vocational program (see Oakes, 1985; O'Connor, Lewis, & Mueller, this volume; Olsen, 1997).

To categorically characterize U.S.-born Mexican youth as emanating from cultures that do not value achievement is to at once treat them as if they were a monolith and to promote an invidious distinction. Key institutional mechanisms such as tracking—and, as I shall shortly argue, subtractive schooling—mediate and have always mediated achievement outcomes. That most minority youth, however, are not located in the college-bound track should not keep us from recognizing the power of such placement: It is there where they acquire privileged access to the necessary skills, resources, and conditions for social ascendancy within schools, and ultimately, within society.

Beyond the "blind spot" in the assimilation literature overlooking the significance of tracking, the limitations of assimilation theory to account for differences in achievement between immigrant and U.S.-born youth becomes further apparent through a close examination of the subtractive elements of schooling. The theoretical question that emerges from the framework I have elaborated is not whether we bear witness to "downward assimilation," as Portes (1995) suggests, but rather *how schooling subtracts resources from youth.*

The Concept of Subtractive Schooling

I derive the concept of "subtractive" in the phrase *subtractive schooling* from the sociolinguistic literature that regards assimilation as a non-neutral process (Cummins, 1981, 1986; Gibson, 1988; Skutnabb-Kangas & Cummins, 1988). Schooling involves either adding on a second culture and language or subtracting one's original culture and language. An additive outcome would be fully vested bilingualism and biculturalism. Whenever Mexican youth emerge from the schooling process as monolingual individuals who are neither identified with Mexico nor equipped to function competently in the mainstream of the United States, subtraction can be said to have occurred.

There is no neutral category for schooling because the status quo is subtractive and inscribed in public policy: the Texas Bilingual Education Code is a transitional policy framework.[7] The state's English as a Second Language (ESL) curriculum is designed to impart to non-native English speakers sufficient verbal and written skills to effectuate their transition into an all-English curriculum within a three-year time period. Under these circumstances, maintaining and developing students' bilingual and bicultural abilities is to swim against the current.

Though "subtractive" and "additive bilingualism" are well-established concepts in the sociolinguistic literature, they have yet to be applied to either the organization of schooling or the structure of caring relationships. Instead, the bulk of this literature emphasizes issues pertaining to language acquisition and maintenance. Merging these concerns with current evidence and theorizing in the nascent comparative literature on immigrant and ethnic minority youth—as I do in this chapter—is fruitful, broadening the scope of empirical inquiry. Currently, the literature addresses differences in perceptions and attitudes toward schooling among immigrant and ethnic minority youth, as well as the adaptational coping strategies they use to negotiate the barriers they face in achieving their goals (e.g., Gibson, 1988, 1993; Matute-Bianchi, 1991; Suárez-Orozco & Suárez-Orozco, 1997). While I address this in my work as well, it is also worthwhile to investigate how the organizational features of schooling relate to the production of minority status and identities, on the one hand, and how these productions relate to achievement and orientations toward schooling, on the other.

I derive the concept of "schooling" in "subtractive schooling" from the social reproduction literature, which views schools as actually "working"—that is, if their job *is* to reproduce the social order along race, class, and gender lines (e.g., Callahan, 1962; Giroux, 1988; Olsen, 1997). Academic success and failure are presented here more as products of schooling than as something that young people do. Of course, the manifest purpose of schooling is not to reproduce inequality, but the latent effect is that with which we must contend.

Segregated and generationally diverse, Seguín proved to be a natural laboratory for investigating reproduction theory. One can see what students are like when they enter school as immigrants and what they look like after having been processed. The combined terms "subtractive" and "schooling" thus bring the school into greater focus than has much of the previous literature on ethnic minority, but especially Mexican, schooling.

The Process of Subtractive Schooling

Language and Culture

"No Spanish" rules were a ubiquitous feature of U.S.-Mexican schooling through the early 1970s (San Miguel, 1987). They have been abolished, but Mexican youth continue to be subjected on a daily basis to subtle, negative messages that undermine the worth of their unique culture and history. The structure of Seguín's curriculum is typical of most public high schools with large concentrations of Mexican youth. It is designed to divest them of their Mexican identities and to impede their prospects for fully vested bilingualism and biculturalism. The single (and rarely taught) course on Mexican American history aptly reflects the students marginalized status in the formal curriculum.

On a more personal level, students' cultural identities are systematically derogated and diminished. Stripped of their usual appearance, youth entering Seguín get "disinfected" of their identifications in a way that bears striking resemblance to the prisoners and mental patients in Goffman's essays on asylums and other "total institutions" (1977). ESL youth, for example, are regarded as "limited English proficient" rather than as "Spanish dominant" and/or as potentially bilingual. Their fluency in Spanish is construed as a "barrier" that needs to be overcome. Indeed, school personnel frequently insist that once "the language barrier" is finally eliminated, Seguín's dismal achievement record will disappear as well. The belief in English as the panacea is so strong that it outweighs the hard evidence confronting classroom teachers every day: The overwhelming majority of U.S.-born, monolingual, English-speaking youth in Seguín's regular track do not now, have not in the past, and likely will not in the future prosper academically.

Another routine way in which the everyday flow of school life erodes the importance of cultural identity is through the casual revisions that faculty and staff make in students' names. At every turn, even well-meaning teachers "adapt" their students' names: *Loreto* becomes *Laredo; Azucena* is transformed into *Suzy*. Because teachers and other school personnel typically lack familarity with stress rules in Spanish, surnames are especially vulnerable to linguistic butchering. Even names that are common throughout the Southwest, like Martinez and Perez, are mispronounced as MART-i-nez and Pe-REZ. Schooling under these conditions can thus be characterized as a mortification of the self in Goffman's terms—that is, as a leaving off and a taking on.

Locating Spanish in the Foreign Language Department also implicates Seguín in the process of subtraction. This structure treats Mexicans as any other immigrant group originating from distant lands and results in course offerings that do not correspond to students' needs. Because Spanish is conceived of as similar to such "foreign languages" as French and German, the majority of the courses are offered at the beginning and intermediate levels only. Very few advanced Spanish-language courses exist. Rather than designing the program with the school's large number of native speakers in mind, Seguín's first- and second-year Spanish curriculum subjects students to material that insults their abilities.

Taking beginning Spanish means repeating such elementary phrases as "Yo me llamo María." (My name is María.) "Tú te llamas José." (Your name is José.) Even students whose linguistic competence is more passive than active—that is, they understand but speak little Spanish—are ill served by this kind of approach. A passively bilingual individual possesses much greater linguistic knowledge and ability than another individual exposed to the language for their first time. Since almost every student at Seguín is either a native speaker of Spanish or an active or passive bilingual, the school's Spanish program ill serves all, though not even-handedly. To be relevant, the curricular pyramid would have to be reversed, with far fewer beginning courses and many more advanced-level courses in Spanish.

Subtraction is further inscribed in Seguín's tracking system. That is, the regular curriculum track is subdivided into two tracks—the regular, English-only, and the ESL track. This practice of nonacademic "cultural tracking" fosters social divisions among youth along cultural and linguistic lines and limits the educational mobility of all youth. A status hierarchy that relegates immigrant youth to the bottom gets established, enabling the development of a "politics of difference" (McCarthy, 1993). That is, immigrant and U.S.-born youth develop "we-they" distinctions that sabotage communication and preclude bridge building.

The sharp division that exists between immigrant and U.S.-born youth is a striking feature, particularly when one considers that many of the U.S.-born students have parents and grandparents who are from Mexico. However, such divisions have been observed among Mexican adults as well (Rodriguez & Nuñez, 1986). This discussion should not be taken to mean that immigrants should not be accorded their much-needed, and often deficient, language support systems. I simply want to express that the broader Mexican community's collective interest to achieve academically gets compromised by a schooling process that exacerbates and reproduces differences among youth.

Regarding mobility, time-honored practices make it virtually impossible for ESL youth to make a vertical move from the ESL to the honors track. Never mind that many immigrant youth attended *secundaria* (known more formally as *educación media*) in Mexico. Since only 16.9 percent of the total middle school-age population in Mexico attends *secundaria,* any *secundaria* experience is exceptional (Gutek, 1993). Though members of an "elite" group, they are seldom recognized or treated as such by school officials, including counselors who either do not know how to interpret a transcript from Mexico or who are ignorant about the significance of a postprimary educational experience. Such negligent practices helped me understand immigrant youth who told me, "I used to be smarter." "I used to know math."

Ironically, the stigmatized status of immigrants—especially the more "*amexicanados*"—endures vis-à-vis their Mexican American peers, enhances their peer group solidarity, and protects them from the seductive elements of the peer group culture characteristic of their U.S.-born counterparts. Immigrant students' proschool, esprit-de-corps ethos (that explains their ESL teachers' affectionate references to them as "organized cheaters") finds no parallel in the schooling experiences of U.S.-born youth. Immigrants' collective achievement strategies, when combined with the academic competence their prior schooling provides, translate into academically productive social capital.

Disassociation and deidentification with immigrant youth and Mexican culture have no such hidden advantage for Mexican American youth. The English-dominant and strongly peer-oriented students who walk daily through Seguín's halls, vacillating between displays of aggressiveness and indifference, are either underachieving or psychically and emotionally detached from the academic mainstream. Hence, for U.S.-born youth, to be culturally assimilated is to become culturally and linguistically distant from those among them who are academically able. Thus eroded in the process of schooling is students' social capital. Within a span of two or three generations, "social decapitalization" may be said to occur. Under such conditions, teachers become highly influential and even necessary gatekeepers. Hence the significance of caring relations.

Caring Relations

Regardless of nativity, students' definition of education, embodied in the term *educación,* gets dismissed. Interestingly, the concept of "*educación*" approximates the optimal definition of education advanced by Noddings (1984) and other caring theorists. Being an educated person within Mexican culture carries with it its own distinctive connotation (Mejía, 1983; Reese, Balzano, Gallimore, & Goldenberg, 1991). *Ser bien educado/a* (to be well educated) is to not only possess book knowledge but to also live responsibly in the world as a caring human being, respectful of the individuality and dignity of others. Though one may possess many credentials, one is poorly educated (*mal educado/a*) if deficient in respect, manners, and responsibility toward others, especially family members.

Following from students' definition of education is the implicit notion that learning should be premised on *authentic* caring, to use Noddings' (1984) terminology. That is, learning should be premised on *relation* with teachers and other school adults having as their chief concern their students' entire well-being. In contrast to their teachers' expectations, Seguín youth prefer to be *cared for* before they *care about* school, especially when the curriculum is impersonal, irrelevant, and test driven. U.S.-born students, in particular, display psychic and emotional detachment from a schooling process organized around *aesthetic*, or superficial, caring. Such caring accords emphasis to form and nonpersonal content (e.g., rules, goals, and "the facts") and only secondarily, if at all, to their students' subjective reality.

The benefit of profound connection to the student is the development of a sense of competence and mastery over worldly tasks. In the absence of such connectedness, students are not only reduced to the level of objects; they may also be diverted from learning the skills necessary for mastering their academic and social environment. Thus, the difference in the ways in which students and teachers perceive school-based relationships can have direct bearing on students' potential to achieve.

Caring becomes political, however, when teachers and students hold different definitions of caring and the latter are unable to insert their definition of caring into the schooling process because of their weaker power position. Mexican American youth frequently choose clothing and accessories such as baggy pants and multilayered gold necklaces that "confirm" their teachers' suspicions that they really do not care about school. Withdrawal and apathy in the classroom mix with occasional displays of aggression toward school authorities. This makes them easy to write off as "lazy underachievers."

U.S.-born youth indeed engage in what Ogbu calls "cultural inversion" whereby they consciously or unconsciously oppose the culture and cognitive styles associated with the dominant group (Fordham & Ogbu, 1986). However, they do so mainly in the realm of self-representation. In contrast to what Fordham and Ogbu (1986) and Matute-Bianchi (1991) have observed among African American and Mexican American youth in their studies, strong achievement orientations among youth at Seguín are never best interpreted as attempts on their part to "act white." Instead, proschool youth are simply dismissed as "nerdy" or "geeky." Rather than education, it is *schooling* they resist—especially the dismissal of their definition of education.

Some of the most compelling evidence that students do care about education despite their rejection of schooling lies with the great number of students who skip most classes chronically but who regularly attend that one class that is meaningful to them. Without exception, it is the teacher there who makes the difference. Unconditional, authentic caring resides therein.

Seguín's immigrant students often share their U.S.-born peers' view that learning should be premised on a humane and compassionate pedagogy inscribed in reciprocal relationships, but their sense of being privileged to attend secondary school saps any desire they might have to insert their definition of education into the schooling process. Immigrant students therefore respond to the exhortation that they "care about" school differently from U.S.-born youth. Immigrant students acquiesce and are consequently seen by their teachers as polite and deferential. Their grounded sense of identity further combines with their unfamiliarity with the Mexican American experience to enable them to "care about" school without the threat of language or culture loss or even the burden of cultural derogation when their sights are set on swiftly acculturating toward the mainstream. U.S.-born youth in Seguín's regular track, on the other hand, typically respond by either withdrawing or rebelling. *Caring about* threatens their ethnic identity, their sense of self.

Frank's story illustrates one student's resistance to schooling, the productive potential of a caring relationship at school, and the debilitating effects of a curriculum that fails to validate his ethnic identity. He is an unusually reflective ninth-grader. As a "C-student," he achieves far below his potential. His own alienation from schooling accounts for his poor motivation:

> I don't get with the program because then it's doing what *they* [teachers] want for my life. I see *mexicanos* who follow the program so they can go to college, get rich, move out of the *barrio*, and never return to give back to their *gente* (people). Is that what this is all about? If I get with the program, I'm saying that's what it's all about and that teachers are right when they're not.

Frank resists caring about school not because he is unwilling to become a productive member of society, but rather because to do so is tantamount to cultural genocide. He is consciously at odds with the narrow definition of success that most school officials hold. This definition asks him to measure his self-worth against his ability to get up and out of the *barrio* along an individualist path to success divorced from the social and economic interests of the broader Mexican community. With his indifference, this profoundly mature young adult deliberately challenges Seguín's implicit demand that he derogate his culture and community.

Frank's critique of schooling approximates that of Tisa, another astute U.S.-born, female student whom I came across in the course of my group interviews. When I ask her whether she thinks a college education is necessary in order to have a nice house and a nice car and to live in a nice neighborhood, she provided the following response: "You can make good money dealing drugs, but all the dealers—even if they drive great cars—they still spend their lives in the 'hood. Not to knock the 'hood at all. . . . If only us *raza* (the Mexican American people) could find a way to have all three, money . . . *clean* money, education, and the 'hood."

In a very diplomatic way, Tisa took issue with the way I framed my question. Rather than setting up two mutually compatible options of being successful and remaining in one's home community, Tisa interpreted my question in *either/or terms*, which in her mind unfairly counterposed success to living in the 'hood. That I myself failed to anticipate its potentially subtractive logic caused me to reflect on the power of the dominant narrative of mobility in U.S. society—an "out-of-the-*barrio*" motif, as it were (Chavez, 1991).

Thus, for alienated youth such as Frank and Tisa to buy into "the program," success needs to be couched in additive, both/and terms that preserve their psychic and emotional desire to remain socially responsible members of their communities. These findings bring to mind the ethos that Ladson-Billings (1994) identifies as central to culturally relevant pedagogy for African American youth. Specifically, effective teachers of African American children see their role as one of "giving back to the community." For socially and culturally distant teachers, such discernment and apprehending of "the other" is especially challenging and can only emerge when the differential power held by teachers of culturally different students is taken fully into account (Noddings, 1984, 1992; Paley, 1995; Ladson-Billings, 1994).

Conclusion

Schools such as Seguín High School are faced with a special challenge. To significantly alter the stubborn pattern of underachievement, they need to become authentically caring institutions. To become authentically caring institutions, they need to at once stop subtracting resources from youth and deal with the effects of subtraction. Although it is up to each school to determine what a more additive perspective might entail, my study suggests that an important point of departure is a critical examination of the existing curriculum.

The operant model of schooling structurally deprives acculturated, U.S.-born youth of social capital that they would otherwise enjoy were the school not so aggressively (subtractively) assimilationist. Stated differently, rather than students failing schools, schools fail students with a pedagogical logic that not only assures the ascendancy of a few but also jeopardizes their access to those among them who are either academically strong or who belong to academically supportive networks.

Although the possession of academically productive social capital presents itself as a decided advantage for immigrant youth, analytical restraint is in order here as well. However "productive" it may be, social capital is still no match against an invisible system of tracking that excludes the vast majority of youth. Strategizing for the next assignment or exam does not guarantee that the exclusionary aspects of schooling will either cease or magically come to light. Even should it come to light, the power to circumvent regular-track placement remains an issue, especially for the more socially marginal. Most sobering is the thought that in some ultimate sense, schooling is subtractive for all.

Notes

This chapter is based on a talk that the author gave at the University of Texas at Austin on February 25, 1998. The presentation was sponsored by the Center for Mexican American Studies and the Department of Curriculum and Instruction. It originally appeared as Angela Valenzuela. "Subtractive Schooling: U.S.-Mexican Youth and the Politics of Caring." *Reflexiones 1998: New Directions in Mexican American Studies* (Austin: Center for Mexican American Studies, University of Texas).

1. All names used herein are pseudonyms.
2. I use the term *Mexican,* a common self-referent, to refer to all persons of Mexican heritage when no distinction based on nativity or heritage is necessary.
3. My extensive observations of Seguín's CTE program have led me to conclude that the acquisition of work skills is compatible with students' college-going aspirations because it reinforces the academic curriculum. The CTE program is effective because the teachers enjoy higher salaries, small class sizes, access to career counselors, and, in the higher level courses, the ability to select their students.
4. I administered a questionnaire to all 3,000 students in November 1992. It included questions about students' family background. English and Spanish language ability, generational status, school climate, teacher caring, and academic achievement. With a 75 percent response rate, a sample of 2,281 students for analysis resulted.
5. My study adopts a conventional generational schema. First-generation students were, along with their parents, born in Mexico. Second-generation students were born in the United States but had parents born in Mexico. Students were classified as third generation if they and their parents were born in the United States. I use the self-referent *Mexican American* and the term *U.S.-born* to refer to second- and third-generation persons. (Fourth-generation youth [i.e., those whose parents and grandparents were born in the United States] were combined with third-generation youth because of their resemblance in both the quantitative and qualitative analyses.)
6. The comparable figures for Mexicans in California and the nation are 11.1 and 10.4 years of schooling completed and dropout rates of 39 and 48 percent, respectively. Mexicans from Texas are thus faring even more poorly than their underachieving counterparts nationwide (Chapa 1988).
7. The Texas Bilingual Education Code (Sec. 29.051 State Policy) rejects bilingualism as a goal: "English is the basic language of this state. Public schools are responsible for providing a full opportunity for all students to become competent in speaking, reading, writing, and comprehending the English language."

References

Buriel, R. (1984). Integration with traditional Mexican-American culture and socio-cultural adjustment. In J. L. Martinez, Jr., & R. Mendoza (eds.), *Chicano Psychology* (2nd ed.). Orlando, FL: Academic.

Callahan, R. E. (1962). *Education and the cult of efficiency.* Chicago, IL: University of Chicago Press.

Chapa, J. (1988). The question of Mexican American assimilation: Socioeconomic parity or underclass formation? *Public Affairs Comment,* 35(1), 1–14.

Chavez, L. (1991). *Out of the barrio: Toward a new politics of Hispanic assimilation*. New York: Basic Books.

Coleman, J. S. (1988). Social capital in the creation of human capital. *American Journal of Sociology, 94*, 95–120.

Coleman, J. S. (1990). *Foundations of social theory*. Cambridge, MA: Harvard University Press.

Cummins, J. (1981). The role of primary language development in promoting educational success for language minority students. In California State Department of Education (ed.), *Schooling and language minority students: A theoretical framework*. Los Angeles, CA: Evaluation, Dissemination, and Assessment Center, California State University.

Cummins, J. (1986). Empowering minority students: A framework for intervention. *Harvard Educational Review, 56*, 18–36.

Fine, M. (1991). *Framing dropouts: Notes on the politics of an urban public high school*. Albany, NY: State University of New York Press.

Fordham, S., & Ogbu, J. U. (1986). Black students' school success: Coping with the burden of acting white. *Urban Review, 18*(3), 176–206.

Gibson, M. A. (1988). *Accommodation without assimilation: Sikh immigrants in an American high school*. Ithaca, NY: Cornell University Press.

Giroux, H. A. (1988). *Schooling and the struggle for public life: Critical pedagogy in the modern age*. Minneapolis, MN: University of Minnesota Press.

Goffman, E. (1977). *Asylums: Essays on the social situation of mental patients and other inmates*. Garden City, NY: Anchor.

Gordon, M. M. (1964). *Assimilation and American life: The role of race, religion and national origins*. New York: Oxford University Press.

Gutek, G. L. (1993). *American education in a global society: Internationalizing teacher education*. White Plains, NY: Longman.

Ladson-Billings, G. (1994). *Dreamkeepers: Successful teachers of African American children*. San Francisco, CA: Jossey-Bass.

Lareau, A. (1989). *Home advantage: Social class and parental intervention in elementary education*. London; New York: Falmer.

Matute-Bianchi, M. E. (1991). Situational ethnicity and patterns of school performance among immigrant and nonimmigrant Mexican-descent students. In M. A. Gibson & J. U. Ogbu (eds.), *Minority status and schooling: A comparative study of immigrant and involuntary minorities*. New York: Garland.

McCarthy, C. (1993a). Beyond the poverty of theory in race relations: Nonsynchrony and social difference in education. In L. Weis & M. Fine (eds.), *Beyond silenced voices: Class, race, and gender in United States schools*. New York: State University of New York Press.

McCarthy, C. (1993b). Multicultural approaches to racial inequality in the United States. In L. Castenell, Jr. & W. F. Pinar (eds.), *Understanding curriculum as racial text: Representations of identity and difference in education* (pp. 225–246). Albany, NY: State University of New York Press.

McQuillan, P.J. (1998). *Educational opportunity in an urban American high school: A cultural analysis*. Albany, NY: State University of New York Press.

Mejía, D. (1983). The development of Mexican American children. In G. J. Powell (ed.), *The psychosocial development of minority group children*. New York: Brunner/Mazel.

Noddings, N. (1984). *Caring: A feminine approach to ethics and moral education*. Berkeley, CA: University of California Press.

Noddings, N. (1992). *The challenge to care in schools: An alternative approach to education*. New York: Teachers College.

Oakes, J. (1985). *Keeping track: How schools structure inequality*. New Haven, CT: Yale University Press.

Ogbu, J. (1991). Immigrant and involuntary minorities in comparative perspective. In M. A. Gibson & J. U. Ogbu (eds.), *Minority status and schooling: A comparative study of immigrant and involuntary minorities*. New York: Garland.

Olsen, L. (1997). *Made in America: Immigrant students in our public schools*. New York: New Press.

Paley, V. G. (1995). *Kwanzaa and me: A teacher's story*. Cambridge, MA: Harvard University Press.

Peshkin, A. (1991). *The color of strangers the color of friends: The play of ethnicity in school and community*. Chicago, IL: University of Chicago Press.

Portes, A., & Zhou, M. (1993). The new second generation: Segmented assimilation and its variants. *Annals of the American Academy of Political and Social Sciences, 530*, 74–96.

Portes, A., & Zhou, M. (1994). Should immigrants assimilate? *Public Interest, 116*, 18–33.

Putnam, R. D. (1993). The prosperous community: Social capital and public life. *American Prospect, 13* (spring), 35–42.

Putnam, R. D. (1995). Bowling alone: America's declining social capital. *Journal of Democracy, 6*(1), 65–78.

Reese, L., Balzano, S., Gallimore, R., & Goldenberg, C. (1991, November). *The concept of* educación*: Latino family values and American schooling*. Paper presented at the Annual Meeting of the American Anthropological Association, Chicago, IL.

Rodriguez, N. P., & Nuñez, R. T. (1986). An exploration of factors that contribute to differentiation between Chicanos and indocumentados. In H. Browning & R. de la Garza (eds.), *Mexican immigrants and Mexican Americans: An evolving relation*. Austin, TX: CMAS Publications, Center for Mexican American Studies, University of Texas at Austin.

San Miguel, G. (1987). *"Let all of them take heed": Mexican Americans and the campaign for educational equality in Texas, 1910–1981*. Austin, TX: University of Texas Press.

Skutnabb-Kangas, T., & Cummins, J. (1988). *Minority education: From shame to struggle*. Clevedon, Canada: Multilingual Matters 40.

Stanton-Salazar, R. (1997). A social capital framework for understanding the socialization of ethnic minority children and youths. *Harvard Educational Review, 67,* 1–39.

Suárez-Orozco, M. M. (1991). Hispanic immigrant adaptation to schooling. In M. A. Gibson & J. U. Ogbu (eds.), *Minority status and schooling: A comparative study of immigrant and involuntary minorities*. New York: Garland.

Valenzuela, A. (1999). *Subtractive schooling: U.S.-Mexican youth and the politics of caring*. Albany, NY: State University of New York Press.

Vigil, J. D., & Long, J. M. (1981). Unidirectional or nativist acculturation: Chicano paths to school achievement. *Human Organization, 40,* 273–277.

Yeo, F. L. (1997). *Inner-city schools, multiculturalism, and teacher education: A professional journey*. New York: Garland.

29

Teacher Experiences of Culture in the Curriculum

Elaine Chan

Preamble

Cultural and linguistic diversity are among the characteristic features describing the Canadian landscape. Eighteen percent of the total population was born outside the country, and 11 percent of the population identify themselves as members of a visible minority group (Statistics Canada 1998, 2003). Not surprisingly, multi-culturalism has been seen as a key educational issue. Yet, despite the importance of multi-culturalism, there are all too few examinations of the interaction of culture and curriculum in school contexts.

There is a wealth of normative prescription about the acknowledgement of culture. Cummins (1996), Igoa (1995), and Wong-Fillmore (1991a, b) have highlighted the academic, emotional, and societal importance of acknowledging diversity by engaging students in learning about their home cultures and languages. Banks (1995) has highlighted the importance of the inclusion of culture in the curriculum as a means of developing positive attitudes among racial and/or ethnic minorities. Rodriguez (1982), Kouritzin (1999), and McCaleb (1994) have explored the dangers of the failure to acknowledge the cultural knowledge of students of ethnic minority backgrounds. Ada (1988) has discussed a project in which the families of students of minority background were engaged in bilingual literacy projects. Paley's (1995) "integrated" curriculum had parents and children discussing values, rituals, and cultural experiences through family stories in order to foster a sense of community within the classroom.

However, although there is much discussion outlining the importance of "information and awareness of the cultural backgrounds of pupils in order to better diagnose strengths, weaknesses, and differences in cognitive styles" (Moodley 1995: 817), there is a lack of consensus about how best to acknowledge this diversity in a school context. In this paper, I examine the challenges and complications that two middle-school-level teachers encountered as they attempted to implement a curriculum event.

Introduction

> The students came into Room 42 after lunch today with all kinds of questions about their upcoming field trip to Boyne River. They wanted to know when they would be leaving, when they would be returning, what they should bring, whether it would be cold at Boyne River, what they would eat, where they would sleep, and so on. They seemed very excited about the trip.

William answered their questions ... [but] when he asked for a show of hands of students from those who would be participating, I was surprised to see that many students did not put their hands up. Sahra, who was sitting directly in front of William, did not put her hand up.

"My father won't let me go" Sahra said. She explained that she could not go on field trips where they would be spending the night. Sahra's family is South Asian and her parents, especially her father, are very strict about the kinds of school activities they allow her to take part in.

"Do you want me to talk to him?" William asked her. "You should be able to go."

I asked some of the students sitting near me whether they would be going on the field trip.

"It's against my religion for girls to go out" Zeynab said.

"I can't. I need to go with my father to the hospital, to help translate for him."

"I need to pick my sister up from school and get my brother from daycare—my parents have to work."

"I work at my family's tea store, and sometimes I need to help them [i.e. my parents] with the forms."

(Field note: November 2000)

I present this field-note documenting student responses to a school field-trip in order to introduce the complexities that two middle-school teachers at Bay Street School, William and Dave, faced as they attempted to acknowledge their students' ethnic, linguistic, and religious diversity in their curriculum and their teaching practices. The field trip to Boyne River, an outdoor-adventure centre, provides a context for examining the intersection of diverse beliefs and values at Bay Street School.[1] This intersection is at the core of the work done by teachers in Canada, and in particular in Toronto, as representatives, and members, of a receiving culture that has a reputation for welcoming immigrants. However, they work with students and families whose values and beliefs about education, and ways of interacting with others, may differ significantly from their own.

In Fall 2000, William and his colleague Dave were preparing to take their combined classes of 71 grade-8 students on a 4-day field trip to Boyne River. I centre this discussion on the planning of this trip, one of many activities and events that occurred during the 3.5 years I spent as a participant observer at Bay Street School.[2]

Despite William's willingness to address issues of diversity in conversations with his colleagues and students, and to be culturally-sensitive in his practices and in his curriculum, there were differences in perspective around the Boyne River trip, and other school activities. Thus, William and Dave found that there were a few parents who did not seem to support activities they undertook; there were tensions between members of ethnic groups in some interactions; and students sometimes did not seem especially interested in sharing aspects of their own cultures, or learning about the cultures of their peers. Given that the teachers at Bay Street School seemed to recognize the value of acknowledging culture by accommodating for differences in the curriculum, these tensions were always surprising.

I use Schwab's (1973) commonplaces of teacher, learner, subject matter, and milieu to explore how differences in perspective around a single curriculum event—the subject matter—were shaped by experiences that teachers, learners, their families, and other members of the school community brought with them to the school milieu.

Research on teachers' professional knowledge landscapes (Clandinin and Connelly 1996, Connelly and Clandinin 1999), the role of schooling in shaping a sense of ethnic identity (Wong Fillmore 1991a, b, Cummins 1996, Kouritzin 1999), experience and education (Dewey 1938, Connolly and Clandinin 1988), and narrative inquiry (Clandinin and Connelly 1994, 2000, Phillion 2002) form the theoretical framework for this study. Given

Dewey's (1938) philosophy of the inter-connectedness between education and experience, I see all that the students' encounter in their school context, as well as all that occurs in their school, home, and neighbourhood, as experience with the potential to contribute to their learning about what a sense of ethnic identity may mean to them. This broad base of potentially-influential interactions highlights the power of schooling experiences, and further reinforces the importance of recognizing and celebrating the diversity that students bring to a school context.

The Boyne River Field Trip

Bay Street School had been placed on a list at the outdoor-education centre to be contacted if another school cancelled their booking. When a call came from Boyne River, the staff at Bay Street School began work to make arrangements in order for their students to participate. They developed an information package complete with translations of notices and waiver forms in different languages, made bookings for buses and supply teachers, and arranged for the teachers remaining in the school to cover the classes of those who would be accompanying the students to Boyne River. These arrangements were made within 3 days of receiving the call; for the teachers at Bay Street School, the field trip was a valuable activity.

Other members of the school community also supported the Boyne River trip. The community-development worker viewed the field trip as an opportunity for students who might not otherwise be able to participate in this kind of outdoor education activity to do so. He spoke about the importance of equality of access for children whose families might not be able to support learning opportunities of this kind outside of a school context.

Dave was the only one of the three grade-8 teachers who was to accompany the students to Boyne River. He spoke of the field trip as an opportunity to interact with the students in a way different from their regular in-school and in-class interactions. His own experience as a camp counsellor and outdoor-education teacher reinforced his personal philosophy in the value of interaction with individual students while participating in outdoor activities.

Marla, the special education teacher who worked with William and Dave, viewed the field trip as an opportunity for the students to gain experiences that were outside of the academic curriculum. She did not understand the unwillingness of some of the parents to send their children: she thought that the field trip was an especially important way for students who were not academically-inclined to excel in a different area. She pointed to one student in particular who had difficulty sitting still, and who struggled academically, and stated that he would likely enjoy something like an outdoor-adventure trip.

Bay Street School Context

William responded to Sahra's statement that she would not be able to participate in a class field trip by offering to speak to her father—to convince him of the value of the field trip and to emphasize to him the importance of female students having educational opportunities equal to those available to male students.

Such criticism by teachers of the unwillingness of some of the parents to permit their children to participate in the Boyne River field trip may suggest a lack of sensitivity to the backgrounds that the students were bringing to the school context. However, throughout my years of work in Bay Street School I saw examples of the teachers' willingness to learn about the cultures of their students, and to accommodate for different practices. William included discussions on cultural diversity and racism in social studies classes, addressing the injustice and prejudice that Native Canadians suffered in New France as his students learned about settlement in Canada. He read passages featuring the experiences of members of the Black community in Canada during Black History Month, and continued to incorporate information about the Black community. He had his students interview their parents in order to write about their childhood in their home countries before immigrating to Canada; he gave his students a family-studies project that involved the preparation of recipes translated from their parents' home language into English. During his first year at Bay Street School, he fasted during Ramadan along with his South Asian students. He supported the integrated international languages classes that are a part of the curriculum at Bay Street School, and demonstrated his desire to learn about the cultures and languages of his students by asking them about specific practices or about vocabulary or expressions in Chinese, Vietnamese, and Spanish.

William and Dave's recognition of the backgrounds of their students was also set in the context of a school community with a history of diversity that began with its establishment over 125 years ago (Connelly *et al.* 2003); the present student population at Bay Street School is highly diverse (Chan and Ross 2002). The school is in a neighbourhood where immigrants settle[3]—in a city identified by the UN as the most culturally-diverse in the world.

In other words, the members of the school community at Bay Street School seemed to be doing what is seen as important in creating a culturally-sensitive curriculum and school context. Nonetheless, the implementation of curriculum events was met with resistance by some students and parents. The difficulties that the teachers encountered as they attempted to be sensitive to the needs of their diverse student population can be explored in terms of Clandinin and Connelly's (1996: 25) distinction between *cover stories, sacred stories*, and *secret stories* about multicultural education and a culturally-sensitive curriculum. Thus, the secret stories of what is actually lived on the school landscape and in classroom are often not presented or explored because they counter a public need to believe that schools are meeting the needs of a culturally-diverse student population. However, these secret stories recognize that the process of acknowledging culture in the curriculum is complicated: good intentions may be misconstrued, or individuals may bring to the school context experiences that shape their interpretations of school events in ways that differ significantly from what was intended.

Differing Student Perspectives

Although the teachers and administrators at Bay Street believed in the value of the field trip to Boyne River, problems around its perceived value became clear when many of the students' parents did not grant permission for their children to participate. Twenty-six of the 71 students did not go on the trip. The reasons were varied. A Pakistani student told me that she needed to accompany her father to the hospital to act as an interpreter; an East Indian student, who had only recently joined the class, did not attend because her parents did not feel comfortable letting her go. Many of the Chinese students did not participate because they had family responsibilities. Kevin was not able to attend because he was responsible for picking up his younger brother from day-care and his sister from school while his parents worked. Bing could not participate because he worked in his family's tea store and was sometimes called upon to complete customs forms and other documents.

I had assumed that the students would want to participate in the field trip, and that those students left behind would feel resentful. The students with whom I spoke, however, did not seem especially resistant to their parents' refusal to allow them to participate. When I shared an earlier draft of this paper with her, a colleague commented that perhaps the sense of self-esteem gained from contributing in important ways to the well-being of the family contributed to their sense of identity in a more significant way than the freedom to take part in a school trip.

Of the Chinese students who participated, Mandy, Elsa, and Annie said that, although they were not usually permitted to attend sleep-overs at their friends' homes, they were permitted to go on school-sponsored field trips: "if it's for school, it's okay!" (Field note: November 2000). They spoke of how their parents had a high regard for school and for their teachers, and school-sponsored activities were viewed in a different light than those initiated outside of school. Nevertheless, although the activities were part of the curriculum and were supported by their teachers, their parents did not show the same commitment to the school's athletic, artistic, or outdoor-education activities as they showed for academic subjects such as science, mathematics, or English.

Teacher Perspectives Interacting with Parent Perspectives

> It's against my religion for girls to go out. (Field note: November 2000)

Sahra was resigned to the fact that she would not be permitted to take part in the field trip. In fact she did not feel that she could even raise the issue with her father since she felt quite certain that such a request would not only be likely to be refused, but would also anger her parents. William offered to speak with her father but, after some consideration, Sahra declined his offer. She explained that her parents had permitted her to participate in an outdoor-education overnight field trip 2 years earlier, but that it had been an exception. Her father had stated explicitly that her participation then had been a one-time exception and that she was not to ask again.

My discussion with William suggested that acknowledging the cultural diversity of his students around the trip by supporting the beliefs and values of their parents conflicted with his personal and professional knowledge. He felt strongly that his students should have the opportunity to take part in school-sponsored events, regardless of gender. It was difficult to support the wishes of some of his students' parents that girls not participate in some school activities and events. And, in the days prior to the departure for Boyne River, it became evident that many of the South Asian girls were not permitted to go. William pointed out that the younger brother of one of his students had been permitted to attend, but that because his student was female, she was not allowed to.

A colleague with whom I discussed this incident responded in a way that was similar to William's reaction. She did not know how a public school could accommodate such differences in perspective around the rights and privileges of the female South Asian students—she is the parent of two daughters. Her husband also felt very strongly that the girls were having their rights infringed upon: as citizens in a democratic society, it is among our responsibilities to protect the rights of the girls and ensure that children are not denied learning opportunities because of their gender.

Thus, the interaction between William and Sahra highlighted the potential for tensions to develop when differences in perspective about the value of specific curriculum events arise. When William offered to speak to Sahra's parents, he hoped he could convince them to permit her to participate in the field trip. He was not aware of the history of Sahra having negotiated permission from her parents to take part in an earlier school field trip, nor was he aware of her agreement not to ask for permission to participate in subsequent overnight field trips.

Nor did William[4] realize the extent to which the parents of some of the South Asian students at Bay Street School are relatively strict with respect to their children's participation in school-sponsored activities away from the school's premises. In the 3 years since this incident, both William and I have learned about some of the practices of the students' families. We are now not surprised when a South Asian student tells us that he or she is not permitted to take part in swimming in physical education classes or go on a field trip. We know how many of the South Asian students fast for a month during the fall, how some of the students and their families regard structured prayer times as a very important aspect of their daily lives, and how some students engage in elaborate washing rituals prior to the prayers held in the library at the school on Friday afternoons. We know—from what some of the female South Asian students in William's class have said—that, with respect to *some* of the South Asian parents, male children are more likely than female children to be permitted to participate in the full range of school activities.

The teachers at Bay Street School realize that their beliefs about curriculum sometimes differed from those of the parents of their students—to the point of conflicting—and that they were faced with the dilemma of how to "accommodate" for such vastly different views. Thus, William was aware that the cultural and social narratives guiding his practices might differ from those guiding the parents of his students, and he was committed to acknowledging the diversity of his students. However, he had not anticipated that his professional identity would come in conflict with values held by some of his students' parents. The Boyne River field trip highlighted the extent to which the implementation of curricular practices seemed to conflict, at times, with his, and his colleagues', beliefs about the "needs" of their students of ethnic minority background. However, it was not until he was faced with a situation where the differences hindered the implementation of an activity he supported that the differences became problematic. When differences in perspective did not have an effect on practice, supporting these differences did not challenge his beliefs, or involve high stakes.

Regardless of the reasons for the parents not wishing their children to participate, we must ask how appropriate it is for a teacher to attempt to influence these decisions. Thus, William had the best of intentions when he offered to speak to Sahra's parents about the Boyne River field trip; he recognized the value of the field trip and wanted to instill in Sahra and his other students an appreciation for the importance of equality of opportunity regardless of gender. He had not realized the potential that his intervention might have to create conflict between Sahra and her parents.

William's offer could also be viewed in terms of his rights and his role as Sahra's teacher in relation to the rights and roles of Sahra's parents as they worked to instill in Sahra the beliefs that they valued. In a situation where her parents and her teachers agreed about the values they would like to instill, Sahra would have had the support of both her parents and her teacher. However, William wanted Sahra to have the opportunity to experience an outdoor-education centre while her parents did not think such a field trip would be appropriate for a young woman. Sahra was caught in the middle: she was a child growing up in an immigrant family whose values differed significantly from those supported in her Canadian school context.

William did not approach Sahra's parents. However, what should teachers do in situations of this kind? What is the formal framework pertaining to student participation in school activities, in general and at Bay Street School in particular? What are the ethics of introducing beliefs and ideas, and engaging students to support these perspectives, when their parents would be opposed to them? Is suggesting to parents that they permit their children to participate in activities they do not value an instance of crossing ethical and professional boundaries? In attempting to convince parents to reconsider their decisions about school activities, are teachers conveying to students, and their parents, that they are more appropriate guides for the development of values and choice of practices than their parents? By stating, openly or tacitly, that they do not support the specific values guiding parents' decisions, are teachers putting students in the middle? A culturally-sensitive curriculum is sine qua non of contemporary schooling; the issues around the Boyne Rover field trip highlight the complexity of these issues.

Differences in opinion around the appropriate behaviour of and towards female students also surfaced on another occasion. After hearing from some of the female students in his class that a grade-7 boy from an adjourning classroom had been behaving inappropriately with them, William scolded them for not telling him about it sooner. He then emphasized to them that they had a right to expect to be treated with respect. As I watched the interaction, I was reminded that some of his students lived such different realities between home and school with respect to ideas about the role of women in society. The students were standing at the door of the classroom, wearing head coverings, preparing to return home to families where they lived with codes of behaviour that define the position of women in the home and society as very different than that of males. Their teacher was telling them that "no one has the right to make you feel less of a person!" (Field note: March 2002). I wondered whether their parents would have encouraged them to take such a stance, or to do so in the way William was suggesting.

The intersection of cultures also became apparent as students and their parents negotiated ways in which their home culture would be adhered to in their school context. As I have indicated, many of the female, South Asian students at Bay Street School wear a head covering, a hijab, when they are outside of the home. I found it interesting that many of the girls who usually wear hijab to school did not wear them for their graduation ceremony, photos, or the party afterwards.

I noticed one day that Miriam, who did not usually wear the hijab, had begun wearing one. She explained that her South Asian friends in her home-room class had pressured her into wearing it because it was Ramadan, the holy month during which many members of the South Asian community at Bay Street School fast during daylight hours. I looked around and indeed all of the South Asian girls in William's class that year were wearing hijab. Miriam said that her mother was not strict about her wearing the hijab and had left it to her to decide whether or not to wear it. She had decided against it; but when her friends started to pressure her, she wore it. She continued to wear the hijab to school, and from that day until one day towards the end of her grade-8 year, I did not see her hair again because it was always covered. She did not, however, wear the hijab for her graduation photos or for her class photos.

Sahra and Miriam told me that wearing the hijab is a serious responsibility. The girls and their families decide whether or not to wear the hijab when the girls are young; once they reach puberty, it is a responsibility that is expected of them. Moreover, once they begin to wear the hijab, they are not to stop. Mrs Mohamed, a teacher at Bay Street School, told me that her older daughter had chosen on her own to wear the hijab when she was very young. "I didn't want her to. I told her, 'Once you start wearing it, you cannot stop'. But she wanted to wear it, and since she was 8, she has always worn the hijab. She was the first of all her friends to wear it." I thought I detected a hint of pride in her voice, which I did not quite understand.

I have been told by members of the Bay Street School community (and read) that some South Asian women find wearing the hijab to be liberating: It provides protection from unwanted attention when out in the streets, and is worn with pride. I had not realized until I began writing about this incident that (I think) I had seen the hijab as a reminder that some opportunities were available to South Asian men but not to South Asian women. I had not understood how it could be liberating to be told to wear something because someone else deemed it appropriate. I might even have believed that those who were wearing the hijab would be more likely to adhere to traditional practices that define the role of women in more restrictive ways than that of men.

In my discussions with William, he also indicated that he sees wearing the hijab as a form of oppression of women. He reasoned that, since women are wearing them because they are being told, or required to, rather than out of freedom of choice, it cannot be a form of liberation. He further argued that if men are not required to wear hijab while women are, then it cannot be viewed as a form of liberation for women. William also indicated how he views South Asian women as having less freedom within their culture than do men: he does not see the need for a man to accompany his wife, or mother, or sister when they are doing errands outside the home, as he sees some of the South Asian men in the community do. As a response to these observations, William's teaching colleague, Lina, suggested that "Maybe it's for their protection"; to which William responded, "If it's the men that are harassing the women, then they are the problem, not the women. Don't you think that it would be a burden, to have someone accompanying you all the time?"

As with the Boyne River field-trip situation, the tensions with respect to the practice of wearing the hijab highlight dilemmas. Thus, William believed that individuals have the right to choose what they will wear, and that the practice of wearing the hijab discriminated against women. At the same time, he wanted to support the parents' attempts to instill their ethnic and religious values in their children. Here we have an interaction of beliefs and values within an individual teacher: He would like to instill in his students values he supports; he also realizes that he may not agree with some of the practices supported by the parents of his students. In a larger sense, there is a tension in that the rights of the individual conflict with the rights of a school to put in place practices and support behaviours that reflect the values respected in the school context but which may conflict with the right of parents to raise their children in ways they deem appropriate.

Confronting Personal Biases to Meet on Landscapes of Difference

The importance of teachers making curriculum decisions and interacting with students and their parents in ways free from bias is a quality that is appreciated in a culturally-diverse society. What is not often acknowledged, however, is that as humans whose beliefs and values have been shaped by prior experiences and interactions, teachers come to teaching with strong views about some aspects of teaching. These strong views may also be interpreted as "biases" in some situations.

For example, I had thought of myself as relatively accepting of difference and tolerant of cultural diversity. However, as I reflected upon how I had written about the role of women in the South Asian community at Bay Street School and about what William and I thought wearing the hijab meant, I realized—with a fair amount of discomfort—that I had judged these practices using my own perceptions of their meaning. I was presenting the practice of wearing a hijab and of "serving men" as examples of ways in which women are valued less than men in South Asian culture, and interpreting in a stereotypical way the role of women in the South Asian community as submissive to that of the men.

I also realized that I was making assumptions about practices without understanding the reasons individuals accepted them, and then judging them by my own beliefs. I overlooked things that I did know that suggested that I needed to reconsider my interpretations. An example: one South Asian woman who works at Bay Street School built a new life in Canada for her three school-aged children and herself after her husband died suddenly shortly after their arrival in Toronto. I also overlooked that Mrs Mohamed, whom I had been judging as very "traditional" in her attitudes—I had heard from William's teaching colleague that she had placed an ad in the local South Asian newspaper in search for an appropriate husband for her 19-year-old daughter—was an architect before immigrating to Canada, and that she supported her daughter's plans to study medicine. She had also raised four children on her own when she had arrived in Canada a few years before her husband was able to emigrate. Thinking about this reminded me that there is much that I do not know about South Asian communities, and that I need to be cautious about judging their practices.

Thus, as I have reflected on the interaction of personal and professional beliefs and values as teachers, students, and parents at Bay Street School live the curriculum, I have to realize the potential of these values and beliefs to shape the work of teachers—as well as their potential role in shaping the work of researchers who undertake research with teachers. I was making generalizations based on an assumption that the behaviours and practices of members of the South Asian community would be uniform. Thus, while I have been contending that Chinese culture cannot be defined by specific traits, characteristics, or practices, I was making assumptions about members of the South Asian community based on generalizations. I was also troubled that my perception of myself as accepting and tolerant was being challenged, and I wondered—and worried about—what this might mean for someone who works with diverse school communities.

Were my feelings similar to those experienced by Dave in the weeks that followed a disagreement during a School Council meeting?[5] Dave felt that he was being perceived as racist when he publicly disagreed with the views of a Black parent about how a Black child who had not complied with school regulations had been disciplined. From conversations with Dave, and from observations of him interacting with students and teaching lessons in which he demonstrated a willingness to address issues of diversity, racism, injustice, I perceived Dave to be supportive of the causes of members of ethnic minority groups. When he expressed an opinion different from that of a Black parent in the School Council meeting, however, he was perceived as racist. Dave expressed frustration at this label, and was indignant that he could not have views that differed from those of someone of an ethnic background different from his own without worrying about offending them. He worried that, as a male of European background, if he took a firm viewpoint, he would be perceived of as representing a privileged position. My reflection upon the incident, and my conversations with members of the school community, lead me to wonder whether his positive attitude towards diversity and willingness to learn about the languages and cultures of his students were sufficient. Sensitivity and tolerance for difference are admirable traits, but they need not be at the expense of the freedom to express differences in opinion without fear that these differences would be interpreted as racist or discriminatory.

This Council meeting led to months of discussion among some teachers at Bay Street School about diversity, racism, school policies pertaining to diversity, and their role as teachers in modelling appropriate behaviours and attitudes. These conversations in turn led me to reflect upon the tensions among the members of the School Council. I have heard individual members of the Council speak with conviction about their commitment to working together to create as positive a learning environment as possible for the sake of the children in the school. In my experience of interacting with members of the School Council, I have found them to be sensitive and supportive of the diversity in the Bay Street School community. However, I wondered what the disagreement meant to the individuals who had been directly involved.

Thus, the difficulties in accommodating for the diverse perspectives and beliefs of those involved in the lived experience of curriculum highlight the need to explore in greater detail what it means to develop, and implement, a "culturally-sensitive curriculum". With respect to the implementation of the Boyne River field trip, the teachers were demonstrating sensitivity to differences in values and beliefs as they sought to accommodate the parents who did not want their children to participate in the activity.[6] However, while it may be perceived as "culturally-sensitive" to accommodate for the parents' wishes, it may also be perceived as culturally-sensitive to raise the awareness of the students involved by highlighting and addressing the differences in perspective. This approach might be likened to Ali's (2004) argument for the importance of acknowledging potentially sensitive issues by raising them such that they may be explored and discussed.

In other words, reflection upon the responses of the teachers, including myself, highlights the complexity of the issues involved in sensitivity to ethnic, religious, and linguistic diversity in a school context, and reinforces the extent to which we are, as the receiving culture, unprepared to deal with some of the issues that arise.

Conclusion

Interaction among students of diverse ethnic backgrounds in a supportive school environment provides a context where positive attitudes towards race and ethnicity may develop (Banks 1995). This approach reinforces the importance of schools in creating opportunities for exposure to, and interaction with, individuals of diverse backgrounds. However William and Dave's experiences of working with their ethnically-, linguistically-, and religiously-diverse students reveals the extent to which mere exposure, and even good intentions and specific ideas about ways in which culture may be acknowledged through school practices, are insufficient and leave some important questions unresolved.

Thus, William's experience around the Boyne River field trip shows how acknowledging cultural diversity can be a challenge. What does it mean for a school community to be "accepting" of diversity? How does a knowledge and an acceptance of differences affect the teaching of values that are normative in the larger community while, at the same time, supporting practices that are important to parents, but may not accord with the larger community's values? While it may be possible to achieve tolerance, how do teachers acknowledge and incorporate conflicting values? Would William, in accommodating for the values of his South Asian students, be indirectly expressing a lack of support for a majority group whose values differ significantly from those of the minority? If he accommodated for a group whose values he does not support, is he nonetheless supporting those values by conceding?

Teachers bring to their teaching beliefs and values shaped by their own experiences of teaching, and being taught. Cohen (1989, see Ball 1990: 274) sees teaching practices and beliefs as "deep-seated dispositions, simmered over the years of a teacher's experience and seasoned by cultural assumptions about and images of teaching and learning". Given the role of experience in shaping perceptions of curriculum, we can expect that teachers' practices and beliefs about incorporating culture in the curriculum would be shaped by their own experiences of culture in their school curriculum. Difficulties arise, however, when we realize that many teachers do not have such curricular experiences to draw on.

Cohen and Ball (1990: 352) raise the question, "How can teachers teach a mathematics that they never learned, in ways that they never experienced?" in their examination of teachers' experiences of mathematics curriculum reform. A similar question emerges around the implementation of a culturally-sensitive curriculum. The changing demographic composition of communities in North America, Europe, and Australia implies that teaching is vastly different than it was 40, or even 20, years ago—when today's teachers experienced schools themselves as students. Teachers working in settings such as Bay Street School are faced with the challenges of acknowledging in a positive way diverse cultures, but many are doing so without a professional knowledge-base, or the personal experience of having themselves lived school contexts of this kind.

In addition, while teachers' beliefs and practices are "simmered over the years of a teacher's experience and seasoned by cultural assumptions about and images of teaching and learning" (Cohen 1989, see Ball 1990: 274), the parents of the students they teach also bring their own "deep-seated dispositions" to the curriculum landscape, simmered over years of schooling in their own cultures, shaped by the interaction of the cultural and social narratives unique to their own situations. These experiences in turn shape their values and beliefs about curricula they interpret as appropriate. In some instances, as with the Boyne River field trip, the beliefs that some families bring to the school context differ in significant ways from the values guiding the practices of others—to the extent that they are in conflict.

These are no easy answers to these questions. However, it is clear that even the teachers who work at Bay Street School—with its tradition of accepting diversity—and who demonstrate a willingness to learn about diverse cultures and languages, and believe in equality and equity for their students regardless of cultural backgrounds and gender need to address and discuss the events that may arise as diverse cultures intersect on their school landscapes, to identify issues of relevance to the particular ethnic communities involved.

The teacher, student, and parent responses to the Boyne River field trip highlight the extent to which the receiving cultures of immigrants need to explore ways of accommodating for this diversity in school contexts. We have the expectation that children of ethnic minority background need to "adapt" to "our" school communities, but we may overlook that, as a host country for immigrants, we also need to explore the extent to which this relationship may be reciprocal. We need to explore ways of accommodating for diverse cultures in ways that are respectful of the differences. At the same time, we need to provide as rich an experience of "our" schooling as possible for the children involved. By addressing potentially sensitive issues, we begin the process of uncovering the "secret stories" (Clandinin and Connelly 1996: 25) that may hinder our ability to meet the needs in our school communities. For example, is a belief in the rights of girls that may lead us to disrespect the views of conservative South Asian parents who are living in another world an example of a secret story that needs to be raised for discussion. Sensitivity to such stories also allows us to explore our role in facilitating the acculturation of individuals of ethnic-minority background through the curricula we implement.

Acknowledgements

I would like to express my heartfelt thanks to F. Michael Connelly of the Ontario Institute for Studies in Education, the University of Toronto and to D. Jean Clandinin of the University of Alberta for their contribution to my research and graduate student experience.

This study was generously supported by a Social Sciences and Humanities Research Council (SSHRC) of Canada Doctoral Fellowship.

Notes

1. This research was part of a larger study examining the ethnic identity of first generation Canadians in a multi-cultural school context (Social Sciences and Humanities Research Council (SSHRC) Doctoral Fellowship 752–2001–1769), which was in turn embedded in F. M. Connelly and D. J. Clandinin's long-term SSHRC-supported programme of research examining the diverse cultural landscapes of experience that students, parents, and educators bring to the professional knowledge landscape of an elementary school (Standard Research Grants—"Landscapes in Motion; Landscapes in Transition; "Landscapes in Transition; Negotiating Diverse Narratives of Experience"; and "Intersecting Narratives: Cultural Harmonies and Tensions in Inner-City Canadian Schools"). As I worked at Bay Street School, my observations and interactions with the teachers were guided by the following kinds of questions: What kinds of curriculum events and activities did the teachers plan? How do the teachers understand the home cultures of the students? How do they accommodate for the diversity of their students in their everyday interactions?

2. To learn about William and Dave's experiences of culture in the curriculum on this multicultural school land-scape, I interacted with them over the course of hundreds of hours of school visits. I began observations at the school during the spring of 2000, and continued until the spring of 2003 for the larger project of which this study is part. Field notes for this study were written during the 2000–2001 school year I spent with William and his teaching colleague, Dave, and their combined classes of 71 grade-8 students at Bay Street School. I wrote field notes following school visits, staff meetings, field trips, classroom observations, school assemblies, and interaction with members of the school community at events such as Multicultural Night, Curriculum Night and School Council meetings. These field notes, along with interview transcripts, researcher journals, and theoretical memos, were filed in an existing project archival system. I also collected documents such as school notices, announcements of community and school events, notices posted on bulletin boards and classroom walls, agendas and minutes from School Council meetings, newspaper clippings of local media coverage, and samples of student work to learn about ways in which the interaction of diverse cultures played out in the school context.

3. The neighbourhood community from which the student population is drawn reflects immigration patterns of recent immigrants into Toronto. Families who have recently immigrated to Canada settle in the community (Makhoul 2000) before moving to suburban communities as they become more established.

4. He was just a few months into his first year of teaching at the time.

5. School Councils were established by the provincial ministry and local school boards, in part, to facilitate the process of parents and teachers working together (Ministry of Education and Training 2004a, b).

6. Although teachers may not have much choice in this matter, since teachers at Bay Street School seem to accept parental decisions about whether their children are permitted to participate in specific curriculum activities or not, the students whose parents did not grant them permission were deprived of the enjoyment and educational value of the activity.

References

Ada, A. F. (1988) The Pajaro Valley experience: working with Spanish-speaking parents to develop children's reading and writing skills through the use of children's literature. In T. Skutnabb-Kangas and J. Cummins (eds.), *Minority Education: From Shame to Struggle*, Clevedon, UK: Multilingual Matters, 223–238.

Ali, N. (2004) Meaning-making for South Asian immigrant women in Canada. Doctoral dissertation, University of Toronto.

Ball, D. (1990). Reflections and deflections of policy: the case of Carol Turner. *Educational Evaluation and Policy Analysis*, 12(3), 263–275.

Banks, J. A. (1995) Multicultural education: its effects on students' racial and gender role attitudes. In J. A. Banks and C. A. M. Banks (eds.), *Handbook of Research on Multicultural Education*, Toronto, ON: Prentice-Hall, 617–627.

Chan, E. and Ross, V. (2002) Report on the ESL survey: sponsored by the ESL Workgroup in collaboration with the OISE/UT Narrative and Diversity Research Team, Toronto: Centre for Teacher Development, Ontario Institute for Studies in Education of the University of Toronto.

Clandinin, D. J. and Connelly, F. M. (1994) Personal experience methods. In N. K. Denzin and Y. S. Lincoln (eds.), *Handbook of Qualitative Research in the Social Sciences*, Thousand Oaks, CA: Sage, 413–427.

Clandinin, D. J. and Connelly, F. M. (1996) Teachers' professional knowledge landscapes: teacher stories—stories of teachers—school stories—stories of schools. *Educational Researcher*, 25(3), 24–30.

Clandinin, D. J. and Connelly, F. M. (2000) *Narrative Inquiry: Experience and Story in Qualitative Research*, San Francisco, CA: Jossey-Bass.

Cohen, D. K. (1989) Teaching practice: plus ça change. In P. W. Jackson (ed.), *Contributing to Educational Change: Perspectives on Research and Practice*, Berkeley, CA: McCutchan, 27–84.

Cohen, D. K. and Ball, D. L. (1990) Policy and practice: an overview. *Educational Evaluation and Policy Analysis*, 12(3), 347–353.

Connelly, F. M., and Clandinin, D. J. (1988) *Teachers as Curriculum Planners: Narratives of Experience*, New York: Teachers College Press.

Connelly, F. M. and Clandinin, D. J. (1999) Stories to live by: teacher identities on a changing professional knowledge landscape. In F. M. Connelly and D. J. Clandinin (eds.), *Shaping a Professional Identity: Stories of Educational Practice*, London, ON: The Althouse Press, 114–132.

Connelly, F. M., Phillion, J. and He, M. F. (2003) An exploration of narrative inquiry into multiculturalism in education: reflecting on two decades of research in an inner-city Canadian community school. *Curriculum Inquiry*, 33(4), 363–384.

Cummins, J. (1996) *Negotiating Identities: Education for Empowerment in a Diverse Society*, Ontario, CA: California Association for Bilingual Education.

Dewey, J. (1938) *Experience and Education*, New York: Simon & Schuster.

Igoa, C. (1995) *The Inner World of the Immigrant Child*, New York: St. Martin's Press.

Kouritzin, S. G. (1999) *Face(t)s of First Language Loss*, Mahwah, NJ: Lawrence Erlbaum Associates.

Makhoul, A. (2000) *Ryerson Community School—Where You Belong*. Caledon Institute of Social Policy. Available online at: http:www.caledoninst.org, accessed 5 May 2005.

McCaleb, S. P. (1994) *Building Communities of Learners: A Collaboration among Teachers, Students, Families and Community*, New York: St. Martin's.

Ministry of Education and Training (2004a) *About the OPC: History and Role of the OPC*. Available online at: http://www.ontarioparentcouncil.org/about_the_opc/default.asp?load=contributions1, accessed 14 September 2004.

Ministry of Education and Training (2004b) *School Councils*. Available online at: http://www.ontarioparentcouncil.org/school_councils/Default.asp?language=English, accessed 14 September 2004.

Moodley, K. A. (1995) Multicultural education in Canada: historical development and current status. In J. A. Banks and C. A. M. Banks (eds.), *Handbook of Research on Multicultural Education*, Toronto, ON: Prentice-Hall, 801–820.

Paley, V. G. (1995) *Kwanzaa and Me: A Teacher's Story*, Cambridge, MA: Harvard University Press.

Phillion, J. (2002) Becoming a narrative inquirer in a multicultural landscape. *Journal of Curriculum Studies*, 34(5), 535–556.

Rodriguez, R. (1982) *Hunger of Memory: The Education of Richard Rodriguez*, Boston, MA: David R. Godine.

Schwab, J. J. (1973). The practical 3: translation into curriculum. *School Review*, 81(4), 501–522.

Statistics Canada (1998) 1996 Census: Ethnic origin, visible minorities. Available online at: http://www.statcan.ca/Daily/English/980217/d980217.htm, accessed 19 September 2005.

Statistics Canada (2003) *Census of Population: Immigration, birthplace and birthplace of parents, citizenship, ethnic origin, visible minorities and Aboriginal peoples*. Available online at: http://www.statcan.ca/Daily/English/030121/d030121a.htm, accessed 19 September 2005.

Wong-Fillmore, L. (1991a) When learning a second language means losing the first. *Early Childhood Research Quarterly*, 6(3), 323–346.

Wong-Fillmore, L. (1991b) Language and cultural issues in the early education of language minority children. In S. L. Kagan (ed.), *The Care and Education of America's Young Children: Obstacles and Opportunities.* 90th Yearbook, Part 1, of the National Society for the Study of Education, Chicago: University of Chicago Press, 30–50.

30

Silence on Gays and Lesbians in Social Studies Curriculum

Stephen J. Thornton

Imagine, as was once the case, that today's social studies curriculum measured all else against a standard of being male, Protestant, and Anglo-Saxon.[1] Women, African Americans, Catholic and Eastern Orthodox Christians, Jews, and Muslims, not to mention other religious, ethnic, and racial groups, would react with righteous outrage. With justification, we can claim that today's social studies curriculum has become more inclusive of a range of groups and perspectives within and beyond the United States.

Although still imperfect, the contemporary K-12 social studies curriculum has moved away from the tacit equating of "American" with, for example, Protestant, or Christian for that matter. At least one major exception to this legitimation of diversity persists: it is still tacitly assumed that everyone is heterosexual until proven otherwise. Despite striking growth in social, political, legal, and media presence of gays in American life, especially in the past decade,[2] few social studies materials appear to have substantive treatment of gay history and issues. Indeed, many of these materials fail to even mention such words as homosexual, straight, or gay. It is as if the millions of gay inhabitants of the United States, past and present, did not exist. Although scholarship studied in colleges is now sometimes rich with gay material, Americans who do not attend college—and the least educated are precisely those who are most inclined to be prejudiced against gay people[3]— are unlikely to hear of such scholarship.

The belief that the archetypal human is straight is called *heteronormativity*. It belies an inclusive curriculum. Moreover, it encourages stereotypes. As James Banks has warned, using a "mainstream" benchmark against which group differences are measured promotes "a kind of 'we-they' attitude among mainstream students and teachers."[4] Banks's observation about multiethnic education seems equally applicable to the study of homosexuals: "Ethnic content should be used to help students learn that all human beings have common needs and characteristics, although the ways in which these traits are manifested frequently differ cross-culturally."[5]

Heteronormativity goes basically unchallenged in teaching materials for K-12 social studies. Unless children are raised in a limited number of locales or have teachers who go beyond what the textbook provides, they may graduate from high school being none the wiser that heteronormativity paints an inaccurate picture of social life and perpetuates intolerance, sometimes with tangibly destructive consequences such as harassment and physical violence.[6]

Curricular Limitations of Current Inclusion

The social studies curriculum, because it must make some attempt at describing the world as it is, has always dealt with "difference." The debate, as Margaret Smith Crocco shows, has centered on what the differences are and how they have been dealt with.[7] The common failure even to mention the existence of lesbians and gay men (let alone bisexual and transgender persons) clearly clashes with gay matters today being a visible part of the public landscape in most of America. Thus, a first step that social studies educators need to take is frank acknowledgment that differences in sexual orientation (and other taboo subjects such as religion) exist in America.[8] To put it another way, educators must answer the question, Does everybody count as human?[9]

One current and widely used U.S. history high school textbook is illustrative of the current failures. In its treatment of postwar African American novelists, James Baldwin is described as writing about "patterns of discrimination" directed toward blacks. This point is placed as a precursor to the struggle against racial injustice in the civil rights era.

The text is silent, however, about Baldwin's being both African American and homosexual. He wrote eloquently of "patterns of discrimination" directed toward gay men. For example, in *Giovanni's Room* and in *Another Country*, which were written in the same postwar and civil rights period of American history, Baldwin explores how young gay men fled prejudice in family and community in the United States for the relative anonymity of Paris.[10]

This silence on homosexual expatriate writers stands in stark contrast to the treatment of heterosexual expatriate writers. U.S. history textbooks routinely discuss the "lost generation" of the 1920s, the group of literary artists such as Hemingway and Scott Fitzgerald who, disillusioned with American materialism, traveled to Paris searching for meaning. Their fictional characters and the motives of these characters are frequently canonized in high school history textbooks, while Baldwin's fictional gay characters and the motives of his characters go unmentioned.

The same silences that characterize the American history curriculum appear in global history and geography. Take the subject of human rights. There has been a great deal of attention, especially since September 11, 2001, to the oppression of Afghan women by the harsh, extremist brand of Islam embraced by the Taliban. Properly, this denial of basic human rights to women has widely stood condemned both in the West and in the Islamic world. But no such condemnation of systematic persecution of gay men (or allegedly gay men) in parts of the Islamic world, such as recently in Egypt, appears in the curriculum although, as with Afghan women, the persecution rests on these men simply for being who they are.

Social studies courses most directly devoted to citizenship, such as government and civics, routinely extol the freedoms Americans enjoy because they are Americans. That such freedoms still extend only to some people and not to others, however, is likely to go unmentioned in textbooks. For example unlike important allies such as the United Kingdom, of whose armed forces in Afghanistan and the Persian Gulf we have heard so much recently, U.S. armed forces legally discriminate against lesbians and gay men. Although American youngsters will certainly study American freedoms in social studies courses, they may never be told or question that other closely associated nations also extend freedoms to gays that are denied them in the United States. American history and government texts justifiably vaunt our belief in self-evident rights dating back to at least

1776; they omit that some of these rights are selectively available depending on a person's sexual orientation.

The limitations of the current curriculum, however, run deeper than exclusion from history and other courses. Although acknowledgment of the humanity of gay people and democratic tolerance for them should be fundamental, these aims fail to strike at the heart of heteronormativity. While it is generally acknowledged that the social studies should prepare young people for citizenship, gay people are vulnerable to the way freedom to participate fully in the affairs of the state is defined. At present, as Nel Noddings writes, it seems that "to improve their status, the vulnerable must either become more like the privileged or accept some charitable form of the respect taken for granted by those acknowledged as full citizens."[11] In other words, even if gay people were identified as gay people in the curriculum, this begs the question of what should be said about them and from what perspectives.

The Hidden Curriculum Everybody Sees

The hidden curriculum of schools rigidly patrols the boundaries of sex role behavior. Homophobia is common in American schools.[12] Although unmentioned in the publicly announced curriculum, all young people learn that sex role deviance, actual or perceived, exacts a heavy price. It is surely one of the most successful exercises in social training that schools perform. Moreover, this unannounced curriculum functions in practically all schools regardless of racial and ethnic composition, social class, and so forth. Indeed, young people who are themselves oppressed by poverty, crime, or racial mistreatment frequently become oppressors of peers perceived to be gay.[13]

Whether by choice or neglect, school professionals are implicated in patrolling sex role boundaries.[14] In corridors and classrooms, for example, few if any taunts are more common than "fag," and embedded in history textbooks are messages about what it means to behave in a "masculine" fashion.[15] In other parts of school grounds such as parking lots, bathrooms, and locker rooms, where youngsters are frequently unsupervised by adults who know them, sex role deviations sometimes meet with physical violence.

There seems to be a variety of motives for how teachers respond to all of this. Some teachers may be afraid of being labeled "gay" if they correct students for bigoted behavior. Disturbingly, some teachers appear to agree with condemnations of perceived departures from "normal" sex roles; girls must be "feminine" and boys must not be "effeminate." They may ignore, and sometimes even encourage, harassment of students perceived to be gay. Administrators and teachers may counsel harassed students to avoid "flaunting" their allegedly deviant behavior, in effect, blaming the victim.[16]

What is clear is that administrators and teachers are not being neutral or impartial when they ignore this hidden curriculum. Silence, far from neutral, implicitly condones continuation of the persecution. Studies have long shown that depression and suicide are far more common among youngsters who are gay than among their straight peers.[17] School professionals—classroom teachers, administrators, counselors, and librarians—are frequently the only responsible adults to whom these at-risk children can turn for both needed support and equal educational opportunities.

Toward More Inclusive Curriculum

It is too easy for educators to feel absolved of responsibility because authorities have frequently omitted gay people and gay issues from curriculum documents and materials. Moreover, censorship of gay material is commonplace. Ominously, these forms of neglect exist alongside a persistent countermovement. Every step forward for the well-being of gay students and a curriculum more inclusive of lesbian and gay experience has been doggedly challenged by anti-gay groups.[18]

Teachers have choices. All teachers are curricular-instructional gatekeepers—they largely decide the day-to-day curriculum and activities students experience.[19] How teachers enact curriculum, even with today's constraints such as standards and high-stakes tests, still matters both practically and ethically. Opportunities to incorporate at least some gay material into the standard curriculum exist; in many instances, all that is required is the will to call attention to aspects of standard subject matter that heretofore went unmentioned.

Quite a few inclusion opportunities in mainstay secondary school courses such as U.S. history, world history, and geography present themselves. No U.S. history survey textbook that I have seen, for instance, omits Jane Addams. She is rightly portrayed as one of the nation's greatest social and educational thinkers and activists, not to mention her formidable work for world peace. Addams never married. She chose to spend her adult life among a community of women and had a long-time special relationship with one woman.[20] This may raise ample opportunities for properly directed class discussion: What did it mean that a considerable number of educated women of Addams's means and generation chose to forsake marriage and pursue careers beyond domesticity? Were they models for gender equity for later generations of women's rights and equity advocates?

Note, we have not directly addressed Addams's sexual orientation. (The evidence, in any case, seems inconclusive.) Perhaps more important than a rush or need to judge, however, is to ask if this woman's accomplishments would be diminished or enhanced by such knowledge. Or a primary educational objective could be to understand how Addams, who rejected some gender conventions for her day, helped shape her times and her legacy for today. Her significance, in this scheme, incorporates the complexities and controversial aspects of her life as well as speaking to different but nonetheless related questions today.

Other topics such as the ancient world in global history courses provide different pathways to incorporate the gay experience. Again, let me underscore that we are still working with standard material in the curriculum. No new instructional materials are required. Specialist knowledge, while as desirable as ever, is unessential.

Take the topic of Alexander the Great. One high school world history textbook I examined, for example, shows how, through his military genius and statesmanship, Alexander built a "multicultural" empire. Although adjectives such as "multicultural" (and "gay" for that matter) are anachronistic here, the point for today's readers seems plain enough: Alexander was a leader, probably before his time, in building what we might call today an inclusive society.

Here we might pause to challenge how inclusive (or "multicultural") this textbook treatment is. No mention is made of Alexander's homosexuality. Teachers, however, could readily place Alexander's homosexuality in its cultural and temporal context. In those terms, his sexual orientation was relatively unremarkable. Sensitively approached, such a perspective may lead students to rethink stereotypes of both warriors and homosexuals.

Classical Greece provides numerous opportunities to explore beyond the information given. Textbooks routinely feature photographs of idealized male images such as Greek athletes and actors. Why did the Greeks so prize the male form? What does it reveal about their culture? How does it relate to today's notions of athleticism and the arts? How is the ideal of male community perpetuated by today's college campus fraternities?

Of course, gay materials may also be an instructional focus rather than ancillary to the main part of a lesson or unit. In U.S. history courses, a unit on the civil rights struggle of the 1950s and 1960s is standard. These days a wide range of groups in addition to African Americans are often featured in this unit, such as Latinos, women, Native Americans, and so forth. But seldom does this extend to gay people. Such a unit could be made more genuinely inclusive if it also included a lesson devoted to a turning point in civil rights for gay people, such as the 1969 Stonewall riots in Greenwich Village, New York City.

Although much more the exception than the rule, teachers in some parts of the country have designed instructional sequences on gay topics longer than a lesson or two. One civics teacher, for example, as part of a nine-week unit on "Tolerance and Diversity," included a two-week mini-unit on "Homophobia Prevention." He has written of the experience and materials he used.[21]

Current events instruction is also a ready site for dealing with gay material. By way of illustration, recently published secondary school American history textbooks are silent on the "history" of former U.S. President Bill Clinton's "don't ask, don't tell" policy for gays in the military. Teachers, however, could still treat this rights topic in the classroom because the media report on it with some regularity. A good issue for critical thinking might be why the number of persons discharged from the armed forces for their homosexuality has continued to rise in the decade since the supposed implementation of the policy.[22]

Conclusion

Even concerned and willing educators face some significant obstacles to incorporating gay material in the curriculum. Many veteran teachers may never have studied gay material during their preservice teacher education programs, either in academic or professional courses. As noted, this situation has changed somewhat in the academy today in courses in history, the social sciences, and literature. In teacher education, too, the situation has altered. "Student sexual diversity guidelines for teachers" now appear in some teacher education textbooks, for instance.[23] Furthermore, explicit training for and sensitivity to inclusion is now common in teacher education programs in diverse regions of the nation. We probably shouldn't expect, however, in-service workshops devoted to gay subject matter to arise everywhere in the nation any time soon. But nearly everywhere the legal realities of protecting the rights of gay students, if nothing else, may compel some staff development.[24]

Heteronormativity is also a concern because many students in our schools now have parents who are gay or lesbian. These children have the same rights to an equal education as do their peers whose parents are heterosexual. About ten years ago, however, a storm of controversy erupted in New York City when it was suggested that the children's book *Heather Has Two Mommies* even be allowed as an option to be included on a several-hundred-page list of curriculum ideas on diversity from which teachers might choose.[25]

Although it is now most noticeable in large cities, many schoolchildren across the nation have lesbian or gay parents. Yet only "traditional" families tend to be included in the curriculum. Despite *Heather's* apparent sensitivity to appropriate treatment for the intended age group, this failed to prevent its being removed from the list of suggested (not mandated) books. However, at least some more encouraging reports of teachers addressing the issue of nontraditional families have appeared more recently. For example, one New York City teacher reported on positive outcomes from teaching a novel to middle school students that concerned a boy coming to terms with his father's being gay.[26]

If we are to be inclusive in the social studies curriculum, then the kinds of changes I have sketched here are vital first steps. The alternative, if many educators perpetuate heteronormativity, is that most young people will continue to learn about homosexuality through a popular prejudiced lens.

Notes

1. Frances FitzGerald, *America Revised: History Schoolbooks in the Twentieth Century* (New York: Vintage, 1980).
2. Suzanna Danuta Walters, *All the Rage: The Story of Gay Visibility in America* (Chicago: University of Chicago Press, 2001).
3. Patricia G. Avery, "Teaching Tolerance: What Research Tells Us," *Social Education* 66, no. 5 (2002): 270–275.
4. James A. Banks, *Multiethnic Education* (Boston: Allyn and Bacon, 1988), 177.
5. Ibid., 175.
6. Human Rights Watch, *Hatred in the Hallways: Violence and Discrimination against Lesbian, Gay, Bisexual, and Transgender Students in U.S. Schools* (New York: Human Rights Watch, 2001).
7. Margaret Smith Crocco, "Dealing with Difference in the Social Studies: A Historical Perspective" *International Journal of Social Education* (in press).
8. Rahima Wade, "Diversity Taboos: Religion and Sexual Orientation in the Social Studies," *Social Studies and the Young Learner* 7, no. 4 (1995): 19–22.
9. Stephen J. Thornton, "Does Everybody Count as Human?" *Theory and Research in Social Education* 30, no. 2 (2002): 178–189.
10. See James Baldwin, Giovanni's Room (New York: Modern Library, 2001) and Another Country (New York: Dial Press, 1962).
11. Nel Noddings, "Caring, Social Policy, and Homelessness," *Theoretical Medicine* 23 (2002): 441.
12. For an analysis of this state of affairs, see Margaret Smith Crocco, "The Missing Discourse about Gender and Sexuality in the Social Studies," *Theory into Practice* 40, no. 1 (2001): 65–71 and "Homophobic Hallways: Is Anyone Listening?" *Theory and Research in Social Education* 30, no. 2 (2002): 217–232.
13. Kevin C. Franck, "Rethinking Homophobia: Interrogating Heteronormativity in an Urban School," *Theory and Research in Social Education* 30, no. 2 (2002): 274–286.
14. Human Rights Watch, op. cit.
15. Jeffrey J. Kuzmic, "Textbooks, Knowledge, and Masculinity: Examining Patriarchy from Within," in *Masculinities at School*, ed. Nancy Lesko (Thousand Oaks, CA: Sage, 2000).
16. Perry A. Zirkel, "Courtside: Gay Days," *Phi Delta Kappan* 84, no. 5 (2003): 412–413.
17. Human Rights Watch, op. cit., 75.
18. See, for example, People for the American Way, "Right Wing Watch: Back to School with the Religious Right," www.pfaw.org/pfaw/general/default.aspx?oid=3652, accessed February 4, 2003.
19. For elaboration of this point, see Stephen J. Thornton, "From Content to Subject Matter," *The Social Studies* 92, no. 6 (2001): 237–242 and "Teacher as Curricular-Instructional Gatekeeper in Social Studies," *Handbook of Research on Social Studies Teaching and Learning*, ed. James P. Shaver (New York: Macmillan, 1991).
20. Jean Bethke Elshtain, *Jane Addams and the Dream of American Democracy: A Life* (New York: Basic Books, 2002).
21. Brian K. Marchman, "Teaching about Homophobia in a High School Civics Course," *Theory and Research in Social Education* 30, no. 2 (2002): 302–305.
22. David Harris has developed a scoring rubric for classroom discussions of controversial issues, in which he uses this issue as the running example. See David Harris, "Classroom Assessment of Civic Discourse," in *Education for Democracy: Contexts, Curricula, and Assessments*, ed. Walter C. Parker (Greenwich, CT: Information Age, 2002).
23. See, for example, Myra Pollack Sadker and David Miller Sadker, *Teachers, Schools, and Society* (Boston: McGraw Hill, 2000).
24. Zirkel, op. cit.
25. Leslea Newman and Diana Souza, *Heather Has Two Mommies* (Boston: Alyson Publications, 1989).
26. Greg Hamilton, "Reading 'Jack,' " *English Education* 30, no. 1 (1998): 24–39.

31

Curriculum and Teaching Face Globalization

David Geoffrey Smith

Globalization is a term now circulating frequently in both popular media as well as formal academic disciplines. It has many meanings, some of which are contestable, others simply descriptive. This chapter attempts to lay out the general parameters of the term as it has evolved historically and, in the process, explore some implications of globalization for the field of curriculum studies. Basically, my argument is that there are three forms of globalization operating in the world today: Globalization One, Two, and Three. Globalization One is the dominant form arising from what can broadly be called the revival of radical liberalism, or neoliberalism, dating back to the administrations of Ronald Reagan and Margaret Thatcher in the 1980s. Globalization Two represents the various ways that people around the world are responding to Globalization One through acts of accommodation or resistance. Globalization Three speaks to the conditions that may be emerging for a new kind of global dialogue regarding sustainable human futures. Especially in this last context, I restrict my remarks to the realm of curriculum and pedagogy.

The 1995 ninth edition of the *Oxford English Dictionary* contains no elaborated definition of *globalization*, noting it only as a noun drawn from the adjective *global*, meaning worldwide. This speaks of how the density of the term as now used is a relatively recent phenomenon, signifying the coalescence of a number of important developments within the political economy of world affairs. The late semantic arrival also speaks of how globalization does not refer simply to such things as trade between peoples and groups, or other kinds of intercultural exchange, because these have been part of human experience from the earliest of times. Instead, globalization has specific reference to fairly recent developments that may in turn be acting to form a new kind of imaginal understanding within human consciousness. As a species, we may be imagining ourselves in new ways, especially with respect to issues of identity and citizenship.

To say this, of course, displays in itself a certain intellectual conceit with its own history. After all, who has the right to speak for the world, for others? In terms of raw numbers, most people in the world have never heard of globalization and maybe never will. Those who participate in its discussions do so out of privileged access to communications, travel, and information technologies, which are tied to various politics of representation, with legacies from the period of Euro-American colonialism extending from the 15th century to the present. Thus, although the technologies may be new, their production and use still reflect nonresolutions inherent within those legacy relationships. Eighty-five percent of all information about Africa, for example, lies in U.S. and European data banks (DeKerckhove, 1997). In a way, then, contemporary globalization is an old phenomenon in a new guise.

Globalization may especially refer to a particular kind of tension in the world, arising from what Arnove and Torres (1999) called "the glocal" (p. 14). Human self-understanding is now increasingly lived out in a tension between the local and the global, between my understanding of myself as a person of this place and my emerging yet profound awareness that this place participates in a reality heavily influenced by, and implicated in, larger pictures. This calls forth from me not just a new sense of place, but also a new kind of response to the world. It is a response I may feel uneasy about making given that so much about what seems to be going on is experienced preconceptually precisely because no one, no authority, can tell me exactly what is happening.

So it is that globalization is fraught with various new kinds of identity crises, ranging from eroding senses of national identity to unprecedented losses of indigenous languages and cultures under the homogenizing pressures of global capital. Within these crises of identity lie conundrums especially relevant for curriculum studies, difficult questions about epistemological authority, about how knowledge is produced, represented, and circulated, and perhaps especially about the auspices of curriculum work. Within the dominant mode of globalization theory, neo-liberal market theory, Herbert Spencer's classic question in the 19th century about what knowledge is of most worth has been replaced by another: How much is knowledge worth? In turn, another question is begged: Is knowledge to be the ultimate arbiter of worth?

A final introductory remark is needed on the importance of positionality as a marker within globalization debates. What Marshall McLuhan (cited in Benedetti & Dehart, 1996) once said of technology may also be true of globalization; whether it is good or bad in some philosophical sense may be beside the point. The real point is to carefully examine its effects within the life structure of human experience. Doing this, it can easily be seen that what is happening today in the name of globalization is benefiting certain rather small groups enormously, whereas for others the influence may be nothing short of catastrophic. In between are the many people simply trying to make a life together in new kinds of conditions. Within all of this is woven a form of economic theory that, in the words of political philosopher John McMurtry (1998), is embedded in "an acculturated metaphysic that has lost touch with the real world outside of its value program" (p. 136). The most important challenge for curriculum work in the new millennium may be to develop the ability to deconstruct precisely as theory the unquestioned assumptions underwriting regnant forms of global economic procedure. Without this, curriculum work, even in the name of justice and equity, will hit its head against a wall. The key is to find a way through the wall to change the thinking that constructs it. As economic historian Karl Polanyi (1944/1989) said earlier in this century, this is the age of *Homo Economicus*, economic man (sic). At least for those in power, everything has come to be defined in economic terms (Kuttner, 1996). Conflicts over globalization in the contemporary world may be driven by nothing less than the determination to put *Homo Economicus* in his place. All these and other issues are taken up later. First, however, attention is given to how globalization has arisen as a defining trope—not just for curriculum studies, but for everyone concerned about the future of the Blue Planet.

Globalization One — *dominant form from liberalism or neoliberalism*

To think about the future, it is best to work backward, tracing trajectories to the present moment, carefully working out the lineages that have brought current conditions into being.[1] Only then can thoughts of "what is to be done" be meaningful. Most immediately, the language of globalization began to emerge in the late 1980s with the collapse of the binary logic of the cold war, a political dualism that had defined the international balance of power since the end of World War II. If in the mouths of its espousers the language of globalization is today aggressively triumphalist in tone, this is because a moral and intellectual victory has been claimed, a certain right to speak and act in a way deemed vindicated by current events. This of course is short-sighted because the situation is not so simple. Especially dangerous is the historical amnesia suffered by those claiming "the road ahead" to be clear (Gates, 1996), that history has come to an "end" (Fukuyama, 1993), or that "there is no alternative" (Thatcher, 1995).

The cold war was a legacy of a particular struggle within the Euro-American empire dating from the Industrial Revolution of the 19th century. Contrary to popular opinion, constructed through Western media, the West did not win the cold war. Its conclusion was much more a compromise settlement to discontinue counterproductive policies that were draining the economies of both sides. The Eastern bloc had begun to suffer seriously from one form of implosion, the West from another. For the East, state control of a planned economy had produced high employment but limited innovation and stagnation of markets, with a consequent rise in social anomie ameliorated only by mythic patriotism and escalating militarization.

For the West, self-confidence was eroded by a number of converging factors: the failure to sustain public support for colonial venturing (Vietnam war); the determination of Middle Eastern states to assume greater control over their petroleum resources (OPEC oil crisis, 1971); the emerging economies of Asia (Japan, Korea, Taiwan, Malaysia, etc.) being able to produce goods for U.S. and European markets well below the cost of those produced at home; the computer and technology revolutions that essentially gutted the middle class running paper-driven ships of state and Fordist manufacturing systems since World War II; and the emergence of *post* theory (poststructuralism, post-colonialism, etc.) that served to threaten both the autonomy and authority of the entire narrative underlying Western civilization.

The end of global binary logic made possible in the minds of some a vision of opening markets worldwide within a new borderless world guided not by states and nations per se, but by the newer institutions of global reach, such as the International Monetary Fund (IMF) and the World Bank (WB) along with the United Nations (UN) and the North Atlantic Treaty Organization (NATO). This vision, which was the foundation of both the Reagan and Thatcher administrations of the United States and United Kingdom, respectively, during the early 1980s became the lynchpin of the economic theory now known as *neo-liberalism*. Based on the ideas of Milton Friedman and Fredrick von Hayek, neo-liberalism redefined the rules of obligation between governments and peoples to privilege the free operation of a global market system over the state as the primary means for solving social problems. This policy turn provided the basis for an assault on public services especially in those countries falling under the orbit of Anglo-American influence (the United Kingdom and the United States, along with New Zealand, Canada, and Australia), with the application of business principles to most sectors of the public domain. Privatization of public services was emphasized, along with the cultivation of *enterprise culture* (Keat & Abercrombie, 1990).

For education, the application of neo-liberalist principles has resulted in a host of actions designed to change both the nature and delivery of educational work. Some of the more important features can be noted as follows:[2]

[handwritten: neo liberals principles]

1. vigorous attempts to delegitimize public education through documents such as *A Nation at Risk* and *The Holmes Report*, highlighting the failures of public schools rather than their successes;

2. treating education as a business with aggressive attempts to commercialize the school environment as well as make it responsible to outcomes or product-based measures;

3. emphasizing performance and achievement indicators as a way of cultivating competitiveness between schools and districts;

4. privileging privatization initiatives through strategies of school choice and voucher systems;

5. giving strict financial accounting procedures precedence over actual pedagogical need;

6. assaulting teacher unions to deregulate teacher labor to make it more competitive;

7. downloading educational management to local board authorities (site-based management) while retaining curricular and policy authority within state (hence now market) hands;

8. tying the financing of education to target projects, such as the technologization of instruction and the privileging of science and technology subjects in schools and universities to serve the needs of global industrial competitiveness;

9. adopting a human capital resource model for education, whereby curriculum and instruction work should be directed at producing workers for the new globalizing market system;

10. invoking the language of life-long learning to abate concerns about the end of career labor (expect to lose your job frequently, and reskill, as companies need to perpetually restructure to remain globally competitive);

11. aggressive generating of curriculum and educational policies by noneducation *[handwritten: Yikes]* groups such as the Business Council on National Issues (Canada), the Business Roundtable (U.S.), the Trilateral Commission, the International Monetary Fund, and the World Bank (thereby accelerating efforts to harmonize curricula across nations and states to enhance the mobility of workers and bring more states into the globalizing web of the new economy);

12. separating debate and discussion of pedagogical issues, such as how children best learn and how teachers can best teach humanely from issues of educational management; and

13. pressuring governments around the world into accepting these actions as a condition for joining the new international trade cartels such as the World Trade Organization (WTO).

During the cold war, curriculum work was ideologically and rhetorically linked to the effort of producing citizens who would support one path over another. International aid programs in education were couched in the language of *development*; they were thinly veiled attempts to win ideological loyalty within a dichotomous structuration of global power. It may well be asked what shall be the organizing principle for curriculum work today? Many writers (Greene, Giroux, McLaren, Apple, etc.) speak to the need for more widespread vigilance in the protection of democratic principles, calling for increased participation of all the world's people in the decision-making processes that ultimately affect them. It is precisely on this point, however, that neo-liberalism, as the rallying call for global market liberalization (Globalization One), runs into difficulty.

Usually *market liberalization* is linked in a semantic pair with *democracy*, but in actual practice the two terms are contraindicative. For example, the installation of the various free trade agreements in the Americas since the late 1980s (The Free Trade Agreement [FTA]; The North American Free Trade Agreement [NAFTA]) made education linked to the language of tradeable goods and services. These agreements were both negotiated and implemented largely without public debate and certainly without due popular consent (McMurtry, 1998). Indeed, various writers have suggested that democracy is a problem for market liberalization because democratic process impedes the speed of decision making necessary for gaining and maintaining commercial advantage. Ian Angel (cited in Gwyn, 1996), professor of Information Systems at the London School of Economics, recently said that "(since) the disposable income of the majority is being reduced, the big question of the coming decades is how to find an acceptable means of scaling back democracy" (p. 16).

The Freidman/von Hayek argument that freedom of the market means freedom of persons is questionable on numerous grounds, not least of which is the way true freedom of thought is compromised when the results of thinking are judged by assumptions deemed to be beyond the scrutiny of thinking. Under such a condition, the end always justifies the means. Tight media control of information, subjugation of alternative knowledges, to say nothing of electoral fraud within constitutional democracies to produce desired results: All these are symptoms of the contemporary crisis of democracy under the reigning dispensation of neoliberalism.[3]

According to British writer, John Gray (1998), it is important to see the neo-liberalist version of globalization as essentially an Anglo-American vision that is attempting to haul the rest of the world into its rules of operation. Historically, it is linked to the history of the European Enlightenment ("The U.S. is the world's last great Enlightenment regime" p. 27), in which it was assumed that (a) because the operation of human reason is the same everywhere, (b) all reasonable people will abide by the version of reality that reason draws and maps for them. According to Immanuel Kant, the chief proponent of this view in the 18th century, any other response, such as that based on emotion, intuition, or deference to convention or other authority, is a sign of "self-incurred immaturity" (Schmidt, 1996).

Historically, it can be argued that the dream of the universality of a single logic (the Enlightenment ideal) is primarily a religious conception tied to monotheism and, in the European context, to Christianity and the vision of a unified Christendom that guided Europe from the days of Roman emperor Constantine in the 4th century C.E. (after his conversion to Christianity) to the breakdown of Christendom under scientific secularism in the 20th century. What we are left with today under Globalization One is a secular residue of the Christendom ideal, with economic theory providing a theological (Loy, 1998) justification for the new universal operation of The Market as God (Cox, 1999).

It is by this logic that a fundamental bifurcation is occurring within the global imaginary. Within the agenda of Globalization One, anything that does not fit the formula of its operations is described as an *externality* (McMurtry, 1998)—an anomaly that will eventually disappear through atrophy or irrelevance, but never to be addressed as bearing any pedagogical news, so to speak, something that could/should be engaged creatively. For example, one can think of neo-liberalism's appropriation of the postmodern emphasis on the ambiguity of language and the dynamic pluralism inherent in the human condition. Within the operation of neo-liberalism, ambiguity and pluralism get folded into another fetish of commodification, whereby the play of meaning becomes a rationale for the endless display of semiotic referentiality under the code of commercial innovation. A more creative response, pedagogically and globally speaking, might be to open the possibility of deconstructing economic theory to show not just how it subjugates alternative knowledges and ways of being, but also how its survival depends on the continuance of such subjugation.

The agenda of Globalization One has had a number of interlocking results that continue to reshape the landscape of both local communities as well as international human understanding. Control of the international economy is increasingly concentrated in fewer and fewer hands through the operation of giant multinational firms such as General Electric, IBM, Ford Motor Company, and Royal Dutch Shell. The largest 300 multinational corporations control 25 percent of all the world's productive assets, 70 percent of all international trade, and 99 percent of all direct foreign investment (see Clarke, 1997). The loyalty of these huge firms is less to the country of their national origin than to new virtual communities of international stockholders. The result is a diminishment of the tax bases that national governments are able to wrest from commercial ventures, which in turn affects the quality of social programs local communities can offer citizens.

The competitiveness of international enterprise also means that firms move frequently to take advantage of labor market conditions, regardless of the politics of local regions, so that in the name of market freedom and democracy, the corruption of local political regimes is often ignored.[4] Firms now enter into joint venture contracts with countries whose policies only 20 years ago would have been regarded as abhorrent. This has led critic William Greider (1997) to ask:

> What was the Cold War really all about? Was it about securing freedom for enslaved peoples, as every patriot believed, or was it about securing free markets for capitalism, as Marxist critics often argued? The goal of human rights that leading governments once described as universal has (now) been diluted by a new form of commercial relativism. (p. 37)

The technological innovation that has been pivotal in the development of globalization processes carries with it new kinds of moral consideration that especially arise when the impact of technology on struggling economies is revealed (Rifkin, 1996). For example, until recently, the islands of Madagascar, Reunion, and Comoros used vanilla production as their export ticket to the global economy. From the tropical climbing orchid, they produced 98 percent of the world's vanilla, selling it on global markets for U.S. $1200 per pound. By 1996, Escagenetics Co. of America was able to produce vanilla genetically for U.S. $25 per pound. The economies of three Indian Ocean islands have thus been completely undermined.

The most important influence of the new technologies of information has been the virtualization of international finance or the development of the new globalized "Casino Economy" (Clarke, 1997). Today, financial transactions of more than $3 trillion are conducted daily by banks, financial services institutions, and speculative market funds. The operation of the international economy is now profoundly disembodied. Entire countries like Brazil, Thailand, and Mexico have been bankrupted in a matter of days through the virtual flight of financial speculators. Although regulations are now in place to prevent the kinds of global collapse that seemed imminent in the mid-1990s, the vulnerability of the new international virtualized market system cannot be underestimated. Again, virtualization means neglect of the needs of concrete existence at the local level.

Other impacts of Globalization One that cannot be elaborated on here include: (a) the new feminization of labor through global electronics and garment industries,

and women's politicization in developing countries (Sassen, 1998); (b) population migra-
tions by political refugees, migrant workers, and postsecondary students who are changing
the ethnic composition of Euro-American communities (e.g., in England, English is no
longer the native tongue of the numerical majority; Pennycook, 1996); and (c) the emerging importance of global cities involving the transformation of traditional urban-rural
linkages (Sassen, 1998).

Finally, brief but important mention needs to be made of the influence of the new
information technologies as vehicles for the production and dissemination of knowledge
under Globalization One. The Internet is a product of Euro-American technical development, and it is rapidly transforming traditional understandings of knowledge and
pedagogy. Access to information (at least certain kinds of information) may be becoming
more democratized at the same time as the Web is becoming a place of alternative kinds of
community building and personal networking.[5] The long-range impact of these developments on curriculum and policy is difficult to assess at the present time. However, it is fair
to say that, by and large, teachers are intimidated by the new technologies, and the costs
of maintaining the technical infrastructure of Web-based instruction are proving prohibi-
tive for local schools. If the 20th century was predicted by late 19th and early 20th century
social planners to be "The Century of the School" (Tomkins, 1976), it may be safely
predicted today that what survives of the school into the 21st century will be quite different from what currently prevails.

Globalization Two   — how people respond to globalization !

If a radicalized interpretation of Market Logic is now providing the theoretical underpin-
ning for social development of all kinds around the world, it is important to register
that this interpretation is not univocally or unproblematically accepted.[6] Media control as
a deliberate strategy of Globalization One (Schiller, 1989) has meant that citizens within
the Anglo-American nexus have, to a large extent, been shielded from facing the true
complexities, contradictions and contestations that are at work within the actual unfolding
of globalization processes. This is partly because the orthodoxies of Globalization One rest
on one important and troublesome assumption to which allusion has already been made,
which is the belief that because history has been transcended by a new universal logic,
history should be forgotten or rendered irrelevant to the true requirements of the
contemporary situation. This is a problem that is endemic to the logic of power: Once
power has been achieved, the process of getting there suffers amnesia. Slavery; subordination of women, gays, lesbians, and people of color; colonial history; genocide of
aboriginal groups; environmental degradation—all these remain as mnemonic ghosts
within the imperial tale, either waiting in the wings for their own moment of truth or
pushing hard against the grain of dominant interpretive frames.

In terms of economic theory alone, there are many different models at work in the
world today, each connected to long traditions of civic obligation. Each plays into the
emerging system of Globalization One, but on its own terms fighting to protect the rights
of its citizens against the assumptions of radical monetarism. For example (see Broadbent,
2001), for most countries of the Organization for Economic Cooperation and Development, technical innovation and globalization forces have produced ever-widening gaps in
income between social classes and regions. Anglo-American governments have allowed the
disparities to deepen and become even more entrenched. Continental governments like

Sweden, France, and Germany, in contrast, have taken steps to remain internationally competitive while maintaining strong social charters. In Canada today, child poverty levels stand at 25 percent; in Sweden, only 2.5 percent of children live in poverty. While the government of Ontario in Canada embarks on a program of dismantling its public education system in favor of privatization, the governments of Germany and the Netherlands have increased spending to enhance already fine public education systems.

Asian countries like Japan, China, and Korea have strong Confucian traditions that make loyalty to family and state virtually coterminous, in such a way that the state economy holds strongly to its social obligations (Gray, 1998). Full employment is more important than high GNP even if much employment is menial and could easily be replaced by technology, such as the operation of department store elevators.

In terms of curriculum policy, Singapore provides the example of preparing citizens who can work for the new multinational corporations that have set up in the country (Spring, 1998). Emphasis is on learning new international languages (English, German, etc.), but also on social attitudes of tolerance and harmony arising from Confucian values. As a reward for citizens, the government eliminated all individual taxes.

In the new South Africa, the path taken by the government for economic regeneration has meant forced compliance with educational and social policies dictated by the IMF and the WB, emphasizing an open door policy to educational institutions from overseas countries, especially England and the United States. The University of Lancashire, for example, now offers degree programs in different parts of the country. This creates new kinds of tensions for South Africans. As one teacher reported recently (Nwedamutswu, 2001), "We have only just won the war against the colonial oppression of apartheid. Now almost immediately our ability to produce and teach our own knowledge is being taken away from us again." This was not meant as a repudiation of globalization processes per se, but as a request that sensitivity be shown to the specific histories of people, and that concern for ownership of the means of knowledge production cannot be separated from those histories.

Japan, long admired in the West for an educational model based on a strict examination system producing high results on international math and science tests, has now acknowledged the human cost of such a system (Asanuma, 2000). Lack of creativity, severance of learning from learning to live, and the production of debilitating stress among students are all products of the old educational priorities. Today, a reform movement is afoot to make learning more relevant to learning to live: to live healthily, with respect for nature, and within a more harmonious rhythm balancing intellectual and social needs. A New Course of Studies has been developed, in which students learn how to grow their own vegetables, cook and sew, visit with the elderly and handicapped, and practice other basic life skills as part of a curriculum designed to foster a more well-rounded understanding of citizenship.

In Latin America and the Caribbean, under the Structural Adjustment policies (SAPs) of the IMF and WB (Globalization One), spending on education in the poorest 37 countries declined 25 percent between 1984 and 1994. Costa Rica, for example, once had the highest literacy rate in the Caribbean due largely to a public education drive between 1950 and 1980. In 1981, the government was given an IMF loan on condition that education expenditures be cut.

Mexico once had a public education system safeguarding equality of access for all students and staffed by teachers who had one of the strongest unions in the hemisphere. Most teachers were of peasant origin and were committed to land reform and other attempts to democratize Mexican life. In return for debt relief, Mexico was one of the first *yikes again* ✗

this is just unethical!

to inaugurate social reforms under the mandate and surveillance of the WB and IMF. Teacher salaries, already low, were cut by 50 percent. The public education system began to be dismantled, with industry-school partnerships put in place to transform education to serve the needs of industry (Barlow & Robertson, 1994).

Resistances are now growing against these kinds of Globalization One developments (Lemus, 1999). The Trinational Coalition (Canada, United States, and Mexico) in Defense of Public Education was formed to lobby governments to protect public education as a social right. The Coalition participated in the civil unrest surrounding the meetings of the World Trade Organization (WTO) in Seattle in 2000. Of particular concern was the potential under Globalization One practices for control of education to be taken over by foreign educational services companies, ostensibly to assist in the building up of the knowledge economy globalization processes are thought to require. What happens, then, to national identity when non-nationals take charge of education?

☆ As John McMurtry (1998) suggested, the "knowledge based economy" might better be termed "the ignorance-based economy" because under it, "rationality" and "knowledge" become "absurd expressions" (p. 187). What genuine knowledge development requires quintessentially are conditions of impartiality and wider comprehension. A commercially based education system cannot provide these because the first canon of such a knowledge economy is that "what does not sell [directly or indirectly] corporate profits is refused communication" (p. 181). "As public education is increasingly stripped of its resources and bent to the demands of the global market, the only remaining institutional ground of human intelligence and reason is undercut" (p. 192).

The Pembina Institute of Canada has undertaken work to show that the standard measures of prosperity used by governments as yardsticks of civil progress—the Gross National Product (GNP) and Gross Domestic Product (GDP)—do not actually provide a realistic measure of the overall health of a population (see *www.pembina.piad.ab.ca*). For example, for both GNP and GDP, marriage breakdown is a positive contributor to the economy. Many sectors of society benefit economically from divorce (e.g., counseling services, legal professions, furniture companies, automobile companies, the real estate industry, etc.); all these stand to gain from the troubles of family breakdown. But what is the human cost of such troubles, even into the second and third generations, as capacities for trust and commitment are imperiled by experiences of betrayal and the breaking of faith between persons? The Pembina Institute developed what is called the *Genuine Progress Indicator* (GPI), which attempts to more realistically balance the social gains and losses from the different economic policies that governments put into effect.

Richard Sennett's (1998) excellent study of the effects of the new workplace under Globalization One ("Just in Time" production processes, the need for a highly mobile contract-based labor force instead of career-based labor, the need for constant reskilling as technology changes, etc.) illustrates that the most fundamental change in human experience currently underway may concern the experience of time. As Sennett expressed it: "The conditions of time in the new capitalism have created a conflict between character and experience, the experience of disjointed time threatening the ability of people to form their characters into sustained narratives" (p. 31). What is created is a new kind of character that is "both successful and confused"; monetarily successful perhaps, but highly confused over the question of what it means to live well with others. The idea of *lasting values* that can sustain a character over time remains nothing but an idea—something to discuss with vigor and passion, but also something completely disconnected from personal experience.

It is on this question of values that the enduring issues of globalization will be worked out. If *Homo Economicus* is just one *homo* among many, and one whose values are increasingly seen as problematic, what shall be the source and nature of alternative values? This is a matter of central preoccupation for writers in the field of globalization studies. Burbules and Torres (2000) have linked this to "the question of governability in the face of increasing diversity" (p. 22).

Responses to the issues surrounding governability and values vary. Huntington (1999) suggested that uncertainty inherent in the current situation may lead to a *clash of civilizations* as global power blocs fight for dominance in a time when no one bloc seems capable of maintaining control over the totality.

Another response is to retreat into the perceived security of past responses—what may be named as the response of *fundamentalism* (Marty & Appleby, 1994). Fundamentalism today takes many forms, from religious fundamentalism, to neo-tribalism, to a dogmatic entrenchment in the realm of pedagogy of such notions as *back to the basics* and *tough love*. Fundamentalism always thrives in times of cultural confusion, offering clear and simple [*interesting*] answers to questions that are difficult and long range in implication.

In the next section, under Globalization Three, some suggestions are made regarding how the future may best be engaged during this time of permeable borders, increased worldwide mobility, and media and technology that are changing the shape and character of human self-understanding. The remarks are organized and sketched out specifically around issues of curriculum and pedagogy, and some personal examples are provided.

Globalization Three   *— conditions emerging from New global dialogue → sustainable human futures*

In the 1980s, East Indian social theorist Ashis Nandy (1988) undertook a study of assumptions about childhood that can be perceived in various global contexts. He then developed a taxonomy for those assumptions—a heuristic that can be useful in exploring directions for curriculum and pedagogy in the age of globalization. According to Nandy, children and the young around the world are typically used and abused in four different ways:

1. When they are used as projection targets for unresolved adult desires and conflicts (i.e., when parents, teachers, and significant adults use children to complete their own personal senses of lack);

2. When *childhood* is used in a semantics of dystopia against the utopian logic of development. In such a case, terms like *childish, infantile*, and *immature* are used against an idealized and mythical binary of *adult* maturity as a way both to discipline the young as well as protect adulthood within a static and contained self-definition. This was/is a primary strategy of colonial domination, in which the colonized were/are infantilized within the power logic of the "adult" colonizer;

3. When children and childhood are used as the battleground of cultures. A key example of this is when school curricula are written specifically to induct the young into a particular ideological viewpoint or historical perspective. For example, as part of its new neo-liberal agenda, the Grade 3 Social Studies curriculum for Alberta, Canada defines *community* as "a place where people trade in goods and services." Current Palestinian textbooks do not depict Israel on maps of the Middle East as a way of teaching that the Middle East is an Arab-Muslim world (Steinitz, 2001). Until recently, Japanese textbooks legitimized Japanese imperial

invasions of Asia during World War II as acts of liberation against Western domination; and

discuss 4. When, in technical/rational cultures like the West, the *idea of childhood* takes precedence over *the real child.* Here, a number of things can happen. For example, children become isolated as a sociological variable that can then be used by social engineers within a calculus of social and capital development. Within this set of assumptions, children have no interlocutionary power within the overall social framework. Also under this assumption, the specific flesh and blood needs of specific children can be ignored under generalized theories of childhood, perhaps the most insidious being the romanticization of the young, which leaves them abandoned to the cage of their own subjectivity.

As a political psychologist, Nandy suggested that, instead of using children as projection targets, as a model of dystopia against adult maturity, as ideological puppets, or as the object of scientific research and management, adults and children best live together in a condition of *mutuality*. It is in recognition of this condition of mutuality between adults and children that may lie the unique contribution of the field of pedagogy to discussions of globalization and curriculum.

Donald Tapscott (1998), an influential writer about the Digital Age, suggested that if schools are to survive at all, they should be places not of teaching and pedagogy in the usual senses, but gathering places for people wanting both information and a place where information can be shared and deliberated.

> Teaching is becoming a less unidirectional process and much more collaborative and heuristic. I've heard many tales of students and teachers working together to implement technology in the classroom and more important new models of learning. All this gives evidence to the view that one of the most powerful forces to change the schools is the students themselves. (pp. ix–x)

Indeed, one of Tapscott's main arguments is that it is the Net Generation of young people who are leading the way in globalization's *techne*. From this viewpoint, globalization is a generational issue.

Here we see an inversion of the orthodox understanding of pedagogy as being always adult driven. Instead, there is a recognition of the young as partners in the journey toward a mutual maturity. This does not mean a relinquishment of responsibility of elders for the young, but a noting that one of the key responsibilities is to try to genuinely hear the young, to engage them conversationally about the affairs of life so that the world between them might be a truly shared one. This can be suggested in response to the findings of a recent documentary film team of the Public Broadcasting System (2001) for the program "Frontline." The film, *Lost Childhood*, documents the youth culture of a suburban Georgia community in the United States (see *http://www.pbs.org* for details) ironically just prior to a shooting incident at the school that received international attention. One of the most outstanding features of the culture was the apparent abandonment of the young by the adult community under a logic of self-interest. Each person, adult and youth, is given the right to follow his or her own interests, but the human consequences are astonishingly somber. There seems to be no basis for an ethic of mutual caring under a rubric of radical autonomy. No common meals: pick up your food and go to your own private bedroom to watch your own private TV. In this condition, both adults and children are lost to each other.

"Adultomorphism," as David Kennedy (1983) described it (endeavoring to turn children into replications of the adult self to serve the needs of that self) is a foundational strategy of conservative culture, whether that culture be religious, ethnic, economic, or pedagogical. The most notable characteristic of all educational reform prescriptions coming from Globalization One institutes and think tanks is indeed their adultomorphic nature: They show virtually no interest whatever in the impact of their formulations on the lives of children and youth. Nor do they show any interest in what possible contribution the young might make to any shared future, other than the future imagined within the neo-liberal agenda. It is on this point that further work is needed, the point of mediation between old and young with respect to how to proceed together, how to share a life. It is a point on which experienced teachers may have some important things to say. Here, two aspects are noted and then elaborated as examples.

First, in any condition of healthy living together, humanly speaking, there must be a sharing of the horizons of understanding among the people involved. Second, the subjects and practices of study must be taken not as inert and self-contained (e.g., commodifiable), but as always and inherently conversational, open-ended, and teleologically oriented to overcoming the alienation between human beings and between humans and the larger world (the sense of Self as different from Other and from World). In other words, successful study is oriented to peace, which is not to prescribe a suffocating absence of conflict, but to acknowledge that all learning involves resolving the resistances that demarcate the line between what is known and what is yet to be known. True learning means breaking the barriers and chains of ignorance and entering a new world in such a way that I and the Other become understood as One, as participating in a reality whose commonness transcends us both. In this case, Other can be understood as curriculum, as other person, as tradition, even as enemy. Learning to share a life together involves acknowledging and accepting that the work of this sharing, and the labor of coming to a mutual understanding of it, is never over, always ongoing, and sustainable only under the shadow of love. These points can be elaborated as follows.

Curriculum and Pedagogy as a Sharing of the Horizons of Understanding

As a teacher, I enter the pedagogical relationship through my own biography, which includes my formative experiences in the world, my training, and my aspirations for both myself and my students. So too does each of my students enter the pedagogical relationship in such a way. Unless there can be a sharing of these stories as a condition of our coming together, there can be no basis for our mutual advancement because it remains perpetually impossible to know who is talking; without such knowledge, what is present to be learned can only remain detached and alienated from those involved. Biographical stories do not need to be shared all at once, but their presentation within the ongoing work of the pedagogical journey is what makes the difference between a pedagogy of domination/subordination and one based on a relation of trust and mutual engagement. In the Advanced Curriculum Research course for doctoral students at the University of Alberta, for example, both students and professor participate in the Who Is the One Researching? (WITOR) project. Members work together to clarify the relations between their own biographies and the respective research projects that holds their interest.

The effect of such efforts is twofold. On the one hand, actually hearing the stories of others becomes a liminal reminder of the impossibility of corralling all of these stories into one conceptual or interpretive schema, except of course the schema of difference. On the other hand, it is precisely the schema of difference that brings people to an awareness of the need for deep tolerance and acceptance—the qualities without which there can be no community, no sense of common belonging. Sometimes the conundrum inspired by the irony is the site of provocation—a prelude for hermeneutic breakthrough. This was the case, for example, in another class discussing an article on gay and lesbian experience. Students from China reacted in horror to the possible sociocultural acceptance of gays and lesbians, relating stories from their own cultures of how such people are treated. Facing a lesbian student in the class, someone who had already gained their respect and trust before *coming out* induced a genuine sense of bewilderment and puzzlement, a new genuine openness to learning, and a reciprocal sharing of assumptions and understandings about sexuality generally.

The sharing of horizons can easily become stuck in a kind of self-aggrandizing narcissism if an effort is not vigilantly made to show how the dynamic at work in the pedagogical situation has reference in the broader world. That is, the sharing of horizons points to the way my horizon is never just *my* horizon, but one that opens out onto that of another and, as such, is in a condition of perpetual revision toward a more comprehensive understanding and appreciation of the broader world. In this instance is gained the appreciation for how no one story can tell the whole story, and that hermeneutic suspicion is best directed at pretensions to the same—pretensions to a univocal and monological theory of globalization, for example. The economistic determinism at the heart of the neo-liberal agenda of Globalization One must be exposed for the way it limits other ways of human expression and common living (e.g., through aesthetics, spirituality, and altruism).

The sharing of horizons within communities of difference helps break down the dichotomy between the private and public spheres, and may serve as a kind of prelude to a theory of justice that honors difference while holding every difference accountable to its influence in the broader public realm. It is one thing to hold private views and to honor the right to privacy for those views. Yet in the age of globalization, where persons and groups now rub shoulders in new and unforeseen ways, the time may soon be near when more open expression of personal convictions is necessitated by the requirement to understand more fully and more publicly the lived-out implications of privately held (including privately held by groups and communities) beliefs. In my graduate seminar on religious and moral education, for example, each person is encouraged to publicly articulate the convictions of their own faith community regarding other faith communities. This becomes a means of facing difference, lifting it out of the realm of abstraction and conceptualization, and embodying it in relations between persons. It is one thing for a Seventh Day Adventist student to state as an abstract principle of theology for his faith community that "the Pope is the Antichrist"; it is quite another to state it while facing directly a Roman Catholic friend and colleague in the class, surrounded by others now deeply invested in the outcome of such facing. These others are invested partly because the future of the class—its tone, its pedagogical receptiveness, its future possibilities as a place of secure freedom—depends on it. They are also invested because they recognize in such a confrontation an exemplification of their own relations of difference, so that the outcome of this specific case becomes prototypical for the resolution of their own personal challenges.

This kind of *outing* of difference also assists in helping students better understand the way their assumptions about others are historically constructed; as such, they must be reexamined and reinterrogated for their time boundedness. Of course, historicization as a strategy for opening dialogue contains its own theory of history, and it must be recognized that it does not work well within and among communities where history is taught as a rigid anamnesis—a memorization of how we got to this point as a way of legitimizing why at this point we should never change. Resolving that difficulty must be reserved for another day; here the pedagogical assumption is that history is open or better, that the future is always open, and that an orientation in the present to an open future is an absolutely necessary precondition not only for a world that is more fair and just, but also for one that may be inspired by hope.

One of the conditions, then, that the sharing of horizons brings into the classroom can be called the condition of *mnemonic reparation,* which has special relevance for curriculum in the age of globalization. Nigerian playwright, essayist, novelist, and poet, Wole Soyinka (2000), has called for an international movement to make possible a new kind of reparation in the world for past wrongs, past injustices. This new kind of reparation would not be monetary ("Reparation is not monetary recompense"), but a recovery and making public of the subjugated memories of oppressed peoples. For an *interesting* example, Soyinka pointed to the UNESCO commitment to the preservation of the slave routes in West Africa, establishing a scientific committee to document, preserve, and open up the landmarks of the slave routes for posterity. In such a way, Africans around the world can better concretize their history to turn it into a living voice within the emerging global community. Also, such mnemonic acts reveal the interdependent nature of every identity.

Curriculum and Pedagogy as Being Oriented to Peace

The best way to understand this is through a kind of phenomenology of learning, which may be exemplified through attending closely to the learning act. Good examples can be found in the practice of learning to play a musical instrument. Contrary to conventional Western theories of musical practice, which are oriented by the desire for personal pleasure, performance, or even aesthetic achievement narrowly understood, the Confucian tradition of ancient China always taught music as a way of shaping character—helping students understand something important about relations in the world. In Confucianism and Chinese, *wen* denotes "the arts of peace" (Waley, 1992, p. 39), and they include music, dance, and literature.

How is learning to play a musical instrument an art of peace or an act of peacemaking? One does not need to be an expert to come to appreciate this; every diligent student has moments of realizing what is happening through good practice. To every student, beginner or experienced, come occasional moments of sensing deeply that what is at work in the playing can be ascribed to neither the instrument nor the practitioner nor the musical score alone. Instead, a mysterious unity has been achieved when all three seem to participate in a reality, a truth even, that transcends any of the individual aspects. It truly is a moment of peace, a moment of letting go—of ego, culture, worry, or otherness. It becomes an entry into quiet wonder—a sense that as a human being one participates in a most amazing and wonderful mystery. In piano playing, sometimes simply striking a single note and listening deeply and carefully to its reverberation into the broader world can produce a sense of participating in something that is large and beyond easy conceptual rationalization. In flute playing, there come moments when the breath seems to lose all resistance to the instrument, so that breathing into the instrument becomes the perfect extension of breathing naturally. It is an experience of amazing freedom, in which as a player one feels completely in communion with the instrument, and the air seems pure, clean, cool, and fresh.

Other examples are easy to find. Suddenly discovering the sheer beauty of a Wordsworth poem, the elegance of a quadratic equation, or the wonderful variegation of wood grain in a shop class: All of these experiences constitute a new kind of reconciliation with the world. The finding of the poem not to be brute and inert perhaps as expected, the equation not to be simply a mad random puzzle, and the wood to speak its own story: This kind of finding is a form of self-finding, a finding of oneself in the things of the world, indeed a finding of the world to be a place where I can find myself to be truly at home. This is what is meant in saying that genuine learning is oriented to peace.

Such learning, however, has its own requirements, and it is precisely these that find little support in a view of education driven solely by commercial or economic interests. For one thing, such learning requires the nurturing of sustained attention. Staying with the subject or object of study until it begins to reveal itself to you so that you may engage it requires discipline (<L. *discere*, "learn"), which also means the ability to follow something to its true end—that is, to the end of its revelation. In this sense, true learning is a life's work. Margaret Atwood, Canada's leading novelist and writer, recalled once being at a cocktail party talking with a famous heart surgeon, who proclaimed, "When I retire I'm going to write a novel," to which Atwood replied, "When I retire I'm going to perform heart surgery!" Real learning can never be fickle or supercilious; it involves deep attunement to the Way of life.

Commercial culture is built on a phenomenology of distraction, and children who are raised in it lose the capacity for sustained attention. The principle of lifelong learning that undergirds the new economy depends on keeping people off-balance, ready to move at a moment's notice, ready to leave one job to take another, to reskill for this, then that. What is undercut is the capacity for a job to be not just a job, but a life—a place to grow, develop character, learn about living, share relations with others deeply, and complexly. "Having a job," without being able to "make a living," is a recipe for social disaster, the manifestations of which first present themselves in the lives of children and youth.

For the classroom to be a place of peace seeking and peace finding, privilege must be given to it being a place where people can find themselves through their inquiries and through their relations with one another. Above all, it must be a place of care, having its own requirements. There needs to be an adequate material base; the size of the group must not be allowed to intrude on the possibility of forming healthy relations; the teacher must be possessed of true hermeneutic skill, to show the essential openness of life, and its conversational character; there must be a balance of relations between speech and silence; the curriculum must address real human issues and problems, connected hermeneutically to the lives of the students; and the teleological purpose of learning must not be determined in advance of its creative engagement, or at least its given auspices must be held up for regular reexamination. Perhaps above all, pedagogical living in the classroom oriented to peace operates in the tension between completion and incompletion, between knowing and what is yet to be revealed. Such is the foundation of hope.

Conclusion

It is in the nature of such a broad discussion of globalization and curriculum that *conclusion* is a misnomer. Yet what may be said by way of drawing things to an informal summation? Perhaps the most relevant thing to say about globalization in the contemporary context is to note it as a topic of widespread discussion. Indeed, the fact that people everywhere are using the term as a new kind of backdrop to discussions about a multitude of different issues may signify a new kind of awareness about the underlying singular comprehensiveness of the human condition—a condition in which, to paraphrase a principle from the field of ecology, each one of us is connected irreducibly to every other one. This may be taken as a new foundation for ethical relation in a human world increasingly aware of itself as sharing a common home on the earth, and any efforts to regress into older more parochial visions must be noted with alarm. *agreed!*

Notes

1. For a more detailed elaboration, see Smith (1999, 2000).
2. These are discussed more fully in Spring (1998); Ball (2000); Peters (1996); Barlow and Robertson (1994) and many other sources.
3. The Internet has become the place of gathering for alternative research and interpretation of events in the public domain. By way of example, for evidence of the ways the U.S. Republican Party obtained the presidency for George W. Bush through tampering with the electoral rights of African American voters, see the website *www.GregoryPalast.com.*
4. The support that the Canadian oil and exploration company, Talisman, indirectly gives to the government of the Sudan, and hence to its civil war with the local Muslim population, has been a topic of great controversy in Canadian media in recent years.
5. Outstanding sources of news include the Canadian Centre for Policy Alternatives (*www.policyalternatives.ca*) and the Black Radical Congress (www.blackradicalcongress.org).
6. For an excellent survey of organizations and movements that are attempting to define civil life alternatively to the scripts of Globalization One, see Starr (2000).

References

Arnove, R., & Torres, C. (1999). *Comparative education: The dialectic of the global and the local.* Lahman, MD: Rowman and Littlefield.

Asanuma, S. (2000, October 14). *The Japan educational reform for the twenty first century: The impact of New Course Studies toward post-modern era in Japan.* A paper presented at the Internationalization of Curriculum conference, East China Normal University, Shanghai, China.

Barlow, M., & Robertson, H.-J. (1994). *Class warfare: The assault on Canada's schools.* Toronto, Canada: Key Porter Books.

Benedetti, P., & Dehart, N. (eds.). (1996). *On McLuhan: Forward through the rearview mirror.* Toronto, Canada: Prentice-Hall.

Broadbent, E. (2001, May 25). It is all about rights. Political direction: The future of the left. *The Globe and Mail,* p. A11.

Burbules, N., & Torres, C. (eds.). (2000). *Globalization and education: Critical perspectives.* London: Routledge.

Clarke, T. (1997). *Silent coup: Confronting the big business takeover of Canada.* Ottawa, Canada: Canadian Centre for Policy Alternatives.

Cox, H. (1999, March). The market as God: Living in the new dispensation. *Atlantic Monthly,* 21–27.

DeKerckhove, D. (1997). *Connected intelligence: The arrival of web society.* Toronto, Canada: Somerville House.

Fukuyama, F. (1993). *The end of history and the last man.* New York: Avon.

Gates, W. (1996). *The road ahead.* Harmondsworth, England: Penguin.

Gray, J. (1998). *False dawn: The delusions of global capitalism.* London: Verso.

Greider, W. (1997). *One world, ready or not: The manic logic of global capitalism.* New York: Touchstone.

Gwyn, R. (1996, October 6). Voice of Angell provides hard truths. *The Toronto Star,* p. A17.

Huntington, S. (1998). *The clash of civilizations and the remaking of world order.* New York: Touchstone.

Keat, R., & Abercrombie, N. (1990). *Enterprise culture.* London: Routledge.

Kennedy, D. (1983). *Toward a phenomenology of childhood.* Unpublished PhD dissertation, University of Kentucky.

Kuttner, R. (1996). *Everything for sale: The virtues and limits of markets.* Chicago: University of Chicago Press.

Lemus, M. (1999, Fall). The millennium round and the social right to education. *Journal of Curriculum Theorizing*, pp. 97–103.

Loy, D. (1998). The religion of the market. In H. Coward & D. Maguire (eds.), *Visions of a new earth: religious perspectives on population, consumption and ecology* (pp. 55–78). Albany: State University of New York Press.

Marty, M., & Appleby, S. (eds.). (1994). *Fundamentalisms observed*. Chicago: University of Chicago Press.

McMurtry, J. (1998). *Unequal freedoms: The global market as an ethical system*. Toronto, Canada: Garamond.

Nandy, A. (1988). Reconstructing childhood. *In Tradition, tyranny and utopia*. Delhi: Oxford University Press.

Nwedamutswu, H. (2001, May 21). *Challenges in South African Education today*. A talk given to the Department of Secondary Education, University of Alberta.

Pennycook, A. (1996). *The cultural politics of English as an international language*. Toronto, Canada: Addison-Wesley.

Peters, M. (1996). *Poststructuralism, politics and education*. New York: Bergin & Garvey.

Polanyi, K. (1944/1989). *The great transformation: The political and economic origins of our time*. Boston: Beacon.

Public Broadcasting System. (2001). *Frontline: Lost childhood*. A documentary film.

Rifkin, J. (1996). The new technology and the end of jobs. In J. Mander & E. Goldsmith (eds.), *The case against the global economy and for a return to the local* (pp. 108–121). San Francisco: Sierra Club Books.

Sassen, S. (1998). *Globalization and its discontents: Essays on the new mobility of people and money*. New York: The New Press.

Schiller, H. (1989). *Culture inc.: The corporate takeover of public expression*. New York: Oxford University Press.

Schmidt, J. (Ed.). (1996). *What is enlightenment? Eighteenth century answers and twentieth century questions*. Berkeley: University of California Press.

Sennett, R. (1998). *The corrosion of character: The personal consequences of work in the new capitalism*. New York: W.W. Norton.

Smith, D. (1999). Economic fundamentalism, globalization and the public remains of education. *Interchange, 30*(1), 93–117.

Smith, D. (2000). The specific challenges of globalization for teaching and vice versa. *The Alberta Journal of Educational Research, XLVI*(1), 7–26.

Soyinka, W. (2000). Memory, truth and healing. In I. Amadiume (ed.), *Memory: The politics of truth, healing and social justice* (pp. 21–37). New York: Zed.

Spring, J. (1998). *Education and the rise of the global economy*. Mahwah, NJ: Lawrence Erlbaum Associates.

Starr, A. (2000). *Naming the enemy: Anti-corporate movements confront globalization*. London: Zed.

Steinitz, Y. (2001, June 2). It is an existential conflict about the very existence of the Jewish state. *Edmonton Journal*, p. H3.

Tapscott, D. (1998). *Growing up digital: The rise of the net generation*. Toronto, Canada: McGraw-Hill.

Thatcher, M. (1995). *The path to power*. New York: HarperCollins.

Tomkins, G. (1976). *A common countenance: Stability and change in Canadian curriculum*. Toronto, Canada: Addison-Wesley.

Waley, A. (1992). *Confucianism: The analects of Confucius*. New York: Book-of-the-Month Club.

32

Gender Perspectives on Educating for Global Citizenship

Peggy McIntosh

Defining Global Citizenship

The 21st century requires us to think about citizenship as extending far beyond the "city" from which the word derives, and the state and the nation with which it has also been associated. Throughout the history of the United States, the matter of what citizenship entails has been contested. But a citizen is generally defined as a person having duties, rights, responsibilities, and privileges within a political unit that demands loyalty from that person and extends protection in return. Since we are living on a shrinking planet and are made contiguous with others by technology, commerce, conflicts, international networks, and the environment, the question arises of how citizenship could be redefined if one of its dimensions were felt membership in a political and social unit that is the whole globe.

The very definitions of citizenship need to be changed before the political and social unit can be conceived of as the globe itself. Political definitions of citizenship would need to be augmented by more affective definitions. The ideas of loyalty, protection, duties, rights, responsibilities, and privileges would need to be expanded and multiplied to the point where one's loyalty and expectation of protection come not only from such units as the living place, province, or nation, but also from a sense of belonging to the whole world. Within this vast world, the marks of citizenship would need to include affection, respect, care, curiosity, and concern for the well-being of all living beings.

What would it take to be global citizens? I can answer only from my own experience and perceptions. I associate the idea of a global citizen with habits of mind, heart, body, and soul that have to do with working for and preserving a network of relationship and connection across lines of difference and distinctness, while keeping and deepening a sense of one's own identity and integrity.

I associate global citizenship first with several capacities of mind: 1) the ability to observe oneself and the world around one, 2) the ability to make comparisons and contrasts, 3) the ability to "see" plurally as a result, 4) the ability to understand that both "reality" and language come in versions, 5) the ability to see power relations and understand them systemically, and 6) the ability to balance awareness of one's own realities with the realities of entities outside of the perceived self. These capacities of mind may be developed through daily life anywhere and fostered in many ways. They do not require literacy. But in our technologically interconnected world—and through experience in reading, writing, imagining, and traveling—such mind capacities can become well developed. They do not fit well with the world of formal education as it is carried on in the

United States. But for me, they are key constituents of global awareness and they point toward values of transglobal communication and peaceful coexistence.

I also associate global citizenship with several capacities of heart: 1) the ability to respect one's own feelings and delve deeply into them, 2) the ability to become aware of others' feelings and to believe in the validity of those feelings, 3) the ability to experience in oneself a mixture of conflicting feelings without losing a sense of integrity, 4) the ability to experience affective worlds plurally while keeping a gyroscopic sense of one's core orientations, 5) the capacity to wish competing parties well, 6) the ability to observe and understand how the "politics of location" affect one's own and others' positions and power in the world, and 7) the ability to balance being heartfelt with a felt knowledge of how culture is embedded in the hearts of ourselves and others. These heart capacities can, I believe, be strong in many people who are not literate, and I observe that they are often quite weak in people who have a great deal of formal education. It is as though strengthening the muscles that allow one to compete in the economic realms of the capitalist world weakens the muscles needed for entertaining multiple emotional connections balancing many complexities of life.

I further associate global citizenship with related capacities of the physical body and the spiritual soul. The global citizen knows his or her body not as a tool for mastery or beauty, but as a body in the body of the world. We have both unique individuality and intricate, inevitable connection with other bodies in the local and global habitats we share. Knowledge of self and other, comparison and contrast between the self and others, plural understanding of the integrity of all beings, and a sense of balance between dependence and interdependence in the physical world are all elements in the development of a global citizen's sense of inhabiting and using a body. Knowledge of our mortality, knowledge that being born entails dying, is part of the wisdom of the body. Respect for our own and others' physical needs is part of the wisdom of the body.

I feel that the soul needs a certain sweetness to be that of a global citizen. Observing turbulence and stillness, comparing and contrasting the outcomes of various kinds of human desire and behavior, I think that the global soul seeks the nondestructive as it seeks to preserve the bodies that house souls. Yet I also see souls of global citizens taking part in the dangerous conflicts of the contentious world, engaging rather than withdrawing, in order that the personality may be put in the service of something larger than itself, and that danger and suffering may be alleviated.

What I have sketched here goes beyond most discussions of citizenship and bears the strong marks of my own experience working with women and doing research on gender relations. It seems to me that many of the qualities that I am defining as essential to global citizenship are qualities that are gender-related. That is, they have been especially delegated to, conditioned in, and rewarded in women. When females bring forth children or do the caretaking that is expected of us, we are automatically placed in obvious relation to other beings and must develop many capacities for plural seeing and feeling: capacities for comparison and contrast, hearing more than one voice, understanding more than one version of self-interest, being empathic persons who have the capacity to hold and to internalize, as our own, more than one version of reality. Women have been charged with caring about the decent survival of all. This charge deeply affects our development.

I do not know, and other researchers do not know, the extent to which these capacities in women are biologically based, and it is very hard to find this out through empirical research. Some must be, in part, biologically based. But if we observe changes over the last century in women's and men's lives in the industrialized world, it is possible to conclude that many forms of gender socialization in the past were based on invented notions of what is appropriate to males and females. Experimentation has shown that these notions can change. Only continuing experimentation can tell us now what the actual limits of male and female capacity are. I do not feel that the capacities for global citizenship and plural competency that I am describing are the purview of women alone, or that they should be. In U.S. society, this openness is, for example, common in small boys before the society delivers messages to them such as "boys don't cry," which weakens their sense of self-knowledge and undermines their ability to feel empathy or acknowledge vulnerability.

In any case, women's ascribed roles in all societies especially require attentiveness to others, and the capacity to hear and take in many voices, stories, and versions simultaneously. Without these capacities women cannot do well the tasks of caretaking they have been assigned. They entail what Jean Baker Miller terms "the emotional housekeeping of the world," and they are crucial to human survival (Miller 1976).

I believe that the transpersonal care and understanding that women have been asked to do is central to history and to citizenship. It is not, however, central to the discussion of citizenship that focuses on rights, responsibilities, and public duties. Insofar as the public world has been assigned to men, as men's definitions of what citizenship is about have prevailed in its definitions. Within patriarchy, male definitions of reality trump female experience. Behind the scenes of what is presented to us as "history," women make and mend the fabric of society. "Lower-caste" men are likewise expected to make and mend the fabric. Those who wield the most public power are seen to be the leaders of citizens, but in fact the alternative fabric of day-by-day maintenance of citizens exists in a world more or less out of sight of public discussion. This lateral work requires a patience and sensibility focused on "getting through" and "getting on," rather than "getting ahead." The nurturance of each generation depends on this lateral, ongoing way of sustaining life in the world.

Educating Global Citizens

I feel that in order to educate global citizens, we need to give young people in school training and support in the little-named skills of what Miller once called, in an unpublished talk, "finding one's development through the development of others," that is, the skills of working for, and wanting, the commonweal, the well-being of all. Young people need rewards for and experiences of caring as a vital part of citizenship and a vital aspect of themselves. In other words, they all need to respect and develop qualities in themselves and in the culture as a whole that were conditioned into women or lower-caste men, who were expected to make and mend the fabric of the society behind the scenes. For the whole point of making and mending the fabric is to keep the self and the habitat, social or ecological, alive and whole.

When the emphasis is put on making and mending the social fabric as a central value for all citizens, then the emphasis can shift, as I feel it should, away from "rights" to "needs" as the basis for local and global policy and care. I feel that "rights" are an invention by 18th-century European thinkers and are not biologically demonstrable. The hand of the Creator did not descend and present us with rights. Human needs, on the other hand, are empirically verifiable and are in all of us. Water, food, clothing, shelter, and meaningful connection with other human beings are basic needs without whose fulfillment we die. The ethos of global citizenship, I believe, must start with providing, and caring about providing, these basic human necessities, and the protections for the sustaining ecosystems that humans depend on.

Can U.S. educators muster the character needed to widen the sense of loyalty and care in themselves and in students beyond the units of family, team, class, school, town, city, state, and nation? At present, most teachers and their students have not been educated to think that good character might require thinking or feeling so broadly or plurally. For most, the United States as a nation is the outermost ring of the series of concentric loyalties suggested above. Beyond this national margin are other peoples and nations mostly seen as competitors, threats, or unknowns, none of them measuring up to the United States. Technology, however, insistently reminds us of our commonalities with others beyond our borders. The national values have not yet caught up.

Another obstruction to bringing what I see as empathetic and plural-minded global citizenship into education is that many educators and parents today in the United States would see compassionate values as undermining the society by undermining the innate nature of boys and men. A myth persists that male and female are "opposite" sexes, and a patriarchal conviction persists that male and female are not equally valuable. In fact, the sexes overlap; in many ways men and women are similar physiologically and psychologically. Either sex can be shown to demonstrate an edge in ability and capacity. Nevertheless, the myths of oppositeness and of male superiority require that males be protected from developing attributes that have been projected onto women. These attributes are seen to undermine, and even to contaminate, masculinity. Males, especially young males, may have strong competencies in the caring, the relationality, and the plural seeing that I think are essential for global citizenship. What is rewarded in them, however, is solo risk-taking and individualism, and if they are white males, a go-it-alone and "damn-the-torpedoes" kind of bravery without a balanced regard for, or awareness of, the outcomes for other people of one's behaviors. Resistance against the kind of global education that I favor is to be expected in the United States in this day and age, since it seems to undermine the values of white male individualism. I favor, however, a balance in all citizens between virtues that have been projected differentially onto people of different groups, on the theory that all of our human virtues carry some validity, and that relational aspects of our personalities are needed in everyone because our world needs plural-minded citizens with capacities for concern and compassion in every citizen.

Gender Roles and Global Education

It is my opinion that both men and women hold within them the capacities that have been projected onto those of the "opposite sex," or "opposite" races or ethnic groups. These capacities in and of themselves are neither negative nor positive. For example, in terms of gender among white people in the United States, individuation and bravery are important human qualities that both sexes would do well to cultivate, as both may be needed at some time in one's life and in the life of one's community. But patriarchy and white supremacy are strong societal frameworks in the United States. Each keeps rules, perceptions, standards, definitions, and control in the hands of a dominant group. Whether or not the members of the dominant group are nice people has no bearing on these dynamics. Within patriarchy, white supremacy, or any other hierarchical system, a power imbalance is inevitable; the attributes projected onto and rewarded in the dominant group count for more than the attributes projected onto and rewarded in members of a subordinate group. Roles projected onto and expected of women—like being attentive to and protective of vulnerable things—are not valued alongside of valor and acquisition of power for the self, as projected onto men, especially white men, in the United States. Cultural restrictions on developing into "whole" persons interfere with the development of global citizens who have individual integrity as well as cosmopolitan attentiveness to the existence and well-being of others. This balance, though I see it as wholeness, would be seen by many as "not strong enough, not male enough" within a U.S. context. So I see a need within school curricula to explore strength and courage more broadly and deeply, to offset the individualistic presentation of heroism, as it is frequently studied in our schools, with the study of goodness and strength in making and mending the fabrics of culture.

A related difficulty in educating global citizens in the United States may reside in the tepid response of many Americans to the idea of citizenship itself. The concept of leadership has had more appeal, as something muscular, tough, interesting, stimulating, and rewarding. And although patriotism has been a very strong emotion in the nation since September 11, 2001, I think that citizenship still has less appeal, being associated with obligations, docility, obedience, and good behavior. It could be that in the popular white mind, citizenship is to women as leadership is to men. Citizenship is not necessarily heroic, expressive, or creative. It is seen as involving responsibilities, duties, and what must be done without the status of social reward. Leadership is seen to enable individuality and special status, whereas citizenship is seen as a social leveler. The United States government prides itself on global leadership, on being out in front as the sole superpower. But in my view, as the 21st century begins, the administration of George W. Bush shows no capacity for, nor understanding of, global citizenship; that is, of belonging within an entity larger than the nation itself. It is hard to press for education of global citizens in a nation whose government is acting out the role of the independent, dominant, unapproachable, individualistic, lone power whose self-interest is seen as the ethos that should prevail throughout the world.

Despite the dominant cultural values of U.S. society and education, many valiant teachers have construed education more broadly and have attempted to do global teaching in the light of their own understandings of intelligence, growth and development for their students. I received some formal global schooling myself in the 1950s that is illuminating for me to think back on now. Remembering both its content and my resistance to the content sheds light on dynamics that I believe persist in the minds and hearts of many white U.S. citizens. This global education occurred because my parents were appalled when the United States dropped the atomic bombs on Hiroshima and Nagasaki in 1945. They became Quakers and pacifists and transferred me to a Quaker school when I was 15 years old. I thought that the plural and gender-fair education I received there was annoying and ridiculous. For example, I had a weird teacher by the name of Mr. Cleveland who taught World Religions, with an "s." It seemed to me that Mr. Cleveland wasted our time. He taught about Buddhism, Hinduism, Islam, Taoism, and Confucianism. I was in school to learn about "the best." I felt that he diluted the class with extraneous books and people. I was filled with scorn when he said there were many paths up the mountain of religious belief. I felt he should take an interest only in "the right path."

Having inflicted comparative religions on us, i.e., comparative "seeing" of a kind that I now believe that global citizens need, Mr. Cleveland went on to teach Semantics, which I also resisted intellectually and emotionally. In fairness, I should empathize with the self I was in those days. World War II had just ended, a war that may be considered a simpler war, morally, for the United States than any subsequent war we have been involved in. I was in a bipolar mode of thinking: win/lose, right/wrong. Mr. Cleveland complexified all that simplicity with the study of semantics. It upset me to be told that "what I say" may not be "what you hear." I believed there was or should be a direct transfer from one mind to another, and that given two different interpretations of what had been said, only one of the two could be right. And if we were right in World War II and the Germans and Japanese were wrong, why on earth did this teacher and his colleagues at my new school hold work camps in Germany and invite Japanese students to attend the school?

Another problem with Mr. Cleveland was that he introduced us to Theories of History. I wanted to hear only one theory, which went approximately this way: People encounter problems in their climb toward perfection. Wars and depressions are such problems, or setbacks. We are now in a post-Depression and postwar time and are making progress toward the millennium, when history will be further along toward perfection. Mr. Cleveland, however, gave us bizarre alternative versions: pendulum theories, spiral theories, progress theories, and descent theories. He said we could think about history as "coming down through the ages" or "coming up through the ages," and that each was a different conceptualization and that the differences were interesting. I was so impatient with this man's attention to differences!

The crowning stupidity, I thought, came when our class put on a play and instead of directing it himself, as head of the Drama Department, he appointed a student director. Though I was the student director, I thought this was a result of the fact that Mr. Cleveland simply didn't know what he was doing. John Dewey might have given several years of his life to know that teachers would actually do this kind of teaching in which students' growth and development are placed at the center of instruction. And I am now aware that his decision to empower a girl in the role of director was unusual in its time.

Moreover, the school had a policy of coeducation in all student offices. A boy and a girl must hold each office. This radical policy enforced coeducational sharing of power. It delivered a message that the school assumed boys and girls should have equal power, and that the school would be better if they did. As it happens, the Quaker Meeting for Worship, a one-hour silent meeting each week at which anyone might speak, had a correspondingly power-sharing feel to it. I found it a rather homespun event, since there was no pulpit and no male authority to preach to us as there had been at the other places of worship I had attended. I remember my particular embarrassment when women stood and spoke in Meeting. What did they know?

The pattern that I see here is that of a representative 1950s small-town, small-minded white middle-class "good girl" challenging everyone who was trying to give her a democratic and, in fact, a global education. Through internalized sexism and classism, I was rejecting teaching that offered us lateral answers to the question of who was competent, who was important, who had knowledge. The answer was everybody. Mr. Burton, the physics teacher, put it in so many words when he said, on the first day of class, "Physics is nothing but common sense wrapped around things you've seen all of your life. Ever since you were a baby hitting balls around your playpen, you have understood inertia and momentum. I just give you the names." So we were already in physics, and it was already in us. He made it seem as though we could all "do physics," because we already had. He also had us build batteries before we studied electricity, on the theory that in this way the boys would not feel they started out ahead of the girls, with a male affinity for science.

Mr. Burton seemed to me "too nice" for a Physics teacher. I heard that in another school a physics teacher said, "Physics is like Mt. Everest. Only a few of you will make it." I thought that made sense. Physics required heroism, and only a few survivors would live to tell the tale. In that other school students indeed fell off the mountain of physics, and if they lived to tell the tale, they compared their wounds, slings, casts, and scars, but they didn't love physics. Mr. Burton had a way of producing students who entered math and science fields, and my very shy lab partner, Ken Wilson, went on to win the Nobel Prize in Physics. It was not Mr. Burton's aim to produce Nobelists, but to be enabling for all of us. Everybody should be engaged and everybody should know that they brought to physics the authority of their own experience, even their infant experience, in the physical world. Now when I hear continual top-down comparisons made between industrialized nations and other nations, or between technological cultures and more indigenous cultures, I remember how the strong base of knowledge in all people was recognized by my Quaker teachers in a way that was impressive and exemplary for global education.

The Challenge for Teachers

This kind of education need not be confined to private schools. What it requires is the professional development of teachers who have cultivated a global sensibility or, in some cases, merely been given permission to bring their global sensibilities into school. Will this nation's domestic culture dare to produce students and teachers who practice thinking and connecting laterally? I think it is possible. It takes courage and imagination to bring to schooling more than we were taught to bring. But I feel that our current crises call for repair of a system that has settled for solipsism and a narrowly functional definition of citizenship that produces people who are employable and do not ask broader questions.

Moreover, I have found that teachers suffer from the same confinements that their students do. Many long to repair the damage done to them by the requirement that they leave their whole selves at home each day and teach from a very narrow segment of their perceptions and capacities, which too often means preparing students for standardized tests and unspeculative, normative ways of thinking. Though it may be hard to change schools and educational ideals, I have found through my experience that it is not so hard for teachers themselves to change if they feel they are recovering something they lost: their human breadth and their longing to help shape a world that is not torn apart.

For the last two decades, I have been working on professional development of teachers from my base at the Wellesley College Center for Research on Women. My main work is with the National SEED Project on Inclusive Curriculum, which I founded 17 years ago and have been codirecting with Emily Style since 1987. SEED stands for Seeking Educational Equity and Diversity. The program establishes teacher-led seminars in K-12 schools. Each seminar involves 10 to 20 committed teachers who meet each month to discuss questions like "What are we teaching?" and "What messages does our teaching deliver with regard to gender, race, class, culture, region, nation, and the world? What outcomes do we want of education? What works for students' and our own growth and development? Can we give our students a more complete picture than we were given ourselves, of the self and the world in their many dimensions? How can we make school climate, teaching methods, and curricula more gender-fair, multicultural, and global?" SEED seminars are powerful, and teachers are deeply changed by them. In some ways they resemble the format and assumptions of Quaker Meeting about the worth of all participants. They create space in which everybody speaks. There is no leading authority and there are no required texts, though there are piles of resources of many kinds. Teachers bring the authority of their own experience. They bring their life stories. The facilitators, whom we prepare for these seminars, receive many books and materials and videos, but it is up to them whether they want to use any of these. When teachers are in lateral spaces psychologically and are allowed to have their own conversations about what they know without outside pressure, then I think SEED replicates some elements of my Quaker schooling: comparative curriculum, reflective listening, and empowering assumptions about where knowledge resides.

But SEED seminars do not depend on any one spiritual tradition, and they improve on my own Quaker experience by teaching systemic seeing. They counter the usual U.S. ideology of individualism, in which the individual is seen as the unit of society, and the belief is that whatever one ends up with is what one wanted, worked for, earned, and deserved. SEED seminars acknowledge systems of power working both within our psyches and in the world outside us. They call forth participants' own deep experience of power. In the balance between testifying to one's own experience and hearing the testimony of others, those qualities that I define as belonging to a capacity for global citizenship are brought forth. The technique that I have named Serial Testimony is particularly relevant to global perspectives. Each member of a group speaks in turn, within a set amount of time, very often 1 minute, or at most 3 minutes. During a serial testimony there is no interruption, no "cross-talk." After a serial testimony there is no debate. The aim is to speak and to listen, to hear and be heard, to compare, contrast, and deepen one's understanding of oneself and others. The modes of Serial Testimony undercut politics-as-usual. For educators, they provide a rare and welcome relief from faculty meetings and other forums in which the talkers talk, the listeners listen, and a general feeling of malaise prevails.

SEED seminars have now been led in the United States, Canada, Latin America, and 10 Asian countries, and may be led in any language with any materials. Many international schools that had an entirely U.S.-based curriculum before teachers engaged in SEED seminars have developed curricula, including language study, that are respectful of their host countries. On the more immediate level, within the seminar, the respectful interactive mode includes everyone of every nationality and cultural group as an authority on his or her own experience. Cultural chasms are bridged in SEED seminars. By balancing what codirector Emily Style calls "the scholarship on the shelves" with "the scholarship in the selves," they do inner and outer work. The program was devised by women and bears the imprint of our plural socialization. It reflects the balance of self and other that is asked of all people doing relational tasks. In another metaphor of Emily Style, the curriculum is like an architectural structure built around students. Ideally it provides a balance of "windows" out to the experience of others and "mirrors" of the students' own reality and validity. When curriculum serves as both "window" and "mirror," students are helped to become whole-souled, complex people. I imagine them as potential citizens of the world, having developed both identities of their own and interconnectedness with others. We have found that when the curriculum serves students as both "window" and "mirror," their alienation and anger decrease, together with their violence toward themselves and others.

Interactive Phases and Global Citizenship Education

United States educational institutions merely replicate the power relations of the rest of U.S. society unless we intervene with correctives. One corrective lens that SEED seminars often use is a Phase Theory I developed in 1983. It is a typology called "Interactive Phases of Curricular and Personal Re-Vision." I devised it after observing changes in college faculty members as they brought Women's Studies perspectives into their liberal arts courses.

I saw that traditionally trained white faculty members in any discipline were likely to move from what I called a Phase I frame of mind, which is womanless and all white, to a Phase II frame of mind, which admits "exceptional others" to the discipline, but only on the terms already laid down. Both frames of mind are challenged by what I identified as Phase III thinking, in which all women, and men of color, are seen as a problem, anomaly, absence, or victim, both in the academic world and in the aspect of the world that the discipline encompasses. Phase III is about coming to see systemically, and to understand local and global issues of, racism, sexism, classism, homophobia, anti-Semitism, nationalism, militarism, colonialism, and other kinds of power dynamics.

I see Phase III as an improvement on the womanless and all-white Phase I and the "exceptional others" flavor of Phase II. It is far wider and more accurate than teaching based on the ideology of individualism. It observes power systems and brings in issues of justice and care. It calls for and inspires action, including intellectual action. But Phase III can be polarizing and get arrested in victim studies. It can reduce people who suffer into mere cyphers with deficit identities. The systemic vision of Phase III makes an important advance into analysis of global problems, injustices, and mal-distribution of goods and resources. But its stories can all sound the same, as in oppressor/oppressed; victims/victimizers; winner/losers.

Phase III improves when it partakes of, and rests on, the detailed narratives, the moving, grounded, daily, and plural stories of Phase IV, the phase of experience, everyone's experience, anywhere in the world. In Phase IV everyone is a knower. Everyone's daily life is history, politics, literature, drama, economics, psychology, and ecology. Within Phase IV, binary thinking is seen as too simple.

The four first interactive phases point toward an eventual Phase V: a version in which the world of knowledge is redefined and reconstructed to include us all, which I consider will take us 100 to 200 years to conceive, depending on the political choices the world makes in this and coming decades. I feel that we desperately need thinking that goes back and forth across the interface between Phase III issues and Phase IV experience, that is, in the interface between systemic issues of power and policy, seen abstractly, and the actual poignant stories of human beings' textured, relational, and interdependent lives as makers and menders of the fabric of life.

Most of education in the United States at present is stuck in Phases I and II. Standardized testing has intensified the value placed on womanless and all-white versions of reality, with a few "exceptions" allowed in. Phase I is about studying government, management, laws, wars, and winners, whether in the arts, sciences, or social sciences. Phase I courses ignore almost all of the world's population. In Phase II, the standardized textbooks bring in a few "others" who are seen as unlike their kind and therefore worth studying. The standardized tests bring in Frederick Douglass or Harriet Tubman, neither as living the actual daily life of an enslaved person, and each seen as modeling heroism in a way that more of their people "should have done." Though the United States in the last three decades paid lip service to critical thinking as a skill to be developed in students, and though it relates to what I see as the need for minds that can compare and contrast evidence from many sources, in recent years the call has been for basic literacy, with no attention paid at all to developing analytical minds, which of course might turn countercultural. Preparation for standardized testing squeezes out both the Phase III critical faculties and the Phase IV method in which student voices may be heard bringing in their own experience. These suppressions are no accident within an administration working toward centralized control. For if students or teachers are encouraged to tell what they know, their deep memories will lead them away from single and simple loyalties and right/ wrong views of the world.

As I have written in my interactive Phase Theory, stories told by those who go back to their early childhood reveal that the multicultural globe is interior; the multicultural worlds are in us as well as around us. Early cultural conditioning trained each of us as children to shut off awareness of certain groups, voices, abilities, and inclinations, including the inclination to be with many kinds of children. Continents we might have known were closed off or subordinated within us. The domains of personality that remain can and do fill the conceptual space like colonizing powers. But a potential for pluralized understanding remains in us; the moves toward reflective consciousness come in part from almost-silenced continents within ourselves. Greater diversity of curriculum reflects not just the exterior multicultural world but the interior self that in early childhood was aware of, and attuned to, many varieties of experience. Recovery of that connectedness is a powerful aid to global citizenship. It can be a source of disorientation and anxiety, even shock, when one first remembers early connectedness that we were made to break off, as our educations or families shaped us for narrower class, race, and ethnic lives than our hearts inclined to.

Phase IV teaching dares to bring students' experience into the classroom and to derive new understanding from hitherto excluded or overlooked sources. Phase IV is the only frame of mind within the first four in my typology in which the student's own life counts. In its ability to educate and engage students, Phase IV goes far beyond the top-down oppressiveness of Phase I, the "exceptional others" framework of Phase II, and the focus on disembodied issues and polarities of Phase III.

Most traditionally trained white teachers started and continue to teach within the framework in which they were themselves taught: Phase I mono-culturalism, in which U.S. white culture is the chief reality. In this frame of mind a teacher is oblivious of the racial and gender elements in his or her actual life, and ignores her/his Phase III issues and Phase IV relational experience while doing his or her paid work. Most teachers teach about conflict and wars, and accept bullying on the playground, or sexual harassment in the hallways, while they think of themselves as desiring peace. There is a gap between the avowed ideals of being peaceful and the actual practice of teaching, with teachers operating as if vertical conflict were inevitable and hierarchical competition were the only logical framework within which schooling could occur. Jane Roland Martin's call for the three C's of care, concern, and connection to balance the three R's of reading, writing, and 'rithmetic has scarcely been answered.

In SEED seminars, when we ask teachers to remember vivid vignettes from their own schooling as children and teenagers, nearly all of the memories are negative, and nearly all involve competition, loss, humiliation, and mortification. When the exercise shifts and we request that they recall positive moments from their own schooling, what they usually remember is working together, in connection, on projects, or sitting in peaceful places, talking. Their positive memories rarely involve beating others or winning, but they do sometimes involve pushing oneself beyond one's usual limits. If educators learn from such testimony and wish to work for a world that is peaceful, they will arrange to balance the win-lest-you-lose paradigm that schooling now takes for granted as "normal" with a paradigm emphasizing students' growth and development in connection. Most schoolchildren testify that they like to work on collaborative projects more than they like to work alone. Recently many schoolchildren have been greatly interested in Internet hookups with children of other countries. They are responding to global education.

Hope for the Future

Writing this chapter during the spring of 2003 is very taxing because of the disconnect I feel between the ideal of educating U.S. students for global citizenship and the behavior of the U.S. government. To me, U.S. citizenship does not feel equated with God's particular approval. I see the United States as a place with a rare and wonderful dream of unity in diversity and a promise of the good life that has not yet been realized within its boundaries. I see the "American Dream" as set back severely by the acts of the Bush administration. It has enforced white, male-led Euro-American power and class dominance, when we need more global unity in diversity to hold the international fabric together. I feel that the Iraq war and its many costs do violence to the daily work of upkeep and maintenance every-where, even in the United States. I fear that the United States's "good vs. evil," "us against them" thinking has weakened global cohesiveness over the long term, disrespecting men and women all over the world, rupturing the fabric of trust and the hope of more tolerant life between differing religions and cultures. It assumes the top-down, either/or Phase I model of life as War: every warrior for himself; every group of warriors for themselves; women and children can deal with their terrors and trials alone, while being expected to take care of daily provisioning for all of us behind the scenes. Though some women are in the U.S. armed services, these are wars conceived by and led by men. The U.S. media present women in the armed services as borrowed from their families; the media do not present generals as borrowed from their families.

While the situation in the United States in the first few years of the 21st century feels like living with an abusive, unbalanced, controlling father who is a bully at home and a bully in the neighborhood, I take hope from numerous sources. One is the interest of many U.S. citizens in wisdom from indigenous and non-Western cultures, including Asian cultures. Learning from people of color in the United States and learning from Asian people in Asia has given me a feeling of hopefulness, as they teach from a less exclusive base of thinking and acting. There is not such a sense of spiritual or social loneliness, nor such stratification based on money and possessions. Acquisition and greed are not such prime values, and the sense of community seems to me far stronger than in the communities of white capitalism that I know best, in which "community" was and still seems to me an empty, disembodied idea. In U.S. African-American, Latino, Native, and Asian-American cultures, I feel that the sense of community is stronger than in my white worlds. The United States has had increasing opportunities to study and learn from more plural value systems and skills, as the schools and the society have become more diverse in their populations. Usually the differences I see in cultures less powerful than my own correspond to values I was taught to hold as a woman in my particular part of patriarchal white U.S. culture. In doing multicultural study I am both revising what I see I am and recovering some of what I was encouraged to give up to fit into the place designated for me in U.S. social and gender structures.

Another source of hope for me is the change toward global education that has slowly but very surely occurred at Wellesley College, where I work. Though Wellesley is not very self-conscious or even verbal about its changes, they are remarkable to me. Nearly half of the students are U.S. students of color or international students who come from some 40 nations. Courses are offered in many languages. Eight or nine religious faiths from around the world are mentioned in the weekly calendar of events. Performance groups and social organizations have many cultural bases. Consultants, lecturers, and visitors come from around the world. New faculty members are hired from outside the United States. Curricula have become more and more international, cross-cultural, and serious about women. Women's Studies is thriving. The values of the college have shifted over the last 50 years, from promoting education for women who would marry powerful white men to promoting the development of students who will matter to themselves and to others in the world. I would not claim that the students are global citizens in the sense that I have defined global citizenship. The values of soloistic behavior, materialism, and personal power once conditioned chiefly into men are strong in the sensibilities of the female students I work with. But they are being educated to know that there is more out in the world than their individual ambitions will encompass or affect for the better. I think their frames of reference and values will widen in later years, as mine did, in part because those teachers of my 15-year-old self did not give up on me. I take as a given, now, that I should not give up on young people even if they do not want to become global citizens. Neither did I.

I was also very heartened by a poem and the woman who wrote it at the time of the inauguration of William Jefferson Clinton as President of the United States in 1992. It seemed wonderful to me that Clinton asked Maya Angelou to write the inaugural poem, which she entitled *On the Pulse of the Morning*. The poem's global dimensions were spiritually uplifting to me. I remembered Robert Frost reciting his sonnet "The Gift Outright" at the time of John Kennedy's inauguration. Beautiful though it seemed to me, I found it on rereading to be deeply racist in its assumption that this land was empty until English people arrived. I saw Frost's poem as ignorant: in a characteristic U.S. history textbook way. Its language was intricately filled with legalistic double meanings about deeds and ownership of the land. By contrast, Maya Angelou used as her primary metaphors The Rock, The River, and The Tree, which are in all lands and speak to all people. She invoked all of the peoples who live or lived in the United States and in every other culture in the world. She recognized deep suffering and inhumanity, and also looked to a new morning. That a poem of such reach and power would grace the inauguration of a U.S. president gave me and others whom I spoke with a great surge of hope in the future of the world.

Another source of hope for me has been the four U.N. Women's conferences of 1975, 1980, 1985, and 1995. The sharp divisions between the two sections of each signals to me that change is possible. In the official U.N. conference, women represent their nations' governments, or are represented by men in those governments, and the arguments and contentions are predictable and orchestrated by rules, rights, privileges, and responsibilities of membership in one's nation and in the conference. But in the Nongovernmental Forum, women come together with much more of a sense of a shared and global agenda. In 1995 thirty thousand women came to the Forum in Beijing. I would trust them to run the world far more than I trust our present leaders, and to devise global education that would help us to live together better. Of course the women contend and fight, but the underlying plural sense of holding and being held in the midst of complexities is there. Our deep training is against either/or thinking and the violence it leads to. Since women and our dependents are the majority of any population and have had at least half of the world's lived experience, with responsibility for so many beyond ourselves, I feel we could in the aggregate be decent global judges of wise distribution of assets. Our policy concerns and skills have certainly been visible at these United Nations conferences. I used to scorn, as inefficient, the bureaucratic U.N. processes of inching toward a plural and multicultural agreement. Now I wonder how the world will survive without these U.N. processes and the empowerment of women's perspectives within them, which was started off so many years ago by the plural imagination and inclusive vision of Eleanor Roosevelt.

That we as a nation moved, for a while, into more global thinking than we had 50 years ago, before the U.N. was founded, is a source of hope for me despite the Bush administration's incapacity and disregard for plural understanding and its lack of intercultural skill. Its ignorance of other cultures reminds me of a more benign moment in the 1950s when my retired uncle from Middlebury, Connecticut, invited me to join him and his wife for a meal at the stately Savoy Hotel in London on the way home from their first trip outside the United States. In a booming voice heard all over the red-velvet Victorian dining room, my uncle proclaimed, "I've been all over Europe, seen seventeen capitals in twenty one days, and I don't think they've improved on us in any way, shape, or from!" His wife sat silently. He seemed to me a stunningly ignorant, loud, rich, blind American. He was very badly educated. The White House today is not about lessening arrogance, ignorance, greed, chauvinism, or patriarchy through education. But educators themselves can still choose to change the mindset and heartset of the system that produced my uncle and his silent wife. They can, among other efforts, work to bring out her voice, so that a man does not speak for both parties. In her voice I think I would have heard at the very least that beyond her husband there were other people in those 17 capitals of Europe.

I remember my schoolteachers' fears of the House Committee on Un-American Activities in the 1950s. Citizens accused of having communist leanings were blacklisted and lost jobs and public protection. Many teachers who refused to take loyalty oaths to the United States were fired. At the time I did not know why my teachers were quite so upset. In response to many policies of the Bush administration, the forces for repression of dissent are strong, and once again many college students seem to be ignorant of why any of their professors are upset about silencing of academic discussion of our foreign policy, and about the silencing of commentary on the Iraq war's local and international race, gender, and class dimensions. Most students have trouble seeing the war or U.S. government policy globally or systemically. In this regard they are good students of what the culture at large has taught them: that there are no large power systems in or around us. I feel that to educate global citizens we will need to support teachers to prepare students and themselves not only for what the United States has considered "standard," but also for "nonstandard" awareness and appreciation of the connected global ecosystems we are in, and the many ways in which human beings can make meaning of our lives without killing each other.

Global travel can be a great introduction or reinforcement to global awareness, though it has class parameters and limitations. Closer to home, even travel down the road can pluralize the mind and heart. In this technological age, much vicarious experience can be had through Internet travel and international exchanges. But students need to develop critical faculties with which to see, and heartfelt connections with which to feel what they are traveling into. In school, sometimes it is the heartfelt trust of a teacher in the worth of a student in a completely local situation that produces a faith within the student that he or she is connected to the world in a way that matters, and that the world is worth caring about. Often it is the day-by-day exchanges that open our capacities to care about, seek to understand, and work for that which is beyond our immediate view, that which is larger than us, but includes and holds us. The global sense for belonging and making spaces for all to belong can be developed close to home by teachers bringing the wholeness of their emotions and capacities into classrooms, unafraid to help students also to develop the plural capacities and the wide-ranging awareness that caretakers absolutely depend on when they work for the decent survival of all.

Reference

Miller, J. B. (1976). *Toward a new psychology of women.* Boston: Beacon Press.

33

The Classroom Practice of Commons Education

C. A. Bowers

Just as helping students to recognize that ecologically problematic cultural assumptions should be part of classroom discussions, learning about the cultural and environmental commons should also be an integral part of every area of the curriculum. Little will be gained in terms of educational reforms that contribute to reversing the cultural trend-line of degrading the self-renewing capacity of natural systems if learning about the cultural and environmental commons is treated as a separate subject. By integrating different aspects of the cultural and environmental commons into other subject areas, and by keeping in focus the different ways in which the commons are the basis of a less money-dependent and less environmentally destructive lifestyle, subjects that many students now find irrelevant will have greater personal meaning—and will even be understood as sources of empowerment. Keeping in focus the many ways in which both the cultural and environmental commons are being brought into the industrial system of production and consumption will also help students recognize that their silence or focus only on personal self-interest may have political implications that may later contribute to a life of poverty. If this sounds too alarmist, consider how few people were aware of the political decisions that led to the foreign outsourcing of local jobs or the local impact of automation.

Before identifying the aspects of the cultural and environmental commons that need to be given special attention, several points need to be reiterated. The first is that learning about the cultural and environmental commons is, unlike many areas of the curriculum, based on making explicit the actual cultural activities and patterns, as well as environmental conditions that are part of the students' too often unexamined experience. That is, learning about the cultural and environmental commons is not an ideologically-driven representation of a new form of society, such as Dewey's vision of societies around the world adopting the scientific method of problem solving as the one-true approach to knowledge. Nor is it based on the culturally uninformed romantic idea that all forms of social injustice will become a thing of the past if students are allowed to construct their own knowledge of the world. The cultural and environmental commons that should be the focus of learning, including being subjected to critical reflection about what needs to be changed and what needs to be intergenerationally renewed, are part of people's everyday experiences. It also needs to be recognized that the nature of the commons will differ from culture to culture, and from bioregion to bioregion. Given that this focus on actual cultural practices and environmental conditions, which goes against the grain of high-status forms of knowledge where the emphasis is too often on context-free generalizations and abstract (that is, print-based) descriptions, classroom teachers and university professors need to be especially mindful about not allowing their own ethnocentrism to get in the way of recognizing differences in cultural and environmental contexts. This more phenomeno-logical approach will be a safeguard against universal prescriptions.

The other point that needs to be kept in mind is that modern forms of enclosure are increasingly dependent upon creating a rootless form of individual subjectivity where memory and long-term perspective are overwhelmed by the steady stream of consumer fads. Many youths are now filling evangelical and fundamentalist Christian churches that combine the emotional release of a rock concert with the ontological certainties that come from declaring Jesus as their personal savior. Their rootlessness has simply taken on a different form of expression. That is, their subjective search for identity and instant gratifi-cation further marginalizes the collective memory of the history of struggle for social justice and a democratic society. In place of memory of the social justice achievements that must be carried forward and further expanded, the merging of consumer and religious fundamentalism orientates youth toward a future where all believers will be saved, regard-less of whether they are good environmental citizens or not. In effect, the dominance of what the future holds, as well as the literal interpretations of the *Bible* about the fate of those who have not declared Jesus as their personal savior, creates special challenges for getting students to take seriously the historical perspective that is necessary in order to understand the many traditions that enabled people to live less money dependent lives, and to recognize the degree to which the self-renewing capacity of natural systems are being undermined.

There are aspects of the cultural and environmental commons that continue to survive because the consumer-oriented culture has not been entirely successful in overwhelming the still ethnically-rooted cultures that exist on the fringes of the dominant culture. More-over, the dominant culture has not been entirely successful in replacing the need of some youth and adults to develop their own interests and talents in more intergenerationally-centered activities. But the efforts of the promoters of a consumer-dependent lifestyle continue unrelenting. Nearly every activity—from playing cards, dancing, cooking, sex, gardening, reading, house repair, hiking, bird watching, conversations, physical exercise, education, to healing nearly all manner of psychological and physical problems, have been turned into exploitable markets—with the latest being the placing of television style adver-tising on the screens of cell phones and movies. An even more egregious example of the total lack of moral limits of what can be exploited as a new market is the example of a corporation named Team Baby Entertainment which develops DVDs that highlight college athletic teams. The market for these DVDs is the pre-school population, and the hook is that in addition to being exposed to the culture of university football the children are encouraged to count and spell. The company lists 20 DVDs, with "Baby Irish" (University of Notre Dame) and "Baby Longhorn" (University of Texas) being among the top sellers. These and thousands of similar examples of turning every aspect of the cultural and environmental commons, and every age group, into an exploitable market indicate just how dominant market liberalism has become—and just how difficult it will be to put the country on a sustainable pathway.

There are signs of hope. While market liberal politicians and corporations big and small continue their assault on what remains of the cultural and environmental commons, a minority of youth and adults continue to find meaning as well as development of personal talents in face-to-face relationships—with mentors in the arts, healing practices, garden-ing, environmental restoration projects, and so forth. Another positive sign is the growing interest among some members of the middle class in cutting back or dropping out entirely from their previously chosen career path that held out the promise of life at the upper level of the consumer pyramid in order to live less hurried and less externally controlled life-styles. This small trend of adopting a life of voluntary simplicity is now being strengthened by what can be called the lifestyle of involuntary simplicity as automation, outsourcing of jobs (even for white-collar workers), and corporate decision makers abandon what remains of older notions of a social contract that provided for retirement benefits in exchange for a life of work and loyalty to the corporation.

The cycle of working in order to consume is now beginning to be replaced by a new cycle where growing unemployment and the loss of retirement and health benefits will lead to less consumerism. Even though market-liberals and fundamentalist Christians promote the idea that poverty reflects personal weaknesses, along with the re-emergence of the Social Darwinian idea that the poorly adapted genes of individuals as well as the memes of businesses, will lead to their extinction, there is still the existential question of how to sustain daily existence when sources of money begin to fail. The dominant ideolo-gies, in effect, can no longer be relied upon to use the instruments of government to distribute wealth in a more socially just manner, nor can government be seen as safe-guarding local communities from the destructive impact of international corporations that exploit the local environmental commons and local economies. Without a knowledge of the nature of the local cultural and environmental commons, and thus of how to re-orient daily life toward what is a more sustainable existence, people faced with a life of involuntary simplicity will spend more hours in front of the television, playing computer games, and experiencing various forms of depression—which will continue to pour money into the coffers of the medical and pharmaceutical industries. Involuntary sim-plicity, in effect, is too often a life of poverty that goes beyond the lack of the material basis of existence. That is, their poverty includes not knowing how to participate in the activities of the cultural commons that would develop their personal talents and lead to the under-standing that the more enduring form of wealth is in mutually supportive relationships. This form of wealth cannot be outsourced!

The following are possibilities for curriculum reform that will provide students with the language for making explicit the various expressions of the cultural and environmental commons that still exist in their communities—as well as the knowledge of why the diversity of the world's cultural and environmental commons needs to be sustained. The following curriculum proposals address what needs to be learned in a post-industrial world—one in which the market and its underlying technologies are viewed as supporting the commons rather than as further enclosing them. An example of how modern tech-nologies can support the cultural commons without further degrading the environmental commons is the introduction of solar powered LED lamps that are replacing kerosene lamps in rural India. The micro-banks that support local producers and markets, as well as a wide range of energy efficient technologies, are other examples that point the way to understanding that post-industrial cultures will need to shift from an emphasis on profits and the autonomous individual required by a market-oriented culture to cultures that are more intergenerationally connected and thus more aware of their responsibility for not undermining the mutual support systems that future generations will need to rely upon. The following discussion of curriculum reforms is also based on the recognition that fostering an understanding of cultural and natural systems as interdependent ecologies will not likely be taken on as a responsibility of churches, most families, businesses, or the media—which leaves formal education as the one possibility that might rise to the chal-lenge, as it did after long delays in addressing the deep cultural assumption of a male dominated culture.

Themes and Issues in a Cultural Commons Curriculum

Initially, many classroom teachers and university professors may have difficulty identifying the different expressions of the cultural commons that need to be brought to the attention of students. In not being able to easily recognize the cultural commons they will have difficulty engaging students in discussions of the many forms of enclosure. Even the professors who have made the criticism of capitalism a central focus seem unable to recognize the commons as an "on-the-ground" alternative. This initial lack of awareness and only marginal interest is likely to replicate how educators initially responded to the efforts of feminists who were critical of those aspects of the cultural commons based on cultural assumptions that privileged men over women. What we can learn from that centuries-long inability to recognize unjust taken-for-granted cultural patterns is that the process of naming is the first step in transforming consciousness from a condition of existence-based formulaic beliefs and practices to becoming explicitly aware—and to critical reflection. If classroom teachers and university professors take seriously the impact of our hyper-consumer culture on the viability of natural systems (and this is a big if), and if they recognize the current rate of dependence upon consumerism, they will find that the easiest way of identifying the cultural commons that are being targeted as new niche markets is to look at the number of magazines used to advertise how different commons activities can be upgraded through the purchase of new products.

The preparation of food, which varies from culture to culture, is represented in a variety of magazines as being elevated in social status by acquiring the latest appliances, cooking utensils, and following the most exotic recipes. Outdoor activities ranging from gardening, fishing, hiking, bird watching, camping, tennis, as well as other sports, are targeted markets of magazines that reinforce the message that purchasing the latest products will increase performance and communicate to others one's higher social status. Woodworking, house repairs, quilt making, weaving, healing practices, and so on, also have their own magazines filled with advertisements. Even extremist groups are targeted by magazines that promote the latest in lethal weapons, camouflage gear, and hate literature. Indeed, it seems there is nothing in our culture that cannot be turned into a new market opportunity. I am not suggesting that this is the only or even the best starting point for identifying the activities within the community that are part of the cultural commons. Even if this is not the starting point, it would still be useful at some point to introduce students to the activities that are part of the local cultural commons, and to compare the values promoted in these activities with what is being promoted in these special market magazines.

The following is intended as a partial list of the activities and interests that represent the cultural commons in different regions of the country. Because of the diversity of bioregions and ethnic cultures, it is impossible to provide a complete list. Even if the website were to contain such a list, it would still not be the best way to introduce the students to the possibilities of a less consumer existence. If the current educational problem of presenting students with abstract knowledge that appears to them as irrelevant to their lives is to be avoided, then the introduction to the local commons should not begin with an abstract list. Rather, the introduction should be based on a more ethnographic approach that will bring the students into face-to-face relationships with the different mentors and other people engaged in cultural commons activities. This involves going into the community, as well as bringing people into the classroom, with the purpose of enabling students to hear personal stories of how interests and talents were discovered, how they were dependent upon intergenerational knowledge shared by mentors, how their activities give them a sense of community, and how they are dealing with the market forces that are attempting to enclose the intergenerational continuities by substituting consumer products for the development of personal skills and interests.

The key point is that the discussions by different members of the community, as well as their activities that help to renew the cultural commons, should not involve reading textbooks or relying upon computer websites—as both have a limited usefulness. Learning from people who are participants, and who have a clear understanding about the differences between consumerism and community self-reliance, will help the students to think more deeply about what areas of the cultural commons are most relevant to their own talents, interests, and need for supportive relationships. This more ethnographic, face-to-face approach to learning can only take students so far in understanding the cultural forces that have contributed to the widespread ignorance of the commons, and that are promoting their further enclosure. Students also need to learn about how various groups beyond their local communities, both in the past and currently, have promoted in the name of progress and other higher values the enclosure of the world's diverse cultural and environmental commons. The students also need to confront the double bind that is inherent in the Western approach to progress where the further enclosure of the cultural and environmental commons is equated with achieving greater progress.

Depending upon the students' maturity, the initial step in introducing them to the cultural commons is to provide a brief explanation of the difference between money-dependent activities and those that are less or entirely free of a monetized relationship. This basic difference needs to be connected with activities and relationships that are part of the students' daily experience. This initial vocabulary, where the words "commons" and "market" (that is, what has to be purchased or paid for), contains the fundamental tension that needs to be explored further as the students move through the educational process. This limited vocabulary, in effect, provides the initial understanding of what separates the activities and relationships that strengthen the commons from the many ways in which the student is dependent upon the market—with some forms of dependency being valid while most others create artificial dependencies that limit the students' personal development and connectedness with community. In both commons and market-dependent relationships, there are key features of the students' experience that need to be made explicit. This can be achieved by providing the verbal space that will enable students to articulate the following: the sense of meaning they experience in both commons and market-dominated activities and relationships, their feeling of dependency or development of personal skills and talents, and how commons-based experiences differ from market-dominated experiences in terms of their impact on natural systems. Consider the ecological impact of their activities should become second nature, and thus begin to replace the cultural myth that humans can survive the destruction of the environment they depend upon by further technological developments.

Skeptics who doubt that young students can understand how language illuminates and hides the cultural patterns that need to be made explicit need to consider how many teachers in the early grades provided an equally limited yet powerful vocabulary for identifying the gender based relationships, activities, and social roles that had been ignored for hundreds of years. To reiterate a key point, it's at the later stages of the educational process that the cultural differences in the nature of the cultural commons can be introduced, as well as the economic, ideological, and scientific/technological forces that are enclosing the commons. Support from members of the community needs to be gained before the forces that are enclosing the commons become the focus of the classroom discussions. What many educational reformers do not understand is that they need to establish that they are helping to conserve intergenerational traditions that strengthen community and that help to ensure the prospects of future generations. This will help to counter the faux conservative critics who are actually in the market-liberal tradition that is committed to expanding markets by further exploiting both the cultural and environmental commons.

Here is an initial list of activities and interdependent relationships that fit the definition of the cultural commons, as well as a brief description of how they are being enclosed—that is, how they are being integrated into a money-dependent economy. The list, which should be expanded or revised in terms of the local culture, might be especially useful for teachers who, having introduced students to the nature of racial and gender prejudice, take on the task of introducing students to the even more daunting challenge we now face in pursuing community-centered alternatives to an economic system that is ecologically unsustainable. All of the suggestions for incorporating learning about the commons and the processes of enclosure are dependent upon introducing students to an ethnographic approach as the starting point in the process of inquiry. The emphasis of this approach on the description of experiences that previously went largely unnamed and thus not thought about, and can later move to the more theory-based examination of ideologies and economic practices—as well as examining why highly educated people continue to promote in the name of progress and freedom the practices that are degrading the environment.

Food

If teachers go to the website of Slow Food USA or the website of the Center for Ecoliteracy, they will find a number of helpful resources for introducing students to a deeper understanding of the issues that are already being contested in public schools across the country. That is, whether industrially prepared foods, which have already influenced most students' eating habits by the time they enter the first grades, should be allowed in schools. Depending upon the students' maturity and background knowledge, other issues need to become part of the discussion of the various cultural traditions in the students' community, such as the growing, preparation, and sharing of food—including how these traditions differ from the more individualized experience of eating at an industrialized fast-food outlet. The Slow Food website is especially useful for providing a larger cultural context for discussing the difference between intergenerational and industrial approaches to the growing, preparation and sharing of food—as well as how industrial approaches are enclosing this important part of the cultural commons.

The larger cultural context includes how the characteristics of the bioregion in which the student's community is situated have influenced what have become the traditional foods of a cultural group—including their knowledge of where and in which season the sources of food are grown or found. The early methods of preservation as well as knowledge of how to prepare food in ways that reduced risks to health and to ensure a balanced diet also need to be compared with the industrial, chemically dependent, and now genetically engineered approaches to agriculture. Learning about different cultural contexts will foreground other aspects of the cultural commons, such as the ceremonies connected with the planting and harvest, as well as narratives that carry forward family and community memories of mistakes in exploiting or acting out of ignorance of natural systems. Narratives still passed along within the students' community, which among many cultures were often sources of wisdom as to how to live in ecological balance, need to be discussed. The absence of these narratives within the student's family and community is an important entry point for a discussion of how industrialized approaches to food contribute to the enclosure of this aspect of the cultural commons—thus, adding further to the students' dependence upon a consumer relationship with food.

At a later stage in the student's education there needs to be a discussion of the history of the industrialization of food, including developments in technologies, scientific discoveries, marketing strategies, and the legitimating ideology that promotes industrially prepared food as healthier than the culturally diverse food that had been refined over generations of living within the limits of the bioregion. This complex and diverse set of traditions is also part of the cultural commons that are now under threat by market liberals who are attempting to globalize what food should taste like, with its excessive reliance on salt, sugar, and other artificial chemicals. As the differences are examined between intergenerationally influenced and industrial approaches to food (probably at the high school and university level), students also need to consider how each approach relates to the issues of community self-reliance, how the monetizing of food contributes to the spread of poverty both here and abroad, and the impact on natural systems of transporting food over thousands of miles. A point that needs to be considered is the role that science, technology, and ideology play in further enclosing the ethnic traditions of growing and preparing food, and how the genetic engineering of seeds is contributing to the loss of diversity of native foods in different regions of the world. There is also the question of how industrial foods are contributing to health problems that did not exist when cultures relied on local sources of food. For example, in the 1930's the diet of the Tohono O'odham (who live on a reservation near Tucson) relied heavily upon the locally grown tepary bean, and no one in the tribe had heard of diabetes. As the members of the tribe became more dependent on processed food, diabetes became a major problem that now affects nearly fifty percent of the adult population. Obesity is now being discussed as a problem that arises in different parts of the world where young people are increasingly eating fast food.

An activity that would help ground the discussion of the differences between traditional and industrially processed foods would be to have students investigate the variety of foods relied upon by indigenous cultures that lived in the bioregion before they were displaced by Anglo and Euro-Americans. This discussion needs to highlight how the variety of foods developed by indigenous cultures enriched the diet of the Europeans as well as the range of food that we now take-for-granted in America. Another activity would be to identify the varieties of fruit trees that the settlers planted when they established their farms and planted their gardens—and to compare the varieties that existed then with what exists today. Another activity would be to check out the list of 700 endangered American foods on the website of Renewing America's Food Traditions, and to investigate which foods on the list still exist in their bioregion. Relying more on individual and community gardens, as well as traditional sources of food that are raised by different ethnic groups, will become increasingly important as the post-industrial culture adapts to a less money-dependent and less environmentally destructive lifestyle.

Creative Arts

An individual who sat in on my talk on how market liberal politicians are undermining the cultural commons while at the same time privatizing poverty sent me an email that described how a group of local musicians were an example of a commons approach to one of the arts—in this case the playing of traditional Irish music. As he explained, "People who wish to play Irish music can come to the jam session and play whatever notes they can. Hopefully, someone at the session will give them an occasional pointer. In a kind of musical gift economy, no money exchanges hands for instruction." The generosity he described is often present in relationships where intergenerational skills are being passed on to the next generation—but found less often in monetized relationships.

A survey of the other arts in the community can begin by identifying the mentors and groups that promote various forms of artistic expression that are only minimally dependent upon the money economy. Who are the women and men in the community who have developed their talents as musicians, potters, weavers, dancers, actors, poets, painters, and sculptors? To what extent has their development depended upon being mentored—often in situations similar to the description of learning from others performing traditional Irish music? And how many local artists who have been mentored are willing to mentor others? What is the difference between paying a fee to mentors who are not totally independent of the money economy and purchasing a ticket to watch a play or another form of artistic performance? Young students can be introduced to this aspect of the cultural commons by inviting various artists to give demonstrations for the class as well as to guide students in their first efforts to express themselves through an artistic medium. This can lead to a discussion of how they were attracted to being a potter, painter, actor, and so forth. It would also be useful to have the artists talk about what they think their contribution is to the community—as well as how being part of a community of artists is different from being an individual consumer of the arts. These early discussions, which may be elementary and general, nevertheless provide students with what may be their first encounter with a different vocabulary than what they encounter through the media. It is the vocabulary of the artist that will enable them to be more discriminating observers of the difference between the arts that represent personal talent and aesthetic judgment that strengthen community ties, and the arts that are used to promote products and to differentiate social status between groups.

As the students progress to the point where they begin to grapple with how this aspect of the cultural commons differs from the arts that are now being used, along with sex, to promote consumerism, it would be useful for them to be encouraged to think about the difference between folk art (including what has been integrated into built environments and local festivals) and the high-status art that is promoted through various media and by experts that make public judgments about the difference between significant and insignificant art. Again, if students are encouraged to connect their classroom discussions to what they have observed in their communities, distinctions will begin to emerge that will be important to them as individuals.

Still later in their learning about this aspect of the cultural commons, they should be introduced to the role that the arts play in ecologically-centered indigenous cultures. This would involve learning how ceremonies in many cultures involve participation of the entire community—in the performance of the dance, music, dress, and so forth. For example, it would be useful for students to consider the cultural importance of how these participatory arts give individuals the opportunity for self-expression, carry forward in highly symbolic form the collective memory of the community, as well as provide for an atmosphere of thanksgiving for nature's bounty (such as the rain ceremonies of the Hopi, and the dances that celebrate the renewal of other members of the human/Nature community). Considering how other non-consumer oriented cultures use the arts to transform the everyday experiences in ways that connect the members of the community to a more intergenerationally connected symbolic world will provide a basis for thinking about what is being reinforced in the different artistic performances in the student's culture.

At the high school and university level, students should begin to think about the social messages that are implicit in films, television programs, video games. How do these hidden messages influence individual consciousness and thus expectations in daily life? Do they promote consumerism, the quest to be glamorous, the need to surround oneself with the consumer products that communicate success and achievement of higher social status? How do the industrial uses of the arts contribute to the silences that lead so many adults to be unaware of the various arts that are part of the cultural commons—and do not require a huge income to participate in? There is also a need to begin thinking about how different ideologies influence what constitutes good art—as well as its social purpose. There is also a connection between how non-Western cultures use the arts as part of daily life, including their role in the local economy. An important question is what happens to these artists when their communities become increasingly dependent upon tourism in order to participate more fully in a money-dependent economy?

Ceremonies and Narratives

Ceremonies and narratives are an important part of the cultural commons, and in many cultures they play an important role in the intergenerational renewal of the culture's environmental ethic. The values and ways of thinking they carry forward differ from culture to culture. They may carry forward the environmental wisdom accumulated over generations of learning from the life-cycles that characterize the bioregion they depend upon, and they may carry forward the moral values that are to govern both relationships with strangers and with members of the community. As recent history reminds us, ceremonies and narratives may also reinforce the idea of racial superiority, the national sense of how wrongs can be reversed by conquering other countries, and the vision of an imperialistic future.

The differences in the values reinforced by cultural ceremonies and narratives can be seen in how some indigenous cultures of the Pacific Northwest, as well as the Ainu (the indigenous people of Japan) understood the spiritual significance of the salmon, and how the return of the salmon in the rivers would be celebrated for providing moral guidance for how humans should live in the world. In these cultures, the appearance of the first salmon would lead to days of ceremony, including feasting and dancing. As no salmon were caught during these days, a large number of salmon were able to navigate their way to their traditional spawning grounds. In effect, not only did the ceremony renew moral/spiritual connections between the practices of the cultural and environmental commons, it also ensured the continuation of the cycle of life that the salmon and people shared together. The ceremonies and narratives in such cultures as Nazi Germany and the American Ku Klux Klan represent how the pathologies of the human mind are also constituted, renewed and passed on to future generations. As Alasdair MacIntyre pointed out in *After Virtue* (1984) narratives connect the individual to the culture's memory in ways that influence both the values that the individual holds but also the individual's moral reference points for establishing a self-identity.

As is the case with most aspects of the cultural commons, it is necessary to begin with identifying the various ceremonies and narratives that are central to the various groups in the students' community. In certain instances it may be wise to raise the more controversial issues later in the students' education. It needs to be emphasized that recognizing the different traditions of ceremonies and narratives establishes a basis of community support for when the controversial issues become part of class discussions. The starting place for students in the early grades, however, is with introducing them to different traditions of narrative that some students will have already encountered in a more surface way in children's literature books. These would include the classic narratives that go back to the early Greeks, the Norse and Germanic tribes, and the narratives of indigenous cultures in North America. The forms of narrative can be discussed, as well as the moral messages they were intended to convey. The similarities and differences between these traditions and the modern narratives that the students are likely to have encountered in animated film can also be discussed. What students are learning is that narratives are part of the cultural memory, that they represent earlier ways of thinking and that they played an important role in the education of the young before the time of literacy, and that they are the source of human experience that are often used as metaphors for understanding today's world.

It is possible in the early grades to have students collect information on the different ceremonies taking place in the community, and to identify the cultural group that sponsors them. This survey of ceremonies and sponsoring groups brings out yet another tradition that promotes community solidarity and memory. In later grades questions relating to these community ceremonies can be raised. For example: What is the cultural origin of the ceremony, and what was its original purpose—to celebrate a victory, the harvest that warded off starvation, some major cultural achievement or discovery, the end of foreign occupation, etc.? How has the ceremony, which has its roots in the distant past of another country, undergone changes in the American context? Does the ceremony in the American context retain cultural traditions that no longer exist in the country of origin—that is, has it become a communal form of nostalgia and a romanticizing of the past? There are other questions that need to be explored, such as whether the ceremony helps to retain the silences about the injustices carried out by the people whose achievements are the focus of the ceremony? The centennial celebration of the pioneers that made the Oregon Trail an indelible part of the history of the American West, and the recent celebration, with all of its regional ceremonies, of the Lewis and Clark expedition, are prime examples. From the Anglo/European perspective what is being celebrated is the successful completion of their journey, but from the indigenous perspective what is being celebrated is their displacement from their traditional homelands. It is this part of the story that is largely ignored. As the expression of a collective memory of the cultural commons, it's necessary that the students recognize the expressions of courage, self-sacrifice, and mutual support—as well as the wrongs done to others.

The ways in which the ceremonies and narratives are enclosed by market forces also need to be examined before students graduate from or drop out of high school. Enclosure may take the form of a ceremony being taken over by military or corporate interests, and by being turned into a marketing opportunity by local businesses. There are other narratives that have been repressed by corporate interests, such as the stories of the labor movement, and anti-war movements. The narratives about the civil rights and feminist movements are still a vital part of the cultural commons in many communities. There are forms of narrative that are particularly prone to being turned into a commodity—first as a movie and then as a wide range of gadgets, toys, clothes with movie derived logos, and so forth. Enclosure may also result from other cultural pressures, such as the targeting of youth as consumers engaged in the constant struggle to own and display the latest trend dictated by peer pressure. This emphasis on youth as the most receptive market for the latest technological innovation further alienates them from having an interest in the narrative and ceremonial traditions of their parents and grandparents. In effect, the rate of technological change, particularly in areas where the microchip is the basis of the technology, undermines different areas of the cultural commons—with hardly anyone under the age of thirty recognizing the loss, much less its significance. The illusion of being an autonomous individual, which characterizes so much of the culture of youth, serves the interests of market forces. This is further reinforced by the widely held idea promoted in teacher education programs that students should construct their own knowledge and determine their own values.

Another question that needs to be explored by students before they leave the classroom—with its potential for a wide ranging examination of cultural practices that might not be tolerated in other social settings. The question is: What are the narratives and ceremonies that embody the experiences of the current generation that merit passing on to future generations? That is, what is the story line of their generation that might be relevant to future generations of youth that will be facing the more constricted choices caused by a degraded environment and a post-industrial culture? And a second question is: what skills and wisdom would they like to become mentors of?

At the university level, the Enlightenment tradition of ideas have marginalized and in many instances denigrated the positive role that ceremonies and narratives play in carrying forward the collective memories of how to live in morally coherent relationships with others. The sources of these ideas that have helped to create the distinction between high- and low-status knowledge can be traced to the earliest Western philosophers, as well as to the political and economic theorists who articulated the importance of eliminating all moral barriers to the expansion of free markets. It needs to be considered how these traditions of thinking led to the pattern of dichotomous categories where rationality, in its contemporary scientific and critical modes of expression, is upheld as justifying the dismissal of other cultural ways of knowing, particularly those represented in ceremonies and narratives, as sources of superstition and ignorance. Some of these cultural ceremonies and narratives, as mentioned earlier, were indeed destructive, based on prejudices, and privileged the economic interests of local elites. The blanket treatment of all forms of knowledge that are carried forward in ceremonies and narratives as sources of ignorance has led to the failure to assess their worth in terms of the contribution they have made in enabling different cultures to live within the limits of their bioregion and to sustain a process of democratic decision making about which traditions are essential to living less money-dependent lives.

Students need to think about the moral and ecological criteria that are to be used in judging the ceremonies and narratives that are part of their own cultural and environmental commons, as well as how the ceremonies and narratives of other cultures contribute to less environmentally and colonizing patterns of existence. A strong case can be made that the deep cultural assumptions underlying the traditions of Western philosophy, including political and economic theory, have the same messianic (colonizing) tendencies that are found in Christianity. Is the Armageddon that many Americans anticipate based on a narrative that enables people to live in less environmentally destructive and money dependent ways? Are the narratives of current scientists who are predicting that we are entering a post-biological phase of evolution, where humans will be replaced by computer networks, to be taken seriously as more people sink into poverty and a state of hopelessness? What is the significance for our cultural commons of the ceremonies that mark the remembrance of Martin Luther King, Jr.'s achievements and vision? My concern is that there are few opportunities in a university education where these specific questions can be considered from an historical and cross cultural perspective.

Moral and Spiritual Commons

This is an aspect of the cultural commons that is more often practiced in daily life, than understood—except when the moral norms are ignored or deliberately violated. It is also an aspect of the cultural commons that may not be shared by all the members of the community because of ethnic and religious differences. Some groups may have a complex and shared spiritual commons—music, traditions of dealing with various forms of oppression, understanding of what is sacred (including places), ceremonies that celebrate special events in the life of the group, and the personal inspiration derived from a tradition of hope and working for social and ecojustice. Others may be marginalized in the larger community's understanding of who is to be included in the moral commons. Basically, the moral commons, which may differ from culture to culture, involves the shared expectations of moral reciprocity—that is, relationships that are mutually supportive, based on trust, and are non-exploitive. The relationships that Martin Buber referred to in terms of I-Thou would be part of the moral commons—and, in terms of his interpretation, it can also be understood as one of the forms that the spiritual commons may take. Examples of enclosure (that is, turning the moral commons into an exploitive relationship that may lead to monetary benefits) include transforming the I-Thou relationship into an I-It relationship where the Other becomes useful in terms of meeting pre-conceived expectations, or a personal need. Other examples include the moral norms that prevent exchanging information about someone else's personal life into data that can then be sold to various segments of the market culture. It also includes being honest, mutually supportive, and having reliable reciprocal relationships.

As these aspects of the moral and spiritual commons differ widely among members of the community, with certain moral values shared more than others, it is important for people to be explicitly aware of them. Most of the moral commons, as well as the spiritual commons that are shared by different groups, are part of the taken-for-granted cultural patterns—and thus are difficult to be aware of. Thus, the need to name these patterns, and to help students understand why they are important to the well-being of the community— and to each individual's sense of what constitutes meaningful relationships.

Incorporating a discussion of the spiritual commons into the curriculum, which should be delayed until the later grades, is relatively easy in that it involves students learning how different religious and spiritual traditions understand the commons—such as special and highly symbolic days and events that transform the members of the group from the routines of daily life to an awareness of being connected to a broader and more elevated purpose. Learning about the differences in the spiritual commons involves learning from representatives of various religious traditions about what they regard as sacred and what they understand to be included in the spiritual commons. It would also involve learning how the members of the different religious traditions think about the ways in which their traditions are being enclosed. For teachers and professors who share the late Francis Crick's skepticism about the non-measurability of spirituality, I suggest that they read Rabbi Michael Lerner's *The Left Hand of God* (2005) for one of the deeper understandings of the connections between spirituality and the values that sustain the cultural and environmental commons. A starting place for acquiring the background knowledge for helping students to understand how other religious traditions understand the commons is *World Views and Ecology: Religion, Philosophy, and the Environment* (1994), edited by Mary Evelyn Tucker and John Grim. Any discussion of how different religions understand the moral and spiritual commons should also involve learning how they reconcile the adoption of market values and practices with their core religious beliefs.

Learning about the moral commons, which should start in the early grades, begins with not only naming the patterns of moral reciprocity in different social and environmental contexts but also participating in discussions of personal experiences that arise when different norms that are usually taken-for-granted are ignored or deliberately violated. The challenge will be to identify the different situations in which the moral norms govern the relationship and activity—which may range from the moral commons that are an aspect of an athletic event, an artistic performance, a conversation, the encounter with a stranger, the person that has been victimized—and the victimizer, the young and old, and the treatment of animals.

Documenting the many expressions of when the moral commons is being kept alive, and even expanded, should include considering the many cultural forces that are undermining the moral commons—and even the spiritual commons. This may lead to considering the many ways in which the consumer culture, with its emphasis on individualism, progress, and instant gratification, contributes to the enclosing of the moral commons. The enclosure may take the form of indifference toward mutually supportive relationships, communicating contempt for what is regarded as a constraint on individual freedom or the imposition of an unwanted sense of moral certainty upon others. The pressures and cultural assumptions that underlie "road rage" would be a good place to start when helping students understand the cultural roots of a growing disregard for sustaining the moral commons. The excessive claims of scientists who have strayed onto the slippery slope of scientism needs to be examined as a threat to the moral commons—and this area of inquiry should consider the nature of the moral commons that would be the outcome of taking seriously that natural selection determines which expression of moral reciprocity is the better adapted. To put this another way, this would involve considering the moral implications of assuming that nature selects the better adapted behaviors (that is, memes).

Landscapes

This word is used to refer to many aspects of the cultural and environmental commons. While the word has a specific meaning for artists, it can be more accurately understood as the patterns of cultural and natural phenomena that we encounter with all our senses. That is, sight, sound, smell, and touch. Thus, the landscapes we move through are experienced as multi-dimensional; they are even part of our memories and stories. Other words often used to refer to different aspects of landscapes include "habitat," "place," "nature," "scenery," and "built environments." Each of these words indicates a particular perspective and tradition that foregrounds what is relevant while putting out of focus other features of the landscape—which is always local in that it is an inextricable part of what humans' experience.

The multiple ways in which landscapes are enclosed by different cultural values and ways of knowing make them an important part of commons education—especially if students are to acquire the vocabulary that will enable them to articulate their concerns about the different ways in which landscapes are being transformed by market forces. In the broadest sense, landscapes include the fields, streams, grasses, trees, mountains, and sky—as well as the built environment of fences, roads, buildings, planted fields, and so forth. Streets lined with in-your-face bill boards and the mixing of architectural styles are also examples of landscapes, as are the rows of nearly identical houses and the lone farm house whose starkness is not softened by flowers, shrubs, and trees.

Rural and urban landscapes possess the combined elements of culture and nature—with their respective forms of enclosure having a direct impact on human experience. Farmers who want to squeeze the maximum profit from the land too often eliminate the vegetation along the sides of their fields, and in the process eliminate the habitat needed for birds, field animals, and other species that make up the local food web. The use of seeds that have been genetically altered to resist herbicides such as Roundup also alter the landscape in multiple ways that affect our experience of the fields as part of the landscape. Its destructive impact on the web of life, which goes deep into the soil, is what should be recognized. Unfortunately when the uniformly planted fields appear free of "weeds" there is little interest in thinking about the true environmental legacy of Roundup. Urban landscapes are also affected by the beliefs and values that have their roots deep in the dominant culture. The urban landscapes may communicate that consumerism is the dominant activity and the basis of human relationships, and they may also be read as the expression of a culture that values the new over the old—which is too often the conscious intent of the architects and business owners. In both rural and urban landscapes, there are constant visual reminders of the power of modern technologies that are imposed on what was a natural landscape.

The complex nature of landscapes, particularly how nature and culture merge together in daily experience, is touched on in only the most superficial way in most environmental education classes. The changes in local habitats, the sources of pollution in nearby streams and lakes, and the strategies for restoring degraded environments such as wetlands which are the main foci, seldom touch on the nature of the cultural commons. The students are given only half of the vocabulary that is needed to address the systemic sources of the deepening environmental crisis. The silences result in a limited ability to exercise communicative competence, especially when the promoters of a further expansion of the industrial, consumer-oriented culture justify new forms of enclosure by invoking the god words of "progress," "freedom," "patriotism," and "innovation."

A number of characteristics of rural and urban landscapes can be introduced in the early grades. These characteristics include what has not been fundamentally altered by cultural practices. What has been altered are often examples of enclosure of the natural environment. Drawing upon the students' experience in different landscapes, such as shopping malls and parking lots, forests, open fields, street corners, etc., can provide the contexts for discussing how different forms of enclosure can be detected through the student experiences of smells, sights, sounds, and tastes. Getting students to pay attention to their own senses in these different landscapes, and to name what they are aware of, is the first step in making them more aware of their surroundings. At this level of education, students might keep a record of the different animals, birds, and insects they encounter in these different settings. What is important is for them to become aware of the environments they inhabit and thus how different environments (high-rise buildings and streets filled with cars, open fields, parks, rows of suburban houses, back-ally dumpsters, etc.) influence which animals and birds will likely be found—and how different environments influence human activity and relationships.

As students move into the middle and upper grades it should be possible to introduce how different cultural ways of knowing have influenced the human impact on the land-scape. Where were the trails of the indigenous cultures, and how do they differ from the modern system of roads and freeways? What cultural assumptions and values account for these differences? How does the modern approach to agriculture differ from how indigenous cultures met their need for food, medicine, and other daily necessities? Perhaps more important would be to have students investigate how modern agriculture, including corporate approaches to agriculture, have contributed to the disappearance of native grasses and other plants. How the use of chemicals have reduced the number of pollinator insects would also be important to investigate.

Other aspects of local landscapes that have been shaped by Western assumptions include how painters have represented landscapes at different times in American history, the source of ideas that led to imposing on the landscape the rectangular grids that are so visible from the airplanes as one crosses the country; the ways in which architects and builders often ignore using local materials and designing buildings that fit the local context; the influence of different religions and ideologies on conserving landscapes or exploiting them for economic purposes. This latter theme needs to be refined so that the question becomes: How do different religions, including non-Western religions, represent humankind's responsibility toward the environment? And a further refinement about the relation of ideologies and landscapes leads to asking: Do ideologies such as market liberalism, social justice liberalism, Marxism, libertarianism, socialism, conservatism (in the tradition of Edmund Burke and Wendell Berry) provide clear moral guidance on what are appropriate and inappropriate ways of relating to the land?

The many ways in which landscapes are enclosed (monetized and privatized) would include examining how they are represented in the media (including the movies and television commercials), the Western tradition of an individual perspective and how this reinforces the experience of being an independent observer of the landscape, the way in which the vocabulary as well as the technologies of the industrial, consumer-oriented culture enclose both the vocabulary necessary for naming and thus recognizing the non-monetized value of local landscapes as well as how technologies such as iPods, laptop computers, and video systems now built into cars reduce awareness of the landscapes their users are moving through. These technologies not only insulate their users from the sounds and smells, but also from the plants, animals and other aspects of the visual landscape. What their attention is focused on are the media products of the consumer culture—which are the result of other forms of enclosure of the cultural commons.

Built Environments and Craft Knowledge

The design, use of materials, and craftsmanship in most of the world's cultures have been dependent upon the intergenerational knowledge that is passed along and added to as each generation introduces its own improvements and modifications. That is, the knowledge basic to vernacular approaches to built environments, such as buildings and the layout of social space for different kinds of human activity, was part of the cultural commons. The design and aesthetic embellishments often were an expression of the culture's religious cosmovision—which reflected the culture's deepest origins in the past, and which provided the moral guidelines for living in the cultural and environmental commons.

The modern industrial approach to the design and construction of built environments is profoundly different from the vernacular approaches that were less influenced by monet-ized relationships. In the modern industrial approach the design team, sources of technologies and building materials, and paid workers often have little or no connection with the local culture. In recent years there has been a reaction to the industrial design and use of building materials, with more attention now being given to local context, achieving greater energy efficiencies, and the use of local building materials. One example of this shift can be seen in what Sim Van Der Ryn and Stuart Cowen advocate in their book, *Ecological Design* (1996). The five principles of design include the following:

First Principle: **Solutions Grow From Place**
Ecological design begins with the intimate knowledge of a particular place. Therefore, it is small-scale and direct, responsive to both local conditions and local people. If we are sensitive to the nuances of place, we can inhabit without destroying.

Second Principle: **Ecological Accounting Informs Design**
Trace the environmental impacts of existing or proposed designs. Use this information to determine the most ecologically sound design possibility.

Third Principle: **Design With Nature**
By working with living processes, we respect the needs of all species while meeting our own. Engaging in processes that regenerate rather than deplete, we become more alive.

Fourth Principle: **Everyone is a Designer**
Listen to every voice in the design process. No one is participant only or designer only: Everyone is a participant-designer. Honor the special knowledge that each person brings. As people work together to heal their places, they also heal themselves.

Fifth Principle: **Make Nature Visible**
De-natured environments ignore our need and our potential for learning. Making natural cycles and processes visible brings the designed environment back to life. Effective design helps inform us of our place within nature.

The fourth principle, "Everyone is a Designer," needs to be qualified in order to take account of the way in which many people raised in an industrial, consumer-oriented culture bring this form of consciousness to how they think about design and to their aesthetic judgments. In reducing people to a wage earner and a consumer, many indi-viduals have become rootless and thus short term inhabitants of place. The result is that their knowledge and commitment to place (in the way Van Der Ryn and Cowan are using the word) is likely to be superficial, leaving them thinking of place as where they live in relationship to schools, freeways, and megastores. When rootless individuals have more money or access to credit cards than knowledge of the local cultural and environmental commons, their sense of good design will more likely reproduce the garish mix of houses and commercial buildings that are often better suited for other climates and cultural traditions.

There are many ways of introducing students to the differences between local knowledge of sustainable built environments that has been accumulated over generations of living in a bioregion, and the knowledge that leads to buildings that reflect the assumptions of the industrial culture. Observing, thinking, and discussing the differences help to develop the vocabulary and awareness necessary for participating in democratic decision making about what is being lost as a result of the further expansion of the market culture.

Like the encounters with other areas of the cultural and environmental commons, developing the concepts that highlight relationships, the vocabulary that fosters awareness of what was previously unrecognized and thus unspoken, as well as introducing students to the differences between a knowledge of a craft and the industrial mode of production can begin in the early grades. Students can discuss the difference between their own experience of assembling something that has been industrially produced and the experience of a craft person such as a weaver or potter whom they have observed and listened to.

This is also the starting point for learning about the different mentors in the community, including the extent that the mentors rely upon a knowledge of local materials, the intergenerational traditions they learned from, and their way of understanding of how traditions of creativity, from jazz to folk music, are both sources of empowerment and individual expression. It should also be possible to introduce in an elementary way the complex nature of context such as weather patterns, physical nature of the environment, the plants and animals, and the traditions of adopting the design and placement of building to the local setting. This can be introduced by showing pictures of rural houses in Japan, of the dwellings that the Dogans have adapted to fit the region of Mali that they have inhabited for generations, and of modern buildings where the temperatures require the use of air conditioning (which can be compared with the approaches to cooling living spaces in the vernacular designed buildings). Through the use of photographs, the differences in aesthetic judgment that lead to the interior spaces and furnishings of a Japanese rural dwelling (including the aesthetic nature of their tools) and the rooms and furnishings of a typical American house can be discussed. Young students are capable of observing and articulating what they see as the differences, and even to begin discussing the differences in cultural values and approaches to individual development.

As students move into the middle grades, it should be possible to begin examining the ecological consequences of relying upon modern, industrially dictated design principles and use of materials that do not take account of the characteristics of the local environment or the traditions of the local culture. The high-rise glass encased buildings, such as the ones built in the new capital of Brazil, in Malaysia, and other regions of the world, require vast amounts of energy to cool them. Students need to consider where the energy comes from, and what impact the dams have on local ecosystems—including the local people. As these people are displaced by the damming of the local river, where are they displaced, and does their loss of knowledge of how to live in communities that are largely outside of the money economy lead to their further impoverishment? The discussion can be made relevant by asking students to compare the differences in how people interact when shopping in a megastore such as Wal-Mart with shopping in small shops along the main street in their local community. In discussing the connections between built environments, spaces in which people interact, and the strengthening or the loss of a sense of community, they are learning to think relationally—which means how the participants in cultural and natural ecologies interact in supportive and destructive ways.

At the university level, students should learn about the impact of different ideologies, including religions, on the local traditions of design and craft knowledge. Which ideologies still promote the industrial system of design and production that continue to marginalize the ability of craft persons to make a living in the local economy? Which ideologies are sensitive to cultural differences in knowledge systems, and which promote the importance of conserving the world's linguistic diversity? This is an especially important concern as many of these languages encode knowledge of how to live within the limits of the local ecosystems (which have been tested over many generations). This knowledge has influenced the nature of the local built environments which, in turn, have influenced the culture's impact on the landscape. In some instances, there is evidence that humans have been living in the same bioregion for hundreds of years without fundamentally altering the capacity of local ecosystems to renew themselves.

The history of ideas that relate to different aspects of built environments as well as the importance of crafts need to be part of the university curriculum. These histories should be approached from the perspective of different cultures. The one theme that connects them is the rise and spread of the West's industrial, market-oriented form of consciousness, and how this form of consciousness continues to undermine the diversity of the cultural and environmental commons. As this theme is brought into focus in these histories, the question that should be raised is: What role have Western universities played in the ongoing process of cultural colonization that we now refer to as globalization?

If teachers feel themselves lacking the knowledge necessary for introducing these and other aspects of the cultural and environmental commons, they can invite speakers such as architects, landscape architects, and urban planners who have different ways of thinking about built environments. They can also invite trades people to discuss their understanding of building materials, the difference between the form of work dictated by an assembly process and a craft such as woodworking, and the traditions they rely upon in framing, wiring, and installing the plumbing system in a house—and how they understand their responsibility. Out of these presentations will come the questions and the issues that should be of central concern to the students who view themselves as future practitioners of these arts and skills.

Technology

All cultures rely upon technologies. As Jacques Ellul points out in *The Technological Society* (1964), there are fundamental differences between the technologies of modern Western cultures and those of non-Western cultures. One of the basic differences is that many non-Western technologies do not undermine the local cultural and environmental commons in the way that many modern Western technologies are designed to do. This difference can be accounted for by the fact that the modernizing technologies of the West are increasingly relied upon as the engine for expanding the economy. While many of these Western technologies have made important contributions to the quality of everyday life in both the West and non-Western countries, some technologies, such as computers, electricity, print, the internal combustion engine, and so forth, have a Janus nature in that they contribute both to the vitality of the local cultural commons while at the same time strengthening the economic forces that are enclosing them.

Historically, public schools and universities have provided the conceptual basis for developing new technologies, including more ecologically sustainable technologies. Unfortunately, there are few classroom teachers or university professors who encourage students to think about the cultural transforming nature of different technologies, how they impact the local commons in different cultures, and how they contribute to the West's market liberal goal of economic globalization. The result is that most students graduate from public schools and universities with the mistaken idea that new technologies are both the expression of progress and are, at the same time, a culturally neutral tool. This taken-for-granted way of thinking about technology effectively depoliticizes for the vast majority·

of people the different uses of technology, as well as the all important question of who benefits from their adoption. Introducing students to thinking about different aspects of the cultural commons (i.e., food, arts, narratives, landscapes, built environments, and so forth) that were discussed earlier will inevitably involve bringing up issues that surround the impact of different technologies. However, if technology is not given special attention, students may get the idea that technology is inherently progressive in nature and thus beyond the need for questioning.

Starting in the early grades, several areas of misunderstanding about the nature of technology need to be addressed directly by raising questions that can be answered as students reflect on their own experiences. Asking students to reflect on their own personal experience with interacting with various technologies is yet another example of students learning to give words to what is too often part of the taken-for-granted background experience. A widely held view is that technologies, such as the cell phone and the computer, are sources of empowerment and convenience. In order to bring out how different technologies mediate human experience (that is, both facilitate and reduce or even eliminate aspects of human experience) students should be asked which aspects of experience are facilitated by different technologies—such as how a cell phone enables them to communicate by voice and now to send pictures. The other question that reflecting upon their own experience will help to illuminate is: What cannot be communicated that is part of face-to-face communication? That is, can the non-verbal patterns of communication that influence how relationships are to be understood, as well as the importance of social context be communicated through a computer? As many of these patterns of non-verbal communication are taken-for-granted by students, the teacher may need to name the different patterns and perhaps even to point out the cultural differences. The question of what other aspects of the cultural commons cannot be stored and communicated through a computer can also be addressed at this level. It is vitally important that students understand the differences between the oral traditions of the cultural commons and what can be stored in and retrieved from a computer.

Another feature of some technologies can be introduced in the early grades, but deserve to be considered in more depth at later stages in the educational process. That is, some technologies alienate people from one another, while other technologies enable people to develop their personal interests and talents. Both assembly line approaches to production, as well as the increasing automation of work, alienate workers from exercising personal judgment and from mastering a craft. An assembly line can be simulated in the early grades in a way where students are responsible for only one segment of the production process. Following this experience, they can be asked to discuss how this affects their relationships with others as well as their sense of responsibility for aesthetic judgment and quality of workmanship that goes into the production process. The assembly line could be set up in terms of preparing a meal, or painting a picture where each student is responsible for using a specific color.

A third feature of technology that can be introduced in the early grades is the way in which some technologies enable people to exercise control over others. The advertising on cereal boxes can be discussed as an example of a non-mechanical technology that influences what children will want to eat for breakfast, and how the images on the box and the use of sugar and other chemicals may lead to rejecting the breakfast based on the intergenerational knowledge of the parents or grandparents (which is an example of the cultural commons). Comparing the technologies that are the basis of "fast food" available in the school cafeteria and at the local McDonalds with the technologies associated with the slow food experience (local gardens, meals prepared by and shared with parents, ethnic tastes, and so forth) will also help students in the early grades to be aware that different technologies are not a neutral tool—and that they may limit important aspects of experience.

As students move into the higher grades the issue of whether new technologies are always the expression of progress needs to be examined. This question should lead to an exploration of the political, economic, and ecological impact of different technologies. Again, the discussion needs to be framed in a way that enables students to assess different ways of thinking about technologies that they have experienced in daily life. These discussions may range from how automation, and the ability to locate the technology in a low-wage region of the world, reduce the need for the parents' knowledge and skills, to how other technologies reduce the need for physically demanding labor that have no redeeming qualities. It might also include a discussion of the forms of knowledge that are made irrelevant when the farmer purchases genetically engineered seeds, and how the use of the iPod reduces important dimensions of the bodily experiences that are part of being aware of the sights, sounds, and smells of the local environment. There are other questions about how different technologies affect interpersonal relationships, where one stands in the social status systems, who benefits and who loses in the use of different technologies, and how different technologies have influenced the use of language and patterns of thinking.

At the university level, the history of ideas that led to marginalizing technology as an important part of cultural studies needs to be given a central place in the students' education. Students need to learn about the differences between the technologies of cultures that have developed in ways that are more centered on living within the limits and possibilities of their bioregion, and the technologies that facilitate the process of colonization and have contributed to massive and possibly irreversible changes in the Earth's ecosystems. How the development and use of different technologies have been influenced by a culture's mythopoetic narratives and, in the West, by different religious beliefs and ideologies also needs to be studied. As modern science has become increasingly a source of new technologies that lead to new markets that further enclose the commons, students need to learn to distinguish between science and scientism, and how the latter leads to the development of technologies and markets that are both ecologically, politically, and morally problematic. The current efforts to explain how cultures are subject to the same process of natural selection that operates in the biological world would be just one example of the growing influence of scientism. Efforts to provide a scientific explanation of consciousness and to develop drugs or to locate the genes that affect both consciousness and memory are other examples that easily come to mind. The proposal to create a "gene-rich" line of humans who will perform the intellectually challenging tasks of society, while the "naturals" will be responsible for the hard work, is yet another example of scientism. As science now has such a direct impact on many aspects of cultural life, the question of what are the limits of scientific knowledge needs to be discussed—especially now that science provides the basis for the rapid advances in the development of surveillance technologies that are threatening our traditional freedoms.

In effect, studying the history of different technologies, their impact on the different cultural and environmental commons, and their role in colonizing other cultures, is essential to developing the vocabulary necessary for being able to participate in democratic debates about which technologies should be adopted and which should be rejected. Possessing the language that makes explicit different aspects of technology is essential to communicative competence, and communicative competence is necessary if people are to begin to democratize technological decisions.

An example of how the public schools and universities have failed to adapt their curricula in ways that enable their graduates to have an informed voice in deciding whether an important part of the cultural commons is being enclosed by recent advances in computer technology is the way in which our personal behaviors (consumer habits, travels, interactions with others), as well as the ideas we communicate over the cell phone or as an email message, are now under constant surveillance by corporations, government agencies, and even by other individuals we do not know. The transformation of what previously was our private life is now being transformed into data that is evaluated by people and computers that use criteria we are unaware of. Increasingly, the evaluations of the data gathered on our personal lives are based on concerns about national security and the marketing of products. Individual privacy, at least in most Western countries, has long been valued as an essential part of the cultural commons.

In most instances, the loss of privacy is directly tied to another tradition of the cultural commons that is also being undermined: namely, the right of the people to vote on what constitutes an appropriate and inappropriate use of this technology. Students need to consider the differences between a democratic and a surveillance society, as well as how a surveillance society impacts the cultural commons. There is also the question of the difference between a surveillance society and a police state—or what more properly should be called a fascist society. This question should lead students back to a consideration of how the diversity of cultural commons across America represents sites of resistance to the many ways computer technologies contribute to the centralization of political and economic power in the governmental agencies and corporations that collect and share the data.

Another issue that needs to be the focus of a discussion by faculty is whether the curricula taken by students going into computer related fields should include in-depth discussions of the moral and political issues that are raised by each new advance in the surveillance capacity of computer-based technologies. Do university graduates working to develop the technologies that will collect information on the products people purchase, that collect data on peoples' searches on Google, that can listen in on our cell phone conversations, understand that there are moral and political issues connected with the introduction of each new technology? Or do they simply assume that all forms of technological innovation are the expression of progress—and that there are no good reasons for questioning progress?

Civil Liberties

The form that civil liberties take in English speaking countries, as well as the different approaches taken in other countries, can be traced to historical events that led to the creation of laws that limited the power of government by codifying the rights of individuals. Among the historical events that contributed to the establishment of civil liberties that are now part of our cultural commons includes the signing of the Magna Carta in 1215 by King John, the abuse of power by a variety of absolute monarchs, the wars in Europe between 1485 and 1789 that were driven by religious differences between powerful despots, and the Enlightenment thinkers that laid the conceptual foundations for democratically elected governments.

As our civil liberties are under attack from a variety of sources, including the growing dominance of market liberalism, the spread of surveillance technologies, and religious fundamentalists who want to overturn the separation of church and state as well as our checks and balances system of government, it is vitally important that students understand how what remains of our civil liberties are being enclosed. They should also understand the consequences that will be faced if we proceed down this slippery slope.

If students do not understand the nature of the civil liberties that previous generations have relied upon and worked to extend to minority groups, the cultural and environmental commons will be further undermined—for the sake of profits and control by authoritarian groups. These civil liberties include habeas corpus which protects against unlawful restraint by government, the rights of individuals guaranteed in the Constitution, the separation of church and state, an independent judiciary (that is, free of market and religious ideology), the presumption of innocence until proven guilty, the rule of law, and so forth. The focus of learning about this critically important part of the cultural commons should be about the nature and origins of our civil liberties, as well as about the different ways they are being threatened and thus enclosed. It is important to reiterate an important characteristic of the political process: if the students (and later as voters) cannot name their civil liberties and do not understand their importance, they will be unable to resist their elimination. It is likely that they will not even be aware that certain of their civil liberties have disappeared. Unthinking patriotism, which serves the interests of politicians who seek power by playing on the fears of the American people as well as pursuing policies that make these fears appear legitimate, leads, as we have just witnessed, to the willing surrender of our rights to privacy to the National Security Agency. The use of Orwellian language contributes to the current trend whereby people who are speaking out in defense of our civil liberties are being accused of being un-American and "appeasers" of the enemy.

When the traditions of civil liberties cease to be part of the cultural commons, decision making will then be centered in the hands of powerful coalitions of political and corporate elites, along religious extremists who will provide the governing moral codes that will justify ignoring the spread of poverty and environmental devastation. Local democracy and the diverse traditions of intergenerational knowledge that are the basis of community self-sufficiency will be replaced by the market forces that will separate the righteous from the unrighteous (for the religious fundamentalists), the better adapted from the less well adapted (for the proponents of natural selection), and those who are driven by competition from those who have been marginalized or do not have the competitive drive to make profits the primary goal in life. The loss of our civil liberties will coincide with the further enclosure of the cultural and environmental commons—and as this process accelerates, the further degradation of the natural systems we depend upon will lead to the kind of economic chaos that will cause people to demand an even greater centralization of power in the government that is responsible for the crises in the first place.

Language

The examples given above of how to connect language and concepts with the different levels of the students' experience and background knowledge also serve as models of how to introduce students to other aspects of the cultural commons that are now being enclosed. An aspect of the cultural commons that is often overlooked as an example of what is shared on a non-monetized basis and available to everyone not limited by the culture's class system and prejudices is the way in which language is being enclosed. The enclosure of language can result from new technologies, from the marginalization of collective memory as a result of an emphasis on progress and the sense that the past (and the language that sustained it as memory) are sources of backwardness, and from different modes of inquiry and the narratives they promote—such as science and its narrative of evolution. Carl Sagan argued that the scientific mode of inquiry is the only one that is self-correcting and thus is universally valid—and that all traditional ways of knowing and valuing are examples of backwardness and superstition. E. O. Wilson, as well as computer scientists such as Ray Kurzweil, argue that evolution should replace all existing religious traditions. Market-liberal and Christian fundamentalists have a different vision of the future. As they came to power we can see how their policies repressed the language used to articulate social justice and environmental issues, as well as the languages of non-Western cultures.

At the high school level it should be possible to examine the words and patterns of thinking that would be silenced or marginalized by taking-for-granted the cultural assumptions about the autonomous individual, a mechanistic model of life processes and relationships, and an anthropocentric way of thinking about human nature relationships. At the university level the way in which disciplines are based on different assumptions, along with the vocabulary that supports them, can lead to asking whose language is being suppressed or marginalized. For example, do disciplines such as psychology and cognitive science marginalize the languages that reproduce the differences in cultural ways of knowing—including the language they use to pass on the intergenerational knowledge of their cultural and environmental commons? How does the theory of evolution, when extended as the basis for understanding which set of cultural memes are better adapted for survival, marginalize the importance of indigenous languages, or the language necessary for clarifying the limits of evolution as an explanatory theory? What does the metaphor of "meme" serve to illuminate and hide? Does it marginalize the language necessary for justifying a democratic form of society, or does it contribute to the revival of social Darwinism? How do courses in economics marginalize the language that is used in mutual support activities where work is returned rather than paid? And does the language of mainstream Western philosophy marginalize the language necessary for thinking and communicating about the commons? Each of the disciplines can be examined in terms of how its vocabulary illuminates and hides—with what is hidden being an example of enclosure.

Other Characteristics of the Cultural Commons

Even the traditions of scholarship that were examples of the cultural commons, (that is shared on a non-monetized basis) are now under threat. One of these long-standing traditions is being enclosed as recent changes in copyright laws now recognize scholarly writing as private property. Other examples of enclosure of the cultural commons that allowed for the free exchange of knowledge and discoveries is being undermined by the merging of scientific research with corporate interests. This has resulted in the early patenting of research results and the growing sense that new knowledge must have market value. Even old knowledge that used to be freely available at the local library is being digitized and sold as a consumer product.

Having students attend a county fair would provide an opportunity to identify the range of knowledge that enables members of the community to grow different kinds of flowers, practice the various needle crafts as well as weaving and fiber arts, preserve a wide range of food—from berry jam to chutney, care and feeding a wide range of domestic animals, and performing on musical instruments. The country fair represents just part of the varied practices of intergenerational knowledge that sustain the local cultural commons. Each area of knowledge and craft skill can be used for examining how the forces of modernity and consumerism is contributing to their enclosure. Other crafts might include boat building, cabinet making, and designing children's toys. The knowledge connected with various games that range from playing chess, many card games, to soccer is passed along from generation to generation—but are now being enclosed by becoming part of the growing computer-mediated market place.

The mutual support systems of the community, which range volunteerism to working on community environmental restoration projects, also need to be examined if the students are to have the experience of "giving back" and of being part of a mutually supportive community. The general silences in the media and most areas of the curriculum at both the public school and university level about these non-monetized forms of personal and community enrichment are a major factor in enclosing these aspects of the cultural commons. The hyper-consumerism, as well as the low paying jobs that force millions of people to work at several jobs in the same day, reduces the time that people have for participating in various activities that sustain the vitality of the local cultural commons. In effect, the growing dependency upon a money economy that is both addictive, and that reduces the free time necessary for non-monetized pursuits, represents yet another form of enclosure. Free time, which we seem to want more of—yet are unable to attain, is a part of the cultural commons that is essential to the continued renewal of the other aspects of the cultural commons. If there is no free time, then it becomes impossible to participate in activities that strengthen the commons.

Education that Sustains the Environmental Commons

When environmental education is treated as a separate course the question of how humans are impacting natural systems is generally approached from a scientific perspective. The larger issue of what is happening on a global scale may be a background concern, but the main focus is generally on the changes taking place in local ecosystems. The curricular focus thus varies with the characteristics of the local bioregion. Specific issues such as the rapid disappearance of sagebrush may be the focus in schools located in the prairie regions of the country, while the pollution of the air is likely to be a focus in densely populated urban areas, and the changes in the chemistry of local lakes, streams, and oceans being the focus in nearby schools. Regardless of the bioregion, there are more general issues that are studied in environmental education classes. These include the nature of invasive species, how the loss of habitat contributes to the loss of species—which, in turn, will focus on different kinds of habitat and species loss.

In the Northwest, the focus may be on changes in the nearby stream beds that limit the ability of salmon to reproduce themselves, how the clear cutting of forests reduces the habitat needed by different species of birds and small mammals, and how the dams and changes in water temperature impact the number of salmon that return to spawn. Across what was formerly the great plains covered with native grasses, the focus now may be on the loss of species that result from the use of herbicides, the impact of irrigation on local aquifers, and the farming techniques that contribute to the loss of topsoil. In other bio-regions, the main focus will reflect essentially the same set of relationships: namely, how the manifestations of the industrial culture, with its reliance upon toxic chemicals and more efficient technologies, impacts the local environment. In the New England states bordering on the Atlantic Ocean, the environmental education class may address the changes in the use of technologies and the chemistry of the water that are affecting the number of lobsters and other species of fish that local economies depend upon. Even though the focus on how changes in local habitats affect the diversity of species may differ from bioregion to bioregion, students are learning how to collect data on changes occur-ring in the local ecosystems and to understanding the characteristics of healthy ecosystems. In many instances they are learning how to restore degraded ecosystems by relying on scientific research.

Increasingly environmental education courses are incorporating what is being learned about mapping green spaces, how to understand the environmental issues that need to be taken into account in various approaches to development, and how environmentally oriented architects are designing buildings that are more energy efficient and less pollut-ing. Some instructors even encourage students to learn how public officials make decisions that may or may not take into account the impact on natural systems. While there are many important issues discussed in environmental education classes, there are silences that reflect the silences in the education of the science professors who teach the courses that constitute the major area of academic concentration and the pedagogy-related classes that are required as part of the environmental education teacher's professional studies.

These silences include a knowledge of the diversity of the world's cultural commons, the nature and importance of what remains of the local cultural commons that are alternatives to the environmentally destructive consumer-dependent lifestyle—that, ironically, scien-tific knowledge has helped to expand on a global basis. As pointed out earlier in the chapter, if environmental education is understood as a stand-alone course it is likely that the silences will be perpetuated. And the result will be that students, when they reach adulthood, will continue to think that environmental issues are important but will not recognize that their consumer dependent lifestyle makes their environmental concerns little more than a ritualistic word game. More importantly, the silence about the nature and importance of the cultural commons, as well as a knowledge of the different forms of enclosure that result from new technologies and the spread of market liberal policies that are packaged under the misleading label of conservatism will reduce the ability to recog-nize when different aspects of the cultural commons are incorporated into the industrial system of production and consumption. In effect, when environmental education does not include the changes occurring in the world's diverse cultural commons, it leaves students with a basic misunderstanding: namely, that working to restore habitats, to reduce pollu-tion, and to introduce the technological changes necessary for limiting the rate of global warming should be the main focus of environmental stewardship.

Unfortunately, these laudable goals leave out the importance of understanding the cul-tural assumptions that still give conceptual and moral legitimacy to the industrial culture that is now being globalized. They also ignore the importance of learning that part of the answer to the global crises we are now facing, which includes growing poverty as more people are forced to live within a money-dominated economy as well as the decline in natural resources that humans depend upon, can be found in the non-monetized, mutual support systems in the local communities. In not understanding the ways in which the industrial consumer-oriented culture, along with its legitimating ideology, are enclosing what remains of the local cultural commons, the possibility of widespread political support for resisting various forms of enclosure will be lacking. This failure of local democracy to protect the local cultural and environmental commons can be seen in the way in which energy-oriented corporations, with the aid of Congress and the President George W. Bush are degrading local environments wherever there is the possibility of finding new sources of energy necessary for the support of the gas-inefficient SUVs and supersized houses. The failure of local democracy can be seen in how the industrial culture is enclosing other areas of the cultural and environmental commons—from intergenerational foods, municipal water systems, to the privacy of individuals. As stated earlier, understanding the cultural assumptions that have marginalized an awareness of the cultural commons as sites of resistance to the industrial culture, as well as the ideas and values that now justify its globalization, require the participation of classroom teachers and university professors who are knowledgeable about a variety of disciplines—including the assumptions these disciplines have been based upon and how they need to be transformed.

References

Ellul, J. (1964). *The Technological Society.* New York: Vintage Books.

MacIntyre, A. (1984). *After Virtue: A Study in Moral Theory.* (2nd ed.) Notre Dame, IN.: University of Notre Dame Press.

Van Der Ryn, Sim, and Cowan, S. (1996). *Ecological Design.* Washington, D.C.: Island Press

34

The Aims of Education

Nel Noddings

People want to be happy and, since this desire is well-nigh universal, we would expect to find happiness included as an aim of education. Its failure to appear among the aims usually stated might be a sign that Western society is still mired in a form of Puritanism or, more generously, it may be generally believed that, as Orwell said, happiness cannot be achieved by aiming at it directly. If the latter is so, what should we aim at that might promote happiness?

Until quite recently, aims-talk figured prominently in educational theory, and most education systems prefaced their curriculum documents with statements of their aims. What functions have been served by aims-talk, and what have we lost (if anything) by ceasing to engage in it? What has taken its place?

I will start this chapter by arguing that we need to talk about aims, and I will fill out that argument with a discussion of aims-talk and the purposes it served in earlier educational thought. Looking at contemporary educational policymaking, we'll see that talk of aims might be considered a missing dimension in the educational conversation. Finally, by discussing aims in some depth, I will set the stage for exploring ways in which education might actively support the pursuit of happiness.

Aims-talk and its Purposes

Suppose we visit an algebra class and watch a lesson on the factoring of trinomials. The learning objective is clear. The teacher has listed several familiar types of trinomials, and the students are occupied in identifying them and performing the factorizations. If we ask Ms. A (the teacher) why she is teaching this topic, she will probably reply that the next topic is combining algebraic fractions, and one cannot easily find the appropriate common denominator without a knowledge of factoring. Now, of course, one could proceed by simply multiplying denominators, but the expressions quickly become unwieldy and, to get the required answer, one would eventually have to factor. Ms. A's response is entirely appropriate if (1) we have already found good reasons for teaching algebra to these students and (2) we have agreed that algebra consists of a certain sequence of topics. When a teacher is asked about a lesson objective, she or he almost always responds with an explanation of how this learning objective fits with others that come before and after it. Today most mathematics textbooks are organized in this way.

An observer might get a somewhat deeper response from Ms. A to the question Why are you spending so much time on this topic? To this, Ms. A might reply that her course of study (or textbook) emphasizes solving equations; many of these involve rational expressions that need simplification—factoring again—and so this topic requires much attention. This answer is unsatisfactory in its apparent circularity, but it does point at a larger goal and not just at the next skill to be mastered.

Without trying to draw a sharp line of demarcation, I will associate objectives with lessons and goals with courses or sequences of courses.[1] Most of our "why" questions are answered within the prescribed system; that is, we explain why we are doing something in terms of other objectives or, occasionally, in terms of goals.

Such answers assume, as noted previously, that we have good reasons for teaching algebra to these particular students and that the course of study we are presenting as algebra will be recognized and approved by mathematics educators. The second criterion is easily tested by submission to a group of experts who are in a position to say whether a given course of study is adequate as algebra. Experts may, of course, differ on whether the course is appropriate for gifted, average, or slow learners, but that analysis brings us back to the first question: Do we have a good reason for teaching algebra to *these* students?

Discussion of aims, in contrast to that of objectives and goals, centers on the deepest questions in education. What are we trying to accomplish by teaching algebra? Who benefits? Should our efforts be designed to enhance the society (or state) or should they be directed at benefits for the individual? If we are concerned with something like self-actualization, what does this mean? Do we have to say something about human nature? If we are concerned with the welfare of the state, must we describe the sort of state in, and for, which we will educate? Is there an inherent conflict between individuals and societies? This is just a sample of the questions that must be considered when we engage in aims-talk.

Some people object to wasting time on aims-talk. Wasn't all this settled long ago? People have been debating questions concerning the aims of education since the days of Plato and, in our times (within a century or so), talk of aims has not changed schooling dramatically. Why not avoid such useless talk and get on with the practical business of educating children? Even teachers talk this way and seem to have little patience for conversations that do not culminate with something useful for tomorrow's lessons.

In response, one might argue that aims-talk is to education what freedom is to democracy. Without freedom, democracy degenerates into a form quite different from liberal democracy. Similarly, without continual, reflective discussion of aims, education may become a poor substitute for its best vision. Moreover, just as freedom takes on newer and richer meanings as times change, so must the aims of education change. Even if they might be stated in fairly constant general terms, the meaning of those constant words will take on new coloring as conditions change. To be literate today, for example, is different from being literate in the days of Charlemagne (who could read but not write) or in colonial America, where people did not need the forms of visual literacy required by present-day media.

It has always been one function of philosophers of education to critique the aims of education in light of their contemporary cultures. It has been another of their functions to criticize the society with respect to a vision of education. In the next section, we will see that some philosophers have started with a description of ideal or actual states from which they have derived recommendations for education. Others have started with a vision for the education of individuals and asked what sort of state might support that vision. Simply accepting the state as it is and the system as it is (merely pushing it to perform its perceived function more vigorously) is a dangerous (and lazy) strategy. I will argue that this is the policy we have followed for the past two decades, and it is likely to prove ruinous.

Another objection to aims-talk is that it often culminates in asking too much of schools.[2] This was an objection raised against the aims suggested in 1918 by Clarence Kingsley in the famous Cardinal Principles Report.[3] Herbert Kliebard comments:

> By far the most prominent portion of the 32-page report was the statement of the seven aims that would guide the curriculum: "1. Health. 2. Command of fundamental processes. 3. Worthy home-membership. 4. Vocation. 5. Citizenship. 6. Worthy use of leisure. 7. Ethical character."[4]

happiness

Oddly, while more radical educators such as David Snedden thought the report was still far too academic, later critics blamed it for laying the foundation of *life adjustment* education, asking the impossible of schools, and making the academic task of the schools more difficult. People in the latter camp wanted to reduce the responsibility of the schools, to academic learning. They insisted that no institution could take on such a broad array of responsibilities.

more objections to early attempts

Whether the task is possible depends on how it is understood, and it is a function of aims-talk to deliberate and come to a useful understanding on this. I have always found the Cardinal Principles quite wonderful. Indeed, I do not see how schools can operate as *educational* institutions without attending to at least these aims, and obviously I want to add another—happiness. Everything depends on the next step: How shall we employ these aims in guiding what we do in constructing a curriculum, in classroom teaching, in establishing interpersonal relationships, in designing school buildings, in management and discipline, and in community relations?

HOW?

If we were to proceed in the way advocated by scientific curriculum makers (for example, Franklin Bobbitt),[5] the task might indeed be impossible, because our next step would be to derive objectives from our aims. Imagine the work required to establish learning objectives for each of these large aims! Where would each objective be placed, and who would teach it? It is not necessary, however, to proceed in this fashion. We might even argue that it is a mistake to do so; specifying the entire curriculum as objectives before teachers and students begin to interact forecloses the freedom of students to participate in the construction of their own learning objectives.

if go by Bobbitt example impossible!

Cannot leave students out of the picture

As we engage in aims-talk, we have an opportunity to question the role of objectives in general. Do our aims suggest that every lesson should have a stated objective and, if so, what form should it take? Must each lesson have a specific learning objective, or is it sometimes appropriate to describe what the teacher will do and leave open what the students might learn?[6] In the midst of our aims-talk, we would pause also to note that some objectives might well be prespecified. When should this be done? By whom?

In earlier chapters, I suggested that Orwell and others might have been right when they said that happiness cannot be attained by pursuing it directly. The same can be said of several other aims in the Cardinal Principles. This does not mean, however, that they cannot function at all as aims. It means, rather, that we must continually reflect upon, discuss, and evaluate what we are doing to see if our objectives and procedures are compatible with our aims.

need constant reevaluation

A little later, I will try to show that failure to engage in vigorous discussion of educational aims has marked the movement toward standardization and high-stakes testing. In that discussion, we will ask what the movement's advocates are trying to do and whether the systems and procedures they have recommended are likely to support or undermine their tacit aims. First, however, to get a better sense of how aims-talk might assist current thinking, let's look briefly at how it has functioned in the past.

Aims in Earlier Educational Thought

Plato's discussion of education is embedded in his analysis of the just state. As Socrates and his companions in dialogue try to create the design for a just state, they inevitably encounter issues concerning education. Plato does not start with the individual; that possibility with respect to the meaning of the term *just* is discarded early in the dialogue as too difficult. Talk shifts from the just man to the just state.[7] Thus, when education becomes the topic of analysis, the needs of the state are paramount. As the discussants consider the needs of the state and its collective people, they decide that the kinds of people needed fall into three categories: rulers, guardians (auxiliaries or warriors), and artisans (tradespeople and other workers).

Plato does not ignore individuals, but he treats them as representatives of classes organized according to their *natures*. Children are to be watched and tested to identify their talents and interests, and then they are to receive an education compatible with their demonstrated natures. Positions in the just state are not inherited; they are distributed through a procedure of diagnosis and education. Poor children from the artisan class may exhibit the "golden" attributes required of rulers, and children of rulers may show the "bronze" qualities typical of artisans.

Socrates brings the needs of the state and the individual together by noting that people will care for what they love. Thus, if the state needs people who will do their jobs well, it should be sure that they are trained effectively in occupations to which they are well suited. Those who love certain forms of work will care deeply about that work and become competent at it. Further, Socrates scorns the dilettante and the jack-of-all-trades. Everyone in the just state is to perform one essential job and do so expertly.

In his comments about the Platonic scheme of education, John Dewey commends the practice of providing different forms of education for children with different interests:

> We cannot better Plato's conviction that an individual is happy and society well organized when each individual engages in those activities for which he has a natural equipment, nor his conviction that it is the primary office of education to discover this equipment to its possessor and train him for its effective use.[8]

But Dewey draws back from Plato's organization of human beings into three classes. For Dewey, "each individual constitutes his own class,"[9] and the processes of education must be dynamic and flexible. Dewey's discussion of education is embedded in that of a democratic state/community, whereas Plato's aims at a perfect (some say totalitarian) state that is unchanging and hierarchically organized.

Plato had two great aims in mind for his system of education. First, for the benefit of the state, he wanted to educate the three large classes he identified, each group trained to the highest degree. Second, for the benefit of the individual, he insisted that education should be aimed at improvement of the soul, and by *soul* Plato meant the harmonious development of three parts: appetite (impulse or desire), reason, and spirit (energy).[10] The parallel to the three classes constituting the population of the just state is striking. In the individual, the three parts are also properly organized hierarchically, and a just soul places reason in the role of ruler, spirit in the role of guardian-auxiliary, and appetite in the role of artisan—one who is necessary to the whole but must be controlled by a wise ruler (reason).

We can draw a limited parallel between Plato's educational aims and those of today's reformers in the United States. First, the standards/testing movement is driven primarily by an aim that speaks to the welfare of the nation. Here the similarity is clear. If anything, the current goal in the United States is even narrower than Plato's because it concentrates almost entirely on the economic status of the country. Second, we see in Plato's plan the elements of what we now call a *meritocracy*. Offices and occupations are to be filled by those qualified, not by inheritance or political preference. This practice is also espoused (if not always enacted) by contemporary democracies.

With respect to individuals, however, the aims diverge. Plato was clear in the way he valued the three classes of individuals, and the high value he placed on rulers came directly from his underlying philosophy. The theory of forms made reason and theory superior to action and practice. Those who work with their minds were thought to be superior to those who work with their bodies. Our own society pretends to reject this ordering on the grounds that it is repugnant to a democratic society, but our actual social ordering suggests a considerable degree of hypocrisy, if not schizophrenia on the issue. The Platonic legacy is still strong, even if kept below the surface of discussion. We say we value all honest, necessary contributions equally, but we allow people who do essential manual work to live in poverty or near-poverty, and we embrace as an educational aim to prepare all children so that they will not have to do such work. We fail to ask an essential question: If we were to succeed in this effort, who would do the work so necessary and yet so despised today?

Not only do we fail to educate children along lines congruent with their *natural equipment*, but we insist that natural differences are so minimal that all children can profit from the education once reserved for a few. Unlike Plato, we do not even ask whether that education is appropriate for anyone, much less for everyone. The use of democratic language suggests that the same education for all is a generous and properly democratic measure when, in fact, it may well be both undemocratic and ineffective. It will be ineffective if Plato was right when he said that people will care for (and do well at) work they love. Many will fail in schools because they are forced to do work they hate and are deprived of work they might love.

Plato's entire discussion of education in *The Republic* is pervaded by aims-talk. He and his companions eventually accept the broad components of a traditional curriculum—music (which then included all forms of literature) and gymnastic—but not without significant modification. They do not simply turn the details over to experts in music and gymnastic. Rather, they ask why these subjects should be taught; that is, they continually return to primary aims—improvement of the soul and benefit to the state. Socrates, Plato's spokesperson in the dialogues, does not want rulers and guardians to become muscle-bound athletes from single-minded concentration on gymnastic, nor does he want them to become *effeminate* (his unfortunate label) through over-concentration on music. Improvement of the soul requires harmony among the three aspects of self.

Referring to those aims directed at establishing and maintaining the just state, Socrates recommends certain constraints on the stories and poems to be heard by children. A discussion of Plato's plans for censorship would take us too far afield. For present purposes, what is important is his continuous attention to aims. The question What shall be taught? is never answered definitively without a thorough exploration of the companion question Why?

Plato also looked at elements of private life that contribute to happiness; he was concerned about how we should live—what virtues should be cultivated and what tastes developed. Today's reformers say little about forms of personal well-being that are aimed at neither the country's nor the individual's economic status. Plato at least argued for a form of happiness that arises in doing one's chosen work well, and Dewey also noted this aspect of happiness. But neither Plato nor Dewey said much about homemaking, parenting, or a host of other everyday occupations significant in personal life. I will argue that these must be included in our discussion of educational aims if we are concerned with the happiness of individuals.

Before leaving this brief account of aims in Plato, I want to emphasize again that I am not defending a hierarchical sorting of children according to specific academic criteria, but I will strongly defend different forms of education for children with different interests and talents. It seems entirely right for a democratic society to reject the elitist scheme offered by Plato, but the rejection must be honest and carefully argued. Have we really rejected Plato's ordering when we decide that all children will be prepared (in effect) for the category once classified as best? By our very designation of that curriculum as best, we may have aggravated the denigration of interests and capacities that do not require traditional academic preparation. At its most arrogant, this attitude says to others, "Now you will have a chance to be just like me, and then you will be worth something."

Another approach to educational aims is found in the work of Rousseau. I will limit the discussion of Rousseau's philosophy of education drastically because my main point is to contrast his approach to aims with that of Plato and to emphasize once again the centrality of aims-talk in any fully developed theory of education.

In contrast to Plato, Rousseau begins his *Emile* with the individual, not the state.[11] The aims of education are derived from the basic premise that the child is born good and will develop best (as nature intends) if education by people and education by things are well coordinated with the education provided by nature. With this basic aim—to produce the best possible (natural) "man"—Rousseau sets out to describe how education by people and things (the forms over which we have some control) should take place. Everything suggested for Emile's education is tested against this aim.

Rousseau does not ignore the needs of the state or society. Recognizing that Emile must live in association with others, he asks how best to prepare him as both a citizen and a man. The citizen Emile will become should be as little different from the natural man as possible. Making enormous assumptions about the natural man, Rousseau aims to produce men who will think for themselves, be models of civic virtue, understand and practice justice, and in general become whatever they are able and willing to become.

The concept on which Rousseau depends so heavily, Nature, is both ambiguous and notoriously problematic as he interprets it. Men and women are "naturally" different, Rousseau declares, and therefore their education should be different. Sophie, Emile's female counterpart, should be obedient, amiable, and useful. She should not think for herself but always seek the approval of proper men and society.[12] Book V of *Emile* is a feminist nightmare. But, although Rousseau's interpretations of nature are questionable and even inconsistent, he is consistent in referring to his stated aims involving nature. We can challenge him intelligently today precisely because we find his answers to the "why" questions unsatisfactory and objectionable. Even if Rousseau were to experience a sort of feminist epiphany and decide, as Socrates did, that there are no relevant intellectual differences between men and women so far as citizenship is concerned, we would still be able to criticize him with respect to the basic aim he has adopted—the natural man (or woman).

When John Dewey discussed aims in education, he said that his account of education "assumed that the aim of education is to enable individuals to continue their education—or that the object and reward of learning is continued capacity for growth."[13] He then went on to claim that such a view of education makes sense and can only be implemented in a democratic society. It takes a book-length discussion to support these claims and to show what they might look like in practice. But Dewey was careful later in the discussion to insist on a multiplicity of aims that change with the needs and beliefs of a society. Not only must these aims be considered together for coherence but each must be judged, we assume, in light of the overriding aim: Is the adoption of Aim X likely to further growth or impede it? Under what conditions?

At a similar level of abstraction, Alfred North Whitehead said that the aim of education should be to produce people "who possess both culture and expert knowledge in some special direction."[14] A bit later, he wrote, "There is only one subject-matter for education, and that is Life in all its manifestations."[15] Again, such statements demand full and lengthy discussion, but they give us a starting point to which we continually return.

As I try to promote happiness as an aim of education. I have to offer a convincing account of happiness, how it connects to human needs, what it means in the society we inhabit, how it might transform that society into a better one, and how it fits with a host of other legitimate aims. Like Dewey with growth and Whitehead with life, I have to show how happiness can be used as a criterion by which to judge other aims and the value of our aims-talk. Indeed, an important function of aims is to encourage the aims-talk that enriches both educational thinking and the wisdom of the race. We continually ask, If you are aiming at X, why are you doing Y? How does Y fit with X?

The Missing Dimension Today

At the beginning of the twenty-first century, educational discussion is dominated by talk of standards, and the reason given for this emphasis is almost always economic. The underlying aims seem to be (1) to keep the United States strong economically and (2) to give every child an opportunity to do well financially. There is something worrisome about both of these aims, if indeed they are the aims that drive the standards movement. First, the idea that schools play a role in making our economy competitive is cast in intemperate language that charges the schools with failure on this task. Why should the schools be accused of undermining the American economy during a time of unparalleled prosperity? The aim of keeping our economy strong seems reasonable, but the demands for accountability and standards at such a time seem oddly out of place. They make us suspect that something else is operating. Second, we should be deeply troubled by the suggestion that economic equity can be achieved by forcing the same curriculum and standards on all children. The question of what is meant by equity is answered hastily and with little justification. Finally, of course, the aims (with no debate) are far too narrow. There is more to individual life and the life of a nation than economic superiority.

The standards movement had its effective start in 1983 with the publication of *A Nation at Risk*.[16] Published toward the end of a significant recession, the report used alarmist language to rouse the American public to the great danger posed by a supposedly failing school system. It spoke of "a rising tide of mediocrity" and went so far as to say, "If an unfriendly foreign power had attempted to impose on America the mediocre educational performance that exists today, we might well have viewed it as an act of war."[17] Response to the alarm was nationwide, and by 2000 every state but one (Iowa) had established new (arguably higher) standards for the achievement of school children at all levels of K-12 education.

It is interesting to note that, without a discernible change in scores on most standardized tests of achievement, the United States moved quickly into a period of unprecedented prosperity—despite its supposedly abysmal schools. Indeed, several careful analysts have challenged the claims of *A Nation at Risk*,[18] but it is not my purpose here to argue the strength of their case. Rather, I want to show what has been missed by failing to engage in a discussion of aims.

One prominent claim of the alarmists was that achievement scores had fallen badly since the late 1960s. This might be something to worry about, and critics of the report set about finding explanations for the drop. For example, it was argued that many more students now take the SATs (one measure of academic achievement) and that, with a substantially different population, we should expect different scores and norms adjusted accordingly. This is entirely reasonable from a statistical perspective.

The debate could have been more thoughtful. Had our aims changed during the period of decline? Clearly, we were trying to prepare many more students for college. Why were we doing this? Did the society need more people with a college education? With a traditional college education? The reason most often offered was that everyone in a liberal democracy should have a chance to obtain the goods of that society. That seems right. But does such a commitment imply that access to those goods must come through successful competition in traditional schooling? What happens, then, to those who do not do well in the only form of schooling we now make available in the name of equity? Suppose instead that we created rich alternative curricula and provided guidance to those students who might welcome and succeed with them? Questions such as these go to the very roots of what we believe about democracy and democratic schooling.

When we neglect these questions, a narrow educational focus is encouraged, and we distract ourselves from the social problems that cannot be solved by schools. For example, all people need adequate medical insurance, livable and affordable housing, safe neighborhoods, and nonpoverty wages for honest work. It is shortsighted and even arrogant to suppose that all people can escape these problems through better education, particularly if that education favors those with specific academic talents or resources. The jobs that today pay only poverty wages will still have to be done and, so long as we measure success in schools competitively, there will be losers.

One can see the value of aims-talk vividly here. When advocates of uniform standards claim that everyone will benefit, we can raise reasonable doubts. As we have seen, it is one function of aims-talk to challenge the existing rules by which a society has organized itself. Can poverty be traced to a lack of good education, or is the causal relation inverted? Why should anyone who works a full week at an honest job live in poverty? If everyone gets a college education, who will do today's poverty-level work? When we ask these questions, we begin to doubt the main argument offered by advocates of uniform standards. We may even be led to ask: What are these people really aiming at?

If the aim is justice—to provide all students with an education that will meet their needs—the solution is likely to involve the provision of considerable variety in school offerings and to include material that might contribute to personal as well as public life. Offering a variety of curricula does not mean putting together a set of courses labeled *easy*, *average*, and *hard* and then equating *hard* with *best*. It means cooperatively constructing rigorous and interesting courses centered on students' interests and talents. It means that the schools should show the society that a democracy honors all of its honest workers, not just those who finish college and make a lot of money.

John Dewey, in lines often misappropriated, said, "What the best and wisest parent wants for his own child, that must the community want for all its children. Any other ideal for our schools is narrow and unlovely; acted upon, it destroys our democracy."[19] Dewey did not mean, however, that the community should give all children exactly the same program of studies. Indeed, he argued so often and so insistently against sameness in the choice of content and curricula that it is hard to understand how anyone could read him this way. The best and wisest parent, Dewey believed, would want an education that is best for each individual child. In direct contradiction to Dewey's hopes, the standards movement keeps pressing for the same education for all.

At the same time, sensitive educators have attacked the tracking system that has been in place for so long in our schools. This system, in which children are placed in *tracks* according to their perceived academic capacities, has had pernicious effects. No reasonable observer could deny this.[20] However, the problem may not be tracking itself but rather the hierarchical values we put on the tracks. There is no obvious reason why students in a commercial or industrial track cannot develop "both culture and expert knowledge in some special direction," as Whitehead advised. The soul-destroying discrimination arises when we regard one track as better than another and place the one loaded with academic information and skills at the top. A bad situation is made worse when we refer to the students in the top track as the "good kids," and teachers often do this. We add insult to injury when we assign the least competent teachers to work with students in the "lower" tracks.

So long as schools value only academic achievement (narrowly defined as success in standard school subjects), this problem will be intractable. I have considerable sympathy for those who, observing the suffering of lower-track students, recommend total abandonment of tracking, but surely this cannot be the answer if our aim is to educate each student to a standard compatible with his or her abilities and purposes. Students who seek careers that require knowledge and skills very different from the standard academic material are not given a fair chance by simply placing them in academic courses with those who actually want these courses. How fair is it to ignore students' own legitimate interests and coerce them into competing with students whose interests lie in the area of coercion? This issue goes to the very heart of democratic education, and I will devote considerable space to it in later chapters. The questions asked here are simply skipped over in the rush to standardized solutions.

Consider the way in which the National Council of Teachers of Mathematics (NCTM) begins its draft of *Standards 2000*.[21] No Socrates-like character asks "And shall we teach mathematics?" Even if the answer is a preordained "Of course, Socrates," asking the question raises a host of others: To whom shall we teach mathematics? For what ends? Mathematics of what sort? In what relation to students' expressed needs? In what relation to our primary aims? And what are these aims?

After a brief statement on "a time of extraordinary and accelerating change"[22] and the widespread use of technology, the document launches into "principles," the first of which is "The Equity Principle." It is worthwhile to examine this principle in some detail. It states as a basic assumption that "all students can learn to think mathematically."[23] It does not even try to make a convincing argument for this claim. It does not tell us what this means or why students should do so. Instead, it says:

> An emphasis on "mathematics for all" is important because of the role that school mathematics has historically played in educational inequity. A student's mathematical proficiency is often

used as a basis for decisions regarding further schooling and job opportunities. Furthermore, mathematics has been one of the subjects frequently associated with "tracking," a practice in which students are sorted into different instructional sequences that often results in inequitable opportunities and outcomes for students.[24]

Therefore, everyone must become proficient in mathematics. Without further argument, this is a non sequitur. Writers of the report do not pause to consider other, more generous ways of alleviating the inequity that has historically been associated with mathematics. For example, why not abandon the requirement that all college-bound students, regardless of their interests and abilities, present academic credits in mathematics? Why not consider ways to improve non-college courses so that the mathematics actually needed is taught sensitively and practically within those courses? Why decide that the road to equity is established by coercing everyone into becoming proficient in mathematics? A thorough discussion of aims might lead in a different direction.

We need a careful analysis of what is meant by equity, and we need a discussion of educational aims that moves in two directions—toward the aims we hold as a liberal democracy and into the actual activities we will provide in classrooms. Educational aims always reflect the aims—explicit or implicit—of the political society in which they are developed. A totalitarian state will engender educational aims that primarily benefit the state. A liberal democracy should generate aims more focused on the needs of individuals. Indeed, it must do this because it depends for its legitimacy on the capacity of its citizens to freely endorse and maintain it. And how is such a capacity developed? Surely, it grows, at least in part, out of guided practice in making well-informed choices. Thus we have an important argument against coercion right from the start.

Another argument against coercion is that coercion makes people resistant and unhappy. If we are serious about promoting happiness, we will recognize that every act of coercion raises a question. There are times when, after considering the question raised, we will still have to use coercion, but there are many times when, because we have paused to think, we will be able to use persuasion or even abandon the end toward which we planned to coerce. As we consider whether or not to coerce, our deliberation will almost always involve an analysis of needs and a commitment to negotiation.

Reviving Aims-talk

I have argued that we need to talk about aims because aims provide criteria by which we judge our choices of goals, objectives, and subject content. Aims-talk can also be directed at the larger society and its policies. Both functions are important.

During the twentieth century, we made considerable progress in humanizing our schools. Corporal punishment has fallen into disfavor (and is illegal in many states), more students go to high school and more graduate, girls are encouraged to take courses in mathematics and science, programs are designed for children with disabilities, and meals are provided for poor children.

American education can be rightly proud of these attainments and aspirations. Still, we could do better in securing these goals and others by analyzing the aims that gave rise to them. Why, for example, have we decided to encourage young women to study math and science? Well, because it's the fair thing to do! Equity seems to require it. If equity is the aim, however, why are we not concerned that so few young men become nurses, elementary school teachers, social workers, early childhood teachers, and full-time parents? The response to this is that equity refers to equitable financial opportunities, and the occupations traditionally available to women do not pay well. But are they important? Well, of course. Why not pay appropriately for them, then, and strive for a balanced form of equity?

As we ask deeper questions about our aims—why are we doing X?—we uncover new problems and new possibilities for the solution of our original problem. In the case under consideration here, we are also led to use caution in encouraging young women to choose careers in math and science. If they want to study in these areas, our encouragement should be backed by generous support, but very bright young women are sometimes led to believe that any other choice is beneath them. Some girls interested in elementary school teaching, for example, have been told, "You're too good for that!" Their self-worth comes to depend on their rejecting traditional female roles. Inferred needs and internal wants are then in conflict, and the joy of doing something wholeheartedly may be lost.

Consider next the goal of providing a free, appropriate education to every child in the least restrictive environment compatible with that goal.[25] Trying to meet this goal has turned out to be enormously expensive, and it has also led to a proliferation of services and demands for services. Are too many children now labeled *learning disabled*? Why did we establish such a goal? Again, the answer seems to be equity. But what is meant by equity in this area?

Unless we ask this question, we are likely to engage in foolish and harmful practices. For instance, in some states, children labeled learning disabled (even those in special classes) must now take the standardized tests required of students in regular classes. It certainly makes sense to monitor the progress of these students and to ask continually whether we are doing the best possible job with them. Are we catching errors in labeling? Are we working hard enough to move capable students out of special education—to relieve them of any possible stigma attached to the label?[26] Are all the children learning something? Granted that these questions should be answered conscientiously, forcing all children to take these tests seems counterproductive. Some probably should be encouraged to take them, with only positive stakes attached. It is outrageous, however, to force these tests on all students in special education. From all over the country, we hear stories of sick stomachs, trembling hands, and wet pants. If by *equity* we mean providing an appropriate education for every child, it is dead wrong to expect the same performance from each child. Having forgotten our aim, we act as though all children are academically equal and can be held to the same standard.

We could analyze each of the goals I listed as admirable from the perspective of underlying aims, and it would be useful to do so. Sometimes the goals themselves require such analysis (as in the two cases just discussed). In other cases, we have to look at the outcomes associated with the goals and then go back to the original aim to see where we might have gone wrong. It seems entirely right, for example, to forbid corporal punishment and sexual harassment in schools, but does that mean that a teacher should never touch a student? Are appropriate hugs ruled out? Is a firm restraining hand on an angry arm ruled out? In the widespread use of zero-tolerance rules, good judgment is often sacrificed. The original aim is forgotten.

Even in the matter of feeding hungry children, we too often lose sight of our aim. Many people claim that we feed children because "hungry children can't learn." A better answer would be this: We feed hungry children because they are hungry! That answer helps us to direct attention to social problems beyond the classroom. Should we stop feeding hungry children if, after being well fed, they still do not learn as well as we think they should?

I want to turn now to an examination of practices that should raise questions about the aims of education. It is often helpful to see a familiar scene through the eyes of an intelligent and sympathetic stranger,[27] so let's pretend that a visitor from another world has visited our schools and wants to share his or her observations with us. The visitor talks with a representative educator, Ed.

Visitor: It struck me as odd that, although your people spend much of their time in homemaking, parenting, and recreation, these topics are rarely addressed in your schools.

Ed: That's because we regard the school as a somewhat specialized institution. Its job is to teach academics—the material that cannot easily be taught at home. Homemaking, parenting, and worthwhile forms of recreation are taught at home. Indeed, most of us believe that it would be an improper intrusion into family life for schools to teach such topics.

Visitor: Ah, yes. This is part of your liberal heritage, is it not? But what is done about the children who come from homes where these matters are not taught well? From what I've seen, there are many such children.

Ed: You're right, and this does worry us. However, we believe that people who have a thorough command of the fundamental processes will be able to learn these other matters on their own. They will have the skills to do so. And they will qualify for good jobs, so they will be able to provide the material resources characteristic of good homes.

Visitor: Hmm. Well, of course, there is something to that. But if children from poor homes (not necessarily poor in the financial sense, you understand) have great difficulty learning, it would seem that a society ought to attack the problem at all levels—do something to eliminate poverty, encourage adult interest in homemaking and parenting, and teach these things in school.

Ed: But parents don't want us to do this! They don't want the schools to prescribe methods of parenting or to pronounce one way of homemaking better than another. We have a hard time teaching any sort of values in our schools.

Visitor: You would not want to indoctrinate, I understand. But these topics need not be presented dogmatically. In your English classes, high school students could read and discuss children's literature. In social studies, they could study the development of the home and forms of housing. In art, they might study the aesthetics of homemaking. In science, child development. In foreign language, patterns of hospitality might be studied. In mathematics, they might look at statistical studies that show the high correlation between socioeconomic status and school achievement. These are just examples, of course.

Ed: And very good examples! However, our schedules are already so full that I don't see how we could make room for all these things.

Visitor: Perhaps, if you will forgive my saying so, you haven't thought deeply enough about what you are trying to do.

Ed: We want to give all children the opportunity to learn what they need to succeed in our society. All children!

Visitor: That is commendable, very fine. But how do you define success? Have the schools failed a child if he wants to become an auto mechanic? Do they help a girl who wants to be a beautician?

Ed: We believe they should make those choices later. First, get a sound, basic education.

Visitor: In watching many classes and talking to many students, it seems that—because their interests and talents are ignored in school—many young people fall into these occupations instead of choosing them proudly. They feel they are not good enough for more desirable work. There is an injury inflicted on them. ⟶ *wow !*

Ed: We are getting off the subject. What has this to do with teaching homemaking and the like?

Visitor: It has to do with happiness, and that was my reason for bringing up those topics in the first place. If happiness is found in domains other than salaried work, shouldn't those other domains be treated in education? And since one's occupation also influences happiness, that too should be included in education. But I was just getting started. . . .

Ed: I hesitate to ask.

Visitor: It seems that your society, your government anyway, has been waging a losing war on drugs—

Ed: Now I've got you! We *do* teach about the dangers of drug abuse.

Visitor: Yes, yes. But your television commercials are filled with ads for drugs, some of them quite dangerous. Do you help students to see how they are being manipulated?

Ed: Well, we worry most about illegal drugs.

Visitor: Have you noticed that many teenagers from low socioeconomic status neighborhoods wear expensive name-brand clothing? They could clothe themselves for far less money and perhaps avoid taking part-time jobs that keep them from their studies.

Ed: So you want us to engage in consumer education as well as homemaking, parenting, and—you're not finished, are you?

Visitor: Perhaps we should let it be for now. It just seems so sad that, when everyone seeks happiness, the schools do so little to promote it.

Ed: Well, I promise to think more about it. (Shaking his head) I just don't see what we can do.

In this chapter, I have argued that aims-talk plays a vital role in sustaining a rigorous and relevant program of education, and I've tried to show how it has done this in the past. Today, with recent changes in social thought and massive changes in technology, it is more important than ever to consider why we are promoting certain goals in schooling and why we continue to neglect education for personal life and for happiness in our occupations.

Notes

1. William Schubert argues, rightly I think, that there is no settled hierarchy of educational purposes, but he notes that aims, goals, and objectives are widely thought to represent a sequence of decreasing generality. See Schubert, *Curriculum: Perspective, Paradigm, and Possibility* (New York: Macmillan, 1986).
2. See Schubert, pp. 190–191, on this.
3. See National Education Association, *Cardinal Principles of Secondary Education* (Washington, D.C.: U.S. Government Printing Office, 1918).
4. Herbert M. Kliebard, *The Struggle for the American Curriculum* (New York: Routledge, 1995), p. 98.
5. See Franklin Bobbitt, *How to Make a Curriculum* (Boston: Houghton Mifflin, 1924).
6. For an excellent analysis of the problems involved in establishing objectives, see Elliot W. Eisner, *The Educational Imagination* (New York: Macmillan, 1979).
7. See Plato, *The Republic*, trans. B. Jowett (Roslyn, NY: Walter Black, 1942), Book II.
8. John Dewey, *Democracy and Education* (New York: Macmillan, 1944/1916), p. 90.
9. Ibid.
10. See *The Republic*, Book III.
11. For an introduction to *Emile*, see William Boyd, ed., *The Emile of Jean Jacques Rousseau: Selections* (New York: Teachers College Press, 1962).

12. For informative analyses of Rousseau's recommendations for Sophie's education, see Jane Roland Martin, *Reclaiming a Conversation* (New Haven, CT: Yale University Press, 1985); also Susan Moller Okin, *Women in Western Political Thought* (Princeton, NJ: Princeton University Press, 1979).

13. Dewey, *Democracy and Education*, p. 100.

14. Alfred North Whitehead, *The Aims of Education* (New York: Free Press, 1967/1929) p. 1.

15. Ibid., pp. 6–7.

16. See National Commission on Excellence in Education, *A Nation at Risk* (Washington, D.C.: U.S. Government Printing Office, 1983).

17. Ibid., p. 5.

18. See David Berliner and Bruce Biddle, *The Manufactured Crisis: Myths, Fraud, and the Attack on America's Public Schools* (New York: Perseus, 1996); also Gerald Bracey, *Setting the Record Straight: Responses to Misconceptions about Public Education in the United States* (Alexandria, VA: Association for Supervision and Curriculum Development, 1997).

19. Dewey, *The School and Society* (Chicago: University of Chicago Press, 1900), p. 3.

20. See Jeannie Oakes, *Multiplying Inequalities: The Effects of Race, Social Class, and Tracking on Opportunities to Learn Mathematics and Science* (Santa Monica, CA: Rand, 1990); also Oakes, *Keeping Track: How Schools Structure Inequality* (New Haven, CT: Yale University Press, 1995). But for an argument on both the positive and negative effects of tracking, see James E. Rosenbaum, "Track Misperceptions and Frustrated College Plans: An Analysis of the Effects of Tracks and Track Perceptions in the National Longitudinal Survey," *Sociology of Education* 53, 1980: 74–88.

21. See National Council of Teachers of Mathematics, *Principles and Standards for School Mathematics*, Discussion draft (Reston, VA: NCTM, 1998).

22. Ibid., p. 15.

23. Ibid., p. 23.

24. Ibid.

25. For a comprehensive review of the problems involved in meeting this goal, see James Paul, Michael Churton, Hilda Rosselli-Kostoryz, William Morse, Kofi Marfo, Carolyn Lavely, and Daphne Thomas, eds., *Foundations of Special Education* (Pacific Grove, CA: Brooks/Cole, 1997); also Paul, Churton, Morse, Albert Duchnowski, Betty Epanchin, Pamela Osnes, and R. Lee Smith, eds., *Special Education Practice* (Pacific Grove, CA: Brooks/Cole, 1997).

26. For powerful accounts of how difficult it can be for children to escape the label, see Theresa A. Thorkildsen and John G. Nicholls, *Motivation and the Struggle to Learn* (Boston: Allyn & Bacon, 2002).

27. This is a familiar technique used in describing utopias. Two well-known examples are Edward Bellamy, *Looking Backward* (New York: New American Library, 1960/1888), and Samuel Butler, *Erewhon* (London: Penguin, 1985/1872).

Permissions

Bobbitt, Franklin, "Scientific Method in Curriculum-Making." Public Domain, Preface and Chapter VI in Franklin Bobbitt, *The Curriculum*. Cambridge, MA: The Riverside Press, 1918.

Montessori, Maria, "A Critical Consideration of the New Pedagogy in its Relation to Modern Science." From *The Montessori Elementary Material: The Advanced Montessori Method* by Maria Montessori © Bentley Publishers, 1734 Massachusetts Avenue, Cambridge, MA 02138. www.BentleyPublishers.com. Reprinted with permissions.

Dewey, John, "My Pedagogic Creed," from *Journal of the National Education Association*, Vol. 18, No. 9, pp. 291–295, December 1929. Reprinted by permission of the National Education Association.

Addams, Jane, "The Public School and the Immigrant Child," from *Journal of Proceedings and Addresses*, 1908, pp. 99–102. Reprinted with permission from the National Education Association.

Counts, George S., "Dare the School Build a New Social Order." Chapters 3 and 4, in George S. Counts, *Dare the School Build a New Social Order?* New York: John Day, 1932. Copyright renewed 1959 by George S. Counts. Reprinted by permission of Martha L. Counts.

Kliebard, Herbert M., "The Rise of Scientific Curriculum-Making and its Aftermath," from *Curriculum Theory Network*, Vol. 5, No. 1, 1975, pp. 27–38. Reprinted with permission of Blackwell Publishing.

Tyler, Ralph W., "Basic Principles of Curriculum and Instruction." From Ralph W. Tyler, *Basic Principles of Curriculum and Instruction*, 1949, pp 1–7, 16–19, 25–33. Reprinted with permission of the University of Chicago Press

Bruner, Jerome S., "Man: A Course of Study." Reprinted by permission of the publisher from *Toward a Theory of Instruction* by Jerome S. Bruner, pp. 73–101, Cambridge, Mass: The Belknap Press of Harvard University Press. Copyright © 1966 by the President and the Fellows of Harvard College.

Popham, James W., "Objectives." Public domain, Chapter 2 from James W. Popham, *An Evaluation Guidebook: A Set of Practical Guidelines for the Educational Evaluator*. Los Angeles: The Instructional Objectives Exchange, 1972.

Eisner, Elliot W., "Education Objectives—Help or Hindrance." Reprinted by permission of the University of Chicago Press, from *School Review*, Vol. 75, No. 3, 1967, pp. 250–260. Copyright © the University of Chicago Press.

Jackson, Philip W., "The Daily Grind." Reprinted by permission of the publisher. From Phillip W. Jackson, *Life in Classrooms*, New York: Teachers College Press, © 1990 by Teachers College, Columbia University. All rights reserved.

Schwab, Joseph J., "The Practical: A Language for Curriculum." Reprinted by permission of the University of Chicago Press, from *School Review*, Vol. 78, No. 1, 1969, pp. 1–23. Published by the University of Chicago Press.

Excerpts from Paulo Freire, *Pedagogy of the Oppressed*. New York: Continuum, © 1970, 1993 by Paulo Friere, pp. 75–86, 95–100. Reprinted with permission of the publisher, The Continuum International Publishing Group.

Greene, Maxine, "Curriculum and Consciousness," from *Teachers College Record*, Vol. 73, No. 2, 1971, pp. 253–270. Reprinted with permission.

Pinar, William F., "The Reconceptualization of Curriculum Studies," from *Journal of Curriculum Studies*, Vol. 10, No. 3, 1978, pp. 205–214. Taylor & Francis Ltd, http://www.informaworld.com, reprinted by permission of the publisher.

Adler, Mortimer J., "The Paideia Proposal." Reprinted with the permission of Scribner, an imprint of Simon & Schuster Adult Publishing Group, from *The Paideia Proposal: An Educational Manifesto* by Mortimer J. Adler. Copyright © 1982 by the Institute for Philosophical Research. All rights reserved.

Noddings, Nel. "The False Promise of the Paideia: A Critical Review of *The Paideia Proposal*," from *Journal of Thought*, Vol. 18, No. 4, 1983, pp. 81–91. Reprinted by permission of Caddo Gap Press.

McLaughlin, Milbrey Wallin, "Implementation as Mutual Adaptation: Change in Classroom Organization," from *Teachers College Record*, Vol. 77, No. 3, 1976, pp. 339–351. Reprinted with permission.

Apple, Michael W., "Controlling the Work of Teachers," from *Teachers and Texts*, by Michael W. Apple. New York: Routledge & Kegan Paul, 1986, pp. 31–53. Reprinted with permission of Routledge, a member of Taylor & Francis Books.

American Association of University Women, "How Schools Shortchange Girls: Three Perspectives on Curriculum," from part four of *How Schools Shortchange Girls: The AAUW Report*, American Association of University Women, Educational Foundation Washington, D.C., © 1992 by AAUW. Reprinted by permission.

Silin, Jonathan, "HIV/AIDS Education: Toward a Collaborative Curriculum." Reprinted by permission of the publisher. From Jonathan Silin, *Sex, Death and the Education of our Children*, New York: Teachers College Press, © 1995 by Teachers College, Columbia University. All rights reserved.

Doll, William E., Jr., "The Four R's—an Alternative to the Tyler Rationale." Reprinted by permission of the publisher. From William E. Doll, *A Postmodern Perspective on Curriculum*, New York: Teachers College Press, © 1993 by Teachers College, Columbia University. All rights reserved.

Hlebowitsh, Peter S., "Generational Ideas in Curriculum: A Historical Triangulation," from *Curriculum Inquiry* Vol. 35, No. 1, Spring 2005, pp. 73–87. Reprinted with permission of Blackwell Publishing.

Au, Wayne, "High-Stakes Testing and Curricular Control: A Qualitative Metasynthesis," from *Education Researcher* Vol. 36, No. 5, June/July 2007, pp. 258–267. Copyright 2007 by Sage Publications Inc. Journals. Reproduced with permission of Sage Publications Inc. Journals in the format Textbook via Copyright Clearance Center.

Sleeter, Christine and Jamy Stillman, "Standardizing Knowledge in a Multicultural Society," from *Curriculum Inquiry* Vol. 35, No. 1, Spring 2005, pp. 27–46. Reprinted with permission of Blackwell Publishing.

Siskin, Leslie Santee, "Outside the Core: Accountability in Tested and Untested Subjects," from *The New Accountability: High Schools and High-Stakes Testing*, edited by Martin

Carnoy, Richard Elmore, and Leslie Santee Siskin. New York: Routledge, 2003, pp. 87–98. Reprinted with permission of Routledge, a member of Taylor & Francis Books.

Eisner, Elliot W., "What Does it Mean to Say a School is Doing Well?" from *Phi Delta Kappan*, Vol. 82, No. 5, 2001, pp. 367–372. Reprinted by permission of Phi Delta Kappa International.

Valenzuela, Angela, "Subtractive Schooling, Caring Relations, and Social Capital in the Schooling of U.S.-Mexican Youth." Reprinted by permission from *Beyond Silenced Voices: Class, Race, and Gender in United States Schools, Revised Edition* edited by Lois Weis and Michelle Fine, the State University of New York Press. © 2005 State University of New York. All rights reserved.

Chan, Elaine, "Teacher Experiences of Culture in the Curriculum," from *Journal of Curriculum Studies*, Vol. 38: No. 2, 2006, pp. 161–176. Taylor & Francis Ltd, http://www.informaworld.com, reprinted by permission of the publisher.

Thornton, Stephen J., "Silence on Gays and Lesbians in Social Studies Curriculum," from *Social Education*, Vol. 67, No. 4, 2003, pp. 226–230. National Council for the Social Studies. © National Council for the Social Studies. Reprinted by permission.

Smith, David Geoffrey, "Curriculum and Teaching Face Globalization," from *International Handbook of Curriculum Research*, edited by William F. Pinar. Lawrence Erlbaum Associates, 2003, pp. 35–51. Reprinted with permission of Routledge, a member of Taylor & Francis Books.

McIntosh, Peggy, "Gender Perspectives on Educating for Global Citizenship." Reprinted by permission of the publisher. From Nel Noddings, Editor, *Educating Citizens for Global Awareness*, New York: Teachers College Press, © 2005 by Teachers College, Columbia University. All rights reserved.

Bowers, C.A., "The Classroom Practice of Commons Education," from *Transforming Environmental Education: Making the Renewal of the Cultural Commons the focus of Educational Reform*, Ecojustice Press 2006, pp. 51–87. Reproduced with permission of C.A. Bowers. Additional sources on the how to introduce cultural commons and sustainability issues into the classroom can be found at www.http://cabowers.net

Noddings, Nel, "The Aims of Education," from Nel Noddings, *Happiness and Education*. Cambridge: Cambridge University Press, 2003, pp. 74–93. Reprinted with the permission of Cambridge University Press.

Index

Please note that references to Notes will have the letter 'n' following the note. Page references to Tables will be in *italic* print.

eBooks

eBooks – at www.eBookstore.tandf.co.uk

A library at your fingertips!

eBooks are electronic versions of printed books. You can store them on your PC/laptop or browse them online.

They have advantages for anyone needing rapid access to a wide variety of published, copyright information.

eBooks can help your research by enabling you to bookmark chapters, annotate text and use instant searches to find specific words or phrases. Several eBook files would fit on even a small laptop or PDA.

NEW: Save money by eSubscribing: cheap, online access to any eBook for as long as you need it.

Annual subscription packages

We now offer special low-cost bulk subscriptions to packages of eBooks in certain subject areas. These are available to libraries or to individuals.

For more information please contact webmaster.ebooks@tandf.co.uk

We're continually developing the eBook concept, so keep up to date by visiting the website.

www.eBookstore.tandf.co.uk